LISTENING TO ICONS

LISTENING TO ICONS

Vol. I

Indian Iconographic & Iconological Studies

Doris Meth Srinivasan

Aryan Books International
New Delhi

LISTENING TO ICONS
Vol. I: Indian Iconographic & Iconological Studies

ISBN: 978-81-7305-551-5

Published in **2016** by
Aryan Books International
Pooja Apartments, 4B, Ansari Road, New Delhi-110 002 (India)
Tel.: 23287589, 23255799; Fax: 91-11-23270385
E-mail: aryanbooks@gmail.com
www.aryanbooks.co.in

Designed and Printed in India by
ABI Prints & Publishing Co., New Delhi

Foreword

I first met Doris Srinivasan when she visited the Varanasi Center of AIIS; it was sometime in 1979. I was present at the Planning Sessions she had arranged for the Seminar on Mathura with the title "The Cultural History of Ancient Mathura". The Seminar was sponsored by the American Institute of Indian Studies (AIIS), Varanasi, for eight days, precisely from 7th to 15th January, 1980. The venues

1979 Planning Session of the Mathura Seminar. Doris Meth Srinivasan with U.P. Shah, N.P. Joshi, A.K. Narain, M.A. Dhaky, D.C. Sircar, R.C. Sharma and others.

were Mathura and the AIIS, New Delhi. The learned papers, 36 in number, that covered eight different disciplines, read at the Seminar were compiled in categories that were carefully edited and next published in a monumental volume with the title "Mathura: The Cultural Heritage", New Delhi, 1989. Doris was the General Editor of those contributions at the Seminar she conceived and convened. Qualitatively and from the research point of view, it is a long lasting achievement for which art and cultural historians will long be grateful to her.

She is now getting published 16 learned articles which reflect a high level of scholarship and profound erudition. At the base of it is the very rigorous methology she employs. Using a multidisciplinary approach, she attempts to understand why an image was made and what it meant at the time it was made to persons worshipping the image (which may or may not be the same as what it meant to craftsmen who fashioned the image). In pursuit of this central concern, she tries to place the icon into its historical and cultural orbit.

The result is seen in these insightful research articles which have appeared in reputed journals, or read in seminars and congresses, or have appeared in different kinds of monographs. Most of these publications are not known nor readily available in India. In numerous cases, the author has brought information up-to-date by attaching addenda to some papers. So her compilation—Listening to Icons, Volume I: Indian Iconographic and Iconological Studies—will prove a most useful volume for reference and study for the art historians in India, and of course the world over.

The studies fall into four main categories: Saiva Themes, Vaisnava Themes, Secular and Folk, and lastly, Narrative Themes. They represent in-depth analyses covering as they do a broad range of topics from Indus seals to Gupta and post-Gupta icons. The author's aim is to allow the objects to define their meaning. That aim is highlighted in the title of Volume I, and Volume II, forthcoming. The researches of this distinguished scholar will impress the reader for the thoroughness and originality of approach and for the sophistication of her inimitable style.

M.A. Dhaky

Contents

Listening — My Way

Early art from South Asia fairly bursts with the urge to communicate. The forms are dictated less by aesthetics and more by an intent to inform, that is, to share ideas of a religious, spiritual, talismanic, societal or ritualistic nature.The enormous excitement in dealing with the iconography of these ancient icons is to try and discern their internal discourse by listening.

An icon speaks. It speaks in the language of its time, which may also reflect the past. Of course, I do not mean that by a study of philology or linguistics, one hears the icon's message—although both these disciplines may contribute towards this end. An icon's message is made audible through investigation of its *gestalt.* A South Asian icon, whether produced for a sacred site or an individual patron in antiquity expresses ideas of a group and not an individual's personal predilections. Today and yesterday, the village storyteller played a part in contextualizing an icon and its message to a rapt group of listeners. The papers in this volume all try to listen and understand why an image was made and what it may have meant to those in a particular group who sought it out, long, long ago.

Is it an overweening aim for an historian alien to South Asia's culture, to attempt to find meaning in images removed thousands of years and miles from her own cultural sphere? Let me first clarify that I wish to witness more than to interpret an image. The studies in this volume will hopefully demonstrate that I have tried, as best as I can, to shed my biases and put myself in the shoes of the ancients in order to get not only a scholastic but an intuitive awareness of what may, or may not, be possible—what may be sought for—during the time and place associated with the object.

Many of the studies in this volume concern the earliest art of Mathurā, especially the Brahmanical or ancient Hindu art forms. For years I have immersed myself so deeply in the physical aspects of that site that at times I began to feel as if I walked Mathurā's ancient streets. This immersion yielded some unexpected results. Perhaps the most direct example is detailed in the paper which concludes that the god Saṃkarṣaṇa/Balarāma was associated with Mount Govardhan prior to his younger brother Kṛṣṇa, whose feat of lifting up this Mountain is integrated into purānic lore. (Paper No. 12) I was prompted by an 18th century Kangra miniature to find a connection between 'mountain and Saṃkarṣaṇa/Balarāma'. Without going to Braj villages surrounding Mathurā where Balarāma is still worshipped and stepping inside shrines to 'Dāūjī' (Braj for 'elder brother' to Kṛṣṇa, thus an affectionate local name for Balarāma), I would never have had that 'lightbulb' moment. For on Dāūjī's altars I saw sanctified pieces of Govardhan stones, with the presence of that sacred mountain ritually installed. Insight from these contemporary scenes gave me the confidence to work backward to try and trace—via studies in ancient religious thought, rites, rituals, folk beliefs and folk art—the ideas that originally tied the god to that Mountain.

Such an approach can only work in a traditional society. "Nothing ever gets lost in Indian culture" is one of the maxims I remember from my Penn graduate days—and though the Indian subcontinent is not a static cultural zone—it may recycle, rephrase or reconfigure and add—but indeed, it often does thread the old into the new cultural fabric. One of the main realizations that has filtered into my own approach, because it has become apparent from so many of my findings, is the enormous longevity and vitality of the Vedic tradition. The earliest deities corporealized in art are either Brahmanical, that is, they have a close relation to Vedic beliefs and rituals or they have an adverse relationship to this tradition (as do, for example, Buddhist themes). In either case, for the art historian of early Indian art there is great advantage to knowing well that tradition for it establishes a listening base.

That hypothesis underlies an investigation into the nature of the god Rudra-Śiva, and resulted in finding that he is not an "outsider" to the Vedic tradition as is so often postulated because of his dark nature. Rather, precisely because of his ambivalent nature, he shares basic characteritics with the most powerful and ancient stratum of the Vedic pantheon (Paper No. 2). The flip side to this finding, namely that Rudra-Śiva is an "insider" to Vedic norms, is explored in the study of the (infamous) Indus Valley seal which is found to have no connection to a proto-Śiva (Paper No. 1). The "insider" theory has considerable reprocussions for the development of early *śaiva* art. If Hinduistic Śiva stems (even in part) from Vedic antecedents, then initial *śaiva* icons could well reflect or be based upon the Vedic (even Indo-Aryan) traditions. (See topic in Vol. II). And such is the case : a Vedic ritual helps explain the forms of the *mukha liṅga* (Paper No. 3); Brahmanic texts are a guide to its significance, as well as the significance of the *liṅga*. This approach clarifies why these typologies were among the earliest plastic conceptualizations marking the supremacy of Śiva (Paper No. 4).

In addition to knowledge of a terrain and its cultural history as part of my listening techniques, my first trip to India made me aware of another desideratum, which was posted right on the doors of numerous institutes of learning that are called Department of Indology; Department of Ancient Indian History, Culture and Archaeology; Center for India Studies etc. These door markers make an important assumption: an holistic grasp of the dynamics of historical events and their cultural reprocussions, or traces thereof, is needed when delving into the past. Researching historical issues through one academic discipline will not prepare the scholar for penetrating conceptual, humanistic problems.This is especially true for certain problems in art history.

There are topics in art history that can, of course, be tackled through the classic art historical approach involving descriptive remarks on 'style and iconography '; such topics are hardly found herein. I am less interested in the 'what' of an object and more in the 'why'. To answer 'why' an image was conceived and used in a social, religious or magical context is to enter into human history which cannot be neatly divided into separate academic disciplines. The human history into which a South Asian icon fits is multidimensional and thereby its 'why' is multidisciplinary. I have always believed that in South Asia the art of a certain age represents the pulse of that age. It is the final product churned up by the multidimensional energies of human experience employed at a certain time by a certain (sub-)group of the population.The more disciplines an art historian can control the greater the span of fundamental problems dealing with an icon's *raison d'être* can be addressed. And even then, multivalent viewpoints within the group, and certainly outside of it, are a possiblity. Perhaps one cannot be absolutely sure that every shade of meaning has been captured in an assessment of an icon's original meaning, but at least a fairly close approximation can be attained by going inside the cultural context which gave it birth.

Several papers in this volume develop from my inquiry into the basic reason for ascribing multiple bodily parts to certain Brahmanic/early Hindu divinities, right from their initial conceptualization. The division among icons using the multiplicity convention is striking; it is absent in early Buddhist and Jain images. To grasp why this convention is only present in Brahmanic/early Hindu icons, I started a philological analysis of certain terms in the earliest Veda and then in the rest of Vedic and epic literature. The outcome proved noteworthy : one general, and three discreet definitions more or less inform the use of the convention throughout. Building upon this finding plus further textual and philological studies helped penetrate forms as diverse as a *caturvyūha* Viṣṇu (Paper No. 8), an eight armed Viṣṇu (Paper No. 10), and the way *śaiva* forms unfold on the walls of some temples (Paper Nos. 5 and 6). In all these cases, I did not start out with a theory as to the meaning of the multiplicity convention, nor a possible ideology behind later visual expressions. The theory came by way of textual, philological and visual evidences. Subsequently, I went further. Using a fuller palette of disciplines, I attempted to answer why the production of icons with the multiplicity convention should have originated at one place, Mathurā.

There are numerous other seminal questions in Indian art history awaiting resolution But not all good questions are ready to yield up their answers. Perhaps the 'Mother' of such questions is the perennial one asking where and why the emergence of the figure of the Buddha first occurred; another is the correlation (if any) between the symbols and signs on the Indus Valley seals and whether these signs actually represent a language; my own involvements have caused me to wonder why the images of Mathurā's own deified Vṛṣṇi heroes (or Vīras), apparently rulers in that town, are not first found there, but are found instead way up North in present-day Chilas, Pakistan, and on coins in an excavated stratum in Ai-Khanoum, Afghanistan, some 200 years before they occur in Mathurā, the cradle of Hindu imagery. These questions are unanswered because some conclusive evidence—whatever that might prove to be—has not yet turned up. Sometimes one has to wait a long time for such evidence. For years I have also wondered why the earliest icons of Śiva in the Northwest are exceedingly different from those conceived concurrently at Mathurā, although the Northwestern ones have some characteristic Hindu traits found at Mathurā. The decisive pieces of needed evidence, at least to my mind, have recently appeared, allowing me to offer a provisional answer (see the paper on Śiva in Vol. II).

A certain threshold of information has to be reached, I believe, before an icon may be ready to open up its ancient intent to a contemporary scholar. The papers in both volumes could not have been attempted without much prior work by others, usually cited in the many references associated with each paper. For over a decade now, the Center for India Studies at SUNY-Stony Brook has been the place giving me needed access to research facilities. I wish to thank F. Jason Torre (Preservation Department; SUNY-Stony Brook Libraries), for the excellent preparatory work he did. My good friend and colleague Dr. Vishakha Kawathekar, Programme Coordinator, M. Arch. [Conservation], School of Planning and Architecture, Bhopal, read my mind when she sent me the photograph I used for the cover of the book.

In so many cases, my work comes only after reports convincingly establish authenticity (often by archaeologists, scientific conservationists and/or art historians); after comprehensive corpuses on the theme have been compiled by others; after broad cultural outlines of a period have been studied by historians, historians of religions and the social scientists; after dating and direct quotes of humanistic action or literary expressions have been resurrected by linguists, numismatists and philologists working with the prevailing scripts and languages. I stand on the shoulders of all these when I attempt to witness why an icon was made and what it may have meant to say. These scholars are mentioned within papers, but three enormous influences have not.

I am extremely fortunate to have been guided in my graduate studies by teachers in the Department of Oriental Studies at the University of Pennsylvania. If ever an education was geared towards learning to generate and solve future multidisciplinary problems, there it was, formulated by my extraordinary thesis adviser, William Norman Brown. Opportunities to put this type of learning into practice continued at the Institute he founded. It is due to the visionary generousity and acumen of Pradeep Mehendiratta, Director of the American Institute of Indian Studies, New Delhi, that so many of my projects and thoughts could flourish. And then there is the initial institution which instilled in me an intellectual curiosity and confidence at a time when women were not generally pushed in that direction—my high school, Hunter College High School in New York City. An all-girls school when I attended, it sent me and my classmates into the world with the absolute unspoken assurance that whatever we would chose to do would matter.

I can never thank all enough.

Westhampton, New York **Doris Meth Srinivasan**

Abbreviations

AAA	-	Archives of Asian Art
AIIS	-	American Institute of Indian Studies
ASI	-	Archaeological Survey of India
BEFEO	-	*Bulletin de l'École Française d'Extreme Orient*
B.M.A.U.P.	-	*Bulletin of Museums & Archaeology in U.P.*
EW	-	*East and West* (Rome)
J.B.R.S.	-	*The Journal of the Bihar Research Society*
J.I.S.O.A.	-	*Journal of the Indian Society of Oriental Art*
SAS	-	*South Asian Studies*
SBE	-	*Sacred Books of the East*
ViDhP (also *Vdh*)	-	*Viṣṇudharmottara Purāṇa*

Additional Abbreviations are listed at the beginning of the paper "Vedic Rudra - Śiva".

Addenda

Recent additions are noted two ways in the papers:

1. With an asterisk (*)
2. With a footnote number plus asterisk

Pl. 1. Balarāma diverting the course of the Yamuna River with his plough, Punjab Hills, Chamba, *c.*1760-65 (© Brooklyn Museum inv. no. 36.250). [**Fig. 12.1**].

Pl. 2. Balarāma seated on a terrace, Kangra, *c.*1780, private collection (© Mr. Jeff Chandler). [**Fig. 12.3**].

Pl. 3. A piece of Govardhan rock on the altar, modern Dāūjī shrine, Mathurā City (© author). [**Fig. 12.8**].

Pl. 4. The Tokyo Nāginī in Fig. 15.2, prior to cleaning. Photograph courtesy Anna Maria Rossi and Fabio Rossi. [**Fig. 15.10**].

1

Unhinging Śiva from the Indus Civilization[1]

When books on Hinduism begin with a discussion of the Indus Valley Civilization, one of the main postulates to illustrate the influence of the Indus upon Hinduism is that Śiva originates from this prehistoric civilization. The postulate is based on three types of objects found in the Mature Harappan context (*c.* 2500–1900 BC) which strongly evoke the personality of the great Hindu god. These objects are phallic emblems and baetyls, seals, and some sculptures. As to the first, conical-shaped objects of stone, shell, faience, paste or clay were found in the Indus cities and an outpost, and these emblems are found to bear considerable resemblance to the later conventionalized Śiva-*liṅgas.* So too the Indus ring stones are likened to the later *yonī-rings,* objects representing the female organ and located at places holy to the Goddess (her *pīṭhas*). Regarding the second, a seal from Mohenjo-Daro portraying a central figure with ithyphallic and tricephallic features, seated in yogic fashion and surrounded by four animals is identified as a proto-Śiva figure whose *paśupati* nature is already recognized. This famous seal, Mohenjo-Daro seal No. 420, incorporates the most extensive range of symbols shared by a set of Indus seals, which are, on that account, all thought to exhibit proto-Śaivite symbolism. Lastly, two sculptures are suggestive evidence that the Indus region visualized something akin to the aspects that later comprise Śiva's nature. As such, a small, broken stone sculpture from Harappa is conjectured, when its missing limbs are reconstructed by modern scholarship, to assume a dancer's pose; in consequence the piece is understood as evocative of a Śiva Naṭarāja.[2] Another small figure from the HR area of Mohenjo-daro has female

Originally published in the *Journal of the Royal Asiatic Society of Great Britain and Ireland,* No. 1, 1984; pp. 77-89. Reprinted with stylistic changes, addenda and with permission of the Royal Asiatic Society.

breasts and male sex parts, though not in *ūrdhvaliṅga.*[3] Thus the broken, clay figurine is a hermaphrodite, and although the unification of sex attributes is rendered in a mode different from that in later Hindu art, the figurine shows an emphasis on sexual symbolism as does the later Śiva Ardhanārīśvara.[4]

The theoretical implications of these interpretations are enormous. If these remains are considered proto-Śaivite, then the Indus Valley Civilization becomes a valid source for the interpretation of any later development in Śaivite thought and art. Moreover, an *a priori* condition is established whereby subsequent interpretations must take into account and harmonize with the proposition that the Śiva-idea originated in a non-Vedic culture which precedes the advent of the Hindu tradition. To state it another way, Śiva as *yogi,* Śiva as the erotic god, Śiva as Naṭarāja, Śiva as Paśupati, Śiva as Ardhanārī, Śiva as the polycephallic Mahādeva, and Śiva as *liṅga,* all would trace their origins to beliefs conceived outside of the Hindu tradition.

The main elements of this postulate were first advanced by Marshall in the brilliant chapter on religion in his monograph *Mohenjo-daro and the Indus Civilization.*[5] Although it was published over fifty years ago, the theory has proven to be attractive ever since. However, as there has been a steady, recent amassing of pertinent information from archaeological findings as well as from studies in art history and the history of religion, it is a good time to review this interpretation.

The review will concentrate on the two types of objects for which new information is available: the so-called phallic emblems and baetyls, and the seals, especially seal No. 420 from Mohenjo-Daro.

A. MOHENJO-DARO SEAL NO. 420 (Fig. 1.1)

Marshall identified a proto-Śiva on seal No. 420 because he viewed the figure and the surrounding field as replete with proto-Śaivite iconography.[6] He saw the figure's head as tricephallic and associated this feature with the later Hindu iconographic convention of multiple heads, especially as it appears in the iconography of Śiva Mahādeva. He noticed the figure's *yoga*-like posture and recalled Śiva's position as the *yogi par excellence;* he suggested that an erect phallus may characterize the figure, though he conceded that what seems to be a phallus may be "the end of a waistband".[7] The figure's ornate headdress reminded him of Śiva's later emblem, the trident. The four wild animals in the field prefigured for him Śiva's aspect as Lord of Animals, or Paśupati. It is these four criteria – the headdress, the posture, the face and the animals—which need to be re-examined in the light of recent findings.[8]

For a clearer understanding of the headdress a terracotta "cake" from the Harappan levels at Kalibangan offers valuable insight.[9] Kalibangan is a site about 120 miles south-east of Harappa. On the obverse side of the "cake" a human figure is crudely incised. The figure wears a headgear composed of two large upward curving horns and a central branch-like configuration. The shape of the horns is nearly identical to those on seal No. 420; the only major difference is that the Kalibangan horns are devoid of the transverse striations which decorate the horns on seal No. 420. The central branch motif on the Kalibangan "cake" is basically similar to the central portion belonging to the headdress on the seal, though the "cake" shows a naturalistic rendering and the seal shows a stylized rendering. Indeed there can be little doubt that the headdresses on the "cake" and the seal are composed of the same elements, though the former exhibits a graffito quality and the latter an engraver's skill. As such, the figure on seal No. 420 wears a mitre composed of the branch and horn motif. Actually the mitre on this seal appears to be the most stylized version among a series of more naturalistic examples found on several other so-called proto-Śiva seals from the Mature Harappan phase at Mohenjo-Daro; the mitres on seals Nos. 222 and 235 display designs more transparently derived from horns, leaves and plants.[10] Moreover, there is evidence for a pre-Harappan phase of development of these forms. On the painted pottery of Balakot, a site near Karachi and a seaport of the ancient Indus period, examples of intertwined animal horns and plant forms appear.[11] One fragment of a plate of orange-red paste shows the floral motif, painted in black and entwined with horns "perhaps of a water buffalo".[12] There is also the tendency, on several other sherds, to associate "a head" with this combination of elements, imparting thereby a suggestive anthropomorphic quality. All these ceramic pieces come from the Early (i.e. pre-Mature) Indus phase, and as such may possibly have, according to the excavator, George Dales, a generic and stylistic relationship to the Mohenjo-Daro so-called proto-Śiva figures of the succeeding phase.[13] These archaeological findings strongly indicate that it is not necessary to go outside of the prehistoric period for the meaning and development of the forms comprising the mitre on seal 420 and the related seals mentioned above. In fact, the horn and branch mitre is not particularly uncommon in the ancient world of the second millenium BC. Such components form, for example, the mitres worn by gods on Mesopotamian cylinder seals dating to the Akkadian period (*c.* 2330–2180 BC).[14] In the Mesopotamian context, this type of mitre is emblematic of divinity.[15]

Turning next to the posture of the figure on seal 420, opinions have divided themselves on whether or not the posture is as peculiarly yogic as Marshall believed. The posture has been seen by some investigators as a natural mode of sitting and therefore devoid of religious significance.[16] For others it represents a *yoga* posture, and one writer even states that it attests the *Yogīśvara* aspect of the god Śiva.[17] Probably the significance lies somewhere between these two views, as a survey of other seated figures on Indus seals shows.

When other seated positions are compared to the posture on seal 420, they convey a greater ease of pose than the one on seal 420, whose stance is more formal, possibly even cultic. It is, however, the occurrence of kneeling personnages in conjunction with a figure in the *yoga*-like posture that suggests that the yogic posture may be a mark of divinity. Examples come from both Harappa and Mohenjo-Daro.[18] A most interesting example is seen on a Mohenjo-Daro faience sealing which shows two kneeling "worshippers" flanking the "yogi" seated on a dais; behind each "worshipper" is a serpent.[19]

It may therefore be inferred that the "yoga" posture is emblematic of divinity, just as the plant and horn mitre is emblematic of a fertility figure[19a(*)]. There is however nothing in the posture or the headdress which may conclusively identify the figure as a proto-Śiva.

The four animals grouped around the figure have fostered the idea that the *paśupati* concept, frequently associated with Rudra-Śiva from the Vedas onwards, is already prefigured in the nature of the proto-Śiva. This hypothesis cannot, upon closer inspection, be fruitfully pursued.

It is critical to observe that the animals depicted on the seal are all wild animals, being the elephant, tiger, buffalo and rhinoceros. In surveying the term *paśupati* in the *Rig Veda* and *Atharva Veda*, especially as it relates to Rudra, it is to be concluded that a *paśupati* does not protect wild animals.[20] Verses in the *Atharva Veda* make it quite clear that a *paśupati* protects the domestic animals upon which the agrarian economy and ritual depend.[21] The Vedic evidence would therefore not support the interpretation that the animals on seal 420 are within the domain of a Paśupati. Indeed there is further textual evidence in the *Rig Veda* and *Atharva Veda* that Rudra injures precisely those creatures under the protection of a Paśupati.[22]

Fig. 1.1. Impression of seal no. 420 from Mohenjo-Daro. Reprinted with permission from Sherman E. Lee, *A History of Far Eastern art*, New York, 1964, p. 22. Fig. 6. Enlarged.

As the probability for a proto-Śiva identification lessens, we may begin to ask ourselves who the figure on seal 420 may be. The posture, headdress and surrounding animals hint that this may be a fertility god whose power is as strong as that of wild animals, or whose domain of power includes them. Greater precision is attained by an analysis of the face.

A close look at the facial characteristics reveals that the long and rather rectangular face is marked by a set of unusual features (Fig. 1.1). The eyes are placed high and slant downward. The nose is prominent and elongated. A double-line contour, suggestive of a pendulous fold of skin, extends from the eyes around the face. The face appears to grow directly out of the shoulders. On either side of the face occur lateral projections consisting of a long pointed flap over horizontal strokes. It is these projections which Marshall considered to be the profiles of a three-headed proto-Śiva. However, the projections as well as the entire group of features correlate well with archaeological remains recently found within the Indus context itself.

Again from the Harappan period at Kalibangan comes evidence which clarifies the seal's iconography. A terracotta bull, very similar to the typical Mohenjo-daro bull figurines, is of interest on account of the way its dewlap is depicted.[23] The folds of skin hanging loose below the neck of the Kalibangan bull are indicated by a series of wavy incised lines that closely resemble the lines which contour the face on seal 420. Does the face on seal 420 also have a dewlap? It is indeed likely, as quite a number of other bovine features have been subtly integrated into the face.

The degree to which bovine features and proportions are integrated is best seen when the face on seal 420 is compared to several horned masks also from Mohenjo-daro.[24] The masks are in the main anthropomorphic and theriomorphic. A certain type of mask however seems to fall between the two categories. That is, this type of mask is different from the set of human horned masks because it has a more animal-like look. However, when compared to the masks of a typical Indus bull, certain human features and proportions can also be discerned. Apparently, this type of mask depicts a humanized bucranium whose features compare very well with those on the face of seal 420. Both show the vanishing brow, the small lozenge-shaped eyes, the snout-like nose and the slight indication of a dewlap.

The face on seal 420 shows additional points of comparison with another humanized bucranium head painted on a vessel from Kot Diji, a site 25 miles northeast of Mohenjo-Daro; the vessel comes from the site's pre-Harappan occupation deposits. The painted design shows a head adorned with huge stylized horns, the upward curving striated tips of which nearly touch. Within the curvature of each horn is a large six-petalled flower. "From the junction of the horns seems to 'hang' down an elongated human head, its chin and cheeks shown in black dots, the low forehead, and the upper part of the long drooping ears in solid black".[25] Sankalia considers the design to represent a humanized bucranium head. He identifies the horns as those of a bull and considers the type as the direct predecessor of the figure on Mohenjo-Daro seal No. 420. A comparison may also be ventured between the ears of the painted humanized bucranium and the flap-like projections on either side of the 420 face. To consider these projections as ears of the humanized bucranium is of course very suitable; however the significance of the extension below the ears remains unresolved.

Even so, the weight of the evidence goes counter to Marshall's idea of a tricephalic proto-Śiva, wearing, in his *paśupati* aspect, an enigmatic headdress. Instead there emerges the manly face of a bucranium whose headdress distinguishes him as a fertility figure and whose human body is poised on a dais in convincing yogic fashion[25a(*)]. The question whether he is a bull-man or a buffalo-man is becoming resolved in favor of the latter. Based on the Balakot evidence noted above, and that cited by Hiltebeitel,[26] it is more likely that the horns worn by the deity are those of a buffalo.

Perhaps the Indus Civilization will some day reveal the identity of this divine buffalo-man. For the moment only one thing seems clear to those who have studied and commented upon the seal in the last few years[27]—the figure can no longer be considered a 'proto-Śiva'. Rather, as Stella Kramrisch has recently proposed in her book, *The Presence of Śiva,* the figure, by whatever name it is called, represented in the Indus context "power". The bovine power is symbolized by the horns; the yogic power is symbolized by the posture. Together they coalesce to convey the superior power possessed by this prehistoric deity.[28]

B. THE SO-CALLED LIṄGA AND YONĪ STONES FROM INDUS CENTERS (Fig. 1.2)

Marshall's initial glossing of the dome-shaped pieces as *liṅga*-shaped stones has been virtually accepted ever since. As recently as 1979, Raymond Allchin, in a seminar paper on the legacy of the Indus Civilization, speaks of the presence of stone or terracotta *"liṅga"* at sites such as Mohenjo-daro, Harappa and Surkotada, and builds upon that supposition.[29] But here too problems arise, as Sankalia may have suspected when several years ago he noted that the *"liṅgas"* of Mohenjo-daro were found in streets and in drains and were not enshrined in rooms as one would expect sacred objects to be.[30]

Before outlining the problems, it may be well to describe the nature of these objects. Marshall distinguished two types.[31] The first type separates the domed top from the base by a groove or ridge (Fig. 1.2, Nos. 2, 4, 5); the second type shows no separation (Fig. 1.2, Nos. 1, 3). The first type can measure between half an inch and a foot; the second type can also be very small, or can measure up to two or three feet. On the whole, the smaller ones much predominate over the larger ones. They are all, to some degree, conventionalized in shape; this is particularly true of the smaller ones which resemble a thimble. Some have a hole at the base and Marshall conjectured that it served to affix the *liṅga* stone to the *yonī* base. It is clear however that Marshall was not very happy with the two types he was able to distinguish. He considered it unlikely that two different conventionalized forms should have been produced during the Mature Harappan period at a given site. He writes that he nevertheless chose to interpret the second, more abstract, shape as a phallic emblem, because its shape is so similar to the majority of phallic stones found in medieval and modern India. He illustrates his

Fig. 1.2. Indus cones and ringstones.

point with a photograph of a modern Śiva-*liṅga* such as can still be found in Indian bazaars, in his time and ours.[32]

It is certainly true that from the Gupta and post-Gupta periods onward, to the end of the medieval period and into modern times, the form of the Śiva-*liṅga* is predominantly an abstract and conventionlized form.[33] For example, the *liṅga* installed in the Śiva temple assumes an uninterrupted silhouette, composed of three parts which merge into each other. The fully developed tripartite *liṅgas* have a circular upper part, an octagonal central portion and a square base which is usually hidden within the *yonī-pīṭha.*[34] There is also a successive reduction in size so that the later ones appear as "inconspicuous small *liṅgas* of thimble size".[35] In essence, the *liṅgas* from about the fifth or sixth centuries AD onward provide scant if any reference to the phallic form.

However, this had not always been the case. Post-Gupta *liṅgas* evolved from a very different type, and that is why problems arise. Unlike the later ones, the earliest *liṅgas* are anatomically realistic, huge, and found mainly in those regions that, unlike the Indus Civilization, are strongholds of the Vedic tradition.

A brief survey of important pre-Gupta *liṅgas* is most instructive.[36] The earliest *liṅga,* the Gudimallam *liṅga,* is undoubtedly also the most realistic. It is housed in the Parasurāmeśvara Temple, District Chitoor in Andhra Pradesh. Discovered in 1903, it has recently received intense re-examination as a result of an excavation and conservation project undertaken by the South-Eastern Circle of the Archaeological Survey of India. The project entailed digging beneath the temple's *garbhagṛha* and exposing the hidden part of the icon.[37] The excavator, I.K. Sarma, would date the icon to the 2nd century BC. A date of the 1st century AD has been recently proposed by von Mitterwallner in her careful stylistic analysis of the piece.[33] Although these and other opinions regarding the date differ markedly, all acknowledge the Gudimallam *liṅga* to be both the earliest and the least conventionalized form. The *liṅga* stands 5′ in height above the ground. The cylindrical shaft is 1′ thick. The nut is not an abstract dome, rather it is anatomically realistic. It projects considerably beyond the shaft and its edge is turned slightly upward. The raised ridge on the upper shaft enters the triangular portion of the nut. The seven-sided shaft is undivided for its entire length down to the square portion which fits—without benefit of holes—into the circular ring stones of varying diameters.[38] In fact, the Gudimallam icon is the earliest *liṅga-pīṭha* known to date. What is more, it is the earliest known Śiva-*liṅga* which closely resembles a phallus.

It is not within the scope of this paper to consider the other iconographic elements of the Gudimallam *liṅga.* We should however not leave this icon without observing the point first made by D.R. Bhandarkar, namely that the connection between phallicism and Śaivism had perhaps not then been definitely established, since the artist felt it necessary to carve the figure of Śiva upon this huge *liṅga.*[39]

Slightly later than the Gudimallam *liṅga,* other realistic *liṅgas* which I would date *c.* 1st century BC, have been found. There is the free-standing plain *liṅga* found at Mathurā (U.P.) and now housed in the State Museum, Lucknow (SML No. Hl).[40] It features the projecting nut with a central fold and decorated with a wide band. The top is evenly rounded off. The shaft is cylindrical. The *liṅga* measures 38.2" in height above ground, and is 10.2" in width. The *liṅga* has a rectangular socle intended for insertion into the ground. There are no base holes here, or on any of the early *liṅgas* described here. A similar *liṅga* is depicted on a relief showing a scene of *liṅga* worship. The relief comes from Mathurā and is now found in the Government Museum of Mathurā (No. 3625).[41] The worshippers, fantastic composite creatures, approach the *liṅga,* which corresponds in realism to the Gudimallam *liṅga,* and of which, like the preceding free-standing Mathurā *liṅga,* a simple band decorates the nut. Another example, again from Mathurā, belongs to the Philadelphia Museum of Art (No. 70.221.1).[42] It is an *ekamukha liṅga,* that is a *liṅga* displaying one head of Śiva upon the shaft. Noteworthy is the combination of the abstract, dome-shaped top of the glans, and the more realistic lower portion. The stone sculpture probably dates around the time of the Christian era and shows that tendencies towards conventionalization are beginning to appear.

Liṅgas from the next phase (*c.* 1st–3rd century AD) illustrate further changes, though realism continues to dominate. As in the preceding phase, the main examples stem from a limited geographic area. There is a colossal (5′ in height) Ekamukha Liṅga from Aghāpura (District Bharatpur, Rajasthan), a site close to Mathurā's cultural climate in antiquity.[43] It continues the same realism seen in the plain and *ekamukha* Mathurā *liṅgas* of the previous phase. From Mathurā itself, come several *liṅgas.* (i) A free-standing *liṅga* measuring 2′8" in height (Government Museum, Mathurā No. 2885). (ii) A huge stone *liṅga* attaining a height of 6′6" (Government Museum, Mathurā No. 15.652).[44] It has a roughly-squared lower portion which was probably inserted into the *yonī-pīṭha.* The shaft rises from a floral base. The nut or glans is 2′ across, and is decorated with two thick jewelled bands which are joined together by a lotus medallion. (iii) Another large *liṅga* comes from Chauma (District Mathurā); it has a lion, a jar, *śrīmukha* and a *gaṇa* at the base.[44] (iv) A plain *liṅga* set on an altar is depicted on a Mathurā relief (Government Museum, Mathurā No. 36.2661)[45] showing foreign (i.e. Indo-Scythian) worshippers bringing garland offerings to the *liṅga.*[45a(*)]

All these free-standing *liṅgas* appear to be quite large. All except the Chauma *liṅga* have the nut projecting beyond the shaft. Though the *liṅga* in worship nearly dispenses with the projection, it nevertheless differentiates the glans from the rest of the phallus by two distinctly incised curves meeting at a point and called the Brahmasūtras. Thus the second phase in the evolution of the *liṅga*-form begins the course leading to the later uninterrupted silhouette and unrealistic shape. These characteristics become dominant in the third phase, dating to the Gupta age,[46] and are established by the fourth, the last phase comprising approximately the fifth century AD to the end of the medieval period.[47]

The first conclusion to be drawn from this quick survey is that the earlier the *liṅga,* the more realistic and larger its form. That is, the closer the time the *liṅga* approaches the prehistoric period, the less it looks like the cone-shaped Indus objects.

The second conclusion stems from the discreet geographical distribution of the early *lingas.* If the find-places of these *liṅgas* are plotted on a historical map, then the region of all, except the Gudimallam *liṅga,* is precisely the area identified as Āryāvarta ("the country of the Aryans") by the *Mānava Dharmaśāstra.*[48] Further, if we confine ourselves to examples in stone,[49] the provenance narrows to a small group of urban centers around the Doab, having the Mathurā region as centre. This region in the centuries around the Christian era was "the acknowledged standard bearer in the propagation of brahmanical life".[50] The *Mānava Dharmaśāstra* specifies that the tract in the Doab comprising the region around Delhi to Mathurā, capital of the ancient Śūrasena, is designated as the country of the Brahmanical seers *(brahmārṣideśa;* II.19).

On the other hand, in the entire region north of Mathurā, extending northwards and northwestwards—into Sind, the Punjab, the Hindu Kush – to southern Bactria and the Indo-Iranian borderlands, no representation of *liṅgas* are found in any medium during the early periods.[51]

To maintain that the Indus stones are the prototypes of the later *Śiva-liṅgas* one would need to explain not only their abstract shape vis-à-vis the realism of the early undisputed *Śiva-liṅgas,* but also the absence of *liṅgas* in the North for more than two millennia. Especially their absence in the North during the time of their presence in Āryāvarta, a totally distinct culture, would need considerable explanation. This explanation would probably need to take into account the implications stemming from the site of Bhagwanpura in Eastern Punjab. This site shows stratigraphic connections between late Harappan pottery and Painted Grey Ware, the ware usually associated with the Aryans.[52]

Finally an important buttress for the *liṅga* identification has also given way. I refer to the Mohenjo-Daro chert or limestone ring stones, so often interpreted, as Marshall did, as the *yonī*-rings associated with the *liṅga* stones (Fig. 1.2, No. 6). When the archaeologist E. Mackay first described the 27 ring stones found in the HR area, he hesitatingly suggested their possible architectural use;[53] in his later report, he clearly considers them as architectural stones, perhaps as parts of stone columns.[54] The possibility for yet another function is introduced by George Dales in a forthcoming paper which discusses these stones. He reports that Dr. Michael Jansen, head of a German team making architectural studies at Mohenjo-Daro, measured and studied all these ring stones in detail and feels that the rings may have been used in making astronomical calculations.[55] Dales correctly observes that if the stone objects, cones and rings, had cultic or religious functions within the Harappan religion, then one would expect that such stones would be found at all Harappan sites. But they are not. Dales does not consider the ring stones as *yonī*-rings and indeed concludes that "there is no archaeological evidence to support claims of special sexually oriented aspects of Harappan religion.[56]

The argument for Śiva's origin in the Indus civilization has always rested mainly on the interpretation of the seal, and of the stones – both the cones and the ring stones. The case presented here is that this argument should be dropped.

NOTES AND REFERENCES

1. An earlier version of this paper was presented in the AAR Hinduism Group's panel "The Indus Valley and Hinduism: an update" at the annual meeting of the American Academy of Religion in December 1981. I wish to express my appreciation to Thomas J. Hopkins, panel chairman and John S. Hawley, coordinator of the Hinduism program, for providing the context in which these ideas could be shared.
2. See Sir John Marshall, *Mohenjo-daro and the Indus civilization I,* London, 1931, 46; Pl. XI and Fig. 1.
3. Marshall, *Mohenjo-daro III,* Pl. 94, Fig. 11.
4. Stella Kramrisch, *The Presence of Śiva,* Princeton, 1981, 12.
5. Marshall, *Mohenjo-daro I,* Ch. V.
6. Marshall, *Mohenjo-daro I,* 52–56.

7. Marshall, *Mohenjo-daro I*, 52.
8. For a lengthier discussion and re-examination of these criteria, see my "The so-called Proto-Śiva seal from Mohenjo-daro: An Iconological Assessment", *Archives of Asian Art*, XXIX, 1975–76, 47–58. It will be in *Listening to Icons*, Vol. II.
9. See Srinivasan, "So-called Proto-Śiva seal", Fig. 4.
10. Srinivasan, "So-called Proto-Śiva seal", Figs. 2 and 3.
11. George F. Dales, "Excavations at Balakot, Pakistan, 1973", *Journal of Field Archaeology*, I, 1974, 3–22. I am grateful to George Dales for drawing my attention during the panel discussion to the comparative material at this site.
12. Dales, "Balakot", 14.
13. Dales, "Balakot", 14–17.
14. See Edith Porada (ed.), *Corpus of Ancient Near Eastern Seals. The Collection of the Pierpont Morgan Library*, Washington, D.C., 1948, I, Pl. XXX, No. 198E.
15. Edith Porada, *Mesopotamian Art in Cylinder Seals of the Pierpont Morgan Library*, New York, 1947, 34.
16. e.g. H. P. Sullivan, "A Re-examination of the Religion of the Indus Civilization", *History of Religions*, IV, 1964, 120.
17. See A.D. Pusalker, *Vedic Age*, Vol. I in R.C. Majumdar and A.D. Pusalker (ed.), *History and Culture of the Indian People*, London, 1951, 187.
18. See Srinivasan, "So-called Proto-Śiva seal", 55.
19. *Ibid.*, Fig. 12.

19a. ADDENDUM: Since this paper was written, it is becoming more difficult to maintain that the pose on Seal 420 is a yoga or proto-yoga pose. The hands are held too loosely to fit a yoga posture. The position of the crossed legs occur in a variety of subjects on early coins and sculpture. A sitting posture with crossed legs can be seen with royalty on early Indian coinage. Maues (early 1st century BC) the first Indo-Scythian king is depiected seated in this manner, as is Azes (who initiated a dynastic era in 58/57 BC). Among the Kuṣāṇas, Wima Khadphises and Huviṣka sit with their legs loosely crossed on coinage they issue. Religious personages, especially Buddhist deities also assume this posture. Two well known and dated examples, among many others that could be cited, are the Buddha on the Bimaran reliquary (early 1st century AD) and the Bodhisattva Maitreya (on a Kaniṣka I drachm from Taxila, thus datable to 127–150 AD).

The cummulative evidence indicates that the crossed legged position is evocative of authority, be it political, ascetic, etc.; it is also a pose that promotes stability and erectness of the upper body. The resultant effect is one of power, authority, prestige and immutability. The figure seated in this manner on the Indus seal ought to be a divinity, an identity buttressed by the aforementioned imagery on the faience Mohenjo-daro sealing.

20. *Ibid.*, 56.
21. *Ibid.*; Alf Hiltebeitel, "The Indus Valley 'Proto-Śiva', reexamined through reflections on the goddess, the buffalo, and the symbolism of *vāhanas*", *Anthropos*, LXXIII, 1978, especially 769–70.
22. Srinivasan, "So-called Proto-Śiva seal".
23. *Ibid.* Fig. 6.
24. For details see Srinivasan, "So-called Proto-Śiva seal", 51–5 and Figs. 7–11.
25. H.D. Sankalia, "Kot Diji and Hissar III", *Antiquity*, XLIII, 1969, 142.

25a. ADDENDUM: Please refer to updated information in footnote 19a.

26. Hiltebeitel, "Proto-Śiva, reexamined", 771–73.

27. Hiltebeitel, "Proto-Śiva, reexamined"; Walter A. Fairservis, Jr., *Excavations at Allahdino I: Seals and Inscribed Material, Papers of the Allahdino Expedition* 1976, New York, 1976, 14–15; Cf. Stella Kramrisch, *Śiva,* 11 ff.; Srinivasan, "So-called Proto-Śiva seal", 47 ff.
28. Kramrisch, *Śiva,* 14.
29. F.R. Allchin, "The legacy of the Indus civilization", in Gregory L. Possehl (ed.), *Harappan Civilization,* Warminster, England, 1982, 325–33.
30. H.D. Sankalia, *Proceedings of the 57th Indian Science Congress,* Kharagpur, 1970, 182–83.
31. Marshall, *Mohenjo-daro,* I, pp. 59–61; 63; Pls. XIII and XIV.
32. Marshall, *Mohenjo-daro,* I, pp. 59–60; Pl. XIII, No.8.
33. For a recent stylistic analysis of the development of the *liṅga* form see Gritli v. Mitterwallner, "Evolution of the Liṅga" in Michael W. Meister (ed.), *Discourses on Śiva: Proceedings of a Symposium on the Nature of Religious Imagery,* Philadelphia, 1984, pp. 12-31.
34. v. Mitterwallner, "Liṅga".
35. v. Mitterwallner, "Liṅga".
36. Additional art-historical and textual information is given in D. Srinivasan, "Significance and Scope of Pre-Kuṣāṇa Śaivite Iconography" in Michael W. Meister (ed.), *Discourses on Śiva: Proceedings of a Symposium on the Nature of Religious Imagery,* Philadelphia, 1984, pp. 32-46. This paper appears in this volume; see pp. 48-73.
37. See I. K. Sarma, "New Light on Art through Archaeological Conservation", *Journal of the Indian Society of Oriental Art,* New Series, X, 1978–1979, 48–54; Pl. XIV–XV.
38. See Sarma, Pl. XV, 11, 12.
39. J.N. Banerjea, ("The Phallic Emblem in Ancient and Mediaeval India", *Journal of the Indian Society of Oriental Art,* III, 1935, 39) states that Bhandarkar suggests this in the Carmichael Lectures, 1921, p. 20.
40. N. P. Joshi, *Catalogue of the Brahmanical sculptures in the State Museum, Lucknow,* Lucknow, 1972, 103.
41. It is illustrated in N. P. Joshi, *Mathurā sculptures,* Mathurā, 1966, Fig. 10 and p. 80.
42. It is illustrated in Stella Kramrisch, *Manifestations of Shiva,* Philadelphia, 1981, Pl. 1.
43. See Shiv S. Lal, *Catalogue and Guide to the State Museum,* Bharatpur, 1960–61, 9.
44. Illustrated in Joshi, *Brahmanical Sculptures,* Figs. 33–35. It should be noted that No. 15.652 is incorrectly cited as No. 15.657.
45. Published in John M. Rosenfield, *The Dynastic Arts of the Kushans,* Berkeley and Los Angeles, 1967, Fig. 41.

45a. ADDENDUM: The latest study of this relief shows that it has been recarved from an initial Buddhist subject.

46. v. Mitterwallner, "Liṅga", observes that in this phase, the head of the *liṅga* is differentiated from its shaft only by shallow, incised lines, that is, the head no longer projects beyond the shaft.
47. See v. Mitterwallner, "Liṅga".
48. *MDhs* 2.22: "The wise call Āryāvarta the land which lies between these two mountain ranges (i.e. the Vindhya and the Himavat) and which extends to the eastern and western oceans".
49. The *liṅga* may be found on coins from Ujjain prior to the Christian era. On the obverse of Allan's "variety e," of class I Ujjayinī coppers, the *liṅga* is seen between two different trees in railings. See John Allan, *Catalogue of the Coins of Ancient India,* London, 1936, 243, No. 19; Pl. 36, No. 15. A humped bull faces the *liṅga* on the reverse of the Ārjunāyana copper coin-type, "variety b". See Allan, *Catalogue,* 121, Pl. 14, No. 11. The land of the

Ārjunāyanas probably lay within the Delhi-Jaipur-Agra triangle, and the coins date to circa 2nd century AD.

50. Norvin Hein, "Kālayavana: a key to Mathurā's cultural self-perception", in D. Srinivasan (ed.), *Mathura: The Cultural Heritage*, South Asia Publications; American Institute of Indian Studies, New Delhi, 1989.
51. See Srinivasan, "Pre-Kuṣāṇa Śaivite Iconography" (cf. n. 36 above).
52. For a summary, assessment and relevant further bibliography on this site, see Jim G. Shaffer, "The Protohistoric Period in Eastern Punjab: A Preliminary Assessment" in A.H. Dani (ed.), *Indus Civilization: New Perspectives*, Islamabad, 1981, 81–3. I am grateful to Jim Shaffer for informing me about this significant site.
53. See his discussion in Marshall, *Mohenjo-daro*, II, 473–5.
54. E. Mackay, *Further excavations at Mohenjo-daro*, I, Delhi, 1938, 595–8; II, Pl. CXIV.
55. George F. Dales, "Sex and Stones at Mohenjo-daro", in B.B. Lal and S.P. Gupta (eds.), *Frontiers of the Indus Civilization*, New Delhi, 1984, pp. 109-115. I wish to express my thanks to the author for generously making this paper available to me.
56. Dales. "Sex and stones".

2

Vedic Rudra-Śiva

In the study of religious phenomena leading up to the development of Hinduism, the idea has long been held that Śaivism arose largely out of a non-Aryan context, and that the Vedic forerunner of Śiva, namely Rudra, reflects a hesitant accommodation between Aryan and non-Aryan beliefs in many Vedic passages which describe him. Several factors have contributed to this point of view. Undoubtedly a major impetus was provided some seventy years ago by a proposal to interpret the figure of an engraved Indus Valley seal as an ithyphallic, tricephallic "yogi," who on that account offered marked similarities with post-Gupta Śiva icons. In effect, this interpretation postulated a proto-Śiva arising from a pre- and non-Aryan sector of Indian civilization. Although there had been periodic dissatisfaction with this position, the seal's identification has only recently been reassessed from the perspectives of several different disciplines. Findings from the domains of religion,[1] art history and philology[2] conclude that this position is no longer tenable. Recent writings in the fields of archaeology and Indology also no longer work with this premise.[3] Freed thus from the proposition of a proto-Śiva already existing in a non-Aryan society prior to the Vedic age, and from the consequent need to attempt harmonizing the Vedic descriptions of Rudra with Indus material remains, this seems like the right time to look afresh at the Vedic descriptions. An evaluation can now be considerably furthered by works in the last several decades which permit refinements in our understanding of what is predominantly pre-Vedic, Vedic-Aryan, non-Vedic Aryan and post-Vedic Aryan. These distinctions were certainly made in ancient times. The *Manusmṛti*

Originally published in the *Journal of the American Oriental Society*, Vol. 103, 3, 1983; pp. 543-56. Reprinted with stylistic change, addenda and with permission of the American Oriental Society.

(II. 17–23), in discussing the sources of sacred law, distinguishes different regions in northern India graded according to their adherence to the law. In this way, the tract of non-Aryans *(mleccha-)* is set apart from the country of the Aryans (Aryāvarta), which is further distinguished by regions which are strongholds of Brahmanism, or the Vedic Aryans. Manu's distinctions, based on geography, culture and purity are becoming somewhat more clear to us. Thanks to comparative studies in linguistics, religion, philology and history as well as new archaeological findings, there is a greater awareness of those features which may be central to Vedic thought, those which are tangential and those which are unrepresentative.[4] As such, this paper considers a basic question: Is Rudra "the outsider" reluctantly brought into the Vedic fold, or is he "an insider" closely related to distinctive components of Vedic thought. The study does not consider anew the identification of the original character of Rudra in the Vedas; Gonda's hypothesis on the essence of the Rudra-power in the *Rig Veda* is found to be eminently workable for that text[5] and a sound basis for Rudra's development in post-Rig Vedic texts. Instead, the aim of the paper is to determine whether that transcendental power experienced as Rudra and manifesting itself in the god's features and functions is alienated from, or allied to the core of the Vedic tradition.

Previous analyses of Rudra in the Vedas have been mainly concerned with identifying his original character.[6] In weighing his particular traits against those of Vedism, a wide discrepancy has been noted which has been explained by Rudra's non-Vedic origins. To summarize, it is often noted that Rudra plays an insignificant role in the Vedic *śrauta*-sacrifices and that he is absent in the Soma sacrifice.[7] His radical ambiguity, consisting of a benign aspect and a wrathful aspect, is seen as atypical;[8] that is, both his twofold nature and the darker side of that nature are deemed sharply different from most other Vedic gods.[9] Rudra's anthropomorphism is considered rather unusual. In contradistinction to other Vedic gods, a considerable number of his physical traits have been recorded and these are judged to be uncharacteristically Vedic. Thus, he is thousand-eyed (*AV* 11.2.2,7); his belly is blue and his back is red (*AV* 15.1.7,8). He is blue-necked (*VS* 16.7) and blue-tufted (*AV* 2.27.6). He is copper colored, red and brown (*VS* 16.6 = *TS* 4.5.li). His hair may by braided and knotted like a cowrie shell[10] (*RV* 1.114.1, 5; *TS* 4.5.5d; 5.9c). Rudra's distance from Vedic gods and rites is believed to be signaled by these points, together with his association with chthonian creatures,[11] his protection of nefarious beings (such as assailers, robbers, burglars and pilferers, see *TS* 4.5.3a,c,d,f) and his worship among the Vrātyas, an Aryan group outside of the Brahmanic culture (*AV* 15.1,5).

Most of these points will be answered below under two sections: "Rudra-Śiva and the Vedic pantheon" and "Rudra-Śiva and the Vedic ritual." However, as the question of Rudra's appearance and his protection of dangerous and seemingly undesirable ritual groups is better reserved for consideration elsewhere,[12] the general outline of the argument may be met here. An intensification of Rudra's appearance and an amplification of his domain occur mainly in the post-Rig Vedic Saṃhitās.[13] In those texts, Rudra is decidedly on his way to becoming *the* great god promulgated by the *Śvetāśvatara Upaniṣad*. In this process, Rudra's features and affiliations are no longer meant to convey mythic or literal images. Rather, the sum of his traits is meant to impart a theological statement on the absoluteness of the Supreme, experienced as God. Such a god encompasses everything, gives rise to everything and is Lord of everything. A benchmark in this process is of course the Śatarudrīya litany of the *YV* (i.e., the *TS* 4.5 and *VS* 16. citations noted above).[14] Indeed it has been recognized that this litany appears to be a literary description of Rudra in his *viśvarūpa*-form.[15] Accordingly Rudra's seemingly negative characteristics are the necessary counterpoise which together with the benevolent characteristics represent for the Yajur Vedins the concept of divine totality. An example of this principle of opposites working to define God in the Śatarudrīya is found in the sections immediately preceding and succeeding section 4.5.3 in the *Taittirīya Saṃhitā* which mentions Rudra's lordship over dangerous societal elements (i.e., lord of assailers, etc.). *TS* 5.4.2 and 4 praise him as lord of such favorable environmental elements as cattle, food, fields, forests, chariots, etc. The Atharva Vedins, in attributing to Rudra heightened ambivalency, omniscience, multiple forms and fusion with Agni, further increase his majesty.[16] The radical intensification of Rudra's appearance and actions may thus be viewed as speculative attempts within the Vedic tradition to define the nature of the all-encompassing Supreme God.

1. RUDRA-ŚIVA AND THE VEDIC PANTHEON

This section analyses the various gods sharing significant philological and/or religious features with Rudra-Śiva. These gods, it will be observed, are the most well known of the Vedic divinities. There is thus no need in this study to provide the sort of overview of the gods' general traits as may be found in the standard surveys on Vedic religion and mythology.[17] The ensuing discussion is comprehensive only with respect to those features that Rudra-Śiva has in common with other Vedic gods. Greatest emphasis is placed on comparative material from the Saṃhitās.

1.1 *Varuṇa and Mitra-Varuṇa*

The god Varuṇa as well as the dual divinity Mitra-Varuṇa belong, as does Rudra, to a special group of gods called Asuras. In the Saṃhitās, the Asuras are a primordial group which include both gods and demons possessing the potential to create the truly wondrous, including life itself. The *Rig Veda* states that the *asura* power is an intrinsic part of Rudra's nature.[18] But of all the Vedic gods, the title of Asura belongs pre-eminently to Varuṇa. In the *RV*, he is most often called *asura-* than any other god;[19] he continues to be the Asura *par excellence* in the

AV[20] and the *TS* repeats the appellation.[21] The dual divinity Mitra-Varuṇa likewise belongs to this group; the highest and everlasting *asura*-power is theirs.[22] Indeed they are the Asuras of the gods *(devā́nām ásurā),* the lords *(aryā́).*[23]

An ambiguous nature, well recognized as the integral feature of Rudra's divinity, is also characteristic of Varuṇa and Mitra-Varuṇa. With respect to Rudra, the union of opposites, or *coincidentia oppositorum,* is expressed throughout the Vedas by breaking up his twofold nature into myriad refractions. The *RV* already recognizes the ambiguities; he is described not only as *ugrá* ('powerful, formidable' 2.33.9,11), but also as *mīḍhvas* ('the bounteous one,[24] 1.114.3), *śivá* ('auspicious' 10.92.9) and having a merciful hand (*mṛḷayā́kur hásta* 2.33.7). By the time of the Śatarudrīya hymn, his twofold nature becomes his two 'bodies' *(tanū-,* i.e., manifestations). One body is *śiva,* not terrible *(ághora-)* and appears free from evil *(apāpakāśin-);*[25] the other is, by implication, wrathful *(manyu-* cf. *TS* 4.5.1a). These qualifiers may also be used as appellations in the god's worship; he is Ugra (The powerful One) and Bhīma (The fearful One, see *TS* 4.5.8c) as well as Śiva and Śivatara (The more auspicious One, *TS* 4.5.81). This is of course quite well known.[26] Equally well known to Vedic scholars,[27] though not emphasized sufficiently in works dealing with Rudra, is that Varuṇa is also an ambiguous god. Varuṇa has some awesome qualities in common with Rudra. Varuṇa shows his wrath *(manyu- RV* 1.24.6) towards transgressors of the law (cf. *RV* 7.86.3), and his snares (*RV* 1.24. 15) and spies (*RV* 7.87.3) bespeak of his role as punisher of sinful man. The dual divinity Mitra-Varuṇa also has a dreaded side: the sacrificer who stints with offerings risks incurring consumption (cf. *RV* 1.122.9). Varuṇa also has a gracious aspect. He can remove sin like a loosened rope (cf. *RV* 2.28.5; 5.85.7,8); he can be merciful (✓ *mṛḍ* RV 7.89.1–4) and grant forgiveness (cf. 7.89.5). Just as Rudra's auspicious aspect dwells on his healing powers (*RV* 2.33.2; *VS* 3.59 ≃ TS 1.8.6g) so is Varuṇa the lord of physicians (*VS* 21.40). Varuṇa has a hundred, a thousand remedies and can drive away death (*RV* 1.24.9); he can increase a lifespan (*RV* 1.25.12) or take it away (*RV* 1.24.11). Likewise can Mitra-Varuṇa be called upon to save the sacrificer (*RV* 5.70.3) and give wealth, welfare and happiness to his offspring (*RV* 5.69.3).

Just as Rudra is associated with North (e.g., *ŚB* 2,6,2,5 and 7; 5,4,2,10), so too is the dual deity. In a section dealing with the reverence paid to the Fire in piling up the bricks of the Fire-Altar (*Ap ŚS* 17.7.6), *TS* 5.5.8.3 says, 'With the northern direction I place you down, with the Anuṣṭubh meter, with Mitra-Varuṇa as deity ...'. The association between the dual deity and the North occurs repeatedly in the Saṃhitās and Brāhmaṇas.[28] Since the vast majority of Vedic gods abide in the East, the place of the rising sun, the regularity with which Rudra and Mitra-Varuṇa are coordinated with the North is somewhat unusual. Moreover, a wider network of interconnections between other gods and other directions can be established. Soma too is connected with the North (*AV* 3.27.4). The pair Soma-and-Rudra are called regents of the North in ŚŚS 6.3.4. In addition, Soma is cited in connection with the western quarter (*AV* 12.3.9) as are Mitra-Varuṇa and Varuṇa.[29] These interconnections do not seem to be fortuitous; they imply conceptual affinities which need to be further analysed.

Another shared characteristic is receival of a sacrificial offering which is less than perfect. Rudra may receive that which is injured (*ŚB* 1,7,4,9). Mitra and Varuṇa may be proffered a barren cow. The reason why, explains *ŚB* 4,5,1,6 is that Mitra takes the well-offered part of one's sacrifice and Varuṇa the ill-offered part.[30]

Lastly, the power of omniscience is attributed to Rudra and Varuṇa by way of referring to their all-comprehensive sight (i.e., knowledge).[31] Thus Varuṇa is ascribed 'a thousand eyes' in the *Rig Veda* (7.34.10) and the *Atharva Veda* continues to assume the god's capacity for total knowledge.[32] As for Rudra, he is descibed as having 'a thousand eyes' more frequently than any other deity in the *AV*,[33] and the Śatarudrīya continues to mention this particular attribute (*TS* 4.5.1i; 11; 5e).

It may be assumed that the considerable number of shared characteristics between these sets of gods implies that some sort of conceptual link was understood to exist between them. Indeed, this linkage seems to be directly affirmed in one *RV* hymn (5.70) where the noun *rudrā-* is repeatedly applied to the dual deity Mitra-Varuṇa.

For our purposes, the most interesting aspect of this comparative data is its cultural implications. Varuṇa and Mitra-Varuṇa can be traced to an Aryan context which predates the Vedic period in India. The well-known inscription of the Mitanni Aryans mentions side by side Mitra and Aruna (generally understood to signify Varuṇa); thus the Aryan historicity of these two gods goes back to the Middle East of 1380 BC. Regarding their Indo-Iranian background, the many associations and similarities between Vedic Varuṇa and Avestan Ahura Mazda have received consistent notice, even though Varuṇa's name does not occur in the *Avesta*. Mitra is, of course, as Mithra mentioned in the *Avesta* and has a number of traits in common with the Vedic counterpart.[34] Direct evidence of an Avestan equivalent for the Vedic Mitra-Varuṇa is lacking although Gonda in his study on dual deities concludes that both gods "were already in the Indo-Iranian period and consequently also in prehistoric India more closely allied to one another than to many other members of the pantheon and than many other deities which had associated themselves with one another."[35] The Aryan antiquity of these gods has significant bearing upon the problem of Rudra's cultural source. The first conclusion to be drawn is that in the earliest stratum of Vedic texts, the Saṃhitās, Rudra shares numerous features with deities who are not only important in the Saṃhitās, but whose Aryan roots go back farther than the *RV Saṃhitā*. Second, the shared features are central to Rudra's nature. The possibility thus arises that some primary Vedic Aryan traits may belong to Rudra from the outset.

1.2 Indra

Several of the similarities between Rudra and Indra are the same as those between Rudra and Varuṇa, and Mitra-Varuṇa. Indra too is an *asura* in the *RV*, though he is more frequently called *deva*.[36] Evidently he belongs to a category of gods known as Asura Devas, a category to which Rudra (*RV* 5.42.11) and Mitra-Varuṇa (*RV* 8.25.4) also belong. Then too, Indra has a kindly and a fearful side, distinguished by terminology already noted for Rudra's two aspects. Thus Indra is *mīḍhvas* ('bounteous, merciful' in *RV* 8.76.7; 10.85.25) as well as *ugrá, ghorá* ('fearful, awesome' in *RV* 7.28.2; cf. 2.12.5). The implication is that Indra (whose ability to project phenomenal manifestations is affirmed in the Saṃhitās)[37] emits outer manifestations *(rūpa-; tanū-)*[37] of a bipolar nature. Indeed the twofold nature of his manifestations is indicated in a number of instances. *RV* 1.4.1 speaks of Indra's "auspicious or good form" *(surūpa-)*,[38] and verse 10 of *RV* 8.85/96 describes him as both *ugrá* as well as *śivátama-* ('most auspicious'). Indra too has an ambivalent relation to the Vedic ritual, resulting no doubt from his dreadful act of killing a Brahman. A *Taittirīya Saṃhitā* tale (2.5.1,2) recounts how Indra beheads Viśvarūpa, the priest of the Gods and Asuras, and how he is excluded, on that account, from the Soma rite performed by Viśvarūpa's father, Tvaṣṭṛ (*TS* 2.4.12). Analogous exclusions occur in the mythology of Rudra. The *Taittirīya Saṃhitā* indicates that the gods barred Rudra from the sacrifice (2.6.8.2), and the *Aitareya Brāhmaṇa* (3.34) recounts how the gods deprived Rudra of his part of the offering. These Vedic accounts are no doubt forerunners of the well-known epic legend of Śiva's exclusion from Dakṣa's sacrifice (*MBh.* 12.274.2–58).

Some similarities between Indra and Rudra are distinctively theirs. For example, the Maruts who are most closely allied to Indra are also called the sons of Rudra and are often named Rudras in the *RV*.[39] Noteworthy too is the number of physical similarities that are shared. Both deities are fair-lipped *(suśipra-;* Indra: *RV* 1.9.3, etc.; Rudra: *RV* 2.33.5), thousand-eyed'[40] *(sahasrākṣa-;* Indra-Vāyu: *RV* 1.23.3; Rudra: *AVŚ* 11.23.7,17; *TS* 4.5.5e; *ŚB* 9.1.1.6, etc.), golden armed *(hiraṇyabāhu-;* Indra: *RV* 7.34.4; Rudra: *TS* 4.5.2a), and decked with bow and arrows[41] (Indra: *RV* 8.66/77.6,7,11; 10.103.2,3; Rudra: *TS* 4.5.1 b,k,l,m,n,p).

The importance of these similarities in the present context lies in Indra's unquestionable Vedic importance and pre-Vedic Aryan position. Indra's popularity and centrality in the earliest Indo-Aryan hymnal, the *Rig Veda*, is too well known to warrant further elaboration. The occurrence of references to an Indra in the *Avesta* also needs little repetition.[42] The deity can also be traced back to the 14th century BC; an Indara (Indra) is mentioned immediately after Mitra and Aruna on the Mitanni inscription. As such, Rudra is again seen as having numerous features in common with a deity of the most ancient Aryan stock.

1.3. VĀYU

It may be noted in passing that the minor Vedic wind god, Vāyu, whose Indo-Iranian prehistory is well attested, has several salient traits in common with Rudra. The use of the term *śiva-* (already referred to in connection with Indra; cf. also *RV* 8.52/63.4) is also applied to Vāyu. This is not to place undue importance on the term *śiva-* which has little, if any, discreet value in this period;[43] rather it is to introduce the possibility of Vāyu's inauspicious nature as a correlative to his stated *śiva* nature. Indeed the probability of an Indo-Iranian belief in wind having both good and bad traits which crystallized into a wind deity having a bi-polar nature has been suggested by Gonda.[44] In support it may be noted that Duchesne-Guillemin not only finds indication in the *Avesta* for a double Vāyu (i.e., Yašt 15.5 etc.) but also identifies a dicephalic figure on an Achemenian seal as representing the god Vāyu.[45] The cumulative evidence, based on the brief survey of Vāyu, Indra, Varuṇa and Mitra-Varuṇa strongly indicates that Rudra's pronounced ambivalence, the hallmark of his Vedic "personality" is in actuality a trait he shares with the oldest of Vedic gods.

Vāyu is allied in other ways to the above mentioned gods, implying once again that we may be dealing with a group bonded by some basic commonality. Indra-Vāyu, as noted above, is "a thousand-eyed" deity. Vāyu and Īśāna (Rudra) are mentioned together in a sacrificial context.[46] Vāyu can also father the Maruts (*RV* 1.134.4) and again like Rudra, Vāyu is ascribed healing power, perhaps expressive of the purifying character of the wind.[47] Unlike the aforementioned gods, Vāyu is not specifically called *asura-* in the Saṃhitās. However, it is interesting to observe with Gonda that a considerable number of Vedic references to Vāyu indicate that some of his qualities are distinctive of a high god.[48]

1.4 AGNI

The strongest bonds exist between Rudra and Agni with respect to the characteristics outlined so far. Agni's *asura*-nature is emphasized throughout the Saṃhitās. To the *RV* and *AV* passages cited elsewhere,[49] passages from the *Yajur Veda Saṃhitā* may be added (e.g., *TS* 1.6.6r = 3.1.11 b = *MS* 1.4.3,8 = *KS* 5.6; 32.6 = *RV* 4.2.5; *TS* 4.1.8b; *VS* 27.12).

Agni too has a gracious side as well as a fearful side, evidenced by terminology already given in connection with the bipolar nature of Rudra, et al. Agni is *mīḍhvas* in *RV* 3.16.3; *śiva* in *RV* 7.34.15; 4.11.6; *ghora* in *RV* 4.6.6; *aghora* in the *Gopatha Brāhmaṇa* (1.2.18,2). The dual character of Agni's manifestations is accepted as a religious reality from the *Rig Veda* onwards.[50] *RV* 4.6.6 succinctly notes: "auspicious is your aspect O good-looking Agni, equally esteemed when you become a different, fearful aspect." Knowledge of Agni's fundamental polarities pervades the *Yajur Veda*. The *VS* (12.32 = *TS* 4.2.3c) recognizes that Agni's flames can be both auspicious and harmful. Another example of the doctrine of *coincidentia oppositorum* defining Agni's nature occurs in *VS* 17.11 (= *TS* 4.6.1m);

the Adhvaryu addresses Agni with the request that only one sort of flame come in contact with the sacrificer: "Homage to your flame, your glow; let homage be to your light. May your missiles heat another than us, be purifying and auspicious to us."

Beyond the pronounced bipolarism intrinsic to both Agni and Rudra, these deities have even more in common. There is evidence in the Vedas that one of Agni's aspects, the fearful or *ghora* "body" is in fact Rudra himself.[51] *TS* 2.2.2.3 says it quite clearly: 'Rudra indeed is his [i.e., Agni's] fearful body' *(ghorā tanūr);* the passage goes on to explain that Agni also has a "healing body" *(bheṣajyā tanūr* 2.2.2.4) and states how it may be propitiated. *TS* 5.7.3.3 expands upon the identity of the two; "Agni is indeed Rudra. Two are his bodies, the one fearful *(ghora-)* the other auspicious *(śiva-).* When he offers the Śatarudrīya, he pacifies with it (i.e., the Śatarudrīya) his fearful body; when he offers 'the Stream of Wealth' *(vasor dhārā),* he soothes with it (i.e., the Vasor-Dhārā) the auspicious body." This passage thus not only identifies Rudra as Agni's fearful form or aspect, it also specifies that the Śatarudrīya offering functions to appease the *ghora-* aspect. It is worthwhile to remember that the offering is done upon completion of the Fire altar, the Agnicayana; the offering is accompanied by the litany addressed to the hundred Rudra forms (lit., *śata-rudrīya*). The brāhmaṇa portion (*TS* 5.4.3.1) belonging to the *TS* Śatarudrīya (in 4.5) opens with the same pronouncement, namely that Agni is Rudra, born when the fire altar has been completely piled up. And *TS* 5.5.7.4 reiterates: "Agni is Rudra; just as a tiger stands angry even so now this (god stands); when piled up, he conciliates (him) with these; thus he pacifies him with adorations." In the *ŚB* (9.1.1–44), Rudra is also the metamorphosis of Wrath, mixed with Prajāpati's tears (6), who comes into being when Agni, or the fire altar, has been completed (I). Related conceptualizations remain valid in the *sūtra* literature; if for example, a sacrificer's cattle are being killed by Rudra, it is prescribed that certain offerings together with homage to Agni be made in the Agnihotra rite in order to stop the killing.[52]

Agni's powers lend themselves extremely well to multiplicity imagery. Some of these references to multiple body parts and forms indicate a fusing of Agni and Rudra.[53] It is instructive to compare Agni's description as "thousand-eyed and hundred-headed" in *VS* 17.71 (= *TS* 4.6.5g) with the same description for Rudra in *ŚB* 9.1.1.6. Further, *ŚB* 6.1.3.1–19, in re-counting a myth on the eight forms of Agni, names each form by an appellation closely associated or identified with Rudra-Śiva.[54]

These affinities between Agni and Rudra do not however reveal the complete nature of the latter. Vedic Rudra is not Wrathful Agni alone.[55] Already *TS* 5.5.9i (≘ *AV* 7.87.1) cautions against placing limitations upon the Rudra power: "The Rudra who is in fire *(agni-),* in waters, in plants, that Rudra who has entered all beings, let homage be to that Rudra." That is, the divine power conceptualized as "Rudra" is not just in fire, etc., but in all phenomenality. The pervasiveness of the "Rudra power" is not the only noteworthy point here. Equally significant is the extent of correlation and/or fusion between Rudra and Agni, the god who is the personification of the sacrificial fire. In effect, the affinities between the two gods relate Rudra to the very heart of Vedism. In addition, Agni is another god whose antiquity dates from Indo-Aryan migrations in the Near East. Mentioned on Hittite documents, Agni seems to have been borrowed by the Hittites from the Aryans.

1.5 *Soma*

Rudra has a special relation to the god Soma. Soma is the only god to join as dual deity with Rudra. One hymn in the *RV* (6.74) is dedicated to Soma-Rudra. In the first verse the dual deity is entreated to hold fast to its *asura*-nature, which is characteristic of each god individually.[56] The hymn continues with a plea to Soma-and-Rudra to drive away disease (vs. 2) provide medicines (vs. 3), remove all sins (vs. 3), and wielding sharp weapons, they are asked to be gracious to the adorants (vs. 4). A healing ability, already mentioned in connection with Rudra is separately associated with Soma, who, when embodied in the divine oblation, is believed to be a powerful remedy (e.g., *RV* 8.72.17; 8.79.2; 10.25.11). The last verse of *RV* 6.74 juxtaposes the gods' sharp weaponry, graciousness and agreeableness and suggests that Soma-Rudra possess a twofold nature. Soma alone is likewise known to have both a *ghora*-form (e.g., *RV* 9.89.4) as well as a *mīḍhvas* aspect (*RV* 8.79.9; 9.61.23; 9.85.4). Thus Soma joins the several gods already mentioned in that he has an ambivalent character. Possibly the similarities which caused the formation of the dual divinity Somārudrā also account for Rudra's epithet, Lord of the soma juice (*VS* 16.47 = TS 4.5.10a) in the Śatarudrīya litany. In addition, the litany continues to assume a close connection between the two gods in that homage to both deities is given in the same verse (*VS* 16.39 = *TS* 4.5.8a).

In sum, it is observed that Rudra forms a complementary unit with Soma, the god who manifests his power in the single most important Vedic sacrificial offering. Indeed, the Soma sacrifice is the central Vedic, nay Indo-Iranian sacramental act and in this respect Rudra's coupling with Soma is highly significant. Moreover, it has been argued that the phenomenon of forming copulative compounds should be understood as an Indo-European desire to express the twofold character of fundamental ideas by way of complementary dualities.[57] That Rudra is included in the Vedic expression of the IE feature is also pertinent to our line of inquiry.

When the above evidence is assembled together, some dominant themes emerge which it will be important to emphasize. The set of divinities sharing characteristics with Rudra stem from the oldest stratum of the Vedic religion and reach back either into the Indo-Iranian or Mitanni Aryan context, or both. As such, if the "outsider" theory is to be maintained, some reason must be given to explain why an "outsider god" has the greatest affinity with the most Aryan of the Vedic gods.

Further, the set of divinities described above is closely associated with early Vedic notions of a high god. In the Saṃhitās, such a god may be designated an *asura-*. In the *RV* for example, nearly all the great gods are called Asuras.[58] The term *asura-*, probably derived from *asu-* (m. 'vital energy'), initially meant 'a being endowed with vital energy'.[59] Because an Asura has an uncanny connection with the mysterious and wondrous creative power *māyā*, an Asura seems to be a divinity endowed with the energy to create life.[60] Indeed, in the *RV* an *asura* denotes a High Being capable of creating or projecting life forms into phenominal reality;[61] and the *AV* retains memory of this denotation.[62] Indo-European evidence lends further support. Iranian *ahura-*, preserved of course in the Avestan Ahura Mazda, seems also to denote a high being. Hittite *hassu-* 'king' and *hass-* 'beget, bring forth' are connected, as Vedic *asura-*, with the concepts of "sovereignty and creativity."[63] Thus if the meaning of *asura-* (i.e., 'high being capable of creation') is endorsed, then all the gods described above, with the exception of Vāyu[63a(*)], belong to a very noteworthy Vedic category of divine beings. Were Rudra an "outsider" some rationale is needed to explain why he is counted from the outset among this special group of Vedic "high beings."

The gods described above also share the capacity for ambivalent action. This trait may be related to their *asura*-hood. It is well recognized that the term *asura-* is an amoral, ambivalent term applied to gods *(devas)* and demons alike throughout the Saṃhitās. Thus in the *RV*, there are Asuras who are Devas, and Asuras who are Adevas (i.e., anti-gods).[64] Or some *asura* gods may also be *asurahan-* ('an *asura-slayer*'; said of Indra in *RV* 6.22.4, and Agni *RV* 7.13.1). The term *asu-* is itself an ambiguous term.[65] Perhaps the notion of ambivalence dominant in *asura*-hood accounts for the bipolar nature associated with all the aforementioned *asura* gods. In this way, the trait believed to set Rudra apart from the other gods, may in fact be a trait in common to a set of awesome Vedic divinities. In short, Rudra's ambivalent nature cannot be used to isolate Rudra from other Vedic gods and support the "outsider" theory.

2. RUDRA-ŚIVA AND THE VEDIC SACRIFICE

There is every indication that Rudra is not peripheral to the Vedic sacrifice *(yajña-)*. Already in a Rig Vedic hymn to Rudra (1.114.4), the god is addressed as "promoter of the sacrifice." In the same vein, *RV* 3.2.5d calls the god, identified with Agni, "Rudra of the sacrifices" *(rudráṃ yajñānāṃ)* and states that he promotes the oblation of the rites *(sā́dhadiṣṭim apásām)*. *RV* 4.3.1ab emphasizes the same connection in precise ritualistic language : "... king of the sacrifices, Rudra, the priest of both worlds, true sacrificer." This verse, which identifies Rudra with Agni, is repeated in *TS* 1.3.14, a section containing formulas for special sacrifices. The *Yajur Veda* contains other references to Rudra's position vis-à-vis the rites. In the Śatarudrīya litany, he is styled "the wearer of the sacred thread" *(upavītin- TS* 4.5.2e), tantamount to fitness for inclusion in the Vedic rites; he is paid homage by those possessing *havis* (*TS* 4.5.10f = *TS* 3.4.11 h ≃ *RV* 1.114.8), the most common term for the ritual oblation; he is addressed as "the one of the holy spot" *(tīrthya TS* 4.5.8m = *VS* 16.42) which may have already connoted 'a holy bathing spot' (see *TS* 6.1.1.1-2[66]). Thus when the later *Śvetāśvatara Upaniṣad* (3.4; 4.12) calls Śiva a "maharṣi" or great seer especially in relation to the Vedic tradition, the appellation does seem to build upon such prior associations as outlined above.

Turning next to the specific Vedic rituals performed to honor Rudra, it is well known that these are relatively few. Certain *gṛhya* rites, such as the Śūlagava and the Bauḍhyavihāra, wherein Rudra has a dominant role, can be described as agricultural festivals.[67] The main *śrauta* rites dedicated to Rudra are the Tryambaka Homa and the Śatarudrīya sacrifice.[68] It is probably not necessary to dwell on descriptions of Rudra in these rituals as these are well enough documented elsewhere.[69] What is of interest here is the status of these rituals within the Vedic textual corpus. The Tryambaka rite, essentially for increase in wealth and for gaining a husband, is mentioned in *Kātyāyana ŚS* (5.10.1ff), *Vaitāna sūtra* (9.18–23), *Lāṭyāyana ŚS* (5), *Āpastamba ŚS* (8.17 and 18) as well as in both the *White* and *Black Veda Saṃhitās* (*Kāṭhaka Saṃhitā* 9.7; *Kapiṣthala Saṃhitā* 8.11; *Maitrāyaṇī Saṃhitā* 1.10.4; *Vājasaneyi Saṃhitā* 3.57–61; *Taittirīya Saṃhitā* 1.8.6) and Brāhmaṇas (*Taittirīya* 1.6.10; *Śatapatha* 2.6.2.4–17). As such, the Tryambaka rite has a place in almost all the four Vedic *śākhās.* The Śatarudrīya litany and sacrifice enjoyed wide popularity in the texts of the *Yajur Veda.*[70] The YV *śrauta sūtra* literature mentions the sacrifice fairly frequently (*Āpastamba ŚS* 17.11.3ff; cf. 19.12.25; 19.13.3; *Vaikhānasa ŚS* 19.6: 291.12ff; *Mānava ŚS* 6.2.4.3–7; *Vārāha ŚS* 2.2.3.3; note also *Mānava ŚS* 11.7.1.20ff; 11.7.2.4). Part or all of the text occurs also in several YV *gṛhya sūtras* (*Āpastamba GS* 7.20.8; *Hiraṇyakeśin GS* 2.3.8.11). The prominent position of the Śatarudrīya in the *YV* sūtra literature reflects its integral position in the YV Saṃhitās. It occurs in both the *White Yajur Veda* (*VS* 16.1–66) and the *Black Yajur Veda Saṃhitās,* where it has been handed down in all the basic known versions of that Veda (*TS* 4.5; *KS* 17.11–16; *KapS* 27.1–6; *MS* 2.9.2–9). The centrality of the Śatarudrīya within the YV school is recognized in a passage of the *Mahābhārata* (13.14, 15f) which reads: "Of birds thou art Garuḍa, among the snakes Ananta, of the Vedas of the *Sāmaveda* and of the Yajuṣes the Śatarudrīya ... That means ... that Śiva himself could ... be identified with the text which is devoted to him and which is, at the same time, declared to be the best or most excellent component part of the whole Vedic corpus to which it belongs."[71]

To conclude, those *śrauta* rituals belonging to Rudra, though few and outside the mainstream of the soma cult, can claim extensive incorporation into the Vedas, especially the *Yajur Veda.*

By far the most significant indicator of Rudra's true position in the Vedic ritual is however his relation to the sacrificial remainder. The residue of the offering is, in effect, claimed as rightfully belonging to Rudra, and there are several early accounts which clearly establish that the god demands that part of the offering. The *TS* account of Nābhānediṣṭha, a son omitted from his share of inheritance is a good example (*TS* 3.1.9.4–6). Nābhānediṣṭha is left out, but his father, Manu, tells him how to get the cattle which the Añgirases brought to the sacrifice.

However, Rudra claims the cattle thus bestowed on Nābhānediṣṭha, saying, "Whatever is left at the place of the sacrifice, that indeed is mine." Challenging the right of the Aṅgirases to give as *dakṣiṇā* their cattle to Nābhānediṣṭha, Rudra insists that he will only relinquish the cattle if Nābhānediṣṭha gives him a share of the sacrifice, and Nābhānediṣṭha offers him the remnant of the mixed *(soma)*. Through this exchange, Nābhānediṣṭha is able to keep the cattle. The story of Nābhānediṣṭha is also told in *AB* 5.14, where it varies somewhat from the above account.[71] However it may be observed that Rudra's claim and the reason for it are not altered. Rudra, appearing as a man in black garments coming from the North, lays claim to the cattle on the ground that they were left at the sacrificial site and whatever is left at the site is his share.

With much the same insistence on "what is left at the site" *(vāstu)*, the god demands, in another myth, the animals first created from the charred residue of fire used to protect the creator's fecundating seed. In this creation myth the power to fecundate and generate the cosmos is released in the sexual union between Prajāpati, the Father, and his daughter, whom some say is the sky, others Uṣas (*AB* 3.33).[72] After the seed of the Father poured out upon the earth, it became a lake. So as to preserve the seed and assist the creation process, the gods surround the pool of sperm with Fire (Agni; *AB* 3.34). The implication is that the gods performed a primordial sacrifice upon the Father's spent seed. From that seed and the enveloping Fire arose gods and animals. The animals, fashioned from the remaining ashes, as well as the burnt earth and the extinguished coals are claimed by Rudra. They come from the leftovers of the conflagration marking creation, prompting the god to state again, "Mine indeed is this, mine is the remainder" (*AB* 3.34).

As if to elucidate upon this claim of Rudra's which is in the nature of an absolute truth,[73] the *Śatapatha Brāhmaṇa* contains a myth explaining when and why Rudra received this specific ritual portion. When the gods ascended to heaven by means of the ritual, Rudra was left behind at the site (*ŚB* 1.7.3. I ff); "hence they call him Vāstavya, for he was then left behind on the (sacrificial) site *(vāstu)*."[74] Realizing that he had been excluded, he rose up on the North and insisted upon inclusion in the rite and a share of the oblation (*ŚB* 1.7.3.4). Thereupon the gods instructed the Adhvaryu priest to render once more the offerings fit for ritual usage and to divide the portion so as to insure an extra portion for Rudra. "This then is the reason why he (Rudra) is called Vāstavya, for a remainder *(vāstu)* is that part of the sacrifice which (is left) after the oblations have been made."[75] In effect, the myth connects Rudra doubly with the remainder. Not only does he remain at the sacrificial site *(vāstu)* after the other gods attain heaven, but also he is consigned the remainder *(vāstu)* of the sacrificial oblation.

The close mythic association between the sacrificial residue and Rudra is actualized in the Vedic rites. The daily Bali offering described in *GoGS* (1.4) concludes with an offering to Rudra. One should offer Bali "of chaff, of the scum of boiled rice, and water. This is sacred to Rudra. This is sacred to Rudra."[76] In effect, Rudra's portion consists of chaff and scum, that is the remnants of the ritual food; also, the donation is reserved for the conclusion of the rite as the last remaining offering is the most appropriate one for Rudra. The Rājasūya ceremony gives further illustration of Rudra's association with residues. At the conclusion of the Ratnin Offerings, the *WYV* prescribes that a pap *(caru)* be prepared for the dual deity Soma-Rudra.[77] In the offering to the *devasū*-gods, performed on the eve of the unction ceremony which consecrates the king, a series of eight gods are presented with offerings.[78] The *Yajus* texts may shift the sequence in which some of the gods receive their offering; however the series concludes in all cases with either a *caru*-offering to Rudra, or one to that other awesome and ambivalent Vedic god, Varuṇa, Here again, as in the Ratnin Offering (and the Bali Offering) it is appropriate to honor Rudra with the last offering. This fact is probably related to the idea that the last of a series of offerings is "the bearer of the dangerous aspect of the powers involved in the series."[79] The *caru* prepared for Rudra Paśupati in the *devasū*-offering is likewise strongly infused with symbolism pertaining to the remainder. Notes *ŚB* 5.3.3.7: "Then he offers to Rudra Paśupati a raudra pap *(caru)* of *gāvedhuka* seeds. Thereby Rudra Paśupati imparts [strength?] to his cattle. Now as regards using the *gāvedhuka* seed, this god is indeed (the recipient of) the remainder *(vāstavyà-)*. The *gāvedhuka* seeds are the remainder. Thus the *gāvedhuka* seed is used." The ritual component immediately following the offerings to the *devasū*-gods contains another example linking Rudra to the ritual residue. In the preparation of the unction fluid, sixteen or seventeen different sorts of "water" are used to make the libation which is stored in a collective vessel. From the vessel, the fluids are ultimately poured into the four unction cups. As for the remainder of the unction fluid left in the vessel, it is offered to Rudra in the *āgnīdhrīya*-fire. Rudra's twofold connection with the remainder—final ritual in a ritual series and residue of the ritual oblation—is again in evidence. A parallel ceremony occurs following the unction rite *(abhiṣeka)*. The remaining portion of the unction fluid dripping down from the anointed king is proffered to Rudra in the *āgnīdhrīya*-fire.[80] The *ŚB* (5.4.2.10), in commenting upon this episode, emphasizes the symbolism of the remaining portion, noting its redundant or extraneous nature and that it must be offered in the northern part of the āgnīdhrīya for that is the region of Rudra. The explanation is important for it implies that the remainder "like the extra element in numerical systems it encompasses, expresses the whole and is at the same time the principle of continuity, the seed of a new production cycle."[81] That is, the remainder has a very special significance in the ancient Indian practice of extending the whole by one. The extra one both represents the composite whole, transcends it and thus assures the beginning of the new cycle.[82] Indeed the basic elements of the ceremony dealing with disposal of the remaining unction fluid clearly show that continuity of the royal line is their purpose. Essentially the ceremony assures that the unction leavings are handed over to the heir apparent. The formulas recited when the Adhvaryu hands over the cup containing the leavings underscore the rite's intent. For example, in the *Taittirīya* version the priest says to the heir apparent, "This cup will be your heritage; when I (shall) anoint you, this will be yours."[83] It is implicit that the remainder is a potent substance, and desirable to the sacrificer for his well-being. It is the ritual substance having the power to provide for fertility, renewal and continuity of the royal line. It is the substance containing the essential and germinating power of the whole ritual sequence of which it is the extraneous element. As such, the remainder is both fearful and beneficial, dangerous and helpful. It is this extraordinary element which the Rājasūya-ceremonies consistently offer to Rudra.

The point of this rather detailed analysis, tracing the frequent connections between Rudra and the remainder, is that these connections are often cited to support an interpretation which views Rudra as isolated and removed from accepted Vedic ritual practices.[84] Such interpretations assume that the residue is charged only with connotations reserved for the trivia, the impurity of leftover food, or the refuse of the liturgy. Certainly the prevailing attitude of the *smṛtis* is one of keen repulsion towards food remnants and ambiguity towards ritual remnants considered inferior to the original oblation.[85] However, the significance of the remnant in the Rājasūya hints of other attitudes and values. In order to evaluate with accuracy Rudra's position in the Vedic rites, it will be important to see what range of concepts the *śrutis* associated with the ritual remainder, and this subject is taken up next.

There is considerable evidence from the Saṃhitās onwards that the concluding ritual portion is an element imbued with extraordinary power, considered awesome and dangerous. The power of the sacrificial remainder is already set forth in a hymn of the *Atharva Veda* extolling the *ucchiṣṭa-* (i.e., the remainder; literally "what is left [out]"). The hymn (*AV* 11.7), having as theme the creation and organization of the universe, identifies the *ucchiṣṭa* as the primordial creative principle, ground of all being.[86] The *ucchiṣṭa* is thus the source of all materiality, name and form (vs. 1), the Vedas (see vs. 5), chants (vs. 24), the Rājasūya, the Vājapeya, the Agniṣṭoma, the Aśvamedha (all important *śrauta* rituals; see vs. 7), together with the Agnihotra (vs. 9), other *sattras* (see vss. 10–12), the sacrificial gift *(dakṣiṇā,* vs. 9), etc. In short, the *ucchiṣṭa* is the origin of all things, including the Vedic religious tradition. Whereas this exaltation of the remainder is unique to the *AV*, it does not represent an isolated belief in Indian speculative thought and ritualistic practice.

The recent studies by Gonda[87] and Malamoud[88] on the significance of the remainder in Brahmanism demonstrate that the ancients believed it was imbued with great potency and importance. Especially awesome are the leavings of the sacrificial food as these are considered the bearers of concentrated power leading to success, procreation and regeneration. The authors cite numerous textual passages to show that the ritual remnant is valued as a substance capable of transmitting desirable and esteemed properties related to man's ritual and daily needs, and that the remnant promotes order and cohesion in religion and society.[89] An awareness of the extraordinary power the ancients attributed to the *ucchiṣṭa*- is gained from the myth of Aditi's successful pregnancy, told in *TS* 6.5.6. Aditi, desiring offspring cooked a brahman's mess for the Sādhya gods. When she ate the remains they offered her, she became pregnant. In addition to the remainder's efficacy, the virtue of eating the sacrificial remainder as against eating first, or cooking for one's own enjoyment is being extolled.

The conviction seems to be that sacred power is concentrated in the remainder. As such, the remnant can be exceedingly dangerous and should be disposed of in a definite manner. The ritualists advise casting the remnant into the water or letting a priest eat it, but caution against throwing it into the fire.[90] This practice is prescribed for Rudra's offerings in the Rājasūya ceremonies; the *Baudh. ŚS* 10,56: 59.4 notes that Rudra's *caru* is not offered into the fire with the offering of the other *devasū*-gods, but thrown instead into the water.[91] Likewise, the *ucchiṣṭa* offering to Rudra in the Agniṣṭoma is not cast into the fire; in this case it is offered upon the coals.[92] The fact that the Tryambaka-offering to Rudra makes no use of a fire and that the administering *adhvaryu*-priest touches water at the close of the rite is in keeping with beliefs that Rudra's ritual share possesses a concentrated power.[93]

The concentrated power in the residue is believed to assure the continuation between one successful sacrifice and the next. The remnant thus has the important ritual function of preserving the uninterrupted flow from ritual to ritual and eliminating any bad results which discontinuities would otherwise cause. There is no need to repeat here the interesting Vedic passages cited by Gonda which convincingly demonstrate the connective function of the remnant in the Full and New Moon rites, the Agnihotra, the *śrāddha*, the Soma sacrifice, etc.[94] To these may be mentioned the Rājasūya-component (treated above at some length) dealing with disposal of the remaining unction fluid. In all these instances, emphasis is placed on achieving, by means of the remnant, an unbroken succession of liturgical action. The remnant allows for continuity since it is imbued with a concentration of sacred power.[95]

This function of the remnant has capital importance for the central problem under consideration. As the ritual remainder is a consecrated remnant, being in effect the germinating seed of subsequent efficacious rites, the bearer of the ritual remnant must, accordingly, be the propagator and nurturer of the rite whose remnant he receives.

It is not possible to suppose that these notions were not in effect in those instances where Rudra is receiver of the remnant. The Vedic ritualists concerned with the Rājasūya were well aware of the connective function of the remnant and were also quite consistent in consigning it to Rudra. Thus concomitant with a clarification of the role of the remnant in the ritual, must also come a reappraisal of Rudra's position in the ritual. Of all the gods, he is most closely linked in myth and ritual to the remainder. He is the god *par excellence* known as *ucchеṣaṇabhāga* ('he whose share is the remnant'; cf. *TB* 1.7.8.5). Far from signaling the god's estrangement from the Vedic ritual as has sometimes been assumed, it is here proposed that the epithet probably emphasizes Rudra's ability to sustain the continuation of the rites. His powers and personality are exceptionally suited for the task. Like the substance which is his share, Rudra is a deity both dangerous and beneficial. Further, being a Vedic High God who in the Saṃhitās has the capacity to create, Rudra's nature can accomplish the remainder's regenerative function. By the time of the upaniṣads, the remainder attains increased metaphysical importance in Indian thought... "the ātman or ātman-brahman are repeatedly stated to be the rest or remainder when all things phenomenal have disappeared."[96] In this sense, too, the remainder relates to Śiva's nature: Lord Śiva declares his eternality by describing himself as *ātman, ādiśeṣa* and *śeṣa* (*Tejobindu Upaniṣad* 3.35).

3. CONCLUSION

To answer the question posed at the outset, the features and functions of Rudra can be better explained if the "outsider" theory is dropped. Rudra's ways are found not to be at variance with the representative aspects of Vedism: the Saṃhitās conceptualization of "a high being" and the sacrifice. The surprise is that the very characteristics previously judged to be non-Vedic, turn out on closer examination to knit Rudra into the Vedic fabric. His ambivalent nature does not set him apart from other gods; instead it allies him with the most powerful and ancient stratum of the Vedic pantheon. His consumption of the ritual leftover does not divorce him from the sanctimony of the Vedic rites; instead it attests to his ability to guarantee their continuation.

What are the consequences of working with an "insider" theory? Several. If a Vedic Rudra-Śiva is postulated, then it seems quite reasonable to search for the thrust toward *śaivite bhakti* from within the Vedic tradition. The recognized *bhakti*-tendencies in the *Śvetāśvatara Upaniṣad* would reflect that Vedic thrust and the Śatarudrīya litany would be its harbinger; who else but a *bhakta* would wish to praise the hundred forms of Rudra? Further, a Vedic Rudra-Śiva would necessitate a closer look at the Vedas and Vedāṅgas as possible sources for the symbolism in early *śaivite* iconography. *Śaivite* icons, fashioned in response to *bhakti*-cult practices, begin to appear in the several centuries before the Christian era. If the determining wellspring for Hinduistic Śiva is Vedic Rudra-Śiva, then the forms and significance of early *śaivite* art could arise from ideas within the Vedic cultural milieu. This subject is explored in another publication on early *śaivite* iconography.[97] The findings there show that the most prevalent and important early *śaivite* icon is the *liṅga*. The provenance of these *liṅga* icons indicate that worship of the *membrum virile* is entirely indigenous and that it is most prevalent in those geographic regions that are the most closely associated with Aryan culture.[98] Brahmanical literature also sustains a cogent, non-erotic meaning for *liṅga,* which is applied in passages related to Rudra-Śiva and his capacity to make himself immanent in phenomenality.[98] In consequence, the *liṅga* icon may disavow Śiva's non-Vedic affinities, and indicate instead his Vedic background.

To be sure, the notion that important Vedic meanings reside in the *liṅga* form, in divine ambiguity and in the sacrificial remainder, in short in the aspects of Rudra's personality usually deemed unconventional and wild, continues to be an unusual, paradoxical notion as long as it is applied to the "outsider" theory. Were the "insider" theory adopted, it would settle into place the dominant Vedic traits of Rudra-Śiva, and it would act as a fulcrum wherefrom could be reasoned out, to a greater degree, the developments leading up to Hinduistic Śiva.

NOTES AND REFERENCES

List of Abbreviations: *AB Aitareya Brāhmaṇa; ApŚS Āpastambīya Śrauta Sūtra; AV Atharva Veda Saṃhitā; AVS Atharva Veda Saṃhitā; Śaunakīya recension; BaudhŚS Baudhāyana Śrauta Sūtra; GoGS Gobhila Gṛhya Sūtra; GS Gṛhya Sūtra; IE Indo-European; KapS Kapiṣthala Saṃhitā; KS Kāṭhaka Saṃhitā; Mbh Mahābhārata; MS Maitrāyaṇi Saṃhitā; RV Rig Veda Saṃhitā; SB Śatapatha Brāhmaṇa; SBE Sacred Books of the East; ŚS Śrauta Sūtra; ŚŚS Śāṅkhāyana Śrauta Sūrra: TB Taittirīya Brāhmaṇa; TS Taittirīya Saṃhitā: VS Vājasaneyi Saṃhitā; WYV White Yajur Veda; YV Yajur Veda.*

1. Alf Hiltebeitel, "The Indus Valley 'Proto-Śiva', Reexamined through Reflections on the Goddess, the Buffalo, and the Symbolism of vāhanas," *Anthropos* Band 73 (1978), 767–797.
2. D. Srinivasan, "The So-Called Proto-Śiva Seal from Mohenjo-Daro: An Iconological Assessment," *Archives of Asian Art,* XXIX (1975–1976), 47–58. Also in *Listening to Icons,* Vol. II and paper No. 1 in this volume.
3. E.g., Walter A. Fairservis, Jr. *Excavations at Allahdino I: Seals and Inscribed Material,* Papers of the Allahdino Expedition 1976 (New York, 1976), pp. 14–15; 18; 20–24; 110–11. Cf. Stella Kramrisch, *The Presence of Śiva* (Princeton, 1981), p. 11ff.
4. See for example discussions on distinguishing elements in a brilliant set of interdisciplinary papers contained in *Aryan and Non-Aryan in India,* M.M. Deshpande and P.E. Hook (eds.), Michigan Papers on South and Southeast Asia, No. 14 (Ann Arbor, 1979). For interpretation of recent archaeological data on the Aryan question see Jim G. Shaffer, "The Indo-Aryan Invasions: Cultural Myth and Archaeological Reality," Paper presented at the Ninth Annual Wisconsin Conference on South Asia, Nov. 1980.
5. J. Gonda opines that the essence of Rudra for Vedic man was "the power of the uncultivated and unconquered, dangerous, unreliable, unpredictable, hence much to be feared nature, experienced as a divinity," *Viṣṇuism and Śivaism* (London, 1970), p. 5.
6. A summary of the major previous studies is found in J. Gonda, *Die Religionen Indiens* I (Stuttgart, 1960), p. 88; fn. 17.
7. See Gonda, *Viṣṇuism and Śivaism,* p. 4; R.N. Dandekar, "Rudra in the Veda," *Journal of Poona University* Vol. II (1953), 97; for description of a *śrauta-rite* wherein Rudra plays a dominant role, see Milan Sen, "The Place of Rudra in the Traiyambaka Homa," *The Calcutta Review* N.S. Vol. I, No.4 (Apr.–June 1976), 138–40.

8. For a summary of both his typical and atypical features see A.A. Macdonell, *Vedic Mythology*, repr. (Varanasi, 1968), pp. 74–77.
9. A well recognized exception is the god Varuṇa, whose twofold nature is evident in the *Rig Veda*. On the duality in Rudra's make-up, see Sukumari Bhattacharji, "Rudra from the Vedas to the Mahābhārata," *Annals of the Bhandarkar Oriental Research Institute* Vol. 41 (1960), 85ff; J. Bruce Long, "Rudra as an embodiment of divine ambivalence in the Śatarudrīya" in Fred Clothey and J. Bruce Long (eds.), *Experiencing Śiva : Encounters with a Hindu Deity*, New Delhi, 1983, pp. 103-28.
10. Also said of Pusan in RV 6.55.2.
11. See discussion in Dandekar, "Rudra," 104.
12. The terrifying and ferocious side of his nature describes in part the Almighty in his *viśvarūpa*-form; in this form Rudra assumes all conceivable forms in the universe. This concept and its related imagery are central to the theme of divine multiplicity of bodily parts and is discussed in my monograph, *Many Heads, Arms and Eyes: Origin, Meaning and Form of Multiplicity in Indian Art*, Leiden, Brill, 1997.
13. The chronological place of the *YV Saṃhitā* mantras appears to be after the *Rig Veda* and *Sāma Veda*, but before the Atharva Veda; the brāhmaṇa portions of the TS are among the oldest Brāhmaṇa texts, being earlier than the *Śatapatha Brāhmaṇa* of the WYV. A. B. Keith, *The Veda of the Black Yajus School* I repr. (Delhi, 1967), clxv-vi.
14. Other *YV* texts containing the Śatarudrīya are mentioned on page 16.
15. C. Śivaramamurti, *Śatarudrīya: Vibhūti of Śiva's Iconography* (New Delhi, 1976), p. 3. Cf. J. Gonda, "The Śatarudrīya," *Sanskrit and Indian Studies: Essays in honor of Daniel H.H. Ingalls*, M. Nagatomi, B.K. Matilal, J.M. Masson and E. Dimock (eds.) (Dordrecht, Holland; Boston, U.S.A.; London, England: 1980), p. 82.
16. See R.G. Bhandarkar, *Vaiṣṇavism, Śaivism and Minor Religious Systems* (repr.) (Delhi, 1965), pp. 102–05; D. Srinivasan, "The Religious Significance of Divine Multiple Body Parts in the Atharva Veda," *Numen* Vol. XXV, Fasc. 3 (1979), 224.
17. E.g., H. Oldenberg, *Die Religion des Veda* (Stuttgart, Berlin, 1923); Macdonell, *Vedic Mythology*; A. Bergaigne, *La Religion Védique*, 3 Vols. (36, 53, 54 in Bibliothèque de l'École des Hautes Études), (Paris, 1878–83); Gonda, *Religionen Indiens* I.
18. Cf. D. Srinivasan, "The Religious Significance of Multiple Bodily Parts to denote the Divine: Findings from the Rig Veda," *Asiatische Studien* XXIX.2 (1975), 164.
19. *Ibid.*, 151. See R. N. Dandekar, "Asura Varuṇa," *Annals of the Bhandarkar Oriental Research Institute* 21 (1941), 157–91.
20. D. Srinivasan, "Multiple Body Parts in the Atharva Veda," 198–200.
21. *TS* 1.5.11j = *RV* 1.24.14; *TS* 4.2.10g.
22. Cf. *RV* 7.65.1c.
23. *RV* 7.65.2.
24. See J. Gonda, *Epithets in the Ṛgveda* (The Hague, 1959), p. 127.
25. *TS* 4.5.1 c.
26. E.g., see Long, "Rudra"; Bhandarkar, *Vaiṣṇavism Śaivism*, pp. 102–06; Dandekar, "Rudra," 95–96; cf. Gonda, *Die Religionen* I, pp. 85–89.
27. Bergaigne, *Rel. Védique* lll, 156; F. B. J. Kuiper, "The Basic Concept of the Vedic Religion," *History of Religions* (1975), 113–15; L. Renou, *Religions of Ancient India* (London, 1953), p. 20; J. Gonda, *Rel. Indiens* I, 73ff.
28. J. Gonda, The *Dual Deities in the Religion of the Veda* in *Verhandelingen der Koninklijke Nederlandse Akademie van Wetenschappen*, Afd. *Letterkunde*, Nieuwe Reeks, Deel 81 (Amsterdam, London, 1974), 191–92.

29. *Ibid.*
30. Gonda, *Dual Deities,* p. 195.
31. D. Srinivasan, "Findings from the Rig Veda," 151–52.
32. D. Srinivasan, "Multiple Body Parts in the Atharva Veda," 198–99.
33. Srinivasan, "Multiple Body Parts in the Atharva Veda," 200.
34. Gonda, *Dual Deities,* p. 163.
35. Gonda, *Dual Deities,* p. 169.
36. "See in P. V. Bradke, *Dyaus Asura, Ahura Mazdâ und die Asuras* (Halle, 1885); and H. Grassmann, *Wörterbuch zum Rig-Veda* (Wiesbaden, 1955) under *asura-* and *deva-*.
37. See my "Findings from the Rig Veda," 149–50; and my "Multiple Body Parts in the Atharva Veda," 201–02, especially fns. 41 and 42. Note also *TS* 2.4.2.
38. Translating this verse in my *Concept of Cow in the Rig Veda* (Delhi, 1979), p. 43, I rendered *surūpa-* as 'right form', which does not give the correct emphasis; a connection seems to be made here between Indra's 'good' form and a 'good' milk cow.
39. A.A. Macdonell, *Vedic Mythology.* Section 29.
40. On this and other ties between Indra and Rudra in the epic, see Wendy D. O'Flaherty, *Asceticism and Eroticism in the Mythology of Śiva* (London, 1973), pp. 84–85. However I cannot agree that the main cause for their multiple eyes is an erotic one. The epic image represents a secondary symbolic layering, the primary symbolic meaning occurs in the Vedas where multiple eyes consistently signify 'omniscience' of a cosmic creator.
41. This is not to obscure the fact that whereas Rudra-Śiva is the archer *par excellence* (see S. Kramrisch, "Śiva, the Archer," *Indologen-Tagung* 1971, H. Härtel and V. Moeller [eds.] [Wiesbaden, 1973], 140–150), Indra's characteristic weapon is the *vajra.*
42. However the relationship between Vedic Indra and Avesta Indra still remains an open question. See for example H. Lommel, *Die Religion Zarathustras* (Tübingen, 1930), p. 50; 91 ff; J. Gonda, *Religionen Indiens* I, p. 60; J. Duchesne-Guillemin, *La religion de l'Iran ancien* (Paris, 1962) p. 176ff.
43. The term is also applied to *inter alia* to Agni, Tvaṣṭṛ, etc; see Grassmann, *Wörterbuch,* p. 1395.
44. Gonda, *Dual Deities,* p. 222.
45. J. Duchesne-Guillemin, "De la Dicéphalie dans l'Iconographie Mazdéenne," *Festgabe für Herman Lommel,* B. Schlerath (ed.) (Wiesbaden, 1960), pp. 32–37.
46. See W. Caland, *Das Jaiminīya-Brāhmaṇa in Auswahl* (Amsterdam, 1919), p. 183.
47. Macdonell, *Vedic Mythology,* p. 82.
48. Gonda, *Dual Deities,* pp. 227–28.
49. Srinivasan, "Findings from the Rig Veda," 157 and my "Multiple Body Parts in the Atharva Veda," 203.
50. For an excellent survey of Agni's dual character in the Vedas see Sukumari Bhattacharji, *The Indian Theogony* (Cambridge, 1970), p. 187ff.
51. A. Hillebrandt (*Vedische Mythologie* II, reprint of 2nd ed. [Hildesheim, 1965], 447, fn. 1) had already proposed that Rudra is really a form of Agni on the basis of AV 7.87.1; AV 19.55.5; *RV* 4.3.1, etc.
52. See Āpastamba ŚS 6.14.11–13; cf. R. N. Dandekar, *Śrauta Kośa* I (Poona, 1958), 129 for similar injunctions in the Vārāha ŚS.
53. Cf. Srinivasan, "Multiple Body Parts in the Atharva Veda," 224.
54. The names are: Rudra, Sarva, Paśupati, Ugra, Aśani, Bhava, Mahādeva or Mahān devaḥ and Īśāna. On the relationship between Sarva, Bhava, Īśāna and Rudra in the *AV*, see my "Multiple Body Parts in the Atharva Veda," 200–01. *ŚB* 1.7.3.8 states that Agni is called "Sarva" among the eastern people and Bhava among the Bāhīkas.

55. To understand the meaning of a "wrathful fire" it may be noted that a major distinction was made between a sacrificial fire and a crematory fire. Cf. Bhattacharji, *Indian Theogony,* p. 191. Quite possibly the Rudra aspect of Agni is the crematory fire. See Gonda, *Dual Deities,* p. 360.
56. Mention of Soma as *asura* in the *RV* is discussed in my "Findings from the Rig Veda," 153–56; 177.
57. See Gonda, *Dual Deities,* Chapter I; especially pp. 32–33.
58. Bradke, *Dyaus Asura,* pp. 119–23.
59. See discussion and references in Srinivasan, "Findings from the Rig Veda," 144–46.
60. *Ibid.*
61. *Ibid.*
62. Srinivasan, "Multiple Body Parts in the Atharva Veda," 196–98.
63. See Edgar C. Polomé, "A Critical Examination of Germano-Indo-Aryan Isoglosses and their Significance for the Reconstruction of Indo-European Culture," paper given at the IVth International Conference of Sanskrit Studies, Weimar, D.D.R. May 1979.

63a. ADDENDUM: Vedic Vāyu probably has important features in common with Văyu in the Avesta. The ancient Iranians formulated a complex Wind God. They venerated Vāta who personifies "the wind that blows', thus the physical wind, according to Mary Boyce. The other Wind God, Văyu is more of a cosmological principle than a phenomenal power. Văyu is the life-breath which animates living things, but abandons them at death and thereby causes death. As a result, from ancient Indo-Iranian times onward Văyu has two aspects : "harmful" and in Yašt 15.5 beneficial[1]. Thus the beneficial side of Avestan Văyu includes power to give life. Vedic Vāyu also has a beneficial, and thus supposedly a harmful, side. For more on Vāyu, the Wind God, and the appearance of the Wind God on Kuṣāṇa coinage, see the paper in Volume II on the Oešo/Śiva puzzle and how it impacts Śiva's distinct Gandhāran Imagery.

64. E.g., *RV* 8.25.4; 8.85/96.9. Kuiper ("Basic Concept," 112ff) offers a stimulating hypothesis as to "why" and "how" these divisions occurred.
65. See Srinivasan, "Findings from the Rig Veda," 145.
66. Cf. P.V. Kane, *History of Dharmaśāstra* Vol. IV (Poona, 1953), p. 554.
67. For descriptions of these rites see A.B. Keith, *The Religion and Philosophy of the Veda and Upanishads* Vol. II, reprint. (Delhi, 1976), 364–65. Dandekar ("Rudra," 98), mentions some other *gṛhya* rites wherein Rudra plays a prominent role.
68. Minor *śrauta* rites mentioning Rudra include the Indraturīya (see Dandekar, *Śrauta Kośa* II, 565; 629) and several optional rites *(Śrauta Kośa* II, 625; 628).
69. See Milan Sen, "The Place of Rudra," 138–40; Śivaramamurti, *Śatarudrīya,* J.B. Long, "Rudra"; this paper contains a good bibliography on the Śatarudrīya.
70. On the history of the Śatarudrīya text, its ritual usage and significance, see Gonda, "Śatarudrīya."
71. Both accounts are insightfully analyzed by Kramrisch, *Śiva,* pp. 54–65.
72. An interpretation of the various symbolic levels of the myth is contained in Kramrisch, *Śiva,* Chapters II and III.
73. Cf. AB 5.14.
74. J. Eggeling, trans. *The Śatapatha-Brāhmaṇa* in SBE XII (reprint) (Delhi, 1963), p. 200. For references to other Vedic gods, see J. Deppert, *Rudras Geburt* (Wiesbaden, 1977), pp. 321–27.
75. ŚB 1.7.3.7. Eggeling *Śatapatha-Brāhmaṇa,* p. 201.

76. *GoGS* 1.4.31. H. Oldenberg, trans. *The Grihya-Sūtras* in SBE XXX, reprint. (Delhi, 1964), p. 25. Oldenberg opines (p. 25, fn. 31) that the repetition of the last words makes it probable that at one time Book I ended here.
77. The function of the dual deity is to protect the royal embryo until its safe birth. J.C. Heesterman, *The Ancient Royal Consecration* (The Hague, 1957), p. 57; see also p. 52.
78. Heesterman, *Consecration*, pp. 69–78.
79. Heesterman, *Consecration*, p. 70; fn. 5.
80. Heesterman, *Consecration*, pp. 123–24.
81. Heesterman, *Consecration*, p. 125.
82. See J. Gonda, "Triads in Vedic Ritual," *Ohio Journal of Religious Studies* Vol. II, No. 2 (1974), 5–23.
83. Heesterman, *Consecration*, p. 124.
84. E.g. Dandekar, "Rudra," 97; Gonda, *Viṣṇuism and Śivaism*, p. 4. Hillebrandt, *Vedische Mythologie* II, 434ff.
85. This is well documented by C. Malamoud, "Observations sur la notion de 'reste' dans le Brāhmaṇisme," *Wiener Zeitschrift für Kunder des Sud-Asiens und Archiv für Indische Philosophie* XVI (1972), 5–26. Gonda is of the opinion that belief in the power inherent in the remnant may be compared to beliefs associated with agricultural rituals. He writes, "The rituals are intended to ensure, *inter alia*, that the favorable relations between man and the power of the harvest will continue and that this power is regularly regenerated. The last ears are not reaped, the last few fruits are never taken from the tree, the chests in which the wheat is kept are never completely emptied for fear that this power is exhausted or the vivifying force may be lost"; J. Gonda, "Atharvaveda 11.7," *Mélanges d'Indianism à la mémoire de Louis Renou* (Paris, 1968), p. 313.
86. Gonda, "Atharvaveda 11.7," pp. 301–36. The ensuing remarks are largely based on this study.
87. Gonda, "Atharvaveda 11.7."
88. Malamoud, "La notion de 'reste'."
89. E.g., Gonda, "Atharvaveda 11.7." 313–15; 319–20; Malarnoud, "La notion de 'reste'," 13–15.
90. Gonda, "Atharvaveda 11.7," 314.
91. Heesterman, *Consecration*, p. 70; fn. 5.
92. See Dandekar, "Rudra," 97, fn. 8 where he cites as reference W. Caland and V. Henry, *L'Agniṣṭoma* (Paris, 1906), 210. Cf. TS 2.6.8.2 which indicates that Rudra's *iḍā* should not be offered in the fire.
93. Sen, "Traiyambaka Homa," 138–39.
94. Gonda, "Atharvaveda 11.7" 319–21.
95. Gonda, "Atharvaveda 11.7" 319–21.
96. Gonda, *Dual Deities*, p. 178.
97. D. Srinivasan, "Significance and Scope of Pre-Kuṣāṇa Śaivite Iconography", in M. Meister (ed.), *Discourses on Śiva: Proceedings of a Symposium on the Nature of Religious Imagery*, Philadelphia, 1984. See also "Ritual as Icon in India"; both papers are in this volume.
98. Srinivasan, "Pre-Kuṣāṇa Śaivite Iconography."

3

Ritual as Icon in India

The history of Indian art opens with a well-acknowledged puzzle. While the earliest artistic phase, religious in nature, is archaic in style, the iconography is not primitive. Hindu stone images first appearing in the centuries around the Christian era demonstrate an iconographic language which is direct, stable, and mature. This phenomenon can be illustrated by images of Śiva and Viṣṇu, two major gods in the Hindu pantheon. The earliest-known Vaiṣṇava multi-armed icon is dated by inscription to the first century BC (Fig. 3.1).[1] Wearing a cylindrical crown, the god holds the wheel and mace in the upper left and right hands. The natural hands clasp an object akin to a conch close to the chest. This image, like the one of Viṣṇu eleven hundred years later (Fig. 3.2), stems from central India. In the later image, the same basic iconographic vocabulary is now imbued with majesty, and the icon is carved with perfected skill; the wheel and mace achieve greater elegance in shape, and there is greater clarity in the arrangement of the four arms. The tenth-century image is not an anachronism. The point is that this medieval sculpture depicts a characteristic mode of representing Viṣṇu, and that mode had been worked out in its essentials in the first century BC.

An even earlier image, from Uttar Pradesh and dated by inscription to the second century BC, has already solved a characteristic form symbolic of the god Śiva. The form is of a phallus with five heads (Fig. 3.3). The phallus is the sign of Śiva, heralding the god's capacity for cosmic creation. The Sanskrit term for this

---

Originally published in *World Art*, Themes of Unity in Diversity. Acts of the XXVIth International Congress of the History of Art. Irving Lavin (ed.), Vol. III. Univeristy Park and London, 1989; pp. 557-62. Reprinted with stylistic changes, and with permission by the National Committee for the History of Art.

Fig. 3.1. Multi-armed Viṣṇu. First century BC. Malhār, M.P. (photo: courtesy Donald Stadtner).

Fig. 3.2. Multi-armed Viṣṇu. *c.* tenth century AD. Sultānpur. State Museum, Lucknow (photo: State Museum, Lucknow).

"sign" is *liṅga,* and Śiva's *liṅga* can be an object of worship in two modes of representation. It can be rendered as a plain *liṅga*, or as a *liṅga* encircled by heads. The term for "head" in conjunction with the *liṅga* is *mukha;*[2] so the second mode of representation is called *mukhaliṅga*. Religious theory imputes five heads to every *mukhaliṅga*. Such a *liṅga* is called a Pañcamukha Liṅga, *pañca* meaning "five." The way in which the heads are generally arranged on the shaft of the *liṅga* is as follows: four heads face in the four directions and the fifth occupies the central, uppermost position. The fifth head may "humanize" part or all of the shaft of the *liṅga*. The inscribed, five-headed *liṅga*, being the earliest Pañcamukha Liṅga, is of this type. The central shaft has been shaped into the fifth head with its torso. Under the arms of the torso appear two heads. The head directly below the left hand of the torso has fanged teeth and a mustache. These features identity it as the fearful aspect of Śiva. The next face, under the right hand, is adorned with large globular earrings, a collar necklace, and a fillet around the well-arranged hair. This face is the peaceful, feminine aspect of Śiva. Next follows a head wearing a turban with a topknot, and last is a head devoid of hair and ornamentation (Fig. 3.4); it represents the ascetic nature of Śiva. The heads face in the directions although not directly in the cardinal points.

In subsequent periods, the fifth head is rarely fashioned. Considered to be superior, both physically and metaphysically, the fifth head is said to be beyond the ken of even the yogīs. It came to be symbolized by the dome of the *liṅga* of the *mukhaliṅga* icon. The resultant form consists of the *liṅga* encircled by four heads. Such an icon has persisted throughout the history of Śaiva art. An example of a Pañcamukha Liṅga with four visible heads comes from a former private American collection (Fig. 3.5); in this seventh-century sculpture, continuities are not hard to find. The heads face in the four directions. The fearful mien and the peaceful mien remain, as do the latter's fillet around the hair and the single-strand necklace.

It must be seen as rather remarkable that forms as complex as a phallus with five heads and a god with four arms could burst upon the scene without any artistic precedence whatsoever. After all, both forms are highly idiosyncratic, and what is more, both forms are totally within the mainstream of Hindu religious art. Puzzles of this sort, in Hindu art, are usually approached by an *argumentum ex silentio.* It is postulated that extant icons in stone were preceded by earlier icons in wood. Since wood quickly perishes in the subcontinent's climate, a gap in the historical evidence has occurred. This postulate is well supported by Indian stone architecture, contemporaneous with, or even earlier than, the stone icons considered above.

The first phase of Indian architecture includes rock-cut caves in imitation of wooden forms. The Lomas Ṛṣi Cave of the mid-third century BC is a good example (Fig. 3.6). Situated in eastern India, the cave's facade features an arch shaped on a bentwood prototype. The ends of the beams are carved as they would appear in a wooden structure. The arch rests on pillars that lean slightly inward. The pediment is decorated in two registers, of which the upper band is carved in imitation of wooden latticework. By the mid-second century BC, the entrance arch has developed a more lithic and impressive form, as seen in the rock-cut cave from Bhaja in western India

Fig. 3.3. Pañcamukha Liṅga. Second century BC. Bhītā. State Museum, Lucknow (photo: State Museum, Lucknow).

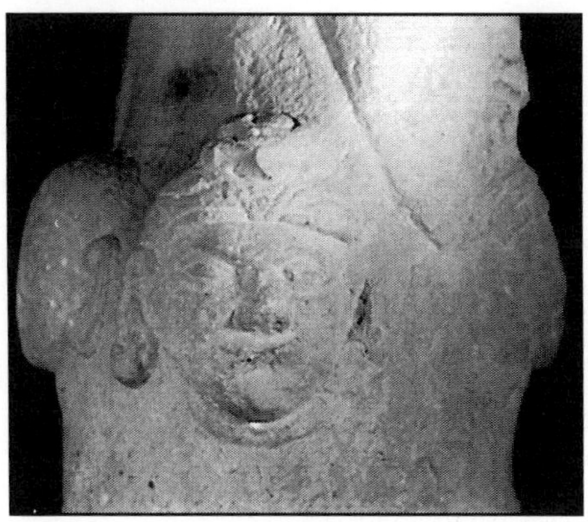

Fig. 3.4. Pañcamukha Liṅga second century BC. Bhītā (detail).

Fig. 3.5. Pañcamukha Liṅga. Seventh century AD. East Rajasthan. Collection Mr. and Mrs. James W. Alsdorf, Chicago. Currently on loan at the Art Institute of Chicago (No. 145.1997).

Fig. 3.6. Lomas Ṛṣi Cave. Third century BC. Bihar (photo: courtesy John C. Huntington).

(Fig. 3.7), but almost every other feature continues to imitate a free-standing wooden structure. It is easy to recognize a wholesale translation from wood into stone in the forms of the beams below the central arch, in the forms of the mock balconies and the false window frames, and in the lattice decoration. These two caves, and others excavated between the third century BC and the beginning of the Christian era, show an evolution wherein forms once dependent upon a wooden prototype develop into forms exploiting the new stone medium.[3] It is hard to detect a similar trend in devotional icons arising during the same period.

There are to date no satisfactory plastic antecedents for the earliest Hindu icons in stone, and this despite vigorous archaeological activity to define materially the ancient form of Hinduism practiced throughout the first millennium BC.[4] Ancient Hinduism is also called Vedism, and a major portion of the first millennium BC is also called the Vedic Age.[5] These names acknowledge that our main source of information about this period and its culture comes from a vast body of religious texts called the Vedas. Compiled throughout the first millennium BC and well into the middle of the first millennium AD, these texts not only codified religious beliefs but also reflected the thinking of society's elite on metaphysics, phonetics, astronomy, grammar, metrics, etymologies, and mythic and magical lore, as well as social customs. In short, though the Vedic texts do not represent all the cultural activities present during those ages, they do represent the ideas of the dominant cultural force during those ages. The Vedic texts abound in hymns of praise to various gods. Ancient Hinduism formulated many gods and they often are addressed in anthropomorphic fashion. The forerunners of Hindu Viṣṇu and Śiva are found in the Vedas. The latter is called Rudra. Yet, no archaeological evidence has surfaced to date to provide us with any iconic prehistoric forerunner for Viṣṇu or Śiva, or any other god for that matter.

Fig. 3.7. Bhaja. Second century BC. Maharashtra (photo: courtesy John C. Huntington).

It can be reasonably argued, and I do so in my forthcoming monograph,[6] that the lacuna is not the result of happenstance digging. There probably will never surface images of the Vedic gods. There are many reasons for this. The main reason, in the present context, is that the focus of the religion lay elsewhere. The axle around which the religious energies of the Vedic Age turned was the ritual.

Ancient Hinduism came to life with the performance of rituals, and these were often events of extraordinary visual power. The full impact of a ritual upon a participant or an observer cannot be gauged from reading one or even several Vedic texts describing it. A ritual, especially a public ritual, is an orchestration of much activity. A given Vedic text indicates only the activity undertaken by one priestly section. What is needed to gauge the impact is an overview of the activities in the total sacred space. Some of that effect is contained in a description of the Horse Sacrifice given in the Indian epic the *Mahābhārata*. The dates for the compilation of the *Mahābhārata* can only be approximate, but the generally agreed upon brackets are between 400 BC and AD 400,[7] placing the epic's material within the historical period of our concern. The Horse Sacrifice is one of the most imposing of Vedic rituals. The actual ritual lasted for three days, but preparations took a year, if not two. Here in the epic's description is some indication of the pageantry, the crowd, the excitement, and the ceremonies for which it took so long to prepare.[8]

> The sacrificial compound is prepared by knowledgeable master-builders, craftsmen and Brahmans who direct the proper ways in laying out the arena. On the selected spot, mansions and a broad avenue were constructed. Apartments decorated in gold and jewels were built for the nobles and their wives. Gateways and pillars of gold and various colours were raised. Nobles were invited from many different regions, bringing gems, women, horses, weapons; when they arrived they saw archways, walkways, seats and couches and very many bejeweled decorations. They saw refreshments in golden vessels. They saw pitchers, vessels, cauldrons, jars, lids. There was not anything to be seen which was not golden. The wooden sacrificial stakes were decorated with gold and erected according to the scriptures. There were dainty things to eat for the Brahman and Vaiśya classes. The nobles were "wonderstruck" upon seeing the sacrificial compound with so many and diverse types of animals tied to the sacrificial stakes. [These were sacrificed prior to the strangulation of the horse.

The passage is our gateway too; it reveals not only the sights to be seen but also who would be likely to see them. The spectators are drawn from the three upper classes of society. These comprise the nobles, the priests, the merchants, the agriculturists, and the artisans. Only persons from the fourth class, which traditionally served the upper classes, could not be in attendance. The upper classes would also perform their own domestic rituals, which were likewise charged with visual appeal.

The visual impact of rituals goes beyond the use of vivid colors, precious gems and metals ornamenting clothes, architectural settings and appurtenances. Ritual altars and consecrated implements themselves had marked iconographic tendencies. A case in point is a clay pot which functions as an icon in a public ritual called the Pravargya. The pot is the most important implement in this ritual; its name is "Mahāvīra," which means "the large man." The vessel is addressed as a supreme god and is set upon a throne which is named the "emperor's throne."[9] The texts speak of the top as "the head," the middle as spheroid,[10] and the bottom as flat and as "the two feet of the sacrifice."[11] One text states that "a mouth" is pinched for the head.[12] The terms used to describe the vessel and its shape suggest to van Buitenen, who studied this ritual, that the fairly tall Mahāvīra vessel was in the form of a large man seated upon a throne (Fig. 3.8);[13] the flat bottom, compared to the feet,

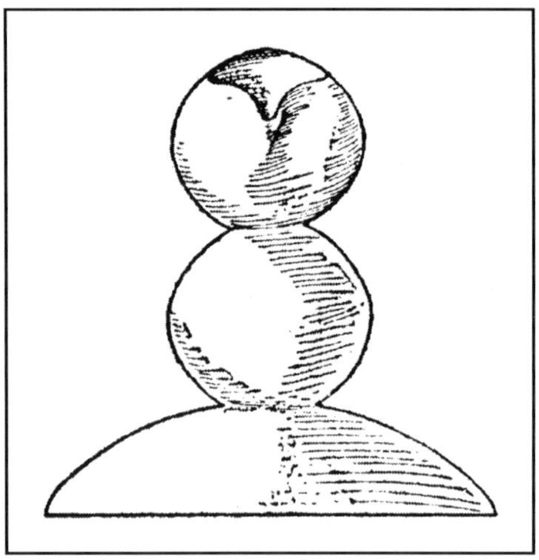

Fig. 3.8. The Mahāvīra Vessel as drawn by van Buitenen (from van Buitenen, *The Pravargya*, p. 11).

Fig. 3.9. "Mother" Pot. *c.* third century BC. National Museum, New Delhi (photo: Horst P. Schastok).

Fig. 3.10. Hāritī *c.* second century AD. Mathurā, U.P. Ashmolean Museum (photo: Ashmolean Museum, Oxford).

could correspond to the cross-legged position, the spherical middle to the trunk, and the pinched top to the head of a man.[14] Enthroned and worshipped, the Mahāvīra pot performed the role of an icon in the ritual.

The ritual manipulation and worship of a pot presumed to be a god and endowed with figural qualities must be kept in mind when trying to comprehend why the dawn of Indian art includes a series of anthropomorphic clay pots. Fashioned in about the third century BC, these vessels comprise both male and female types. A male vessel found in an excavation in Mathura District (i.e., Sonkh, in the Gangetic plains) has a wheel-thrown body; the arms, nipples, and genitals are hand-modeled and attached.[15] A complete female vessel now in the National Museum in Delhi is also composed of a wheel-thrown body whose legs, arms, head, breasts, and ornaments are modeled by hand and attached (Fig. 3.9).[16] The female is a mother holding her baby on the left hip. Between her

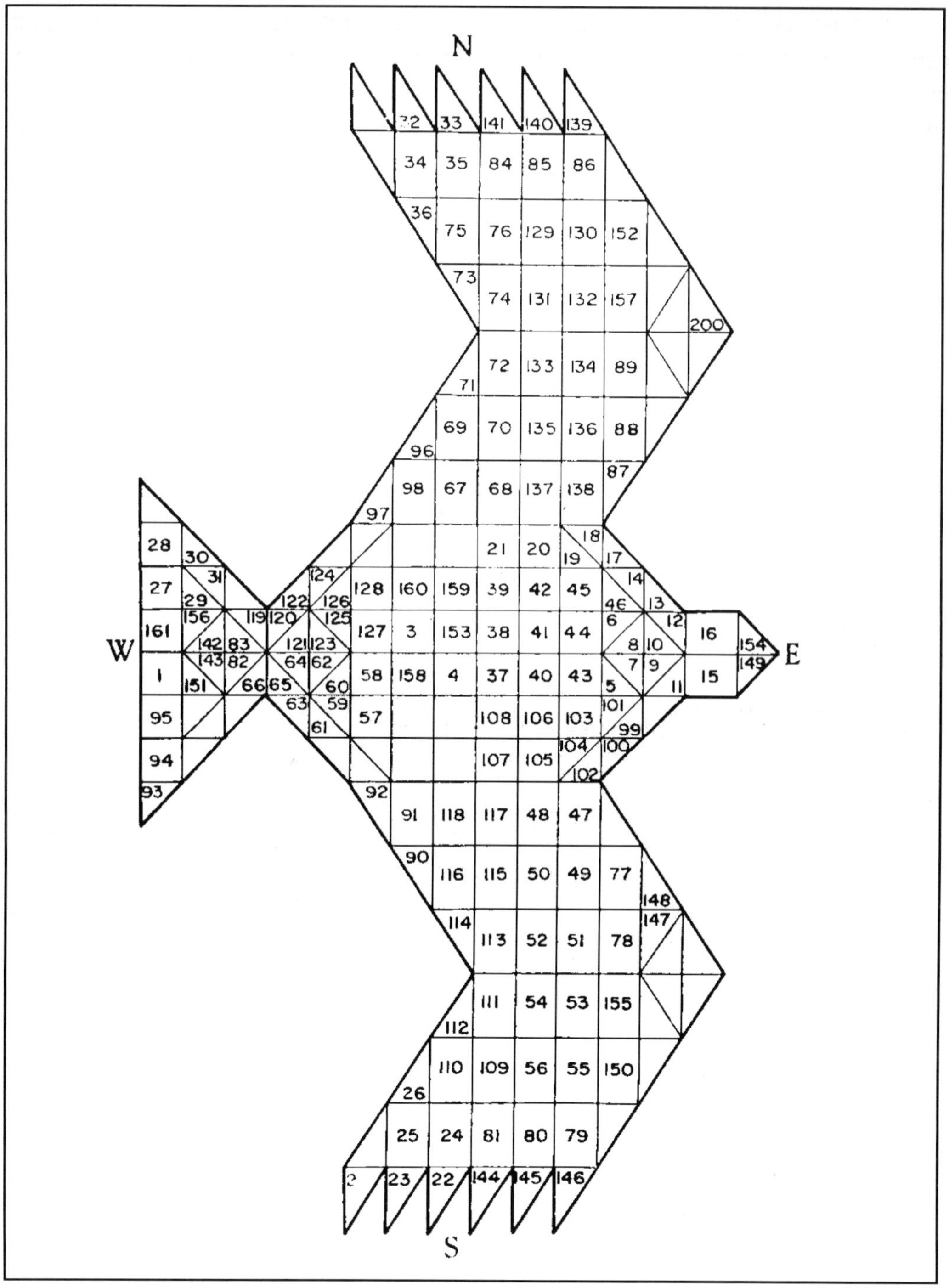

Fig. 3.11. Order of Bricks in the First Layer of the Agnicayana (photo: from Staal, *Agni*, Vol. I, p. 400).

legs, which are splayed and pendant, and at the lowest and fullest part of the vessel, there is a hollow cuplike depression. Either it served as a libation container, or it emphasized some fertility aspect, or, as I suspect, it did both.

The main features of the third century BC "mother" pot are echoed in a second century AD stone image now in the Ashmolean Museum (Fig. 3.10). The carving comes from Mathura; it depicts a particular mother goddess whose name is Hāritī, In drawing a thread between similar plastic expressions of maternity in a stone image and in an anthropomorphic pot whose own existence may have been stimulated by ritual, I approach the main hypothesis of this paper. It is proposed that we look at the ancient Hindu ritual as a three-dimensional, living icon whose properties could provide models from which to construct a devotional icon.

To demonstrate the potential of this heretofore untapped source, I would like to show how another great public ritual helps us to gain an understanding of the iconography and meaning of the Pañcamukha Liṅga. As noted above, we are now quite certain that the *liṅga* of Śiva was devoid of priapric symbolism, whether plain or encircled by heads.[17] A philological perusal of the term *liṅga* in Vedic and early devotional literature determines that *liṅga* is the first "sign" of the transcendental Śiva. It expresses belief in the immanence of the transcendental in nature. The sign is in the form of the phallus to symbolize god's capacity to produce life itself. The significance of the heads has as yet not been fully understood. Here is where the orthopraxy connected with the Vedic Agnicayana ritual is helpful.

The name of this ritual signals its most distinctive feature; Agnicayana means "the piling (of bricks to build for the altar) of fire." The main fire altar is in the shape of a huge bird whose wing span is about forty feet. The altar consists of five layers of baked bricks; in all there are about 1,000 bricks,[18] of various shapes and names specified in the texts. Were we confined to these texts alone, the visual dimensions of this complex twelve-day ritual would be hard to assess, but quite wonderfully a full visual documentation of the ritual is available. The Agnicayana was performed in 1975 by the Nambudiri Brahmans of Kerala. The Nambudiris have made it a chief interest of their community to preserve and cultivate some of the traditional Vedic knowledge. Their entire performance of the ritual was taped, filmed, and photographed by a group of Western scholars.[19] What follows is based on the documentation of the actual performance and the descriptions in ancient texts.

In each of the five layers comprising the great altar are a group of bricks called *mukha* bricks. There are five *mukha* bricks in each of the five layers of the altar. The bricks are piled onto the altar in a specific way. In specifying the manner in which they are laid down in the first layer, the general pattern in all the five layers is known. Bricks numbered 149–153 on the plan of the first layer (Fig. 3.11) correspond to the *mukha* bricks. In following the placement of each brick, it is evident that brick 149 is in the easterly direction and occupies a position in the head of the bird. Brick 150 is in the southern section and occupies a position in the right wing. Brick 151 is in the westerly section and occupies a position in the tail. Brick 152 is in the northern section and occupies a position in the left wing.

Fig. 3.12. Wooden goblets with a face (*mukham*) (photo: from Staal, *Agni*, vol. I, p. 213).

Brick 153 occupies a position in the center of the altar. After the five *mukha* bricks are laid down, the placement of four other sets of bricks follows, each having a distinctive name. In this way the *mukha* bricks initiate a series of bricks with the following names:

aṅga or limb bricks—of which there are five
Prajāpatya—one brick for the god Prajāpati, Lord of Creatures
Ṛṣabha or bull brick—of which there is one
Lokampṛṇa or space fillers—of which there are forty

This schema, repeated in all the layers, has some noteworthy features. It is most interesting that the five *mukha* or head bricks are immediately followed by five *aṅga* or limb bricks. The *aṅga* bricks are also placed in a directional pattern; actually they are placed in close proximity to the *mukha* bricks. No other set of bricks correlates in this manner. Apparently the *mukha* and *aṅga* bricks are meant to define a unit. That unit seems to be a "body" having multiple heads and multiple limbs. From this it may be deduced that the term *mukha* need not simply mean head; it can connote "head (or the first element) when more of the body is forthcoming." The *mukha* bricks usher in more than the anthropomorphic entity; they also usher in a cognate theriomorphic entity to judge from the "bull" brick forming part of the series. This theriomorphic entity evokes the realm of Śiva. In Hinduism, the bull is the theriomorphic form of Śiva. The anthropomorphic entity may well be associated with the Vedic forerunner of Śiva, Rudra.

As soon as the building of the Agnicayana altar has been completed, a liturgical chant and oblation are offered to Rudra. The offering and chant are made over one brick in the fifth layer of the altar—brick 189 in the northern section. This is the appropriate place to give homage to Rudra, for "in that region lies the house of that god."[20] The homage extols Rudra as the creator of life and as the rhythm in life. The good and the bad, the big and the small, the ugly and the sublime are all expressions of him. From this long and powerful litany, here are some excerpts:

> Homage to the turbaned wanderer on the mountains (Fig. 3.4)
> Homage to the wearer of the knotted locks and to him of the shaven hair (Fig. 3.4)
> Homage to the powerful and the fearful One (Fig. 3.3)
> Homage to the auspicious and the more auspicous One (Fig. 3.3)[21]

The Sanskrit of the last stanza reads: *namaḥ śivāya ca śivatarāya ca.* It is of course Rudra's epithet *śiva,* "the auspicious One," which becomes the name of the god in Hinduism.

In sum, physical properties in the Agnicayana reveal many elements suggestive of the iconographic properties found in the Pañcamukha Liṅga of Śiva. First, in both ritual and icon, *mukha* is associated with the number five. Second, in both ritual and icon, the five *mukhas* are placed in the four directions and the center. Third, the heads of the icon seem to answer epithets of Rudra contained in a litany chanted immediately upon the completion of the piling of the altar. Parenthetically, the domain of Śiva is also acknowledged by the presence of the "bull" brick in the series of bricks initiated by the *mukha* bricks. Still, it is a big jump from bricks in an altar to heads on the shaft of a *liṅga.* But perhaps here, too, the ritual was the catalyst for bringing these shapes together. The ritual demands the use of round wooden goblets for some oblations made for the gods. One of the goblets, the *ṛtu-pātra,* is described in another Vedic context as having a head *(mukha)* on both sides.[22] In 1975 the carpenter, under the direction of a Nambudiri, turned out simple cylindrical goblets with one or two heads on the cylindrical shaft (Fig. 3.12).

If we now combine the meaning of *mukha* as derived from the ritual and the meaning of *liṅga* as derived from the ancient texts, then the significance of the Pañcamukha Liṅga icon is that it represents the manifestation of the first part of the body of Śiva projecting out of his own cosmic essence. A *mukhaliṅga* seems to symbolize a theological belief concerning the manifestation of the transcendental god. God moves toward manifestation as a baby moves toward birth: the head projects first.[23 & 23a(*)]

To establish the origins for an iconography seen on an artistic representation, it is usual to seek antecedents in prior artistic representations. In effect, postulating antecedents in perishable wood for the extant early Indian stone icons reflects a desire to continue this approach. But the case of the Pañcamukha Liṅga indicates a different predicament. Here is a form suddenly appearing with a full-fledged iconographic language for which there is no pre-existing artistic model. The second-century BC Pañcamukha Liṅga is an invention. Where did the new form come from? It is the thesis of this paper that the visual aspects of rituals could stimulate the invention of new iconic shapes. There must, however, be present the religious and/or social possibility for influences to move from a performing media to a representational media. In India, during the several centuries around the Christian era, such possibilities existed. Inscriptional evidence indicates that there was little or no barrier between a person's involvement in Vedic rituals and devotional cult practices requiring icons; potential patrons and artisans could experience both.[24] In this accommodating atmosphere, ritual forms charged with symbolic meaning congenial to the new context could be transmitted with ease.

Comparable historical situations, in other areas of world art, exist to support this thesis. For example, quite analogous is the role of the ritual as the starting point for iconographic innovations in twelfth-century English narrative painting. In the early twelfth century, full-fledged picture cycles suddenly make an appearance for which no prior textual or pictorial models exist.[25] Tracing the source of a particular cycle, the St. Albans Psalter, Pächt is able to show that the spoken words of the liturgical drama helped the twelfth-century artist cope with the problem of finding pictorial expressions for subjects never treated before.

Ritual is the enactment of a religious reality needing to be repeatedly experienced.[26] It imparts notions about this reality through words, gestures, postures, and objects and their arrangements. Given the possibility for a historical rapprochement between the two media, anyone of the ritual elements can function as a pictorial model, making available an iconographic language upon which an incipient art form can draw.

NOTES AND REFERENCES

1. D.C. Sircar, "Burhīkhar Brāhmī Inscription," *Proleg. of the Indian Historical Congress* (1953); 39–41.
2. *Mukha* can mean head, face, mouth, front, that is, the forepart or top of something.
3. James Fergusson and James Burgess, *The Cave Temples of India* (London, 1880), 27–94.
4. See Bridget and Raymond Allchin, *The Rise of Civilization in India and Pakistan* (Cambridge, 1982), chaps. 11–13, for a survey of the available information and related problems.
5. In considering Vedism as ancient Hinduism, stressing thereby its importance to, and its continuities with, Hinduism, I follow L. Renou, *Hinduism.* (New York, 1961), 19.
6. *Many Heads, Arms and Eyes: Origin, Meaning and Form of Multiplicity in Indian Art.*
7. *The Mahābhārata,* trans. and ed. by J.A.B. van Buitenen, Vol. I (Chicago/London, 1973), xxiii–xxv.
8. Mahābhārata 14.86.11–26; 87.1–16.
9. J.A.B. van Buitenen, *The Pravargya* (Poona, 1968), 9, 15.
10. van Buitenen 1968, 10.
11. See Stella Kramrisch, "The Mahāvīra vessel and the Plant Putika," *Journal of the American Oriental Society* 95.2 (1975), 231, citing *Āp.Ś.S.*15.2.14; *Tait.Ār.*4.2.6.

12. van Buitenen 1968, 11.
13. This is the position of van Buitenen, who considers the Pravargya an ancient Indian iconic ritual. L. Renous also sees the anthropomorphic tendencies in the vessel; he considers it to have the shape of a "human head"; see his *Vedic India,* trans. from the French by Philip Spratt (Delhi, 1971), par. 209; Kramrisch 1975, 232, argues that the vessel "is not an icon but a symbol in the shape of a vessel."
14. It must be registered that the Mahāvīra pot as it appears now is devoid of anthropomorphic tendencies; see van Buitenen 1968, pl. 3.1; and Frits Staal, *Agni: The Vedic Ritual of the Fire Altar* (Berkeley, 1983), 1: pl. 5B.
15. See H. Härtel, "Pottery of Mathurā," in *Mathurā: The Cultural Heritage,* D.M. Srinivasan (ed.) (New Delhi, 1989), pl. 7.
16. I wish to thank my colleague Sara Schastok for bringing this piece to my attention.
17. See Stella Kramrisch, *The Presence of Śiva* (Princeton, 1981), 162–178; Doris Meth Srinivasan, "Significance and Scope of Pre-Kuśāṅa Śaivite Iconography," in *Discourses on Śiva,* Michael W. Meister (ed.) (Philadelphia, 1984), 32–46, see pages 48-73 in this volume.
18. However, the Śatapatha Brāhmaṇa mentions 10,800 kiln-fired bricks; for an interpretation of this phenomenon, see H. S. Converse, "The Agnicayana Rite: Indigenous Origin?" *Hist. of Rel.* XIV (1974), 81.
19. Staal 1983, 2 vols.
20. *Śatapatha Brāhmaṇa* IX.1.1.10
21. The excerpts cited are from *Taittirīya Saṃhitā* IV.5. 3h; 5d; 8d; 81.
22. *Taittirīya Saṃhitā* VI.5.3.1: *ubhayáto-mukham ṛtu-pātrám bhavati.*
23. This simile, "the birth of god", is valid for the whole unfolding process of Śiva.
23a. ADDENDUM: Hans Bakker in his review of my book (*Many Heads, Arms and Eyes* etc.), fails to give both conceptual and chronological priority to this ritual for the origin and meaning of a *mukhaliṅga.* A later meaning of the term is in the Tilottamā myth. The myth is the *līlā,* the play of the god that develops after the theological position (*veda*) has been established. His review is in *Artibus Asiae* 58, 1999: 339-342. Unfortunately, his student's thesis repeats this error. See Yoko Yokochi, *The Rise of the Warrior Goddess: A Study of the Myths Cycle of Kauśikī-Vindhyāvasinī in the Skandapurāṇa,* Groningen 2004; p. 87, fn. 25.
24. For details, see Doris Meth Srinivasan, "Early Vaiṣṇava Imagery: Caturvyūha and Variant Forms," *Archives of Asian Art* XXXII (1979), 51; and "Early Kṛṣṇa Icons: The Case at Mathurā," in *Kalādarśana, American Studies in the Art of India,* Joanna G. Williams (ed.) (New Delhi, 1981), 132, and n. 77. Both are in this volume.
25. Otto Pächt, *The Rise of Pictorial Narrative in Twelfth-Century England* (Oxford, 1962); see especially chap. III. I acknowledge with thanks the assistance of William Tronzo, Johns Hopkins University, who referred me to this work.
26. Two discussions which helped formulate my definition of ritual are Wade T. Wheelock, "The Problem of Ritual Language: From Information to Situation," *Journal of the American Academy of Religion,* L (1981), 49–71; Richard Schechner, "Wrestling Against Time: The Performance Aspects of Agni," *Journal of Asian Studies* XLV (1986), 359–63; this is a review of Staal 1983 as in note 14.

4

Significance and Scope of Pre-Kuṣāṇa Śaivite Iconography

> A brahmin shall meditate correctly on the three-eyed, five-faced, ten-armed, auspicious, adorned with all ornaments, blue-necked, with a banner with the moon (as hare), similar to pure rock crystal, with a serpent as sacred cord over the left shoulder, a tiger skin as upper garment, a water jar and a rosary in the hand, giving safety, a trident in the hand, a club in the hand, mounted on the shoulder of a bull, bearing half of the body of Umā, flaming, wearing a brown tress with a diadem, causing splendour on the topknot of hair, covered with immortality, excited, worshiped by gods and Asuras, joined with the deities of the quarters, continual and eternal, kind, constant, imperishable, immutable, all-pervading, deceitless, multiform ruler Rudra.[1]

So enjoins the *Mānava Śrautasūtra* (11.7.1.12), an early *śrauta* text, possibly of the pre-Christian era.[2] Is this mental image representative of the earliest actual Śaivite icons? The earliest images of Śiva precede the Kuṣāṇa period (*c.* AD 78)[2a(*)] from which time onward, images both in number and in plastic expression begin to proliferate considerably. Earlier images, more limited in range, are however found in stone and on coins and seals over quite a large region, both within and without the indigenous Indian cultural sphere. That is, the finds can be associated with regions of Indo-Parthian, Indo-Greek, and Śaka suzerainty as well as regions of local rulership in the Himalayan foothills, in the Gangetic valley, and pockets in the south such as Guḍimallam. This vast (Fig. 4.1) terrain has yielded Śaivite iconographic evidence for more than three hundred years prior to the establishment of the Kuṣāṇa kingdom. For a clear understanding of the range and development of these early Śaivite images, it is most instructive to divide the

---

Originally published in *Discourses on Śiva*, Michael W. Meister (ed.), Philadelphia, 1984, pp. 32-46. Reprinted with stylistic changes, addenda and permission from University of Pennsylvania Press.

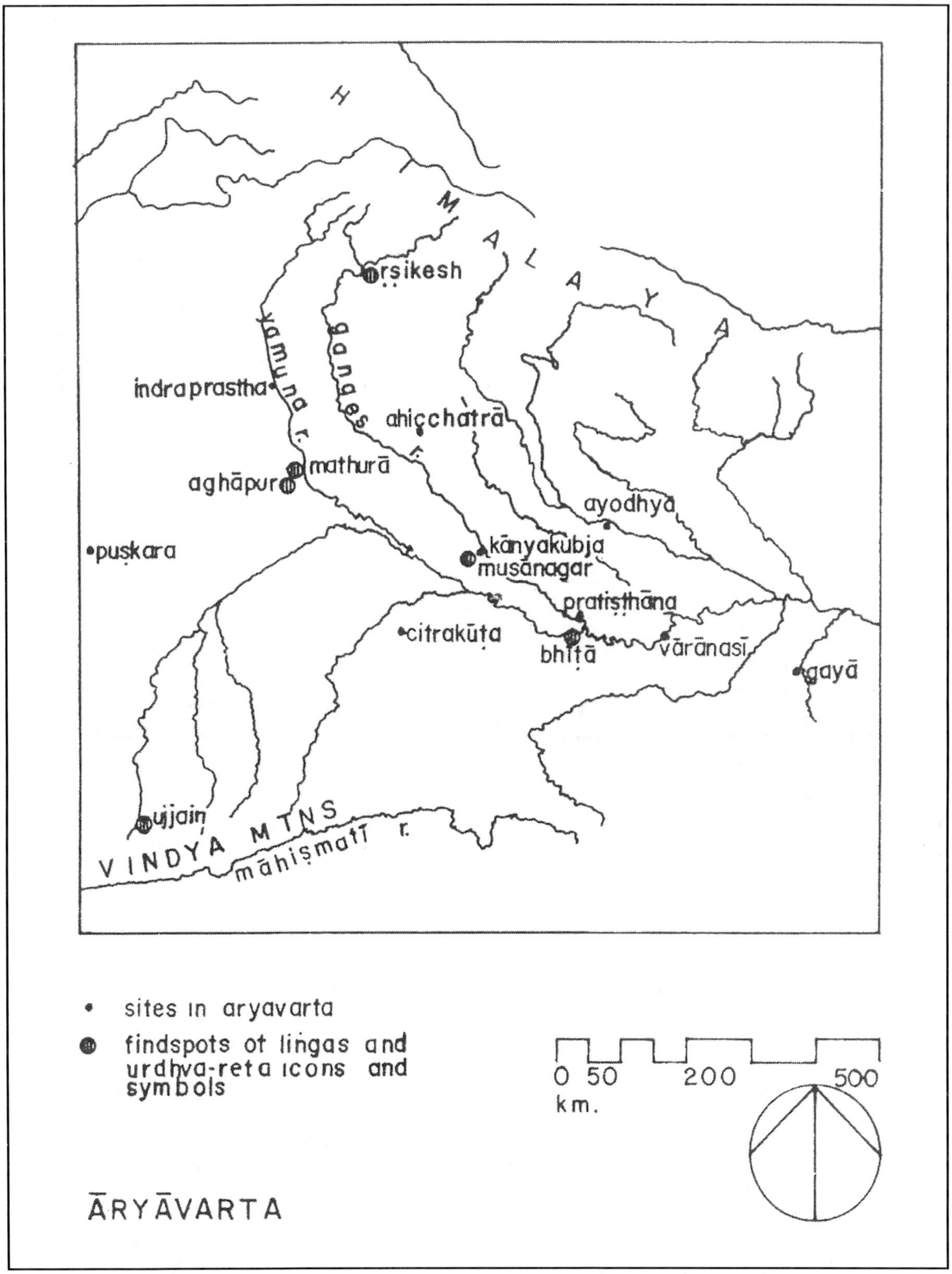

Fig. 4.1. Map of Āryāvarta, early *liṅga* sites.

Fig. 4.2. Guḍimallam, Andhra Pradesh. Paraśurāmeśvara Temple, Śiva *liṅga*, ca. third-second century BC. (Courtesy: Archaeological Survey of India and I.K. Sarma); Phase 1.

material into two broad chronological phases and analyze it as such. Phase 1 comprises findings belonging mainly to the second and first centuries BC, the Śuṅga-Kāṇva ages, and into Phase 2 are placed those pieces dated roughly to the period around the Christian era, beginning with the post-Kāṇva era and including the pre-Kuṣāṇa period of time (i.e. the Śaka-Kṣatrapa period).

PHASE 1

Śaivite iconography probably begins with the Guḍimallam Śiva *liṅga* (Fig. 4.2), very well known since it was first discovered in 1903.[3] It can now be fully appreciated, thanks to a recent excavation and conservation project undertaken by the South-Eastern Circle of the Archaeological Survey of India. The icon, renowned as the earliest image of Śiva and his aniconic symbol, the *liṅga,* is housed in the Paraśurāmeśvara Temple (Chittoor District, Andhra Pradesh). The date, previously determined on stylistic grounds to be ca. second century BC, may be pushed back somewhat as a result of associated strata and finds of the small-scale dig. Digging within the temple's *garbhagṛha* revealed that the *liṅga,* of hard igneous stone and dark brown color, belongs to the temple's earliest phase, that is, the third-second centuries BC.[4 & 4a(*)] Thus it is with renewed interest that a quick survey of the *liṅga's* iconography is undertaken. The *liṅga,* shaft and nut, is ca. five feet in height. The realistic nut is differentiated from the cylindrical shaft (ca. one foot thick) by a deep, slanting groove near the top. The excavation shows that the shaft continues to become square at the bottom and that this section is fitted into two circular ring stones of varying diameters.[5] In effect, the Guḍimallam icon is the earliest *liṅgapīṭha* known to date.

Two-armed Śiva, carved in high relief, stands. astride upon the shoulders of a crouching *yakṣa.* The god holds a small, horned animal in the lowered right hand, a battle-ax and water pot in the left. Wearing only a thin *dhotī,* his lowered *membrum virile* is seen through the delicate drapery folds. Neither the particular patternization of the drapery, the *jaṭābhāra* hair, the ornamentation, or modeling of forms needs to be dwelt upon, since these details can easily be found elsewhere.[6] New is that the excavation uncovered the fish-shaped feet of the *yakṣa*.[7] These, together with his pointed "conch-shape" ears,[8] suggest that the *yakṣa* is associated with the aquatic realm.[9] In effect, the *liṅga* and Śiva arise from the waters. A square railing *(vedikā)*, composed of closely set crossbars *(sūcis)* and uprights *(stambhas)*, has also come to light; it seems devoid of coping stones. Sarma hypothesizes that the *liṅgapiṭha*, within the *vedikā*, stood in the open and was worshiped much like a *vṛkṣacaitya* (the caitya [piled platform] with the sacred tree)[10] in antiquity.[11] The point is well taken. Indeed a Mathurā relief (Mathura Museum no. 3625; Fig. 4.4), probably belonging to Phase 1,[12] shows a plain, realistic *liṅga*, under a tree and inside a similarly compact railing, receiving worship.

Fig. 4.3. Mathurā, Kankālī Tila, free-standing Śiva *liṅga*. Pre-Kuṣāṇa phase 1, *c.* first century BC. (Photo: Doris M. Srinivasan).

This scene of *liṅga* worship appears on a buff sandstone lintel (6 1/4" x 30" x 4 1/2") from Bhūteśvara, Mathurā (Fig. 4.4). But for the simple band which decorates the nut, the *liṅga* corresponds to the Guḍimallam *liṅga*. The Guḍimallam *liṅga* and the later Jaṭeśvara *liṅga* found *in situ* at Mathurā[13] strongly suggest that free-standing *liṅgas* such as depicted on this lintel would have possessed a square socle which was set into ring stone(s) underground. The worshipers approaching the *liṅga* from either side and bearing garlands and flowers are composite creatures. Human up to the abdomen, sporting griffins' wings, their lower portions seem to dissolve into leonine forms. While Mathurā's inventiveness in rendering fantastic creatures is here clearly indicated, their connection with the Śiva *liṅga* cult is less obvious.[14]

A free-standing plain *liṅga*, quite like the one in the above relief, has been found at Kankālī Tila (Mathurā) and is now housed in the State Museum, Lucknow (no. H1; Fig. 4.3). Realistically conceived in red sandstone, it features the nut with the central fold and encircled with a wide band. The *liṅga* measures 38.2" X 10.2" above ground; it has a rectangular socle intended for insertion into the ground.

Numismatic evidence confirms that in antiquity free-standing *liṅgas* were indeed closely associated with trees. On the obverse of Allan's variety e, of class 1 Ujjayinī coppers, the *liṅga* is seen between two different trees in railings.[15]

Fig. 4.4. Mathurā, Uttar Pradesh. Sandstone lintel showing worship of Śiva *liṅga*. (Courtesy: Government Museum, Mathurā); Phase 1.

Already in our Phase 1, the *liṅga* is conceived as a cylindrical chamber wherefrom unfold the different emanations of Śiva. These are plastically expressed as his faces *(mukhas),* and as such, this period sees the development of *ekamukha* and *pañcamukha* Śiva *liṅgas.*

The Philadelphia Museum of Art contains an important *ekamukha liṅga* from Mathurā (no. 70.221.1; Fig. 4.5). It shares the realism of the other stone *liṅgas* discussed so far. An incised rim circles the nut just above the central fold, and above this point the human head emerges. The treatment of the cap of ringlets and the wide open eyes indicate a first century BC date.[16] Of considerable interest is the appearance of a snake slithering among the locks of hair.

The inscribed Bhīṭā (Allahabad District, Uttar Pradesh), *pañcamukha liṅga,* of buff sandstone, serves as a significant iconological benchmark (Fig. 4.6). The central shaft is carved into the shape of a two-armed male, Īśāna, whose straight strands of hair fall on his shoulders. In the left hand, bent at the elbow, he holds a water pot; the right hand was probably raised in *abhaya mudrā.* The oblique parallel lines across the chest could either be the border of a scarf or the *yajñopavīta.* Under the arms of the central male, four different faces are distinguished. The face directly below the left hand represents the terrific Aghora (lit., reassuring) aspect of Śiva; the fanged teeth and moustache identify this aspect. The next face moving counterclockwise, devoid of hair and ornamentation, is the *yogin* or ascetic aspect. Next follows the *kapardin* or *uṣṇīṣin* form represented by a head wearing a turban with topknot. The fourth face, adorned with large, globular earrings, collar-necklace, and a fillet around the well-arranged strands of hair, is likely to portray the female (Strī) nature of Śiva.

Ithyphallic Śiva is also represented in this phase. A unique statue, of the red mottled sandstone characteristic of Mathurā, was found at Ṛṣikeśa (Uttar Pradesh), a decade ago[17] (Fig. 4.7). It is significant that the statue is a colossus (4′ 9" in height) as this strengthens a recent conjecture that Brahmanic colossi, as

Fig. 4.5. Mathurā, *ekamukha liṅga*. Pre-Kuṣāṇa phase 1. (Courtesy: Philadelphia Museum of Art).

Fig. 4.6. Bhīṭā, Uttar Pradesh. *Pañcamukha liṅga* (State Museum, Lucknow). Pre-Kuṣāṇa phase 1. (Photo: Doris M. Srinivasan).

well as Buddhist and folk colossi, were fashioned in these early periods.[18] In most respects, the figure exhibits features belonging to a pan-Indic iconographic program extending over many sects during the two phases considered in this paper; the *abhaya mudrā*, the *kamaṇḍalu* in the left hand, the characteristic draping of *dhotī* and scarf all partake of this pan-Indic vocabulary. The Ṛṣikeśa male,[19] though poorly preserved, may be identified by the still clearly discernible *ūrdhvareta*. Śiva's stolid stance is roughly comparable to early *yakṣas* (e.g., the pre-Śuṅga Parkham Yakṣa from Mathurā; the Śuṅga Vidiśā Yakṣa, etc.), *nāgas* (e.g., pre-Śuṅga Mathurā Nāga, no. 17.1303 in the Mathura Museum) and Vaiṣṇava figures (e.g., Vāsudeva and Pradyumna of the Śuṅga Caturvyūha icon from Bhīṭā, no. 56.394 in the Lucknow Museum). Specifically, this Śiva icon seems somewhat more advanced than the pre-Śuṅga forms and exhibits modeling and forms closer to such Śuṅga *yakṣas* as the one from Palwal (no. 0.107 in the Lucknow Museum) and the one from Biravai, a village about six miles from Noh on the Bharatpur-Agra Road. (This region was included in the cultural sphere of Mathurā during these ages.) The protuberance on Śiva's head could either be the topknot of his locks, as

Fig. 4.7. Ṛṣikeśa, Uttar Pradesh. *Ūrdhvareta* Śiva. (Courtesy: Archaeological Survey of India, Delhi Circle) Phase 1.

reported, or the turban (cf. no. 107 in the Lucknow Museum), signaling his *uṣṇīṣin* form. In any case, the icon bespeaks of the nature of Śiva alone since it predates, by several centuries, the advent of Lakulīśa.[20]

Numismatic evidence widens our knowledge of Śaivite iconography during this phase. The Indian humped bull is surely the bull of Śiva when facing the *liṅga* on the reverse of Ārjunāyanas's copper coin type (variety b).[21] The coins date to *c.* second century BC and the Ārjunāyanas are a tribal oligarchy whose lands probably lay within the Delhi-Jaipur-Agra triangle.[22] This variety may show, on the obverse, a bull facing right before a tree in railing.[23] A bull before a tree in railing also occurs on the-obverse of rare coins found in Almorā (in the Himalayas).[24] Two of the coins bear the names "Śivadatta" and "Śivapālita," indicating that the Almorā chiefs may have given worship to Śiva. Gomitra coins from Mathurā also feature the bull to the right of a tree in railing on the obverse.[25] Some coppers from Kauśāmbī may depict these emblems the same side or on separate sides.[26]

The trident, with or without ax head, is another Śaivite symbol found on coins of indigenous tribes. Audumbari kings with names showing adoration of Śiva (i.e., Śivadāsa, Rudradāsa) issued coins showing a two-storied domed and pillared shrine beside a trident with ax on the right.[27] On the reverse square Audumbara coppers of Dharaghoṣa, a two-storied shrine and trident appear; the legend on these coins includes the word *"mahadeva,"* understood by some as a regal title.[28] It seems better to follow Sircar's suggestion and consider *"mahadeva"* as referring to Śiva. Thus, the coins are understood to be issued in the name of Mahādeva (-Śiva) as well as the ruling chief of the Audumbaras because Śiva enjoyed the special devotion of this Punjabi tribe.[29] On two round silver coins of Dharaghoṣa, the reverse shows the trident with ax and, to the left, the tree in enclosure motif. The obverse shows a bearded figure having a lion's skin over the left arm. The figure is labeled Viśpamitra (i.e., Viśvāmitra)[30] and the marginal legend reads *mahadevasa raña Dharaghoṣasa;* here too, *"mahadeva"* is likely to refer to Śiva in whose name the Audumbari leader struck his coins.

Coins associated with foreign influences show other Śaivite emblems. From Taxila comes a copper type having a lion to the left of a tree in railing.[31] To the best of my knowledge, this combination is rare further south, and may be a variation for the bull and tree in railing seen on the tribal coins. A distinctive anthropomorphic representation of Śiva is found on a rare coin type of the Śaka king Maues; the god is depicted striding and holding both club and trident.[32 & 32a(*)]

Śiva's aspect as Lord of Music and Dance is reflected in a unique Śuṅga terracotta now in the Gopi Krishna Kanoria Collection.[33] Vīṇādhara Dakṣiṇāmūrti is seen seated on a bull, with *gaṇas* below; he is carrying a harp-shaped *vīṇā* in his hand. This important terracotta, whose provenance is not known, attests to the antiquity of Śiva's musical form in the plastic arts.

PHASE 2

The main type which continues into this phase from the previous one is the *ekamukha liṅga.* An example of a colossal (5' high) *ekamukha liṅga,* probably of the pre-Kuṣāṇa period, comes from Aghāpura (Bharatpur District, Rajasthan). Of spotted red sandstone, the *liṅga* (Fig. 4.8) emphasizes the same realism seen in the above mentioned plain and *ekamukha liṅgas* also from the Mathurā region. The Aghāpura *liṅga,* having an undecorated nut, displays Śiva's head upon the shaft, contrasting thereby with the Philadelphia *ekamukha liṅga.* Śiva's *uṣṇīṣin* aspect is represented; the turban, tied in a series of generous folds and adorned with a bejeweled central crest, displays proportions similar to pre-Kuṣāṇa turban styles. Whereas the Kuṣāṇa style from this general region features a large central crest as the most dominant and decorative element, in earlier styles, the size of the central crest is about equal to that of the rest of the turban. Good comparative pre-Kuṣāṇa examples are found on railing pillars from Mūsānagar (Kanpur, Uttar Pradesh); one railpost shows a turbaned *yakṣa* figure (no. 53.123, State Museum, Lucknow; Fig. 4.9); the other, now in the Muktā Devī Temple (see below), depicts a turbaned, seated Śiva.

Fig. 4.8. Aghāpura, Uttar Pradesh. *Ekamukha liṅga* (Government Museum, Bharatpur). Pre-Kuṣāṇa Phase 2. (Courtesy: Archaeological Survey of India).

Another *ekamukha liṅga,* outlining Śiva's head with *jaṭājūṭa,* is carved on an architectural fragment (B 141; State Museum, Lucknow; Fig. 4.10). Stemming from Mathurā, the fragment (13" x 7.5"), can be placed, on the basis of style, to *c.*

Fig. 4.9. Mūsānagar, Uttar Pradesh. *Yakṣa* on railpost (from Muktādevī Temple; now State Museum, Lucknow). Pre-Kuṣāṇa Phase 2. (Courtesy: Archaeological Survey of India).

first century AD. We may consider it briefly, as distinctive elements of our previous phase are evident here. The realistic nut[34] is decorated with a patterned band, tied as if to secure Śiva's face to the *liṅga.* The shaft is installed upon a brick platform, situated before a spreading pipal tree. To the right of the altar are two *yakṣas* who have presumably completed their worship. They stand before a broken figure, perhaps a female, to judge from the remaining drapery folds (cf. Mathura Museum no. H6; State Museum, Lucknow no. J225).

The earliest Śiva Ardhanārī occurs on a Mathurā red-sandstone relief depicting a row of standing divinities (Mathura Museum no. 34.2520; Fig. 4.11). The two-armed Ardhanārīśvara is the first figure on the right of this stele (7 1/2" high x 10" long). The male side, on the proper right, has the hand in *abhaya mudrā,* the raised phallus (*ūrdhvaretas*), and slim hip. Close examination shows that the leg is covered by a lion skin, having the lion's head over the kneecap. A mustache and distinctive ornamentation further differentiate the male from the female side. The female half has a full breast, rounded hip, wide girdle, long drapery, and an anklet around the foot. A mid-first century AD date is suggested on the basis of stylistic and iconographic features. In general, all the figures are stiffer and exhibit greater abruptness in their transitional planes than the more relaxed yet sturdy forms of the Kuṣāṇa period. Specifically, the somewhat heavy and static Ardhanārīśvara with raised female arm differs in these respects from the typical Kuṣāṇa representations (Figs. 4.12–4.13). An early date is also endorsed by details associated with the other figures. The turban of the fourth deity conforms to the above stated pre-Kuṣāṇa proportions. The second deity, Vāsudeva-Kṛṣṇa, holds a flask in his natural left hand. This is another early indicator since the flask,

Fig. 4.10. Mathurā, *ekamukha liṅga* on *vedī* platform (State Museum, Lucknow). (Photo: Doris M. Srinivasan) Phase 2.

though depicted in early Kuṣāṇa images of this god, is ultimately supplanted by a conch, held in the left hand.[35]

Two other extraordinary Śaivite reliefs belong to this phase. They are carved on adjacent sides of the Mūsānagar pillar (height ca. 5′) now in the Muktā Devī Temple.[36] The sides are divided into three panels. The first relief (Fig. 4.14) appears as the top panel, above the two lower panels showing *mithuna* couples. In the center of the top panel, a two-armed male figure crowned with the pre-Kuṣāṇa type of fluted turban is seated, in *lalitāsana,* on an elaborate seat which resembles a throne; the seat rests on bulbous legs and contains a curved backrest. The figure's conspicuous raised phallus clearly indicates that this is Śiva. He holds his right hand in *abhaya* while the left, poised on the folded left leg, holds a jar. He wears a *dhotī* and simple ornaments consisting of earrings and bracelets. Beneath his throne lies a lion. Iconographically, the most interesting features are the three auxiliary male forms emerging from the central figure of Śiva. Two arise from either side of his shoulders; each is two-armed and wears headgear. The middle form emerges directly from Śiva's headdress. His hair is worn *jaṭājūṭa* fashion, and in his arms, bent at the elbows, he holds two objects, one round and the other crescent-shaped. Possibly they symbolize the sun and the moon.[37] The other relief shows a standing Śiva, associated with attributes similar to the seated Śiva.

Fig. 4.11. Mathurā, panel of Brahmanical gods. Pre-Kuṣāṇa Phase 2, *c.* mid-first century AD. (Courtesy: Government Museum, Mathura).

He is ithyphallic, with right hand in *abhaya,* left hand holding a jar near the waist. A lion and *yakṣa* flank him to the right and left respectively (Fig. 4.15).

From the northwest a rather different set of Śaivite iconographic combinations are apparent. Śiva is represented on some silver coins of Gondophares, the Indo-Parthian king. His coinage is marked with a two-armed Śiva, carrying a trident in his right hand and a palm branch in his left;[38] or, the trident may be held in the god's left hand.[39] In both types, Śiva stands with his weight on his right leg, and the left one is relaxed and bent. A round copper seal from Sirkap shows Śiva striding, with the right leg thrust forward. He holds the trident and the club in his left and right hands, respectively. The seal bears the legend "Śivarakṣita" (protected by Śiva) in both Brāhmī and Kharoṣṭhī characters of the early first century AD.[40 & 40a(*)]

The cultural implications of the above assemblage become more sharply defined if we consider next whether this assemblage exhibits any patterns in use or distribution of iconography. The evidence shows that certain symbols are found in certain geographic regions. Probably the most important symbol, the *liṅga,* shows the most discrete usage and distribution. There seem to be no sculptural or

Fig. 4.12. Mathurā, Śiva Ardhanārīśvara. Kuṣāṇa period. (Courtesy: Victoria and Albert Museum, London).

Fig. 4.13. Mathurā, Śiva Ardhanārīśvara (Government Museum, Mathura). Late Kuṣāṇa period. (Photo: Doris M. Srinivasan).

numismatic examples of the *liṅga* in geographic regions outside of the indigenous Indian cultural milieu until the post Kuṣāṇa period. Moreover, except for the Guḍimallam *liṅga,* all the rest come from the region the *Mānava Dharmaśāstra* identifies as Āryāvarta (the country of the Aryans).[41] Further, if we exclude the Ujjayinī coins, the provenance narrows to a group of sites clustering around the Doab.[42] To state it another way, the entire region north of Mathurā, extending northerly and north-westerly to the Indo-Iranian borderlands, the Hindu Kush, and southern Bactria does not fashion representations of the *liṅga* during our time frame.[42a(*)] Instead, the findspots indicate not only that worship of the *membrum virile* is entirely indigenous, but that it is most prevalent in those regions most closely associated with Aryan culture.

The same observation applies to the usage of *ūrdhvareta* images, since the findspots of ithyphallic Śiva likewise cluster in Āryāvarta.

Fig. 4.14. Mūsānagar, Muktādevī Temple, pillar, panel of seated Śiva. Pre-Kuṣāṇa Phase 2. (Courtesy: Gritli v. Mitterwalner).

On the other hand, the northerly regions produced iconographic combinations not found elsewhere. That is, the lion and enclosed tree, the trident and club[42b(*)], and the trident and palm branch do not combine as Śaivite emblems in Āryāvarta and points south.

The assemblage also shows that the animal world associated with Śaivite iconography extends, in pre-Kuṣāṇa times, considerably beyond the expected bull. A horned animal and the snake occur, as well as the lion. Although the lion is not usually considered an important animal in Śaiva iconography, this apparently was not the case in the incipient stages. Not only are the lion and lion's skin seen in the pre-Kuṣāṇa art, but the animal continues to be linked with Śaivism in the Kuṣāṇa period as well. For example, a free-standing *liṅga,* found in the region of Caumā Bundapur (Mathura District), has four different configurations on the bottom of the shaft: an *amṛta ghaṭa,* a female head, a pot-bellied *gaṇa* or *yakṣa,* and a couchant lion (Fig. 4.16).[43] A couchant lion and a *gaṇa* also appear beside the legs of a male statue, broken below the thighs (Mathura Museum no. 214). V. S. Agrawala correctly identified this sculptural fragment from Māt (Mathura District) as a standing Śiva on the basis of the *gaṇa* and lion.[44]

The lacunae in the above assemblage are equally interesting. The important iconographic convention of multiple body parts, to flower in the succeeding age, is rarely evident. Śiva's third eye is not yet depicted; his multiple arms await the realization of the Kuṣāṇa artist. The urge to portray multiple heads is, however, experimentally expressed. Also noteworthy, and different from subsequent iconographic developments, is that Śiva is shown alone. Portrayal of the divine couple or the divine family is absent, and as a corollary, absent is a mythological orientation in the entire assemblage.

Absence of plastic representations of legendary episodes needs further elaboration. It is not that early literature is devoid of Śaivite legends. Vedic literature contains a story to explain how Rudra received his names *(Kauṣītaki Brāhmaṇa* 6.1–9) and another on how Rudra punishes incestuous Prajāpati and distributes the seed (*ŚB* 1.7.4.1–8). Already the *Taittirīya Saṃhitā* indicates that the gods barred Rudra from the sacrifice (2.6.8.2) and the *Aitareya Brāhmaṇa* (3.34) recounts how the gods deprived Rudra of his part of the offering. Another myth in the *Śatapatha Brāhmana* (1.7.3.1–7) relates why Rudra has claim to the remaining portion of the sacrificial oblation. These Vedic accounts are forerunners, no doubt, of the epic legend which tells of Śiva's exclusion from Dakṣa's sacrifice (*Mahābhārata* 12.274.2–58). The epic also narrates Śiva's destruction of Tripura (*MBh.* 8.24.3ff). However, these myths do not receive plastic expression, and the overwhelming impression gained from the material evidence is that it is more concerned with the nature of divinity than divine legends. This emphasis in Śaivite art is matched with developments in early Vaiṣṇavite art. From earliest times through the Kuṣāṇa period, narrative sculptures are few.[45] The minimal use of the narrative in early Śaivite and Vaiṣṇavite art is sharply distinguished from the emphasis on the narrative in Buddhist art during the same periods. Its absence in much of early Hindu sectarian art must have been purposeful and in response to a different religious orientation.[45a(*)] The orientation of early Śaivite art is decidedly theological: the emphasis is on knowledge of god's nature and the translation of this knowledge into forms fit for worship.

Fig. 4.15. Mūsānagar, Muktādevī Temple, pillar, panel of standing Śiva. Pre-Kuṣāṇa Phase 2. (Courtesy: Gritli v. Mitterwalner).

Śiva's nature, according to the art examined, is predominantly linked to the symbolic significance of the phallus. As such, knowledge of the significance of the *liṅga* during the first millennium BC would contribute, more than any other iconographic convention, toward an understanding of the nature of Śiva in pre-Kuṣāṇa art. The symbolic values associated with *liṅga* and *ūrdhvaliṅga* in late epic and Purāṇic sources have been found to encompass a complex range of

Fig. 4.16. Caumā, Uttar Pradesh. *Liṅga:* female face, lion, and *gaṇa* at the base, pre-Kuṣāṇa period. (Photo: N.P. Joshi).

sexual ambiguities of cosmic and mundane dimensions.[46] Such notions are preceded by notions on the *liṅga* and phallus in the earlier literature of the Vedas. It may not be immediately apparent why this literature can be profitably surveyed since it has long been argued that Rudra, the Vedic forerunner of Śiva, is himself an outsider to Vedic traditions, that his ithyphallic nature is prefigured in a pre-Vedic culture, and that the Vedic religion's disdain toward ritualistic sexuality precludes obtaining information on the significance of the phallus from this source. This argument probably can no longer be maintained for prehistoric and proto-historic developments of Rudra-Śiva, and for Vedic ritualism.[47] Several recent studies in religion and art have shown that evidence for the existence of an ithyphallic proto-Śiva in the pre- and non-Vedic Indus civilization is lacking.[48] Further, in a study on the nature of Rudra in the Vedas (especially the Saṃhitās), it is demonstrated that the "outsider" label may need to be considerably revised. For Rudra's most fundamental characteristics—his ambivalent capacity for benign and fearful action, his *asura*-hood, his close association with the most ancient stratum of the Vedic gods, his relation to the Vedic ritual, especially the remnant—bring him into the very center of Vedic norms and ideals.[49] It begins to appear as if the antecedents of Hinduistic Śiva are predominantly Brahmanical, and it therefore seems appropriate to test, below, the validity of this supposition with respect to the meaning and significance of both the term *liṅga* and the phallic form.

The term *liṅga* rarely occurs prior to the Upaniṣads. In the Upaniṣads, the term as well as the privative *aliṅga* are not used in the sense of "male sexual organ." Early Vedic terms having that meaning are *śiśna* and *vetasa*. The oft-cited occurrence of *śiśna* in the compound *śiśnadeva* (*Ṛg Veda* 7.21.5; 10.99.3), is usually understood to refer to phallic worship among non-Aryan groups. The compound, meaning "those who have the phallus as their deity," is, in any event, not associated with Ṛg Vedic concepts pre-figuring Śiva. Beyond these two occurrences it is hard to find mention of phallic worship in Vedic literature from the Saṃhitās through the Upaniṣads.

Not without mention in the older Upaniṣads,[50] *liṅga* is more often found in the "middle" Upaniṣads. The *Kaṭha Upaniṣad* (6.8) speaks of Puruṣa (i.e., the supreme male Being), who is higher than the unmanifest (*avyakta*), as "all-pervading and without any mark" (*aliṅga*); knowledge of him is equated with liberation. In a somewhat similar vein the *Śvetāśvatara Upaniṣad* (6.9) declares that Maheśvara (6.7; i.e., Śiva: 5.14) has no *liṅga* [in the world], [and] he is the [first] cause. Book 6.11 explains this further, saying, "He is the One God hidden in all things..., alone [and] devoid of attributes *[nirguṇa].*" The same Upaniṣad elaborates further on the connotation of *liṅga:*

Just as the material form (*mūrti*) of fire when latent in its source *(yoni)* is not seen even though its *liṅga*[51] is not destroyed, for it is perceptible again by kindling in its source (*yoni*). Similarly both indeed [are found] in the body by Oṁ.[52]

The passage, in clearly distinguishing between *mūrti* and *liṅga,* tells much about the latter concept. Whereas *"mūrti"* is a concrete, apprehensible form, *"liṅga"* is the sign, nonmaterial and therefore unchangeable, which testifies to the existence of something. *Liṅga* is also distinguished from source (*yoni*), the effective cause for the arising of both *liṅga* and *mūrti;* possibly the notion of *yoni* is akin to that of *aliṅga* (see above). In any case, in the process of arising or concretization, the *liṅga* seems to be a "subtle form or body" and it is in this sense that the *Maitrī Upaniṣad* uses the term (6.10).[53]

References to *liṅga* or *aliṅga* in several later non-Vedic works also do not use the term in an erotic sense. According to Caraka, *aliṅga* ("without any characteristic") describes a state attainable by the doctrine of ultimate renunciation.[54] In Aśvaghoṣa's *Buddhacarita, liṅga* denotes "marks" of an ascetic or mendicant (9.18; 12.46).[55]

For our understanding of the religious significance of Śiva *liṅgas,* the most important text is the *Mahā-Nārāyaṇa Upaniṣad,* forming Book 10 of the *Taittirīya Āraṇyaka.* Not only is it close in time to the earliest plastic *liṅga* representations,[56] but it also contains a remarkable series of prayers which correlate *liṅgas* with Rudra-Śiva. Prayers Number 271–316 are dedicated mainly to Rudra-Śiva and contain the formulaic repetition of the term *liṅga.* These formulas are introduced with an opening salutation (No. 270): "Homage to the Lord of destruction, homage to Him who puts an end to destruction" (the translation supposes, as does the *Vedic Word-Concordance III*, p. 448, that *nidhanapatāntikāya* should be *nidhanapatyantikāya*). In effect, Rudra-Śiva is recognized as the universal cosmic power which in its undifferentiated state is both destructive and creative. There follows a set of prayers, Numbers 271–75, having a definite internal pattern. In each instance, homage is first given to a particular power or attribute of the Supreme and then to the *liṅga* of that power or attribute.[57] As such, homage is given to the raised *liṅga,* the golden *liṅga,* the bright *liṅga,* the celestial *liṅga,* the Bhava *liṅga,* the Śarva *liṅga,*[58] the Śiva *liṅga,* the flame *liṅga,* the *ātman liṅga,* the supreme *liṅga,* and the all-*liṅga.*[59]

This set of *"liṅga"* verses is followed by a set of prayers which again have some internal cohesiveness. *Mantras* 277–285 invoke a pentad of names which the later tradition records as the names of the five faces of a *pañcamukha liṅga*.[60] This is the earliest mention of this pentad which later Śaivism considers to represent the emanatory forms of the formless (*niṣkala*) Śiva,[61] or the five forms which represent the fivefold nature of the supernal. Much of the remaining laudations convey specific descriptions on the looks, attributes, and activities of Rudra, and forecast thereby, much like the *Mānava Śrautasūtra* passage quoted at the outset, future developments in Śaivite icons.

In short, there seems to be a fixed progression in which the *mantras* are spoken. That progression, it is proposed, correlates with the unfolding process of the supreme. Thus verse 270 refers to the undifferentiated supreme; verses 271–276 refer to an initial differentiating process of the one into a series of subtle forms, and verses 277–85 refer to a secondary unfolding wherein the five aspects of the supreme arise from subtle form or matter.

Liṅga is thus the first "sign" or evolute of the essence of Śiva, in subtle form or matter. If *liṅga* expresses the theological belief in the immanence of the transcendental in nature, in a subtle form, why does that form take the shape of a realistic phallus? An instructive Vedic passage indicates that already in the Saṃhitās, the phallus is the sign symbolizing the Creator's capacity for unlimited production. The passage occurs in the *Atharva Veda*, hymn 10.7, a hymn to Skambha (lit. "prop, support, pillar"). Skambha is the cosmic generative force whence the entire material world originates.[62] However, Skambha is not postulated as the active demiurge who gives rise to phenomenality. Rather Skambha is the cause which gives rise to the agent who in turn takes over the creative process. As such, Skambha generates Prajāpati. It is thus of more than passing interest that a *vetasá-hiraṇyāya*[63] ("a golden phallus"), standing in the water represents the hidden (*guhya-*) Prajāpati (41). Indeed what is being said is that the first evolute of cosmic creative energy is a hidden, or unperceivable progenitor symbolized by a golden phallus in the water.

The image presages *liṅga* symbolism. It is related in the "Sauptika" Parvan of the *Mahābhārata* (10.17) that Brahmā told Mahādeva to create, but Śiva saw the defects of living creatures and did *tapas* in the water for a long time.[64] After a long time Brahmā decided to create another progenitor, Prajāpati (10.17.16), who proceeded to give birth to many creatures. Śiva rose out of the water and saw that beings had, in the meantime, been created. He tore off his *liṅga* and placed it in the ground. Then he set forth, in anger, to perform *tapas* at the foot of the Muñjavat Mountain. For our purpose, this epic passage is highly important. First, it associates unambiguously the meaning of "phallus" with the term *liṅga*, an association not readily discernible in the texts cited above. Second, Śiva's *liṅga* is emblematic not of his personal sexuality but of his cosmic creative energy. Third, the myth in its specific details contains mythopoeic imagery overlapping with the Atharva Vedic account: the golden phallus *(vetasa)* in the water as sign of the unseen creator has become the phallus (*liṅga*) of Śiva submerged in the water in preparation for creation. Further, in the light of the epic and Vedic passages, it seems reasonable to conclude that Śiva's act of castration is brought about because his *liṅga* had been rendered useless by the *liṅga* of Prajāpati. Thus it appears, Prajāpati's *liṅga* has usurped the function of Śiva's *liṅga;* the story bridges the Atharva Vedic account and other epic and Purāṇic passages associating Śiva's *liṅga* with his potential for cosmic creation.[65]

To conclude, according to Brahmanical literature, *liṅga* is the subtle, recognizable, unchangeable sign of the otherwise unknowable, transcendental, unseen Śiva, and this sign may be in the form of a phallus to symbolize Śiva's capacity to produce life itself.

It must be quickly added that whereas worship of the phallus is non-Vedic, there is nothing inherently non-Vedic in using the phallus (or "maleness" in general) as a metaphor. To cite a few examples occurring in a ritual context: in the New and Full Moon Sacrifice, the after-offerings are three *śiśna* (the penis and the testicles);[66] in the *Cāturmāsya,* the *kraiḍina* oblation is the male organ;[67] in the *Pravargya,* the caldron is the penis and the two handles are the testicles;[68] in the preparation of the Āhavanīya in the *Agnicayana,* the pestle is the *śiśna,* the mortar the *yoni.*[69] Or, when the *Ṛg Veda* assigns "a thousand testicles" to Indra, it is to dwell upon his heroic, creative strength rather than his sexual energy.[70] Upon close analysis, the union between male and female, *mithuna,* is allegorically described throughout the Vedas,[71] and human parturition, in an intensified image, provides the mythic model for a most important creation theory.[72] Thus sexual symbolism is far from foreign to the Vedic religion, and it is from this background that the phallus could develop as the appropriate *liṅga* of Śiva. The textual material therefore cautions against the assumption that sexual symbolism has erotic connotations. Indeed, inasmuch as *liṅgas* may be *mukhaliṅgas* and ithyphallic Śiva is solitary, the plastic material evinces the same caution. Moreover, not only does pre-Kuṣāṇa evidence alert us to the nonerotic significance of *liṅga,* inscriptional evidence also comes to support. The Mathurā pillar inscription of Candragupta II (AD 380) records a donation by the Māheśvara teacher, Uditācārya of two *liṅgas* named after his teacher, Bhāgavat Kāpila, and his teacher's teacher, Bhāgavat Upamita. Uditācārya is described as tenth in descent from Bhāgavat Kusīka, disciple of Lakulīśa, the probable founder of the Pāśupata order.[73] In this inscription, the *liṅga* can hardly be associated with priapism. Mention should also be made of the Kuṣāṇa inscription which describes a Śiva *liṅga* as *jaṭeśvara.* The naming of Śiva *liṅgas* with names ending in *īśvara* continues in the Purāṇas (e.g., the Kāśī Khaṇḍa of the *Skanda Purāṇa*). Such *liṅga* names likewise tend to negate the erotic element. The *liṅga* in Tantrism and Vīraśaivism equally denies a priapic content. In the Tantric tradition, "the ithyphallic condition is not priapic, but represents precisely what the tantric aims to master, i.e. seminal retention in the laboratory setting of tantric ritualistic copulation."[74] For Basava, the founder of the Vīraśaivas, *liṅga* is devoid of erotic meaning, and in the known *vacanas* there is no suggestion that *liṅga* is a phallic symbol.[75] Thus our findings may be seen as part of a distinct religious scheme in India wherein *liṅga* symbolism is not erotic.

These findings likewise reopen the question whether the form and meaning of *liṅga* iconography entered Śaivite art and religion from the fertility beliefs of non-Aryan folk. If this sector had influence, there should have surfaced examples of *liṅgas* and the like among the abundant, extant terracottas of the Maurya and Śuṅga periods; or some *liṅga* representations should have been found in the less Aryanized regions during the periods these forms appeared in the more Aryanized ones. However, to the east, in northern Bihar for example, probably the earliest *liṅga* and *yoni* configuration occurs on a Gupta seal.[76] This contrasts sharply with the (often large) stone examples surveyed above, which bespeak thereby of patronage and acceptance by an established, monied segment of the population.

In drawing the conclusion that the Brahmanic tradition itself fostered depiction of the *membrum virile* and considered it the subtle form of Śiva's cosmic energy, it may be well to look once more at particular icons with a view to seeing whether these define Śiva's nature further. In that the Guḍimallam *liṅga* and Śiva arise from an "aquatic" *yakṣa,* this icon closely answers the *"liṅga-in-the-water"* imagery contained in the *Atharva Veda* and *Mahābhārata* accounts. Śiva standing before his symbol of potency is represented, according to Śivaramamurti, as *yajamāna.*[77] The hand-held attributes relate closely to Vedic worship and culture. Water in the *kamaṇḍalu* is used to make ritual ablutions. The combination of *liṅga* and *yajamāna* could perhaps be read as Śiva, stimulator of the sacrifice. This aspect, already recognized in the *Ṛg Veda* (e.g., 3.2.5d) and implied in his epithet *maharṣi* (*Śvetāśvatara Upaniṣad* 3.4; 4.2; *Mahā-Nārāya Upaniṣad* verse 223), is best expressed by his name Ucchesaṇabhāga ("Lord of the sacrificial remainder"; *Taittirīya Brāhmaṇa* 1.7.8.5) in that the remainder is considered to be an unusually potent force serving as the connective link between the preceding and succeeding sacrifices.[78]

Mukhaliṅgas in general, on the basis of the foregoing, represent a stage in the unfolding process of the supernal which must come after the crystallization of his *liṅga* form, as the *mukha(s)* or aspect(s) issue from his subtle form. This theological notion could be the reason for the occurrence of certain artistic developments which aim to convey the idea that the heads emerge from the *liṅga:* either the carving itself imparts the sense of the head(s) arising from the central shaft, or the head(s) may be held to the shaft by a cord. With respect to the Bhīṭā *pañcamukha liṅga,* bracketed in time by the *Mahā-Nārāyaṇa Upaniṣad* and the *Viṣṇudharmottara Purāṇa* (which correlates the heads with the five faces of Śiva, and with the five gross elements and his ten arms with the ten directions)[79] it may have symbolized Śiva's identity with manifest reality.

The seated ithyphallic Śiva on the Mūsānagar pillar is problematic. The iconography seems to combine Indian and non-Indian influences. The depiction

of a throne chair and the lion may reflect foreign influences; the headdress, *āsana, ūrdhvareta,* and emanating figures are purely indigenous elements. The disposition of the emerging figures is very similar to a Kuṣāṇa icon identified as Viṣṇu Caturvyūha.[80] It is an open question whether these forms bespeak of a Śaivite *vyūha* concept; indeed the postulate for such a Śaivite concept has been recently suggested as a result of the study of a ninth-century Kashmiri-icon.[81] However, until textual evidence on the *vyūha* doctrine in Śaivism is forthcoming, it may be equally possible to consider the fourfold, ithyphallic Mūsānagar Śiva as symbolizing notions congruent with those of a *caturmukha liṅga.* The first *caturmukha liṅgas* occur in the Kuṣāṇa period. The icon features four differentiated heads emerging usually from a central *liṅga*[82] and facing in the four cardinal directions. (In effect, Īśāna of the *pañcamukha liṅga* becomes the central *liṅga* of the *caturmukha liṅga* icon.) Interestingly, two of the Mūsānagar Śiva heads have the same appearance as those of a Kuṣāṇa *caturmukha:* the central turbaned figure prefigures the later *uṣṇīṣin* head and the middle emanating figure prefigures the later *jaṭāmukuṭa* head. As such, the unique Mūsānagar seated Śiva displays similarities in headgear and in emphasis on the *membrum virile* as does a *caturmukha liṅga,* and likewise concentrates upon the fourfold nature of the Supreme.

The Ardhanārīśvara form emphasizes, as do many of the icons discussed above, the creative aspect of Śiva's nature. Divine bisexuality, in effect, is the mythopoeic answer to a probe into the origin of things. The answer given is based on an analogy with human reproduction, but avoids the need for two primordial creators. Śiva as hermaphrodite clarifies the mystery that God though One gives birth to manifold phenomenality. The divine hermaphrodite as First Cause occurs frequently in ancient mythologies;[83] in the Indian tradition, the bisexuality of Rudra-Śiva is already stated in the *Śvetāśvatara Upaniṣad* (4.3). The god is described as both man and woman in a passage offering other polarities to intimate the divine completeness and the underlying unity behind apparent dichotomies. But perhaps the most explicit statement on the meaning of the symbol comes from the *Mahābhārata:* "That god of gods (Rudra), that cause of both creation and destruction displays in his form the indication of both sexes as the One Cause of the creation of the universe."[84]

Pre-Kuṣāṇa Śaivite iconography from the subcontinent reveals a dominant theme: it celebrates the greatness of Śiva by extolling his cosmic energy and the way it stimulates the arising of things. These ages, allied to a heritage seeking above all to know the essential nature of God, show little concern to explore divinity's individuality. Śiva's family and his legends await depiction in future ages. Among Śaivite followers of the subcontinent, regardless of the paucity of a dominant theme in the early evidence from north India, he is worshiped as the supreme cause and source of all creation.

NOTES AND REFERENCES

1. *The Mānava Śrautasūtra,* Jeannette M. van Gelder, trans. (New Delhi, 1963), p. 320.
2. Cf. Louis Renou, *Vedic India, Classical India,* Vol. 3, P. Spratt, trans. (Delhi, 1971), pp. 42–43; Ram Gopal, *India of Vedic Kalpasūtras* (Delhi, 1959), p. 78.

2a. ADDENDUM: It is currently believed that the Kuṣāṇa era begins in AD 127, not in AD 78.

3. It is doubtful that proto-Śaivite material comes from the Indus Valley Civilization. For recent reappraisals on the so-called proto-Śiva seal from Mohenjo-daro, see my paper "The So-Called Proto-Śiva Seal from Mohenjo-daro: An Iconological Assessment," *Archives of Asian Art* 29 (1975–76): 47–58; Alf Hiltebeitel, "The Indus Valley 'Proto-Śiva,' Reexamined through Reflections on the Goddess, the Buffalo, and the Symbolism of Vāhanas," *Anthropos* 73 (1978): 767–797; cf. Walter A. Fairservis, Jr. *Excavations at Allahdino* I: *Seals and Inscribed Material* (New York, 1976), pp. 14–15; 18; 20–24; 110–11.
4. I. K. Sarma, "New Light on Art through Archaeological Conservation," *Journal of the Indian Society of Oriental Art,* n.s. no. 10 (1978–79): 52.

4a. ADDENDUM: On stylistic grounds Gritli von Mitterwallner has dated this *liṅga* to 50 BC–AD 50. See her "Evolution of the *Liṅga*" in Michael W. Meister (ed.), *Discourses on Śiva,* Philadelphia, 1984.

5. Sarma, "New Light," p. 51.
6. E.g., T.A. Gopinatha Rao, *Elements of Hindu Iconography* 2, Pt. 1, 2nd ed. (Madras, 1971), pp. 65–69.
7. Sarma, "New Light," p. 51; see Pl. XV, 11.
8. Ibid., p. 51.
9. On the symbolism of the conch, cf. Jan Gonda, *Aspects of Early Viṣṇuism,* 2nd ed. (Delhi, 1969), pp. 100–101; Ananda K. Coomaraswamy, *Yakṣas* 2, reprint (Delhi, 1971), p. 13.
10. U. P. Shah, "Beginnings of the Superstructure of Indian Temples," *Studies in Indian Temple Architecture,* P. Chandra, ed. (Delhi, 1975), p. 82.
11. Sarma, "New Light," p. 52.
12. This dating, based mainly on the style of carving, has already been suggested by N.P. Joshi, *Mathurā Sculptures* (Mathura, 1966), p. 80.
13. See V. S. Agrawala, "Further New Inscriptions from Mathura," *JUPHS* 12 (1939): 29–31.
14. Perhaps such creatures do not directly comment on a Śiva cult since a very similar type is found worshiping the Buddha's begging bowl (Boston Museum of Fine Arts, no. 26241).
15. John Allan, *Catalogue of the Coins of Ancient India* (London, 1936), p. 243, no. 19; Plate 36:15.
16. Cf. Bodhgayā Indra railing pillar and Mathura Museum figure of a noble (no. E7) for similar treatment of hair and eyes, respectively.
17. W. H. Siddiqi, "Two Newly Discovered Pre-Kuṣāṇa Sculptures from Ṛśikeśa (Uttar Pradesh)," *JISOA, Dr. Moti Chandra Commemoration Volume* (1978): 76–80. I am thankful to Dr. U. P. Shah for informing me about this important finding.
18. See Doris M. Srinivasan, "God as Brahmanical Ascetic: A Colossal Kuṣāṇa Icon of the Mathura School," *JISOA,* n.s. no. 10 (1978–79): 1–16; Doris M. Srinivasan, "Early Vaiṣṇava Imagery: Caturvyūha and Variant Forms," *Archives of Asian Art* 32 (1979): 39–54; see pages 130-152 in this volume.
19. The Śiva image was found together with a female colossus whose identification may need further study; she is conceived on the model of the *yakṣī.*
20. The controversy surrounding the date of Lakulīśa appears to center on whether to place him in the first half of the second century AD or a hundred years earlier. See David

N. Lorenzen, *The Kāpālikas and Kālāmukhas* (Berkeley and Los Angeles, 1972), pp. 179–81.

21. Allan, *Catalogue*, p. 121; Pl. 14:11.
22. Ibid., pp. lxxxii–lxxxiii.
23. Allan notes the uncertainties in the identification; an elephant with uplifted trunk is also noticed (Ibid., p. lxxxii).
24. Ibid., p. 120; Pl. 14: 7–9.
25. Ibid., p. 172; Herbert Härtel reports finding Gomitra coins in Level 28 at Sonkh, assigned to ca. 100 BC; see his "Some Results of the Excavations at Sonkh: A Preliminary Report," *German Scholars on India*, vol. 2 (Bombay, 1976), pp. 69–99.
26. Ibid., pp. 149–52.
27. Allan, *Catalogue*, pp. 122–23.
28. Ibid., p. lxxxiii.
29. D.C. Sircar, *Studies in Indian Coins* (Delhi, 1968), p. 212.
30. On the association between Viśvāmitra and the Audumbaras, see Sircar, *Studies*, p. 210, fn. 1.
31. Allan, *Catalogue*, p. 235.
32. Percy Gardner, *The Coins of the Greek and Scythic Kings of Bactria and India in the British Museum*, reprint (Delhi, 1971), p. 71; Pl. xvii: 3.

32a. ADDENDUM: Joe Cribb has identified the deity on the obverse of this Maues coin as Balarāma. He sees a plow (not a trident) on this coin in The British Museum. See *The Crossroads of Asia. Transformation in Image and Symbol*, E. Errington and J. Cribb, with M. Claringbull (eds.), Cambridge, 1992, p. 80; Coin # 40. But Laura Giuliano (in "Studies in Early Śaiva Iconography: (1) the origin of the *triśūla* and some related problems", *Silk Road Art and Archaeology* 10, Kamakura 2004; Fig. 15, p. 56), considers the figure to be Śiva, with trident and club.

33. See C. Śivaramamurti, *Natarāja in Art, Thought and Literature* (New Delhi, 1974), p. 169, Fig. 4.
34. The majority of Kuṣāṇa *ekamukha liṅgas* lose their realistic appearance and take on a more abstract form. However, the earlier type continues to be fashioned and to be worshiped (see Mathura Museum no. 2661, illustrated as Fig. 41 in John M. Rosenfield, *The Dynastic Arts of the Kushans* [Berkeley and Los Angeles, 1967]).
35. See Doris M. Srinivasan, "Vaiṣṇava Art and Iconography at Mathurā," *Mathura: The Cultural Heritage*, Doris Meth Srinivasan (ed.), New Delhi, 1989, pp. 383–92.
36. A full description is given by N.P. Joshi, "A Unique Figure of Śiva from Mūsānagar," *Bulletin of Museums and Archaeology, in U.P.* 3 (1969): 25–30.
37. Ibid., p. 26; cf. the Umā-Maheśvara terracotta from Rang Mahal in the Gangā Golden Jubilee Museum (no. 228).
38. Gardner, *Coins*, p. 104; Pl. XXII: 8.
39. Ibid., Pl. XXII: 9.
40. For a recent discussion of this legend see G. Fussman, "Documents Epigraphiques Kouchans (2)," *Bulletin de L'Ecole Française de l'Extrême-Orient* 67 (1980): 54–56.

40a. ADDENDUM: The Sirkap, Taxila seal may also not show Śiva, again, according to Cribb (via personal communication). He believes Balarāma is represented with his plow and club. Giuliano, ibid, thinks the figure is Śiva with the trident.
Although it has been usual to identify the figure struck on Gondophares' silver tetradrachm as Śiva, some doubt has been expressed as to whether this is Śiva or Poseidon. See David W. Macdowall, "Coinage from Iran to Gandhāra. With special reference to Divinities on coin types." *On the Cusp of an Era*, Doris Meth Srinivasan (ed.), Leiden, 2007, p. 255.

I believe that the Northwest may suggest linkages between these two gods. For example, a recently published white crystal seal (No. 07.01.06; Inv. # GK g 048) from the Aman ur Rahman Collection seems almost to be a composite Poseiden-Śiva (see Aman ur Rahman & Harry Falk, *Seals Sealings and Tokens from Gandhāra*; Ludwig Reichert Verlag (Band 21 der Reihe Monographien zur Indischen Archaologie, Kunst und Philologie) Wiesbaden 2011. The male holds a trident and a wreath The trident which is somewhat indistinct is clearly marked on seal 07.01.05; Inv. # GK g 033, which seems to be carved by the same hand. The latter seal, a red garnet, also shows a figure with the trident and beribboned wreath. The trident, not associated with Śiva in contemporaneous Gangetic sculpture, reminds of Poseiden's trident. Prominent on the figure on seal 07.01.06 is a large *liṅga* shown is a way it is never shown in Gangetic *śaiva* art, that is, very large and raised outward, not upward. This priapic depiction is at variance with the cosmic symbolism attributed at this time in Hinduism to Śiva's raised *liṅga*. Joe Cribb observes that similar laterally raised *liṅgas* (as on seal 07.01.05; Inv. # GK g 048) occur on Kaniṣka I smal copper coins. In a personal communication dated 5/4/2010, he cites Göbl Nos. 813 and 814. This helpful obervation does not however mitigate the possible interface between Śiva and Poseidon among some Northern populace in the early centuries around the Christian era.

41. *Mānava Dharmaśāstra* 2.221, 22.
42. See Joseph E. Schwartzberg (ed.), *A Historical Atlas of South Asia* (Chicago and London, 1978), p. 165; maps on Pl. 3. B.1.

42a. ADDENDUM: This observation still can be maintained if we set our timeframe to coincide with the pre-through-Kuṣāṇa periods. There is new data for subsequent periods. Ibrahim Shah as part of his (2007) Ph.D. thesis from the university of Peshawar entitled, "Hindu Art in Pakistan: A Study Based on Museums Collections" has collected a few examples of Śiva Liṅgas and Mukhaliṅgas. As far as I can tell, these date from third/fourth to the ninth/tenth centuries AD and can be understood as the result of the cultural interchange between the Northern and Gangetic regions of the post-Kuṣāṇa Empire and beyond.

42b. ADDENDUM: Note: if "the trident and club" attributes are revised as "the plow and club" then the figure with these attributes has iconographic similarity with Saṃkarṣaṇa/Balarāma on the 2nd century BC Agathocles coin found in Afghanistan.

43. R.C. Agrawala, "A Unique Śiva-Liṅga near Bharatpur," *Bulletin of Museums and Archaeology in U.P.* 7 (1971): 22–24.
44. V.S. Agrawala, *A Catalogue of the Brahmanical Images in Mathura Art* (Lucknow, 1951), p. 26.
45. Srinivasan, "Vaiṣṇava Art."

45a. ADDENDUM: When I invited Phyllis Granoff to write a paper on the Pre- Kuṣāṇa *śaiva* narratives in texts and art for my Symposium, she accepted. The Symposium, entitled 'On the Cusp of an Era. Art in the Pre-Kuṣāṇa World', was held in 2000 and most of the papers were published in 2007 (Brill) under the title of the Symposium. Granoff however decided to base her paper largely on early medieval texts with little recourse to artistic evidence (thus she rightly withdrew her contribution and published her work elsewhere). The positions she puts forth to explain why early narrative scenes relating to Śiva are lacking in pre-Gupta art can be itemized: 1) hesitancy to portray the god anthropomorphically, 2) late appearance of Śiva himself in narrative exploits, because, 3) relevant narratives, as early Purāṇas show, have others, especially Śiva's *ganas*, and not Śiva as the main actor in a story. These positions skirt the problems, plus they are at

variance with the art. Therefore they need to be briefly answered here, now that Granoff's explanation is in print and could be used by others.

My present essay shows that anthropomorphic images of Śiva appear at a time when other images of gods begin to appear in India. The fact that the Supreme as Śiva is also represented as *liṅga* and *mukhaliṅga* is due to theological considerations within Śaivism, and not due to a hesitancy to depict Śiva anthropomorphically. (Please see the other *śaiva* papers in this volume, together with other papers in *Discourses on Śiva*, from which the current paper is reprinted.

Granoff bases much of her theoretical approach on several narratives (especially the Andhakāsuravadha, Bhikṣāṭana, and the Destruction of Dakṣa's sacrifice) showing Śiva's lack of engagement in an early *Skanda Purāṇa* (dated 9th century; i.e. c. 810 AD). These are unfortunate choices because they can be contradicted by much earlier art and texts. Already by the mid- sixth century AD, the walls of the Śiva shrine at Elephanta portray Śiva in at least six narratives, including the great Destroyer of Evil in the (mutilated) panel featuring his killing of Andhakāsura. By the Eighth century, a life-size Śiva Bhikṣāṭana stood at Aihole, Karnataka (see *Manifestations of Śiva*, exhibition catalogue; No. 33). The ancient story of Dakṣa's sacrifice goes through several versions and the focus of Granoff's analysis features a passive Śiva and a more aggressive wife. However, D.C. Sircar (*The Śākta Pīṭhas*, pp. 5-6), recounts earlier versions where, (in Kalidasa's *Kumārasambhava* I. 21), an unaggressive Umā commits suicide, and where (in the *Matsya Purāṇa* Chap. 13) Satī forewarns Dakṣa that Śiva will kill him and destroy his sacrifice. Nepal already knew and pictured Śiva's alliance with Umā by 600 AD.

Lack of narrative scenes involving Śiva in Pre-Gupta art certainly needs to be explained more fully. This critique of Granoff's suggestions apply only to her proposals pertaining to that aspect; her analyses of medieval texts have not been addressed in these remarks of mine. I have begun to discuss my views on the topic of Hindu narratives (see *Many Heads, Arms and Eyes*, Brill, 1997, Chapter I, especially pp. 13-15). The theme is explored in my paper entitled "Mathurā's Personality vs. Development of Narrative Art" for a Berlin Workshop on Mathurā in April 2014; pp. 329-51 in this volume. The paper has also been re-published in the Festschrift for Devangana Desai.

Incidentally, there is no need to refer, as Granoff does, to Oesho coins with *śaiva* attributes as additional indication that Śiva is not present on Kuṣāṇa coinage. These coins reflect Iranian culture. They pertain to the method by which *śaiva* iconography could be incorporated on Kuṣāṇa coins (as noted in my oral presentation at the American Oriental Society; 120th Meeting, March 15, 2010, entitled "Unpublished Seals Trace Śiva's Entry into Gandhāran Art"). These coins are out of the mainstream of Indic narratives and therefore irrelevant to *śaiva* naratives in Indian art.

46. See Wendy Doniger O'Flaherty, *Asceticism and Eroticism in the Mythology of Śiva* (Oxford, 1973).
47. Cf. Sadashiv A. Dange, *Sexual Symbolism from the Vedic Ritual* (Delhi, 1979). Note also D. Desai, *Erotic Sculpture of India* (New Delhi, 1975), p. 88*ff.*
48. See fn. 3. These studies cast doubt on Indus-Valley stones described as "liṅga-shaped cones" by Sir John H. Marshall, *Mohenjo-daro and the Indus Civilization* 1 (London, 1931), p. 212; 3, Pl. 153: 21–23. The stones, made of conch shell, average 1.9 inches and come close to resembling thimbles. It seems difficult to maintain the position that a culture engaged in phallic worship fashions nonrealistic phallic shapes, and a culture antagonistic to phallicism in religion allows realistic, colossal phallic emblems to be made.

49. Doris M. Srinivasan, "Vedic Rudra-Śiva" *JAOS* Vol. 103.3; 1983: 543–56; see pages 14-34 in this volume.
50. *Bṛhad-Āraṇyaka Upaniṣad* 4.4.6.
51. Translated as "subtile form" by R.E. Hume (*Thirteen Principal Upanishads*, 2nd rev. ed. [London and New York, 1971], p. 396) and R.C. Zaehner (*Hindu Scriptures* [London, 1966], p. 205).
52. *Śvetāśvatara Upaniṣad* 1.13.
53. J.A.B. van Buitenen, *The Māitrayaṇīya Upaniṣad* (The Hague, 1962). Hume, *Upanishads*, p. 431; see also p. 436.
54. S. Dasgupta, *A History of Indian Philosophy* vol. 1, Indian ed. (Delhi, 1975), p. 217.
55. The *Buddhacarita*, E.H. Johnston, ed. and trans., 2nd ed. (Delhi, 1972), pp. 126, 174.
56. The text is of uncertain date but may go back as far as the third century BC; Jan Gonda, *Viṣṇuism and Śivaism* (London, 1970), p. 42.
57. 271 *ūrdhvāya namaḥ, ūrdhva-liṅgāya namaḥ, hiraṇyāya namaḥ, hiraṇyaliṅgāya namaḥ* 272 *suvarṇāya namaḥ, suvarṇaliṅgāya namaḥ, divyāya namaḥ, divyaliṅgāya namaḥ* 273 *bhavāya namaḥ, bhava-liṅgāya namaḥ, sarvāya namaḥ, sarvaliṅgāya namaḥ* 274 *śivāya namaḥ, śivaliṅgāya namaḥ, jvalāya namaḥ, jvalaliṅgāya namaḥ* 275 *ātmāya namaḥ, ātmaliṅgāya namaḥ, paramāya namaḥ, paramaliṅgāya namaḥ*
58. On Bhava and Śarva in connection with Rudra, cf. the Śatarudrīya litany *(Taittirīya Saṃhitā* 4. 5.2; 5); see also Doris M. Srinivasan, "Divine Multiple Body Parts in the Atharva Veda," *Numen* 25, no. 3 (1978): 200.
59. I.e., *sarvaliṅga* in no. 276.
60. These five names are Sadyojāta, Vāmadeva, Aghora, Tatpuruṣa, Īśāna.
61. Gonda, *Viṣṇuism and Śivaism*, pp. 42*ff*; 48.
62. Srinivasan, "Atharva Veda," pp. 209–15.
63. A *vetasā hiraṇyāya* is frequently cited in Vedic literature (e.g., *ṚV* 4.58.5; *TS* 4.2.9; *Mahā-Nārāyaṇa Upaniṣad* verse 369). *Vetasā* may mean both "stick, reed" and "phallus," and therefore has lent itself to punning such as in *ṚV* 4.58.5, noted by L. Renou, *Hymnes spéculatifs du Veda* (Paris, 1956), pp. 232–33.
64. On this myth see R.G. Bhandarkar, *Vaiṣṇavism, Śaivism and Minor Religious Systems*, reprint (Benares, 1965), p. 113; cf. O'Flaherty, *Asceticism*, p. 131.
65. O'Flaherty, *Asceticism*, pp. 143; 130–32.
66. *Śatapatha Brāhmaṇa (ŚB)* 11.1.6.31.
67. Ibid., 11.5.2.4.
68. *Aitareya Brāhmaṇa* 1.22.
69. *ŚB* 7.5.1.38.
70. *ṚV* 6.46.3; see my paper "The Religious Significance of Multiple Bodily Parts to Denote the Divine: Findings from the Rig Veda;" *Asiatische Studien* 29 (1975): 150.
71. Dange, *Sexual Symbolism*, see pp. 34*ff*; 99*ff*.
72. See Srinivasan, "Rig Veda;" pp. 138–142; Srinivasan, "Atharva Veda," pp. 193; 223–24.
73. See *Epigraphia Indica* 21 (1931–32): 8*ff*; Lorenzen, *Kāpālikas*, pp. 179–80.
74. A. Bharati, *The Tantric Tradition* (London, 1965), p. 296.
75. Raymond Allchin, "The Attaining of the Void—A Review of Some Recent Contributions in English to the Study of Vīraśaivism," *Religious Studies* 7 (1971): 339–59; A.D. Ramanujan, *Speaking of Śiva* (Baltimore, 1973), p. 32, fn. ii.
76. Md. Aquique, "Liṅga Worship in North Bihar;" *Vishveshvaranand Indological Journal* 13 (1975): 6–11.

77. C. Śivaramamurti, *Śatarudrīya: Vibhūti of Śiva's Iconography* (New Delhi, 1976), Fig. 9.
78. Cf. Jan Gonda, "Atharvaveda 11.7," *Mélanges d'Indianisme à la mémoire de Louis Renou* (Paris, 1968), pp. 301–36.
79. J.N. Banerjee, The *Development of Hindu Iconography*, 3rd ed. (New Delhi, 1974), p. 573; cf. Gonda, *Viṣṇuism and Śivaism*, pp. 46–48.
80. Mathura Museum no. 392–95; cf. Srinivasan, "Early Vaiṣṇava Imagery;" pp. 39–40 (see fig. 8.1 in this volume).
81. Herbert Härtel, "Zur typologie einer Kaschmir-Skulptur," *Jahrbuch Preussicher Kulturbesitz, Sonderband, Festschrift Stephan Waekoldt*, Berlin, 1983.
82. One exception is Mathura Museum no. 516.
83. See Mircea Eliade, *The Two and the One* (New York, 1965), p. 108.
84. P.C. Roy, trans., *Mahābhārata* 10 (Calcutta, 1883–1896), p. 57 (*MBh.* 13–14).

5

Śaiva Temple Forms: Loci of God's Unfolding Body

Much scholarly attention has been directed towards Śaiva art during the last few years. A major exhibition[1] and numerous publications[2] focussing on this subject afford an excellent opportunity to assess where advances in our knowledge have occurred and where problems remain. A perusal of the recent writings shows a lack of agreement on a rather basic issue. The issue concerns the identification of a most commanding aspect of Śiva. There seems to be little consensus on when to call an image 'Sadāśiva' and when to call it 'Maheśa'. Some writings use these names as if they were synonymous. Others establish criteria for their differentiation only to have other criteria used by other authors. Therefore a considerable confusion is immediately apparent regarding some of the most well-known and impressive Śaiva forms.

A few examples will situate the problem. A short book of essays and photographs on Elephanta, Cave I[3], published in 1983, describes the colossal triune head under the names "The Eternal Shiva (Mahādeva, Maheshvara, Maheshamurti)"; but the caption under all the relevant photographs uses the name "Sadāśiva—Eternal Shiva". Another publication not drawing a clear distinction between the names 'Sadāśiva' and 'Maheśa' is the 1983 release of selected writings of Stella Kramrisch[4]. The book reprints her famous paper on the image of Mahādeva in Cave I at Elephanta written in 1946. The reprint contains some revisions[5], but continues to call the image 'Mahādeva' even though it had been designated as 'Sadāśiva' by Kramrisch in her 1981 work *The Presence of Śiva*[6]. The Elephanta image is considered a Maheśa by Krishna Kumar in

---

Originally published in *Investigating Indian Art*, Berlin, 1987; pp. 335-47. Reprinted with stylistic changes, addenda and permission from National Museums, Berlin, Prussian Cultural Foundation, Asian Art Museum, Art Collection South-, Southeast- and Central Asian Art.

connection with an iconographic classification of Maheśamūrti images he devised in a 1975 publication[7]. There are two types of Maheśa images according to Kumar; one is the seated variety (Fig. 5.1) and the other is the bust variety (Fig. 5.2). Further subdivisions depend upon the physiognomy of the lateral faces. If the terrific head of Aghora/Bhairava is to the proper right and the peaceful head of Vāmadeva/Umāvaktra is to the proper left of the central face, then the central face is that of Sadyojāta/Mahādeva. If the lateral faces assume the reverse positions, that is, Aghora is on the left and Vāmadeva is on the right, then the central head is that of Tatpuruṣa/Nandin[8]. Although these orientations supersede those offered by Kumar, it is to his credit that the direct relationship between the triune heads of a Maheśa image and those of a Caturmukha Liṅga is established. Kumar observed that a Caturmukha Liṅga can have as its central head any one of four heads, depending upon the view from which it is seen. When viewed from the East, Sadyojāta is in the center, Aghora is to the proper right and Vāmadeva is to the proper left. Since this distribution can also occur on images of Maheśa, Kumar came to the more general conclusion that for each type of Maheśamūrti distribution of faces, there exists a consonant distribution of faces on a Caturmukha Liṅga[9]. The names assigned to the faces of a Caturmukha Liṅga are the names used in the iconographic section of the *Viṣṇudharmottara Purāṇa* (3.48.1–8) to identify the faces of Mahādeva[10 & 10a(*)]. Kumar did not however label a Caturmukha Liṅga as a 'Maheśa'. For him, a Maheśa image must be either a partial, or full, anthropomorphic figure showing three or four faces. Kumar seems to reserve the name 'Sadāśiva' for those images with five visible faces[11]. That is not the way B.N. Sharma, in 1976, classified Sadāśiva images in the only monograph devoted to this deity. A quick perusal of the text and plates can determine that any implicit or explicit five-headed Śaiva form is identified as Sadāśiva. Sharma therefore includes in his book Pañcamukha Liṅgas, Caturmukha Liṅgas, three-headed busts, three-headed full figures, four-headed full figures and five-headed full figures[12]. By implicit or explicit, I mean that Sharma worked with the accepted theory that a relief of a three-headed Śiva and a four-headed

Fig. 5.1. Maheśa image from the temple of Bhujaṅgeśvara (A.P.). (Photo: courtesy Archaeological Survey of India).

Fig. 5.2. Sadāśiva from Lankeśvara, (Photo: courtesy Doris Chatham).

Śiva both represent, in effect, the five-headed or fivefold nature of Śiva which may be called Sadāśiva. It is recognized that the fifth face may be depicted in art but seldom is. Situated in the center of the four faces, and on top, it came to assume a position of superiority not only from the physical point of view but also from the metaphysical point of view. The oft-quoted dictum of the 15th century iconographic text, the *Rūpamaṇḍana*, probably sums up accurately the denotations of the fifth head which led to its infrequent representation; 'the fifth stage *(pañcamañca)* is beyond the range of even the yogīs' (IV.94)[13]. Thus, from a visual standpoint, a three-headed Śaiva figure in a relief, a four-headed Śaiva figure in the round or in relief, or a five-headed Śaiva figure, all represent the same theological concept, namely fivefold Śiva.

This set of equivalencies operates in the background of the three categories for depicting fivefold Śiva images according to T.S. Maxwell's 1982 analysis[14]. First there is the Pañcamukha Liṅga. Here four faces appear around the central *liṅga*. On top of the *liṅga*, facing upwards is the fifth face. Maxwell calls this the 'Caturmukha Liṅga' type although what is described is the Pañcamukha Liṅga. Second, the five aspects may appear as a full figure with five faces. Here too the fifth face is present on the uppermost part of the image. Third, four full-length figures can be joined at the shoulders and form a square, from the center of which emerges the fifth face[15]. Maxwell clearly does not include Kumar's bust type. He also eschews the label 'Sadāśiva' or 'Maheśa' for any of his examples.

Fig. 5.3. Kalyānpur Liṅga (Udaipur Dist. Rajasthan); Eastern side. (Photo: courtesy Frederick M. Asher).

Fig. 5.4. Kalyānpur Liṅga; Western side. (Photo: courtesy Frederick M. Asher).

He prefers the label 'five-faced Śiva' or 'five-bodied Śiva'. He notes an iconographic development of his first, or 'Caturmukha Liṅga' type. This type may combine with the type of *liṅga* showing a full-length deity on each of its four sides. The latter type of *liṅga* is often called a Pañcāyatana Liṅga. According to Maxwell, the combination of the two types (i.e. Caturmukha Liṅga and Pañcāyatana Liṅga) explains a form such as the late 7th century Kalyānpur Liṅga[16]. This Liṅga can be read vertically. For example, Maxwell reads the Eastern view (Fig. 5.3), going from top to bottom as: the rounded portion of the plain *liṅga*, the central head on the *liṅga* shaft belonging to Sadyojāta, and below Sadyojāta the full figure of ithyphallie Śiva standing in front of Nandin[16a(*)]. The Eastern view also makes visible the faces on either side of the central face. As such, the Aghora head is seen on the proper right and the profile of Vāmadeva is on the proper left. The Western view of the Kalyānpur Liṅga shows the face of Tatpuruṣa in the center, with Vāmadeva to the proper right and Aghora to the proper left (Fig. 5.4). The full figure of Sūrya is below the central face. The mid section of the Kalyānpur Liṅga is therefore a true Caturmukha Liṅga. The faces are distributed in the same pattern established for the *mukhas* or faces on a Caturmukha Liṅga, and using Kumar's formula, we may add that the faces are also distributed in the same directional pattern as the *mukhas* of a Maheśa image.

It is not difficult to see that all these writings are dealing with a similar set of iconographic properties, even though there is little agreement on the parameters or the theological definition of these properties. All the discussions deal with Śaiva icons having three, four or five heads as if they belong to some larger unit, namely fivefold Śiva. The fact that there is also variation in the number of arms is not an important factor here. The difficulty surrounds the identification of an image which symbolizes a fivefold Śiva. The *Somaśambhupaddhati* consistently describes Sadāśiva with five faces[17], The *Suprabhedāgama* mentions that Maheśa is five-headed[18]. Are the names synonymous? Should one agree with the conclusion reached by Phyllis Granoff after reviewing the literature in connection with her 1979 study on a unique Kashmiri image which resembles Maheśa from the front? She writes "...the name Sadāśiva seems somewhat arbitrarily selected. Śiva is repeatedly described in texts as five-headed, but he is not always designated as Sadāśiva. See the *Bṛhatstotraratnākara* ... See also the *Śivapurāṇa...* etc.... The selection of either name 'Sadāśiva' or 'Maheśa' thus seems largely a matter of convenience, without necessarily strong textual support"[19].

The first aim of this paper is to show that there is strong textual support for a distinction between the names 'Sadāśiva' and 'Maheśa'. The textual evidence indicates that the distinction occurs in theological expositions on the progressive unfolding of the body of Śiva. In this sequential progression, the two names refer to two distinct stages in the unfolding process. This unfolding process is also represented in Śaiva temple architecture, sculpture and painting. In these representations, images of Sadāśiva and Maheśa are recognizable on the basis of the descriptions in the texts. The second aim of the paper is to demonstrate the difference between Sadāśiva and Maheśa in the art.

The clearest exposition on the sequential unfolding of the body of Śiva occurs in the medieval Śaiva Āgamas. These texts employ the names 'Sadāśiva' and 'Maheśa' unequivocally in an effort to explain the progressive stages whereby the Absolute becomes manifest god. The *Ajita Āgama* is particularly useful since it contains a rather detailed description of the unfolding process in Paṭala 1 (st.25–32)[20]. First the twofold nature of Brahman is declared. The Highest (Para) Brahman, who is beyond word, is also known as the Highest (Para) Śiva. The Brahman which consists of word, or which is definable, is known as Sadāśiva. Sadāśiva stems from the Highest Śiva who is formless. Sadāśiva is the agent (of creation) and the preserver, the Highest Lord. From Sadāśiva arose Maheśvara, from Maheśvara arose Rudra, from Rudra Viṣṇu and from Viṣṇu arose Brahmā. In this way, proclaims the *Ajita Āgama*, the world rulers, Maheśvara, etc. arose from Sadāśiva and from these arose the existence of all creatures. The *Kiraṇāgama* relates the same sequence only in reverse order. The sequence occurs in a description on the path of *yoga* and the successive stages reached, going from lowest to highest[21]. The succession begins with Brahmā, then Viṣṇu, after which follow Rudra, Maheśvara and Sadāśiva[22]. In the chapter on 'Triads' in the

Śaivāgamaparibhāṣāmañjarī[23], the three names defining the triple aspect of god are recounted as follows: "[The supreme reality is triple[24]] and its three parts are Śiva, Sadāśiva and Maheśa". The Āgamas therefore agree that in the progression going from transcendency to matter, there are three stages; first there is Para Śiva, the transcendental Supreme, next is Sadāśiva, last is Maheśa. The gods arising from Maheśa are already mentioned in the *Mahābhārata*. The epic tells how the great god Mahādeva emitted Brahmā, Viṣṇu and Rudra from his own body. He produced Brahmā from his right side, and Viṣṇu from his left (XIII.14.183). The *Śiva Purāṇa* also tells how these deities arose from Maheśa, adding that Rudra is born of his heart[25].

The triple reality of Śiva is characterized in the Āgamas by a series of technical terms relating to the domain of representation. The Para Śiva is *niṣkala,* that is formless or undifferentiated. Maheśa is *sakala,* that is, the aspect with form. And Sadāśiva is between the two, namely *sakala-niṣkala*[26]. This stage is therefore no longer part of the undifferentiated or *niṣkala* stage[27]. This is the stage where *niṣkala* Śiva begins to assume form leading to his eventual, full manifestation. From a fraction of the last emanation of the *sakala-niṣkala* stage arises Maheśa. Maheśa is the manifestation seen by the *bhakta;* he is the creator of all further *mūrtis* of god as well as the other gods[28]. In essence, the traditional teaching in the Āgamas is that the Highest Śiva is without form, that Maheśa is with form, and that Sadāśiva is the formless with form[29].

The most fitting symbol for *niṣkala* Śiva is the plain *liṅga*[30]. Already the *Śiva Purāṇa* acknowledges this, saying that in the *niṣkala* aspect the *liṅga* is appropriate[31]. A *niṣkala liṅga* is plain since it is the sign of the undifferentiated Absolute. The *niṣkala liṅga* is distinguished from the *mukhaliṅga*. The former is said to be "simple" *(kevala)* and the *mukhaliṅga* is said to be *sakala-niṣkala* or "mixed" *(miśra)*[32]. The *mukhaliṅga* thus evokes Sadāśiva, identified with the *sakala-niṣkala* stage. It follows that a *liṅga* showing god's faces portrays that stage in the unfolding process wherein the formless begins to assume form. *Mukhaliṅga* may therefore be understood as a technical term. The weight of the theological significance of this compound is carried by the term *mukha. Mukha* means 'head', 'face', 'mouth', 'front', 'beginning', etc. Elsewhere it is argued that these meanings are extended in Vedic and Sanskrit literature to include such meanings as 'beginning of a progression' and 'beginning of a progression leading towards manifestation'[33]. Therefore a *mukhaliṅga* is a fitting symbol of Sadāśiva since it is the sign of the beginning of the unfolding of god. Unlike Sadāśiva, Maheśa is the fully manifest, anthropomorphic form of god on earth; that is the force of the term *sakala*[34].

Pulling together the textual evidence, the triple Śaiva reality seems to be composed of three entities, each of which is described with concepts strongly related to iconography. They are:

Para Śiva = the plain *liṅga*
Sadāśiva = the *mukhaliṅga*
Maheśa = the full anthropomorphic form

These texts go further. They provide details on the specific appearance of Sadāśiva and Maheśa. It has already been noted that according to the *Somaśambhupaddhati*, Sadāśiva has five faces. The Sadāśiva Reality described in the *Vātuḷaśuddhāgama* is also composed of five emanations[35]. Since Sadāśiva has five faces and is symbolized by the *mukhaliṅga*, it follows that the Pañcamukha Liṅga icon represents Sadāśiva.

It must now become clear why Maheśa, in the *Suprabheda Āgama*, is also described as five-headed. Since Maheśa emanates from the Sadāśiva Reality, he must partake of the characteristics of his predecessor. The main difference between Sadāśiva and Maheśa has nothing to do with the number of heads or arms. It is, according to the Āgamas, a question of the difference between *sakala-niṣkala* and *sakala*. That is, it is the difference between the beginning of the unfolding of fivefold Śiva and the end. Maheśa is the end, the completely unfolded, manifest god. To say that the tradition can arbitrarily designate a five-headed form as Sadāśiva or as Maheśa misses the theological position completely. It is precisely because of their sequential connection in the unfolding process that both Sadāśiva and Maheśa can be described with the same number of heads.

When theology is translated into iconography, five heads may be rendered in a variety of ways. To reiterate, both Sadāśiva and Maheśa may be depicted with three, four or five heads, irrespective of the medium, but depending upon how closely the icon follows the theoretical model. The distinguishing criterion between Sadāśiva and Maheśa is the degree of manifestation. Maheśa is the full manifestation. Sadāśiva is the "mixed" manifestation. He can be designated as "mixed" in the Āgamas because he is neither fully manifest nor fully unmanifest. This notion (i.e. *miśra*) can be rendered by more than the Pañcamukha Liṅga icon. Sadāśiva is to be recognized in art as any partially exposed anthropomorphic form of fivefold Śiva. In short, the type Kumar labeled as the 'bust' form of Maheśa is, in actuality, Sadāśiva.

Before turning to representations of these concepts, it should be noted that these Āgamic speculations can be expected to be known in both Northern and Southern regions of the subcontinent from circa the post-Gupta periods onwards[36]. Kashmiri Śaivas and Śaiva-Siddhāntins in the South consider the Āgama literature their basic authoritative texts. Apparently, the same Āgama could be known in both regions. For example, Brunner-Lachaux reports that there are two manuscript traditions of the *Somaśambhupaddhati*, one of the most ancient ritual manuals. One comes from Devakottai, a small village to the south of Tanjor and the other comes from Srinagar, Kashmir[37].

Perhaps the clearest depiction of the Śaiva tenets outlined above comes from an early 18th century Nepalese painting in the Los Angeles County Museum of

Art (Fig. 5.5). Most of the painting is occupied by a Śaiva temple which rises in three tiers. We know that the *garbhagṛha* is situated beneath the *śikhara* of a Hindu temple; therefore it is with the representations directly under the *śikhara* that we shall be concerned. These are the main deities of the temple and they are three. On the top tier is the *niṣkala* or plain *liṅga*. It symbolizes Para Śiva. The middle tier is occupied by a Caturmukha Liṅga. It represents Sadāśiva. The bottom tier shows a five-headed, ten-handed full anthropomorphic form. It represents Maheśa. To the right of Maheśa is Viṣṇu; Sūrya stands on the left side of Maheśa. The shrine itself is an accurate depiction of a temple design known in the Kathmandu Valley during the seventeenth century. This fact encourages a search into Śaiva temples in India in order to determine whether there are other, earlier temple forms, *in situ*, which represent the loci of god's unfolding body.

Fig. 5.5. Śaiva Shrines in a Landscape, 1700–25; Nepal; Los Angeles County Museum of Art. Gift of Mr. and Mrs. E. Sherwood and Indian Art Discretionary Fund (enlargement in Fig. 6.1).

There are. This paper will concentrate on three examples dating between the 6th–8th century. As may be gaged from the Nepali example, the physical position of an icon in the temple plan can critically assist in the identification of the image. The examples chosen have the merit of still being in the positions assigned to them by the temple planners.

The Lankeśvara Temple at Ellora is the earliest extant temple I know showing all the three aspects of the Śaiva Reality. The Lankeśvara is of course not a free-standing temple; it is an 8th century Rāṣṭrakūtā temple cut into the same living rock as the Kailāsa temple which it adjoins on the northern side. Since Lankeśvara is a rock sanctuary, we may be prepared to find an arrangement other than the three-tiered vertical arrangement for positioning the triple Śaiva Reality.

Lankeśvara is a cave 123′ long from the back of the Nandi shrine to the *pradakṣiṇapatha* and 60′ wide inside the front screen[38]. The low ceiling is supported by 27 large pillars plus pilasters. The *garbhagṛha* is situated at the northern end of the North-South axis (Fig. 5.6). It is a square chamber featuring a *liṅga* placed in

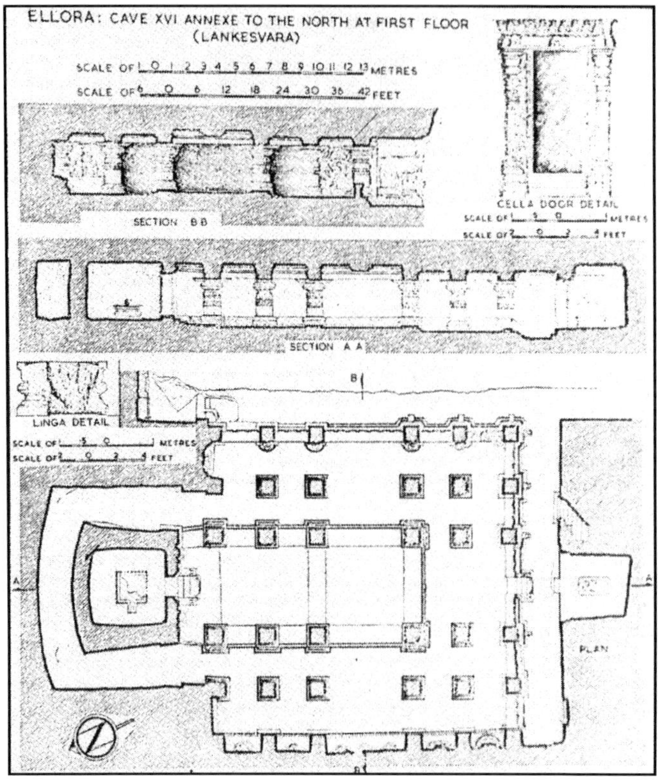

Fig. 5.6. Plan of Lankeśvara, (Photo: from K.V. Soundara Rajan, *Cave Temples of the Deccan*, New Delhi, ASI, 1981. p.182).

a monolithic *pīṭha*[39]. On the back wall of the cella, there is a carving in low relief of a tricephalic anthropomorphic form, partially exposed (Fig. 5.2). This relief may now be identified as Sadāśiva. To the proper left of the central face is the face of Aghora. To the proper right is the face of Vāmadeva. Accordingly, the central face is that of Tatpuruṣa. Aghora has three eyes; the normal two are bulging out. A snake is intertwined in his locks and he holds the characteristic *kapāla*. Vāmadeva has the gentle countenance and seems to hold a flower bud. Three-eyed Tatpuruṣa has four arms. The attributes in the hands, going from left to right are: *nāga, mātuluṅga, khaṭvāṅga* and *vyākhyā-mudrā*. The womb chamber thus houses the *niṣkala liṅga*, symbolic of Para Śiva, and the *sakala-niṣkala* form of Sadāśiva. The fully manifest image of Maheśa is on the back wall of the western end of the cave. The god appears as the central figure in a very wide panel; the width of the panel corresponds to the width of the central nave, going North-South or East-West (see Fig. 5.7). It is the widest panel at Lankeśvara. Indeed, I believe that this panel terminates the East-West axis of the temple just as the *garbhagṛha* terminates the North-South axis. Lankeśvara, I propose, is an 8th century biaxial shrine. Maheśa, standing perfectly straight, has one head and four arms. The upper right hand holds the trident, the upper left the cobra. He stands in front of Nandin. There is a small attendant on the right. Maheśa's lower left arm is held at the hip; the lower right is broken. I have reserved until now the fact that both Sadāśiva and Maheśa may also be described with one head and four arms. For example, the *Uttarakāmikāgama* describes Sadāśiva both with five faces and ten arms, and with one face[40]. The *Vātuḷaśuddhāgama* describes Maheśa with one face[41]. There are two points to stress here. First, it may again be observed that there is a correlation between the number of heads of Maheśa and Sadāśiva because, I propose, they represent the same Absolute at different, but sequentially related, stages of manifestation. Second, I believe that the religious denotations of an *'ekamukha'* are not different from that of a *'pañcamukha'*. Symbolic properties of numbers related to divine multiple bodily parts are analyzed in my monograph[42].

Fig. 5.7. Maheśa panel at Lankeśvara. (Photo: courtesy Doris Chatham).

The analysis leads me to conclude that the number 'one' can signify 'the whole'[43]. 'One' can therefore stand for 'all (the relevant *mukhas*'), that is, for '*pañcamukhas*'. This rationale agrees with the intuitive explanation for the Ekamukha Liṅga type offered by Kramrisch. She writes, "Four of the faces" [of a Pañcamukha Liṅga] "look into the four directions of space; as a rule the fifth face on top of the *liṅga*—symbolically in transcendence—is invisible. It is not even necessary that all four faces be carved; many *liṅgas* have but one face... which implies the others"[44]. It may be noted that other examples occur in Indian art, outside the realm of Śaiva iconography, where 'one entity' stands for that 'whole group' of entities[45]. If doubt still remains that the center figure represents Maheśa, it may be dispelled by the identity of the flanking figures. To the proper right appears Brahmā, and to the proper left appears Viṣṇu. These gods assume the positions corresponding to the sides from which they emanate from Maheśa, according to the early texts. Brahmā has the usual four faces, three of which are visible. He is four-armed. The upper left arm is completely broken; the upper right may be holding a very large palm-leaf manuscript[46]. The lower right hand carries the rosary and the corresponding left holds *kamaṇḍalu* which is broken. The *haṁsa vāhana* of Brahmā is seen below the lower right figure. Four-armed Viṣṇu may be recognized by the characteristic attributes: the *cakra* is held in the upper left; his lower left hand rests on Garuḍa. Gadādevī is on Viṣṇu's right side. Lankeśvara therefore represents the triple aspect of Śiva on one level just as the Nepalese painted shrine does on three; the double axes work together to make this theological statement emphatic.

Fig. 5.8. Elephanta, outside of the *garbhagṛha*. (Photo: courtesy American Institute of Indian Studies, Center for Art & Archaeology).

The Great Cave at Elephanta was hewn out of hard trap rock in about the middle of the 6th century. It is a large pillared cave measuring in the interior about 91′ on a side. There is no need to describe in detail the architectural and sculptural program of this extraordinary temple on which an extensive bibliography already exists. We will wish to concentrate only on those sculptural and architectural elements related to the unfolding of the Śiva Reality. The temple has two main devotional icons; each governs its own axial plane. The East-West axis has the *garbhagṛha* at the Western end of the axis (Fig. 5.8). The square chamber has the *liṅga* installed within. Inside the walls are unadorned. Outside the walls are decorated with colossal Dvārapālas on each side of the doorway. The only other icon in the Main Hall to be guarded by Dvārapālas is the tricephalic head, resting on broad shoulders at the southern end of the North-South axis (Fig. 5.9). This form rises to a height of 20′ 6". Nothing in the temple plan today obstructs the worshipper's gaze upon this gigantic partially manifested god. There are however holes in the corners of both the floor and the lintel "as if to receive doorposts and in the floor is a groove, as if a screen had been used for occasionally concealing the sculpture[47]...". The *liṅga* and the colossal tricephalic sculpture share several features: they are the only forms that could be enclosed. They are the only forms that are guarded. They terminate their respective axes. Here then are the two main icons of the temple. There are eight other sculptural scenes in the Main Hall. In each, the form of Śiva is fully manifest, and in each the god enacts a different divine play or *līlā*. Elephanta holds within the main grotto the *niṣkala* Śiva, *sakala-niṣkala* Sadāśiva and the *mūrtis* of god. The *garbhagṛha* contains the *niṣkala liṅga*. The partially exposed form in the southern recess is that of *miśra* Sadāśiva. The Aghora head is to the proper right; the blissful face of Vāmadeva is to the proper left and the central head belongs to Sadyojāta. A remarkable aspect of this artistic rendering of Sadāśiva is that it melds together the two possibilities for representing this god. The image is at once a *mukhaliṅga* and a partially revealed anthropomorphic form. It is precisely this visual perception of the melding of the aniconic and the iconic which Kramrisch refers to when she states "In Elephanta,

Fig. 5.9. Elephanta, Sadāśiva. (Photo: courtesy Asian Art Archives; University of Michigan).

the heads and chest of Śiva themselves form the *liṅga*"[48]. The Elephanta image is no doubt the most powerful and subtle expression of the quality of *miśra* that identifies Sadāśiva. Elephanta does not contain an image of Maheśa[49]. It does however contain representations of *mūrtis* that arise from Maheśa. These *mūrtis* are assumed by the Supreme for the benefit of his worshippers. These are the forms that bring the faithful into the presence of Śiva. They need no enclosures. They need no guardians. They no longer directly relate to the mystery of the divine unfolding.

The temple of Bhujaṅgeśvara in Andhra Pradesh is an 8th century small, free-standing edifice built during the Rāṣṭrakūtā period[50]. It is a two-storey Śiva temple which faces and opens West. The sanctum houses the *liṅga*, behind which, on the eastern wall appears an image of tricephalic Maheśa (Fig. 5.1). The four-armed god is seated; his legs are folded at the knees. The fiercesome head of Aghora is on the right, Vāmadeva is on the left. The god wears armlets, necklaces and the sacred thread; a girdle secures his *dhotī*. In his upper right hand is the trident; in the upper left is the drum. His natural hands are poised so that the fingers bend inwards. The raised right hand makes this gesture with the palm outward, and the left rests in this manner on the left thigh. The Bhujaṅgeśvara Temple holds the *niṣkala* and *sakala* aspects of the Absolute and leaves out the *sakala-niṣkala*[51]. Failure to represent this link in the sequential progression probably does not indicate a variant theological position. The possibility for coalescing links is indicated in the *Suprabheda Āgama* (Chapter 1.33 ft), which states that Sadāśiva resides in the formless (*niṣkala*) *liṅga* from which the anthropomorphic (i.e. *sakala)* image of the same god emanates for cult purposes[52]. Representational latitude is also borne out by the southern *Rauravāgama;* this text mentions that on the back wall of the Śaiva cella, behind the *liṅga*, there must appear "a representation of the manifest Śiva accompanied with Umā"[53]. The need to represent Sadāśiva is not mentioned. Bhujaṅgeśvara partially answers the prescription of this Āgama. On the one hand, there is the representation of the manifest god Maheśa; but on the other hand, he is alone and not accompanied by Umā.

In conclusion, there is a clear distinction in Śaiva theology between Sadāśiva and Maheśa which is carried through into the art. Possibly the best way to summarize these findings is by looking once more at the Kalyānpur Liṅga which offers the strongest evidence in support of the findings. The Kalyānpur Liṅga, made of a black stone, is now enshrined in a modern temple at Kalyānpur in Udaipur District, Rajasthan[54]. It is correct to read the image from top to bottom, but it is not correct to consider the image as a result of combining two separate images. The Kalyānpur Liṅga condenses into one mass the same program that may be spread out in a three-tiered or a biaxial temple plan. The main view is the Eastern one (see Fig. 5.3). As Maxwell points out, this view comprises the dome of the *liṅga*, the *mukhaliṅga*, having the face of Sadyojāta in the center, and the figure of Śiva. It may now be added that the bottom figure is the fully manifest form of Śiva, called Maheśa. The god is four-armed, having the trident and cobra in his upper hands. Standing thus in front of Nandin, the Kalyānpur Maheśa is of course quite similar to the Lankeśvara Maheśa. The Eastern view charts the process whereby the triple reality of Śiva unfolds—from *liṅga* to *mukhaliṅga* and then to *mūrti* – or to state it another way – from Para Śiva to Sadāśiva and then to Maheśa. Circumambulation of the *liṅga* begins at the East. As the worshipper views the icon from the East[55], he sees the full figure of Viṣṇu to the left of Maheśa and the full figure of Brahmā to the right. Their positions recall the sides from which Viṣṇu and Brahmā arose from the body of Maheśa. The Kalyānpur Liṅga is an extraordinary achievement; it is an icon planned as a temple. Here in one sculptural unit are portrayed all the loci of god's unfolding body. The unfolding proceeds downward, as in a birth. The heads appear first, as in a birth. The fully emerged body ends the process, as in a birth. Be it sculpture, or painting or architectural program, be it condensed or spread out, the theological statement, wherein Sadāśiva and Maheśa take their proper place, remains the same.[55a(*)]

NOTES AND REFERENCES

1. Manifestations of Shiva; Philadelphia Museum of Art, 1981; organized by Stella Kramrisch.
2. A work to be mentioned in addition to the publications discussed below is *Discourses on Śiva,* edited by M.W. Meister, Philadelphia 1984.
3. *Elephanta, The Cave of Shiva,* photographs by C. Berkson, Essays by W. Doniger O'Flaherty, G. Michell and C. Berkson, Princeton, 1983. See page 37 and plates 39–44.
4. *Exploring India's Sacred Art, selected writings of Stella Kramrisch,* edited, with a biographical essay by B. Stoler Miller, Philadelphia, 1983; pages 141ff.
5. The central head is identified as Sadyojāta rather than Tatpuruṣa; see fn. 8.
6. Published by Princeton University Press; see the Appendix, especially pp. 445–48; 451; 453.
7. "A Dhyāna-Yoga Maheśamūrti and some Reflections on the Iconography of the Maheśamūrti Images". In: *Artibus Asiae,* Vol. XXXVII, 105–120. See also K. Kumar, "Maheśamūrti Images at Ellora: Their Typology and Cult-affiliation". In: *Vishveshvaranand Indological Journal,* Vol. XVII, pts. 1 & 2, 1979, 225–37.
8. This orientation is the result of the work of T. S. Maxwell, "The Five Aspects of Śiva". In: *Art International,* Vol. XXV, 1982, 41–57. It reverses the position of the central head such as given in Kumar's analysis in "A Dhyāna-Yoga Maheśamūrti", 107. Maxwell's orientation has been accepted by Kramrisch, see fn.5.
9. Kumar, "A Dhyāna-Yoga Maheśamūrti", 107–08.
10. This text, dated *c.* 6th–7th century, cites the following pentad of names: Sadyojāta/Mahādeva; Vāmadeva/Umā; Aghora/Bhairava; Tatpuruṣa/Nandin; Īśāna/Sadāśiva. See also Maxwell, "Five Aspects", 41 and Appendixes I & II.

10a. ADDENDUM: Since this paper was written and published in 1987, I have concluded that the date of the *Viṣṇudharmottara Purāṇa* is earlier. Previously, I used the date provided by other scholars. However, in the course of studying aspects of the text while writing a review of Parul Dave Mukherji's critical edition of *The Citrasūtra of the Viṣṇudharmottara Purāṇa,* I came to realize that there is both relevant internal and external data to warrant revising the date to around the middle of the 5th century AD. My evidence is cited in the review, please see *Journal of the American Oriental Society*, Vol. 124.3 (2004), pp. 569-72.

11. Kumar, "A Dhyāna-Yoga Maheśamūrti", 107 and fn.10.
12. B.N. Sharma, *Iconography of Sadāśiva,* New Delhi 1976.
13. See the text in Sharma, *Sadāśiva,* p.18, fn.7.
14. Maxwell, "Five Aspects".
15. Maxwell, "Five Aspects", 41–42; see pls. 1–10.
16. Maxwell, "Five Aspects", 42.

16a. ADDENDUM: I should have referred to Śiva's bull, on the 7th century icon, as vṛṣa, and not Nandi. On the distinctions and where they apply, see Pratapaditya Pal, "Revisiting the Vṛṣa/Nandi Issue", in *Prajñādhara: Essays on Asian Art History, Epigraphy and Culture in Honour of Gouriswar Bhattacharya,* Gerd J.R. Mevissen and Arundhati Banerji (eds.), New Delhi, 2009, pp. 413-17. Additional bibliography is on Pal's page 417.

17. H. Brunner-Lachaux, editor and translator, *Somaśambhupaddhati* Vol. I, Pondichéry, 1963; pp.xi; 178–83; fn.2 on pp. 178–80.
18. T.A.G. Rao, *Elements of Hindu Iconography,* Vol. II, pt.II, Reprint. New York, 1968; p. 379 and p. 191 in the textual appendage.

19. Ph. Granoff, "Maheśvara/Mahākāla: A Unique Buddhist Image from Kaśmīr". In: *Artibus Asiae,* Vol. XLI, 1979, 46, fn. 11.
20. N.R. Bhatt, editor, *Ajitāgama,* Vol. I, Pondichéry, 1964; see pp. 3–4.
21. J. Gonda, *Medieval Religious Literature in Sanskrit,* Wiesbaden, 1977, p. 188.
22. After Sadāśiva, the stages are related to Kuṇḍalinīśakti, Paraśakti and Śiva.
23. B. Dagens, editor and translator, *Śaivāgamaparibhāṣāmañjarī de Vedajñāna,* Pondichéry, 1979. This text is an anthology of Śaiva texts in verse compiled in the 16th century by Vedajñana.
24. Dagens supplements the hemistich of vs. 3.54b by a line from the *Vātulaśuddhākya,* the text probably being cited here.
25. J.L. Shastri, editor, *The Śiva Purāṇa,* Motilal Banarsidass, 1970, Vol. I, page 213; st.56 and 57. See also the *Kūrma Purāṇa;* cf. the account of the Liṅgodbhavamūrti in C. Dimmitt and J.A.B. van Buitenen, *Classical Hindu Mythology,* Philadelphia, 1978, pp. 205–06. Note however that in the purāṇa and epic passages, all the gods emanate from Maheśvara, whereas in the *Ajita Āgama* and the *Kiraṇāgama,* a chain is indicated wherein only Rudra arises directly from Maheśvara.
26. E.g. *Śaivāgamaparibhāṣāmañjarī,* vs.3.51; cf. 3.55. Cf. Rao, *Elements,* Vol. II, pt.II, p. 361. Rao summarizes the tenets from the *Vātuḷaśuddhāgama;* the complete text is not available to me.
27. See H. Brunner, "Toujours le Niṣkala-Liṅga". In: *JA,* Vol. 256, 1968, 446.
28. See Rao, *Elements,* Vol. II, pt.II, pp. 367–69.
29. See Gonda, *Medieval,* p. 200, fn.125; H. Brunner, Niṣkala-Liṅga, 446.
30. Brunner, "Niṣkala-Liṅga", 445–47.
31. Shastri, ed., *The Śiva Purāṇa,* Vol. I, p. 50; st.11.
32. See Brunner, "Niṣkala-Liṅga", 445 and fn. 3, citing the *Īśānaśivagurudevapaddhati* and the variation in the *Suprabhedāgama* in fn. 4.
33. Ritual as Icon in India, paper delivered published in the Proceedings of the XXVIth International Congress of the History of Art; Washington, D.C., 10–15 August 1986. This paper is in this volume.
34. So also Brunner, "Niṣkala-Liṅga", 446. She states that *sakala* applies to Īśvara under all his forms. These are the anthropomorphic forms called *pratimā,* 445.
35. Cf. the summary given by Rao, *Elements,* Vol. II, pt.II, pp. 363–366.
36. During the discussion of this paper at the Berlin Symposium, Gérard Fussman pointed out that J. Filliozat (in a paper entitled: Sur le Çivaïsme et le Bouddhisme du Cambodge, à propos de deux livres récents. In: *BEFEO* Tome LXX [1981], 59–99), showed that many of these Āgamic speculations were also known in Cambodia. The paper, arguing for the need to employ Āgamic literature to elucidate Khmer Sanskrit inscriptions, mentions *inter alia* that in Cambodia too, a *liṅga* symbolizes *niṣkala* Śiva; the *sakala* form of Śiva refers to images, to statues "pourvues de parties": and a Sadāśiva relief at Vat-Phu has five heads.
37. Brunner-Lachaux, *Somaśambhupaddhati,* Vol. I, p.xl.
38. J. Fergusson and J. Burgess, *The Cave Temples of India;* London 1880, p. 458.
39. Cf. K.V. Soundara Rajan, *Cave Temples of the Deccan,* ASI, New Delhi, 1981, p. 187.
40. Rao, *Elements,* Vol. II, pt.II, p. 372; see Appendix, Sadāśivādimūrtayaḥ, p. 187 for the *Uttarakāmikāgama* text.
41. Cf. Rao, *Elements,* Vol. II, pt.II, p. 369.
42. *Many Heads, Arms and Eyes: Origin, Meaning and Form of Multiplicity in Indian Art.* Brill, Leiden, 1997, chapter XII.

43. For IE citations of 'one' with the sense of 'the whole', 'alone', see J. Gonda, *Reflections on the Numerals "One" and "Two" in ancient Indo-European Languages,* Utrecht, 1953, p. 80. There is a special connection between 'one' and 'five' in IE. The five fingers of a hand represent 'a unit' or 'a whole'. Cf. Gonda, *Reflections,* p.23, citing Kathās. 5,8ff. Also the "morpheme [penk^w], applying to the whole hand when all five fingers are being counted, may be assumed in the case of '5' according to E. Polomé, The Indo-European Numeral for 'Five' and Hittite *panku-* 'All', *Pratidānam* edited by J.C. Heesterman, The Hague, 1968, p. 100.
44. *Manifestations of Shiva,* Philadelphia, 1981, page xvi.
45. E.g. see painting No. 15 in *Painted Delight, Indian Paintings from Philadelphia Collections,* by Stella Kramrisch, Philadelphia, 1986.
46. Soundara Rajan, *Cave Temples,* p. 189.
47. Fergusson and Burgess, *Cave Temples,* p. 476.
48. Stella Kramrisch, "The Great Cave Temple of Śiva in Elephanta: Levels of Meaning and Their Form". In: *Discourses* ed. M.W. Meister, p. 4.
49. Another 6th century Deccan cave temple also features only the first two aspects of Śiva. The Ankai-Tankai Temple east of Nasik contains the image of tricephalic Sadāśiva on the back wall of the cella which still contains the plain *liṅga*; see Fergusson and Burgess, *Cave Temples,* p. 480. I wish to thank Walter Spink for drawing my attention to this cave site.
50. The discussion which follows is based on the field work of B. Dagens, *Entre Alampur et Śriśailam,* Tome I, Pondichéry, 1984, pp. 562–68; Tome II, Photos 832–41.
51. The *sakala-niṣkala* aspect, it may be noted in passing, can be the main object of worship in a temple. For example, the Caturmukha Liṅga from the 7th century Muṇḍeśvarī Temple (Shāhābād Dist., Bihar), should have been the main cult object of this temple. See F.M. Asher, *The Art of Eastern India, 300–800,* Minneapolis, 1980, pp. 39–40; plates 50 and 43.
52. H. Brunner, "Analyse du Suprabhedāgama". In: *JA,* Vol. 255, 1967, 38.
53. Rauravāgama 34. 1–2 and Vol. II, p.viii–ix; see B. Dagens, *Les enseignements de l'Ajitāgama et du Rauravāgama,* Pondichéry, 1977, p. 107.
54. This *liṅga* has also been discussed by F. M. Asher, "Pañcāyatana Śiva Liṅgas: Sources and Meanings". In: *Kalādarśana, American Studies in the Art of India,* editor J.G. Williams, New Delhi, 1981, p. 2. The findings in this paper agree with Asher's belief that the Liṅga is not a syncretistic sculpture; they do not agree with his observation that Viṣṇu has been placed under the *Aghora* head to underscore "the rivalry between the devotees of the two principal deities, and according to the Śaiva view, the ultimate dominance of Śiva..."
55. Maxwell in "Five Aspects" perceptively argues for the need to keep in mind the ritualistic context when interpreting icons.

55a. ADDENDUM: I have not made a concerted effort to look for other Śaiva temple forms after writing this essay. However, one example in an exhibit was so unusual that it caught my eye. It is a brush drawing from Mandi (Punjab Hills) included in an exhibit of *Indian Paintings and Drawings from the Collection of Howard Hodgkin.* The Catalogue with this title is by Andrew Topsfield and Milo Cleveland Beach (New York; 1991). Fig. 30, dated to *c.* 1710–20, shows the image of a five-headed, ten-armed deity, seated in *padmāsana* and represented as a *yogī.* The deity's aspects are preponderantly Śaiva: the third eye is on each visible head and the five-attributes in the five right arms bespeak of Śiva (trident, hand-drum, skull cup, sword and cobra). But the five in the left hands hold Viṣṇu's attributes. The drawing's title (given I suppose by the authors of the Catalogue since there is no inscription on the drawing), caught my attention. They call it Harihara Sadāshiva.

The title seems incorrect, although it follows previous nomenclature for similar iconographical depictions (see p. 80 and footnotes in the Topsfield, Beach Catalogue for references). Therefore it is useful to review the analysis for this sort of depiction and propose a different identification.

As discussed in this essay, Āgamic texts agree that Sadāśiva is the Śiva reality in the process of unfolding. Sadāśiva is not a fully manifested form whereas Maheśa is. Since the Mandi drawing shows a fully manifested form, I consider it unlikely that it represents Sadāśiva and believe it is a form of Maheśa. (I do realize that the Kandariyā Mahādeva temple, Khajuraho, has a fully manifested figure with six heads and four feet, inscribed as "Sadāśiva". See Devangana Desai, *The Religious Imagery of Khajuraho*, Mumbai, 1996). There are also several full figures called "Sadāśiva" made in the Sena Period. See "From Transcendency to Materiality", in this volume. Further, when in a ritual the worshipper tries to visualize Sadāśiva's weapons, the *Kamikāgama* assigns a group to the right hand that disagrees with those depicted in the drawing (cf. Richard H. Davis, *Ritual in an Oscillating Universe*, Princeton University Press, 1991; Chapter IV). As for the Harihara designation, to date I have not found a visual or textual example of five-headed, ten-armed composite Harihara. I am not convinced therefore that the Mandi five-headed depiction is a Harihara which usually shows a clear vertical demarcation—absent here—between a Hari (Viṣṇu) and a Hara (Śiva). The case for a "Harihara Sadāśiva" identification is therefore quite weak. However, there are five-faced, ten-armed fully manifest figures of a seated Maheśa; one is pictured in a beautiful Pahārī painting in the National Museum, New Delhi (see D.C. Bhattacharyya, *Iconography of Composite Images*, New Delhi, 1979, Fig. 12). The best example in the present context is, of course, the standing Maheśa in the Nepalese painting illustrated in Fig. 5.5 of the present essay. I am not sure how to interpret the *vaiṣṇava* aspect of the plausible Mandi Maheśa. Possibly an allusion is being made to the arising of the god Viṣṇu from the side of Maheśa. But this is unlikely since there is no reference to the arising of Brahmā from the other side of Maheśa.

More likely is that the region wrote its own iconographic formulae. Mandi and Pahārī are in a region suffused with unusual medieval Śaiva temple forms. (See Madanjeet Singh, *Himalayan Art*, Greenwich, 1968). The 14th century AD Pāñcavaktra Temple at Mandi with its carving of a five-faced Śiva seated with his consort indicates the importance of this form. Unlike our drawing, that statue is composed of four identical Śivas facing the four directions, plus a fifth head on top, in the center. Mandi also contains a Trilokanātha temple (16th century), again showing Parvatī with Śiva. In the Pahārī style, there is an Ardhanārī temple at Mandi also dating to the 16th century. A natural consequence of the composite form could have been to fashion another composite of Śiva as Maheśa and Viṣṇu. The Mandi painting, and others like it (see Topsfield and Beach, above), may be giving expression to a regional vision, combined with the syncretic spirit or liberal inclination of the patron.

6

From Transcendency to Materiality: Para Śiva, Sadāśiva, and Maheśa in Indian Art*

For all Śaivites, knowledge of the Supreme through devotion to god is the goal. The Supreme is the unmanifest transcendental. It has the potential for creation of the universe by the expulsion of forms out of its essence. God is the Supreme as manifested form. God actualizes the potential by creating the material world. Śaivite theology, from its beginnings, has probed the relationship between the Supreme, god, and the world. These probings involve a concern for the structure of forms emitted from the Supreme, beginning with that of god himself.

A concern for structures and their interrelationships appears with the formulation of the personal god Rudra-Śiva in Brahmanical literature. The relationship between the Supreme and god in texts of ancient Hinduism, including the Upaniṣads and Epics (i.e. in the *Śvetāśvatara* and the *Mahānārāyaṇa* as well as the *Mahābhārata)* is triadic[1]; that is, a threefold sequence explains how the all-pervasive, transcendental Supreme is connected to the material form of god. The first stage in this sequence is that of the formless (i.e., *niṣkala, arūpa)* Supreme; it is called Brahman. Third is the stage of god's material form (i.e., *tanū);* it may be referred to as *mūrti.* In between is the stage of the subtle form of god; it is the sign (i.e. *liṅga)* of that which is without sign (i.e., *aliṅga),* the transcendental source, and it is also the prototype of all subsequent material forms (cf. *Śvet. Up.* 1.13). Vedic speculative thought recognizes that each stage is linked to the preceding one. Thus, the material form of the godhead, the *mūrti,* has as its ultimate source the formless *(niṣkala)* Brahman. Upaniṣadic speculation has a name for the one

Originally published in *Artibus Asiae,* Vol. L, ½; 1990; pp. 108-42. Reprinted with stylistic changes, additions and with permission of *Artibus Asiae.*

who actualizes the potentiality of Brahman; he is called Maheśvara, or simply Īśvara (as well as Īśa or Īśāna; cf. *Śvet. Up.* 4.10). The *Mahābhārata* gives notice that even the gods spring from Maheśa. The first gods to be emitted are Brahmā, Viṣṇu, and Rudra. Brahmā emanates from the right side of Maheśa and Viṣṇu from his left (see xiii.14.183).

There is surely a considerable time span between speculations in the texts of ancient Hinduism and those in the medieval Śaiva Āgamas. Nonetheless, the outline of the ancient thoughts remains and there develops a doctrine defined in terms having iconographic implications.[2] In the Āgamas, the triple Śiva Reality is composed of three elements having three names. These are: Para Śiva, Sadāśiva, and Maheśa. Para Śiva is *niṣkala* and can be viewed as the theistic equivalent of the formless Brahman. From Para Śiva begins a process of unfolding whereby the transcendental moves towards manifestation. The fully manifested form (i.e. *sakala*, lit. 'consisting of parts') of the creator god is the third Reality, Maheśa. Sadāśiva is the godhead on the way to full manifestation. He is the formless as it begins to assume form. The Āgamas also distinguish three entities, each symbolic of one of the stages constituting the Śiva Reality. The plain *liṅga* refers to the undifferentiated, formless Para Śiva. The *liṅga* is symbolic of the unmanifested Supreme empowered with cosmic creation. A *mukhaliṅga* refers to Sadāśiva. It evokes the manner in which the formless begins to assume form. Out of the cosmic essence that is Para Śiva (i.e. the *liṅga*), the body of god begins to reveal itself and the head projects first. There follow a series of projections leading towards full manifestation. When the full figure is revealed, that is Maheśa. That figure can be described with five heads in the Āgamas.[3]

Being links in a chain, the three forms of the Śiva Reality share ultimate identity and potency. The third or last element is but the effective means to realize the potency inhering in the other two. As such, Āgamic Maheśa creates and does so in a manner recalling the description in the *Mahābhārata;* first to arise from Maheśa are the gods Rudra, Viṣṇu, and Brahmā. The Purāṇic tradition also knows that these three deities arise from Maheśa.[4]

Śaivite iconography employs the symbols emblematic of Para Śiva, Sadāśiva and Maheśa. When two or more of these symbols occur together in a visual context, it may be assumed that the doctrinal unfolding of the triple Śiva Reality is being expressed. Perhaps the clearest visual expression of the unfolding process is found in an early eighteenth century Nepalese painting in the Los Angeles County Museum of Art; the painting depicts śaiva shrines (Fig. 6.1). The chief śaiva shrine in the painting is three-tiered, each tier having a central niche containing the main icon of that tier. In the niche on the top tier is a plain *liṅga*; it symbolizes Para Śiva. Below, in the second niche is a *mukhaliṅga* showing three visible heads; it symbolizes Sadāśiva. In the bottom, third niche is a five-headed, ten-armed fully manifest, anthropomorphic figure. He represents Maheśa. The three entities

Fig. 6.1. Nepalese painting, Śaiva Shrines in a Landscape, 18th century. Los Angeles County Museum of Art, M76.20. Reproduced by courtesy of the Museum.

Fig. 6.2. *Liṅga* with partial body of Sadāśiva, brass with silver and copper inlay, eighth-ninth centuries. Formerly Pan-Asian collection.

symbolizing the Śiva Reality, their sequential relationship and their distinctive structural properties, are immediately apparent in this painting. Less apparent but equally present is the question of equivalencies in the number of bodily parts. Maheśa's five heads are clearly depicted, but those of his predecessor are not. Theoretically there should be structural parity between Maheśa and Sadāśiva since the former is the latter, fully revealed. Indeed, Sadāśiva, just like Maheśa, is described with five heads in the Āgamas, and the Pañcamukha Liṅga is his theoretical cognizance. But Sadāśiva may also be represented with one, three, or four heads depending upon how closely the representation follows the theoretical model. In the case of the Nepalese painting, we may understand that the three visible heads of the *mukhaliṅga* refer in fact to a Caturmukha Liṅga, The latter, the four-headed Śiva Liṅga, is understood to stand for a Pañcamukha Liṅga, since the fifth head, in the center, is rarely represented.[5]

The painting, like the Āgamic teaching, illustrates the fact that the main difference between Sadāśiva and Maheśa relates not to the number of depicted bodily parts, but to the degree of bodily manifestation. Sadāśiva begins the unfolding process with the emergence of the head(s); then more of the body appears. In that way, Sadāśiva could be represented by more than the *mukhaliṅga;* a partially exposed anthropomorphic body of god also represents Sadāśiva. Both iconic types convey the same theological message in visual terms: god is in the process of moving towards manifestation. Thus it is Sadāśiva whose tricephalic, partially exposed form appears at the southern end of the north-south axis of Cave I at Elephants.[6] It is also Sadāśiva whose single head and partial body emerge from the *liṅga* on the eighth-ninth century Kashmiri icon formerly in the Pan-Asian Collection (Fig. 6.2).

Aspects of the doctrine exhibited in the eighteenth century painting and described in the medieval Śaiva Āgamas already existed in different parts of India from the post-Gupta period onwards. For example, a Sanskrit inscription, written in late Brāhmī characters, and dated on palaeographic grounds to the sixth-

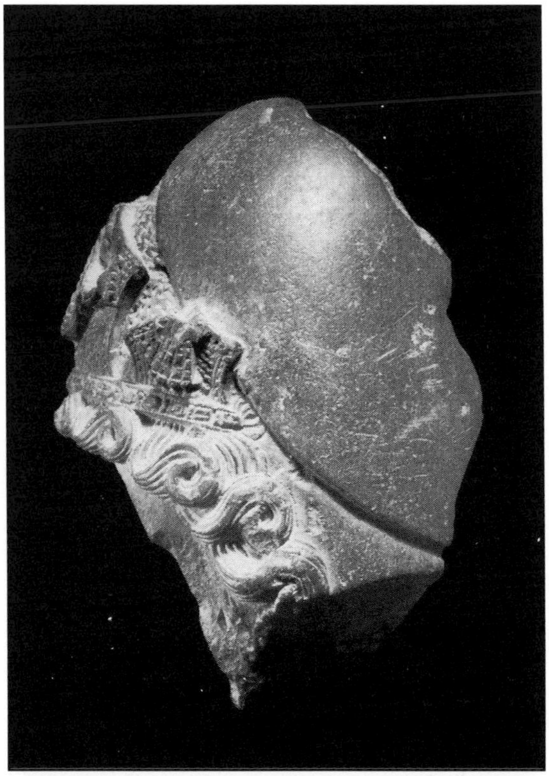

Fig. 6.3. Exterior of left leaf of damaged stone diptych, probably showing head of Sadāśiva. Northwest India, Śāhi period. Formerly S. Eilenberg collection, now Metropolitan Museum of Art. Reproduced by courtesy of the Museum.

Fig. 6.4. Interior of left leaf of damaged stone diptych, showing standing Maheśa. Northwest India, Śāhi period. Formerly S. Eilenberg collection, now Metropolitan Museum of Art. Reproduced by courtesy of the Museum.

seventh century AD refers to the doctrine;[7] the inscription is found on the pedestal of a marble carving of Umā-Maheśvara unearthed during the excavation of Tepe Skandar, 30 km. north of Kabul. The opening part of the inscription states that a single form *(ēka-mū[r]ttis)* became triple *(tridhā)* in the shapes of Brahmā[8], Viṣṇu, and Maheśvara, the latter being the (first) cause *([k]āraṇan)*, presumably of the other two.[9] This inscription, just like the Epic, Purāṇic, and Āgamic passages, represents Maheśa as the creator of the other gods. In using the word *mūrti*—a technical term in the *Śvetāśvatara Upaniṣad* 1.13 (signaling the material form rising out from *liṅga;* i.e. subtle form), the inscription introduces the possibility that more than the *mūrti* stage of the unfolding may have been known at that time in this northern region. This possibility is supported by the supposition that the earliest Āgamas in both the North and the South may be assigned to the seventh or eighth centuries AD.[10] All this suggests that representations of these ideas may have occurred prior to their codification in the mediaeval Āgamas. A previous paper[11] has already indicated as much: Śaiva temple forms between the sixth and eighth centuries do, in fact, portray the unfolding of Para Śiva.

This paper attempts to go further, to show that the doctrine was represented all over India by the sixth to eighth centuries.

To reiterate, by doctrine I refer to a process; specifically it is the process whereby the triple Śiva Reality unfolds from transcendency to materiality. The method I have used to identify the depiction of the doctrine is derived from the Nepalese painting. Therein, identification of the entities, their interrelationship and their distinguishing structure is possible because the icons are seen in their architectural context. The demonstration that follows begins with the pan-Indic representations of the doctrine in the earliest extant Śaiva shrines. Only by analyzing sculpture in an architectural context can there be amassed a body of criteria permitting identification of pieces no longer *in situ;* identification of some isolated pieces no longer *in situ* completes the demonstration.

After noting that an early inscription indicates some knowledge of the doctrine in the Northwest, it is perhaps appropriate to begin with an example from that region. The example comes from a seventh to eighth century (probably closer to the seventh century) portable shrine. Only the left leaf of this heretofore unpublished diptych remains (Fig. 6.3). It is a *liṅga*-shaped diptych (4–1/2" high) of hard stone, and carved on both sides. The outer side, quite damaged, shows the top of the *liṅga* and a portion of the head below. The deep groove of the *glans penis* separates the two. The portion of the head that remains is a crown with large locks of hair descending along the brow[12]. The crown is a decorated band topped with crests; these crests somewhat resemble crenelated turrets.[13] From the center of each crest hangs a tassel (a bunch of jewels? ribbons?) The shape of the crown is the single most important clue to identify the subject of the diptych. The crown worn by the Ekamukha on the outer side matches the shape of the crown worn by the four-armed, fully anthropomorphic figure on the inner side (Fig. 6.4).[14] Clearly, the intent is to establish by visual means a formal connection between the outer head and the inner figure. The latter is also in poor condition. It is not possible to determine the attributes held in the hands. All that can be said is that the extra, raised left arm follows the curve of an arch under which stands the male figure. The figure wears a *dhotī* and is sparsely and simply adorned, with earrings, armlets, and necklaces.[15] In spite of the few details and the damaged condition, the identity of the figure is unproblematic. This is Maheśa, the Ekamūrti form of the triple Śiva Reality. He stands as the finale of a process initiated on the outer side, having iconographic analogies with the Kalyānpur liṅga (analysed elsewhere, see fn. 2 above). In both cases, the top of the *liṅga* evokes Para Śiva, and the *mukha*, or head, projecting from the *liṅga* evokes Sadāśiva. Were the diptych complete the outer right leaf would depict the right-hand parts of the *glans penis* and the *mukha*. It is not possible to predict the motif on the inner right side since there are no right-hand examples available. Still, the general theme of the diptych—probably an example of Śāhi art[16]—is above conjecture. This portable shrine displays the unfolding process in such a manner as to exploit the properties of a diptych.

Fig. 6.5. Interior of left leaf of damaged stone diptych, showing the Umā-Maheśa pair. Northwest India, Śāhi period. Formerly S. Eilenberg collection, now Metropolitan Museum of Art. Reproduced by courtesy of the Museum.

The process is illustrated by the unfolding of the diptych itself. This is not the only known Śaiva diptych from the north to touch upon the doctrine. Another *liṅga*-shaped diptych of the Śāhi period has been published by Taddei[17] and Goetz.[18] Taddei's analysis of a bronze mould for a stone piece now in the Metropolitan Museum of Art, allowed him to date the piece to the seventh-eighth centuries. Again the left side is the one preserved, and it shows an Ekamukha Liṅga.[19] The interior contains the Umā-Maheśvara pair (Fig. 6.5).[20] Maheśvara is

Fig. 6.6. Bhujaṅgeśvara Temple. Andhra Pradesh, eighth century. Image of seated Maheśvara on east wall of sanctum. Photograph: Archaeological Survey of India.

three-headed and four-armed. The middle head with the third eye is larger than the lateral heads; its hairstyle is similar to that seen on the outer Ekamukha. Again, thereby, a formal connection between the two beings (i.e. Sadāśiva and Maheśvara) is stated in visual terms. The nature of the lateral heads is somewhat problematic, although the head on the left may be feminine. Maheśvara holds a trident in the upper right and a water pot *(kamaṇḍalu)* in the upper left hand; the lower right and left hands hold the rosary and *gaḍā* respectively. Leaning towards his consort, Maheśvara stands cross-legged in front of Nandin in a manner recalling the stance of Oēšo in front of the bull on coins issued by Vāsudeva II.[21] Parenthetically, this diptych permits further insights into numerical equivalencies. Sadāśiva, on the outer side, is represented with one head; Maheśa, the same god now fully revealed, is shown with three (= five) heads. These are not iconographic inconsistencies. They are iconographic realities drawing upon conceptual connections between the number one and the number five.[22]

These two portable shrines from the northwest extend the possibility that in the future early structural temples illustrating the doctrine may be identified in this region.[23]

An early structural temple from the southeast displays the manifestation of Śiva. The sanctum of the eighth century Śaiva temple of Bhujaṅgeśvara (Andhra Pradesh) holds the plain *liṅga*, symbolic of Para Śiva.[24] Behind it, on the eastern wall, is a carving of a three-headed, four-armed full figure. This is Maheśa. He is seated with his legs folded at the knees (Fig. 6.6). The tricephalic god shows the Aghora head on the right side and the Vāmadeva head on the left; the central head is that of Sadyojāta.[25] He holds the trident and drum in his upper right and left hands, respectively. (The numbers of heads, arms, and the trident associated with this Maheśa are also associated with the Maheśvara on the interior of the second diptych discussed above). Outside the sanctum, in niches around the ground floor of the temple, are reliefs of the eight Dikpālas. On the second story, images of Dakṣiṇāmūrti and Harihara are carved. There is, however, no representation of Sadāśiva in this temple.[26] Absence of an icon representing the second stage in the unfolding process may be due neither to an artistic anomaly, nor to a doctrinal shift. The possibility for coalescing the second stage with the first stage can be gleaned from the *Suprabheda Āgama*.[27] The Southern *Rauravāgama* gives further evidence for possible coalescing. This text states that on the back wall of the Śaiva cella, behind the *liṅga*, there must appear "a representation of the manifest Śiva accompanied with Umā."[28] The need to represent Sadāśiva is not mentioned. It remains for future investigations to determine to what extent coalescing is an actual feature in south Indian Śaiva temples. As for the Bhujaṅgeśvara temple, the doctrinal statement is unambiguously made, despite absence of an image of Sadāśiva. One glance cast within from the threshold of the *garbhagṛha* can locate Para Śiva and Maheśa. Both the source and its material form are present in the sanctum.

Fig. 6.7. Parāśurāmeśvara Temple, Bhuvaneśvara, Orissa. View of *śikhara* above sanctum roof. Śailobdhava period, seventh century. Photograph American Institute of Indian Studies (AIIS).

To the east, a much more developed program delineating the doctrine is found on the seventh century Paraśurāmeśvara Temple at Bhuvaneśvara, Orissa. The *garbhagṛha* contains the *liṅga;* other than it, the sanctum is bare. The drama of divine unfolding is reserved for the exterior of this temple. The Paraśurāmeśvara temple is of the *rekhā* type, inasmuch as the spire above the sanctum has a curvilinear shape (Fig. 6.7). The spire, or *śikhara,* has central projections *(rāhās)* and it is on these that the doctrine is portrayed. In that the temple faces west, it may be assumed that the western central projection of the *śikhara* is the most important. Here are the sculptural motifs, in ascending order, on the western *rāhā:* first, the Rāvaṇānugrahamūrti, in the largest *caitya* arch (which is situated just above the clerestory of the *jagamohan);* above, Śiva Nateśa in a slightly smaller *caitya* arch which is crowned by a *kīrtimukha;* above, Lakulīśa seated in a meditative pose (Fig. 6.8).[29] He is not framed by a *caitya* arch. Also, he is the last of the fully anthropomorphic figures, though not the last relief on this central

Fig. 6.8. Paraśurāmeśvara Temple, details of carving on west face of the *śikhara*. Photograph AIIS.

projection. Above Lakulīśa, in the same vertical alignment and within ever decreasing *caitya* arches, are portrayed: the partially visible form of a tricephalic Sadāśiva, having "the fierce side face on the viewer's left standing for Aghora-Bhairava and the placid side face on the right standing for Umāvakta-Vāmadeva;"[30] immediately above is the single-headed, three-eyed, partial form, presumably again of Sadāśiva (Fig. 6.8). The central projection ends abruptly with a flat course (i.e. the *bisama).* Śaiva symbolism however does not stop here, although the non-anthropomorphic shapes that follow contrast markedly with the preceding figural reliefs. Raised above a joining are the topmost elements of the spire: a large, flattened and fluted stone disc (the *āmalasāraka),* the moon cap *(candrikā* or *khapūri),* and an *ākāśaliṅga* surmounted by Śiva's trident (Fig. 6.7). There probably was no *ākāśaliṅga* when the temple, in disrepair, was scheduled for restoration. The report filed by M.H. Arnott, who supervised the restorations undertaken between 1899 and 1901, makes no mention of it.[31] Reconstruction of the top order as seen today, with the *ākāśaliṅga,* could have resulted either from a broken piece lying on the ground or from the presence of an *ākāśaliṅga* in the top order of the contemporaneous Svarṇajāleśvara Temple also at Bhuvaneśvara (Fig. 6.9)[32]. In either case, the probability is good that the Paraśurāmeśvara temple originally had an *ākāśaliṅga* (lit. *liṅga* of ether) as finial. As such, the temple would

Fig. 6.9. Svarṇajāleśvara Temple. Bhuvaneśvara as recently reconstructed. Seventh century. Photograph: AIIS.

have originally had two *liṅgas*, one on its summit and the other in its sanctum. They could be regarded as brackets containing a series of forms dramatizing the unfolding of god.

The unfolding is contained within a vertical axis which, like a spine, upholds the doctrine. Along the western axis the unfolding can be espied, as it were, through openings in the *caitya* arches along the central projection as well as by the topmost order pointing heavenward. The latter, consisting of forms open to the sky, begins the sculptural program. In that way, the program begins with the form least visible from the ground and not with the form most visible on the *rāhā*, the Rāvaṇānugrahamūrti (Fig. 6.7). This relief is not the biggest because it is the most important; it is the biggest because it displays a form of god pertaining more to gross materiality than the forms which precede it. In the context of the theological doctrine portrayed on the western vertical axis, it is the least important form. The program probably begins with the finial at the summit of the temple, the *ākāśaliṅga*. Anchored only at one point and thus almost unbound, the *ākāśaliṅga* is the sign of "the first departure into manifestation from the unchanging Pure Principle or Essence..."[33] The *ākāśaliṅga* is a symbol meant to evoke the first evolute from the Pure Principle (Para Śiva), namely the subtle aspect of Sadāśiva; this is Īśāna, the fifth and uppermost head of the evolving Sadāśiva.[34] The *ākāśaliṅga* enters the center of the *āmalasāraka* which "symbolizes the passage to heaven; it is the architectural symbol of the celestial world."[35] In concert, these non-figural forms represent the heavenly sphere with its various subtle levels. The figural forms unfold subsequently. Through a small *caitya* window near the top can be seen the bust of Sadāśiva having one head; it is followed by a tricephalic bust of Sadāśiva (Fig. 6.8). Possibly the two representations of Sadāśiva are meant to indicate a sequential unfolding of the god's subtle form. There is no reason to consider these two as depictions of different gods. It is more likely that two stages, invested with the self-same revelatory power of Sadāśiva, are evident through the *gavākṣas*.[36] It may seem unusual for Lakulīśa to be the first fully manifest body of god on the *rāhā*. From the foregoing, Maheśa is to be expected and not Lakulīśa, the historical teacher who founded the Pāśupata order. It must therefore be quickly pointed out that by the seventh century, the Orissan cult of Lakulīśa-Pāśupata no longer considered him to be a human teacher. Lakulīśa was deified and recognized by the sixth-seventh centuries as an incarnation of Maheśvara.[37] Already in the Gupta age his deification was acknowledged. The *Vāyu Purāṇa* (probably no later than the fifth century), enumerating the 28 incarnations of Maheśvara, mentions Nakulin (Lakulin or Lakulīśa) as the 28th, and also mentions the first four disciples.[38] The *Liṅga Purāṇa* (Chapter 24) also recounts how Maheśvara told Brahmā of his various incarnations, including that of Lakuli, the 28th (see 124b–133). Therefore the appearance of Lakulīśa directly below Sadāśiva on the central projection must be in recognition of his identification with Maheśvara, who was worshipped by the Śailodbhavas under whose rule the Paraśurāmeśvara temple was built.[39] In the next *caitya* window, god as cosmic creator is seen; this is ten-armed Nateśa. A manifestation, the

Fig. 6.10. Svarṇajāleśvara Temple prior to reconstruction. Photograph: AIIS.

Fig. 6.11. Temple at Kusumā, Śirohī District, Rajasthan with inscription of 636-637. View through sanctum doorway. Photograph AIIS.

Rāvaṇānugrahamūrti, terminates the divine unfolding traced along the course of the western *rāhā*.[40]

The unfolding is also evoked by the symbolism adhering to temple architecture. The *śikhara* represents heaven; its finials soar toward the highest heaven. The body of the temple is considered the atmosphere, and the temple's foundation is the earth.[41] From the womb chamber enclosing the sign of Para Śiva germinate the myriad manifestations of the god and all the earthly transformations of his energy; they are seen on the outer walls.

Also in the seventh century, but in the West, a different combination of architectural elements was utilized for essentially the same purpose. In Rājasthān, the Śiva temple at Kusumā (Śirohī Dist.; probably dating to 636–37 by an inscription of that year),[42] displays the doctrine with great economy. The *garbhagṛha* and the door which frames it join together to become one sculptural program; that program, expressing the doctrine, is perceived in its entirety at the doorway of the *garbhagṛha* (Fig. 6.11). At the doorway there comes into view (1) the plain *liṅga* inside the *garbhagṛha;* (2) the tricephalic, partially revealed form of Sadāśiva carved on the wall behind the *linga;* (3) the central portion of the doorway's lintel where originally the image of Lakulīśa-Maheśvara should

Fig. 6.12. Temple at Kusumā, view inside sanctum showing *yoni/liṅga* on floor and tricephalic relief of Sadāśiva on rear wall. Photograph: AIIS.

have appeared (see below). The plain *liṅga*, symbolic of Para Śiva, is grounded in the *yoni pīṭha*, which is situated in the center of the sanctum (Fig. 6.12). Behind it, on the western wall is a relief of Sadāśiva manifested up to the chest (Fig. 6.12). The degree of manifestation and also the distribution of the faces (Aghora on the right, Vāmadeva on the left, Sadyojāta in the center) recall the iconography of the Elephanta Sadāśiva, as does the hint of a *liṅga*-shape in the piled-up *jaṭas* of the central head.[43] In spite of these similarities, the level of artistry of the Kusumā Sadāśiva nowise matches up to the image at Elephanta. The full figure of the god is no longer in its place today. When Michael W. Meister visited the site in 1974 he noted an image at the site which "probably was the missing central image over the door."[44] The figure is ithyphallic, a characteristic of Lakulīśa; he sits on the same type of lotus as do the lateral figures. From the 1917 photograph showing the doorway with its lintel more complete than it is now (Fig. 6.11), it is easy to recognize Brahmā seated to the right of the central space and Viṣṇu seated to the left.[45] Thus these gods assume positions equated with the sides from which they emanated out of Maheśvara. As at the Paraśurāmeśvara temple, Lakulīśa is introduced at Kusumā because he is the embodiment of Maheśa. And again as at the Paraśurāmeśvara temple, the symbolism of architectural members appears to confirm the significance of the images. A doorway, especially the lintel, is reserved for depictions pertaining to celestial regions.[46] The center of the lintel is reserved for an image of the god enshrined within. Thus the movement towards manifestation begun in the womb chamber is completed in an architectural space, associated with the heavens, which frames that chamber. The symbolism of the architecture seems to imply that god, though fully manifest, is not yet fully enmeshed in the world of matter.

Elsewhere in western India, Lakulīśa as Maheśa's incarnation is depicted during times roughly contemporaneous with the Śiva Temple at Kusumā. Icons coming from the Karvan area of Gujarat (dating between the sixth and eighth centuries) show Lakulīśa in front of the *liṅga*.[47] A distinctive manner of depicting Maheśa in the formative phase of Śaiva iconography is to show him in front of (i.e. conjoint with) the *liṅga*, his ultimate source of being.[48] This manner of portraying Lakulīśa is still seen in the Karvan area in the medieval period.[49] Quite possibly the reason why icons at Karvan, and the western region in general, emphasize Lakulīśa as Maheśa incarnate is because Karvan is the locale associated with "the descent."[50] This is the place where the incarnation of Lakulīśa was supposed to have taken place, and reverence to him has endured. Much later than Kusumā, the temple at Aṭrū (Koṭāh District, Rājasthān) displays an arrangement seen at Kusumā. In 1906, the Aṭrū temple was described as dilapidated, but on the lintel of the sanctum's doorway could still be seen Lakulīśa seated in the center "with Brahmā and Viṣṇu to his right and left respectively."[51]

The evidence from the West indicates that under certain circumstances, there may be sufficient information to associate pieces no longer *in situ* with the doctrine. The most accurate guidelines for identifying such pieces usually come from sculpture and constructs *in situ*. There follows below a reappraisal of several sculptures no longer *in situ* which can, in light of the above, be reidentified. The ensuing analyses are neither exhaustive nor paradigmatic. They are meant to illustrate future possibilities in understanding Śaiva art forms, should the symbolic representations of the doctrinal theory, as outlined above, be accepted.

1. FROM THE NORTH

Recently the Metropolitan Museum of Art acquired a small (5½"h., 5½" w.) Kashmiri stone relief dating eighth-ninth centuries (Pl. 13, No. 1985.85).[52] Three multi-armed, multi-headed male gods surrounded by plain banded nimbuses, stand on a plain pedestal. Each god assumes the *tribhaṅga* posture in this heretofore unpublished relief. The god in the center with three visible heads is Maheśa; the Aghora head is on the right; the Vāmadeva head is on the left. Crowned, regally dressed and ornamented, Maheśa stands in front of Nandin. He holds the trident in the extra right hand while the natural right is held in *abhaya-mudrā*. The attributes in the left hands are too rubbed to be identified. This representation of Maheśa, it may be noted, has some iconographic features in common with the Maheśa on the interior of the second diptych discussed above (Fig. 6.5; e. g. number of arms and heads; probably types of lateral heads; position of trident and Nandin). Brahmā, whose ascetic nature is emphasized, stands to the right of Maheśa. *Jaṭas* are on each of his three visible heads. Four-armed, the god holds the *kamaṇḍalu* in the lowered right; the attributes in the other three hands are too damaged to be identified. By the side of his feet appears Brahmā's *vāhana*, the *haṁsa*. Viṣṇu

Fig. 6.13. Relief of three standing gods, centering on Maheśa. Kashmiri, eighth-ninth century. Metropolitan Museum of Art. Reproduced by courtesy of the Museum.

Caturmūrti, showing the lateral heads of the boar and the lion, stands to the left of Maheśa. He too is crowned, richly attired, and rests his two lowered hands upon the heads of Gadādevī and Cakrapuruṣa. A lotus is held in Viṣṇu's natural right hand. Bhū Devī emerges between the god's feet. Even though Viṣṇu, Brahmā and Maheśa are the same size and have similar postures, haloes, and multiple bodily parts, they are not of equal importance. From sculptural programs *in situ,* the Śaiva doctrinal significance of this arrangement of figures may be proposed. The lintel arrangements at the temples of Kusumā and Aṭrū come quickly to mind. In these architectural settings, Brahmā and Viṣṇu flank (Lakulīśa)-Maheśvara on the right and left respectively because they issue from those sides of Maheśa. Further architectural evidence exists to show that in this seeming triad, it is Maheśa who is the superior god. The evidence comes from the eighth century Lankeśvara shrine at Ellora.[53] Lankeśvara is a biaxial shrine. At the end of the east-west axis, on the western wall, is a very large relief showing three gods of equal size. Maheśa is in the middle; he stands, four-armed, in front of Nandin. The trident is in his upper right hand. Maheśa is flanked by Brahmā to the right and by Viṣṇu to the left. The Lankeśvara relief, like the Kusumā lintel, must be seen as part of a larger sculptural program in order to arrive at its proper understanding. In the larger context it is clear that the Lankeśvara relief depicts Maheśa together with the gods that emanate from his sides. At Lankeśvara, just as in the Kashmiri relief (Fig. 6.13), size, nimbuses, postures, or pedestal do not establish divine hierarchies; the program does this. Thus, by superimposing upon the isolated piece the evidence gleaned from analogous programs *in situ,* the significance of the Metropolitan Museum of Art relief may be established: it represents Maheśa together with the godlings he created from his sides.[54]

2. FROM THE SOUTH

A series of magnificent Chola stone images exist that have been considered representations of Brahmā[55] or, most recently, of Brahmā/Śiva. The second identification goes to the heart of the iconographic problem posed by the series.[56] The images show a four-headed, four-armed seated deity; these features relate, of course, to Brahmā. Since the rosary *(akṣamālā)* appears in the upper left hand, the likelihood that it is Brahmā goes unchallenged. However, a third eye appears on the forehead of the image and therein lies the problem. Brahmā is not adorned with this mark, Śiva is. The series comprises the following large tenth century examples: an image (63½" h.) in the Museum of Fine Arts, Boston (Pl. 14; No. 42.120); an image (64" h.) in the Albright-Knox Art Gallery, Buffalo; and an image (58³/₈" h.) in the Worcester Art Museum (No. 1964.16).[57] Since a four-headed Hindu image whose ascetic nature is emphasized ought to be either Brahmā or Śiva, and since there is no satisfactory religious evidence to justify the appearance of the third eye with Brahmā, he cannot be the subject of the series. Within the Śaiva

Fig. 6.14. Seated image of four-headed deity, here identified as Maheśa. Stone, Chola, tenth century. Boston Museum of Fine Arts. Reproduced by courtesy of the Museum.

context, there is no problem; Maheśa could well be the subject. The presence of the four-armed, three (=five)-headed seated Maheśa in the Bhujaṅgeśvara temple quickly reminds us that the South could fashion large icons of this aspect of the Śiva Reality. Like the Bhujaṅgeśvara Maheśa, the images in the series wear armlets, elaborate necklaces, the sacred thread, and the *dhotī* (secured by the girdle). The Boston image (Fig. 6.14), just like the Bhujaṅgeśvara Maheśa (Fig. 6.6), portrays the god's natural left hand resting on the left leg, with the palm up and fingers bent inward. The *sukhāsana* posture assumed by the Chola images can be observed not only on a related tenth century image from Khajuraho (discussed below) but more importantly on a Maheśa icon fashioned within the incipient phase of Śaiva art.[58] Even so, it should not be forgotten that an *āsana* is not a critical factor in the iconography of a Maheśa image: the comparatively rare posture portrayed in the Kāveripākkam stone image did not prevent T.A. Gopinath Rao from calling it a Maheśamūrti.[59] What distinguishes Maheśa, according to the Āgamas, is what these Chola images display: a fully manifest form of the Śiva Reality having (theoretically) five heads. Other iconographic details, though subordinate, work to assist this identification. With regard to the Boston Maheśa, the *akṣamālā* could well refer to the god's ascetic nature.[60] The lotus held in the lower right hand could be emblematic of Maheśa's creative power, signifying as it does the essentially "playful character of the divine operation."[61] Asymmetrical earrings, seen on the front of the image, are not infrequently seen on Śaiva icons, including *mukhas* of a Caturmukha Liṅga.[62] Dissimilar earrings may focus on the inherently biune, androgynous nature of Śiva, and could emphasize, in the Boston image, the distinctiveness of each of the lateral heads of Maheśa, as the Aghora – Vāmadeva heads are wont to do.

3. FROM THE CENTER

The Khajuraho (Madhya Pradesh) sculpture just referred to, is reproduced by B. N. Sharma *(Sadāśiva,* New Delhi, 1976, Pl. IV), who considers it to represent Sadāśiva. The god has five faces, three of which are visible. He is seated in the *sukhāsana* pose, having the right pendant leg resting on a lotus issuing from the base. He wears necklaces, *yajñopavīta,* and a *dhotī.* Originally the god should have had eight arms; Sharma notes that the attributes held in the natural hands are indistinct. That does not matter for purposes of identification. In this icon, what matters is the degree of divine manifestation and the identity of the two small godlings on either side of the nimbus. On the right side is a seated, multi-headed, bearded Brahmā; on the left a much broken Viṣṇu. The main god thus ought to be Maheśa, The Khajuraho Maheśa has a large protruding abdomen reiminiscent of the bellies characterizing *yakṣas* in early Indian art. (The symbolism of the *yakṣa's* belly, considered elsewhere,[63] would not be inappropriate for Maheśa, were one inclined to minimize, as I am, the intervening span of time.)

4. FROM THE EAST

An impressive twelfth century Sena sculpture in the Indian Museum, Calcutta, shows a three (=4 = 5)-headed, ten-armed figure seated on a lotus base in the *padmāsana* pose (Fig. 6.15).[64] As such, it could in a general way recall the five-headed, ten-armed standing figure in the bottom tier of the Śaiva shrine in the Nepalese painting (Fig. 6.1). That standing figure as we have seen is identifiable as Maheśa. The seated figure, from Rajibpur, Bengal, carries an inscription on the pedestal below the lotus base, which refers to the installation of Sadāśiva (literally Sadāśiva's feet, *Sadāśivapādāḥ*).[65] If this fully manifest form is Sadāśiva, and there seems no other way to interpret the inscription,[66] then it contradicts the hypothesis advanced in this and my previous study, that Sadāśiva is a partially manifest form of god. It is the only exception I have encountered so far.

Fig. 6.15. Sculpture, named by inscription Sadāśiva, from Rajibpur, Bengal. Stone, Sena, 12th century, Indian Museum, Calcutta. Photograph by courtesy of the Museum.

Since the Rajibpur sculpture has often been cited and described,[67] only the details pertaining to the identification need be discussed. In addition to the *āsana* and the number of multiple bodily parts, the attributes pertain to the identification. The natural hands are held close to the chest in the teaching *(vyākhyāna) mudrā*. The right hands are in *varada* and hold the club *(khaṭvāṅga)*, the *triśūla*, the *śūla* (or *śakti);* the left hands hold the *sanāla-padma*, a drum *(ḍamaru)* a snake, and the citron *(bījapūra*, etc.) A figure similar to the Rajibpur Sadāśiva occurs on several copperplate grants of the Sena kings. Two of these copperplates identify the figure in their inscription. The Idilpur copperplate of Keśavasena (second quarter of the twelfth century) states that it has, riveted to the plate, the mark of Sadāśiva *(Sadāśiva-mudrā);*[68] the Madanpada copperplate inscription of Viśvarūpasena states that it has been stamped with the mark of Sadāśiva *(Sadāśivamudrayā mudrayitvā)*.[69] The same inscription also informs us that Viśvarūpasena is a most devout worshipper of Maheśvara. On the Barrackpur Grant of Vijayasena, which also bears the figure, Maheśvara is mentioned in the same way: the grant is given "in honor of Lord Maheśvara."[70] These figures and others on the grants do not agree in every detail with the Rajibpur Sadāśiva, but they agree typologically.[71] All are fully manifest figures with equivalent numbers of multiple heads and arms, seated in *padmāsana.* They all appear to be Sena representations of Sadāśiva.

The Sena kings were not native to eastern India. They came to Bengal from the south. There exists in the Āgamic tradition known in the south, another conceptualization of Sadāśiva which attributes to him the *sakala* qualification usually reserved for Maheśa. Section III, 57–60 of the *Somaśambhupaddhati,* a Śaiva text, demonstrates the other conceptualization.[72] The first part of *śloka* 57 addresses the god, pure as a bright crystal *(devaṁ śuddhasphaṭikanirmalam)* and immediately proceeds to invoke the form of god having a body. The body has ten arms, five faces, and sits in *padmāsana,* The right hands hold *śakti,* sword *(asī), śūla,* club *(khaṭvāṅga),* and make the *varada* gesture. The left hold the drum *(ḍamaru),* the citron *(bījapūraka),* the snake, the rosary *(akṣasūtra),* and the blue lotus. The *Somaśambhupaddhati* calls this body 'Sadāśiva'. The commentators' reaction to this section is as follows: most of the commentators divide the first part into two. First the invocation is to the subtle, luminous essence, being without substantive form; and then the invocation is to the concrete body. The commentator Nirmalamani cites a *śloka* from another Āgama (presumably from the South) which qualifies Sadāśiva as consisting of parts (i.e. *sakala).*[73] Thus the commentaries recognize that the concrete form usually named 'Maheśa' is in this text called 'Sadāśiva'.

The importance of the evidence from the *Somaśambbupaddhati* is that its description of the *sakala* body called 'Sadāśiva' is very similar to descriptions of Sadāśiva in the *Uttarakamikāgama* and the *Garuḍa Purāṇa,* two texts influential in Bengal.[74] Therein the five-headed, ten-armed god is described as seated in *padmāsana;* his right hands show *abhaya* and *varada-mudrā,* and hold *śakti, triśūla* and *khaṭvāṅga.* The left hands hold the snake, rosary, drum, blue lotus, and citron.

It is immediately apparent that the Sena Sadāśiva from Rajibpur (Fig. 6.15), closely follows the description of Sadāśiva in the *Garuḍa Purāṇa* and the *Uttarakamikāgama.* The Rajibpur Sadāśiva can be considered an East Indian representation whose antecedents could well stem from an Āgamaic tradition known in the South; this tradition calls the fully manifested body 'Sadāśiva' instead of the more usual name 'Maheśa'.[75] The Rajibpur Sadāśiva need not be considered an exception. Instead it may be an East Indian icon representing an alternate, or second, Āgamic tradition.[76] Since this is not the only Śaiva representation peculiar to East Indian art,[77] it serves notice that this region may indeed have followed or developed such a distinctive tradition.

5. FROM THE WEST

The last example is in the form of a figural hood placed ceremoniously over the *liṅga* in order to effectuate the transformation of god from spirit to matter. Such hoods have a wide distribution and are known from fairly recent times onwards.[78]

I am concentrating on contemporaneous Goan examples because their ritual usage has been witnessed and well described by Gritli von Mitterwallner. Without knowledge of their ritual usage, their significance would be hard to assess. Even with this knowledge, their significance may be elusive. von Mitterwallner writes.

> The plain form of the *pūjyabhāga*[79] of the *liṅga*, devoid of *sūtras*, apparently did not satisfy the patrons, priests, and worshippers of the past few centuries. Their urge for anthropomorphization of the *liṅga* head may have been the reason why in more recent Śiva temples of Goa and other regions of India, hoods of metal or even wood, in the form of heads and busts of Śiva, were made to be put over the plain stone *liṅgas*, subsequent to the performance of lustration ceremonies.[80] These heads and busts... are often placed on rackets or in niches of the rear walls in the *garbhagṛhas* of Śaiva temples in Goa, so as to have them readily at hand. We witnessed the climax of the trend towards anthropomorphization of the plain and small *pūjyabhāga* in the Saptakoṭīśvara Temple at New Narve, Bicholim Taluk. The *liṅga*, projecting merely nine centimeters above the surface of the square *pīṭha*, is regularly camouflaged after *abhiṣeka* ceremonies by the draped, seated figure of Śiva, whose face, hands, and feet are made of hammered metal and whose gown consists of a dark-colored cloth, all dextrously joined together.[81]

Contained in this account is yet another mode of representing the doctrine. The progression is neither painted nor sculptured here. It is liturgically enacted. The enactment occurs by placing, over the *liṅga*, layer(s) which symbolize the different stage(s) in the progression.

Perhaps the following liturgical sequence may be visualized: worship commences in the *garbhagṛha* with appropriate homage paid to the *liṅga*, The sanctum may contain, in addition to the *liṅga*, the forms of the layer(s) to be placed over the *liṅga*. Layering begins after the *abhiṣeka* ceremony has been completed. Thus the hood is kept in the sanctum not for the sake of convenience but in preparation for the ritual enactment of an ontological truth. Representing part of the Śiva Reality, a hood *belongs* in the sanctum, as does the carving of Sadāśiva in the Kusumā temple, for example. After the layering of the *liṅga* has been completed, it may be presumed that worship of the resultant form of Śiva occurs.

von Mitterwallner illustrates her account with some contemporary Goan objects used to cover the *liṅga*. These are: (1) a plain *liṅga* on which Śaiva features have been permanently stuck;[82] (2) hoods;[83] (3) the figure draped over the *liṅga* of the Saptakoṭīśvara temple.[84] The hoods are partial anthropomorphic forms (the "heads and busts" in von Mitterwallner's account). When placed over the *liṅga* in the liturgy, these hoods become the representations of Sadāśiva. In the same way, the full figure draped over the *liṅga* "whose face, hands and feet are made of hammered metal and whose gown consists of dark-colored cloth" becomes the representation of Maheśa. It cannot be adduced from this account whether the face, hands, feet, etc., are kept in the *garbhagṛha* when not in use, the same way the hoods are kept. Nor can it be surmised whether it is the custom to place one or two layers over the *liṅga* in the Goan temples, or whether this varies from temple to temple. However, the proffered identification of the hoods (and the figural accessories) does not depend upon this additional information. The identification, together with the premise that layering is yet another way to represent the doctrine, rests on the shapes of the hoods themselves, their repositorium, and their placement over the *liṅga* after the *abhiṣeka.*

The relevance of the last point becomes sufficiently clear from an analogous circumstance in the south Indian Śaiva worship which follows the *Somaśambhupaddhati.*[85] After completing the initial rites which purify both worshipper and *liṅga*, etc., god's presence is invoked. God must first be given a body in order to be present in the ritual. The worshipper constructs, as it were, a bodily form by invoking certain mantras. As mentioned above, in this text, the body is called Sadāśiva.[86] Once the body of god is constructed in the imagination, homage to Sadāśiva and *abhiṣeka* are performed. After *abhiṣeka,* flowers, clothes, jewels, etc., are offered and the ritual continues. We can, however, stop at this point to summarize part of an elaborate set of ritual actions: adoration begins with the *liṅga,* continues with the mental construction of god's body and its lustration. After *abhiṣeka* has been completed, actual decoration and dressing of the *liṅga* can occur while prayers are offered to Śiva.[87] Thus completion of *abhiṣeka* in both the Āgamic text and the Goan service signals the commencement of the layering of the *liṅga.* It can therefore be assumed that the Goan hoods are ritually required. They certainly do not answer an urge to anthropomorphize or to camouflage the *liṅga.*

For the worshipper, the Śaiva ontological symbols discussed above proclaim the supremacy of Śiva and god's will to become bodily present in the world of man. The ontological symbols—*liṅga, mukhaliṅga,* full figure—may vary somewhat since equivalencies can occur (e.g., Sadāśiva may be evoked by an Ekamukha as well as a Pañcamukha Liṅga; Maheśa may be evoked by his *avatāra* Lakulīśa, etc.), but the basic typologies change little. Combinatorial usages of the symbols do however change, as the above demonstration has shown. Indeed the usages of these symbols are sufficiently distinct to warrant classifying them as different programs. To summarize these is to become aware of their breadth and innovative nature. Outlined below are the different Śaiva programs derived from studies in this and the previous paper.[88]

A. Biaxial Temple Floor Plan[89]

1. Lankeśvara shrine, Ellora

Northern end of the north-south axis has the *garbhagṛha* containing the *liṅga* and the relief of Sadāśiva.

Western wall of the east-west axis has the panel carved with Maheśa flanked by Brahmā and Viṣṇu, to his right and left, respectively.

2. Cave I at Elephanta

Western end of the east-west axis has the *garbhagṛha* containing the *liṅga*.

Southern end of the north-south axis has the large relief of Sadāśiva. Manifestations of Śiva are in the grotto's chapels.

B. Sanctum and its Doorway

1. Śiva Temple at Kusumā

The *garbhagṛha* contains the *liṅga* and the image of Sadāśiva. The lintel of the sanctum's doorway originally would have shown Lakulīśa-Maheśa in the center, flanked by Brahmā and Viṣṇu to his right and left, respectively.

2. Śiva Temple at Aṭrū

There remains, essentially, the same program as at Kusumā. However, it is not stated in the *ASI Report of 1906–07* whether an image of Sadāśiva existed in the interior of the *garbhagṛha.*

3. Śiva Temple at Bhujaṅgeśvara

The *garbhagṛha* contains the *liṅga* and the image of Maheśa. There may be coalescing of the doctrine; in any case, the program is abbreviated and confined to the sanctum.

Addendum

Śiva Temple at Bodh Gāya

A Bodh Gāya door lintel inscribed in the reign of Dharmapāla (c. 770–810 AD) records the installation of a Caturmukha Mahādeva in the temple. The lintel shows Lakulīśa in the center, flanked by Sūrya and Viṣṇu.[90] Only further research may determine whether this lintel testifies to a Śiva Temple at Bodh Gaya having the program "Sanctum and its Doorway."

C. Architectural Sculpture

1. Śaiva Diptych from the Northwest

The outside shows the *liṅga* and the *mukha* of Sadāśiva. The inside shows the full figure of Maheśa on one leaf. He may be shown alone or together with Umā. It is not possible to conjecture what the scene on the other interior leaf would have been.

2. Śiva Liṅga from Kalyānpur[91]

The main side of the four-sided *liṅga* is the eastern side. The eastern side must be read downward to obtain the following progression: dome of the *liṅga;*

Fig. 6.16. *Mukhaliṅga* metal hood, covering *liṅga* resting on *pīṭha*. Not earlier than late 18th century, Goanese. Collection of Mandala Gallery, Milan.

multiple faces of Sadāśiva issuing from the *liṅga*: the full figure of Maheśa. On the same level as Maheśa, but on the worshipper's right (when facing the *liṅga*) is Brahmā; Viṣṇu is on the left.

D. Layering the Liṅga

1. Contemporary Goan Hoods

The "Nagesi" Temple at Priol has the *liṅga* in the *garbhagṛha* covered with a hood symbolizing Sadāśiva. When not in use, the hood is kept in a niche on the rear wall of the *garbhagṛha*.[92]

2. Contemporary Goan Figural Accessories

The Saptakoṭīśvara Temple at New Narve covers the *liṅga*, set in the *pīṭha*, with face, limbs, and dress.

Addendum

Recent Metal Hoods from Maharashtrian Temple Altars

The Collection in the Mandala Gallery, Milan, contains numerous examples of *mukhaliṅga* hoods. In a letter from the collector (of 20/1/87) he states, "The *mukhaliṅga* are hollow and did, in fact, cover cylindrical *liṅga* on the temple altar... On occasion, they may, quite simply, have been placed on the altar, retaining their symbolic content notwithstanding the absence of the *liṅga*... Judging by the stylistic treatment of the facial features and the type of metal used, I do not think they [i.e., the examples in the Mandala Gallery Collection] can date earlier than the second half of the eighteenth century." An example from this collection, not previously published, is illustrated in Fig. 6.16; it is a *mukhaliṅga* hood covering a *liṅga* resting on the *pīṭha*. Other examples from the same collection are illustrated in *FMR* 16, September 1983, 54–68; *Arts of Asia* 17, No. 1, Jan.-Feb. 1987, 134–37.

E. Temple Tiers and Towers

1. Paraśurāmeśvara Temple at Bhuvaneśvara

The *garbhagṛha* contains the *liṅga*. The main side of the temple is the western side. The western tower must be read downward to obtain the following progression: the evolving form of Sadāśiva (from ether to one-headed to three (= five)-headed god); Lakulīśa-Maheśa; Śiva Nateśa, the Progenitor; the manifestation, the Rāvaṇānugrahamūrti terminates the progression.

2. Three-tiered Painted Nepalese Śaiva Shrine

The painting shows the cross section of the interior of the three-tiered shrine. Each tier has a central niche containing an icon. When the tiers are read downward, the following progression is noted: plain *liṅga* symbolic of Para Śiva; Caturmukha Liṅga symbolic of Sadāśiva; the full figure representing Maheśa.

Reading the programs, the predominant movement of god's unfolding is downward, even though life as we know it grows upward. A baby grows tall. Grasses and flowers shoot up. A tree climbs high.

"The trees, like longings of earth, stand a-tiptoe to peep at the heavens."[93]

Trees, like longings, originate from earth. Not so does god. His otherness is conveyed in many ways. One is his downward progression from transcendency to materiality.

NOTES AND REFERENCES

* This paper is based on a lecture, "Para Śiva, Sadaśiva, et Maheśa dans l'art de l'Inde," prepared for delivery in March 1988 at the Collège de France, Paris. Many discussions on critical aspects of this study occurred while I was in India in connection with another project supported by a short-term fellowship from the American Institute of Indian Studies (summer 1987).

1. Details are in my monograph, *Many Heads, Arms and Eyes: Origin, Meaning and Form of Multiplicity in Indian Art,* Leiden, Brill, 1997, chapters 9 and 10.
2. What follows is a summary of findings contained in my paper, "Śaiva Temple Forms: loci of god's unfolding body," in *Investigating Indian Art,* M. Yaldiz, W. Lobo eds., Berlin 1987, pp. 335–47; Reprinted in this volume, see pages 74-90.
3. "Śaiva Temple Forms", pp. 338–40; pages 78-79 in this volume.
4. "Śaiva Temple Forms", p. 339 and fn. 25; see page 79 and fn. 25 in this volume.
5. For details on the iconography of the fifth head and the symbolic equivalencies, see "Śaiva Temple Forms", p. 335; see pages 82-83 in this volume.
6. See reproductions in *Exploring India's Sacred Art, Selected Writings of Stella Kramrisch,* edited by Barbara S. Miller, Philadelphia, 1983, pls. 7.1–7.7.
7. In using this date I follow D.C. Sircar, "Umā-Maheśvara Image Inscription from Skandar (Afghanistan)," *Journal of Ancient Indian History* (Calcutta), VI, 1973, Pts. 1–2, pp. 3, 294. This dating is also followed by G.S. Gai, "Umā-Maheśvara Image Inscription from Skandar," *Studies in Indian Epigraphy* (Mysore, 1975), I, p. 1 ff. S. Kuwayama would date the sculpture to the seventh-eighth centuries, see his "The Turki Śāhis and relevant Brahmanical sculptures in Afghanistan," *East and West,* n.s. 26, 1976, pp. 375 ff.
8. I translate the (Bra)hmā" of the inscription as Brahmā (as does Gai) and not as Brahman (as does Sircar) in the works cited in fn. 7 above.
9. The complete translation of the opening part reads: "The single form became triple in the shapes of Brahmā, Viṣṇu, and Maheśvara; Viṣṇu [is] the doer, Brahmā the doing, and Maheśvara the cause [i.e., the origin]."
10. Jan Gonda, *Mediaeval Religious Literature in Sanskrit,* Wiesbaden, 1977, p. 165.
11. "Śaiva Temple Forms", see fn. 2, above.

12. The diptych leaf formerly in the Samuel Eilenberg Collection is now at the Metropolitan Museum of Art (No. L1986.9.60). The same full curls can be seen on the post-Gupta terracotta head of a youth from Tapa Shotar, Afghanistan. The head, also from the Eilenberg Collection and now in the Metropolitan, is illustrated in Amy G. Poster, *From Indian Earth,* Brooklyn Museum, 1986, p. 135. Cf. also the terracotta head from Ushkur in the British Museum, illustrated in Douglas Barrett, "Sculpture of the Shāhi Period," *Oriental Art,* III, 1957, p. 56, No. 5.
13. The shape of the crown is distinctive and apparently uncommon. The closest parallels I could find come from two other small Northwestern pieces formerly in the Eilenberg Collection, and now in the Metropolitan. One is a trilobed crown worn by Viṣṇu (No. 1984, 491.8), possibly of the sixth century. The other is a similar crown worn by Viṣṇu on Garuḍa (No. L198 5.151.10). Both these crowns fail to show the central tassels featured on the crown of the diptych (see below). I wish to thank Dr. Martin Lerner, Curator, Far Eastern Art at the Metropolitan Museum of Art, for making available all these pieces for my inspection, as well as No. 1985.85, mentioned below.
14. The number of arms is based on the evidence from the left side. It may be observed that what looks like a trifurcation on the left shoulder is in actuality the indistinct remains of the *ajina,* or animal skin, over the god's shoulder.
15. The larger necklace compares with the shape of collars seen on early Kashmiri bronzes. See P. Pal, *Bronzes of Kashmir,* Graz, 1975, Pls. 15, 19, 20.
16. It is rather difficult to date and place this piece. The date is based on criteria found in fns. 12, 13, 15. The Śāhi period is determined largely on the distinctive physiognomy of the full figure, although the crown may also be a factor. The round, full face, high cheek bones, small eyes, and pursed lips resemble the Śāhi facial type. See Diana P. Rowan, "Reconsideration of an unusual ivory diptych," *Artibus Asiae* Vol. XLVI, 4, 1985, pp. 281–82.
17. M. Taddei, "A Liṅga-shaped Portable Sanctuary of the Śāhi Period," *East and West,* N.S., 15, 1–2,1964–65, pp. 24–25.
18. The fact that Taddei was describing the "bronze mould" of the same chlorite stone piece discussed by H. Goetz, "A Kāshmīrī Liṅgam of the 10th century," *Artibus Asiae,* 27, 1965, pp. 275–79, is not sufficiently emphasized in the paper by Rowan, "Ivory diptych."
19. For stylistic details and analyses, see the papers by Taddei and Goetz cited in fns. 17 and 18.
20. Taddei, writing when little comparative material was known, suggested that the inner scene represented "Kalyāna-Sundara or Vaivāhika Murti (?)," 24; but there is no harm in now revising this suggestion.
21. See Robert Göbl, *System und Chronologie der Münzprägung des Kuśānreiches,* Wien, 1984, p. 44, No. 14, Series 525, 526.
22. This topic is touched upon in "Śaiva temple forms," p. 342; see pages 82-83 in this volume. It is more fully considered in Chapter XII, Vol. I in my monograph (see fn. 1).
23. Possibly an example may turn out to be the Lākhamaṇḍal Temple discussed by T. S. Maxwell, "Lākhamaṇḍal and Trilokināth: the transformed functions of Hindu architecture in two cross-cultural zones of the Western Himalaya," *Art International,* Vol. XXIV. 1–2, 1980, pp. 9 ff. This building started out as a Śiva temple. The tiny *garbhagṛha* still contains the central liṅga. The oldest building phase is of the fifth or sixth century; the second building phase can be placed by inscriptional evidence to the seventh-eighth century AD. A proportionately large sculpture of four-armed Maheśa (dating to the second phase) is now stacked against the wall of the *garbhagṛha,* along with other loose pieces. Maxwell calls the piece a Śiva Vṛṣabhavāhana; its iconography

is, however, reminiscent of the Maheśa figure on the east side of the Kalyānpur Liṅga (see my "Śaiva Temple Forms," p. 338, see page 77 in this volume), and must be identified as such. There exists a panel of the partially revealed Sadāśiva in the godown of the temple (see Fig. 12 in Maxwell's article). It shows the three (=five) heads of the god, with the Aghora head to the left. Maxwell concludes that during the last building phase this panel was deliberately removed from the front (east) side of the temple's tower because it was "... the outward sign of the Śaiva identity of the temple" (p. 24). The last phase has had, according to Maxwell, a tribal rather than an orthodox Hindu orientation. The remains of the temple seem to include a *liṅga*, a partial representation of god, and a full figure of Maheśa. Whether all these remains date from the same period, and whether indeed the panel in the godown can be called a main icon (versus one of several such panels distributed in less central areas around the temple) can only be determined by an on-site investigation. Maxwell mentions "many such panels stored... in the godown" (p. 24), but only one is illustrated.

24. For details see Bruno Dagens, *Entre Alampur et Śriśailam*, Pondichéry, 1984, I, pp. 562–68, II, photos 832–41.
25. On the recent work determining when the central face is Sadyojāta and when it is Tatpuruṣa, see my "Saiva Temple Forms," p. 335 and fn. 8; see p. 75 and fn. 8 in this volume.
26. It may, however, be that there exists another tradition in the South wherein the fully manifest body is called Sadāśiva (see the discussion of the Rajibpur Sadāśiva under 4. "From the East," above. Further study of relevant Śaiva icons is needed to determine whether the fully manifest body may be called Sadāśiva when there is evidence of coalescing the second stage in the unfolding process with another stage.
27. See "Śaiva Temple Forms," p. 344; see page 86 in this volume.
28. *Rauravāgama*, 34.1–2 and Vol. II, pp. viii–ix; see Bruno Dagens, *Les enseignements de l'Ajitāgama et du Rauravāgama*, Pondichéry, 1977, p. 107.
29. For an analysis of Lakulīśa here and in other early Orissan temples, see Debala Mitra, "Lakulīśa and Early Śaiva Temples in Orissa," *Discourses on Śiva*, edited by Michael W. Meister, Philadelphia, 1984, pp. 103–18.
30. D. Mitra, "Lakulīśa", p. 117, fn. 31.
31. M. H. Arnott, *Report with Photographs of the Repairs Executed to Some of the Principal Temples at Bhūbannēsvar and Caves in the Khandagiri and Udaigīri Hills, Orissa, India, between 1898 and 1903*, London 1903; see photograph No. 24.
32. This rationale emerged from discussions with Shri M.A. Dhaky whose assistance I gratefully acknowledge. According to Shri Dhaky, an *ākāśaliṅga* must be part of the original plan of Svarṇajāleśvara temple since an *ākāśaliṅga* is seen as the crowning finial of the temple prior to its reconstruction (Fig. 6.10). The temple would have stood hundreds of years in disrepair and no one would climb to the top during its years of decay, to install a fresh liṅga. Also, the liṅga seen in Fig. 6.10 shows signs of weathering only at the rounded top, exposed to the elements. This is exactly as it should be since the photo shows how most of the *liṅga*'s octagonal shaft would be hidden by the *āmalaka* and the covering stone, thereby protecting it from the elements. So the Svarṇajāleśvara temple at Bhuvaneśvara, which is contemporaneous with the Paraśurāmeśvara temple, most probably had an *ākāśaliṅga* finial. This and the fact that another fairly early Orissan temple, the 10th century Gandharaḍi temple, also had an *ākāśaliṅga* finial, indicate that such a tradition existed in Orissa and that there is a good likelihood that the Paraśurāmeśvara temple originally had an *ākāśaliṅga* too.
33. Stella Kramrisch, *The Hindu Temple*, I, Calcutta, 1946, p. 164.

34. See M. A. Dhaky, "The 'Ākāśaliṅga' Finial," *Artibus Asiae*, 36, 1974, p. 310.
35. Kramrisch, op. cit., Vol. II, p. 351.
36. Ibid., Vol. II, pp. 318–21, for an interpretation of the significance of the *gavākṣa.*
37. D. Mitra, "Lakulīśa," p. 105.
38. *Vāyu Purāṇa,* Chapter XXIII. The section is entitled *Maheśvarāvatāra-yoga,* Cf. D.R. Bhandarkar, "An Eklingji stone inscription and the origin and history of the Lakulīśa Sect", *Journal of the Bombay Branch of the Royal Asiatic Society,* Vol. XXII, 1908, p. 154.
39. See Sri Satyanarayan Rajaguru, *Inscriptions of Orissa* (300–700 AD), Vol. I, Pt. ii, Berhampur, 1958. See Inscriptions No. 33 (p. 164) and 45 (p. 240). D. Mitra, "Lakulīśa," considers Lakulīśa to represent on the walls of Orissan temples "the graceful and placid *(saumya)* aspect of Maheśvara as repository of *jñāna* (knowledge) and expounder of the *Śāstras* (Jñānavyākhyānamūrti)", p. 115. It is interesting to observe with Mitra (p. 114) that attributes assigned to Lakulīśa by the *Viśvakarmāvatāra Vāstuśāstra,* namely the *mātuliṅga* and the *daṇḍa,* are the two attributes ascribed by the *Viṣṇudharmottara Purāṇa,* 48, for the hands of the Bhairava face of Maheśvara or Mahādeva.
40. It is not clear to me whether the sequence of images on the courses of the other three *rāhās* follows a program relating to the theological program depicted on the western *rāhā.* On the south, going upward may be seen Śiva as Bhikṣāṭanamūrti, a bust of Śiva, a Nateśa, a seated figure which may be Sūrya. On the east may be seen Lakulīśa with his four disciples, Umā-Maheśvara, a figure in *yogāsana.* On the north are Mahīṣasuramardiṇī, a head of Śiva, a Nateśa, and Śiva in *yogāsana.*
41. Cf. Kramrisch, *Hindu Temple,* I, pp. 40–43, 176, *passim.*
42. See Michael W. Meister, "A Field Report on Temples at Kusumā," *Archives of Asian Art,* XXIX, 1975–76, pp. 23–46.
43. Cf. the description in "Śaiva Temple Forms", p. 343; see pages 84-85 in this volume and other references given there.
44. Meister, "Kusumā", p. 28, fig. 10. The image dates to the seventh century. In recent conversation with Meister, he further observed that the size of the image fits that of the central space and the style of the image is like that of the Brahmā and Viṣṇu images that flanked the central space, Fig. 6.11. I wish to thank Michael Meister for providing me with this important additional information.
45. In Meister's preliminary report ("Detective archaeology: A Preliminary Report on the Śiva Temple at Kusumā", *Archives of Asian Art,* XXVII, 1973–74, p. 83), the positions of Brahmā and Viṣṇu are given from the viewer's point of view and are therefore reversed.
46. See Kramrisch, *The Hindu Temple,* II, pp. 314–15, and fn. 40.
47. See U.P. Shah, "Lakulīśa: Śaivite Saint", *Discourses* (full ref. in fn. 29), Pls. 85–87.
48. A series of pre-Gupta icons, identified as Maheśa conjoint with the liṅga, is discussed in Chapter XIX, in *Many Heads* (see fn. 1).
49. See D. R. Bhandarkar, "Lakulīśa", *Archaeological Survey of India, Annual Report* 1906–07, Calcutta, 1909, figs. 4 and 5, pp. 185–86.
50. There exists a *Karvan Māhātmya,* in which the opening verse of Chapter I invokes the blessings of Lakutapāṇi, who is said to be Maheśa incarnated in the Kaliyuga. See Bhandarkar, "Lakulīśa" p. 179 ff.
51. Bhandarkar, "Lakulīśa", p. 186.
52. Cf., for example, the Viṣṇu in this relief to the Kashmiri bronze of Viṣṇu dated c. 800 AD by Pal (P. Pal, *Bronzes,* Pl. 9).
53. For details, see "Śaiva Temple Forms," pp. 341–43; see pages 81-83 in this volume.
54. Another so-called Brahmanical triad from Kashmir has recently been reassessed as a Śaiva stele. Stella Kramrisch *(Manifestations of Shiva,* Philadelphia, 1981, No.8, p. 9)

entitles the relief, "Liṅga flanked by Brahmā and Viṣṇu." The title and description recognize that the *liṅga* has theological dominance over the lateral figures.

55. E.g. Aschwin Lippe, "Divine images in Stone and Bronze, South India, Chola Dynasty (c. 850–1280)," *Metropolitan Museum Journal*, Vol. IV, 1971, 29 ff; see pp. 38–41. P. Pal, "South Indian Sculptures: A reappraisal," *Boston Museum Bulletin*, 67, 1969, p. 151; A.K. Coomaraswamy, "An Indian Image of Brahmā," *Bulletin of the Museum of Fine Arts, XI*, 1942, pp. 40–41.
56. See Kramrisch, *Manifestations*, p. 54, where the icon from the Albright-Knox Art Gallery is labeled Brahmā/Śiva. Also see this entry for other bibliographic references. On a recent trip to Boston (Feb. 1987), I noticed that the Boston image has now been labeled Śiva/Brahmā.
57. Mention should also be made of the image in the Metropolitan Museum of Art (No. 27.79); it belongs to the same period. This sculpture features the third eye only on the front head and the head on the proper left; the other pieces in the series show the third eye on all the four heads.
58. This is the Maheśa on the Musanagar pillar dated to the Kṣatrapa period. For identification and analysis, see Gerd Kreisel, *Die Śiva-Bildwerke der Mathurā-Kunst*, Stuttgart, 1986, pp. 143–48.
59. *Elements of Hindu Iconography*, Vol. II, Pt. II, 2nd edition, Delhi, 1971, pp. 380–81.
60. On the iconography pertaining to Hindu asceticism, see D. M. Srinivasan, "God as Brahmanical Ascetic: A Colossal Kuṣāṇa Icon of the Mathurā School," *J.I.S.O.A.*, N.S., X, 1978–79, pp. 1 ff, contained in this volume.
61. Coomaraswamy, "Brahmā," p. 41 and fn. 1.
62. Some examples seen in the catalogue, *Manifestations of Shiva*, are: No. 22, Vīṇādhara; No. 82, Sadāśiva symbolized by the Caturmukha Liṅga: No. 85, Vīṇādhara Dakṣiṇāmūrti, No. 88, Candraśekharamūrti; No. 105, Umā-Maheśvara-mūrti,
63. See *Many Heads*, Chap. 15.
64. Actually a fourth face has been carved on the back of the sculpture; see Susan L. Huntington, *The "Pala-Sena" Schools of Sculpture*, Leiden, 1984, p. 70.
65. The use of the plural, according to Shri Krishna Deva, who looked at the inscription anew, is a sign of respect.
66. The readings of four scholars on this inscription are provided in Huntington, *"Pala-Sena,"* pp. 234–35; No. 52. Shri Krishna Deva and Richard Salomon, whom I thank for reviewing the inscription once more, both concur with Sircar's reading.
67. R.N. Banerjea in *History of Bengal*, edited by R.C. Majumdar, I, Dacca, 1943, p. 444; B.N. Sharma, *Sadāśiva*, New Delhi, 1976, pp. 8–II; S. Huntington, *"Pala-Sena,"* pp. 69–70, 177–78; also her "Epigraphy from Art History; Studies in the Art of the Pāla Period," *Indian Epigraphy*, edited by Frederick M. Asher, G.S. Gai, New Delhi, 1985, pp. 178–79.
68. J. Prinsep, "Copperplate Grant from Bakerganj," *Journal of the Asiatic Society of Bengal*, VII, 1838, p. 50; see figure p. 38.
69. N. Vasu, "On a Copperplate-grant of Viśva-rūpa, one of the Sena Kings of Bengal," *Journal of the Asiatic Society of Bengal*, 65.1, 1896, p. 8.
70. R.D. Banerji, "Barrackpur Grant of Vijayasena: the 32nd year," *Epigraphia Indica* XV, 1919–20, p. 286.
71. Note H. Mitra's observation on the lack of agreement among the figures on the seals and the stone figures and the descriptions of Sadāśiva found in the literary texts in "Sadāśiva Worship in Early Bengal: A Study in History, Art and Religion," *Journal of the Asiatic Society of Bengal*, N.S. XXIX, 1933, p. 172.
72. What follows is contained in Hélène Brunner-Lachaux, *Somaśambhupaddhati*, I, pp. 178–82 and esp. fn. 2, p. 178.

73. Brunner-Lachaux cites this *śloka* from the *Kiraṇāgama* given in the work by Nirmalamani (see her *Somaśambhupaddhati* I, v. 57 f, p. 181). If I understand the contents of the text correctly from the synopsis given by the same author (see her "Analyze du *Kiraṇāgama*", *JA* 253, 1965) then this is but one view expressed in the text. The other is the more usual view, namely that Sadāśiva's form is perceived by the three or four faces visible on the *vyaktāvyakta-liṅga*, or *mukhaliṅga* (p. 325). This is the *sakala-niṣkala* aspect typically associated with Sadāśiva. For an example of this aspect in a Southern architectural context see P.Z. Pattabiramin, *Sanctuaires Rupestres de l'Inde du Sud, Andhra,* 1971, Publication de l'Institut Français d'Indologie, Pondichéry, 42.1, Pl. LII, fig. 1. The illustration shows Cave 4 at Bhairavakoṇḍa (c. seventh century AD). The small sanctuary contains a small black stone *liṅga*; carved on the wall behind it and facing east (as does the cave) is a bas-relief of a three-headed, partially manifest Sadāśiva, probably a later addition according to A.H. Longhurst, *Pallava Architecture,* (Memoires of the Archaeological Survey of India, 17, 1924) Pt. 1. pp. 34–35.
74. Banerjea, *History* I, p. 444. I wish to thank Dr. Debala Mitra for drawing my attention to this work.
75. A possible tendency in the South to coalesce Sadāśiva with another form of the tripartite Śiva Reality could perhaps account for this.
76. This observation, could also explain why the Bhujaṅgeśvara temple (cited above) lacks a representation of the second Śiva Reality.
77. The theme of the Birth of Śiva from Parvatī is peculiar to Eastern Indian art. Examples from the Pala-Sena school are: No. 25210/GR1 in the Indian Museum; No. 59.34 in the National Museum; No. 53 in the Burdwan University Museum; No. 68 in S. Kramrisch, *Manifestations.* From the easternmost region of U.P., namely Kasia, comes No. G. 398 in the State Museum, Lucknow. The uniqueness of the theme and its application to the discussion of the Rajibpur Sadāśiva became apparent in talking with Dr. N.P. Joshi, who has collected 15 examples from Eastern India, all between the tenth and twelfth centuries AD. Cf. on this subject N.K. Bhattasali, *Iconography of Buddhist and Brahmanical Sculptures in the Dacca Museum,* Dacca, 1929, p. 136 ff.
78. See *FMR* No. 16, pp. 55-68 (full ref. see under D. Layering the Linga); see also Robert Göbl, *Documents zur Geschichte der Iranischen Hunnen in Baktrien und Indien,* III, Wiesbaden, 1967, Tafel 97 and 98.
79. The topmost part of the *liṅga.*
80. The *abhiṣeka* ceremonies.
81. Gritli v. Mitterwallner, "Evolution of the *Liṅga,*" *Discourses* (full ref. fn. 29), pp. 24–25.
82. Mitterwallner, "*Liṅga*", Pl. 14.
83. Mitterwallner, "*Liṅga*", Pls. 15–16.
84. Mitterwallner, "*Liṅga*", Pl. 17.
85. H. Brunner-Lachaux, *Somaśambhupaddhati,* Première Partie, Pondichéry, 1963, pp. xxvi–xxvii; *SŚP* III, 57–83a.
86. See Brunner-Lachaux, *idem,* Première Partie, III, pp. 57–60 and fn. 2.
87. See Brunner-Lachaux, *idem,* Première Partie, p. 204, fns. 1 & 2.
88. See citation in fn. 2.
89. This program is treated in "Śaiva Temple Forms," with specific reference to Elephanta and the Lankeśvara shrines.
90. D. Mitra, "Lakulīśa," p. 116, fn. 16, where further reference is cited.
91. This program is fully treated in "Śaiva Temple Forms."
92. Mitterwallner, "*Liṅga,*" fn. 67.
93. Rabindranath Tagore, *Whisperings,* Kansas City, 1973, p. 41.

7

Bhagavān Nārāyaṇa: A Colossal Kuṣāṇa Icon

In 1977, the Mathura Museum acquired a colossal statue (Acc. No. MTR 77.4), quite unlike any other known Kuṣāṇa colossus. (Fig. 7.1, Nos. 1 and 4) The image came to the Museum from Nadan (near Firozabad, Distt. Agra) and represents a male originally standing over 8′ tall. The unusual aspect of this image is that it is not a Yakṣa, nor a Buddha, nor a Tirthankara. That means that it does not compare with any of the known colossal types fashioned from the time of the Mauryan period through the Kuṣāṇa period. I analyzed this colossus in a paper published in 1981.[1 & 1a(*)] The analysis arrived at four conclusions: 1) that the colossus represents a divine Brahmanic Ascetic; 2) that the well-known gods modeled on the Brahmanic Ascetic (i.e. Śiva Agni, Brahmā), have, in Kuṣāṇa times, iconographic traits not shown in this colossus; 3) that the only other Brahmanic divinity modeled on the ascetic type and important enough to have a cult was Bhagavān Nārāyaṇa, and, 4) that Nārāyaṇa is the god represented in the unique Kuṣāṇa colossus.

The reaction to these conclusions has been mixed. It is generally agreed that the statue must represent a Brahmanic ascetic. However, there has been hesitancy to identify it as Bhagavān Nārāyaṇa. The reason is not hard to find. There is, to date, no other Kuṣāṇa image of this god. So, when it is a question of a unique image, coupled with an unfamiliar identification, there is bound to be hesitancy.

Since 1981, I have found additional information, coming from Central Asia, the Punjab and places in India, to support my initial findings. The new evidence is the subject of the present paper.

Originally published in *Pakistan Archaeology*, Vol. 1; No. 26, 1991; Dr. Ahmad Nabi Khan (ed.); pp. 263-71. Reprinted with stylistic changes, addenda and permission from the Department of Archaeology & Museums; Govt. of Pakistan.

In case the publication containing my first analysis is not easily available, I shall, at the outset, briefly summarize how the image looks. The head has several distinctive features (Fig. 7.1, Nos. 2 and 3). To begin with, the face is conspicuously covered with hair. A thick mustache extends above the rounded lips; below there is a pointed beard. At the base of the brows appears a plain tilak[2] (*bindi*)[2a(*)]. Much of the nose, forehead and parts of the hair are damaged. Enough of the hair remains to indicate the way it was worn: the strands were gathered up on the crown and twisted laterally around the head above the ears. The ears are unadorned and judging from the unpierced lobes, the ears were never decorated with earrings. Over the god's left shoulder is the skin of an antelope. Also suspended from the left shoulder is the sacred thread (*yajñopavīta*). The figure was originally two-armed; the left arm is now broken. The fracture on the left hip indicates that initially the left hand rested at this point and held a water pot (*kamaṇḍalu*). The right arm, bent at the elbow, is raised to the level of the shoulder. The hand, though partially broken, clearly displays a rosary (*akṣamālā*) between the thumb and the rest of the outstretched palm. The lower garment, tied at the hip by a knotted rope, hangs in even strips which do not resemble cloth. It seems to be made of a fibrous substance. Apparently, it is meant to represent the typical garment of an ascetic which is made of bark, hemp or *kuśa* grass. Much of the portion below the garment no longer remains. As such, the figure now measures 88" in height and 34 1/2" in breadth.

The iconography of the figure offers the best indication as to its identity. While such iconographic elements as the tilak, rosary[3], and water pot[4] occur with images of different religions in South Asia, it is the particular combination of these elements together with the long matted hair twisted on top of the head (*jaṭā*), the beard, mustache and *yajñopavīta* which precludes attributing the colossus to the Buddhist, Jain or folk traditions[5]. Rather, the combination of these attributes together with the ascetic's garb, the black antelope resting on the shoulder, the unadorned ears plus the absence of jewels and other ornaments are specific to one personage only: the Brahmanic ascetic[6].

In my earlier analysis, I discussed stone examples of the Brahmanic ascetic dating from the Śuṅga through the Pala times, and I emphasized that the conventions noted above are kept throughout. This stable iconography is seen not only in sculpture but also in the painted medium. A most interesting example occurs on a Pala palm-leaf painting now in the Cleveland Museum (Wade Fund No. 55.49). The manuscript painting illustrates an episode from the Mahāyāna Buddhist text, the *Gandavyūha.* The figure on the left may be a Ṛṣi encountered by Sudhana[7]; the figure is endowed not only with a stylized antelope skin, but also with a combination of such other ascetic attributes as short unadorned earlobes, hairy countenance, matted hair curled and twisted on the crown of the head, tilak on the brow, and total absence of ornamentation.

Fig. 7.1.

The fact that the Mathurā Brahmanic ascetic once stood over 8′ tall mandates that he is a god. This is a critical point. It has been proposed that the image represents a great human sage or some revered legendary seer[8] (i.e. Ṛṣi). While seers and ascetics are represented on pre-Kuṣāṇa and Kuṣāṇa reliefs, they are not portrayed as colossae. I consider it most improbable that a colossal male image be made of a mortal—no matter how venerated he may have been in the Kuṣāṇa period.

Since some of the most distinctive iconographic characteristics of the gods Śiva, Agni and Brahmā are absent in the Mathurā image[9] (MTR 77.4), this image must be of some other god. To my knowledge, there is only one other divinity, modeled on the ascetic, with whom the colossus may be profitably associated. This is the god Nārāyaṇa. Nārāyaṇa is an important cosmic god in the Vedic Brāhmaṇas and Āraṇyakas, and he is the Cosmic Soul in an Upaniṣad[10]. In the *Mahābhārata* and the Purāṇas, Nārāyaṇa continues to be mentioned as the supreme cosmic creator. The god was sufficiently prominent to have his own following of worshippers in the centuries around the Christian era. His nature and the nature of his cult are well described in the *Mahābhārata (Mhbh.)*. *Mhbh.* III. 186. 90–117 describes the god's supreme cosmic power. This section tells how Mārkaṇḍeya goes into the mouth of Nārāyaṇa and sees the whole universe inside his body. This unusual image—all materiality in the interior of the divine – is, from the time of the *Rig Veda*, the main symbolic expression for the creative power of the Supreme[11].

Nārāyaṇa appears to be the divine embodiment of the Brahmanic ascetic. Numerous passages in the Nārāyaṇīya section of the *Mahābhārata* indicate that the Supreme Lord, Nārāyaṇa, is an ascetic god and represents spiritual perfection expressive of Vedic religion and culture. For example, in XII.325[12] wherein Nārāyaṇa is praised by the sage Nārada, the devotee attributes to the god the creation of Vedic sacrifices, texts, rituals, mantras, and identifies him with the great Vedic sacrificial elements, Vedic ritual practices, a class of Vedic seers and the god of the Brahmans. Specifically, the sage addresses Nārāyaṇa as the *yajña* (the Vedic sacrifice personified), the *mahāyajña* (the great Vedic sacrifices), *yajña-saṃbhava* (the Cause of the sacrifice), *yajñayone* (the Origin of the sacrifice), *yajñagarbha* (the Womb of the sacrifice), *yajñahṛdaya* (the Heart of the sacrifice), *yajñastuta* (the One hymned in the sacrifice), *yajñabhāgahara* (One who takes the share of the sacrificial offering presented to him), *susnāta* (He who has performed the ritual ablutions), *oṃkara* (The syllable oṃ), *ṣaḍaṅgavidhāna* (the six works auxiliary to the Veda), *vaikhānasa* (a hermit; a Brāhman in the third stage of life), *brāhmanarūpa* (He who has the form of a Brāhman), *brāhmaṇapriya* (He who is dear to Brāhmans), *brāhmanyadeva* (the god of the Brāhmans). When Nārāyaṇa speaks of his own nature he claims to be the embodiment of the Vedas and the supplementary texts to the Vedas[13]. Accordingly, Nārāyaṇa's image is based upon the earthly Brahmanic ascetic, that is the Ṛṣi. The *Mahābhārata* says it best, 'Those persons of wisdom who are the authors of the scriptures say that Nārāyaṇa, who is a Ṛṣi, is the one object of reverent worship in the universe'[14]. An epiphany section in the Nārāyaṇīya provides an excellent literary description of the god. A vision of Nārāyaṇa is granted on the White Island, to his true devotee, the sage Nārada. The god appears before Nārada holding a sacrificial altar, a rosary, a bundle of *kuśa* grass, a jewel, a pair of wooden (?) sandals, some stones, a wooden staff, an antelope skin and a blazing fire[15]. The Nārāyaṇīya also makes clear reference to a cult of Nārāyaṇa. It is a devotional, or *bhakti,* cult expounded by the Supreme Nārāyaṇa himself (*Mhbh.* XII. 323.48 49; 326.11,12,19ft).

It is of course a well-accepted fact that *bhakti* cults established modes of worship necessitating the use of icons. Textual references describing icons relevant to Nārāyaṇa are not wanting. The *Lalitavistara,* a work perhaps coeval with the Kuṣāṇa phase of Gandhāran art[16], contains a most interesting reference in Chapter VIII. In a passage enumerating the different divine images *(pratimā)* seen by the young Siddhartha on his visit to a temple *(devakula-),* that of Nārāyaṇa is included[17].

Inscriptional evidence likewise attests to a *bhakti* cult of Nārāyaṇa. The well-known Ghosūṇḍī stone inscription (near Nagarī, Rajasthan), records the erection of a stone enclosure for the purpose of worship, in the Nārāyaṇa compound, for the blessed Saṃkarṣana and Vāsudeva[18]. The inscription, dated to the second half of the 1st century BC testifies to the presence of a sacred precinct dedicated to Nārāyaṇa. Reference to Nārāyaṇa also comes from Inner Asia[19]. A Kharoṣṭhī inscription from Darshai in the West Pamirs has been read as 'Nārāyaṇa be victorious' by J. Harmatta[20]; he dates the inscription to the end of the 2nd, beginning of the 1st century BC. His reading and dating have not been completely accepted; a Kuṣāṇa dating has also been proposed[21]. A 3rd century AD stone inscription of Ābhīra Vasusheṇa (Nāgārjunakoṇḍa, Guntur Distt., Andhra Pradesh), opens with a salutation to Bhagavān Nārāyaṇa as Supreme god, as well as the Primeval Puruṣa[22]. A 4th century AD copperplate inscription from Guṇṭūr Distt speaks of a shrine *(devakula)* dedicated to Bhagvān Nārāyaṇa[23]. Another Nārāyaṇa *devakula* is mentioned in an inscription coming from the Śaivite site of Mundeśvari. It is dated the 22nd Karttika of the year 30, which is attributed by some scholars to the 7th century AD, by others to the 4th century AD. The inscriptions speak of the building of a Nārāyaṇa temple close to the Vinitesvara temple.[24]

I can now support the inscriptional and textual evidence with many more ancient examples of actual Nārāyaṇa temples and representations than I cited in the first paper. Evidence for a Nārāyaṇa temple comes from the ancient ruins of Sunet in Ludhiana District, Punjab; "... some of the terracotta sealings found here show that in the Kuṣāṇa and Gupta periods the site must have been adorned with important Brahmanical religious edifices. One of these was dedicated to Śaṅkara and Nārāyaṇa together, while two other sealings would appear to have belonged to separate temples of the same deities called in the inscriptions Sthanu ... and Bhagavat[25] ...", that is Śiva and Nārāyaṇa[26]. Medieval temples dedicated to Nārāyaṇa may be found in the villages of Beur and Belur[27] in present Mysore State. Recently there was published an icon of Nārāyaṇa still under worship at Badarī. The god is seated and has four arms; long strands of matted hair are piled on top of his head[28]. Near Badarinath, at Pandukeśvara, there is an icon of Yoga-Nārāyaṇa dating to the medieval period. Here too the god is four-armed. He holds the conch and the wheel in his raised right and left hands respectively while the natural hands are in *dhyāna-mudrā*[29]. A large Gupta (?) Nārāyaṇa image was noted briefly by Cunningham in his report on the site of Rūp Bās (in former Bharatpur State)[30]; in antiquity this area formed a cultural continuum with the Mathurā region. Cunningham reports seeing an erect image about 9′ high, of Nārāyaṇa with Lakṣmī kneeling at his feet. He also notes three recumbent sculptures of huge dimensions; one, 20′ and 6" in length, is supposed to represent Yudhiṣṭhira with Nārāyaṇa standing on his shoulders and surrounded by the Five Pāṇḍavas.

It is of course highly appropriate for the supreme Nārāyaṇa to be depicted as a gigantic male (lit. *mahāpuruṣa*). He is, it should be remembered, closely associated in Vedic and Epic literature with Puruṣa, the male Cosmic Giant of the ancient Vedic tradition. The Cosmic Giant in the Puruṣasūkta (*Rig Veda* 10.90), is a creative force envisioned as a huge primeval Male *(puruṣa);* the image exerted an extraordinary influence on Vedic and Hindu speculative thought[31]. Nārāyaṇa comes to be identified with Puruṣa, a development which contributes importantly to his cult as well as to the growth of Hindiustic Viṣṇu[32]. Evidence for the merging of Puruṣa with Nārāyaṇa is found in Vedic literature and beyond[33]. In the *Śatapatha Brāhmaṇa* (*ŚB*) XIII, 6, 1,1, the Ultimate Reality, Puruṣa is called Nārāyaṇa; Puruṣa Nārāyaṇa is also mentioned in *ŚB* XII.3,4,1; XIII, 6,2,12. The hymn in the *Atharva Veda* ascribed to one Nārāyaṇa, and dealing with the human body, describes in actuality the Cosmic Giant[34]. The *Mahā-Nārāyaṇa-Upaniṣad,* in quite a number of verses identifies Nārāyaṇa with Puruṣa[35]. In the Nārāyaṇīya of the *Mahābhārata*, Nārāyaṇa too is considered to be Puruṣa in the following sections: XII. 325.4; 326.41; 327.24. A domestic ritual belonging to the post-Vedic period shows how these associations merged into Viṣṇuism, as evidenced by daily ritual practices. A portion of the *Gṛhya-Pariśiṣṭa-* or *Gṛhya-Śeṣasūtra* describes the Viṣṇuite daily worship of Mahāpuruṣa, "requiring a formula in which the god is addressed with twelve names, Keśava, Nārāyaṇa, Govinda, etc., and referring to sanctuaries which possess an image of the Mahāpuruṣa (2, 14)..."[36]

An icon over 8′ tall is the literal translation of 'Mahāpuruṣa' into apprehensible form. This Mathurā image of Mahāpuruṣa (MTR 77.4), epitomizes the Brahamnic ascetic. I once again submit that, on the basis of the evidence presented in this and the previous paper, the image be identified as Bhagavān Nārāyaṇa. The god appears in the Mathurā icon in much the same guise, basically, as he appeared before his devotee on the White Island.

NOTES AND REFERENCES

1. "God as Brahmanical Ascetic: A Colossal Kuṣāṇa Icon of the Mathura School", *Journal of the Indian Society of Oriental Art* N.S., (1978–79). 1ff

1a. ADDENDUM: Note that the dates given in that paper may need recalibration since they had been based on dating the Kaniṣka era to 78 AD. This date is now less in favor than the date of 127 AD.

A smaller (H. 0.77 m), headless Kuṣāṇa torso of a brahmanic ascetic was acquired by the Musée Guimet (Inv. MA 12135). It forms the subject of a paper by Amina Okada, "Un torse d'ascète brahmanique d'époque kushāna au musée Guimet", *La Revue des musées de France; Revue du Louvre*; No. 2–2006; 24–30. The author adequately describes this Mathurā sculpture and recognizes that it has iconographic similarities with the Nadan colossus I designate as Nārāyaṇa. I had proposed this identification in my 1978–1979 analysis of the same colossus (cited in footnote 1) and this is the only article which Okada read. Okada does not accept the Nārāyaṇa identification. She says that there is nothing to corroborate such an identification and prefers Pramod Chandra's description of the colossus as a simple brahmanic ascetic who cannot be identified.

There are two problems with Okada's position. First, it is nearly inconceivable that the Mathurā school during the Kuṣāṇa Period would fashion a simple, nameless brahmanic ascetic standing over 8′ tall; colossal size implies that the figure is divine. Second, Okada did not read the present 1991 paper giving more textual and sculptural evidence to buttress the Nārāyaṇa identification. Admittedly, one would not expect to find further discussion of this subject in an issue of *Pakistan Archaeology*, and that is one reason why the paper is included in this anthology. I withhold comment as to the identification of the Musée Guimet's smaller torso (without limbs and head).

2. A plain tilak is portrayed on Mathurā's Tīrthankaras (e.g. Mathura Museum No. B63); Buddhas (e.g. Mathura Museum No. 76.17); Bodhisattvas (e.g. B26 in the State Museum, Lucknow; No. 59.530/1 from Ahicchatra in the National Museum, New Delhi); Nagas (e.g, Mathura Museum No. 439); and Yakṣas (e.g. Mathura Museum No. C30).

2a. ADDENDUM: A recent and very fine survey of south Asian tilaka should be noted: Chandreyi Basu: "Tilaka: Traditional Body Markings in India", in Joan Evans Pim, Sergey A. Yatsenko and Oliver T. Perrin (eds.), *Traditional Markings Systems: A Preliminary Survey*, Dover Dunkling Books, 2010, pp. 241-66. Basu consider the mark on statue MTR 77.4 a tilak, but probably not a sectarian mark.

3. A probable Jain statue of Sarasvatī (J24 in the State Museum, Lucknow), shows the goddess holding the *akṣamālā* in her right uplifted hand.

4. The water pot can be found in the left hand of a Naga (e.g. Mathura Museum Nos. C20; C21) and a Bodhisattva (e.g. The National Museum Maitreya, No. 59. 530/1).

5. To be sure, even matted hair (*jaṭā*) and *yajñopavīta* may be found with Maitreya (e.g. No. 59.530/1 in the National Museum). But the whole series of attributes—tilak, *akṣamālā, kamaṇḍalu, jaṭā*, beard, mustache, and *yajñopavīta*—is not associated, to the best of my knowledge, with any deity outside of the Brahmanical tradition.

6. For descriptions of the Brahmanic ascetic which clearly set forth his appearance, see Srinivasan, "God as Brahmanical Ascetic".

7. In a personal communication, Dr. Jan Fontein suggests that the episode depicted may be Sudhana's visit to the Ṛsi Bhīsmottaranirghosa, at Nalayur, who makes him see a vision by touching his forehead.

8. U.P. Shah, 'The Badari-Nārāyaṇa Image' in *Vaisnavism in Indian Arts and Culture,* Ratan Parimoo (ed.), New Delhi, 1987; p. 306.
9. A detailed analysis of the iconography of these gods in the Mathurā school during the Kuṣāṇa period is found in Srinivasan, "God as Brahmanical Ascetic".
10. Jean Varenne, *La Mahā Nārāyaṇa Upaniṣad,* Vol. I (Paris 1960), pp. 59–67.
11. D.M. Srinivasan, "The Religious Significance of Multiple Bodily Parts to Denote the Divine: Findings from the Rig Veda" *Asiatische Studien* XXIX (1975), 137–79.
12. All *Mhbh.* citations are according to the Poona critical edition.
13. *Mhbh.* XII. 330. 32–35. See J. Gonda, *Medieval Religious Literature in Sanskrit* (Wiesbaden 1977), p. 8 and fn. 10 for important additional references to brahmanic tendencies in the Nārāyaṇīya.
14. *Mhbh.* XII. 337. 35; P.C. Ray, *The Mahābhārata,* Eng. trans. (Calcutta 1893), Vol. 8; 859. The trait of 'ṛṣi' can be traced back to the Vedic conception of Nārāyaṇa. A passage in the *Śatapatha Brāhmaṇa* (XIII,6,2), hyphenates his name with that of Puruṣa (the Cosmic Male of the Vedic tradition) and mentions Puruṣa-Nārāyaṇa as the Ṛṣi of the Puruṣasūkta namely *Rig Veda* 10.90. Sāyaṇa in his commentary on the Rig Veda also attributes the authorship of Rig Veda 10.90 to a Ṛṣi Nārāyaṇa. Hymn number 10.2 in the *Atharva Veda* is also attributed to Nārāyaṇa.
15. *Mhbh.* XII. 326.9.
16. This text is difficult to date; cf. Sir Charles Eliot, *Hinduism and Buddhism* II (London 1921), p. 53. A 4th century AD Chinese translation of the *Lalitavistara* is mentioned in Nanjio Bunyio, *A Catalogue of the Chinese Translation of the Buddhist Tripitaka* (Oxford 1883), No. 160.
17. Translations by R. Mitra, *The Lalita-Vistara* in *Bibliotheca Indica* (Calcutta 1881), p. 175. Ph. Ed. Foucaux, *La Lalita Vistara* in *Annales du Musée Guimet,* Tome 6 (Paris 1884), p. 108. The Sanskrit text available to me is: S. Lefmann, *Lalita Vistara* (Halle 1902), p. 120.
18. D.C. Sircar, *Select Inscriptions* Vol. I, second ed. (Calcutta 1965), pp. 90–91. H. Lüders, *A List of the Brāhmī Inscriptions.* Appendix to *Epigraphia Indica* Vol. X (Calcutta 1912), No. 6.
19. B. Gafurov, M. Asimov, G.M. Bongard-Levin, B. Ya. Stavisky, B.A. Litvinsky et. al. *Kuṣāṇa Studies in U.S.SR.* (Calcutta 1970). p. 63.
20. J. Harmatta, "The Oldest Kharosthi Inscription in Inner Asia", *Acta Orientalia Academiae Scientiarum Hungaricae,* Vol. XIX, No. 1 (Budapest 1966), 1–12.
21. B. Gafuro et al., *Kuṣāṇa Studies,* p. 63. See also B. Ja. Stavisky, *La Bactriane Sous les Kouchans,* (Paris 1984), p. 202. fn. 28
22. Sircar, *Select Inscriptions,* pp. 525–26.
23. Sircar, *Select Inscriptions,* pp. 467–69.
24. Cf. *Archaeological Survey of India,* Annual Progress Reports. Bengal Circle. (1903–04). Note also *ASI,* Ann. Rep. (1902), Bengal Circle; 19–20. I wish to acknowledge the profitable talks I had on this subject with my colleague, Michael W. Meister.
25. *Archaeological Survey of India: Annual Progress Report of the Superintendent. Hindu and Buddhist Monuments.* Northern Circle for the year ending 31 March 1917; Lahore, p. 7.
26. The Sunet and Mundeśvari examples would seem to imply a deliberate proximity between Śiva and Nārāyaṇa structures. Quite possibly the appropriateness of such structural associations relies on a conceptual identification between these two deities accepted at that time. Certainly the *Mahābhārata* knows of their identification. In one long passage (XII, 328), wherein the significance of Nārāyaṇa's various names is explained, the Supreme Lord himself says that he and Rudra (the Vedic antecedent of

Śiva), form a conceptual unity. He who worships Maheśvara (i.e. Rudra/Śiva), worships Nārāyaṇa; Rudra is Nārāyaṇa's self or soul *(ātman)* and Nārāyaṇa worships Rudra. Rudra is Nārāyaṇa, the One displayed in two different forms (cf. XII. 328. 19–24). The *Mahānārāyaṇa Upaniṣad* probably earlier than the epic, also sustains a very close relationship between Rudra and Nārāyaṇa (v. 470).

27. *Archaeological Survey of India,* Annual Progress Report, Western Circle (1920–21), 121–23.
28. V.P. Shah, The Badari-Nārāyaṇa Image; pp. 305–06.
29. Information from Shri M. C. Joshi. Archaeological Survey of India, in a personal communication.
30. A. Cunningham, *Archaeological Survey of India,* Report; 1871–72; 1872–73, Vol. 6 (Calcutta), p. 21.
31. The theme of Puruṣa, according to L. Renou *(Hymnes spéculatifs du Veda* [Paris 1956], p. 12), forms the major link between the cosmological speculations of the *Rig Veda* and the *Atharva Veda*. The theme resurges in the Brāhmaṇas, the Upaniṣads (Renou, *Hymnes spéculatifs,* pp. 12, 248; cf. J. Gonda, *Viṣṇuism and Śivaism* [London 1970], pp. 31–32), the *Mahābhārata* (Gonda, *Visnuism and Śivaism,* pp. 31;154), and ultimately becomes central to Viṣṇuite philosophy (Gonda, *Viṣṇuism and Śivaism,* pp. 32; 153–54).
32. Cf. Gonda, *Viṣṇuism and Śivaism,* Chapter 11.
33. For example, the 3rd century AD Nāgārjunakoṇḍa inscription mentioned above. Note also the later associations between Puruṣa and Viṣṇuite elements in general cited by J. Gonda. *Viṣṇuism and Śivaism,* pp. 32–33.
34. Renou, *Hymnes spéculatifs,* p. 12.
35. J. Varennue, *La Mahā Nārāyaṇa Upaniṣad,* vss. 25; 71ff; 238; 263; 536.
36. Jan Gonda, *The Ritual Sūtras,* Wiesbaden, 1977; Vol. I in the *History of Indian Literature,* J. Gonda; p. 586.

8

Early Vaiṣṇava Imagery: Caturvyūha and Variant Forms

Students of the arts of Hindu India are closely familiar with evolving traditions of Vaiṣṇava imagery from the Gupta period onward at such prominent sites as Udayagiri near Besnagar, Deogarh, Badami, Aihole, and Mamallapuram. The origins of these artistic traditions are less well known, however, and it is the purpose of this paper to suggest that examples of Vaiṣṇava figural sculpture and cult imagery may be dated as early as the second century before Christ. Also presented here is a description of the theological principles that gave rise to the early Vaiṣṇava images, and an attempt is made to distinguish between such concepts as *vyūha* and *avatāra* by which Vaiṣṇava theologians designated different nuances of the process of divine manifestation. This study thus touches upon a major theme in the history of Hinduism, the formation of the cult of Viṣṇu out of three distinct schools of religious thinking.

Vaiṣṇavism developed its own theological doctrine to explain the nature of the Supreme. The concept of *vyūha* (literally, "placing apart; orderly arrangement") attempts to outline the fundamental nature of the supreme God as well as the relationship between God and his personal manifestations. As numinous Power, God is identified with the all-pervading Brahman. However, this Power makes itself manifest in a series of four successive emanations (Caturvyūha[1]) that are both identical to the numen and, at the same time, are the cause for the creation of the phenomenal world. In this way, the *vyūha* doctrine affirms a causal relation between the numinous and the phenomenal, without assigning limitations conditioned by time, change, form, or will upon the Supreme who is the creator of all these delimitations. In this system, Vāsudeva, literally,

Originally published in *Archives of Asian Art*, Vol. XXXII, 1979; pp. 39-54. Reprinted with stylistic changes, additions and with permission of The Asia Society, Inc.

"the indwelling deity," is the first emanation and the fountainhead of the successive emanations, which may be represented either anthropomorphically or theriomorphically in Hindu art.

It has recently been recognized that the Caturvyūha concept was plastically portrayed in the Mathura school of art in the Kuṣāṇa period.[2] The icon comes from the Satsamudri Well situated on the compound of the Mathura Museum, and is now housed in the Museum. Though fragmentary, enough remains of this important statue to identify the central crowned image as Vāsudeva (Fig. 8.1). He wears a necklace, a garland of flowers, armlets, and bracelets. His high *mukuṭa* is decorated with overlapping circles. Vāsudeva is four-armed. The natural right hand is in *abhaya-mudrā*; the raised right hand rests on a highly ornamented mace. (The sculpture fragment of the mace, although of the same buff sandstone as the other three fragments comprising this sculpture, is not joined correctly with the other parts.) Vāsudeva's raised left hand is broken; the natural left hand holds an object identified as a conch by R.C. Agrawala (see note 2). One emanating form is seen projecting from Vāsudeva's right shoulder (Fig. 8.2). This manifestation, wearing a single earring, is shown holding a wine cup in his left hand; his right arm

Fig. 8.1. Viṣṇu Caturvyūha (Mathura Museum no. 392-95). Photograph: Government Museum, Mathura.

Fig. 8.2. Viṣṇu Caturvyūha. Photograph: Doris Srinivasan.

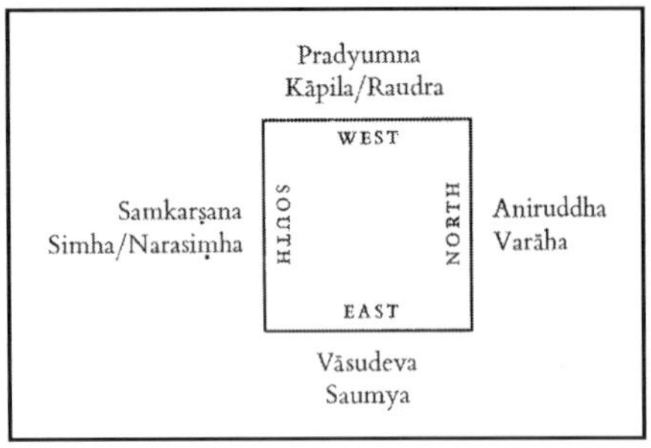

Fig. 8.3. Vaiṣṇava Caturvyūha, from Bhīṭā, disposition of *vyūhas* (State Museum, Lucknow, no. 56.394).

Fig. 8.4. Eastern side of 56.394. Photograph: State Museum, Lucknow.

should have been raised in front of the existing serpent-hood canopy. Two other forms originally projected from Vāsudeva. One emanated from his crown; the head and right arm of the form are now broken. The fragment of a shawl remains draped over the left shoulder. A fourth figure, completely lost, should have emanated from Vāsudeva's left side; this may be inferred from the break above the god's left shoulder.[3] A Gupta-period textual reference to this sort of emanating type, in the *Viṣṇudharmottara-Purāṇa*[3a(*)], assigns the right or southern side to the emanation known as Saṃkarṣaṇa (also called Baladeva or Balarāma[4]), represented in his theriomorphic form as a lion.[5] In the Kuṣāṇa sculpture Saṃkarṣaṇa is represented anthropomorphically. The identification is not problematic; a snake canopy, wine cup, and single earring are characteristics regularly associated with Kuṣāṇa-period icons of this god.[6] Rather puzzling, however, is the clear and direct visual expression of a complex theological notion; this clarity of expression implies a prior phase of artistic experimentation and conceptual familiarity wherefrom a meaningful synthesis of religious, iconographic, and stylistic idioms could result. It is therefore of considerable interest that a fourfold image in the State Museum, Lucknow, represents a formative, pre-Kuṣāṇa portrayal of the Caturvyūha concept (see Figs. 8.3–8.7).

The piece in question comes from Bhīṭā (District Allahabad in Uttar Pradesh), and was acquired by the Museum in 1956. It is a colossal (167 cm high and 58 cm wide) buff-colored sandstone image sculpted on four sides. Each sculpture appears above an undecorated plinth approximately 46 cm in height. Perhaps the plinth of this upright was placed into the ground, leaving the carved sides exposed for the purpose of circumambulation and adoration.[7]

On one side stands a corpulent figure who seems to be more important than the others because he wears a crown and heavy earrings (Fig. 8.4). The figure raises the right arm, adorned with several bracelets; the hand is in *abhaya-mudrā*, emblematic of divinity. The left arm, also decked with bracelets, is posed in a somewhat relaxed manner; a decorated jar is held in that hand.

Fig. 8.5. Western side of no. 56.394.

Fig. 8.6. Southern side of no. 56.394.

Fig. 8.7. Northern side of no. 56.394.

The deity wears additional ornamentation in the form of a broad, flat necklace with a large central amulet. An upper garment (*uttarīya*) is draped over the shoulders. The drapery folds of the *dhotī* fall in the center and indications of the cloth are still visible on the thighs. The *dhotī* is held by a girdle fitting tightly around the loins and accentuating thus the lower portion of the abdomen.

On the reverse side appears another full standing figure which may be sharply distinguished from the one on the obverse (Fig. 8.5). The personage wears no crown and, except for a bracelet on his left wrist, the body is starkly devoid of ornamentation. Nevertheless, there are some noteworthy features. The figure's hair is parted in the middle and falls in strands onto either side of the shoulders. Both hands are broken but probably the right was raised in *abhaya-mudrā* while the left may have held a flask (the object is too effaced to be properly identified). The figure is bulkier than the crowned one, and the belly protrudes even more over the constricting waistband.

Fig. 8.8. Pratapgarh Yakṣa. H. 1.150 m, w. 0.440 m. Allahbad Museum., AM 1. Photograph: American Institute of Indian Studies, Varanasi.

Adjacent to the right side of the crowned figure occurs, at the level of the crowned face, another face; it is completely damaged[8] (Fig. 8.6). There are no other corporeal details. However, the entire lower portion of this side, corresponding roughly to the region between the hips and feet of the crowned figure, is allotted to the frontal image of a seated lion.

Adjacent to the left side of the crowned figure, a similar alignment exists. Another damaged face occurs in the upper portion; only traces of the ears, earrings, and a heavy V-shaped necklace remain[9] (Fig. 8.7). The lower portion also contains an animal. The profile view is that of a boar standing with hind legs on a high pedestal. The animal raises his head in the direction of the crowned figure and his paws come together in a gesture approximating *namaskāra*.

The second-century BC date that N.P. Joshi assigns to this piece seems to be the most reasonable.[10] The image compares well with other colossal Śuṅga-period figures from north central India. Indeed, when compared to a series of colossal *yakṣas*, the dating of the piece may be further refined. For example, the two standing figures of the Bhīṭā icon show, in the modeling of masses, a slight advancement over the static, bilateral Śuṅga Yakṣa from Pratapgarh (District Pratapgarh, Uttar Pradesh). The stiff posture of the Pratapgarh Yakṣa (Fig. 8.8), its blockish contour, and abruptly protruding abdomen relate more closely to the pre-Śuṅga Parkham Yakṣa in the Mathura Museum (Fig. 8.9) than to the Bhīṭā figures.[11] Likewise the faces of the Bhīṭā figures—especially the crowned head—are slimmer than the Parkham Yakṣa or the Noh Yakṣa of approximately the same age[12] (Fig. 8.10). Further, the Bhīṭā standing figures, though affixed to a central core, exhibit a greater sense of roundness than the aforementioned free-standing *yakṣas*. On the other hand, the Bhīṭā figures anticipate the stylistic developments found in the Vidiśā Yakṣa of the second half of the second century BC[13] (Fig. 8.11). The Vidisa Yakṣa displays more subtle skin tonalities, a greater relaxation and naturalism in hand gestures, and a more convincing and unified flow of corporeal masses. The Bhīṭā figures are likely to be earlier than the Vidiśā Yakṣa and probably later than the Pratapgarh

Fig. 8.9. Parkham Yakṣa. H. 2.6 m. Mathura Museum C-1. Photograph: Government Museum, Mathura.

Fig. 8.10. Noh Yakṣa. Photograph: Frederick M. Asher.

Yakṣa. Even though none of these works can be given a narrowly precise date, it may be suggested that the Bhīṭā icon belongs to the first half of the second century BC, and possibly to the second quarter of that century.

Perhaps the stylistic affinities between the Bhīṭā image and the *yakṣa* model caused Joshi to consider the Bhīṭā colossus as a fourfold *yakṣa* image. Joshi observes, however, that certain iconographic peculiarities are indicative of Śaivite and Vaiṣṇavite tendencies. The figure on the reverse, unadorned and with loosely falling hair, may, he suggests, have some connection with Śiva. And the figure on the obverse, together with the two lateral images, may illustrate "some earlier practice of depicting Viṣṇu with his boar and lion forms ...."[14]

It is possible to develop these interesting suggestions further. In this paper it is proposed that the crowned image be identified as the first *vyūha*, Vāsudeva; that the head and seated lion panel to the right of Vāsudeva, combining anthropomorphic and theriomorphic elements, be identified as Saṃkarṣaṇa,[15] the second *vyūha*; and that the reverse full figure, together with the head and boar panel, be identified as the third and fourth emanations, respectively, of the

Fig. 8.11. Vidisa Yakṣa. Photograph: Frederick M. Asher.

fourfold division of the supreme Godhead.[16] Seen as such, the emanations are distributed and represented in a manner akin to both the Mathura Museum Caturvyūha (see Fig. 8.1) in that each emanation has a human face. They also are related to later textual prescriptions of the more developed icons of Viṣṇu Caturvyūha that come to be called Vaikuṇṭha (literally, "the keen, the penetrating irresistible") and Viṣṇu Caturmūrti. The name Vaikuṇṭha, according to the textual evidence, should be reserved for those four-faced Viṣṇu images where the god, either alone or with his consort, rides on Garuḍa. When Garuḍa is absent, as for example in the Kashmiri type to be discussed below, the designation Caturmūrti (four-faced image) is appropriate.[17] The designation Caturvyūha is applied to those icons that also omit Garuḍa and the consort and that focus on the theme of divine emanation by depicting a fourfold Vaiṣṇava image.

To demonstrate the close correspondence between the Bhīṭā image and the Vaiṣṇava textual sources, it is instructive to quote the aforementioned *Viṣṇudharmottara* passage in full: "Viṣṇu, the god of gods, should be represented as seated on Garuḍa, wearing a celestial yellow garment, with Kaustubha brightening his bosom and with all sorts of ornaments. His complexion would be like that of a cloud, laden with water. He has four faces and eight arms. The eastern face is called Saumya [i.e., placid], the southern Nārasiṃha [man-lion] .... the western Kāpila[18] [the fierce face], and the northern Varāha [the boar face]...."[19] This type of icon is called Vaikuṇṭha Viṣṇu in another chapter of the same text.[20] The iconography of the Vaikuṇṭha image is corroborated in the *Jayākhya Saṃhitā*, a *Pāñcarātra* text also dated to the Gupta period that describes the four-armed Vaikuṇṭha type as follows: "The Lord, creator of the universe, is to be meditated upon as having four faces—Vaikuṇṭha [Vāsudeva?], Nārasiṃha, Varāha, and Kāpila—and four hands holding the conch-shell, the disc, the club, and the lotus... mounted on Garuḍa ...."[21] The *Viṣṇudharmottara* also assigns the following names to the four faces of Viṣṇu: Vāsudeva, Saṃkarṣaṇa, Pradyumna, and Aniruddha.[22] These are the names of deified heroes belonging

Fig. 8.12. Viṣṇu Caturmūrti. H. 61 cm. Obverse. Photograph: Prince of Wales Museum of Western India.

Fig. 8.13. Viṣṇu Caturmūrti. H. 61 cm. Reverse. Photograph, Prince of Wales Museum of Western India.

to the Vṛṣṇi clan, prominent in the Mathura region at the beginning of the Christian era. In combining the information in *Viṣṇudharmottara* III.44, III.78, and III.79, it is possible to determine the directions prescribed for the faces. These are (given in the same order as the above names): east, south, west, and north. Banerjea seems to have erred in identifying the left or northern (boar) face as that of Pradyumna and the western one (kāpila or raudra, the terrific or fierce) as that of Aniruddha.[23]

A comparison between Viṣṇu Vaikuṇṭha and Caturmūrti icons and the fourfold Śuṅga image from Bhīṭā shows many iconographic parallels.[24] Vaikuṇṭha and Caturmūrti icons from Kashmir offer the closest reflections of the textual descriptions, and seem to have enjoyed a special popularity during the early medieval period. A ninth-century AD fragmentary Viṣṇu Caturmūrti in the Prince of Wales Museum, Bombay, illustrates the classic Kashmiri type[25] (Fig. 8.12). The central figure has a human face wearing an elaborate triple-crested crown. The body is ornamented with earrings, a necklace, the yajñopavīta, and the śrīvatsa mark on the chest. To the right projects the face of a lion; to the left that of a boar. On the reverse appears the fierce-looking face called Kāpila[26] (Fig. 8.13). This face, devoid of ornamentation, sports only simple circular earrings and a plain chain around the neck. The hair is worn as jaṭāmukuṭa, that is, twisted and gathered upon the head, with loosely falling locks cascading on either side of the

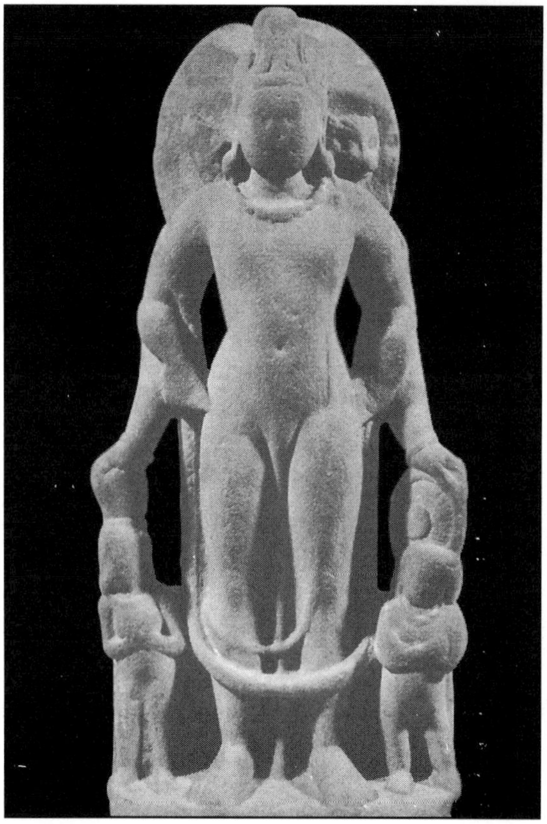

Fig. 8.14. Viṣṇu with lion and boar heads. H. 29 cm. Photograph: Government Museum, Mathura.

Fig. 8.15. Viṣṇu Caturmukha. Vaikuṇṭha. Photograph: Gwalior Museum.

shoulders. Clearly each of the four mūrtis of this image displays iconographic traits that correlate with those of the Bhīṭā image.[27] It is only in the placement of the forms, especially in the elimination of the rectangular dispositioning, that the major iconographic innovation occurs.

The placement of forms seen in the Kashmiri Viṣṇu Caturmūrti may stem from a type developed in the Mathura school during the Gupta period. Gupta images from Mathura show a certain flexibility regarding the position of the animal heads. A small statuette of a standing Viṣṇu (Fig. 8.14) in the Mathura Museum, coming from the village of Khammi (six miles from Mathura city) may be cited as an example. The front visage is human; the side faces are those of a lion and a boar. There is no fourth face.[28] Two of Viṣṇu's four arms are broken; the remaining two hold a wheel and mace placed, respectively, on the heads of a *cakrapuruṣa* and *gaḍadevī*.[29] In this icon, however, the lion and boar positions are reversed, being to the left and right, respectively, of the central figure.[30] The more conventional arrangement, with the lion on the right, etc., occurs equally well in Gupta Mathura images.[31]

There is an interesting Viṣṇu-Caturmukha in the Gwalior Museum that reflects vestiges of the iconography considered in this paper.[32] One side shows a

Fig. 8.16. Viṣṇu Caturmukha. Trivikrama. Photograph, Gwalior Museum.

Fig. 8.17. Viṣṇu Caturmukha. Nārasiṃha. Photograph, Gwalior Museum.

four-armed, well-ornamented Viṣṇu seated on Garuḍa (Fig. 8.15). Viṣṇu wears a *mukuṭa, vanamālā,* and *yajñopavīta*. Although the attributes are considerably mutilated, it is possible to discern that a sword was held in the upper right hand and a disc in the upper left hand. As such, the image has similarity with several Vaikuṇṭha images discussed by Desai;[33] indeed, in that the god is mounted on Garuḍa, the image adheres to the prescribed mode of portraying Vaikuṇṭha in the *Jayākhya Saṃhitā* and the *Viṣṇudharmottara*. On the three other sides, continuing counterclockwise, are representations of Trivikrama, Nārasiṃha, and Varāha; a lotus configuration is carved on top (Figs. 8.16–8.19). The icon, measuring 77½ cm x 45 cm x 45 cm, comes from Badoh and dates approximately to the eighth century AD. It cannot be called a Vaikuṇṭha Viṣṇu, nor is it like the Kashmiri Caturmūrti discussed above; it seems to represent. a development related to both the Vaikuṇṭha and *avatāra* themes.

Although the aforesaid Vaikuṇṭha and Viṣṇu Caturmūrti icons display numerous iconographic variations, they do not disagree in the area of religious thought. They are all expressions of the *vyūha* doctrine, and in each case the four configurations represent emanations of God.[34] The *vyūha* doctrine emphasizes the distinction between God as supernal power and the concretized emanations proceeding from that power. In postulating the fourfold personal emanations of

Fig. 8.18. Viṣṇu Caturmukha. Varāha. Photograph: Gwalior Museum.

Fig. 8.19. Viṣṇu Caturmukha. Lotus top. Photograph: Gwalior Museum.

the One, the doctrine insists that God makes himself known in the universe through a process of emission. The assumption is that the eternal, all-encompassing One has the potentiality to bring forth from out of himself that which he encompasses. In realizing this potentiality, a chain of emanations is emitted from God. The first four of these, the *vyūhas*, are emitted to cause creation of the phenomenal world and give form to the otherwise formless source of creation in order to provide man with objects of devotion.[35]

The process by which the *vyūhas* arise is clearly represented in two types of early Vaiṣṇava images. Basically there are two ways in which the emanative process is indicated. The first is represented by the Mathura Caturvyūha icon dated to the Kuṣāṇa period (see Figs. 8.1–8.2). In this icon, the *vyūhas* quite literally spring from the fountainhead, that is, from the central figure of Vāsudeva. This seems to have been the prevalent manner of depicting the emanative process during the Kuṣāṇa period; it can be noticed on several other Kuṣāṇa pieces in the Mathura Museum.[36] Although the process of emission is forcefully indicated in nos. 392–95, lost is the notion of successive emanations (that is, one entity arising directly and only from the preceding entity). This notion, however, is well symbolized in the second manner of representation. This schema allows for a quadrilateral disposition of forms such that 'a' (Vāsudeva) is adjacent to 'b' (Saṃkarṣaṇa, the *vyūha* emitted by 'a'), which is adjacent to 'c' (the vyūha emitted by 'b'), etc. Interestingly, this disposition of forms can follow the *pradakṣiṇapatha* orientation.[37] The classic Kashmiri Caturmūrtis re-reflect this orientation even though the forms are not disposed on adjacent rectangular panels. The Gwalior Caturmukha exhibits the quadrilateral disposition although in this case all the

Fig. 8.20.

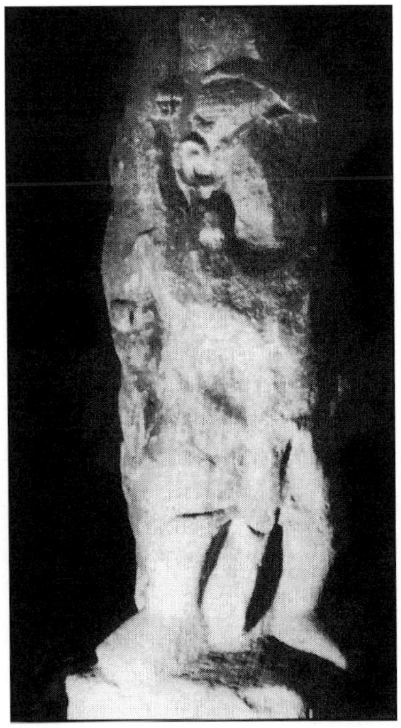

Fig. 8.21.

Fig. 8.22.

Figs. 8.20, 8.21 & 8.22. Rājghāṭa Threefold Yakṣa Image. Photographs: Bharat Kala Bhavan.

vyūhas are not represented. Actually the clearest depiction of the second mode is found in the Bhīṭā image (see Fig. 8.3).

Two factors contribute to the disposition of forms in the Bhīṭā image. The first is purely formal or functional. By the second century BC, it had become common practice to carve figures on the sides of an upright. Bharhut offers several examples. A cornered pillar, described by Cunningham as part of the outer railing of the stūpa, has "a single human figure on each of the two outer faces ...."[38] The figures, dressed in *dhotī* and turban and well ornamented, stand with hands in *añjali-mudrā*.[39] On the corner pillar of the North Gate at Bharhut, three of the sides contain figures of *yakṣas* and a *yakṣī*.[40] Important examples also come from other sites. The Allahabad Museum contains a late second-century BC corner post (no. AM 68) of a railing from Nagod (Satna District, Madhya Pradesh) which relates to this iconographic theme.[41] On two adjoining sides stand nearly identical *yakṣas* holding their hands in *añjali-mudrā*. They are similar to the two *yakṣas* on the Bharhut outer railing pillar. From Rājghāṭa comes a threefold *yakṣa* image that shares a noteworthy feature with the Bhīṭā upright. The plain, square base supports an upper portion that is carved with figures on all sides. On the Rājghāṭa upright, one *yakṣa*, perhaps the main one, straddles the axis in a squatting posture (Fig. 8.20). The other two squatting *yakṣas* (Figs. 8.21–8.22) span the remaining two corners in such a way that they occupy the rest of the space. The Rājghāṭa threefold *yakṣa* image (no. 97 in the Bharat Kala Bhavan) is likewise to be dated to the Śuṅga period.[42] These examples show that there existed in north central India, during the second century BC, the practice of depicting two or three addorsed figures on the sides of an upright; it thus seems altogether artistically appropriate that all the sides of an upright should have been chosen to depict a notion such as the *caturvyūha*.

The second factor to influence the disposition of figures on the Bhīṭā image is a religious one. The *vyūha* doctrine postulates the fourfold form of the supreme God where every *vyūha*, being God, is identical with Him.[43] This identity is well symbolized by the disposition, as each of the four *vyūhas* face in each of the four cardinal directions. Indeed the notion of extending into the four quarters is associated with the verb *vy/ūh* (the verb from which the noun *vyūha* is derived) in the vocabulary of the Vedic ritualists.[44] Further, the *vyūha* doctrine maintains a strictly monotheistic view on the nature of God; accordingly the four emanations together represent cosmic completeness. From the time of the *Rig Veda*, the idea of 'facing in the four directions' is connotative of spacial and cosmic totality; Agni in *Rig Veda* 5.48.5 is four-faced because the god, as flaming fire, extends into all the directions on earth and possibly beyond.[45] The idea of cosmic completeness expressed by the *vyūhas* is well translated into stone by the disposition of the fourfold Bhīṭā figures. In sum, the Bhīṭā image is a felicitous result of prevailing sculptural practices and accepted religious symbolism. These are used to convey the belief that the essential Oneness of the Supreme may be realized through contemplation of the quadruple outer forms emitted by Him.[46]

The identification of the Bhīṭā image as a Caturvyūha icon cannot be finally accepted, however, unless it can be shown that the *vyūha* theory, together with its core notion of cosmic emanation, were known in certain circles during the Śuṅga period. Before discussing that point, it should be noted at the outset that a full flowering of the *vyūha* doctrine is a development characteristic of the Pañcarātra system, whose texts (beginning ca. AD 600–800) give clear descriptions of this doctrine.[47]

However, the first statement of the basic doctrine occurs prior to the Pañcarātra texts; it is already found in a section of the Śānti Parvan of the *Mahābhārata* called the Nārāyaṇīya (XII.321–338).[48] The Nārāyaṇīya enounces the basic tenets of the *vyūha* doctrine in connection with the epiphany of the Supreme Nārāyaṇa; the divine manifestation is granted to the Sage Nārada on the White Island (Śvetadvīpa). Nārāyaṇa grants a vision of his universal self to Nārada because the latter, as a true bhakta, is with all his heart devoted solely to the Lord.[49] The supernal Nārāyaṇa reveals his personal aspect, which he declares to be of quadruple form. These forms are called his *mūrtis*,[50] the first being that of Vāsudeva, the Supreme Soul and Creator who originates the chain of successive conditioned forms: from Vāsudeva springs Saṃkarṣaṇa, representing the living soul; from Saṃkarṣaṇa comes Pradyumna, the mind; and from Pradyumna comes Aniruddha, self-consciousness.[51]

It is highly significant and worthy of closer scrutiny that this early statement of the *vyūha* doctrine is made in connection with the Supreme Nārāyaṇa. To state it another way, in defining the personal aspect of Nārāyaṇa, the doctrine is expounded in connection with but one out of three possible divinities that merge, in a series of stages, to give rise to the syncretic Hindu god, Viṣṇu. Although a comprehensive, philological analysis tracing the merger of the three major strains forming God in sectarian Vaiṣṇavism is greatly needed, the general character of these strains is well recognized.[52 & 52a(*)] Viṣṇu, as known from the Purāṇas onward, is the amalgamation of myths, philosophic notions, and religious doctrines associated with Vedic Viṣṇu, Vāsudeva-Kṛṣna of the Bhāgavata school,[53] and Nārāyaṇa, an important cosmic god in the Brāhmaṇas and Āraṇyakas, who continues in the *Mahābhārata* and Purāṇas as a supreme god, especially in connection with creation.[54] Of importance for the present study is that in the Nārāyaṇīya account, the *vyūha* doctrine defines the essential nature of the god of one Vaiṣṇavite strain (Nārāyaṇa), but associates the actual *vyūhas* with the names of four deities belonging to another Vaiṣṇavite strain (the Bhāgavata school). It thus appears as if the Nārāyaṇīya account brings two strains together in promulgating an early statement of the fundamental doctrine.[55] This remarkable feature of the statement in the Nārāyaṇīya dictates the method by which we may attempt to answer the question posed above. In order to determine whether aspects of the *vyūha* doctrine were already in existence in the second century BC, it is necessary to see whether aspects of the doctrine may be traced back to the two Vaiṣṇavite strains that come together in the Nārāyaṇīya. And this we propose to do next.

Nārāyaṇa, a divine being of rather early Vedic occurrence, is in some way connected with the primeval Waters (*Laws of Manu* I, 10). He comes to be identified with the Upaniṣadic Brahman (*Taittirīya Āraṇyaka* X.11; *Laws of Manu* I, 9, 10). Passages in the *Śatapatha Brāhmaṇa* (XII.3.4.1 ff and XIII. 6.1.2) enable better apprehension of the developments leading up to Nārāyaṇa's becoming the Supreme Principle. In this text, his name is hyphenated with that of Puruṣa, the Cosmic Male of the ancient Vedic tradition.[56] Accordingly, *Śatapatha Brāhmaṇa* XII.3.4 states that Puruṣa-Nārāyaṇa, having thrice offered sacrifice, sent forth from that place the Vasus, Rudras, and Ādityas. When Prajāpati told him to sacrifice again, then Puruṣa-Nārāyaṇa placed himself in all the worlds, gods, Vedas, and vital airs, and they were placed in him (XII.3.4.11). This passage indicates that Puruṣa-Nārāyaṇa is a generative force. In placing himself into apprehensible forms, he is, as it were, creating them. That these created forms are also 'placed' in him is a way of conceptualizing a correspondence felt to exist between the creative force and the forms he creates. This sort of conceptualization grows out of a Vedic school of thought that considers creation to occur by a process of emission.[57] The idea is that cosmic creation may be viewed as an analogue of human parturition. That is, the creator, believed to contain all forms inside his belly, causes creation when he 'gives birth' to forms.[58] This notion continues to be associated with Nārāyaṇa in parts of the *Mahābhārata*. For example, in *Mahābhārata* III.186.90–117, Mārkaṇḍeya goes into the mouth of the cosmic god and sees the whole universe inside his body. There is additional indication that the idea of cosmic emanation is connected with Nārāyaṇa. *Śatapatha Brāhmaṇa* XIII.6.2 suggests that Puruṣa-Nārāyaṇa is the author of the Puruṣasūkta (*Rig Veda* 10.90). The Vedic commentary tradition also considers a Ṛṣi Nārāyaṇa as author of *Rig Veda* 10.90[59] For the present study, this attribution has particular significance. The Puruṣasūkta postulates that the whole universe takes shape as Puruṣa emits materiality from out of himself.[60] Therefore the *Śatapatha Brāhmaṇa* passage implies that the concept of cosmic emanation originates from Puruṣa-Nārāyaṇa. The implications of these ideas are not lost in the later discussions of the *vyūha* theory contained in the *Pañcarātra* texts. The *Ahibudhnya Saṃhitā*, for example, in chapter 59, connects the Puruṣasūkta with the origin of the *vyūha* theory.[61]

To summarize, the evidence from Vedic and post-Vedic literature shows that the idea of creation by emanation—the sine qua non of the *vyūha* doctrine[62]—relates consistently to the Nārāyaṇa strain within Vaiṣnavism.

On the other hand, however, the names of the *vyūhas* in the Nārāyaṇīya account do not come from the Vedic tradition.[63] The names of Vāsudeva, Saṃkarṣaṇa, Pradyumna, and Aniruddha are the names of important hero-gods in the Bhāgavata tradition. The Bhāgavata religion, in contradistinction to the Vedic religion, emphasizes bhakti: intense personal devotion to a godhead (called Bhāgavat, the worshipful One). The manner of worship differs from the Vedic sacrificial rites. Bhāgavat may be represented and worshiped in a concretized form (*mūrti*), sheltered in a sanctuary. He may also be represented aniconically, as a plant or symbol, or theriomorphically, and in these forms likewise receive worship. As part of the intense devotionalism to the personal god, dramas or religious performances may take place to recount his glories and experience his presence.

The gods of the Bhāgavata religion may have been human heroes who came in time to be deified. This development is discernible when information from the Morā Well inscription now in the Mathura Museum, dating to the early decades of the Christian era,[64] is taken together with information gleaned from the *Brahmāṇḍa* and *Vāyu Purāṇas*. The Morā Well inscription refers to a stone shrine in which were placed five images (*archās*) of the blessed (*bhāgavat*) five heroes (pañcavīras) of the Vṛṣṇi clan.[65] Vāyu Purāṇa 97.1–2 states that these five heroes were originally human and named Saṃkarṣaṇa, Vāsudeva, Pradyumna, Sāmba, and Aniruddha. They are all closely related to each other, being related in one way or another to Vāsudeva-Kṛṣṇa: Saṃkarṣaṇa (Balarāma) is the older brother of Vāsudeva-Kṛṣṇa; Pradyumna and Sāmba are his sons; and Aniruddha is his grandson, being the son of Pradyumna. Although the worship of Sāmba declined, the worship of the remaining four eventually brought them into contact with the

Fig. 8.23. Agathocles Coin. Vāsudeva. Photograph: Délégation Archéologique Française en Afghanistan.

Fig. 8.24. Agathocles Coin. Saṃkarṣaṇa. Photograph: Délégation Archéologique Française en Afghanistan.

vyūha notions. In tracing a general overview of this contact, it is useful to determine the pre-Christian-era trends pertaining to three religious phenomena: (1) deification of the Vṛṣṇi heroes; (2) their association with the god Nārāyaṇa; and (3) the association of the *vyūha* notion of successive emanation with the four Vṛṣṇi hero-gods.

Evidence for the deification of some of the Vṛṣṇi heroes exists from the time of Pāṇini (ca. 400 BC) onward. Sūtra IV.3.98 in the *Aṣṭādhyāyī* has been interpreted by several scholars as a reference to the worship of Vāsudeva.[66] The *Milindapañha* includes the Vāsudeva cult in a list of cults centering around folk deities;[67] the core of this text may go back to pre-Christian times although in its present form it is several centuries later. Patañjali's *Mahābhāṣya* (*c.* mid-second century BC to the beginning of the Christian era[68]) is very informative on the growth of the Vāsudeva-Kṛṣṇa cult. In commenting on Pāṇini's sūtra IV.3.98, Patañjali states that Vāsudeva is the name of Kṛṣṇa, whose worshiper is called Vāsudevaka;[69] he also speaks of the existence of temples dedicated to Keśava (Vāsudeva-Kṛṣṇa), Rāma (Balarāma), and Kubera.[70] References in the *Mahābhāṣya* to the binding of Bali, the killing of Kaṃsa by Kṛṣṇa or by Vāsudeva, the narration and presentation of dramas depicting Kṛṣṇa's life and deeds[71] show that Patañjali knew Vāsudeva as Kṛṣṇa and also he knew of an expanded Bhāgavata cult containing elements already considered old at the time of Patañjali.[72]

Evidence in support of developments noted in the *Mahābhāṣya* comes from a series of coins issued by the Indo-Greek king Agathocles (reigning *c.* 180–165 BC).[73] The two divinities on the obverse and reverse of this coin type have been associated with Vāsudeva-Kṛṣṇa and Saṃkarṣaṇa.[74] Each figure stands under an umbrella (Figs. 8.23–8.24). Vāsudeva-Kṛṣṇa holds a *cakra* and a pear-shaped vase (*kamaṇḍalu*); Saṃkarṣaṇa holds the plow[75] (*hala*) in his left hand and a club (*musala*) in his right hand. The same attributes are associated with another second-century BC representation of (Saṃkarṣaṇa-) Balarāma, namely the well-known Śuṅga sculpture in the State Museum, Lucknow.[76] The Lucknow Balarāma, the Agathocles coins, as well as the famous Heliodoros pillar inscription at Besnagar[77] (also of the second century BC) corroborate the textual evidence. It seems very likely that in the several centuries before the Christian era at least two of the Vṛṣṇi heroes were deified. Further, the advent of devotionalism to Bhāgavata gods stimulated Bhāgavata icons, and the cult had become sufficiently established to attract Yavanas and/or other people under their rule.

The Ghosūṇḍī Stone Inscription[78] (near Nagarī, Chittorgarh District, Rajasthan) of about the second half of the first century BC, testifies to the association of two Bhāgavata gods with the Vedic cosmic god Nārāyaṇa. The inscription records the erection of a stone enclosure for the purpose of worship in the Nārāyaṇa compound for the blessed (*bhagava[d]bhyām*) Saṃkarṣaṇa and Vāsudeva. That is, within the sacred precinct of the god Nārāyaṇa was set up a sacred object[79] dedicated to the two Bhāgavata gods. The inscription thus goes a long way in documenting the gradual merger of the two Vaiṣṇavite strains. The order in which the names of the Bhāgavata gods occur in the compound of the Ghosūṇḍī inscription is also noteworthy. In that, Saṃkarṣaṇa is mentioned before Vāsudeva, the genealogical order is being given and not the metaphysical order, valid in the *vyūha* doctrine. The same order occurs in the Nānāghāṭ (Maharashtra) inscription of about the same period.[80]

These inscriptions may lend support to my earlier observation that the *vyūha* doctrine originates from outside of the Bhāgavata tradition. Were it otherwise, then it would seem to me that the metaphysical order should have been recorded, given the Bhāgavata religious climate of the first century BC. The chief text of the Bhāgavatas, the *Bhagavad Gītā* (*c.* second century BC – second century AD) substantiates this view. The Gītā displays no knowledge of the *vyūha* doctrine, though its teachings also do not go counter to it. It is my understanding that *vyūha* notions stemming from the sphere of Nārāyaṇa came to be associated with the Bhāgavata gods as a result of the gradual merging tendencies within Vaiṣṇavism itself.[81] That these tendencies had already begun in the late pre-Christian period can be deduced from the following passage in the *Mahābhaṣya*, in which Patañjali probably alludes to the *vyūhas* in his commentary on Pāṇini VI.3.5.[82] The passage reads: *janārdanas tv ātmacaturtha eva*—"Janārdhana, whose self is fourth." Janārdhana, another name for Kṛṣṇa, is here cited as one member presumably of a group of four. It is likely that the reference is to the Caturvyūha concept.

In conclusion, both the artistic and religious traditions of the Śuṅga period allow for the possibility of a plastic expression of the *caturvyūha* concept. Some brief remarks concerning the political climate may be in order here. The Śuṅgas (*c.* 185–75 BC), as is well known, were brahmans and strong adherents of Brahmanical traditions. Puṣyamitra, the founder of the dynasty, celebrated, according to the Ayodhyā inscription of Dhanadeva,[83] two Vedic *Aśvamedha* sacrifices. Indeed this period witnessed a variety of Vedic rites; the *Mahābhāṣya* mentions domestic sacrifices as well as large Soma sacrifices such as the Agniṣṭoma, Rājasūya, and Vājapeya. Not only Brahmanic ceremonies but also Bhāgavata ones gained prestige. To the aforementioned iconic, textual, and inscriptional indicators of Bhāgavata activity in this period, additional evidence may be cited. Another stone pillar from the region of Besnagar carries an inscription, dated to the second century BC,[84] recording the setting up of a Garuḍa flagstaff of the Lord Puruṣottama by ... a worshiper of Viṣṇu. Apparently the political atmosphere in north central India favored the marked artistic and religious readiness to formulate a Caturvyūha icon. The Bhīṭā image, it is proposed, is the result of these cultural currents.

NOTES AND REFERENCES

EDITOR'S NOTE in "Archives of Asian Art". *Transliterations from Sanskrit and other Indian languages are given with complete diacritical marks in the first usage. Thereafter a simplified form may be used.*

Research for this paper was supported by a fellowship, in 1977, from the American Institute of Indian Studies.

1. In a brief survey of the Vedic usages of the term *vyūha*, Gonda concludes, "... the idea of *vyūha* implied an effective arrangement of the parts of a coherent whole. In this connection, the number four ... appears to have been of cosmic significance." J. Gonda, *Viṣṇuism and Śivaism* (London, 1970), p. 51.
2. Kalpana S. Desai, *Iconography of Viṣṇu* (New Delhi, 1973), p. 40. Cf. R. C. Agrawala, "Four-Faced Siva and Four-Faced Viṣṇu at Mathura", *Vishveshvarānand Indological Journal*, III.1 (1965): 107–110.
3. I wish to thank Professor J. Rosenfield for drawing my attention to the stylistic similarities between this Viṣṇu Caturvyūha and a Kuṣāṇa Kārttikeya (Mathura Museum no. 42.2949) inscribed in the eleventh year of the Kuṣāṇa era. Professor Rosenfield would date the Viṣṇu Caturvyūha to the early third century AD.

3a. ADDENDUM: On the date of *Viṣṇudharmottara Purāṇa* here and in subsequent papers (e.g. 11 and 13), please see my review of Parul Dave Mukherji, *The Citrasūtra of the Viṣṇudharmottara Purāṇa*, Delhi, Indira Gandhi National Centre for the Arts, 2001, in *Journal of the American Oriental Society* 124.3 (2004), pp. 569-72.

4. Baladeva or Balarāma is known as the elder brother of Kṛṣṇa, who is the eighth avatāra of Viṣṇu.
5. *nārasiṃhaṃ tu dakṣinn*, III.44, v. 11 in *Viṣṇudharmottara-Purāṇa*, Priyabala Shah (ed.), Oriental Institute (Baroda, 1958), Vol. I. The literal translation is: The southern [face] is Nārasiṃha. The emanation Samkarṣaṇa may be symbolized both by a manlion (nārasiṃha) and by a lion (*Viṣṇudharmottara-Purāṇa* III. 85.45).

6. For example, Mathura Museum nos. C15 and 14.406.4; Lucknow Museum no. 57.457.
7. The Gautama Dharma-Sūtra, dated between the sixth and the fourth centuries BC, speaks of devotional circumambulation of a temple (9.66). On the dating of this text cf. P.V. Kane, *History of Dharmaśāstras,* Vol. II, pt. 1 (Poona, 1941), p. xi, and M.A. Mehendale in *The Vedic Age,* R.C. Majumdar (gen. ed.) (London, 1957), p. 477.
8. N. P. Joshi, in "Some Unnoticed Finds of Iconographic Interest", *East and West* (Rome), n.s. XXII, nos. 1-2 (1972): 42, suggests that the angular portion below the chin may indicate that the face was originally bearded.
9. Joshi, ibid.
10. Joshi, ibid., 41. The piece is considered to be no earlier than the first century BC by Debala Mitra in her study "Viṣṇu Chaturmūrti Image in the Hari Rāi Temple at Chamba" in V.C. Ohri, *Arts of Himachal* (Simla, 1975), p. 3. My attention was drawn to this interesting paper by Dr. P. Pal, whom I wish to thank.
11. V.S. Agrawala, *A Catalogue of the Brahmanical Images in Mathura Art* (Lucknow, 1951), pp. 75–77.
12. R. C. Agrawala, "Yakṣa Torso from Bharatpur Region", *Oriental Institute Journal* (Baroda), XVII (1967): 64–65.
13. Pramod Chandra, "Yakṣa and Yakṣī Images from Vidiśā", *Ars Orientalis* VI (1966): 157 ff.
14. Joshi, "Some Unnoticed Finds of Iconographic Interest", pp. 41–43.
15. The Bharat Kala Bhavan has a pre-Kuṣāṇa fragment of Balarāma (no. 279) with a couched lion on top of his plow. In Mathura sculpture of the Kuṣāṇa period, Balarāma-Saṃkarṣaṇa is associated with a staff topped by a sejant lion. Cf. Mathura Museum no. C19; Lucknow Museum no. 758.
16. Debala Mitra (Viṣṇu Chaturmūrti Image in the Hari Rāi Temple at Chamba, pp. 1–12) briefly discusses this Bhīṭā image, and concludes that it represents "the earliest sculpture so far discovered ... to render the form of Chaturmūrti ..." (p. 3). I prefer to label it as a Caturvyūha image. She also identifies the boar panel as symbolic of Aniruddha, and the Kāpila figure as that of Pradyumna, on the basis of *Viṣṇudharmottara* III.78.1 and III.79 (see below).
17. P. Pal points out these distinctions in *Bronzes of Kashmir* (New Delhi, 1975), p. 17.
18. For the significance of this name, see note 62.
19. III.44.9–12. For the text, see *Viṣṇudharmottara-Purāṇa,* P. Shah (ed.), vol. I, pp. 158–59. See vol. II (Baroda, 1961), p. 141, for a translation.
20. *Viṣṇudharmottara-Purāṇa* III.85, especially vv. 43–45. The text is in Shah (ed.), ibid., vol. I, pp. 225–226; the translation is in vol. II, p. 163. It should be emphasized at this point that the lion and boar faces are, in this icon, associated with the *vyūha* and not the avatāra theory. I would differ with K.S. Desai's opinion in "Vaikuṇṭha Caturmūrti", *Journal of the Indian Society of Oriental Art,* n.s. II (1967–1968): 22 ff., that iconographically the Vaikuṇṭha Caturmūrti "is an attempt at synthesizing, under the principal form of Viṣṇu, some of his incarnations."
21. VI.73–76 of *Jayākhyasaṃhitā of Pāñcarātra Āgama,* E. Krishnamacharya (ed.), in Gaekwad's Oriental Series, no. 54 (Baroda, 1967). The dating is discussed on pages 26–34 of the Foreword.
22. *Viṣṇudharmottara,* see III.47.
23. J. N. Banerjea, *The Development of Hindu Iconography* (Calcutta, 1956), p. 409.
24. For recent surveys of Vaikuṇṭha Viṣṇu icons see the following: K.S. Desai, "Vaikuṇṭha", pp. 22 ff; R.C. Agrawala, "Unusual Icons of Vaikuṇṭha Viṣṇu with Aśvamukha", *Journal of the Oriental Institute Baroda* xxv (1976): 387–89; R.C. Agrawala, "Nṛsiṁha-Varāha—

Viṣṇu Images and Some Allied Problems", *Lalit Kala* XVI (1974): 11–21; V.S. Parch, "A Rare Sculpture of the Consort of Vaikuṇṭha", *Journal of the Oriental Institute Baroda* xxv (1976): 390-92.

25. Moti Chandra, *Stone Sculpture in the Prince of Wales Museum* (Bombay, 1974), p. 29; pl. 85 a and b.
26. On Kāpila, cf. Desai, Vaikuṇṭha, p. 24. She notes that the later Silpaśāstras prescribe the fourth face as that of a woman instead of Kāpila.
27. Cf. also another ninth-century Viṣṇu Caturmūrti from Kashmir in the Prince of Wales Museum (no. 73.5; see Moti Chandra, *Stone Sculpture in the Prince of Wales Museum*, p. 30, pl. 86 a and b). This sculpture, like no. 73.4, portrays the obverse central human figure wearing an ornamental crown and numerous decorations; the reverse fierce face features similar simple earrings, necklace, and jaṭā with cascading locks. An unusual feature in this icon is that both the lateral faces are those of a lion.
28. The Kāpila face can also be absent in Kashmiri images, as in the Viṣṇu bronze in the Museum für Indische Kunst, Berlin, discussed by H. Härtel, "Zur Datierung einer alten Viṣṇu-Bronze", *Indologen-tagung* (Göttingen, 1960), pp. 165–78; also in *Indische Sculpturen I* (Berlin, 1960), pp. 73–74, plates 42–43. Härtel dates the piece to the seventh century. Arguments for a sixth-century AD dating are presented by Pal, *Bronzes of Kashmir*, pp. 64–65. The bronze is also discussed by C. Sivaramamurti, *Indian Bronzes* (Bombay, 1962), who assigns it to the fourth or fifth century. D. Barrett (*Lalit Kala* XI) says it is post-Gandhāran.
29. Viṣṇu does not hold a conch as is mentioned in both the J. Ph. Vogel and V. S. Agrawala Mathura Museum catalogues.
30. See also Mathura Museum no. 771.
31. For example, Mathura Museum no. 34.2525.4.
32. I wish to thank Dr. C. Sivaramamurti for informing me about this piece.
33. K. S. Desai, *Iconography of Viṣṇu*, pp. 42–43.
34. Cf. J. N. Banerjea, "Mediaeval Viṣṇu Images from Kashmir and Some Viṣṇudharmottara Passages", *Proceedings of the Indian Historical Congress* IV (Lahore, 1940): 61–64.
35. On the *vyūha* doctrine, see R. G. Bhandarkar, *Vaiṣṇavism, Śaivism and Minor Religious Systems*, reprint (Varanasi, 1965), p. 165; F. O. Schrader, *Introduction to the Pāñcarātra and the Ahirbudhnya Saṃhitā* (Madras, 1916), chap. II; Gonda, *Viṣṇuism and Śivaism*, pp. 49–62 and notes on pp. 164–71.
36. Mathura Museum nos. 382; F2; 47.3259; 44.3161 (which may date to the late third to early fourth century AD).
37. Cf. note 7.
38. A. Cunningham, *The Stūpa of Bharhut*, reprint (Varanasi, 1962), p. 13.
39. Cunningham, ibid., pl. v.
40. They are: Kuvera Yakṣa, Candrā Yakṣī, Ādyakala Yakṣa. See A. K. Coomaraswamy, *La Sculpture de Bharhut* (Paris, 1956), p. 42, pl. VII.
41. See P. Chandra, *Stone Sculpture in the Allahabad Museum* (Bombay, 1970), p. 59, pl. 32.
42. The significance of the piece is problematic. Because each yakṣa squats with uplifted arms, they may have originally supported a common object. That form may not have been a sculptured component, for the upright contains neither socket nor projection on top.
43. Gonda, *Viṣṇuism and Śivaism*, p. 50, and see the references cited in his fn. 216. Cf. J. Gonda, *Die Religionen Indiens* (Stuttgart, 1960), vol. I, p. 275; Sanjukta Gupta, "The Caturvyūha and the Viśākha-yūpa in the Pāñcarātra", *The Adyar Library Bulletin*, 35, parts 3–4 (December 1971): 189–94.

44. Gonda, *Viṣṇuism and Śivaism*, pp. 50–51.
45. See D. Srinivasan, "The Religious Significance of Multiple Bodily Parts to Denote the Divine: Findings from the Rig Veda", *Asiatische Studien* XXIX.2 (1975): 162.
46. Gupta, "The Caturvyūha and the Viśākha-yūpa in the Pāñcarātra", pp. 189 ff., discusses the formulation of the Viśākha-yūpa concept in the Pāñcarātra system as an aid in meditation. The *yūpa* (pillar) to be visualized is that of the Caturvyūhas; each *vyūha* occupies one side of the pillar. The *Lakṣmī Tantra* specifies that Vāsudeva is to be visualized on the eastern section; Saṃkarṣaṇa faces south; Pradyumna, west; and Aniruddha, north. The central hiatus is considered to be filled with his all-encompassing, transcendental Self (Brahman). An earlier Pāñcarātra text, the *Satvata Saṃhitā*, already has an allusion to the envisioning of the four *vyūhas* in connection with the Viśākha-yūpa concept. Could the plastic representation of the Caturvyūha concept in the pre-Christian period be related to the later meditative device, the Viśākha-yūpa?
47. Gonda, *Die Religionen Indiens,* Vol. I, pp. 247–284. Cf. O. Schrader, *Introduction to Pāñcarātra,* pp. 14–19.
48. G.A. Grierson dates the Nārāyaṇīya to ca. AD 200–400 in "The Nārāyaṇīya and the Bhāgavatas", *The Indian Antiquary* 37 (1908): 258. Cf. S. Chattopadhyaya, *Evolution of Hindu Sects* (New Delhi, 1970), p. 55.
49. *Mahābhārata* XII.326.9.
50. *Mahābhārata* XII.321.8.
51. See *Mahābhārata* XII.326.31–41.
52. The three elements and their influence on the development of Viṣṇu are well treated in J. Gonda, *Die Religionen Indiens* I, pp. 236–54; Bhandarkar, *Vaiṣṇavism, Śaivism, and Minor Religious Systems,* see part I, esp. pp. 1–46; cf. Chattopadhyaya, *Evolution of Hindu Sects,* Section B.
52a. ADDENDUM: See D.M. Srinivasan, "Becoming Viṣṇu" in *Viṣṇu: Hinduism's Blue-Skinned Savior*. Exhibition Catalogue. Ahmedabad and Ocean Township, 2010, pp. 24-33.
53. The same school is designated around the Christian era as Sātvata, after the clan that worshiped Vāsudeva-Kṛṣṇa as the Supreme Being. See Bhandarkar, *Vaiṣṇavism, Śaivism, and Minor Religious Systems,* pp. 8–13; cf. *Viṣṇu Purāṇa* 17.15.
54. See Bhandarkar, *Vaiṣṇavism, Śaivism, and Minor Religious Systems,* chap. VII.
55. Bhandarkar (ibid., p. 32) emphasizes this point strongly in stating, "The burden of the whole Nārāyaṇīya section seems to be this identity between Nārāyaṇa and Vāsudeva."
56. For example, *Śatapatha Brāhmaṇa* XII.3, 4; XIII.6.1. For a bibliography on important studies of the Rig Veda Puruṣasūkta, see D. Srinivasan, "The Religious Significance of Multiple Bodily Parts to Denote the Divine: Findings from the *Rig Veda*", p. 171, fn. 142.
57. Similar sets of correspondences are already set up in hymns of the Atharva Veda. In these hymns, creation is an emanative process. The Creator emits or emanates from his own Being the outer forms comprising materiality. See D. Srinivasan, "The Religious Significance of Divine Multiple Body Parts in the Atharva Veda", *Numen,* 25.3 (1979), concerning the Skambha Hymns.
58. See Srinivasan, "The Religious Significance of Multiple Bodily Parts to Denote the Divine: Findings from the Rig Veda", pp. 143–47; and "The Religious Significance of Divine Multiple Body Parts in the Atharva Veda".
59. The attribution comes from Sāyaṇa's commentary on *Rig Veda* 10.90.
60. Srinivasan, "The Religious Significance of Multiple Bodily Parts to Denote the Divine: Findings from the Rig Veda", pp. 171–72.

61. See Schrader, *Introduction to the Pāñcarātra and the Ahirbudhnya Saṃhitā*, p. 143. It is most interesting that, in the *Śatapatha Brāhmaṇa* XIII.6.1, Puruṣa-Nārāyaṇa is associated with a pāñcarātra sacrifice. The passage declares that Puruṣa-Nārāyaṇa perceived the Pāñcarātra sacrifice (a sacrifice lasting five days) and performed it in order to obtain supremacy over everything in the universe. For a brief survey of the indebtedness of the Caturvyūha notion to the Puruṣasūkta, see Gupta, "The Caturvyūha and the Viśākha-yūpa in the Pāñcarātra", pp. 194–96.
62. One name of the western face of the Viṣṇu Vaikuṇṭha and Caturmūrti icons affirms the integral nature of the emanation theory in the *vyūha* doctrine. The face called Kāpila probably is associated with the sage Kāpila, reputed founder of the Sāṃkhya school of philosophy. Sāṃkhya believes that the world came into being through the successive emanation of a chain of elements. See S. Dasgupta, *A History of Indian Philosophy*, reprint (Cambridge, 1951), vol. 1, chap. VII; G.J. Larson, *Classical Sāṃkhya* (Delhi, 1969), esp. chap. II. The doctrine of emanation, as described in the Sāṃkhya system, had a profound influence on cosmogonic theories developed in the *Mahābhārata* and Purāṇas; see P. Hacker, "The Sānkhyization of the Emanation Doctrine Shown in a Critical Analysis of Texts", *Wiener Zeitschrift für die Kunde Süd- und Ostasiens* V (1961): 75–112.
63. The present study does not attempt to trace the origin of Kṛṣṇa worship, or the association of the name Kṛṣṇa with that of Vāsudeva, and it does not explore the fact that a sage Kṛṣṇa is mentioned in Vedic literature from the time of the *Rig Veda* to the time of the *Chandogya Upaniṣad*; see Bhandarkar, *Vaiṣṇavism, Śaivism, and Minor Religious Systems*, p. 11. Whether this is the Kṛṣṇa who comes to be associated with Vāsudeva is not very clear. R.N. Dandekar, in *Some Aspects of the History of Hinduism* (Poona, 1967), p. 95, doubts it, discerning three separate religio-ethical trends combining to produce Hindu Kṛṣṇa.
64. The inscription dates to the time of Śoḍāsa. On the relative dating, and other inscriptions of Śoḍāsa, see H. Härtel, "Some Results of the Excavations at Sonkh", in *German Scholars in India* (Bombay, 1976), Vol. 2, p. 84; and D.C. Sircar, *Select Inscriptions Bearing on Indian History and Civilization* (Calcutta, 1965), nos. 24–26B.
65. See V.S. Agrawala, *Mathura Museum Catalogue* IV (Varanasi, 1963), pp. 130–32.
66. V.S. Agrawala, *India as Known to Pāṇini*, 2nd ed. (Benaras, 1953), pp. 361 ff.; Gonda, *Die Religionen Indiens* I, p. 237; P.V. Kane, *History of Dharmaśāstras* (Poona, 1941), vol. II, part II, pp. 705–40; R.N. Dandekar, *Ramakrishna Gopal Bhandarkar as an Indologist* (Poona, 1976), p. 27, cf. p. 29.
67. See V. S. Agrawala, *Ancient Indian Folk Cults* (Varanasi, 1970), p. 10.
68. Mid-second century BC is the date generally ascribed to Patañjali's *Mahābhāṣya*. The date of this text has recently been studied by S.D. Joshi and J.A.F. Roodbergen, *Patañjali's Vyākaraṇa-Mahābhāṣya* (Poona, 1976); see Introduction. It is suggested that Patañjali may be dated to the first century AD (p. xxix).
69. Agrawala, *India as Known to Pāṇini*, p. 360. Cf. H. Raychaudhuri, *Materials for the Study of the Early History of the Vaishnava Sect*, 2nd rev. ed. (Calcutta, 1936), pp. 23–24; R.G. Bhandarkar, "Allusions to Kṛṣṇa in Patañjali's *Mahābhāṣya*," *The Indian Antiquary* III (Jan. 1874): 16.
70. *Mahābhāṣya*, I. 436.
71. Bhandarkar, "Allusions to Kṛṣṇa in Patañjali's *Mahābhāṣya*", pp. 14–16; cf. Raychaudhuri, *Materials for the Study of the Early History of the Vaishnava Sect*, pp. 37 and 105.

72. Bhandarkar, ibid., p. 16.
73. The coins are part of a "treasure" found in room 20 of the administrative quarters at the site of Ai-Khanum, on the borders of the Soviet Union and Afghanistan; see A.K. Narain, "The Two Hindu Divinities on the Coins of Agathocles from Ai-Khanum", *Journal of the Numismatic Society of India,* 35 (1973): 73–77.
74. A.K. Narain, ibid.; J. Filliozat, "Représentations de Vāsudeva et Saṃkarṣaṇa, en IIe siècle avant J.C.", *Arts Asiatiques* XXVI (1973): 113–123.
75. The name Samkarṣaṇa may mean 'the plowing one'; he is identified with Balarāma or Baladeva, called Halāyudha, 'the one who has a plow for his weapon.' Gonda, *Viṣṇuism and Śivaism,* p. 52.
76. The piece (no. G215) comes from Jansuti, District of Mathura. See N.P. Joshi, *Catalogue of the Brahmanical Sculptures in the State Museum of Lucknow;* part I (Lucknow, 1972), p. 90, fig. 13.
77. As is well known, the inscription records the setting up of a Garuḍa pillar by Heliodoros to honor Vāsudeva, the god of gods. Heliodoros of Taxila and an ambassador from King Antialkidas to King Kāśiputra Bhāgabhadra calls himself a Bhāgavata. Near to the Heliodoros pillar has been discovered an approximately third-century BC Viṣṇu temple; see M.D. Khare, "Discovery of a Viṣṇu Temple near the Heliodoros Pillar, Besnagar, District of Vidisha (M.P.)", *Lalit Kala* XIII (1967): 21 ff.
78. Sircar, *Select Inscriptions Bearing on Indian History and Civilization,* pp. 90–91.
79. K.P. Jayaswal, in "The Ghosūṇḍī Stone Inscription", *Epigraphia Indica,* XVI (1921): 25 ff., suggests that it was a railing of slabs of stone.
80. Sircar, *Select Inscriptions Bearing on Indian History and Civilization,* pp. 192 if. The inscription, no. 1 in a large cave, is of the Sātavāhana queen Nāganikā. It attests to the spread of the Bhāgavata cult further south. The progress of Bhāgavatism southward into Andhra Pradesh is witnessed by the second-century AD Chinna inscription cf Yajña-Śātakarṇi (D.C. Sircar, *Studies in the Religious Life of Ancient and Medieval India* [Delhi, 1971], p. 21), and the late third-early-fourth-century AD Kondamotu sculptured panel depicting the Pāñcavīras on either side of Viṣṇu's *avatāra,* Nārasiṃha (see Md. Abdul Waheed Khan, "An Early Sculpture of Nārasiṃha", *Andhra Pradesh Government Archaeological Series,* no. 16 [Hyderabad, 1964]).
81. The *Mahābhārata* illustrates these tendencies. For example, Āraṇyaka Parvan, chap. 12, identifies (Vāsudeva-) Kṛṣṇa with Nārāyaṇa. In chaps. 65 and 66 of the Bhīṣma Parvan, Viṣṇu as the Supreme Spirit is addressed as Nārāyaṇa and identified with Vāsudeva-Kṛṣṇa. The *Mahānārāyaṇa Upaniṣad,* in a modification of the Gāyatrī mantra, identifies (in III.78) Nārāyaṇa with Vāsudeva and Viṣṇu. This work, of uncertain date, may go back as far as the third century BC according to Gonda, *Viṣṇuism and Śivaism,* p. 42.
82. See also Raychaudhuri, *Materials for the Study of the Early History of the Vaishnava Sect,* p. 98, fn. 1; Sircar, *Studies in the Religious Life of Ancient and Medieval India,* pp. 32–33; Dandekar, *Ramakrishna Gopal Bhandarkar as an Indologist,* p. 33.
83. See Sircar, *Select Inscriptions Bearing on Indian History and Civilization,* pp. 94–95.
84. J. Agrawal, "Vidisha Stone Pillar Inscription of the Reign of Mahārāja Bhāgavata, Dated Regnal Year 12", *Vishveshvarānand Indological Journal* III, part 1 (1965): 99–100.

9

Viśvarūpa Vyūha Avatāra: Reappraisals Based on an Inscribed Bronze from the Northwest Dated to the Early 5th Century AD*

I. THE PROBLEM (DMS)

The hitherto unpublished bronze image in a private Asian collection is the first known example to bear an inscription giving the identification of a well-recognized but problematic type (Fig. 9.1)[1]. That, together with the fact that the image can be accurately dated[1a(*)], distinguishes the bronze. For the problem raised by this Vaiṣṇava type deals precisely with its identification, its theological meaning, and its chronological development in religion and art.

The type features a male deity with multiple heads and arms. The central head is human and the side heads are of a lion *(siṃha)* and a boar *(varāha)*. The earliest examples, both from the Gangetic Valley and the Northwest, show only these three heads—as does our bronze. (See Fig. 8.14 and fn. 28 in the paper in this volume "Early Vaiṣṇava Imagery") From the 9th century onwards (perhaps even earlier), a fourth head is added in back of the human head in examples from Kashmir. Four arms customarily belong to the central figure; the natural hands hold the conch and lotus, while the two extra hands rest on the god's attributes, namely the mace and the wheel. These attributes become personified sometime during the Gupta period as Gadādevī and Cakrapuruṣa, respectively[2].

Scholarly reference to the visually unmistakable type is far from uniform. It has been called Viṣṇu Caturānana ('four-faced') whether the image has four faces[3] or three[4]. It has been called Viṣṇu Caturmūrti ('having four forms') when the image has one body with four heads and arms, a label considered by some to be almost synonymous with Viṣṇu Caturānana[5], but by others to be almost

Originally published in *East and West*, Vol. 47, Nos. 1-4 (Dec. 1997); pp. 105-70. Reprinted with stylistic changes, additions and with permission from IsIAO, Rome.

* Section II written by Lore Sander.

Fig. 9.1. Para Vāsudeva-Nārāyaṇa. 427 AD Himachal Pradesh. Private Collection.

synonymous with, or expressive of Viṣṇu Caturvyūha ('four [successive, cosmic] emanations')[6]. It has been called 'Vaikuṇṭha' (literally 'the keen, the penetrating irresistible') because the *c.* 8th century *Viṣṇudharmottara Purāṇa* (III.85.43–45), a Kashmiri text, calls the composite, four-faced type by this name; but the same text does not assign the name 'Vaikuṇṭha' to a four-faced, eight-armed god seated on Garuḍa (III.44.9–13) which is the form receiving the name 'Vaikuṇṭha' in the later Pāñcarātra texts[7]. It is apparent that no scholarly consensus exists on when to apply this name. Indeed, scholars designate examples from Kashmir, and from all over India, by the name 'Vaikuṇṭha' regardless of their anachronistic positions vis-à-vis the *Viṣṇudharmottara* and posterior texts, and, regardless whether these examples are three-faced[8], four-faced[9], or whether they include Garuḍa[10].

There is consensus that the type expresses beliefs of the Pāñcarātra sect within Vaiṣṇavism. The name a scholar assigns to the type invariably reflects which Pāñcarātra beliefs he attributes to the type. The sect believes in one Supreme, transcendental great Being (*mahā puruṣa*) who represents cosmogonic totality[11]. This is Nārāyaṇa.

Cosmogony begins to unfurl when the transcendental Nārāyaṇa first manifests himself in his undivided glory. That manifestation is called Para Vāsudeva. Cosmogony continues as Para Vāsudeva differentiates himself into four emanations (Caturvyūha). The first is *vyūha* Vāsudeva, who may be distinguished from Para Vāsudeva[12]. The three subsequent and successive *vyūhas* are: Saṃkarṣaṇa, Pradyumna and Aniruddha. The four *vyūhas* head the cosmogonic process. They initiate pure creation which is the creation of all divine forms. All deities other than the *vyūhas* are *vibhava* or *avatāra* deities and they belong to the subsequent stage in the process of pure creation. Thus the names Caturānana, Caturmūrti and Vaikuṇṭha permit, either directly or by default, that the type could be interpreted according to the *avatāra* doctrine, since the lateral heads showing the lion and boar, could be taken to represent two of Viṣṇu's *avatāras*. Only the name Caturvyūha insists that none of the heads are primarily *avatāras* but must primarily symbolize emanations *(vyūhas)*. Specifically, the lateral heads are understood to refer to the second and fourth *vyūha*. If the four heads correspond to the four *vyūhas,* the type relates to the essential nature of Nārāyaṇa, being manifest totality, as it were. If the heads are identified as *avatāras,* then the type must belong to the lower, secondary level of pure creation, containing incarnations that are partial aspects of god.

The theological significance of the side heads has consistently confounded art historical interpretations even though J.N. Banerjea provided a cogent methodology in perhaps the earliest serious consideration of the type[13]. Summarizing the details on Vaikuṇṭha from the *Viṣṇudharmottara Purāṇa* (III.85)[14], he joins that description to two other relevant passages elsewhere in the same text (III.47, especially verse 10 which describes the four *vyūhas,* Vāsudeva, Saṃkarṣaṇa, Pradyumna and Aniruddha, and III.44.11–12 which places the *saumya* face to the front or east, the face of Narasiṃha to the south, that of Kāpila to the west and Varāha to the north). Coordinating the data results in the following disposition: the front or eastern (human/*saumya*) face is that of Vāsudeva, the right or southern face (lion) is that of Saṃkarṣaṇa, the back or the western one *(kāpila* or *raudra,* the terrific) is that of Pradyumna; and the left or the northern one (the boar) is that of Aniruddha. Banerjea concludes, 'The lion- and the boar-faces are thus primarily associated with the Pāñcarātra Vyūhas and not the Nṛsiṃha and Varāha incarnations, though the latter might have helped to some extent the formation of this concept'[15]. De Mallmann unequivocally agrees with Banerjea's conclusion, '[...] il paraît certain qu'à l'origine, la forme et la représentation de Viṣṇu aux quatre faces ont illustré les Quatres Grandes Manifestations' (i.e. Caturmahāvyūha), 'en une seule personne [...]; les faces animales ne seront que tardivement assimilées aux Avatāra [...]'[16]. She makes this observation in connection with her analysis of *Agni Purāṇa,* 49.21–23. This Purāṇic section contains a description of Viṣṇu Viśvarūpa whom de Mallmann considers to be a syncretic aspect of the *caturvyūha* forms of Para Vāsudeva[17]. These arguments convinced Gonda. He associates the four faces of the early medieval Kashmiri images, which include lateral animal heads, with the four *vyūhas* and he considers the type to represent the idea of 'One in Four'[18]. I, too, was persuaded that these Kashmiri images express the *vyūha,* and not the *avatāra* doctrine when I first analyzed the iconography pertaining to the *caturvyūha* belief. I refrained from designating the Kashmiri images as 'Caturvyūha' images, mainly because they do not feature the effective separation of the One into Four, but rather the inherent capacity for the One with four forms (i.e. Caturmūrti) to do so[19]. Different views of the side heads are represented by the works of Adalbert J. Gail and Thomas S. Maxwell. Gail mentions that the Pāñcarātra texts describe the *vyūhas* as four distinct anthropomorphic entities, an observation leading him, no doubt, to consider as *avatāras* the lateral boar and lion heads in the Gupta three-faced images from Mathurā in the Gangetic Valley. However Gail should have considered the evidence from the Gupta Pāñcarātra text, the *Jayākhya Saṃhitā,* which mentions animal heads in a context highly suggestive of a *vyūha* description (see section VI). The Kashmiri four-faced type, according to Gail, adds yet another *avatāra* head. But Gail hesitates to advance a hypothesis for understanding the resultant Kashmiri figure: 'This four-faced Viṣṇu might have been interpreted by several Pāñcarātrin as a representation of their four *vyūhas*, but not even that is to be verified on the basis of one single *Vdh.* verse'[20]. Maxwell considers the side heads as *avatāras;* indeed he considers all the four heads as *avatāras.* However he asserts that they are to be understood as *avatāras* in terms of Pāñcarātrin ideology, and not primarily in terms of the *avatāra* doctrine. Maxwell explains that in the Pāñcarātrin system each *vyūha* emanates specific *vibhavas* or *avatāras,* and he refers the reader to Schrader's discussions of those Pāñcarātra texts mentioning which *avatāras* spring from which *vyūhas.* Thus, he proposes 1) that the Vāsudeva, Narasiṃha, Kāpila and Varāha *avatāra* faces could be taken as visible, earthly manifestations of the four *vyūhas,* and 2) that in the Kashmiri four-headed images, the 'avatāras and their associated vyūhas can be worshipped without the need of separate icons [...]'[21]. The difficulty with his proposition is that the relevant Pāñcarātra texts, cited by Schrader, do not distribute the heads, deemed by Maxwell to be *avatāra* heads, among *all* the four *vyūhas;* therefore it is misleading to suggest that the latter can be associated, *in toto,* with the former. Schrader discusses three Pāñcarātra texts; two (the *Viṣvakṣena Saṃhitā* and the *Lakṣmī Tantra)* claim that all the *avatāras* spring from one *vyūha* alone: Aniruddha. The third *(Pādma Tantra)* distributes the *avatāras* over the four *vyūhas,* but the text neither mentions the Kāpila *avatāra,* nor that this *avatāra* (or any other *raudra* form) springs from the *vyūha* Pradyumna.

Into the web of the problem posed by this type, the inscription on the base of the hitherto unpublished bronze (Figs. 9.2–9.5) injects pertinent information. The

Fig. 9.2. Inscription on base of Fig. 9.1. Front.

inscription, dated to the early 5th century, states that the image is called 'Nārāyaṇa'. Both the script and the icon can be assigned to the Northwest, but not to Kashmir. Accordingly, the inscribed bronze image is, to date, the earliest complete example of the Vaiṣṇava type found in the Northern areas 1) being approximately four hundred years prior to the earliest Kashmiri figures and 2) being allied to the formulation and development of the type at the Gangetic site of Mathurā. This means that the earliest (three-headed) examples described below can be identified as mainly images of 'Nārāyaṇa'; they come from the Northwest and the Gangetic area and date between the 3rd/4th century AD–7th/8th century. But the identification cannot be proffered without further discussion. Nārāyaṇa is not a name previously assigned by any scholar to the early images of this type[22]. Moreover, it is not at all obvious how a visible manifestation with multiple bodily parts can symbolize a transcendental Being. Therefore, the theological position of the type within the Pāñcarātra's system of cosmogony needs to be examined, and this is done subsequent to a close scrutiny

Fig. 9.3. Inscription on base of Fig. 9.1. Proper right side.

Fig. 9.4. Inscription on base of Fig. 9.1. Back.

Fig. 9.5. Inscription on base of Fig. 9.1. Proper left side.

of the inscription, and the technical as well as art historical analyses of the 'Nārāyaṇa' bronze.

II. THE INSCRIPTION (LS)

The Brāhmī inscription is well preserved. The *akṣaras* are engraved in the middle of the pedestal with the help of a sharply pointed instrument. Pointed *akṣaras* are confined to metal inscriptions (i.a. the Shōrkōt inscription, Table of Comparison, column 2), but even there they are rare. In India this practice is attested to in Kharoṣṭhī inscriptions from the time of the Kuṣāṇa rulers, as, for example, on the Kalawān copperplate inscription (near Sirkap)[23], the Taxila silver scroll[24], and on the Wardak (Afghanistan) vase of the time of Huviṣka[25].

Most of the *akṣaras* are clearly readable; only some, especially a few at the rear, are faint. The arrangement of the inscription around the pedestal is rather strange. The following diagram may illustrate it:

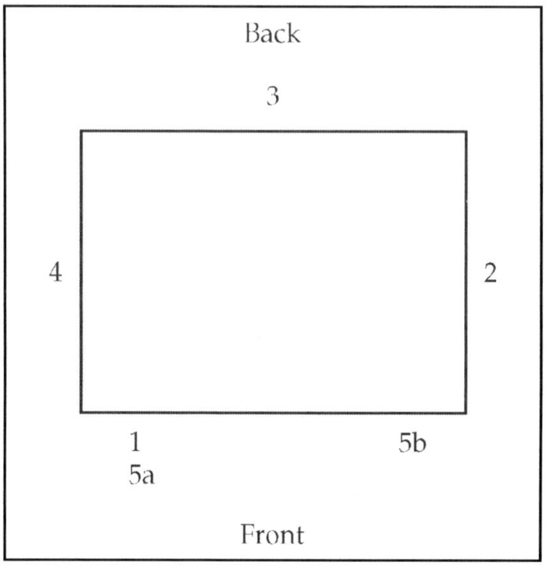

It begins to the left of the front side which is split into two parts by the figure of the earth goddess arising from a lotus. The first line (front, left side, line 1) ends at the outspread right arm of the goddess (No. 1 in the diagram). The inscription is not continued on her left side, as expected, but around the corner on the right side of the pedestal (diagram, No. 2). The one ascending line on the left side of the goddess (front, right side) contains the end of the inscription (diagram, No. 5b) and is the continuation of the second line on her right (diagram, No. 5a; front, left side, line 2). In fact, it is not only the strange arrangement which can hardly be explained. The inscription raises several grammatical and syntactical questions which have to be commented. Therefore the following translation has to be regarded as being tentative.

Reading

Square brackets [ ] indicate uncertain *akṣaras*

front, left side, line 1: *sa[m]vacchare trayo*
right side: *aṣāḍhamasa dīvase pañca-*
rear: *mi [atra dī]vase nārāyaṇapratimā pratitthāvita*
left side: *bhīmāsthāne gharaṭṭamaṭṭhe śrī vaï(ḥ?)likā-*
front, left side, line 2: *yā devadharma[yaṃ?]*
front, right side: *tya śrī variṣāyā*

Translation

In the year three, in the month of Āṣāḍha, on the fifth day, on this day the image of Nārāyaṇa was installed at Bhīmāsthāna in (or at) Gharaṭṭamaṭṭha of the honorable *(śrī)* Vaï(ḥ)likā. It is a religious gift of ... the honorable *(śrī)* Variṣā[26].

Commentary[27]

There are some open questions concerning the reading, which is based on photos only, and the translation. To begin with the date of the inscription, there are two points which have to be discussed. The first concerns *sa[m]vacchare trayo* (front). The *-m-* in the ligature of the Middle Indic form for 'year' *sa[m]vacchare* (cf. Linguistic analysis, below) is not quite sure because it is partly engraved on the upper rim of the pedestal. Clearly readable is *trayo* which is unusual. One would expect the ordinal number *tṛtīye* (cf. *dīvase pañcami*) or as in most inscriptions of the Kaniṣka and the Gupta era the numeric sign for three, but not the cardinal number.

The second expression in question is the reading *atra dīvase* (rear). It is written in that portion of the inscription which is rather faint. Instead of *atra* one would expect *su ti = śukla tiṭhi*[28], the bright half of the month, but in this type of Brāhmī script, typical for the Northwest of ancient India, *A* is clearly discernible from *su*, because of its prominent hook at the left side of its top (cf. Table of Comparison). Another argument against *su ti* is the close relationship in formulaic rendering of our inscription to that of the Kuṣāṇa inscriptions, in which the bright or the dark half of a month are not mentioned. In the ligature *tra* only *t-* is fairly sure. The subscribed *-ra* is very faint. [*at*]*(i)°* instead of [*atra*] seems to be possible. But *atra* is more likely; it is not only preferable for the shapes of the *akṣaras* suggest this reading, but also for *atra divase* occurs in Kharoṣṭhī inscriptions, e.g. the much sanskritized Sui Vihār inscription (South West Pakistan), which is dated into the eleventh year of Devaputra Kaniṣka[29]. S. Konow[30] explained *atra* as being an orthographical error or misunderstanding for *ayatra*[31] in the same manner as *tatra* is from *tat*. The normal formula in these Kharoṣṭhī inscriptions is the Gāndharī *iśa* or *iśe* (Skt. *asmin) divase*, meaning the same: 'on this day'[32]. The formula corresponds also to the Sanskrit *asmiṃ divase* in the famous inscription from

Dalpat-ki-Khirki Mohalla (Mathurā) dating of the year 14 of Kaniṣka[33]. The formulaic rendering of the date of our inscription follows that of the Kharoṣṭhī inscriptions of the Kuṣāṇa period and not that of most of the Brāhmī inscriptions from Mathurā which is *(et)asyām pūrvāyāṃ*[34], with the exception of the inscription of the year 14 of Kaniṣka.

The names of places occurring in our inscription are *bhīmāsthāna* and *gharaṭṭamaṭṭha.* Both places are difficult to locate. To begin with *bhīmāsthāna:* The second member of the compound °*sthāna* indicates a small place[35], most probably a holy place *(tīrtha)*, not a village *(grāma)* or town *(nagara)*. The name *bhīmā*° can be connected with the Devī, the highest Śivaitic deity[36]. In attempting to interpret the compound, the possibility that *bhīmā*° could be an orthographic error for *bhīma*° needs to be taken into consideration. In our inscription long and short vowels are not always distinguished according to the rules of classical Sanskrit (cf. Linguistic analysis, below). In the case of an orthographical error, *bhīma*° may refer to the Pāṇḍava hero of the *Mahābhārata* whose cult is and was very popular in the Northwest[37] (For literary evidence cf. Section IV, below).

More obscure is *gharaṭṭamaṭṭha. gharaṭṭa*° is known from the *Rājataraṅginī* to mean 'grindstone' and 'handmill'[38]. In the *Rāj.* it is translated by Stein as 'handmill'[39]. In Sheth's Prākrit Dictionary the meaning 'waterwheel or °mill' (*pānī kā carikhā*) is also attested. °*maṭṭha*[40], the second word in the compound, corresponds to Sanskrit °*mṛṣṭa* 'pure'. This meaning tallies better with 'waterwheel' or 'mill' than with 'grindstone' or 'handmill'. The meaning of the name of the location, whatever it was, is probably 'pure by a watermill'. The following name Śrī Vaïlikāyā or Vaḥlikāyā suggests a possessive meaning: 'in (or at) the Gharaṭṭamaṭṭha of Śrī Vaïlikā or Vaḥlikā'.

The reading of the name is not absolutely sure. It may be read as Śrī Vaïḥlikāyā or Vaḥlikāyā. The left point of the initial *I* is engraved flatter than the other two. If this point is not the original, the name must be read Vaḥlikā, but Vaïlikā seems to be more likely. The reading is not the only difficulty of this portion of the inscription. Professor Fussman drew my attention to the fact that in almost all Kuṣāṇa inscriptions the formula 'the image was installed' is connected with a person in the instrumental case. Because the ending of feminine *ā*-stems *-āyā* often represents the instrumental[41] the translation could possibly be: 'on this day the image of Nārāyaṇa was installed at Bhīmāsthāna, in (or at) the Gharaṭṭamaṭṭha by Śrī Vaïlikā'. Against his hypothesis speaks, besides the difficulty of having two donors, Vaïlikā and Variṣā, that normally the name of the donor in instrumental case preceeds the announcement of the gift[42]: 'by N.N. the image of N.N. (or another gift) was installed'. For syntactical reasons the lady Vaïlikā should be connected with *gharaṭṭamaṭṭha,* and *-āyā* should represent the genitive gender with omission of the visarga.

The origin of the name, whether read as Vaïlikā or Vaḥlikā, is likely Iranian[43], perhaps meaning 'the lady from Balkh (Baktria)'. In our inscription it is a personal name, clearly indicated by Śrī. It is not probable that the name refers directly to the original homeland of the lady[44].

The name of the female donor of the Viṣṇu bronze is Śrī Variṣā. Professor von Hinüber[45] kindly informed me about the same name occurring in a graffito from Ōshibāt, a place in the Upper Indus Valley. In this inscription the son of Upala-variṣā announced his presence at this remote place (*upala* [skt. *utpala*]-*variṣā-putra*) in one of the rare Hybrid Sanskrit inscriptions found in this area. However, the occurrence of the same name in two different inscriptions is not a proof for the identity of the ladies.

The last peculiarity of our inscription concerns the *devadharma* formula at the end of the inscription. The reading °*yaṃ* in *devadharmayaṃ* is not sure from the photo. There is just enough space for °*yaṃ* in front of the figure of the earth goddess. Conjecturing °*yaṃ* means that *tya,* the first *akṣara* on the right side of the earth goddess, is isolated. But *devadharmatya* is not attested and gives no sense, despite one thinks of an elimination[46].

Summarizing, the main difficulties of the inscription concern the part in the front of the pedestal. It is not only the strange arrangement on this side, but also the isolated *tya* in the *devadharma* formula[47] which suggests that this side may have been engraved from the same copy after the three others. It appears as if the engraver had difficulties to arrange the parts of the last portion of the copy on the front of the pedestal.

Linguistic Analysis

The inscription is written in a language named by Th. Damsteegt 'Epigraphical Hybrid Sanskrit'. It encompasses different grammatical forms resulting from the differing degree of Sanskritization of the inscriptions from the time of the Kuṣāṇas. Although the language of our inscription is not Gāndhārī, it shares some orthographic and formulaic pecularities with the Kharoṣṭhī inscriptions of this time. The use of the Middle Indic form *samvacchare* 'in the year' is rare, even in the Kuṣāṇa inscriptions. The Sanskrit equivalent is *saṃvatsare* which is the standard word in the Mathurā inscriptions, while in the Kharoṣṭhī inscription *saṃvatśare* is preferred[48]. According to von Hinüber[49] the change of *tsa* (also *tśa;* the author) to *ccha* is well attested in Middle Indian languages and is only a writing variant[50] for the same or very similar sounds[51]. Other influences in our inscription are common to Kharoṣṭhī inscriptions from the times of the Kuṣāṇas, as the formulaic date ending with *atra dīvase* (see 'Commentary'). Furthermore, compared with the correct Sanskrit forms short and long vowels are often confused which is characteristic for the 'Epigraphical Hybrid Sanskrit'. *a* stands for *-ā* (cf. *aṣāḍha* for Sanskrit *āṣāḍha, masa* for *māse*[52], *pratitthāvita* for *pratiṣṭhāpitā*[53], *devadharmayaṃ* for *devadharmāyāṃ),* and *-ī* is used instead of *-i* in *dīvase*[54]. The ending of the loc. sg. *-i pañcami* for Sanskrit *pañcame* is attested mainly in the Kharoṣṭhī inscriptions[55], and also the change from Sanskrit *p* to *v* in *pratitthāvita*[56].

Analysis of the Script (see 'Table of Comparison')

Our inscription (column 1) is written in a northwestern Gupta variety, similar to that of the Buddhist Sarvāstivāda inscription (column 2) found at Shōrkōt[57], near the banks of the river Chenāb north to Multān in ancient Pañjab, modern Pakistan[58], on one of the old roads to Kashmir following the river Chenāb. The inscription is incised round the shoulder of a copper cauldron in the same pointed technique as used for our bronze. The Shōrkōt inscription is dated into the year 83, which was assigned by J.Ph. Vogel[59] to the Gupta era, corresponding to 403 AD. Opposite to our inscription, it is composed in a fairly good Sanskrit. The main difference of letters is the form of the medial vowel *-ā,* which, in the inscription under examination, is always added to the top, while in the Shōrkōt inscription it is added to the right side (Pṛṣṭhamātra) of those Mātṛkās and ligatures having a triangle-shaped head (cf. *cā, tthā, rā*), and also *mā.* This is hardly an indicator for the age. *-ā* was added to the right side of most of the Mātṛkās already in the Kuṣāṇa era[60].

The *akṣaras* in the third column belong to two Mathurā inscriptions of the time of Kumāragupta I, dated into the Gupta years 107 and 135 (427/28 and 455/56 AD) respectively[61]. The two inscriptions are composed in classical Sanskrit. Most of the *akṣaras* show a close affinity to those of our inscription. The main differences concern the shape of *A* which does not have such a pronounced hooklet to the left; the medial *-ā* in *mā* which is, as in the Shōrkot inscription, always added to the right side where it is sometimes bent up to the bottom of *ma;* the sign for the medial vowel *-i* which is bent in the same manner to left side *(vi);* the *akṣara ṇa* which has in rare cases the Kuṣāṇa form, but not in the Nārāyaṇa inscription which shows the normal Gupta form; the letter *ra,* the vertical of which is always straight while it is curved or looped in the inscription under discussion.

The inscription of Toramāṇa in column four belongs to the late 5th century AD. It was found in Kurā, Salt Range, Punjab (Pakistan)[62]. It is written in a Prakritized Sanskrit. Although it has many similarities with our inscription—e.g. the same shape of *A*—there are some differences also in comparison with the inscriptions already examined: the waved form of *-e (de),* and the cursive form of *sa;* the *akṣara la,* the vertical of which does not rise above the upper line of the other Mātṛkās. Such differences point towards a later state of development. The Kurā inscription shares these features with the script of the Kashmirian Bower manuscript—especially with the script of parts V–VII—which draws the line between the northwestern Gupta script and the more elaborate 'Siddhamātṛkā' or 'Kuṭila' type[63] occurring in India for the first time in the middle of the 6th century AD. For paleographic reasons our inscription should be earlier than the Kurā inscription. The paleographic analysis leaves no doubt about the 5th century as being the time when our inscription was written.

Date and Location According to the Script

The inscriptions in the 'Table of Comparison' give not only an idea about the approximate date of our inscription but also about the possible area of origin of our bronze. Except for the inscriptions from Mathurā, all other examples belong to the northwestern frontier of ancient India. Especially characteristic for this region is the *A* with the pronounced hook. This is also found on several graffiti of the Upper Indus Valley, examples from them are joined to the 'Table of Comparison' (column 5)[64].

Two possible eras come into question for our inscription: it is the Gupta era beginning with 320/21 AD and the Laukika of Saptaṛṣi of the lost 100. If we date our inscription according to the Gupta era, the year 3 coincides with 323/24 AD. This is not in accordance with the paleographical evidence which points, as detailed, to the 5th century. As to the Saptaṛṣi era its date can be calculated as follows:

Year 3 + [4]00 + 24[65] = 427 AD[66]

The day of the week is missing. Therefore the exact date cannot be ascertained. Professor Claus Vogel from the University of Bonn was so kind to calculate the possible days on the basis of the Pūrṇimānta and the Amānta systems. It is Wednesday, the 15th of June for the light *(śukla, su ti)* half of the month, for the dark half *(bahala, ba ti)* it is Tuesday, the 31st of May in the Pūrṇimānta system, and Thursday the 30th of June in the Amānta system. According to this date the Nārāyaṇa bronze was installed at Bhīmāsthāna in (or at) the Gharaṭṭamaṭṭha of the honorable Vaï(ḥ?)likā at the 15th or 31st of May or the 30th of June 427 AD respectively, this means in the golden age of the Gupta empire under Kumāragupta I.

The formulaic similarities of expressing the date, the language, and also the technique of engraving with the help of a pointed instrument, all this reminds of Kharoṣṭhī inscriptions from the late Kuṣāṇa period. This script was already on the retreat in the Indian subcontinent during the reign of the Gupta kings, who favored the classical Sanskrit written in various forms of Brāhmī script. The Brāhmī of our Nārāyaṇa bronze is characteristic for the northwestern provinces. But not only for those. The northwestern Gupta Brāhmī was in use in the valleys of the Himālayas as far as Ladakh, where graffiti of approximately the same time were discovered[67]. Moreover, it spread north up to Merv and east up to Xinjiang[68]. This type of script in combination with linguistic and formulaic rendering to inscriptions from the late Kuṣāṇa period at a time, when on the Indian subcontinent classical Sanskrit was on advance, suggests a remote region in the Northwest of ancient India as being the place of origin of our Nārāyaṇa bronze. It is corroborated by the name of the place Bhīmāsthāna, and also by the Iranian names of the two ladies. Technical and stylistic analyses have to define from where our bronze comes.

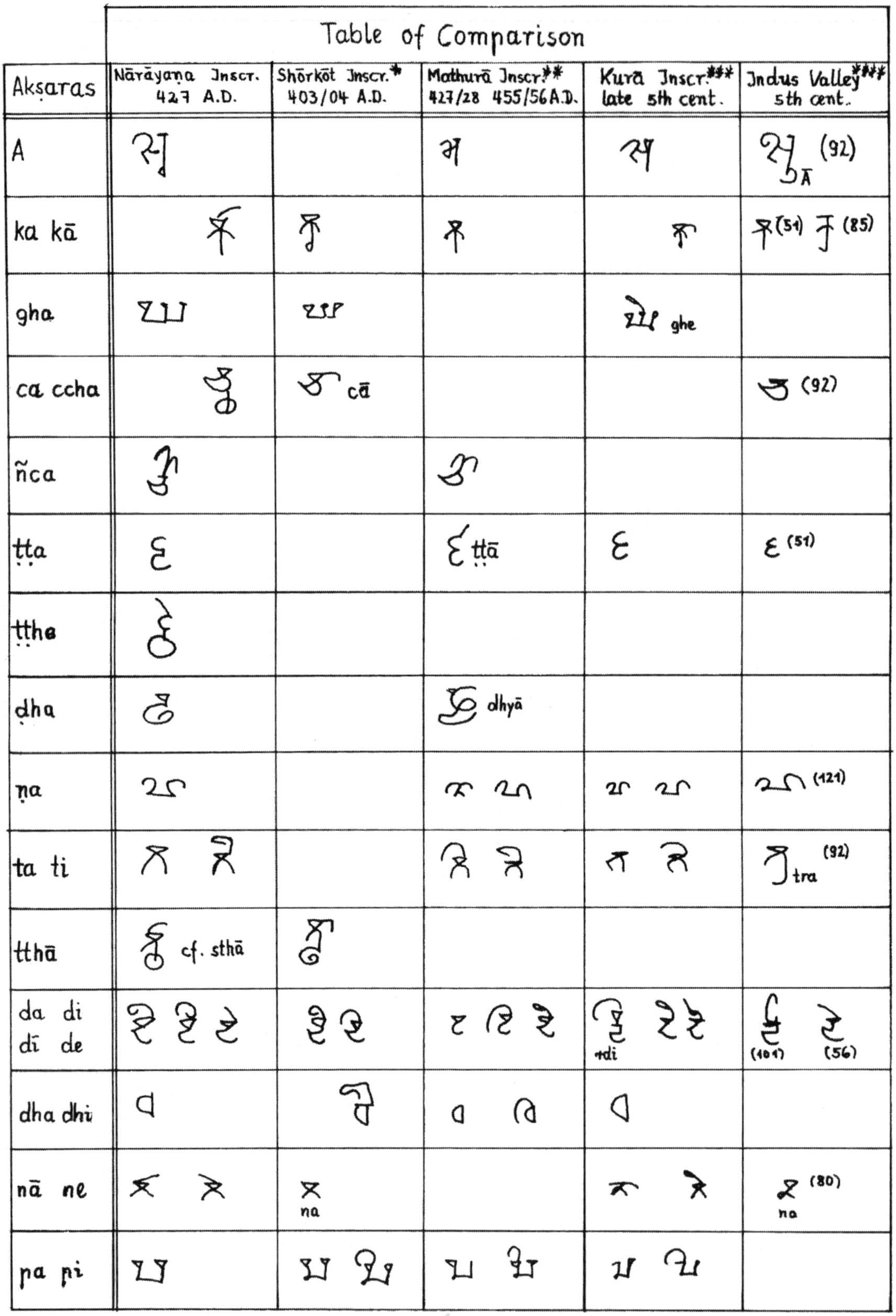
Table of Comparison
Akṣaras
Nārāyaṇa Inscr. 427 A.D.
Shōrkōt Inscr.* 403/04 A.D.
Mathurā Inscr.** 427/28 455/56 A.D.
Kurā Inscr.*** late 5th cent.
Indus Valley**** 5th cent.
A
ka kā
gha
ca ccha
ñca
ṭṭa
ṭṭha
ḍha
ṇa
ta ti
tthā
da di
dī de
dha dhi
nā ne
pa pi
Ā
(92)
(51)
(85)
ghe
cā
ṭṭā
dhyā
(121)
tra
cf. sthā
+di
(101)
(56)
na
(80)

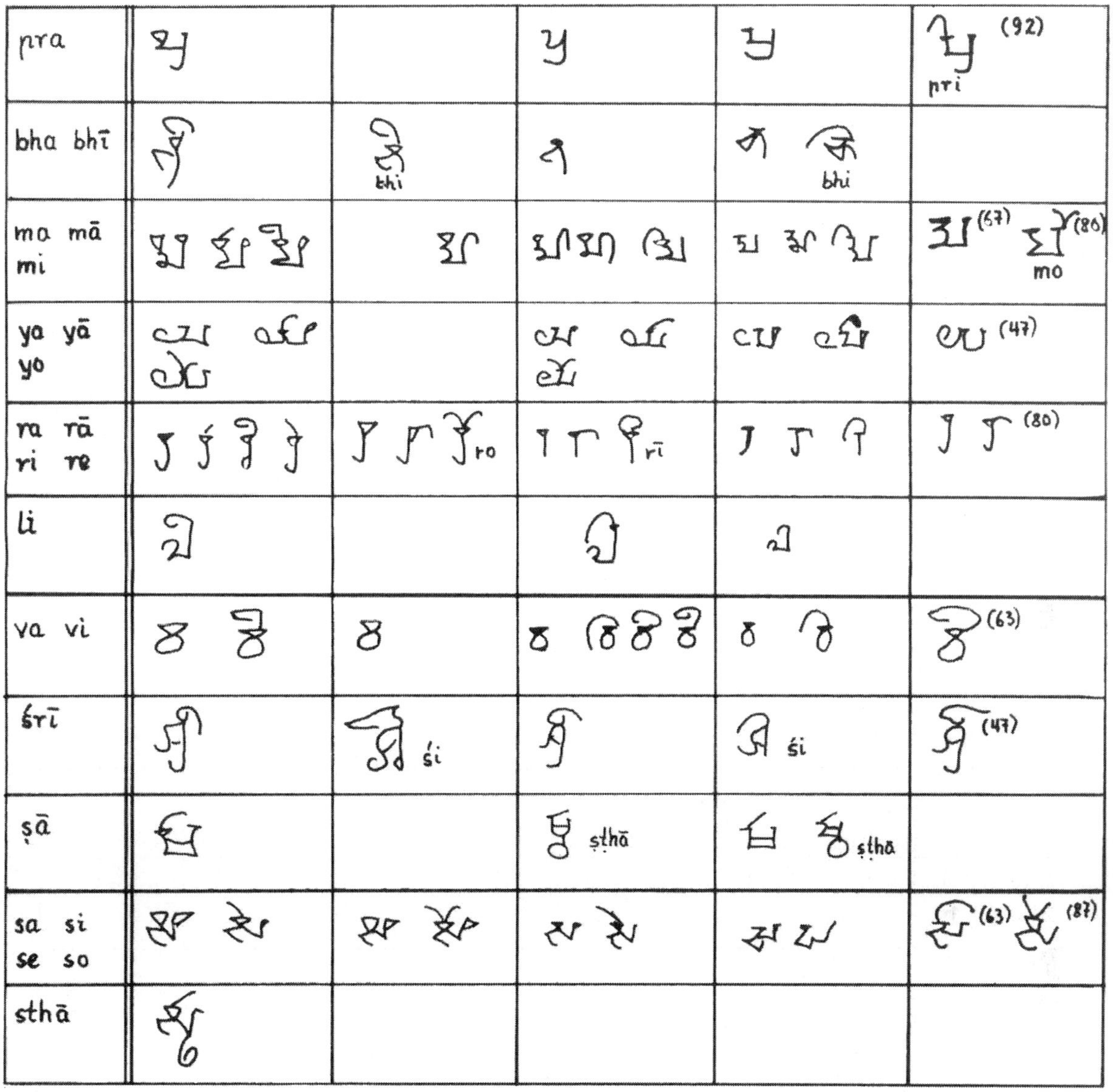

* J.Ph. Vogel, 'Shorkot Inscription of the Year 83', *Epigraphia Indica,* Vol. XVI, 1921–1922, pp. 15–17.— The table contains *akṣaras* from Northwest-Indian inscriptions (cf. A.H. Dani, *Indian Palaeography,* Oxford 1963, Table XII). Only such inscriptions are used for comparison which are close in ductus and form to the inscription in question.

** J.F. Fleet, *Inscriptions of the Early Gupta Kings and Their Successors.* Corpus Inscriptionum Indicarum, Vol. III, Calcutta 1888 (repr. Varanasi 1963), pp. 262–64; revised ed. by D.R. Bhandarkar, ed. B. Chhabra & G.S. Gai, *Corpus Inscriptionum Indicarum,* Vol. III, New Delhi, 1981, pp. 272–73.

*** G. Bühler, 'The New Inscription of Toramana Shaha', *Epigraphia Indica,* Vol. I, Calcutta, 1892, pp. 238–41.

**** The Arabic numbers refer to the plates in K. Jettmar, ed., *Antiquities of Northern Pakistan. Reports and Studies,* Vol. 1: *Rock Inscriptions in the Upper Indus Valley.* Heidelberg Academy for Humanities and Sciences. Research Unit: Rock Carvings and Inscriptions along the Karakorum Highway, Mainz, 1989.

III. DESCRIPTIVE ANALYSES

A. Technical Considerations (DMS)

The following discussion on the technical aspects of the 'Nārāyaṇa' bronze is based on visual assessments rather than laboratory testing[69]; the latter is not deemed necessary because the physical properties that can be visually ascertained appear to be unproblematic.

The composition of the 'Nārāyaṇa' bronze is copper to which tin has been added. Moreover, it looks to be a high tin bronze. This metal alloy is prevalent in Gandhāra copper-based sculptures. For example, about 70% of the Gandhāra copper-based sculptures in the recent exhibition 'The Crossroads of Asia' have tin added[70]. A copper object with a high tin content may also be found further afield to judge from a bronze vase in the same exhibit; it is the 1st century BC vessel found in Himachal Pradesh whose silvery appearance and brittleness suggest a high tin content[71]. Few Kashmiri bronzes are of high tin content, '[...] technical studies of 60 Kashmiri sculptures of the medieval period showed that only 22% had added tin [...] This is in strong contrast to 90% of contemporary sculptures with added tin contents [...]'[72].

Copper could have been mined in the northern areas but tin had to be imported. Small copper deposits can be located in Gilgit and Swat[73]; however no early mine workings have been reported from northern Pakistan and probably copper was imported from Afghanistan in the pre-Islamic period[74]. Kashmir seems to have had sizeable copper deposits along the Valley's western periphery[75]. Copper mining is also recorded in Himachal Pradesh[76]. Sources for tin would come from Afghanistan or India[77]. Importation of tin into the Gandhāran region probably was from Afghanistan rather than India; if the source were India then Kashmiri sculptures ought to have made more use of tin as an alloy in their bronzes. It still needs to be determined, however, whether or not the region of Himachal Pradesh, below Kashmir, received tin from Indian mines.

Another technical feature of the "Nārāyaṇa' bronze reduces the probability that it comes from Kashmir. The hole seen in the back of the head (Fig. 9.6) is present in almost all bronzes attributed to northern Pakistan (though not actually found in excavations). Whereas about 95% from northern Pakistan show this hole, about 20% from Kashmir do. Too few icons from Himachal Pradesh or the Punjab predating the medieval period have been analyzed to provide a useful basis for a comparison of this feature. The hole is the result of a particular casting technique: a rod is put in the back of the head to stabilize the figure during the casting process.

Next may be addressed the important question whether the four separate parts, comprising the entire image, go together. These parts are: the central figure, the two side figures and the pedestal. A close-up view of a section of the base and the feet of the central figure show that the degree of corrosion is the same for both (Fig. 9.7). Further, the central figure appears to have been cast to fit well into the pedestal. The fit occurs under the thin platform on which rest the feet of the central figure. Posts, attached under the platform, fit into holes in the base. It is hard to cast pieces to fit exactly into holes in a base. Therefore if the central figure (and also the side figures) were not originally conceived for this particular pedestal, the joinings would be ill-fitting. Corroboration that the figures belong together comes from stylistic comparison contained in Section III.B; these comparisons strongly suggest that the central figure and the two side figures are a unit. Lastly, the pedestal and the statue show similar remains of earth deposits, indicating that they were buried at the same time. Thus, on the basis of all these factors it can be assumed that the four parts of the image are the genuine pieces belonging to the original composition.

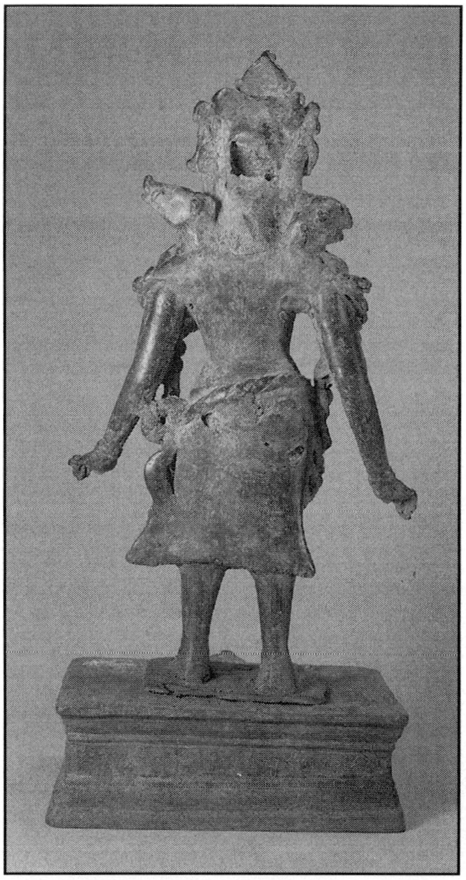

Fig. 9.6. Back view of Fig. 9.1.

B. Art Historical Analysis (DMS & LS)

The three separate figures stand on the same pedestal, showing Bhū Devī as she emerges from the pericarp of a flower (Fig. 9.1). The base measures 19 cm (w.) by 6.5 cm (ht.). 'Nārāyaṇa', the central figure, is 34 cm (ht.). To his right and left stand, respectively, Cakrapuruṣa (12.5 cm in ht.) and Gadādevī (11.5 cm in ht.); were the top of her *gadā* not broken off, the entire figure of the goddess would probably measure around 12.5 cm and fit securely underneath the palm of the central figure.

The iconography of the central deity conforms to the type as stated above (see Section I). The male deity stands authoritatively, with both feet equipoised on the thin platform whose posts insert into holes in the pedestal. His oval face looks youthful, having large, alert eyes under arched brows, a full mouth beneath a slight mustache, round cheeks and chin, a prominent, fleshy, nose and a distinct *ūrṇā* gracing the smooth forehead. From the front, the eyes are the god's most distinctive facial feature; they are heavy lidded yet sufficiently open to disclose the entire pupil as well as the concave iris. From the side, the nose, especially the way it juts out from a receding brow and chin, becomes the most distinctive feature (Fig. 9.8). A crown, tied around the god's locks, has a diamond-shaped crest decorated with knobs at each of the four points and in the center; the knobs are connected to each other and to the central one by raised radial and perimetral links. Profiles of the animal heads arise from 'Nārāyaṇa's strong, straight shoulders,

Fig. 9.7. Close-up of Fig. 9.1, showing a part of the base and feet of the central figure.

and extend up to the ornamented ears; the lion (*siṃha)* is on the right and the boar *(varāha)* is on the left. The deity's bare torso, swelling softly, is marked by a clearly etched *śrīvatsa* emblem and two simple necklaces, one close to the throat, the other looped below the *śrīvatsa.* Armlets with discs circle under the armpits. The god's waist is well defined but the navel is not. Neither is there emphasis on the musculature of the chest or the upper abdominal area. The deity is four-armed. A rather long *vanamālā,* composed of uncertain leafy buds or flowers, extends from the upper arms and reaches almost to the knees. From the front view of the image, it appears as if the natural and extra arms share the upper arm and bifurcate only at the elbows. The side view indicates that this is not quite the case since the upper arm already divides (but does not split) into two at the shoulder (Fig. 9.8). The natural right and left hands, adorned with plain double bangles at the wrists, bend up from the elbows and hold the lotus stalk and the conch, respectively. The extra hands spread downward to rest on the personified attributes. The right hand cups over the rim of the Cakrapuruṣa's wheel; the left palm would have rested on the *gadā* of the Devī, as indicated by the remains of the *gadā* in the palm of the god (slightly visible in Fig. 9.6). The god wears a *dhotī* gathered by a round pin below the waist; folds descend on his left thigh and in between the legs. Drapery folds are indicated by thinly incised double lines as well as raised, curved ridges at the hemline below the knees. A twisted sash circles the hips; ending in a large knot and streamer on the left, the sash helps to secure the *dhotī* (see Figs. 9.1 and 9.6).

Considering that the complete image is composed of three separate figures, each standing on a small platform that fits into the pedestal, it is reassuring to note that some of the same features of the central figure reappear in the ancillary, side figures. Cakrapuruṣa, standing with raised chin and arms folded across the chest, exhibits an equally short *dhotī* draped in much the same fashion as that of the central figure. Also similar are Cakrapuruṣa's full, fleshy features within the oval head. Gadādevī's facial features likewise conform to the general characteristics of the males. Her jewelry—the simple necklace, armlets and bangles—remind of those associated with the central figure. So too is her *dhotī* like his, being not only marked by the same type of drapery folds but also by the same evasive panel on each side at the hemline. These artistic considerations indicate that the three separate figures are likely to belong together. (An unattached, *c.* 10" ht. Bhū Devī in The Kronos Collection serves notice that it is theoretically possible for this type of an image to be composed of four separate figures).

Fig. 9.8. Side view of Fig. 9.1.

The pedestal has a rectangular shape. It is quite simple and plain, having two mouldings on the top and again at the bottom. The inscription runs along its middle portion which is framed by upper and lower thin bands intermittently decorated with double vertical lines. This order, neatly maintained on all four sides of the base, may be conditioned by the dedication, inscribed on all the four sides. The image, to the contrary, is to be viewed mainly from the front; the back has received a minimum of artistic attention and is left in rough condition (Fig. 9.6).

The style and iconography of the 'Nārāyaṇa' bronze is eclectic. It intermingles characteristics found over a very large area and over several centuries. Some of facial characteristics illustrate this intermingling; the full, rounded features, the heavy lidded, open eyes with the depressed iris, and the oval-shaped head are not unlike early terracotta faces, allegedly from the Gangetic area[78]. The way these features occur in early Gupta stone icons is faintly (perhaps fortuitously), evident in a recently published Mathurā relief of the 3rd/4th century AD (now housed in the Harn Museum of Art, University of Florida, Gainesville), depicting a three-headed 'Nārāyaṇa'[79] (Fig. 9.9). The mustache, absent on this Mathurā 'Nārāyaṇa' and on all Gupta Viṣṇu icons, is a Northwestern trait, and as such appears on our bronze. A similarly shaped mustache occurs on a head wearing a crown nearly identical to the one worn by 'Nārāyaṇa' (cf. Figs. 9.10–9.11). The shape and decoration of 'Nārāyaṇa's crown are uncommon; indeed I could find

Fig. 9.9. Para Vāsudeva-Nārāyaṇa. Late 3rd-early 4th century. Mathurā area. The Harn Museum of Art; University of Florida, Gainesville (S-82-1-UFG). Photograph by Dr Roy C. Craven, Jr.

no comparable example until Dr Martin Lerner (Curator, Asian Art; Metropolitan Museum of Art), alerted me to the head illustrated in Fig. 9.10; it is my pleasure to thank Dr Lerner for his assistance. The head, offered for sale in the 1988 Spinks' Catalogue, seems to be a metal mask. It has other similarities with the bronze

Fig. 9.10. Hollow mask. 5th century. Cast Bronze. 6" x 4". Provenance: Spink and Son Ltd. in 1988.

Fig. 9.11. Close-up of upper portion of Fig. 9.1.

'Nārāyaṇa'. Note the similarity in the shape and rendering of the eyes, the eyebrows, the nose, chin, *ūrṇā* as well as the flat necklace ornamented with indented knobs. The many idiosyncratic similarities between the bronze 'Nārāyaṇa' and the head from Spinks' convince me that the Spinks' head should also date to the 5th century and originate from an area near to the bronze 'Nārāyaṇa' (see Section IV)[80]. A Gangetic element seen on Gupta Viṣṇus[81] as well as our central figure, is the twisted sash, knotted generously on the left. Its source is to be found in the pre-Gupta art of Mathurā[82]. Also, the rendering of the four arms in our 'Nārāyaṇa' bronze reflects a trend underway in the art of Mathurā. In Mathurā art of the early Gupta period, the extra arms can bifurcate either at the shoulder, or at the elbow[83], or as the Florida 'Nārāyaṇa' shows, the arms can be divided (but not split) for a considerable length before bifurcating close to the wrists (Fig. 9.9). The divisions in arms of the Florida 'Nārāyaṇa' from Mathurā and our Northern 'Nārāyaṇa' may illustrate an early and a later tendency within the same trend. The pattern of the *śrīvatsa* symbol on 'Nārāyaṇa's chest resembles most closely the *śrīvatsa* engraved on a Gupta bone seal from Rajghat (Varanasi, U.P.); in both cases, the configuration consists of an arrow-like, central upright flanked by devices resembling an'S' and an inverted 'S' all of which rests on a double platform (Fig. 9.11)[84]. The Rajghat seal does not exhibit the earliest *vaiṣṇava śrīvatsa* in the Gangetic area. The symbol with a slightly different shape can be

Fig. 9.12. Para Vāsudeva-Nārāyaṇa. Beginning of the 7th century. Swat, Pakistan. Photo copyright: National Museums Berlin, Prussian Cultural Foundation, Asian Art Museum, Art Collection South-, Southeast-, and Central Asian Art.

found on a Vaiṣṇava Kuṣāṇa relief from Mathurā, and in Gupta Vaiṣṇava contexts predating the 427 AD bronze 'Nārāyaṇa'[85]. Accordingly, both the style and usage of the *śrīvatsa* on the 'Nārāyaṇa' bronze, where it seems to be the earliest Northern appearance of this symbol, is due to the Gangetic influences. Influence from the Gangetic Valley, specifically Mathurā, is again reflected in the way the conch is held. A late Kuṣāṇa Mathurā sandstone relief of four-armed Vasudevā-Kṛṣṇa, now in the Museum für Indische Kunst, Berlin (No. I 5878), is a rare early example still having intact the natural left hand holding the conch[86]. The fingers of the left hand wrap around the conch and enter into the opening of the shell. This is the way the conch is held in our 'Nārāyaṇa' bronze, as well as in a series of post-Gandhāran stone sculptures of four-armed Vāsudeva-Kṛṣṇa, two of which can be assigned provenances. One comes from the Dharmarājikā compound, Taxila, and the other from Bijbehāra, Kashmir[87]; Paul dates both sculptures to the 6th century AD. Early Vaiṣṇava images from the Northwest need not, however, hold the conch in this manner. A case in point is the famous 7th century Berlin three-headed, four-armed Vaiṣṇava image, which can now be called an image of 'Nārāyaṇa' (Fig. 9.12)[88]. Though the Berlin image shares essential iconographic similarities with our 'Nārāyaṇa' bronze, it also shows numerous variations, one of which is the conch, cradled in a somewhat different manner. Also the Berlin 'Nārāyaṇa' is brass, made mainly of a copper and zinc alloy[89], not copper and tin. Turning next to Cakrapuruṣa on our 'Nārāyaṇa' bronze, it is seen that some of his iconographic traits also pertain to the Gangetic region. First, there is his unusual position to the right of the main figure. It is customary, in post-Gandhāran and Gupta representations for Cakrapuruṣa to stand to the left[90]. However, a Gupta terracotta of a seated three-headed 'Nārāyaṇa' from Mathurā shows Cakrapuruṣa to the right of the god[91]. And the Florida 'Nārāyaṇa' from Mathurā dating *c.* 3rd–4th century AD (Fig. 9.9) has the non-personified *cakra* to his right. Thus when this positioning occurs in the Northwest, as it does in our bronze and in a British Museum image of Vāsudeva-Kṛṣṇa[92], we may be fairly certain that its occurrence is under the influence of Gupta India, specifically Mathurā. Cakrapuruṣa's stance with folded arms equally reflects artistic influence from the southern regions. A quick comparison between Northern and Gangetic representations of the godling reveals that the pose seen on our bronze can at present be located in the 5th century art around Mathurā and Allahabad, and at the 6th century temple of Deogarh[93]. The poised and peaceful mien of these Cakrapuruṣas contrast markedly with the agitated posture, open gestures and lively expression seen on the 7th century Cakrapuruṣa appearing in the Berlin 'Nārāyaṇa', possibly from Swat (Fig. 9.12). But that is not to say that our 'Nārāyaṇa' bronze is devoid of characteristics from the Northwest. Not at all. Compare, for example, the figure of Gadādevī to two small bronzes of females likely to come from Bannu (NWFP, Pakistan) and probably dating *c.* 100 AD[94]. Their overall resemblance rests on a similar concept of femaleness, expressed in the posture, the pose of the right arm, the ornaments, the sash suspended on the left hip and the flaring hem (whose folds are indicated by double parallel horizontal lines). So too, the presence of Bhū Devī seems to be a Northwestern convention as she does not appear in the early 'Nārāyaṇa' images from Mathurā[95]. Again, the Berlin 'Nārāyaṇa' is the closest parallel to our 'Nārāyaṇa'. Both show Bhū Devī coming out of the pericarp of the flower[96]. But here the comparison stops. Whereas the Bhū Devī on our bronze appears on the front of the pedestal with arms lifted upward as if to support the ground underneath the deities, the 7th century Berlin Bhū Devī is winged and appears between the legs of the central figure; with her arms lowered, she seems to balance (or raise) herself. Although the Berlin brass image offers the only early Northwestern example of Bhū Devī in an identical context, the partial form of the Earth Goddess can be noticed between the legs of the sculpture of Vāsudeva-Kṛṣṇa housed in The British Museum[97]. Precedence for an emerging Earth Goddess located on the platform underneath a deity can be found in Gandhāran art. In a Gandhāran relief depicting the Buddha's conquest over Māra, the upper body of the Earth Goddess is carved in the middle of the pedestal upon which the Buddha sits[98]. Another Northwestern innovation may be the introduction of the lotus in

Fig. 9.13. Gajendra Viṣṇu, 6th century. Darel, Pakistan. Eilenberg Collection, Metropolitan Museum of Art.

the right hand of the central figure, although this point is difficult to prove conclusively. The difficulty lies in the fact that none of the Gupta 'Nārāyaṇa' reliefs from Mathurā still have the natural right hand intact. Kuṣāṇa reliefs of Vāsudeva-Kṛṣṇa, including the late Kuṣāṇa reliefs[99], do not features the *padma,* nor apparently do the Gupta Viṣṇu images from north central India[100]. The situation is different in the Northwest although not diagnostically different. The Berlin 'Nārāyaṇa' holds a lotus in his natural right hand; however the flower's depiction differs from that of our 'Nārāyaṇa' bronze since the lotus is held much higher, has a longer stem, and a raised seed-pod. Other early Vaiṣṇava images both from the Northwest and Kashmir also show the lotus carried in the natural right hand of the god; however, even though the stalk can be shorter than that of the Berlin flower, they all seem to feature the raised seed-pod[101]. All these examples, it must be quickly underscored, are one to two hundred years later than the 'Nārāyaṇa' bronze. For the present, the 'Nārāyaṇa' bronze of 427 AD has the distinction of being the earliest Vaiṣṇava image to display the *padma.*

These comparisons suggest a trend. Although our bronze may share some of the distinctive innovations of both the Northwest and the Gangetic Valley, its style and iconography are more an intermingling of the two regions than the predominant expression of one. The image also does not reveal the aesthetic subtleties associated with sculptures from either of the regions. The crispness and the naturalism of Gandhāra stone carvings or the graceful litheness of Gupta stone carvings cannot be discerned.

Post-Gandhāra bronzes, especially from Swat, do not have much more in common with the 'Nārāyaṇa' bronze than Gandhāran stone carvings. A group of 20 Buddhist bronzes were recently attributed to Swat on the basis of technical studies and art historical criteria. It is important to note that the point of departure of the technical studies is the use of 'art historically defined groups of plausible attribution'[102]. The results of the studies indicated that Swati bronzes produced between the 5th and 7th century have a couple of technical features in common with the 'Nārāyaṇa' bronze, namely a high tin content and probably the hole in the back. However these early Swati examples (Reedy's Figs. 9 and 13; 10 and 6) use inlay and exhibit physiognomic traits, pedestals and ornamentation unlike those associated with the 'Nārāyaṇa' bronze. Focus on the two earliest Swati bronzes from this study clarifies the issues. Reedy's Fig. 9 is the oldest, dated to the 5th century[103]. The small bronze (ht. 7.5 cm.) depicts Śākyamuni Buddha seated on a very constricted base on top of a simple lotus. The features in his oval face appear much effaced, although it is possible to discern the narrow eyes[104], the copper inlay in the lips and the silver inlay in the eyes. The Buddha's shoulders droop and the general proportions of this seated figure do not appear unusual (e.g. the head is not too big for the body). Reedy's Fig. 13 of a seated Vairocana is dated to the 5th–6th century on the basis of carbon-14 testing[105]. The god's face is broad, the eyes are narrow, the mouth is small and thin. Silver is used to inlay the eyes and copper for the lips. The god's shoulders are straight; the waist is small. The impression that the head is too large for the body is created by the high, elaborate crown displaying the five Buddhas. Vairocana's other ornaments—the pearl necklace, floral earrings and armlets—are in keeping with his gorgeous headgear. He sits on a tasseled cushion placed on the backs of a row of lions which rest atop a double lotus throne. Clearly, neither these Buddhist bronzes nor the Northwest Vaiṣṇava images discussed thus far offer persuasive evidence for selecting the Gandhāran-Swat heartland as the provenance of the 'Nārāyaṇa' bronze.

Kashmir is another unlikely provenance. Now that at least two 6th century Kashmiri images of four-armed Vāsudeva-Kṛṣṇa can be used for comparative purposes[106], it is possible to exclude Kashmir on art historical grounds, in addition to the foregoing paleographic and technical criteria.

But the pedestal of our 'Nārāyaṇa' image opens up new geographic spheres. It is remarkably similar to a series of bronze bases dating between the 4th–7th century AD and found over a vast territory, stretching from Gandhāra eastward and southward to lands below the Vindhya Mountains in central India. The earliest, to date, is a late Gandhāra Buddhist reliquary; dated to *c.* the 4th century AD. It features a decorated *stūpa,* with a circular drum, resting upon a small pedestal which, in turn, is stacked upon a larger pedestal[107]. The bronze, cast in several pieces, was allegedly discovered in the Swat Valley. Both pedestals of the reliquary already exemplify the distinctively simple design that characterizes the series: a rectangular shape, framed, on all sides, by a few, plain mouldings that leave a wide central space bare (or inscribed). The pedestal supporting the bronze Buddha found at Dhanesar Khera (U.P.) and dated *c.* 400 AD is virtually identical to ours, except that it is raised on four lion claws. Whether this piece, in the collection of the Nelson-Atkins Museum of Art (No. 44–13), ought to be assigned to the northwest or to central India had been unclear[108] until the comparatively recent find of another 5th century bronze Buddha from Ramtek in Vidarbha (Nagpur district, Maharashtra)[109]. Stylistically the Ramtek Buddha, including the pedestal (devoid of the lion claws), is very similar to the image from Dhanesar Khera. From Phophnar, a village on the border of Madhya Pradesh and Maharashtra, were found other 5th century Buddhist bronzes, some of which rest on pedestals with the same characteristic order noted above[110]. For our purposes, the pedestals of these central Indian Buddhist bronzes made during the height of Gupta-Vākāṭaka artistic traditions, together with the Late Gandhāran pedestals illustrate the extensive terrain wherein this sort of pedestal was popular already by the 5th century. A post-Gandhāran bronze of the Buddha, allegedly from Sahri Bahlol and dated between the 5th–7th century, shows a slight variation of the same type of pedestal[111]. The wide central section between the mouldings, has oblique rather than vertical edges. The tendency for oblique contours is found on the bronze pedestal of the 5th–6th century Buddha in the Norton Simon

Collection[112], and on the 7th century Berlin 'Nārāyaṇa' image. As such the shape of these 5th/6th and 7th century pedestals vary slightly from our 'Nārāyaṇa' pedestal. But it must straightaway be acknowledged that the Berlin pedestal also shows a significant similarity to our pedestal; it shows the same double vertical lines intermittently decorating the thin band (Fig. 9.12; see the lower band). Another variant of this pedestal comes from Kashmir. The inscribed pedestal is underneath a seated bronze Buddha whose late 6th century date has recently been proposed by Fussman on the basis of paleographic and linguistic arguments[113]. It is interesting to observe with Fussman that this sort of simple, rectilinear pedestal is similar to those found under seated Buddhas on the petroglyphs at Chilas I, assigned to the same date[114]. It may be added that simple, rectilinear bases also occur under *stūpas* at Chilas I where they are stacked as they diminish in size[115]. As such, they show some similarity to the above mentioned Late Gandhāra reliquary, featuring a small *stūpa* raised on two stacked pedestals. In short, the pedestal of our 'Nārāyaṇa' bronze though simple in design, yields two major insights. First, it confirms the paleographic analysis: on balance, our bronze could well date to the early 5th century AD. Secondly, it opens up the possibility that the provenance for the piece could be north or east of Swat and Taxila, that is in some region closer to the cultural and artistic zone of Chilas/ Kashmir. This is indeed a welcome possibility as it is becoming progressively clear that the aggregate of technical, artistic, and paleographic characteristics of this image do not quite gel around either a Gandhāran, Kashmiri, or a Gangetic attribution.

IV. OTHER NORTHERN REGIONS WITH EARLY VAIṢṆAVA IMAGERY (DMS)

CHILAS

Chilas itself contains very early Vaiṣṇava imagery. On the western face of a rock at Chilas II, there are engravings of two male figures and an inscription naming them as 'Rama[kri]ṣā', that is, Balarāma and Kṛṣṇa. The attributes and positioning of the two figures leave little doubt that they represent Saṃkarṣaṇa/Balarāma and Vāsudeva-Kṛṣṇa. The shorter figure holds the wheel and club; this is Vāsudeva-Kṛṣṇa and he stands to the left of Saṃkarṣaṇa/Balarāma who is taller and holds the club and plough. These petroglyphs, dated to the first half of the first century AD on the basis of the paleography of the inscription[116], are not depictions of the first and second *vyūha*. The *vyūha* doctrine emphasizes the theological pre-eminence of Vāsudeva. At Chilas II, however, Vāsudeva-Kṛṣṇa cedes eminence to Saṃkarṣaṇa/Balarāma in both height and position. Nor do the engravings represent Balarāma and Kṛṣṇa as *avatāras*. In the several centuries around the Christian era, very few *avatāras* are depicted in the subcontinent; the few that are depicted all have four arms. None of these can, with certainty, be identified as Vāsudeva-Kṛṣṇa and Saṃkarṣaṇa/Balarāma. The portrayals at Chilas II are typical, however, for the way the two gods appear as objects of worship in a hero-cult. The cult centers on devotion to Vāsudeva-Kṛṣṇa, his elder brother, Saṃkarṣaṇa/Balarāma and other personages in their lineage, the Vṛṣṇi lineage. The worship of the Vṛṣṇi Vīras (i.e. heroes), originating, no doubt in Mathurā, gives evidence of the initial exaltation of Vāsudeva whose apotheosis culminates in the sects of the Bhāgavatas and the Pāñcarātrins. Paradoxically, for the historian wishing to trace the ascendancy of Vāsudeva, his earliest unambiguous representations as one of the deified Vṛṣṇi Vīras are, for the present, found not in Mathurā, but in the North[117]. In the mid 1st century AD, worship of Vāsudeva was established in the Upper Indus, having penetrated into the Northwest several centuries earlier[118] and attained a permanent foothold there. Thus when searching for the likely provenance of the 'Nārāyaṇa' bronze, it is to the Vaiṣṇava legacy in regions North, West, and South of the Chilas/Kashmir zone and the Vaiṣṇava images produced there between the 5th and 7th century AD, that one must look.

Darel

Above Chilas, but in the same district, lies Darel wherefrom is said to come a Vaiṣṇava stone relief of four-armed Viṣṇu as liberator of Gajendra, lord of elephants (Fig. 9.13). Its *c.* 6th century date is proposed on the basis of its similarity to a group of Vaiṣṇava potstone sculptures analyzed by Paul and assigned to that date[119]. As such, the Darel Viṣṇu, wearing a *vanamālā* composed of stacked rectangles, holds the conch in his lower left hand in precisely the same manner as the 6th century images of Vāsudeva-Kṛṣṇa from Dharmarājikā and The British Museum. Further, his upper left hand carries a round shield edged in much the same way as the circular rims of the haloes surrounding these two images. Viṣṇu's large hoop earrings, his broad shoulders, inflated chest, muscular upper arms and comparatively slender legs compare favorable with these two images and others related, by Paul, to the series. However, these features cannot be found in our 'Nārāyaṇa' bronze. 'Nārāyaṇa' looks almost childlike in comparison to the Darel Viṣṇu and the Dharmarājikā and The British Museum images of Vāsudeva-Kṛṣṇa. The childlike quality resides not only in the undeveloped musculature; it mainly resides in the proportions of the central figure. The face is somewhat too large for the body and the upper torso is somewhat more elongated than the lower limbs. The degree to which this is a stylistic rather than a conceptual phenomenon can be quickly demonstrated. From the Dharmarājikā compound in Taxila comes a potstone representation of the youthful Skanda/Kārttikeya, executed in a manner very similar to the Vāsudeva-Kṛṣṇa image from the Dharmarājikā; the style and proportions of Skanda/Kārttikeya have not been altered to convey youthfulness[120]. In other words, when there is a need to depict a divine youth, it can be done in the Northwest by way of iconography and not

Fig. 9.14. Vaiṣṇava image. 6th century. Possibly Taxila region. J. Sherrier Collection.

necessarily via a stylistic shift in bodily proportions.

Taxila Region

A three-headed god, executed in a style associated with a series of c. 6th century Vaiṣṇava images found in the region of Taxila-Gandhāra, as well as Kashmir, is published here for the first time (Fig. 9.14). The steatite fragment (4" ht.; 3 1/4" w.), is in the Collection of J. Sherrier. The fragment may represent a Gandhāra 'Nārāyaṇa' image. The tricephalic head of the Sherrier fragment has one unusual variation. The National Museum in New Delhi has another example reputedly from Kashmir, but I have not seen the piece. (See *JASB*, XVIII, 1951–53, pp. 251–53, pl. III). The lateral heads are of the same animal, the lion. The significance of this iconographic anomaly is unclear. The piece allegedly originates from Charsada, but the central human head looks like the Vāsudeva-Kṛṣṇa head from the Dharmarājikā and the one from The British Museum. The Sherrier piece also features a detail in the headdress of the lateral animals seen on another sculpture from the Dharmarājikā, namely the Skanda/Kārttikeya. The device looks like a crescent with a center rod inside; in all the cases, the device is located in the front and center of the headdress.

The Sherrier 'Nārāyaṇa' (if this is the correct identification) is cited here to show that, in the 6th century, Brahmanical images, especially *vaiṣṇava* images, are not as rare in Northern regions outside of Kashmir as is sometimes supposed (on this point, also see below)[121]. Moreover, Northern 'Nārāyaṇa' images may also not be so unusual, for when the Sherrier 'Nārāyaṇa' is added to our inscribed 'Nārāyaṇa' bronze, the Berlin 'Nārāyaṇa', and (probably) a polycephalic terracotta first published in 1898[122], the total number of 'Nārāyaṇa' images from the North, thus far described, comes to four. That number will augment when the evidence from Kangra, Kulu and Chamba is counted. The Sherrier 'Nārāyaṇa' is not cited to reopen the possibility of a Taxila-Gandhāran provenance for our inscribed 'Nārāyaṇa' bronze. The Sherrier 'Nārāyaṇa' and the inscribed bronze 'Nārāyaṇa' exhibit no similarities in the shape of the faces, the facial features, ornamentation—including crown, necklaces, earrings,—the modelling of the chests, nor even in the employment of specific *vaiṣṇava* symbols: the *kaustubha* is found on the Sherrier

'Nārāyaṇa' (Fig. 9.14) and the *śrīvatsa* is on Fig. 9.1.

It can straightaway be reiterated that the 'Nārāyaṇa' bronze is not at home in the Taxila-Gandhāra region.

Bannu District

The region to the west of Chilas/ Kashmir can also be excluded as the home of our 'Nārāyaṇa' bronze. A rather spectacular Varāha, carved on a 92 cm limestone stele, has recently come to light in Lakki Tehsil, Bannu District, NWFP, Pakistan. This is an area not known for Gandhāran sculpture. The relief has been quite thoroughly described and convincingly dated to the mid-4th-early 5th century by Farid Khan[123]. There is no need to repeat his details here other than to remark that the figure combines influences from Sassanian art, local traditions, and Gupta art growing out of Kuṣāṇa iconographic and stylistic innovations conceived, most notably, at Mathurā. This combination of artistic influences does not characterize the 'Nārāyaṇa' bronze. The 'Nārāyaṇa' bronze does, of course, reflect a combination of influences, but the Sassanian factor is absent. So too, is a Parthian factor absent. Accordingly, it is unlikely that the bronze originates from a region bordering on, or influenced by, western Asia.

Fig. 9.15. Para Vāsudeva-Nārāyaṇa. *c.* 2nd half of the 7th century. Masrur, Himachal Pradesh. Photograph by Mme Hélène Diserens.

The remaining Northern region producing Hindu art between the 5th and 7th century AD is below Kashmir, in what is now called Himachal Pradesh. Three main areas of artistic activity are Kangra, Kulu and Chamba and it is to these that we must now turn.

Kangra

Among the Hindu deities carved on the rock cut temples at Masrur, Kangra, it is possible to identify a figure somewhat similar to the bronze 'Nārāyaṇa' (Fig. 9.15)[124]. The sandstone temples have greatly deteriorated and details on the sculpture are not easily discernible. Nonetheless, the type we are tracing can be spotted effortlessly in a niche on the eastern side of the central, principle temple. This is, states Mme Diserens, the oldest part of the temple complex, and could not be earlier than the mid-or second half of the 7th century AD; the entire complex took a very long time to excavate[125]. The tricephalic Masrur 'Nārāyaṇa' has the lion face to the right and the boar face to the left. Two of his four arms can be seen without difficulty, they are lowered and reach out to touch the upper part of Gadādevī's *gadā,* on his right, and the top of Cakrapuruṣa on his left. The similarity between this figure and the bronze 'Nārāyaṇa' is limited to the general configuration of the body. The waist of the Masrur figure is defined, the hips are noticeably round, the body tends towards squatness, the legs spread slightly as do the lower arms; the outline thereby created is not unlike that of the bronze. However, it cannot be said that the Masrur head is disproportionately larger than the body, as is the case with the bronze figure. A dating for this temple complex has been proposed on the basis of style alone; there is no inscription associated with the site. The post-Gupta stylistic traits of the sculptures and some of the architectural ornamentations have been noticed by Hargreaves[126], and Ohri, who also points out that lingering Gandhāran influence combined with local traits[127]. Hargreaves, writing in 1915, placed the temple in the 8th century which is also Ohri's date. Vincent Smith who saw photographs of Masrur made in 1913 put the date at the 7th century, which is where I, too, would date the Masrur 'Nārāyaṇa'. The stance of 'Nārāyaṇa's body (though not its general configuration), the remaining traces of the god's *dhotī* and *vanamālā* together with the stance of his attendants can be compared to a 7th century Viṣṇu image from Bijbehāra now in the Sri Pratap Singh Museum, Srinagar[128]. Local tradition assigns the excavation of the Masrur shrines to the Pāṇḍavas who are said to have executed the work during a night of six months' duration occurring at the time they were exiled in the forest[129]. This legend is of interest in the present context because the inscription on the 427 AD. 'Nārāyaṇa' bronze mentions that the image was installed at Bhīmāsthāna (the holy place of Bhīma). Bhīma is one of the Pāṇḍavas. Bhīma is associated with a sacred spot in Kangra. Remains of a fairly large *stūpa,* known as Bhīma-ṭīlā exists near the village of Chaitru[130 & 130a(*)]. It is not uncommon in the hills for old monuments to be linked with the Pāṇḍavas[131]. For example, a large number of temples in Hatkoti, situated in southeastern Himachal Pradesh are attributed to the Pāṇḍavas. Singh illustrates a stone sculpture of the figure of Bhīma from a Pāṇḍava Temple in Rohru Valley, just North of Hatkoti[132]. I am not aware that other Northern regions outside of present-day Himachal Pradesh put similar emphasis on Bhīma.[132a(*)]

Kulu

Quite a number of the earliest *vaiṣṇava* sculptures surviving from Bajaura, Nirmand and neighboring regions in Kulu, have things in common with the

'Nārāyaṇa' bronze. The earliest *vaiṣṇava* image, a four-armed, life-size sculpture of Vāsudeva-Kṛṣṇa from Nirmand, is now in the State Museum, Simla (Fig. 9.16). Ohri, calling it a 'Viṣṇu' image, describes it as free standing and having a flat back. The god's stance is frontal with the weight equally distributed so that there are no bends in the body. The extra hands of the god are placed over his attributes, the wheel on the right and the *gadā* to the left. Noting the broad, inflated chest and the belly's gentle protuberance, especially as it bulges due to the constriction of the tight lower garment, Ohri rightly associates the style with the vigorous images produced in the Gangetic Valley during the 1st–2nd century AD. However, not all of the sculpture's features stem from north India; notable in this respect are the crown, the treatment of the hair and the ornamentation. Ohri opines that the sculpture was produced locally because the stone used is only available there and not in the lower hills or the plains; he dates the image to the 6th century[133]. To one familiar with imagery of Vāsudeva-Kṛṣṇa in the Gangetic area, this image resembles the equally large statue of Vāsudeva-Kṛṣṇa in Gayā District which reflects stylistic developments of the late Kuṣāṇa-early Gupta period in Mathurā (Fig. 9.17)[134]. Similarities between the two sculptures focus on their size, stance, degree of modelling of the bodies, the shape of the faces, the simple ornamentations, the manner of holding the conch and, in each instance, the portrayal of the *dhotī;* the tendency towards squatness and compacteness in the Nirmand statue is more of a local trait (cf. Figs. 9.16–9.17). The Nirmand Vāsudeva-Kṛṣṇa certainly exhibits an interplay of local and Gangetic characteristics. It may be that influence from the Gangetic plains to Nirmand traveled faster than Ohri's dating would suppose. Direct routes connected the two regions and helped spread the stylistic achievements of Uttar Pradesh deep inside areas of the western Himalayas[135]. The Vāsudeva-Kṛṣṇa of Nirmand looks as if it could date between the 4th–6th century AD.

Fig. 9.16. Vāsudeva-Kṛṣṇa from Nirmand. *c.* 4th–6th century. State Museum, Simla. Photograph by Mme Hélène Diserens.

Also from Nirmand is a second sculpture of Vāsudeva-Kṛṣṇa that shows new elements mixed with those of the earlier image seen in Fig. 9.16. Ohri, who describes it sufficiently, dates it to the 7th–8th century[136]; I would not go as high as the 8th century. The feature of greatest interest in the present context is that

Fig. 9.17. Vāsudeva-Kṛṣṇa of the Gayā Trio. Late Kuṣāṇa-Early Gupta Period. Gayā District. Patna Museum (No. 11299). Photograph Patna Museum.

the weapons, personified here, are arranged, just as in the previous Nirmand image: Cakrapuruṣa is on the right and Gadādevī is on the left of the deity. A third human size image of Vāsudeva-Kṛṣṇa from Nirmand, perhaps belonging to the early 8th century, also depicts the personified weapons in these positions[137]. Evidently, this arrangement, seen in the Nirmand images and in the inscribed 'Nārāyaṇa' bronze, is unusual in most places but not so in Kulu. Moreover, this arrangement can be documented in the art of Kulu at about the same time, or a little later than it occurs in the art of Mathurā (cf. Figs. 9.16 and 9.9). Parenthetically, a 6th century architectural fragment of Govardhana Kṛṣṇa also comes from Nirmand; evidently this site sustained a community of *bhaktas* to Vāsudeva during the Gupta and post-Gupta periods[138].

In the village of Nirath, a few kilometers from Nirmand, exists a 13th century temple to Sūrya-Nārāyaṇa which, according to Ohri, must have been built in the place of an older temple, since the 13th century temple incorporates sculptures of a period 'about five centuries earlier'[139]. One of the older sculptures depicts what we may now call the 'Nārāyaṇa' type of figure[140].

The stone Viśvarūpa from Bajaura, *c.* 7th century[141], has some iconographic similarities in common with the type exemplified by the 5th century inscribed 'Nārāyaṇa' bronze. The similarities have caused Mallmann to believe Viṣṇu Viśvarūpa is a syncretic aspect of the Caturvyūha forms of Para Vāsudeva. A discussion of what that may mean in terms of the theological connections between Viśvarūpa, the Caturvyūha forms of Para Vāsudeva and Nārāyaṇa, will be explained in Sections V and VI. For now, it is the iconographic connections that are of interest. The iconographic core of the Bajaura Viśvarūpa, it will be noticed, is based on the type called 'Nārāyaṇa' throughout this paper. The core reduces to a four-armed human figure with lateral heads of the lion and boar to the right and left. Traces of Gadādevī and Cakrapuruṣa remain on the pedestal of the Bajaura Viśvarūpa. One noteworthy detail is the presence of a horse's head over the crown worn by the human head. But a complete description of this famous and oft-described stele is not necessary[142], as only those details relating to the provenance of the 'Nārāyaṇa' are being pursued. In this connection, two details can be mentioned. First, the lotus is held by Viśvarūpa in a way that is similar to the way 'Nārāyaṇa' of the bronze holds the flower. Second, the head of the boar on Viśvarūpa's left side is raised at an angle similar to the boar on 'Nārāyaṇa's' left. The raised position of the head of the boar is likely to be another item influenced by the art of Mathurā, where this position is noticed in the Florida 'Nārāyaṇa' of the late 3rd-early 4th century (Fig. 9.9), in the (early?) 5th century 'Nārāyaṇa' in the Boston Museum of Fine Art, and in the Viśvarūpa from Bhankari, Mathurā[143].

This paragraph is no longer relevant here.[143a(*)] [Bhīma is well known in Kulu Valley; a Kulu Rākṣasī, Hirimbā/Hiḍimbā fell in love with Bhīma. Their love story and mating all over the Himalayan region, including the shores of the legendary Lake Mānasa in Kashmir, is told in the Ādi Parva of the *Mahābhārata*[144]. Although she is infrequently met with in other parts of the subcontinent, Hiḍimbā seems to have entered the Hindu pantheon; a temple in Kulu was constructed for her habitation and worship. In Kulu Valley more than the epic legend are associated with Hiḍimbā and Bhīma[145]. She and Bhīma appear to be connected with the preservation of the Kulu royal line; from an inscription and local legends, Pott has proposed that a royal marriage took place in the 16th century wherein the groom and bride personify the epic lovers to ensure analogous progeny[146]. A Chamba *rāja* took on the role of Bhīma, the only surviving princess of Kulu that of Hiḍimbā, and their union was sanctioned to ensure the continuance of the Kulu Badānī dynasty. For our purposes it is important to note that a medieval analogy to an epic legend could not have been enacted had not the epic hero and Hiḍimbā been raised to some sort of cult status during the intervening centuries.]

In sum, a concentration of elements similar to the bronze 'Nārāyaṇa' comes from Kangra and Kulu. To summarize them, two other pre-Kashmiri 'Nārāyaṇa' images; images that likewise reflect an intermingling of lingering Gandhāran and Gangetic influences upon a local product; a preference for a squat bodily type; the repeated occurrence of Cakrapuruṣa to the right of 'Nārāyaṇa'.

Chamba

Chamba adds to the list of similarities coming from Himachal Pradesh. Indeed, Chamba clinches the argument favoring Himachal Pradesh as the likely source for the 427 AD 'Nārāyaṇa'. It will be shown that Chamba has strong links to the worship of Nārāyaṇa. Further, its early phase of Hindu art, fashioned during the Gupta and post-Gupta periods, shows a similar intermingling of late Kuṣāṇa (both from Mathurā and Gandhāra) and later Gupta characteristics as does the 'Nārāyaṇa' bronze. The physiognomy of Chamba imagery is close to the facial characteristics of the bronze 'Nārāyaṇa'. Lastly, one term used in the inscription of the 'Nārāyaṇa' bronze arguably implicates the general region of Himachal Pradesh.

The oldest antiquities from Chamba date around the 6th century; they include the platform of a brick temple (in the Bhuri Singh Museum) and the Sūrya image

Fig. 9.18. Skanda/Kārttikeya. *c.* 5th–6th century. *In situ* in the Śakti Devī Temple. Chhatrarhi, Chamba. See pl. 4.2 in V.C. Ohri, *Sculpture of the Western Himalayas*, Delhi 1991.

Fig. 9.19. Para Vāsudeva-Nārāyaṇa. Early 8th century. *In situ* at the Śakti Devī temple, Chhatrarhi, Chamba, Himachal Pradesh. Photograph by Mme Hélène Diserens.

from Gum[147]. This image, variously dated between the 6th–7th century[148], is a good example of the intermingling of styles and iconography in the early art of Chamba. Sūrya's dress is at home in the northern regions; his close trimmed beard is also peculiar to the Northwest, according to Ohri[149]. Yet the style of the sculpture is in the Gupta idiom, and the manner in which Sūrya squats within his horse-drawn chariot is a convention already well-established in Mathurā art of the Kuṣāṇa period[150]. The significance of Sūrya's squat, or *bhadrāsana* pose, can be determined from the context of a Mathurā relief depicting the life of the Buddha; here it symbolized lineage, specifically the Sūryavaṃśa or Solar lineage[151]. The stone sculpture of Skanda-Kārttikeya (Fig. 9.18), which may be even earlier (i.e. 5th–6th century), has the same short legs and somewhat too large head as seen in the 'Nārāyaṇa' bronze. The Skanda-Kārttikeya image is still under worship at the Śaktī Devī temple at Chhatrarhi, Chamba, where presumably it was made. Some of Skanda/Kārttikeya's facial features also tally with those of the bronze 'Nārāyaṇa'. Both have a short brow, but large almond shaped eyes set in heavy, pronounced upper and lower lids; also both have full lips and a well-developed

Fig. 9.20. Śiva mask. Uncertain date. Chamba, Himachal Pradesh. Philadelphia Museum of Art: Gift of the Friends of the Philadelphia Museum of Art (No. 1980–99–1).

Fig. 9.21. Left profile of Fig. 9.20.

chin that is small. Still *in situ*, at the same temple, is a wooden relief of 'Nārāyaṇa' showing essentially the same physiognomy, though the carving is several centuries later (Fig. 9.19)[152]. The central human head of 'Nārāyaṇa' does not accentuate the lower eyelid as much, but the head has the same strong, fleshy nose and round, youthful cheeks as does the bronze 'Nārāyaṇa'. In addition, it is interesting to note that his mace presents a ribbed profile not unlike the mace held aloft by Vāsudeva-Kṛṣṇa from Gayā District (Fig. 9.17). Similar facial features are found on two more pieces, allegedly from Chamba. The first is a bronze 'mask' *(mohra)*, possibly of Śiva. It is in the collection of M. Postel who describes the mustached face as follows: 'The face is [...] with heavy cheeks, a thick protruding underlip, a well-defined chin, almond-shaped eyes with upper eyelids projecting from the soft, rounded eyebrows[153]. This description contains features seen in the bronze 'Nārāyaṇa'. Postel dates the bronze mask to *c.* the 6th century and assigns it to eastern Himachal Pradesh. The last related facial type is a brass *mohra* of Śiva

(Fig. 9.20) whose countenance displays the same raw dynamism as the bronze 'Nārāyaṇa' (cf. Figs. 9.20, 9.11). The vitality of Śiva's face, as well as its anatomical similarity to 'Nārāyaṇa' is best captured by the words of Stella Kramrisch: 'The young, round, firm face—with its full, detailed lips; strong, sensitive nose; and wide-open, commanding, demanding eyes [...] gazes [...] far beyond the world that the nose scents and the mouth relishes'[154]. To best appreciate the likeness of these two faces is to see them both in profile (cf. Fig. 9.21 with Fig. 9.8). Then the same expression arising from the same physiognomy is seen in sharp relief. I am inclined to think that the sort of visage seen on the several pieces from Himachal Pradesh is due to a local physical type. One need only look at the devotee, photographed sitting at the feet of the 7th century icon of Śakti Devī kept in her Temple at Chhatrarhi, to see a face that is similar to that of Śakti Devī herself, as well as the 427 AD 'Nārāyaṇa', and in some respects to the Śiva *mohra*[155]. The Śiva *mohra* is dated by von Schroeder to 450–550 AD and assigned to Chamba[156]. Kramrisch revised her dating several times; her first dating was *c.* 450 to 550, then she placed it into the '6th–8th century(?) and Chamba(?)'[157], but in 1990 she assigned it to *c.* 800–900[158]. Postel et al. consign the Śiva mask to the 9th century and to the Middle Sutlej[159].

Literary evidence may also help to situate the 'Nārāyaṇa' bronze into what is now Himachal Pradesh. The inscription on the 'Nārāyaṇa' bronze states that the image was installed at Bhīmāsthāna. A *tīrtha* called Bhīmāsthāna is mentioned in *Mahābhārata* 3.80.100 *(bhīmāyāḥ; sthānam)*; the name occurs in a description about making a pilgrimage of sacred sites. By noting the sites mentioned before and after the (Holy) Place-of-Bhīma[160] in this account, it is possible to gain a rough approximation of the location of this *tīrtha.* Here is the sequence of sites immediately surrounding Bhīmāsthāna (3.80.99–105): Pañcanada, Bhīmāsthāna, Girimuñja (cited as Girikuñja in several mss.), Vimala, Maladā. Pañcanada is the region of the five rivers, namely the Punjab[161]. Girimuñja cannot be geographically located[162]. Both Vimala and Maladā are *tīrthas* in Kashmir[163]. The general direction, therefore, of this segment of the tour seems to be from the Punjab, northeasterly, to Kashmir. This direction could well cut through a part of Himachal Pradesh. As a result, Bhīmāsthāna could lie either in the Punjab, or someplace between the Punjab and Kashmir, such as Himachal Pradesh. Kashmir is also a possible choice for the location of Bhīmāsthāna. From among these choices, the bronze itself favors some areas over others: 1) The script of the 'Nārāyaṇa' bronze, it will be remembered, is similar to the script found at Shōrkōt, in Punjab; 2) Part of the formulaic expression of the date in the inscription (i.e. *atra/ayatra dīvase)*, together with appearance of dotted *akṣaras*, remind of occurrences on the Sui Vihār inscription from southeastern Punjab; 3) Both Shōrkōt and Sui Vihār are in the general neighboring region, being South and West of Himachal Pradesh; 4) The aggregate of the Bronze's stylistic, iconographic and cultural (see also below) indicators favour Himachal Pradesh over the Punjab; 5) Technical considerations do not rule out this general region. The Bhīmāsthāna of the inscription ought, therefore, to be located somewhere between eastern Punjab and western Himachal Pradesh. If we assume that the bronze was installed near the place that it was made, then the probable provenance of the 'Nārāyaṇa' bronze ought to be in this same area. I am inclined to place the bronze more towards Himachal Pradesh because strong religious and cultural forces, concentrating on 'Nārāyaṇa' operate there (see below). Of course, the possibility exists that Bhīmāsthāna refers to the (Holy) Place-of-Bhīmā (a female goddess who may be associated with the goddess Hiḍimbā[164 & 164a(*)]. This goddess attained the rank of the Mother Goddess in Kulu and is addressed as 'Bhīmākālī', among other names[165]. The name, Bhīmā, is the feminine of the name of the god with whom she is connected, (much like the individual names of the Hindu Saptamātṛkās, the seven mother goddess, are formed). Were this the case, mention of a Bhīmādevī of Himācala in the early *Mārkaṇḍeya Purāṇa* (Chapt. 91, see verses 45–48), would appear to implicate the same general region.

Followers of the Pāñcarātra sect ought to have inhabited the region of Himachal Pradesh to judge by the three early 'Nārāyaṇa' images (excluding the 427 AD bronze), mentioned above. These images in style and iconography draw upon Gangetic models, especially models developed from the Mathurā idiom. The prominence, and precedence, of Gangetic models for this type suggest that the beliefs also originated in the Gangetic Valley and spread from there to the Himalayan valleys, but the latter supposition is rather conjectural. Probably Pāñcarātra originated in the North of India, though where in the North is somewhat unclear[166]. It is clear that Pāñcarātra Viṣṇuism enjoyed great popularity in the Himalayan valleys, as seen by the increased number of 'Nārāyaṇa' icons in Chamba and Kashmir from the 8th century onwards[167]. Indeed, one inscribed 'Nārāyaṇa' image can assuredly be attributed to medieval Chamba. The Museum at Chamba preserves a 12th century stone image of Lakṣmi-Nārāyaṇa riding on Garuḍa bearing an inscription which names the icon as 'Nārāyaṇa'[168].

Sectarian ideology may not be the only reason for the popularity of 'Nārāyaṇa' images in this region. The lineage of local rulers can descend from Nārāyaṇa and thus add to his importance here. For example, the rulers of Chamba trace their descent from Nārāyaṇa. The Chamba Vaṃśavalī, in the form published by Vogel[169], is a *c.* 17th century text charting the lineage of the rulers of Chamba. The text opens with a declaration that god Nārāyaṇa is the progenitor of the Sūryavaṃśa (i.e. the Solar lineage) from which ultimately stem the rulers of Chamba. That is, the 34th on the list is Campa, the mythical founder of the town of Campa. The testimony from this late text could be handily dismissed for the early period, were it not that its declaration explains numerous artistic phenomena in Chamba and other Himalayan valleys dating to the early period. The testimony could confirm that the 6th century Gum Sūrya image makes symbolic reference to the Sūryavaṃśa and has therefore the same significance in Chamba as in the

Kuṣāṇa art of Mathurā, a not unlikely supposition in view of the fact that early Chamba art and iconography exhibit unquestionable influence from Mathurā. (The significance of the Sūrya from Masrur who assumes the same low squatting position, would also fall into place)[170]. The testimony could explain why a Kulu temple such as the one at Nirath, dating back to *c.* the 8th century[171], would be dedicated to Sūrya-Nārāyaṇa (and it may explain the presence of 'Nārāyaṇa' imagery on the great 8th century Sūrya temple at Martand, Kashmir)[172]. To conclude, it is not unlikely that two stimuli fostered images of Nārāyaṇa in the region of Himachal Pradesh: Nārāyaṇa's role as royal progenitor and his position as supreme Being of the Pāñcarātrins, who were prevalent in the area.

An unexpected source evincing the popularity of 'Nārāyaṇa' images in the Northern regions is the Buddhist texts, the *Lalitavistara.* A passage included in Chapter VIII, tells that the young Siddhārtha visited a temple *(devakula),* and viewed a number of divine images there; Nārāyaṇa is one of them. The interesting aspect of this passage is that the *Lalitavistara* is believed to be a Buddhist text composed in the North. The text probably was in the process of formulation somewhere between the 4th century to *c.* the 8th century AD[173]. Here then is a literary passage which elegantly corroborates the popularity of Nārāyaṇa's worship in the North as indicated by the Northern icons, beginning with the 427 AD 'Nārāyaṇa'.[173a(*)]

In the course of this lengthy exploration of Northern *vaiṣṇava* art in order to determine the provenance of the 427 AD bronze, quite another issue has arisen. Art of the Northern areas made during the 5th–7th century is essentially an art that is post Gandhāran and pre-Kashmiri. The probings made above comment upon existing enclaves of art during this time and wherefrom come their influences. It is usual to ground analyses of the art of this time on comparisons with Swati and early Kashmiri art, especially in the case of bronzes. If the proposed provenance of the 'Nārāyaṇa' bronze is accepted, then the region of Himachal Pradesh must be recognized not only as a producer of a very early *vaiṣṇava* bronze, but the earliest 'Nārāyaṇa' type image known to date to originate in the North. Moreover, Himachal Pradesh seems to have been an active enclave for Hindu art during this time, receiving influences rather quickly from the Gangetic Valley. The art produced in the Himalayan valleys does not appear to be a pastiche of outside (i.e. Gandhāra and Gangetic) influences; local traditions play a role in artistic expressions. In addition, artistic diffusion need not go only from the artistic centers of Gandhāra and the Gangetic Valley to the Himalayan peripheries; influences can be expected to move among and between the peripheral valleys. The larger theoretical issue raised in the process of finding a home for the 5th century 'Nārāyaṇa' bronze is the possibility that the mountain valleys below Kashmir may be very early repositories of a Hindu art which synthesizes, rather dynamically, divergent influences from North and South.

V. OTHER ICONOGRAPHIC CONTEXT OF THE NĀRĀYAṆA TYPE (DMS)

Not all the 'Nārāyaṇa' icons discussed so far are solitary images devoid of additional iconographic clues to establish the meaning of the type, especially the lateral animal heads. It has already been observed in connection with the *c.* 7th century Bajaura Viśvarūpa that the core of a Viśvarūpa icon can be based on the iconography of the 'Nārāyaṇa' type. Viśvarūpa iconography probably developed in the Mathurā school of art as indicated by the Gupta Bhankari Viśvarūpa with its lateral lion and boar heads[174]. But Viśvarūpa need not have lateral animal heads; lateral crowned human heads can also occur. The association of Nārāyaṇa with Viśvarūpa is not due to Pāñcarātra theology. Already a passage in the *Mahānārāyaṇa Upaniṣad* giving adoration to Nārāyaṇa attributes to him hugeness, the result of being filled with the totality of creation; in a word, the passage attributes to Nārāyaṇa a *viśvarūpa* nature[175].

One Viśvarūpa example that does have lateral animal heads goes a long way towards weakening the suggestion that the lateral heads are associated with the *avatāras*. The Viśvarūpa reputedly from Bhusawar in Rajasthan has been recently published by Maxwell[176]. Bhusawar is in eastern Rajasthan, near to Bharatpur, a town which, in antiquity, was within the cultural orbit of Mathurā. The central Viśvarūpa figure retains the Bhankari iconography showing the lion head on the right and the boar head on the left. The central figure is surrounded, *inter alia*, by a depiction of ten *avatāras* represented in two vertical sets of five. On the right side of Viśvarūpa and second from the bottom is a depiction of Varāha; on the left side, second from the bottom, is a depiction of Nṛsiṃha. For Maxwell, the depiction of the Varāha and Nṛsiṃha twice as *avatāras* (in the lateral heads and in the outer margins of the stele) suggests 'a late phase in the development of the iconographic type'[177]; he dates the image to the 11th century. For me the outer depictions of the Varāha *avatāra* and the Nṛsiṃha *avatāra* hint that the boar and lion lateral heads may not also represent the same *avatāras*.

Happily the Bhusawar sculpture is not the only sculpture with such repetitions. The Devsar halo (Fig. 9.22) from Kashmir, presents a great many relevant details. This magnificent elliptical halo displays a hierarchy of divine manifestations. At the apex stands the cosmic source of these manifestations, a multi-headed, multi-armed *vaiṣṇava* figure whose lowermost three heads are a lion and a boar to the right and left of a human head (Fig. 9.23). Below the multi-headed deity, and on either side of the halo, are a series of *vibhavas* or *avatāras* in roundels. In the two uppermost roundels, to the right and left of the central apex, the Varāha *avatāra* is represented. On the right, Varāha is shown rescuing the Earth; on the left, Varāha kills Hiraṇyākṣa, the cause of Earth's plight. Below this roundel appears Nṛsiṃha destroying the demon who would not worship Viṣṇu, Hiraṇyakaśipu, the brother of Hiraṇyākṣa.

Fig. 9.22. Halo of a Vaiṣṇava image. 8th–10th century. Devsar, Kashmir. Sri Pratap Singh Museum. Śrinagar. Photograph American Institute of Indian Studies.

Fig. 9.23. Detail of halo's apex. Photograph American Institute of Indian Studies.

The halo is older than the Bhusawar sculpture, alerting straightaway to the possible trouble for Maxwell's opinon that a decline in iconographic integrity may be responsible for more than one boar and lion representation in the piece from Bhusawar. J.L. Bhan places the halo in the early 8th century[178]. Goetz dates it between the 9th and 10th century[179], and Pal assigns it to the 10th[180]. Thus the halo is at least a hundred years older than the Bhusawar Viśvarūpa, and, of course, it is from a region considerably closer to Himachal Pradesh, the proposed provenance for the inscribed 'Nārāyaṇa' bronze.

At the apex, the Devsar halo features a figure that incorporates the 'Nārāyaṇa' type; below this figure, it depicts the lower aspects of divine forms. Even this abbreviated description of the halo fits quite well into the Pāñcarātrin schema of higher and lower levels of pure creation. It is therefore advisable to try and determine the halo's larger iconographic program into which the 'Nārāyaṇa' type has been incorporated. If the meaning and significance of the divine forms above and below the 'Nārāyaṇa' type can be determined, the conceptualization of the latter ought to be advanced.

The complete *vaiṣṇava* figure at the apex has ten arms and seven visible heads arranged in three rows (Fig. 9.23). The top row has one head of the horse Hayagrīva. The second row has three human heads with crowns. The third and lowest row, is the one with the typical heads of the 'Nārāyaṇa type'. The figure has many other iconographic characteristics which, throughout this paper have been attributed to 'Nārāyaṇa'. Between the god's feet is a tiny figure of Bhū Devī, 'Nārāyaṇa's' lowermost arms rest on his personified attributes; Gadādevī is on his right and Cakrapuruṣa is on his left. The emblems in the other pairs of hands are (going upwards): lotus and conch, sword and club, stylus and book, sun and moon discs[181].

The figure on top of the halo is some sort of *vaiṣṇava* cosmic deity. One indication of its cosmic nature is the intensification of multiple bodily parts[182], in this case multiple heads and arms. The Devsar halo seems to display a sequence of creation beginning with the cosmic deity at the apex and ending with the series of *vibhavas* or *avatāras.* Indeed, the halo's composition specifies that the entire sequence begins with the entity represented by the horse's head.

There is sufficient evidence to propose that the horse's head (Hayagrīva), symbolizes Nārāyaṇa, the Supreme, all-inclusive god of the Pāñcarātrins. Let me immediately eliminate any confusion by directing the reader's attention to the fact that throughout this paper I have referred to the deity of the inscribed bronze as 'Nārāyaṇa'—in quotes. The point is that the deity of the bronze is Nārāyaṇa's highest *(para)* form in the Highest Heaven (Vaikuṇṭha); as such, the deity is the first of his five modes of existence, but the deity is *not* Nārāyaṇa, the transcendental Being *per se.* Hayagrīva is the alter-ego of God Nārāyaṇa in the *Mahābhārata.* Specifically, in the Nārāyaṇīya section of the *Mahābhārata,* Nārada the devotee of Nārāyaṇa, praises the god in the form with the equine head. And Nārāyaṇa recounts his own exploits in the horse-head form: in the northwestern ocean he drinks sacrificial oblations offered to him with faith (12.326.56); he preaches the wisdom of the Vedas even to Brahmā, who then worships him (12.327 .81–82). In the Ramachandra Shastri edition of the Nārāyaṇīya account, Hayaśiras (i.e. Hayagrīva), is described in terms that recall the Vedic cosmic Puruṣa[183], whose image also inspires the description of Viśvarūpa-Nārāyaṇa in the same text (see below). It is true that already in the *Mahābhārata,* Hayagrīva is an *avatāra* and he becomes a god of learning especially associated with Pāñcarātra knowledge[184]. The *Viṣṇudharmottara* allies him to both higher and lower levels of creation; it states that Hayagrīva is Saṃkarṣaṇa, and that he saved the *Vedas* in a previous age[185]. Admittedly, both the date and place of the *Viṣṇudharmottara'* s composition make it a highly appropriate source for the interpretation of the iconography of this Kashmiri sculpture dating between the 8th–10th century. But I am quite sure that the topmost position of Hayagrīva in a halo whose theme is divine unfolding obviates the possibility for Hayagrīva's identity as the *vyūha* Saṃkarṣaṇa, or as the *avatāra.* Being at the pinnacle, Hayagrīva can only refer to Nārāyaṇa himself, as the Nārāyaṇīya proclaims. Incidentally, Hayagrīva, the *avatāra,* does appear in the Devsar halo, but in the appropriate place. He is seen in one of the roundels, that is, in one of the spaces reserved for *avatāras.*

Beneath the head of Hayagrīva are seen the three crowned heads. They represent Nārāyaṇa as cosmic totality. To state it otherwise, these three heads metonymically express the Pāñcarātra belief that Nārāyaṇa is cosmogonic totality. The image for cosmogonic totality can be a Viśvarūpa image. Therefore we may say that the three crowned heads symbolize Nārāyaṇa as Viśvarūpa. It will be remembered from the above discussion, that a Viśvarūpa image may have lateral animal heads or three (visible, though intentionally four) crowned heads. Perhaps the best examples of Viśvarūpa with the crowned human heads are the 6th century series made in Śāmalājī[186].

It may be well to summarize the symbolism of the two rows of heads on the apex of the halo. The two rows of heads represent the beginning of a cosmic progression leading towards pure creation. The progression begins at the point where all is the One, namely Nārāyaṇa. The first emanation represents the One as omniform Creator; this is the Viśvarūpa form which contains all other forms of creation. The two Beings, namely Nārāyaṇa and Viśvarūpa-Nārāyaṇa, form a unit. This unit, an ideograph for the creative potentiality of the transcendental Supreme, is already represented in the Bajaura relief. Only at Bajaura the horse's head (Hayagrīva), rests above a Viśvarūpa whose lateral heads are animals, not human. (The 5th century Viśvarūpa on the Gadhwa [U.P.] lintel may be coalescing the unit; here Viśvarūpa's central head may be that of the horse while the side heads are of the boar and lion)[187]. The Viśvarūpa recently acquired by the Metropolitan Museum (Fig. 9.24; No. 1986.506.15) also shows the horse's head of Hayagrīva above the human, central head of Viśvarūpa. The Met Viśvarūpa displays some stylistic features reminiscent of Vāsudeva-Kṛṣṇa from the Dharmarājikā and the one from the British Museum (see Figs. 2–3 mentioned in n. 87), together with the group related to these two sculptures. The crown of the Met Viśvarūpa has the shape and interior cross-hatching as in the crowns of this group (cf. Fig. 9.14). Also the lotus with the raised seed pod, observed with some icons in this group, is being held in Viśvarūpa's upper raised right arm. Although the Met Viśvarūpa is later than the above *vaiṣṇava* group assigned to the 6th century, it is unlikely to date beyond the 8th century. Here then is an addition to the growing number of Hindu icons from the Taxila area made between the post-Gandhāra and the pre-Karkoṭa period in Kashmir.

The cosmogonic progression depicted on the Devsar halo continues with Nārāyaṇa's highest or *para* form. As this form precedes even pure creation, it is the embodiment of the undifferentiated Nārāyaṇa. God in this highest form is Para Vāsudeva[188]. The three-headed god with lateral animal heads, appearing beneath the three crowned heads of Viśvarūpa, is Para Vāsudeva. God in his *para* form comes to be mentioned in the original Pāñcarātra literature, although it is intimated earlier. If we assume with Schrader that the *terminus ad quem* of the original Pāñcarātra Saṃhitās is the 8th century[189], and if we remember that the Devsar halo has been dated anywhere between the 8th and the 10th century, then associating this cosmic form with this particular name does not pose a problem. Para Vāsudeva's potentiality to initiate pure creation is declared by his lateral animal heads which represent the second and fourth *vyūhas*.

Avatāras and *vibhavas,* according to Pāñcarātra cosmogony, are deities belonging to a lower category of pure creation than Para Vāsudeva and the Caturvyūhas. This theological distinction is visually expressed in the Devsar halo, again by way of position within the overall compositional schema. Those deities, being partial manifestations of Para Vāsudeva, are shown in roundels which are literally below Para Vāsudeva.

The Devsar halo is thus a splendid and clear expression of the steps in Pāñcarātrin theology leading to, and effectuating, pure creation. The cosmic figure at the apex shows that Nārāyaṇa is both the Supreme and the efficient cause of pure creation. Nārāyaṇa manifests himself as Para Vāsudeva, who in turn emanates the *vyūhas,* who carry out subsequent stages of creation. Beneath the cosmic figure, and in a series of roundels, is the second level of pure creation represented by the *vibhavas* or *avatāras.*

The clarity of the halo's composition is an additional indicator that the lateral animal heads must be *vyūhas* and not *avatāras.* First, the heads occur with Para Vāsudeva, who marks the juncture between primary and secondary pure creation. Second, the double appearance of the boar and lion is analogous to Hayagrīva's upper (i.e. Nārāyaṇa) and lower (i.e. *avatāra)* appearances in the overall compositional schema. As such, the visual distinctions between the upper placement of the lateral lion and boar heads, and the lower occurrence of Narasiṃha and Varāha is logical only if the lateral animal heads are understood to be *vyūhas.*

Perhaps the halo's clarity of expression is related to the fact that the theological progression it portrays is already given, in a rudimentary manner, in a pre- or early- Gupta text. The Nārāyaṇīya section of the *Mahābhārata's* Śānti Parvan (i.e. Book XII), dated *c.* late 3rd-early 4th century AD[190], exposes a system of thought which it labels, quite consciously, as Pāñcarātra. An exposition on cosmogony and the nature of Nārāyaṇa is given to the sage Nārada who witnesses an epiphany of the Supreme Nārāyaṇa on the White Island (Śvetadvīpa). Nārāyaṇa first shows his *viśvarūpa* form (XII.326.1), manifesting his thousand eyes, hundred heads[191], thousand feet, thousand bellies and arms (XII.326.6, 7), etc. This vision of Viśvarūpa-Nārāyaṇa is modeled upon the *viśvarūpa* form of Vedic Puruṣa (in *RV* 10.90), the ancient omniform creator upon whom so much of *vaiṣṇava* imagery is based. Then Nārāyaṇa displays the form of Vāsudeva, who is described as 'the highest Self' *(paramātman),* 'the eternal One' *(sanātana;* XII.326.24). The *vyūhas* emanate next (e.g. see XII.326.35–39; 68–69), and they are called his 'fourfold form' *(mūrticatuṣṭaya* XII.326.43)[192]. After these emanations, the rest of creation proceeds from Brahmā who has arisen from Aniruddha, the fourth *vyūha.* First come the *avatāras,* the Boar *(varāha)* and Man-Lion *(narasiṃha),* heading the list (see XII.326.72–96). The Nārāyaṇīya's cosmological sequence parallels, in its fundamental outline, that of the Devsar halo; both the literary and visual progression proclaim a monotheistic starting point, Nārāyaṇa, for the ensuing

Fig. 9.24. Viśvarūpa; *c.* 8th century. Possibly Taxila region. Metropolitan Museum of Art (No. 1986.506.15). Photography courtesy of the Metropolitan Museum of Art.

divine manifestations. What is more, both intimate that there is a connection between the Supreme Nārāyaṇa and the origin of the universe. Indeed both offer the same two connections: Brahmanic *viśvarūpa* followed by the Pāñcarātra four *vyūhas* (although this term is not in the Nārāyaṇīya). Mallmann considers Viśvarūpa the syncretic form of the Caturvyūha because the texts she analyzed attribute the same animal heads to both. She declares, and I agree, that the four faces of Viśvarūpa correspond to the four directions, the Caturvyūhas, and to the attributes *(guṇa)* of the Supreme Vāsudeva[193]. (I presume she is referring to Para Vāsudeva). It is important also to realize that although the Nārāyaṇīya does not yet specifically refer to Para Vāsudeva, it contains several concepts associated with this form of Nārāyaṇa. First, the form between the Viśvarūpa form and the 'fourfold form' is described as Vāsudeva *paramātman,* Second and most significantly, this form of Vāsudeva is distinguished from the fourfold form wherefrom the *vyūhas* emanate. This distinction is made in the Pāñcarātra literature, although not at all times (see n. 12). The theological distinction between Para and Vyūha Vāsudeva is of course the basis for assuming that the distinction also occurs in the iconography. Both the Nārāyaṇīya and the Devsar halo proclaim that the higher form of Vāsudeva is linked to transcendental 'Nārāyaṇa' and Viśvarūpa. The linkage between these three entities (i.e. transcendental Nārāyaṇa, Viśvarūpa and Para Vāsudeva) is the preservation of the totality of Nārāyaṇa. Each entity is beyond pure creation. The four *vyūhas,* beginning with Vyūha Vāsudeva, initiate pure creation. Therein lies the fundamental distinction.

The correspondence between the Nārāyaṇīya's cosmological progression and the iconographic program of the Devsar halo, though much later in time, assists in solving the problem stated at the outset: the Devsar halo places the iconic type depicted in the 427 AD bronze, into a hierarchical framework similar to the one given in the Nārāyaṇīya, the earliest relevant Pāñcarātra exposition. Fortunately, the Nārāyaṇīya is not the only text which is nearly contemporary—or contemporary—to this bronze. There are other textual references that advance the interpretation of this type of image, and these are considered in the concluding section, below.

VI. INTERPRETATION AND IDENTIFICATION OF THE 427 AD TYPE OF IMAGE (DMS)

A passage in Paṭala 6 of the *Jayākhya Saṃhitā (JS)* describes how the mental image of Nārāyaṇa should be conceived. This is a Pāñcarātra text produced in the later Gupta age, and possibly the centuries following this age. Therefore its prescriptions have relevancy for a Pāñcarātra icon of the 5th century, labeled 'Nārāyaṇa'[194]. *JS 6* 73–75 prescribes that a devotee should meditate on Nārāyaṇa who is four-armed, holds the conch, the wheel, the mace and the lotus, whose four-faces are composed of 'Vaikuṇṭha, Narasiṃha, Varāha, Kapila', and who is mounted on Garuḍa...[195]. Paṭala 6 amplifies upon the conceptualizations and worship of the last three faces (*JS* 6 135-153)[196].

This passage has enormous importance for the interpretation of the iconic type analysed in this paper. On the one hand, we have a text produced roughly around the Gupta period, assigning and naming the four heads of God Nārāyaṇa. On the other hand, we have the 427 AD bronze showing three heads of the god named Nārāyaṇa in the inscription on the bronze. It appears that a three headed image may well represent a four-headed concept[197]. We are clearly not dealing with numerical, but rather symbolic quantities. Still, it is fair to ask why the early period should have represented mainly three-headed images. No definite answer to this question is on record. However, what is on record is an apparent difference of opinion on the correct number of *vyūhas.* The *Mahābhārata's* Nārāyaṇīya may be reflecting the opinion of different Pāñcarātra schools, or different beliefs within a given school when it indicates theoretical divergences on whether there are one, two, three or four *vyūhas* (see XII.336.53). Evidently, the theological codification of four *vyūhas* had still not occurred by c. the 3rd century AD. I am therefore not so sure that too much can be made of the fact that, between the 3rd–5th century AD, there is one four-headed image (from Mathurā, see below) and six three-headed images (from Mathurā, see Fig. 9.9, and in Maxwell, *Viśvarūpa,* figs. 40, 42, 43, 45, and from Himachal Pradesh, Fig. 1). Perhaps this is the time to remember that as late as the 8th century, a passage in the *Viṣṇudharmottara Purāṇa* contains ambiguities on the number of *vyūha* faces (see fn. 7 on my revised date of the *Viṣṇudharmottara Purāṇa*). At this stage in our understanding of the image type, it seems reasonable to conclude that the three heads of the 427 AD bronze (and all the early three-headed images of this type mentioned in Sections III–IV), represent the *vyūha* concept also associated with a four-headed divinity. The names of the heads supplied by the *Jayākhya Saṃhitā* underscore who this divinity is. The Pāñcarātra text mentions that the first face of Nārāyaṇa is that of 'Vaikuṇṭha', that is Vāsudeva, as I already suspected in an earlier study[198]. It is now possible to refine my hunch and add that Vaikuṇṭha refers to *para* (not *vyūha)* Vāsudeva: 'The most prominent figure in the "Highest Heaven" [or Vaikuṇṭha] is God Himself in His *para* or "highest" form, which is the first of his five prakāras or modes of existence, the other four being the Vyūhas and the three kinds of Avatāras [...]'[199]. According to this information given by Schrader, 'Vaikuṇṭha' refers to *para* Vāsudeva alone. To whom do the other faces belong? The answer, given by the *Jayākhya Saṃhitā* and the Devsar halo, is that the other faces represent the *vyūhas,* or the modes of existence coming right after, and out of Para Vāsudeva. The *Jayākhya Saṃhitā* specifies—not once but twice in Paṭala 6—that two of these faces have animal names. Only one conclusion is possible: The animal names cited (i.e. Narasiṃha and Varāha) are names referring to the *vyūhas.* The Devsar halo, it will be remembered, featured animal heads which represent *vyūhas,* and it is thus a visual example of this conclusion.

The *Amarakośa,* a lexicon dated to *c.* 500 AD seems to be aware of the Caturvyūhas. The text mentions Vāsudeva, Saṃkarṣaṇa, Pradyumna and Aniruddha, in that sequence[200]. This sequence is in the *caturvyūha* order, that is, it is the sequential order in which the *vyūhas* emanate. This passage justifies another significant interpretive point. Here the *vyūhas* are all assigned human names. The *Jayākhya Saṃhitā* assigns animal names to the second and fourth *vyūha.* If these two texts manifest alternate ways of referring to the *vyūhas,* it ought to follow that the art could do the same.

It does—in the same place and at about the same time.

For close to thirty years now, there has been scholarly agreement that a late Kuṣāṇa statue made in Mathurā represents Vāsudeva and three *vyūhas* emanating from him (Fig. 9.25). Though this is a fragmentary statue, the fragments all appear to be human forms. Limiting myself only to details relevant to the present problem[201], it is possible to identify the main figure as Vāsudeva[202], to his right (and emanating from him) is the *vyūha* Saṃkarṣaṇa; from Vāsudeva's crown arises a broken bust that ought to represent the *vyūha* Pradyumna, and the broken segment on the left side of Vāsudeva ought to have originally represented *vyūha* Aniruddha. It is but recently that the three-headed Florida image (Fig. 9.9) has been published and therefore it has not yet been compared to the fragmentary form of Vāsudeva and the emanating *vyūhas* (Fig. 9.25). The Florida image was made in Mathurā probably not more than 50–75 years after the image in Fig. 9.25. However in the Florida image the second and fourth *vyūhas* are represented by the alternate lion and boar animal heads. The Florida image, dating to the late 3rd/early 4th century AD raises a question not previously formulated. At the time the image was made (i.e. prior to, or, at the beginning of the Gupta period), are there examples in Mathurā sculpture of the boar and lion in contexts unequivocally indicative of the *avatāra* concept? One relief of a Varāha exists; no examples of Nṛsiṃha are known to date[203]. Isn't this another indication that the right lateral head of the Florida image from Mathurā (Fig. 9.9), cannot represent the Nṛsiṃha *avatāra* since this *avatāra* has not yet been given a separate iconographic reality in Mathurā art by the 3rd/4th century AD?

Fig. 9.25. Vāsudeva with emerging Vyūhas; from Mathurā. Early 3rd century. Mathurā Museum (Nos. 392–95).

In sum, the interpretation of the type represented in Figure 1 can proceed on the assumption that its three heads equal a four-headed concept, and, that its animal heads can signify, just as human heads, the notion of *vyūhas,* a hallmark of Pāñcarātra ideology.

The inscription of the 427 AD bronze states that it is an image of Nārāyaṇa. We know now that Nārāyaṇa allows himself several evolutions before his totality (his Nārāyaṇa-ness) is broken apart into *vyūhas* (lit. orderly arrangements). What evolute of Nārāyaṇa is the bronze?

The cosmic figure at the apex of the Devsar halo portrays an evolute which looks very similar to the form of god depicted in the 427 AD bronze. The theological significance of this form is strongly suggested by the halo's iconographic progression. The form represents god's oneness before it is eclipsed through differentiation into the four *vyūhas.* Extant Pāñcarātra literature justifies calling the halo's form Para Vāsudeva. Can justification be found to call the deity represented in the 5th century bronze by the same name? The answer seems to be 'yes', if we are attentive to the information provided by the *Jayākhya Saṃhitā.* This Gupta text, it is well to reiterate, admonishes the worshipper of Nārāyaṇa to meditate on this god, by meditating, *inter alia,* on Vaikuṇṭha, Narasiṃha, Varāha and Kāpila. The text strongly suggests that the incipient Pāñcarātra ideology is coming into place. Accordingly, it is proposed that meditation on Para Vāsudeva (i.e. Vaikuṇṭha) and the *vyūhas* heads emanating from him is being advanced in the *JS.* Then too, there is the slightly older Nārāyaṇīya passage which mentions Vāsudeva *paramātman* as that form of Nārāyaṇa which precedes the *vyūhas.*

I believe that the main deity in the 427 AD bronze represents the theological notions which the Pāñcarātra texts come to associate with Para Vāsudeva. Because of that and because *vyūha* Vāsudeva can be theologically distinguished from Nārāyaṇa's *para* evolute, the name given to this type should reflect these considerations. Amalgamating, thus, inscriptional and theological evidence, the 427 AD image is of Nārāyaṇa as Para Vāsudeva, or Para Vāsudeva-Nārāyaṇa[204]. There are those who may object to this (cumbersome) name on the grounds that giving an icon a name that appears in texts several centuries later is problematic[205]. I am aware of this concern. However, since numerous features foreshadowing Para Vāsudeva can be documented earlier, it seems far better to call this Pāñcarātra type of image by the name reflecting precisely its theological position in the Pāñcarātra belief system.

An image of Para Vāsudeva-Nārāyaṇa represents the visible form of Nārāyaṇa poised to usher in cosmogony. The god displays this capability by exhibiting the *vyūhas,* instrumental in achieving pure creation. A capability is a potential for some end result; it is different from the end result itself. In the same way, an image of Para Vāsudeva-Nārāyaṇa, displaying the *vyūhas* as they arise from him, ought to be different from an image of the four fully arisen *vyūhas.* An early Nepalese image confirms this assumption. Enshrined in the Nārāyaṇa Hiti, Kathmandu, is a four- sided image. Carved on each side is the full anthropomorphic figure of one of the four *vyūhas;* each is represented with one head and four arms, holding the appropriate attributes. Another iconographically similar image but of the 16th century, names this type of representation *caturvyūhāmaka* in the dedicatory inscription. Slusser, who published the earlier 'Caturvyūha' image in the Nārāyaṇa Hiti dates it to the 7th century on stylistic

Fig. 9.26. Para Vāsudeva-Nārāyaṇa with Vyūhas. *c.* 9th century. Kashmir. Gift of Robert H. Ellsworth to the Nelson-Atkins Museum of Art. In honor of the appointment of Doris Meth Srinivasan as curator.

Fig. 9.27. Para Vāsudeva-Nārāyaṇa; Vyūha.

grounds; she therefore must be rejecting the implications of a textual entry that may refer to this piece and would place it in the mid 5th century[206]. The Nepalese examples suggest that a Caturvyūha image is a fourfold image featuring four fully evolved forms which do not show intensification of multiple bodily parts. Instead each *vyūha* shows only the multiplication of one bodily part. Para Vāsudeva-Nārāyaṇa is quite different. In a theology which emphasizes, by subtle degrees, the evolutionary distance between the transcendental Nārāyaṇa and the first manifestation of the transcendental, the iconography of Para Vāsudeva-Nārāyaṇa affirms his minimal distance from the Supreme Nārāyaṇa. The early imagery consists of one figure with multiple heads *and* arms, that is, the imagery shows intensification of multiple bodily parts which is a sign of a cosmic being[207]. The idea is that Para Vāsudeva is still Nārāyaṇa, the One who is not yet divided into a fourfold arrangement. But division is immanent. The emanating lateral heads are beginning to project. The highest personal god of the Pāñcarātrins,

Para Vāsudeva, or manifest Nārāyaṇa, stands before the devotee as the supreme expression of the unaffected, unchanging One whose very nature augurs the changes leading towards creation. This is the god represented in the 427 bronze made in Himachal Pradesh and fashioned even earlier in the art of Mathurā. This god is also represented in the Kashmiri votive bronze, inlaid with copper and silver, whose figures are arranged in the *sarvatobhadrika* manner (Fig. 9.26). The essential features traced and assigned to Para Vāsudeva-Nārāyaṇa throughout this paper can be attributed to one standing figure; this is the main figure of the fourfold icon; it probably faced East. The other three standing figures can be distinguished from Para Vāsudeva-Nārāyaṇa due to the absence of the multiple heads and Bhū Devī (Fig. 9.27). As in the Nepalese *caturvyūhatmaka,* they do not show intensification of multiple bodily parts; each figure has four arms only. These figures represent *vyūhas.* Therefore I am inclined to call the newly acquired Nelson image 'Para Vāsudeva-Nārāyaṇa with Vyūhas'. To date I know of no other image which combines the *para* aspect of Nārāyaṇa with the fully arisen *vyūhas.* Thus, this small *c.* 9th century Kashmiri image is unique albeit theologically quite unproblematic. That is not its only significance. Recognizing that this image is based upon developments which had been worked out previously in the Mathurā/Himachal Pradesh axis (see below) and in Nepal, this small image gives added support that art in the Himalayan valleys evolved as a result of influences stemming from both local and distant centers.

Is it possible to concretize part of the totality of transcendental Nārāyaṇa? From a Western perspective, giving form to that which is beyond form and can itself create form, verges on the paradoxical. From the Hindu perspective, representation of the transcendental in iconic form does not defy reason; indeed, such an icon enables the most spiritually advanced worshipper to gain realization of the Supreme. Several examples in Śaivism come immediately to mind. There is the *Liṅga* icon which is the symbol of the Absolute, Para Śiva, the transcendental One. There is also the fifth head of the Pāñcamukha Linga, declared to be even beyond the ken of yogis yet rendered, albeit infrequently, in visual form[208]. It therefore comes as no surprise that Vaiṣṇavism may also have icons which concretize certain forms of god that are imperceivable to the ordinary mortal. For the Pāñcarātrins, Nārāyaṇa in his Para Vāsudeva form is one such portrayal.

This paper comes to the conclusion that the art of two localities provides the earliest evidence for the worship of Para Vāsudeva-Nārāyaṇa. The first locality is Mathurā (Fig. 9.9 etc.; perhaps Fig. 9.25). This is to be expected since Mathurā during the first few centuries of the Christian era is the innovator par excellence of *vaiṣṇava* art and iconography[209]. The second locality, Himachal Pradesh (Fig. 9.1 etc.), could be viewed as an unexpected place for *vaiṣṇava* innovations were it seen in isolation. If however, it is viewed as an area in close contact with Mathurā and responsive to the artistic inventions there, then the occurrence of a new *vaiṣṇava* form in the hills not more than a hundred years after its formulation in Mathurā is unremarkable; indeed its occurrence could even be viewed as part of a pattern. In a short addition to this paper, which I hope to write fairly soon, I can demonstrate that not too much time is lost between the formulation of a new *vaiṣṇava* image in Mathurā and its production in some Northerly workshop within Mathurā's radiating sphere of influence.

Would the devotee of long ago, in either locality, recognize Para Vāsudeva in a single guise only? The modern scholar strives to carve out consistencies. Being far removed from the evocative ambiguities and multivalent symbols of a living, growing faith, he seeks definitions in texts and inscriptions, and hesitates before deviations[210]. But early Pāñcarātra displays ambiguities and overlapping symbols which seep into iconography (cf. n. 8, 12, 202 and pp. 191 and 153-156). The scholar sees but three heads or four heads, animal heads or human heads, Para Vāsudeva or Vyūha Vāsudeva. The adept would have seen them too, but—as likely as not—he may have seen more. The devotee may have understood the significance of fluid symbols, allowing for ambiguities. Should we discount the possibility for layered meanings and thereby restrict our scope of understanding?

NOTES AND REFERENCES

1. Research for this paper was made possible by a grant in 1991 from the Asian Cultural Council, to whom I express thanks for their support. Thanks go to Professor Gérard Fussman for going through an earlier draft of this paper and raising significant questions, consideration of which improved the arguments presented in the paper. I also wish to thank Professor Dennis Hudson for reading a draft of this manuscript and providing thoughtful discussion on the Pāñcarātra belief system.

1a. ADDENDUM: The date has been revised from 427 AD to 460 AD by Harry Falk. Lore Sander now shares this opinion. See Harry Falk, "Six Early Inscriptions from Gandhāra", *AION*, 64/1–4 (2004), 144–46. The analysis of the inscribed bronze icon is complex. In addition to the revised date of the icon, its provenance (i.e. where it was made vs. where it was found) and the meaning of '*bhīmāsthāna*' inscribed on its base will be reexamined in the Addenda to this reprint of the 1997 article.

2. See W. Begley, *Viṣṇu's Flaming Wheel: The Iconography of the Sudarśana-Cakra,* New York 1973, pls. 5–7.
3. E.g. P. Pal, *Bronzes of Kashmir,* New York 1975, pl. 9: re a 9th century Kashmiri representation.
4. E.g. J. Siudmak, "Early Stone and Terracotta Sculpture" in Art and Architecture of Ancient Kashmir', *Marg,* 1989, p. 53, fig. 20.
5. E.g. Pal, *Bronzes, cit.*, pp. 17–18.
6. J.N. Banerjea, *The Development of Hindu Iconography,* 3rd ed., Delhi 1974, p. 408; D.M. Srinivasan, 'Early Vaiṣṇava Imagery: Caturvyūha and Variant Forms', *AAA,* XXXII, 1979, p. 45.
7. Pal *(Bronzes, cit.,* p. 17) argues this point on the basis of the later *Rupamaṇḍana* and the *Aparājitapṛccha.* See sections 3.52–54 and 219.25–27 in the respective texts. Also see the *Devatāmūrtiprakaraṇa,* 5.91–93. I have revised the date of the *Viṣṇudharmottara Purāṇa.* See fn. 10a of the paper, 'Śaiva Temple Forms', in this volume.

8. E.g. T.S. Maxwell, 'Vaikuntha', in *Akṣayanīvī*, ed. G. Bhattacharya, Delhi 1991, fig. 13 from the Devsar, Kashmir, bronze frame. D. Handa, 'An Interesting Vaikuṇṭha-mūrti from Pehoa', *Svasti Śrī*, 1984, pp. 297–302. *The Crossroads of Asia*, E. Errington & J. Cribb with M. Claringbull (ed.), Cambridge 1992, see fig. 220 (being the famous Berlin Museum three-headed Viṣṇu, No. MIK I.24); the entry, written by M. Claringbull, cites that her nomenclature follows C. Sivaramamurti and von Schroeder. It must be mentioned that ViDhP 3.85.43–45 which cites Vaikuṇṭha contains areas of ambiguity. Vaikuṇṭha is four-faced and has one form, or body (43); he becomes *caturmūrti* or four-formed (fourfold) when four faces are made (44a). This comment could lead to the supposition that a Vaikuṇṭha could have less than four faces. Indeed, 44b and 45 go on to mention only three faces, namely, the *saumya* (eastern), the *siṃha* (southern), and the *raudra* (western) faces.
9. E.g. Maxwell, 'Vaikuṇṭha', *cit.*, figs. 2–5, 7–10.
10. E.g. R.C. Agrawala, 'Nṛsiṁha-Varāha-Viṣṇu Images and Some Allied Problems', *Lalit Kalā*, XVI, 1974, pp. 11–21; R.N. Misra, 'The Vaikuṇṭha Images from Chamba and Other Centres in North-Western India', chapt. 8 in *History and Culture of the Chamba State*, V.C. Ohri (ed.), New Dehli 1989.
11. Notions in this paragraph are based on O.F. Schrader, *Introduction to the Pāñcarātra and the Ahirbudhnya Saṃhitā*, Madras 1916 and S. Gupta, 'The Pāñcarātra Attitude to Mantra', in *Mantra*, ed. H.P. Alper, Albany 1989, pp. 224–48.
12. Schrader (*Pāñcarātra, cit.*, p. 53) writes that Para Vāsudeva is sometimes identified with, and sometimes distinguished from Vyūha Vāsudeva. Gupta's overview on this point (see 'Pāñcarātra Attitude', *cit.*, pp. 226–27) emphasizes their distinctions.
13. In the overview that follows, I am considering only studies deemed seminal from the methodological point of view.
14. Contents of the relevant sections are in n. 8.
15. Banerjea, *Hindu Iconography, cit.*, p. 409. To avoid confusion, it may be best to remind that Banerjea seems to have switched the positions of the last two *vyūhas* when, in the sentence preceding the quote, he situated Pradyumna in the northern and Aniruddha in the western directions.
16. M.Th. de Mallmann, *Les enseignements iconographiques de l'Agni-Purāṇa*, Paris 1963, p. 21.
17. *Ibid.*, p. 19; p. 21, citing ViDhP.III.47.2–17. I am inferring that de Mallmann has taken 'Para Puruṣa' mentioned at the outset of III.47 as a reference to Para Vāsudeva, whom she refers to as 'Vāsudeva suprême', p. 21.
18. J. Gonda, *Viṣṇuism and Śivaism*, London 1970, p. 58.
19. Srinivasan, 'Caturvyūha', see pp. 43, 45. The same paper includes those early icons I deem expressive of the orderly arrangement (lit. *vyūha-*) pertaining to the cosmic emanation. They are: Fig. 9.25 in the present paper and the Śuṅga Caturvyūha from Bhīṭā, Figs. 4–7 (State Museum, Lucknow No. 56.394). See Figs. 8.5-8.7 in this volume.
20. A.J. Gail, 'On the Symbolism of Three- and Four-Faced Viṣṇu Images: A Reconsideration of Evidence', *Artibus Asiae*, XLIV, 1983, p. 306.
21. Maxwell, 'Vaikuṇṭha', *cit.*, p. 121.
22. Maxwell comes close in connecting *Jayākhya Saṃhitā*, VI. 59–153 with the type and proposing that the icons would have been known as 'Nārāyaṇa Viśvātman'. However, the only illustrated images he labels as such are from Kashmir and date to the 9th century; see 'Vaikuṇṭha', pp. 133, 146–51 and figs. 17–20.

23. D.C. Sircar, *Select Inscriptions Bearing on Indian History and Civilization*. Vol. I: *From the Sixth Century B.C. to the Sixth Century A.D.*, 2nd ed., Calcutta 1965 (repr. Delhi 1986), pp. 131 ff.
24. S. Konow, *Kharoshṭhī Inscriptions with the Exception of Those of Aśoka*, Corpus Inscriptionum Indicarum, Vol. II, Part I, Calcutta 1929, pp. 70–77, pl. XIV. See also Sircar, *Select Inscriptions, cit.*, pp. 133 f.
25. Konow, *Kharoshṭhī Inscriptions, cit.*, pp. 165–70, pl. XXXIII. See also Sircar, *Select Inscriptions, cit.*, pp. 158 f.
26. For a different translation of the last two lines cf. n. 46.
27. I am very thankful to Professor von Hinüber who made many helpful suggestions. I wish to express my thanks to Professor Vogel who was so kind to calculate the exact date of the inscription.
28. D.C. Sircar, *Indian Epigraphy*, Delhi-Varanasi-Patna 1965, p. 327.
29. The Sui Vihār inscription shares the dotted *akṣaras* with our inscription and the other metal inscriptions in Kharoṣṭhī script mentioned above. Cf. Konow, *Kkaroshṭhī Inscriptions, cit.*, p. 139.
30. Ibid.
31. Cf. also Sircar, *Select Inscriptions, cit.*, pp. 139 f., esp. p. 140, n. 1.
32. Konow, *Kharoshṭhī Inscriptions, cit.*, p. CXV.
33. E.g. H. Lüders, *Mathurā Inscriptions.* Unpublished Papers, ed. K.L. Janert, Abhandlungen der Akademie der Wissenschaften in Göttingen, Philolog.-hist. Klasse, 3. Folge, No. 47, Göttingen 1961, S 81. The normal formula for Mathurā inscriptions is *asyāṃ* or *etasyāṃ pūrvāyāṃ* 'on this date' (Index: p.224).
34. Cf. Th. Damsteegt, *Epigraphical Hybrid Sanskrit*, pp. 195 f.
35. D.C. Sircar (*Studies in the Religious Life of Ancient and Medieval India*, Delhi-Patna-Varanasi 1971, pp. 105–14) refers to an inscribed stone slab from a spring tank near Abbottabad in the Hazara District with a Brāhmī inscription dated 25 of an unknown era. Sircar dates it according to the Gupta era 344 AD. The inscription refers to Kumāra-sthāna which was caused to be made (*kārito kumāra-sthānam*). Sircar considers °*sthāna* to be a temple. The meaning does not suit to *bhīmā-sthāna* in our inscription, because *bhīmā-sthāna* is a common name for holy places. In our inscription *gharaṭṭamaṭṭha* seems to be the locality in which the image found its home.
36. A late reference to a place named after the goddess *bhīmā (bhīmā-devī)* is mentioned in *Kalhaṇa's Rājataraṅginī* (ed. M.A. Stein, Vol. I: *Sanskrit Text with Critical Notes*, Calcutta, 1892 [repr. Delhi 1960], section II, p. 22, v. 135). This reference belongs to the chapter attributed to king Saṃdhimat, who was a devotee of Śiva. He is one of those earlier kings not historically attested. Stein (*Kalhaṇa's Rājataraṅginī. A Chronicle of the Kings of Kaśmir*, transl. M.A. Stein, 2 vols., 1900 [repr. Delhi-Patna-Varanasi 1961], Vol. I, p. 68, n. 135) identifies this place as being the modern Brāṅ (= Bhīmā) in the northeast of Śrinagar in Kashmir. He also refers to the *Haracaritacintāmaṇi* of Rājānaka Jayaratha, a Kashmirian poet of approximately the same time as Kalhaṇa, the 12th century AD: *bhīmā-devī* is described there as a *tīrtha* where many austerities were performed.
37. For general references comparing locations connected with *bhīmā* and *bhīma* see *The Imperial Gazetteer of India, new ed. repro New Delhi, n.d., VIII, pp. 107–9. Cf. also a mountain of the same name situated east to Shāhbaz-garhi (Pakistan). A. Foucher, L'art gréco-bouddhique du Gandhâra*, Vol. I, Paris 1905, map: 'District de Peshwar, Swât, Bounêr'.
38. O. von Boehtlingk, *Petersburger Wörterbuch* and M. Monier-Williams, *Sanskrit-English Dictionary*, where the reference does not agree with the editions of Stein (cf. n. 39).

39. Stein, *Kalhāṇa's Rājataraṅginī, cit.*, Vol. II, 1900; chapt. VII: 1232, 1292, 1576.
40. It is tempting to understand °*maṭṭha* as °*maṭha*, 'hut' or 'hermitage', but to explain the double °*ṭṭha* is difficult, except thinking of an orthographical mistake. For °*maṭṭha* being the pp. of *mṛj* cf. T.W. Rhys Davids & W. Stede, *The Pali Text Society's Pali-English Dictionary*, London 1921–1925 (repr. London 1979). See also H.D.T. Sheth, *Pāia-Sadda-Mahaṇṇavo. A Comprehensive Prākrit-Hindī Dictionary with Sanskrit Equivalents, Quotations and Complete References*, ed. V.S. Agrawala & D.Bh. Malvama, Prākrit Text Society Series, Vol. 7, Varanasi 1963.
41. Cf. F. Edgerton, *Buddhist Hybrid Sanskrit, Grammar and Dictionary*, Vol. I: *Grammar*, New Haven 1953 (repr. Delhi-Varanasi-Patna 1977), p. 64, ¶ 9.48 'Instrumental', ¶ 9.49 'Genitive'.
42. Cf. e.g. numerous examples in Lüders, *Mathurā Inscriptions, cit.* See also S. Shrava, *The Dated Kuṣāṇa Inscriptions*, New Delhi 1993.
43. Cf. Sircar, *Studies, cit.*, p. 108. In the inscription from Abbottabad the name of the donor Gaśura Śāphara is also of Iranian origin.—I thank Professor von Hinüber for having drawn my attention to the most detailed linguistic study on *B(V)ahlika* and its various forms mainly in Indian, but also in other sources: M. Witzel, 'Early Iran and the Atharvaveda', *Persica*, Jaarboek voor het Genootschap Nederland-Iran, Annuaire de la Société Néerlando-Iranienne, IX, 1980, pp. 86–128. Among his quotations neither Vaïlikā nor Vaḥlikā occurs. Assuming the reading Vaḥlikā is correct, the wrong Visarga for the ligature *hla* cannot be explained by linguistic arguments. But, there exists an example for a misunderstood Visarga in the Ratnagiri inscription No. 5 dating from the late 6th century (cf. O. von Hinüber, 'Epigraphical Varieties of Continental Pāli from Devnimori and Ratnagiri', in *Buddhism and Its Relation to Other Religions: Essays in Honour of Dr Shozen Kumoi on His Seventieth Birthday*, Kyoto 1985, pp. 185–200, esp. p. 194). The preferable reading Vaïlikā may be explained with the help of the *svarabhakti* form Vahilikā with omission of the sonant *h*. But, in the light of the studies of S. Konow *(Kharoshṭhī Inscriptions, cit.*, p. CXI) and Th. Damsteegt (*Epigraphical Hybrid Sanskrit, cit.*, pp. 46 f.) sonant *h* is generally preserved in the Mathurā and Gandhāra inscriptions of the Kuṣāṇa period with which our inscription, although younger, shares linguistic and formulaic pecularities. Another Sanskrit origin for the name Vaïlikā is also possible: Vaïlikā = Vailikā from *velikā* (Skt. *velā)*. For the change from *-ai* to *-aï* cf. Konow, *Kharoshṭhī Inscriptions, cit.*, p. XCVI.
44. Despite the improbability that the name Vaïlikā refers directly to her homeland, the discussion about the localization of *B(V)alhika* is of interest to our inscription. K.Ch. Mishra ('Bālhika', *Bhāratī*. Bulletin of the College of Indology, Central Asian Number, A.K. Narain (ed.), X/XI, 1966–68, pp. 210–19) deals with the probable difference of the meaning of Bālhīka, Bālhika and Bāhlika. He states (p. 213): 'Bālhika really stood for a country distant from Kuru land, whereas Bālhīka seems to be a later appellation for the whole of western Punjab and N.W. region when the population in these areas became largely mixed with foreign intruders (*Bahiḥ*)'. He further quotes from the *Mahābhārata* (II.24.21) that 'the Bāhlika country was conquered by Arjuna in the extreme northwest along with Darada, Kamboja etc.' (p. 214). In a 5th century inscription from Chilās-Terrace (Upper Indus Valley) a Dard king Vaiśravaṇasena is mentioned (O. von Hinüber, 'Brāhmī Inscriptions on the History and Culture of the Upper Indus Valley', in *Antiquities of Northern Pakistan. Reports and Studies*, Vol. 1: *Rock Inscriptions in the Upper Indus Valley*, K. Jettmar (ed.), Heidelberg Academy for the Humanities and Sciences. Research unit: Rock Carvings and Inscriptions along the Karakorum Highway, Mainz 1989, pp. 57–

59). Further informations about the Dards cf. Jettmar in the same volume, pp. XXXVII f. D.C. Sircar ('Pāñchāla, Kāmboja, Bāhlīka and Pāṇḍu [Pāṇḍya]', *Bhāratī*, pp. 3–6) tried to locate i.e. Kāmboja and Bāhlīka on the basis of the late medieval work *Śaktisaṅgama Tantra*. He located Bāhlīka 'in the west of Northern Afghanistan' (p. 6). There is another controverse discussion about the homeland of the Vāhlikas in context with the country conquered by Candra in the Mehrauli pillar inscription. S.R. Goyal (*A History of Imperial Guptas*, Allahabad 1967, p. 204, n. 2) summarizes the discussion as follows: 'So far Vaḥlikās are concerned S.K. Aiyangar, R.G. Basak and D.R. Bhandarkar, etc. place them in the Punjab on the strength of a verse of the Rāmāyaṇa. But R.C. Majumdar ("The King Candra of the Meharaulī Iron Inscription", *JASB*, IX, 1943, pp. 179 ff.) and D.C. Sircar (P.V. Kane Volume, Art. No. 64) have conclusively shown that Vāḥlikas, conquered by Chandra belonged to Baktria'. For further discussion cf. M.C. Joshi et al., (eds.), 'King Chandra and the Meharauli Pillar', in *Kusumañjarī, Problems of Indian History* Series No.1, Meerut 1993. Cf. also R.C. Majumdar, *History and Culture of Indian People. The Classical Age*, Bombay 1954, p. 20, especially n. 2: 'For the different view on the identification of Chandra and the location of Vāhlika (with some place in the Beās Valley, bordering Kashmir) cf. *JASB, Letters*, Vol. IX, 1943, pp. 179 ff.'. This location possibly coincides with that of the *tīrtha bhīmā-sthāna* in the *Mahābhārata*, as located by Doris Srinivasan, Section IV, below.

45. O. von Hinüber, 'Zu einigen iranischen Namen und Titeln aus Brāhmī-Inschriften am oberen Indus', in *Studia Grammatica Iranica. Festschrift für Helmut Humbach*, R. Schmitt & P.O. Skjaervø (ed.), München 1986, p. 147. Cf. also M. Bemmann & D. König, *Die Felsbildstation Oshibat*. Materialen zur Archäologie der Nordgebiete Pakistans, 1, H. Hauptmann (ed.), Mainz 1994, p. 46, 13.1.
46. *n*- and *t*- are clearly discernible in this script (cf. Table of Comparison). Therefore the reading *tya* is the only possible. One may think of a substitution like *devadharmaparityaga* for °*parityāga* or simply °*tyāga* 'this is the bestowal of a religious gift' by (or of) Śrī Variṣā.
47. Professor Fussman mentioned that the *devadharma* formula generally stands at the beginning of inscriptions. For *devadharma, deyadharma* cf. O. von Hinüber, 'Die Kolophone der Gilgit-Handschriften', in *Studien zur Indologie und Iranistik*, Heft 5/6, Festschrift Paul Thieme, Reinbek 1980, p. 54.
48. Forms like *samvacchara* are seldom attested, and no example is known to me written with the ligature *-mva* for *anusvāra* (cf. Lüders, *Mathurā Inscriptions, cit.*, ¶ 14, p. 73 [*savacarā*]; for late examples cf. D.R. Bhandarkar, 'A List of Inscriptions of Northern India in Brāhmī and Its Derivative Scripts, from about 200 A.C.', in *Appendix to Epigraphia Indica and Records of the Archaeological Survey of India*, Vols. XIX–XXIII, repr. Delhi 1983, No. 578; Sircar, *Indian Epigraphy, cit.*, p. 327). Three further examples are present in Mathurā inscriptions from the Kuṣāṇa times: one *(svarvacchara)* is occurring in an inscription of uncertain origin dating 299 of a disputed era (cf. R.D. Banerji, 'The Scythian Period of Indian History', *The Indian Antiquary*, XXXVII, 1908 [repr. Delhi 1985], pp. 33–35; G. Fussman, 'Nouvelles inscriptions Śaka: ère d'Eucratide, ère d'Azès, ère Vikrama, ère de Kaniṣka', *BEFEO*, LXVII, 1980, p. 42; G. von Mitterwallner, *Kuṣāṇa Coins and Kuṣāṇa Sculptures from Mathura*, Government Museum, Mathura, Growse Memorial Lectures 4, Mathura 1986, pp. 62–64. von Mitterwallner accepts the reading 199 which, as to my knowledge of number signs, is not correct. A little stroke added to the right of the vertical is visible which indicates the 200). The second (*savāchārā*) is copied by Fussman (1980, pp. 5–25) from an unpublished stone slab in the Russek collection; and

the third *saṃvacṭare* is written on a pillar from Govindnagar (Mathurā) dating to the 12th year of *devaputra* Kaniṣka (R.C. Sharma, *Buddhist Art from Mathurā*, Delhi 1984, fig. 13, the same von Mitterwallner, *Kuṣaṇa Coins, cit.*, p. 70). For general discussion cf. Damsteegt, *Epigraphical Hybrid Sanskrit, cit.*, pp. 192 ff.

49. O. von Hinüber, *Das ältere Mittelindisch im Überblick*, Veröffentlichungen der Kommission für Sprachen und Kulturen Südasiens, Heft 20. Österreichische Akademie der Wissenschaften, philos.- hist. Klasse, Sitzungsberichte, 467. Band, Wien 1986, p. 116, ¶ 237.
50. Cf. also Konow's (*Kharoshṭhī Inscriptions, cit.*, i.a. p. 62) reading *saṃbatśarae.*
51. Cf. T. Burrow, *The Language of the Kharoṣṭhī Documents from Chinese Turkestan*, Cambridge 1937, p. 19. He argues against Konow's reading *saṃvatśara:* 'But it is difficult to see how this *(tśa)* would differ from *c*'. There seems to be no difference. The reading *samvacchare* in our Brāhmī speaks in favour of von Hinüber's view that *tsa, ccha*, and—if the reading is correct—also *tśa* are only orthographic variants.
52. Konow, *Kharoshṭhī Inscriptions, cit.*, p. XCVI. Damsteegt, *Epigraphical Hybrid Sanskrit, cit.*, p. 17.
53. Konow, *Kharoshṭhī Inscriptions, cit.*, p. CI. Examples for *pratittha(ā)pita* without cerebralization are also found in several Mathurā inscriptions, cf. i.a. Lüders, *Mathurā Inscriptions, cit.*, Index, p. 225.
54. Konow, *Kharoshṭhī Inscriptions, cit.*, p. XCVI. Damsteegt, *Epigraphical Hybrid Sanskrit, cit.*, p. 18.
55. Konow, *Kharoshṭhī Inscriptions, cit.*, p. CXIII. Cf. also rare examples Damsteegt, *Epigraphical Hybrid Sanskrit, cit.*, p. 99 and F. Edgerton, *Buddhist Hybrid Sanskrit Grammar*, pp. 53 f., ¶ 8.59.
56. Burrow, *The Language of the Kharoṣṭhī Documents, cit.*, p. 8, ¶ 20. Cf. also Damsteegt, *Epigraphical Hybrid Sanskrit, cit.*, pp. 39 f. and rare cases in Buddhist Hybrid Sanskrit, Edgerton, *Buddhist Hybrid Grammar, cit.*, p. 17, ¶ 2.30.
57. Sircar, *Studies, cit.*, p. 106 states for the Abbottabad inscription: 'The characters of the present epigraph resemble those of Shorkot [...]'. For this inscription cf. also n. 35 and 43.
58. *The Imperial Gazetteer of India*, Vol. XXII, pp. 308 f.
59. J.Ph. Vogel, 'Shorkot Inscription of the Year 83', *Epigraphia Indica*, 1921–22, Vol. XVI, p. 17.
60. L. Sander, *Paläographisches zu den Sanskrithandschriften der Berliner Turfansammlung.* Verzeichnis der Orientalischen Handschriften in Deutschland, ed. W. Voigt, Supplementband 8, Wiesbaden 1968, Tafel 1–2, and p. 65, Tafel II.
61. J.F. Fleet, *Inscriptions of the Early Gupta Kings and Their Successors.* Corpus Inscriptionum Indicarum, Vol. III (repr. Varanasi 1963, pp. 262–64). D.R. Bhandarkar, *Inscriptions of the Early Gupta Kings*, revised by D.R. Bhandarkar, B. Chhabra & G.S. Gai (ed.). Corpus Inscriptionum Indicarum, Vol. III, New Delhi 1981, pp. 272–73.
62. G. Bühler, 'The New Inscription of Toramana Shaha', *Epigraphia Indica*, Vol. I, Calcutta 1892, pp. 238–41. Sircar, *Select Inscriptions, cit.*, p. 422, No. 56.
63. L. Sander, 'On the Origin and Date of the Bower Manuscript, A New Approach', *Investigating Indian Art, Proceedings of a Symposium on the Development of Early Buddhist and Hindu Iconography Held at the Museum of Indian Art*, Berlin 1986. Veröffentlichungen des Museums für Indische Kunst, M. Yaldiz & W. Lobo (ed.), Berlin 1987, Vol. 8, pp. 313–23.
64. K. Jettmar, ed., *Antiquities of Northern Pakistan, Reports and Studies*, Vol. 1: *Rock Inscriptions in the Upper Indus Valley*, Mainz, 1989.

65. Cf. F. Kielhorn, "A Note on the Saptarshi Era", *Kleine Schriften,* Teil 2, W. Rau (ed.), Glasenapp-Stiftung, Bd. 3, 2. Wiesbaden 1969, pp. 617–22.
66. Cf. also A. Cunningham, "Book of Indian Eras with Tables for Calculating Indian Dates", *The Indian Antiquary,* Vol. XI, 1882 (repr. 1970), p. 171.
67. Cf. i.a. L. Sander, "A Graffito with the Quintessence of Buddhist Doctrine from Ladakh", in *Festschrift Klaus Bruhn,* N. Balbir & J.K. Bautze (ed.), Reinbek 1994, pp. 561–70.
68. Two manuscripts were found in ceramic vessels near Merv, one at the site of Gjaur-qala in old Merv, and the other in a *stūpa* about 600 m east of Gjaur-qala. The latter contains manuscripts written in different varieties of northwestern Brāhmī of the 5th–6th centuries. Cf. B.J. Stavisky, 'The Fate of Buddhism in Middle Asia—in the light of archaeological data—', *Silk Road Art and Archaeology,* 3, 1993/94, pp. 117 f.
69. The visual assessments benefited from a discussion with Dr Chandra L. Reedy, who was also good enough to send me the pre-publication paper mentioned in n. 74.
70. *Crossroads of Asia, cit.,* Technical Analysis by Ch. Reedy, p. 244.
71. Ibid., No. 163, p. 162. A vase with incised scenes attributed to Gondla, Himachal Pradesh, now in The British Museum. (No. OA 1880–22).
72. Ibid., p. 244.
73. Ibid., pp. 243–44.
74. Ibid., p. 244. Cf. Ch.L. Reedy, "New Evidence for the Attribution and Historical Context of Buddhist Bronzes from Swat Valley, North Pakistan" in *Scientific Research in the Field of Asian Art,* Paul Jett with Janet Douglas, Blythe McCarthy and John Winter (eds.), London, 2003, pp. 134-40.
75. Cf. P.G. Paul, *Early Sculpture of Kashmir,* Leiden 1986, p. 3.
76. See S.S. Charak, *History and Culture of Himalayan States; Himachal Pradesh,* Vol. II, Part 2, New Delhi 1979, p. 8.
77. For specific localities, see Reedy's discussion in *Crossroads of Asia, cit.,* p. 244.
78. A.G. Poster, *From Indian Earth. 4,000 Years of Terracotta Art.* The Brooklyn Museum, 1986, No. 56, p. 122, dated to the 2nd century AD, and No. 76, p. 141 dated to the 5th century.
79. R.C. Craven, Jr., "A Unique Vaikuṇṭha-Style Viṣṇu (*narasiṁha-varāha*) Sculpture from the Mathurā Area", *Oriental Art,* XXXVIII, 3, 1992, pp. 145–53. The author dates the relief *c.* late 3rd to 4th century AD.
80. Based on the decorative device in the crown, perhaps the bronze Avalokiteśvara (P. Pal, *The Ideal Image,* New York 1978, No. 70, p. 117), could be assigned to the same region, but a somewhat later date. The center diamond of a three-peaked tiara on the Bodhisattva shows essentially the same device. Pal rightly expresses doubt that the bronze's provenance is Swat, its reputed findspot. Noting too many Gupta Gangetic stylistic features, he gives a date of 600 AD and leaves the question of provenance open. On the basis of the finding in the current paper, the date and provenance of this Avalokiteśvara may be re-evaluated.
81. See for example J.G. Williams, *The Art of Gupta India,* Princeton 1982, pl. 54.
82. S.J. Czuma, *Kuṣāṇa Sculpture: Images from Early India,* Cleveland 1985, No. 17, p. 74. Cf. *Palast der Götter,* Museum für Indische Kunst, Berlin 1992, pl. 5 (a Sanghol railing post).
83. D.M. Srinivasan, "A Unique Mathurā Eight-Armed Viṣṇu of the 4th Century A.D.", *Oriental Art,* Winter 1988/89, Vol. 34.4, p. 276. See figs. 1-2, in this volume (chapter 10).
84. P.K. Agrawala, *Śrīvatsa, The Babe of Goddess Śrī,* Varanasi 1974, figs. 55 and 57, p. 68. For a similar form on Ahicchatra pottery of the 2nd and 4th century AD, cf. text fig. 52, p. 44. The same sealing is dated between the 1st and 3rd century AD by A.L. Srivastava

('The Śrīvatsa Symbol in Indian Art', *EW*, 29, 1979, fig. 3.7). Srivastava uses sketches and does not refer to Agrawala's work.

85. Agrawala, *Śrīvatsa, cit.*, illustrations on p. 6 and pl. 114; figs. 53–54, p. 44.
86. See H. Härtel, 'Archaeological Evidence on the Early Vāsudeva Worship', in *Orientalia Iosephi Tucci Memoriae Dicata*, G. Gnoli & L. Lanciotti (eds.), SOR, LVI 2, Roma 1987, pp. 573–87, pl. Xa. See also the 4th century Mathurā Viṣṇu from the Asian Art Museum of San Francisco, The Avery Brundage Collection, No. B73 S17, in Craven, 'Vaikuṇṭha-Style Viṣṇu', *op. cit.*, fig. 15, p. 152.
87. P.G. Paul, "An Early Kashmiri Viṣṇu in the Peshawar Museum—A Ripple in Crosscurrents of the Northwestern Art Style", *South Asian Archaeology* 1987, Part 2, Rome 1990, pp. 831–46. See figs. 2 and 7, but also fig. 3.
88. H. Härtel & W. Lobo, *Schätze Indischer Kunst*, Berlin 1984, pl. 59; see text by Härtel, p. 114, n.2. Id., 'Zur Typologie einer Kaschmir Skulptur', in *Einblicke—Einsichten—Aussichten.* Festschrift E. Waetzold. Jahrbuch Preussicher Kulturbesitz, Sonderband 1, Berlin 1985, pp. 95–115.
89. *Crossroads of Asia, cit.*, p. 234 and table 2, p. 247.
90. For example, see the Berlin bronze (Fig. 9.12), and the illustrations from Mathurā (noted in n. 2; Figs. 5 and 7).
91. T.S. Maxwell, *Viśvarūpa*, Delhi 1988, fig. 45.
92. Paul, "Early Kashmiri Viṣṇu", *cit.*, fig. 3, p. 834.
93. See Begley, *Sudarśana-Cakra, cit.*, figs. 5 and 18. P. Chandra, *Stone Sculpture in the Allahabad Museum*, American Institute of Indian Studies, Poona, n.d., pl. 203a. Also fig. 15, p. 152 cit. in n. 85.
94. J.C. Harle, "An Early Indian Metal Figure", in *Eastern Approaches. Essays on Asian Art and Archaeology*, ed. T.S. Maxwell, Delhi 1992, pp. 74–80, pls. 23–26.
95. Bhū Devī is not present in the Florida 'Nārāyaṇa' nor in the few Mathurā pieces where the lower portion still survives: see Maxwell, *Viśvarūpa, cit.*, figs. 43, 45; Begley, *Sudarśana-Cakra, cit.*, fig. 7.
96. The flowers are not of the same variety since their petals are quite different.
97. No. 1969 1.15.2; see Paul, "An Early Kashmiri Viṣṇu", *cit.*, fig. 3. Paul compares this sculpture to the one from Bijbehāra and dates it to the 6th century.
98. *Palast der Götter, cit.*, pl. 25, p. 73, being Inv. No. I 10 198 in the Museum für Indische Kunst, Berlin. See also Härtel & Lobo, *Schätze Indischer Kunst, cit.*, p. 70, no. 34.
99. See Härtel, "Early Vāsudeva Worship", *cit.*, pl. Xa; D.M. Srinivasan, 'Vaiṣṇava Art and Iconography at Mathurā', in *Mathurā: The Cultural Heritage*, D.M. Srinivasan (gen. ed.), Delhi 1989, pls, 36.VI.A, 36.V.B, 36.III.A, 36.VIII.B.
100. See, for example, K.S. Desai, *Iconography of Viṣṇu*, New Delhi 1973, figs. 4–5; P. Chandra, *Allahabad Museum, cit.*, pls. 120, 196; Williams, *Gupta India, cit.*, pls. 54,218. These examples span the 4th to 6th century AD.
101. Paul, 'An Early Kashmiri Viṣṇu', *cit.*, figs. 3, 7, 8. Paul has shown that this feature is already seen on the lotus carried by some of the Gandhāran Bodhisattvas. See fig. 10.
102. C.L. Reedy, "Determining the Region of Origin of Himalayan Copper Alloy Statues through Technical Analysis", *A Pot-Pourri of Indian Art*, Bombay 1988, p. 77. For the recent paper, see C.L. Reedy, 'Buddhist Bronzes from Swāt'.
103. It is listed simply as coming from a private collection.
104. The narrowness cannot convey meditation since the Buddha's right hand is in *varada mudrā* and his left hand holds the hem of the robe.
105. This image belongs to the Metropolitan Museum of Art (No. 1987.218.7).
106. Paul, "An Early Kashmiri Viṣṇu", *cit.*, figs. 7–8.

107. See U. von Schroeder, *Indo-Tibetan Bronzes,* Hong Kong 1981, p. 76, no. 2.2. F. H. Ingholt, *Gandhāran Art in Pakistan,* New York 1957, illustrated in fig. 496. Ingholt does not date the *stūpa* but compares an aspect of it to the Dharmarājikā Stūpa, Taxila, see p. 181.
108. E.g. see discussion in Pal, *Bronzes, cit.,* p. 192.
109. See A.R. Mathur (ed.), *The Great Tradition 0/ Indian Bronze Masterpieces,* New Delhi 1988, fig. 4, p. 50. For a complete description, by A.P. Jamkhedkar, of all the bronzes found at Ramtek, see pp. 51–52.
110. For illustrations and literature on these finds, see Mathur, *Bronze Masterpieces, cit.,* pp. 47 ff., figs. 1–2. Note that the bronze in fig. 1 displays a pedestal with an additional bottom register decorated with interlaced four-petalled flowers. See also M. Venkataramayya, "Sixth Century Bronzes from Phophnar", *Lalit Kala,* 12, 1962, pp. 16–20. Cf. P. Chandra, *The Sculpture of India 3000 B.C.-1300 A.D.,* Washington 1985, pp. 97 and 106–7.
111. The piece, currently in the Victoria and Albert Museum, London (No. I.S. 12–1948) is often illustrated. See for example *Crossroads of Asia, cit.,* no. 211, or von Schroeder, *Indo-Tibetan Bronzes, cit.,* p. 81, fig. 4.4B.
112. See von Schroeder, *Indo-Tibetan Bronzes, cit.,* p. 78, fig. 3.3B.
113. G. Fussman, "Chilas, Hatun et les bronzes bouddhiques du Cachemire", in *Antiquities of Northern Pakistan* II, K. Jettmar, ed., Mainz 1993, pp. 29–31, re: 6.2; See Paul, *Early Sculpture of Kashmir, cit.,* pl. 83. The variant consists of placing the inscription on the bottom register, and sectioning this register off from the principle moulding by several thin bands.
114. Fussman, "Bronzes bouddhiques", *cit.,* pl. 13; A.H. Dani, *Chilas,* Islamabad 1983, p. 147, fig. 119.
115. See Fussman, "Bronzes bouddhiques", *cit.,* pl. 15.
116. G. Fussman, "Les inscriptions kharoṣṭhī de la plaine de Chilas", in *Antiquities of Northern Pakistan.* Reports and Studies, Vol. I, ed. K. Jettmar, Mainz 1989, pp. 3–6; see pl. 4.
117. A review of the depictions of the Vṛṣṇi Vīras throughout the subcontinent is contained in chapt. 16 of my monograph, *Many Heads, Arms and Eyes: Origin, Meaning and Form of Multiplicity in Indian Art,* Leiden 1997.
118. R. Audouin & P. Bernard, "Trésor de monnaies indiennes et indo-grecques d'Aï Khanoum (Afghanistan)" *Revue Numismatique,* 16, 1974, pp. 7 ff.
119. Pal has dated the relief to 800 AD. See P. Pal, "Art from the Northwest of the Indian Subcontinent", (Aspects of South Asian Art in the new galleries at the Metropolitan Museum of Art), *Arts of Asia,* 24, 2, 1994, fig. 18, p. 87.
120. See pl. 50 in Paul, *Early Sculpture of Kashmir, cit.*
121. The supposition that Kashmir is by far the main Northern region where Brahmanic worship was practiced during the 6th century is a major reason for Paul to attribute the entire series of early *vaiṣnava* images to Kashmir, even though he concedes that most of the pieces in the series were found in the region of Gandhāra: see Paul, *Early Sculpture of Kashmir, cit.,* p. 120.
122. Fig. 9 in Paul, 'An Early Kashmiri Viṣṇu', *cit.,* p. 843; taken from J. Burgess, "The Gandhāra Sculptures", *Journal of Indian Art and Industry,* VIII, 1898, pp. 23–40.
123. Farid Khan, "Recent Discoveries from the North-West, Pakistan", *SAS,* 8, 1992, pp. 67 ff.
124. I am pleased to acknowledge the gracious assistance given to me by Mme Hélène Diserens on the art of Masrur and Chamba and I wish to thank her for providing me with the photographs for Figs. 9.15, 9.16, and 9.19.

125. Information in a personal communication, dated 25 June, 1993.
126. H. Hargreaves, "The Monolithic Temples of Masrur", *Archaeological Survey of India, Annual Report,* 1915–16, pp. 39–48.
127. V.C. Ohri, *Sculpture of the Western Himalayas (History and Stylistic Development),* Delhi 1991, pp. 58 ff.
128. See B. Malia, *Sculptures of Kashmir (600–1200 A.D.),* Delhi 1990, pl. 9. This comparison was brought to my attention by Mme H. Diserens.
129. Hargreaves, "Masrur", *cit.,* p. 47.
130. Ohri, *Western Himalayas, cit.,* p. 57.
130a. ADDENDUM: It has since been determined that bhimā is fem. See the ADDENDUM to fn. 164.
131. M.G. Singh, *Art and Architecture of Himachal Pradesh,* Delhi 1983, pp. 47, 45. It should be added that folk traditions in other parts of India also associate the Pāṇḍavas to neighboring localities and edifices.
132. Singh, *Himachal Pradesh, cit.,* pl. 85a. Unfortunately Singh provides no further details.
132a. ADDENDUM: Re Bhimā see fn. 164a.
133. Ohri, *Western Himalayas, cit.,* pp. 45–46.
134. D.M. Srinivasan, "Early Kṛishṇa Icons: The Case at Mathurā", in *Kalādarśana, American Studies in the Art of India,* ed. J.G. Williams, New Delhi 1981, see pp. 130–31, or see paper in this volume.
135. Ohri, *Western Himalayas, cit.,* p. 33.
136. Ibid., pp. 46–47; see pl. 2.41.
137. Ibid., p. 49; this image, near the entrance of the Parasurama temple, shows an emerging Bhū Devī between the feet of the god.
138. Ibid., p. 47.
139. Ibid., p. 50.
140. Ibid., pp. 50–51, pl. 2.51.
141. See the reconstructed image, giving an idea of the original proportions, in H. Diserens, "Mahiṣāsuramardinī Associated with Viṣṇu: Rare Iconography on a Stele at Manali", in *South Asian Archaeology* 1989, Madison 1992, fig. 42.2. Regarding my date for this image, I consider, on the one hand, the modeling of the torso, the face, and the type of crown of the Bajaura Viśvarūpa to be more developed than that of the 4th–6th century Nirmand Vāsudeva-Kṛṣṇa (Fig. 9.16) and the Baramula 6th century torso of Viṣṇu (see Siudmak, 'Early Stone... Sculpture', *cit.,* fig. 6). On the other hand, the Viśvarūpa does not have the Kashmiri elements seen in Bajaura 'Nārāyaṇa' sculpture, probably of the late 8th century. (This sculpture is illustrated in Maxwell, 'Vaikuṇṭha', *cit.,* figs. 15 and 16). The silhouette of the body of the Bajaura Viśvarūpa appears more or less comparable to the 7th century Nirmand Vāsudeva-Kṛṣṇa, mentioned above and in n. 136.
142. For example, see the description in Ohri, *Western Himalayas, cit.,* p. 37.
143. See Maxwell, *Viśvarūpa, cit.,* figs. 42 and 49.
143a. ADDENDUM: See Doris Meth Srinivasan, "Childbirth, Childhood and the Magico-Religious World of Transformations", *Annali* 2011; 115-135; Plates I-XII. See fn. 164a ADDENDUM below.
144. I.139.144 in the critical edition.
145. In the shamanistic context, their union guarantees fertility and wealth to the people of Kulu. G. Jettmar-Thakur, "Raksasa Lore in the Kulu Valley", in *Eastern Approaches. Essays on Asian Art and Archaeology,* ed. T.S. Maxwell, Delhi 1992, pp. 107 ff.
146. P.H. Pott, "The Goddess Hirmā in Kulū Valley", *Pratidānam,* F.B.J. Kuiper Festschrift, ed. J.c. Heesterman, G.H. Schokker & V.I. Subramoniam. The Hague-Paris 1968, pp. 556–62.

147. See V.C. Ohri, ed., *History and Culture of the Chamba State,* New Delhi 1989, pl. 9.
148. H. Goetz, "The Antiquities of Chamba State", in *Studies in the History and Art of Kashmir and the Indian Himalaya,* Wiesbaden 1969; see p. 131 where it is dated to the 6th century. Ohri, *Western Himalayas, cit.,* 6th century. In the publication of two years earlier, the same piece is dated by Ohri to the 7th century. See *Chamba State,* V.C. Ohri (ed.), *cit.,* pl. 9.
149. Ohri, "Sculpture of Chamba" in *Chamba State, cit.,* p. 162.
150. See D.M. Srinivasan, 'Genealogy of the Buddha in Early Indian Art', in *Eastern Approaches, cit.,* pp. 38–44; see pl. 4.
151. *Ibid.,* pp. 40–42, see pl. 3. Note that Sūrya in the same low squat is also represented in a relief from Masrur, now in the State Museum, Simla. See V.C. Ohri, *Arts of Himachal,* Simla 1975, p. 136, fig. 9.
152. Like so many of the antiquities from Himachal Pradesh, it is not easy to obtain consensus on the date of the Chhatrarhi temple. Paul, *Early Sculptures of Kashmir, cit.,* p. 32, characterizes the temple as 'post-Gupta'. Goetz, 'Antiquities of Chamba', *cit.,* p. 131, associates the temple with the 7th century. Mme Diserens dates the temple to *c.* the beginning of the 8th century. See H. Diserens, 'La déesse Durgā Mahishāsuramardinī: petite stèle en pierre au musée Guimet', *La revue du Louvre,* Février 1988 - No. 1, p. 19, and n. 14 for additional descriptions of this figure.
153. M. Postel, A. Neven & K. Mankodi, *Antiquities of Himachal,* Bombay 1985, p. 185, fig. 286.
154. S. Kramrisch, *Manifestations of Shiva,* Philadelphia 1981, p. 103.
155. See Postel et al., *Antiquities of Himachal, cit.,* pp. 46–47, figs. 49–50; see also p. 70, fig. 94, for a later image of Tārā from the Śakti Devī temple which exudes the same energy, partially by means of the intensely convex features.
156. U. von Schroeder, *Indo-Tibetan Bronzes, cit.,* p. 25, no. 25C.
157. *Manifestations, cit.,* p. 103.
158. Personal communication of 12 October 1993 from Mrs. Nancy D. Baxter, Collections Manager and Administrator, Indian Art at the Philadelphia Museum of Art. Mrs. Baxter indicates that perhaps Stella Kramrisch's papers and notes, which are to come to the Museum, will shed light on her reasons for the changes in dating.
159. Postel et al., *Antiquities of Himachal, cit.,* p. 187.
160. J.A.B. van Buitenen, transl., *The Mahābhārata,* Books 2–3, Chicago 1975, p. 376.
161. See J.E. Schwartzberg, *A Historical Atlas of South Asia,* Chicago and London 1978, pl. III.C.1. p. 20; also B.C. Law, *Historical Geography of Ancient India,* Paris 1954.
162. P.V. Kane, *History of Dharmaśāstra* IV, Poona 1953, contains a List of Tīrthas. Kane remarks that this is the *tīrtha* where Brahmā lives (p. 753).
163. According to Kane, *Dharmaśāstra* IV, Vimala is a famous spring near the Mārtāṇḍa Temple (p. 821) and Malada is in Kashmir according to *Padma Purāṇa,* I.25.4 (p. 778).
164. Lore Sander opines that *bhīmāsthāna* in this passage may describe a *tīrtha* where a man becomes the son of the goddess after having taken a bath in her *yoni,* probably a spring; the goddess *bhīmā* may refer to an unknown local goddess. I must register an inability to agree with this statement. First, the passage does not qualify the *'yoni'* as belonging to anyone in particular. Second, it needs to be stressed that *yoni* is a term having meanings other than 'female genitalia', and the like, associated with the female. Vedic literature is replete in the references to *yoni* where the term means 'the source', 'the place', (i.e. the place of power, especially creative power). As such, *'yoni'* can be associated with a male god (e.g. *Śatapatha Brāhmaṇa,* 8.2.2.5; *Bṛhad Āraṇyaka Upaniṣad,* I.4.11).

164a. ADDENDUM: Since 1997, inscriptions on seals and vessels from Kashmir Smast mentioning *bhīmā sthāna* have been published, showing that Sander's remarks are on the right track. Harry Falk published "A Copper Plate Donation Record and Some Seals from Kashmir Smast", *Beiträge zur Allgemeinen und Vergleichenden Archäologie*, Band 23, 2003. The new evidence reopens the problem of the bronze's provenance. I too have had access to the Kashmir Smast material and published a study on the 'Bhīmā' seals entitled "Childbirth, Childhood and the Magico-Religious World of Transformations", *Annali* (Napoli), 2011. The paper will be reprinted in Vol. II of *Listening to Icons*. Therefore a summary pertaining only to the bronze 'Nārāyaṇa' is given here: The Kashmir Smast seals' symbols and inscriptions prove that 'bhīmā' is a female divine power, and a *bhīmā sthāna* is a place infused with her power. Footnotes 144-146 will be relevant in the Addendum to that paper.

165. See Jettmar-Thakur, "Raksasa Lore", *cit.*, p. 107.

166. Schrader, *Pāñcarātra, cit.*, p. 16. Schrader thinks of the extreme North, on the basis of the story in the Nārāyaṇīya section in the Śānti Parvan of the *Mahābhārata;* the story suggests that the home of Pāñcarātra worship is in the Northern Śvetadvīpa. However, worship of Vāsudeva, pivotal in the Pañcarātra system, originated in the region of Mathurā.

167. A brief survey is available in K.N. Misra, "The Vaikuṇṭha Images from Chamba and Other Centres in North-West India", in *Chamba State, cit.*, p. 111–21. Additional examples can be seen in Postel et al., *Antiquities of Himachal, cit.*, pp. 99–101.

168. J.Ph. Vogel, *Antiquities of Chamba State,* Part I, Calcutta 1922, pp. 207–8, pl. XXIX.

169. Ibid., pp. 78–95.

170. This sandstone relief, now in the Himachal State Museum, Simla, is illustrated in Ohri, *Arts of Himachal, cit.*, see n. 150.

171. Ohri, *Western Himalayas, cit.*, pp. 50, 151.

172. A figure on the north side of the inner wall of the hall in front of the main shrine is described by Debala Mitra *(Pandrethan, Avantipur, and Martand,* Delhi 1977, pp. 100–101) as follows: '[...] the figure [...] has [...] leonine and boar-like side heads representing Saṅkarṣaṇa and Aniruddha [...] the front placid face stands for Vāsudeva [...] Between the legs appears the bust of Pṛthvī. The attributes in his hands are not very distinct [...] From old photographs of this relief it appears that above the man-lion-boar heads there is a pile of seven more heads in three rows, two rows having three each and the top only one. In that case, the image most probably stands for Viśvarūpa Viṣṇu'.

173. A 4th century AD Chinese translation of the Lalitavistara is mentioned in Nanjio, Bunyio, *A Catalogue of the Chinese Translation of the Buddhist Tripitaka* (Oxford 1883), No. 160. See J.W. De Jong, 'L'épisode d'Asita dans le Lalitavistara', *Asiatica,* Festschrift F. Weller, Wiesbaden 1954, especially p. 313; cited by G. Fussman *(Annuaire du Collège de France* 1989–90, p. 623) to support the 8th century dating of the text.

173a. ADDENDUM: The place where the bronze (in Fig. 9.1) was found can be conjectured on the basis of two bits of information (available thus far). The first is an oral remark made to me much after the publication of this paper by John Siudmak (dealer and researcher) who says that a dealer took him to the site of Kashmir Smast in Pakistan over twenty years ago and informed him that the icon came from there. The second is the site *bhīmā sthāna* named in the inscription of the icon as the place where the icon was installed. Harry Falk argues that *bhīmā sthāna* refers to the place of the icon's find place as well as origin which he believes is Kashmir Smast.

I have argued that a distinction must be made between where the object was made and where it was found—if indeed it was found at Kashmir Smast, the name of an enormous cave on top of a mountain in the Sakra range, Mardan District in the Peshawar Basin of northern Pakistan. Whereas the bronze may have been found at Kashmir Smast, it is difficult to believe that a distinctive casting technique, a traceable intermingling of far-flung but recognizable stylistic and iconographic features expressing a complex theology involving god Nārāyaṇa datable to these times, could have jelled together in a remote sacred site which has no other examples or evidence for such a production. These points (expanded upon below) need to be answered before I can accept that this Nārāyaṇa bronze was made at Kashmir Smast.

New information has come to light that further refines the provenance problem and highlights the likelihood of Himachal Pradesh/Kashmir.

In the original 1997 paper I comment on factors that bode against an origin in Kashmir, namely the high tin metallic content of the piece, the hole in the back of the icon being the result of a particular casting technique and that neither the script nor the stylistic features appear to conclusively assign the image's origin to Kashmir. Whereas I have noted that 'bhīmā' could have been an orthographic error for masculine 'bhīma', Lore Sander cited textual references to a place of worship associated with a goddess named 'bhīmā' which is located in Kashmir (see fn. 36). Further, she notes that the script—in use in the Himalayas as far as Ladakh and beyond—suggests a remote Northwestern region as the origin of the bronze.

My analysis of the bronze's style and iconography arrives at the conclusion that it exhibits diverse elements. The icon appears to fuse Kuṣāṇa through early Gupta influences from the Gangetic Valley with Northwestern characteristics found within a broad area (Gandhāra, Taxila, Himachal Pradesh, Kashmir). Accordingly, I conjectured that the place of origin must be a locality which was open to the artistic influences of both the Gangetic and the Northern Himalayan regions. In the end, I opted for Himachal Pradesh, due to good comparative evidence especially in Chamba. Himachal Pradesh is bordered by Jammu and Kashmir on the North, and Chamba District is in the Northwest of Himachal Pradesh, thus close to the modern geographical region designated as Kashmir.

It is determined that there are other references to a place of *bhīmā* beside the one on the 'Nārāyaṇa' bronze and those occurring on finds from Kashmir Smast. As already mentioned in the original paper, the *Mahābhārata* alludes to 'the place of Bhīmā' among a series of *tīrthas* which suggest the place of Bhīmā the epic has in mind lies somewhere between the Punjab and Kashmir. A Kashmiri text of *c.* the 7th century cites a Bhīmā temple at the modern Kashmiri village of Brāṅ and a medieval Kashmiri poet mentions a Bhīmā Devī *tīrtha* located at Nandiparvata. These can be added to the information contained in fn. 36 of this paper. There is rather frequent mention of Bhīmā's place in mountains within the Himālayan system. I have even conjectured that the toponym Kashmir Smast (Kashmir Cave) could have been given by the locals to link their *bhīmā sthāna* to others within a sacred Himālayan orbit. Further, the theological beliefs expressed by the 'Nārāyaṇa' bronze relate to beliefs of the Pāñcarātra sect within Vaiṣṇavism. Early Pāñcarātra texts, quite possibly contemporaneous with the icon, were composed in Kashmir. In sum there seem to be many aspects that point to the Kashmir region as the provenance of the 'Nārāyaṇa'. In the paper written in 1997, I underestimated the implications from 6th century Kashmiri imagery (e.g. pedestal variant, idiocyncracies pertaining to the conch and possibly the lotus) which are similar to the 5th century 'Nārāyaṇa' and I was guided by strong stylistic and iconographic factors in Himachal Pradesh, especially Chamba.

In conclusion, the provenance of this piece may be situated somewhere between northern Himachal Pradesh and Kashmir. I suspect that more evidence may some day be forthcoming, permitting more work to be done on the precise location of this bronze. Should the reader be confused by the designation 'Nārāyaṇa' in the text for imagery like Fig. 9.1, yet the caption for Fig. 9.1 and other comparable images read 'Para Vāsudeva-Nārāyaṇa', please turn, straightaway, to pages 191-192 and 198 for an explanation.

174. Maxwell, *Viśvarūpa, cit.*, pp. 136–41 can be consulted for a detailed description; however the identification of Agni in the nimbus must be taken with caution.
175. See J. Varenne, *La Mahā Nārāyaṇa Upaniṣad,* Tomes I–II, 2nd ed. Paris 1986, vv. 235–36, 251–252. For an interpretation of this text and the evolution tracing the omniform nature of Vedic Puruṣa unto Nārāyaṇa, see Srinivasan, *Many Heads..., cit.*, chapt. 10, entitled 'Mūrtis and the Mahā Nārāyaṇa Upaniṣad'. In this chapter I discuss the philological and religious evidence to support dating this text to the time around the beginning of the Christian era.
176. See T.S. Maxwell, 'The Viśvarūpa Sculpture from Bhusawar at Bharatpur', in *Eastern Approaches, cit.*, pp. 155–67.
177. Id., "Bhusawar Viśvarūpa", *cit.*, p. 165.
178. See J.L. Bhan, 'Manifestations of Viṣṇu—A Critical Study of an Eighth Century Prabhavali from Devsar, Kashmir', in *Vaiṣṇavism in Indian Arts and Culture,* Ratan Parimoo (ed.), New Delhi 1987, pp. 362–95.
179. Goetz, *Kashmir and the Indian Himalaya, cit.*, p. 84.
180. Pal, *Bronzes, cit.*, p. 70.
181. The sun and moon symbolize eternality; see Srinivasan, *Many Heads..., cit.*, chapt. 20.
182. Ibid., chapters 11, 18, 22.
183. A.-M. Esnoul, *Nārāyaṇīya Parvan du Mahābhārata,* Paris 1979, p. 63, re chapt. XIV *(Mhbh.* XII.347).
184. S. Jaiswal, "The Demon and the Deity: Conflict Syndrome in the Hayagrīva Legend", in *Vaiṣṇavism in Indian Arts and Culture, cit.*, p. 43.
185. P. Shah, *Viṣṇudharmottara-Purāṇa.* Third Khaṇḍa. Vol. II, Baroda 1961, p. 158, re: Adhyaya 80.
186. S.L. Schastok, *The Śāmalājī Sculptures and the 6th Century Art in Western India,* Leiden 1985; see figs. 26, 34, 38.
187. A clear photograph is in J.C. Harle, *Gupta Sculpture,* Oxford 1974, fig. 73.
188. Schrader, *Pāñcarātra, cit.*, pp. 51–53.
189. Ibid., p. 19.
190. The date of late 3rd century is offered by Esnoul, *Nārāyaṇīya,* p. 3, n. 2. A date of 200–400 AD is given by G.A. Grierson; see Srinivasan, "Caturvyūha", *cit.*, p. 53, n. 48. See p. 150 in this volume.
191. 'One hundred' heads signifies 'the ultimate number' of heads. In the artistic rendering of a *viśvarūpa* image, the 'ultimate number' can be expressed by the basic three (= four) faces plus as many other faces as the artist can make. See Srinivasan, *Many Heads..., cit.*, chapt. 11.
192. These are Vāsudeva, Saṃkarṣaṇa, Pradyumna and Aniruddha. It may be pointed out that Vāsudeva is not mentioned twice; thus this passage does not sharply distinguish between *para* Vāsudeva and *vyūha* Vāsudeva. Also noteworthy is that this is not the only fourfold emanation arising from Nārāyaṇa in the account of the Nārāyaṇīya. Nārāyaṇa's fourfold form is also said to be born in the house of Dharma (cf. XII.322.2). These forms have different names; they are Nara, Nārāyaṇa, Hari, and Kṛṣṇa. The difference between these two sets has been well set forth by Esnoul *(Nārāyaṇīya, cit.*, pp. 18, 60). She specifies that the *vyūha* forms are cosmic in nature, whereas the *dharma* forms approach an *avatāra* nature since they contribute to the increase of righteousness

(Dharma) in the world. This digression on Nārāyaṇa's two sets of fourfold forms is made because it may relate to two sets of iconographic conventions in the depiction of Viśvarūpa. The depiction of animal or human heads as *vyūhas* has already been dealt with, above (one more human headed Caturvyūha will be cited below). But some Viśvarūpa icons, notably from Deogarh and Kannauj feature four lateral animal heads that seem to represent the four *avatāras* (i.e. Fish, Tortoise, Boar and Lion); see Maxwell, *Viśvarūpa, cit.*, fig. 5.1, table 6.1 and table 6.2. Recently two more examples, a 9th century one from Bengal and a 10th century one from Bihar have been discussed by G. Bhattacharya, "A Unique Viṣṇu Image from the National Museum of Bangladesh", *South Asian Archaeology* 1989, Madison 1992, pp. 317–26. The fluidity in the iconography of a *vaiṣṇava* Viśvarūpa image could perhaps reflect Nārāyaṇa's multiple fourfold nature as expressed in the Nārāyaṇīya, The digression is not meant to reopen the debate on the lion and boar lateral heads as *avatāra* heads in connection with Para Vāsudeva-Nārāyaṇa or Viśvarūpa. It may be well to reiterate Mallmann's observation, namely that the four faces (two of which she cited as animal faces) in the Caturvyūha and Viśvarūpa icons originally refer to the *vyūhas* and subsequently to the *avatāras*.

193. Mallmann, *L'Agni Purāṇa, cit.*, pp. 19–21.
194. Nārāyaṇa's epithet *viśvātman* (*JS*, 6.69), designates him as 'the universal soul', a designation attributed to other high gods besides Nārāyaṇa. See S. Sorensen, *An Index to the Names in the Mahābhārata*, repr. Delhi 1978, p. 730. Thus I cannot agree with Maxwell (see n. 22), on the expanded name for Nārāyaṇa. The dating of the *JS* is discussed by the editor of the text; see E. Krishnamacharya, *Jayākhyasaṃhitā of Pāñcarātra Āgama*, No. 54 in Gaekwad's Oriental Series, Baroda 1931, pp. 26–34. See also J. Gonda, *Medieval Religious Literature in Sanskrit*, Wiesbaden 1977, p. 54.
195. Other features of Nārāyaṇa which are iconographic in nature are in *JS*, 6.74–76.
196. See Maxwell ('Vaikuṇṭha', *cit.*, pp. 146–51), for the text and translation of Paṭala 6.
197. Now that we have a Gupta three-headed Pāñcarātra icon labelled as 'Nārāyaṇa', the icon must be viewed in relation to the roughly contemporary *JS* (see n. 194). Prior it was unclear whether a precise mental image of a four-faced 'Nārāyaṇa' could elucidate the iconography of Gupta three-faced icons. Therefore Maxwell ('Vaikuṇṭha', *cit.*, p. 128), had dated the *JS* to the 8th century to coordinate with the date that the four-headed icon became integrated with the Pāñcarātra. The fact that the *JS* places the god on Garuḍa and that Garuḍa does not appear on the 427 AD bronze is not sufficiently critical to prevent application of the text's information to the 427 AD bronze.
198. Srinivasan, 'Caturvyūha', *cit.*, p. 44.
199. Schrader, *Pāñcarātra, cit.*, p. 51.
200. D.C. Sircar, chapter on 'Vaishṇavisrn' in R.C. Majumdar et al. (eds.), *The History and Culture of the Indian People*, Vol. III. *The Classical Age*, Bombay 1954, p. 423.
201. Further details, and bibliography are in Srinivasan, 'Caturvyūha'.
202. It has been usual to assume that the figure represents *vyūha* Vāsudeva, and the entire statue is generally identified as a 'Caturvyūha' image. I also identified this piece as a 'Caturvyūha' (see Srinivasan, 'Caturvyūha', *cit.*, 39 ff.). I am no longer so certain that the Vāsudeva figure represents a *vyūha*. It seems to me that the figure could also be Para Vāsudeva and three *vyūhas* which emanate from him. Para Vāsudeva appears to display an intensification of multiple bodily parts, whereas the *vyūha* does not seem to (see below). Perhaps a comparative study of the type called Para Vāsudeva-Nārāyaṇa in this paper, and the type called *caturvyūhātmaka* in the Nepalese dedicatory inscription (see below) will clarify this important point. Such a study would probably commence

with the important bronze recently gifted to the Nelson-Atkins Museum of Art (Figs. 9.26-9.27). It is a small (ht. 2 5/8"), bronze from Kashmir, based on the *sarvatobhadrika* model. Four deities, facing the cardinal directions, surround a central pillar, topped by a lotus. Its importance lies in the fact that it seems to represent an intermediary. The bronze may portray Para Vāsudeva-Nārāyaṇa together with three other standing figures of the type called *caturvyūhātmaka* in the Nepalese example (see below). A number of features of this small bronze tally with the iconographic expression of the Sādhaka's dream state of awareness of the Supreme God in Pāñcarātra practice. (See S. Gupta, "Yoga and *Antaryāga* in Pāñcarātra", in *Ritual and Speculation in Early Tantrism. Studies in Honor of André Padoux,* ed. T. Goudriaan, New York 1992, p. 200).' The expression features a central luminous pillar, topped by a lotus; the four *vyūha* forms are envisaged around the pillar, facing the four directions. Here, the central pillar symbolizes the Supreme God, and the lotus, his *śakti.* To advance theological correspondences in the art forms, it almost seems necessary for a Pāñcarātra specialist to collaborate with an art historian.

203. See D.M. Srinivasan, 'Vaiṣṇava Art and Iconography at Mathurā', in *Mathurā: The Cultural Heritage,* gen. ed. D.M. Srinivasan, New Delhi 1989, pp. 387–88. I do not consider the Varāha image in the Los Angeles Country Museum of Art (No. M72.53.8) to date the Kuṣāṇa Period; it belongs in the Gupta Period.

204. The following aforementioned 'Nārāyaṇa' images may therefore be called Para Vāsudeva-Nārāyaṇa; the Florida 'Nārāyaṇa': the Berlin 'Nārāyaṇa': the Mathurā terracotta 'Nārāyaṇa' *(Viśvarūpa,* fig. 45); probably the Masrur 'Nārāyaṇa' and the Nirath 'Nārāyaṇa': the Boston Museum of Fine Arts 'Nārāyaṇa' *(Viśvarūpa,* fig. 42) assuming the complete image would be like another Mathurā Para Vāsudeva-Nārāyaṇa (fig. 43 in *Viśvarūpa),* and, the Ādi Śakti Devī 'Nārāyaṇa'.

205. This is the position of Dr Lore Sander.

206. Mary Shepard Slusser, *Nepal Mandala,* Princeton 1982, Vol. I, pp. 244-45; Vol. II, pls. 386–88. In a personal communication with Slusser (2.10.94), she informs me that an earlier date is possible for the Nārāyaṇa Hiti Caturvyūha. The 16th century Caturvyūha is illustrated in Gail, 'Three- and Four-Faced Viṣṇu Images', *cit.,* figs. 1–4.

207. E.g. Srinivasan, *Many Heads..., cit.,* chapters 11, 18.

208. The 15th century *Rūpamaṇḍana* is often quoted to explain why the fifth head so seldom is depicted. Yet, it is carved in stone at the earliest stage of Hindu iconography. The Bhīṭā Pāñcamukha Liṅga, dated to the 2nd century BC portrays the fifth head, called Īśāna.

209. Srinivasan, 'Vaiṣṇava Art'.

210. What happens when definitions based on texts and inscriptions are superceded by definitions based on visual distinctions is demonstrated by the paper of G. Bhattacharya, 'Unique Viṣṇu', *cit.* For example, the Mathurā type with emanating figural *vyūha* heads (Fig. 9.25) is considered a type distinct from the Mathurā type with emanating animal heads from the Gupta period (his fig. 38.4). The author calls the Late Kuṣāṇa sculpture (Fig. 9.25), Vāsudeva-Caturvyūha and decides to name the Gupta piece Visnu-Vaikuṇṭha (his fig. 38.4), apparently unaware, or not bothered by the fact that Vaikuṇṭha can be a name of Vāsudeva in Pāñcarātra texts.

10

A Unique Mathurā Eight-armed Viṣṇu of the 4th Century AD

In Sotheby's Catalogue (Indian, Himalayan, South-East Asian Art and Indian Miniatures) of the September 1985 New York Sale, I first saw a photograph of Lot 227 described as "A Central Indian Mottled Pink Sandstone Fragmentary Figure of Śiva, Gupta, 4th/5th Century". The fragmentary relief belongs to a Private Collection (Fig. 10.1). I was able to view the relief at Sotheby's in New York and to register the following details:

The relief, measuring 27½ in., shows a god facing frontally. The four arms on his right side are intact. The torso and part of the right thigh also remain. The god wears a *dhotī* tied with a simple sash. The rest of the body is broken off; it is therefore no longer possible to determine with certitude the position of the left leg. However, due to the lack of movement in either the torso or the right thigh, it is possible to conjecture that the god stood in the *samapāda* pose, that is, with the body's weight equally distributed on the two straight legs.

Although fragmentary, enough of the relief remains to suggest its provenance. The red mottled sandstone indicates the Mathurā area. Further, the iconography of the four arms on the right side as well as certain stylistic elements, to be discussed below, strongly implicate the Mathurā area as the place of origin.

The god's full and spheroid face has large open eyes which do not bulge out as is characteristic of the treatment of the eyes in Mathurā sculpture of the Kuṣāṇa age. The eyes on this piece are somewhat integrated into the curvature of the head, although traces of the heavy Kuṣāṇa eyelids are evident. The god wears earrings, a simple necklace close to the throat, plain armlets and bracelets. This combination of ornaments can be found on early Gupta images, as for example,

Originally published in *Oriental Art*, New Series, Winter 1988/89, Vol. XXXIV. No. 4; pp. 276-281. Reprinted with stylistic changes and with permission of *Orintal Art*.

Fig. 10.1 Viṣṇu Aṣṭadhā Prakṛti. 4th Century. Photo: Courtesy Sotheby's.

Fig. 10.2 Four-armed Viṣṇu. 4th Century. Photo: Courtesy Doris Wiener Gallery.

the early Gupta four-armed Viṣṇu formerly in the Doris Wiener Gallery (Fig. 10.2). The presence of a long *vanamālā* also assures that the god in the relief is Viṣṇu. Viṣṇu wears a crown with a large central crest, from which descend bejewelled loops encircling both sides of the crown. This headdress is not entirely like the typical Kuṣāṇa turban with its large central crest, nor is it entirely like Viṣṇu's bejewelled straight-edged *makuṭa,* but somewhere in between. Other early Gupta Viṣṇu figures have similar crowns (e.g. The Nelson-Atkins Museum No. 62-26 [Fig. 10.3]; cf. Fig. 10.2).

Originally, the relief depicted an eight-armed Viṣṇu each side having four arms. At present only the set on the right remains. The natural arm is bent at the elbow and the extended hand comes to rest on the centre of the nude chest. The three additional arms radiate from different points of the upper portion of the natural arm. The extra arms are all raised and all carry attributes. Going from top downwards, the attributes held are a rock, a sword and arrows. The series of attributes and the disposition of the arms closely ally this image of eight-armed Viṣṇu to a group of eight-armed Viṣṇu images of the Kuṣāṇa period.

There are three Kuṣāṇa eight-armed Viṣṇu images known to date. Two come from Mathurā and one comes from Kauśāmbī. These reliefs are small and preserve the right side better than the left. One of the Mathurā reliefs (Mathura Museum No. 1010, ht 4 in.), shows the god wearing the typical Kuṣāṇa turban (Fig. 10.4). Viṣṇu's natural arm is bent at the elbow and the outstretched hand is placed on the nude chest. In the curvature of this arm appears an unidentified weapon; perhaps it is the mace. The extra three arms extend from the upper portion of the natural arm; they are raised and carry the following attributes, in descending order: a rock, a sword and arrows. The mottled sandstone relief is broken below the waist. The second Mathurā relief (Mathura Museum No. 3550; ht 1 ft 1 in.) has all of the right side and part of the left side and lower portion intact (Fig. 10.5). The head of the god is totally damaged but the breakage indicates that his headdress should have been the typical Kuṣāṇa turban. The natural right arm is bent and the hand on the nude chest holds an unidentified round object. The other three arms assume the same raised positions as seen in both the Kuṣāṇa relief (Fig. 10.4; No. 1010) and the early Gupta relief (Fig. 10.1). Again, the attributes held in descending order in the right set of hands are: the rock, the sword and arrows. The natural left arm rests on the raised left leg and holds a conch. Many more ornamental features are seen on this relief. Viṣṇu wears, in addition to bracelets and armlets, a necklace of beads close to the neck, a thick floral garland around the shoulders[1] and a long, thin *vanamālā* which descends below the knees. His *dhotī* is gathered and tied in a simple knot at the centre. The eight-armed turbaned Viṣṇu from

Fig. 10.3 Head of Viṣṇu. Early Gupta. The Nelson-Atkins Museum of Art, Kansas City, Missouri (Nelson Fund).

Fig. 10.4 Viṣṇu Aṣṭadhā Prakṛti. Kuṣāṇa Period. Photo: Courtesy Government Museum, Mathurā.

Kauśāmbī (Lucknow, State Museum No. 49. 247, ht 6 in.) is more fragmentary than the Mathurā ones. Nonetheless, the same disposition of the four arms on the right side is discernible, as is a bundle of arrows held in the lowermost extra hand. The standardized iconography of the right side of these Kuṣāṇa eight-armed images is obvious. It is not possible to gauge how the left side looked. Nor can it be predicted whether the lower portion, marking the stance of the god, was uniform in all the Kuṣāṇa images.

One thing is clear, that the right set of arms of the early Gupta Viṣṇu is entirely consonant with the iconographic formula developed in the Kuṣāṇa period. This formula is not apparent in any eight-armed Viṣṇu images dating to the 5th–6th century. It is therefore proposed to date the fragmentary relief of eight-armed Viṣṇu (Fig. 10.1), to the 4th century AD. The dating reflects the transitional nature of the piece, showing a pronounced continuation of Kuṣāṇa iconography as well as early Gupta stylistic developments.

The 5th- and 6th-century images of eight-armed Viṣṇu are in a better state of preservation than the earlier ones and it is possible to discern two distinctly different types of eight-armed images.[2] The two types are seen together in Bādāmi, Cave III. The Cave, dating to the last quarter of the 6th century, is fronted by a platform. On the wall at the East, or left end of the platform, is a huge (12 ft 4 in. in ht) relief of an eight-armed Viṣṇu. On the West, or right end of the platform, is an even larger relief (13 ft 1 in. in ht) of another eight-armed Viṣṇu.[3] The figure to the East stands in the *samapāda* pose (Fig. 10.6). The right natural hand rests on the hip and holds a sword. The three extra arms radiate about the natural arm and the following attributes are held, in descending

Fig. 10.5 Viṣṇu Trivikrama. Kuṣāṇa Period. Photo: D. M. Srinivasan.

order: the wheel, arrows, mace. The left natural arm rests against the thigh and on the knot of the garment. The left extra arms echo the positions of those on the right. The attributes on the left side, again in descending order are: the conch, the shield and the bow. In the image on the opposite side, there is little difference in the attributes held in the arms.[4] The major difference occurs in the movement of the arms and in the god's standing position. The left leg is raised high almost to the level of the shoulders. This position reminds us that there are three possible ways to represent the level of the raised left leg in images of Viṣṇu Trivikrama. Rao notes that the left leg can be raised to the level of the right knee, to the navel or to the forehead.[5] It is well known that the relief on the western end represents Viṣṇu Trivikrama. The identifying feature of the uplifted left leg captures the dramatic moment of a narrative whose roots go back to myths in Vedic literature.[6] It is not possible, on account of the difference in pose, to agree with those wishing to identify the eastern image as another rendering of the Trivikrama theme.[7]

Fig. 10.6 Viṣṇu Aṣṭadhā Prakṛti. Bādāmi, Cave III. 6th century. Photo: Courtesy Carol R. Bolon.

A Trivikrama image, to judge from other examples of the 5th and 6th centuries, indicates its narrative content either by movement in the body of god, or by secondary figures relating to the narrative, or by both. The eight-armed Trivikrama carved on a rock at Ramgarth Hill (Vidisha Dist., M.P.), raises the left leg to the level of the navel.[8] The natural arms of this carving, dated to the 5th[9] (possibly 6th)[10] century, extend outward and the hands rest at the hips. The extra arms radiate around the elbows of the natural arms. The right arms, from top downward (1) hold a round object, (2) an object almost totally destroyed, (3) rest at the hip, (4) hold the mace. The left arms from top downward (1) hold a small round object (2), the wheel (3), the

Fig. 10.7 Viṣṇu Trivikrama. Gupta Period. The Russek Collection. Photo: Courtesy R. Russek.

bow (4) the conch at the hip. A Gupta terracotta depicting eight-armed Viṣṇu Trivikrama has lost most of the left side and lower portion (Fig. 10.7; 13¼ in. ht). The movement, however, flowing from the torso into the right set of arms leaves little doubt that the god is engaged in winning the triple regions from the demons. The concentration of weaponry held in the arms underscores the action. Going from top downward are seen (1) a small dagger, (2) an oval wheel with flame-like spokes, (3) a large sword, (4) a small round object held at the hip. A conch is in the hand at the left. In this heretofore unpublished terracotta from the Russek Collection (No. 686), Viṣṇu's face is exultant with joy and his rhythmic body is framed in a *vanamālā* of notable tactile quality. The Pawaya toraṇa lintel, dated to the beginning of the 5th century,[11] shows only a part of the upper right section of Viṣṇu Trivikrama. The narrative content pertaining to Trivikrama is carved to the left of the god; to wit, the sacrifice of Bali is depicted in elaborate detail. The attributes carried in Trivikrama's extra three hands are the sword, the wheel and the bow. The natural arm is bent at the elbow and the open hand rests in the centre of the nude chest. The gesture, in this the earliest of the 5th-century Trivikrama representations, closely parallels that of the 4th-century Viṣṇu (Fig. 10.1) as well as the three Kuṣāṇa eight-armed Viṣṇu images discussed above. Indeed, there can be little doubt that one of these, namely the Mathurā relief showing the god with the left leg raised to the level of the navel (Fig. 10.5), should be identified as Viṣṇu Trivikrama.

The other Kuṣāṇa representations and the 4th-century Viṣṇu show neither movement nor narrative content. The lack of narrative content is especially evident in the 4th-century image; no secondary figures are to be seen on the fragment.[12] Most important, the figure looks hieratic in its stark frontality and (presumably) equipoised stance. As such, the image compares better with the eastern eight-armed Viṣṇu at Bādāmi than with the figure of Viṣṇu Trivikrama at the western end.

It is possible to suggest an identification for the second type of eight-armed Viṣṇu image. The possibility for an eightfold Vaiṣṇava god (who is not Trivikrama) presents itself even within the time frame of our earliest extant eight-armed images.

Śri Bhagavān in the *Bhagavad Gītā (c.* 2nd century BC–2nd century AD), gives Arjuna full insight into both his higher and lower natures. His higher nature is omniform *(viśvarūpa).* God tells Arjuna that his lower nature *(prakṛti)* is his material nature which is eightfold *(aṣṭadhā).*[13] He further explains that this lower nature is the source from which all phenomenal forms are created. Upon analysis,[14] the *Gītā* appears to convey belief in a lower form of the Supreme which is the embodiment of the basic eight elements needed for the production of life. This form is therefore a cosmic form which may be called Aṣṭadhā Prakṛti, or, God as Eightfold Primordial Matter. It is proposed that representations of Viṣṇu Aṣṭadhā Prakṛti were invented in the ateliers of Mathurā during the Kuṣāṇa period, which was a time when Mathurā was THE center of innovation in *vaiṣṇava* art.[15] The 4th-century Viṣṇu Aṣṭadhā Prakṛti (Fig. 10.1), seems to represent the last phase of this innovative tradition in Mathurā; the image also seems to be a forerunner of future monumental forms of Viṣṇu Aṣṭadhā Prakṛti (e.g. the eastern image in Cave III, Bādāmi[16] Fig. 10.6). Therein lies its uniqueness.

NOTES AND REFERENCES

1. This floral wreath compares with the wreaths seen on the following Viṣṇu images from Mathurā: Mathura Museum Nos. 781; 3502; 392-95. These images have all been assigned to the late Kuṣāṇa period. See my paper "Vaiṣṇava Art and Iconography at Mathurā", *Mathurā: The Cultural Heritage,* gen. ed. Doris Meth Srinivasan. 1988. Manohar Book Service. Delhi p.383ff.
2. I have omitted from the ensuing discussion the eight-armed Viṣṇu on the West side of the 5th-century Bhitargaon temple. The two available descriptions of this panel differ significantly. See M. Zaheer, *The Temple of Bhītargaon,* Delhi, 1981, p. 89; J.C. Harle, *Gupta Sculpture,* Oxford, 1974, p. 55. No. 133 and Fig. 133. Not having seen the image myself, it is not possible to determine from these descriptions whether the image represents a true third type, or a variation of one of the two types discussed below.
3. R.D. Banerji, "Basreliefs of Badami", in *Memoires of the Archaeological Survey of India,* No. 25, 1928, Calcutta. Plates 14 and 16, respectively. Banerji's unorthodox numbering of the caves considers this as Cave IV.
4. A slight difference occurs on the left side where the sequence is: conch, bow, shield and hand pointing towards Rāhu.
5. T.A. Gopinatha Rao, *Elements of Hindu Iconography* Vol. I, Pt. I, 2nd Edition, Delhi, 1971, p. 164.
6. Cf. Wendy D. O'Flaherty, *Hindu Myths*, Penguin Books, 1975, pp. 175-79.
7. Banerji, *Bādāmi,* pp. 30-3l.
8. Carmel Berkson, "Some New Finds at Ramgarh Hill, Vidisha District", *Artibus Asiae,* Vol. 40, 1978, 215 ff.
9. Berkson, "Ramgarh Hill", 215.
10. See Joanna Gottfried Williams, *The Art of Gupta India,* Princeton, 1982, p. 53, fn. 106.
11. Williams, *Gupta India,* Pl. 50, pp. 53-55.
12. It is not possible to determine the significance of the background of the relief. The lower right part shows a spray of foliage. On the upper part are cusped arches from which curved lines descend. The reverse of the relief is not carved.

13. *Bh. G.* 7.4.
14. A full analysis is contained in Chapter XI of my monograph, *Many Heads, Arms and Eyes: Origin, Meaning and Form of Multiplicity in Indian Art,* Leiden, Brill, 1997.
15. See Doris Meth Srinivasan, "Vaiṣṇava Art and Iconography at Mathurā".
16. Over the mitre of this Viṣṇu, there is a small effigy of a multi-armed partially exposed being. Its superior position and partially exposed form are indicators that this being is placed above Viṣṇu because it is the source of Viṣṇu. (On the representations of successive emanating Śaiva forms see my paper "Śaiva Temple Forms: Loci of God's Unfolding Body", *Investigating Indian Art,* Festschrift, Herbert Härtel, Berlin, 1987.) According to the theology of the Gītā noted above, the effigy above a Viṣṇu Aṣṭadhā Prakṛti ought to be Viṣṇu Viśvarūpa, the highest nature of the god. P. Pal identifies the effigy as Narasiṃha and notes that it adorns the crown of Viṣṇu ("An Addorsed Śaiva Image from Kashmir and its Cultural Significance", *Art International* Vol. XXIV/5-6, 1981; 38). Strictly speaking, the effigy above does not adorn or even relate to the crown. From a theological point of view, it is hard to justify the form of Narasiṃha in that position. But since Pal mentions the Bādāmi Viṣṇu as one of several examples having a tiny image on top which represents some sort of supreme deity, it may be that we have the same theoretical model in mind. I wish to thank my colleague Carol R. Bolon for drawing my attention to Dr Pal's interpretation.

11

Early Kṛṣṇa Icons: The Case at Mathurā

Writing about thirty years ago, an eminent authority on the art of Mathurā referred to a paradox. Describing a relief in the Mathurā Museum (No. 1344) which he identified as Vāsudeva carrying baby Kṛṣṇa across the Jumnā to the village of Gokula, V.S. Agrawala remarked, "Of the hundreds and thousands of Mathurā sculptures that have come down to us from the Kuṣāṇa period the present relief is the only one about which it can be said that it illustrates an incident from the life-story of Śrī Kṛṣṇa."[1]

This paucity is unusual in two ways. First, Mathurā during the Kuṣāṇa period was the artistic fountainhead from which not only Hindu, but also Buddhist, Jain and folk icons and iconography originated. In consequence, among the "hundreds and thousands of Mathurā sculptures" that Agrawala speaks of, both major sectarian divinities and minor sectarian godlings are represented. Second, according to Purāṇic lore, Kṛṣṇa is the "man in Mathurā,"[2] being born there and returning later in life to punish Mathurā's tyrannical ruler, Kaṃsa, who plotted to destroy him. The association between Kṛṣṇa and Mathurā is of course already recorded in pre-purāṇic literature. The *Mahābhārata* in several passages reveals that Kṛṣṇa considers Mathurā the home from which he had to flee when Jarāsaṃdha attacked.[3] Earlier evidence, though more circumstantial, nonetheless seems to connect Kṛṣṇa with Mathurā. The *Mahābhāṣya (c.* mid-second century BC to the beginning of the Christian era), already mentions the killing of Kaṃsa by Kṛṣṇa, or Vāsudeva, and the narration and presentation of dramas, presumably in Mathurā, on the life of Kṛṣṇa.[4] In effect what has perplexed Agrawala and other art historians is that the most productive center of sectarian art in the Kuṣāṇa

Originally published in *Kalādarśana*, Joanna G. Williams (ed.), (New Delhi, Bombay, Calcutta, 1981), pp. 127-36. Reprinted with stylistic changes, addendum and with permission of the American Institute of Indian Studies.

period would refrain from fashioning icons of an important local hero who was probably deified before the time of the *Mahābhāṣya*.[5]

This lacuna is not confined to Mathurā alone. Representations of episodes in the life of Śrī Kṛṣṇa (Kṛṣṇa-līlās) have not, with the exception of Keśivadha, mentioned in note 1, been clearly recognized from any site prior to the Gupta period. Indeed even the identification of the Kuṣāṇa relief discussed above (No. 1344), cannot be easily accepted. The *Harivaṃśa,* which provides an early description of the events surrounding Kṛṣṇa's removal from Mathurā to escape Kaṃsa, does not mention Vasudeva's crossing of the Jumnā.[6] In accordance with this, there is no depiction of a river crossing in the famous late Gupta panel from Deogarh; it portrays Kṛṣṇa's mother Devakī handing over the babe to Vasudeva on her right.[7] So too the well-known Kṛṣṇa Govardhana from the Gataśram Nārāyaṇ Temple in the heart of Mathurā, though attributed to the Kuṣāṇa period by Coomaraswarny,[8] may be more comfortably assigned, on stylistic grounds, to the post-Gupta period.[9]

The situation changes in the post-Kuṣāṇa period, though not appreciably for Mathurā. During the fourth through sixth centuries AD, several themes relating to the life of Kṛṣṇa as cowherd (Gopāla-Kṛṣṇa) come from western India and Uttar Pradesh. Two Rang Mahal (Bikaner) terracottas depict Kṛṣṇa lifting Mount Govardhana (Govardhana-dharaṇa) and his asking a *gopī* for tribute (Dānalīlā).[10] The Mandor pillars (Rajasthan) show several more episodes, including: the Keśīvadha; Govardhana-dharaṇa; Yaśodā churning milk and Kṛṣṇa stealing butter; overturning of the cart by baby Kṛṣṇa; Yaśodā nursing baby Kṛṣṇa; Kṛṣṇa's elder brother, Balarāma killing Dhenuka; Kṛṣṇa's subjugation of the Nāga Kāliya (Kāliyamardana).[11] The Uttar Pradesh region is innovative in expanding both the size and themes of the Kṛṣṇa-līlā repertoire.[12] The impressive Govardhana-dharaṇa figures from Varanasi and Kara are well known.[13] Three representations of the Kāliyamardana are attributed to the Mathurā school.[14] A Chandausī terracotta plaque shows Pralamba and Balarāma.[15] The Bhitargaon brick temple may, according to R.C. Singh, feature terracotta panels of a wrestling scene; Kṛṣṇa destroying the elephant Kuvalayāpīḍa; possibly Kṛṣṇa killing Kaṃsa.[16] The Garhwa pillar and pillar fragments further amplify the sculptural representations of Kṛṣṇa's youth and astounding feats.[17]

The aim of the foregoing scan is not to treat extensively the development of early Kṛṣṇa-līlā scenes.[18] Rather it is to illustrate the unexceptional role Mathurā played in initiating Kṛṣṇa-līlā motifs even in the Gupta period. On the basis of present knowledge, one may conclude that during the first five hundred years of the Christian era, which mark the school's zenith, the Mathurā workshops did not experiment sufficiently with the theme of Gopāla-Kṛṣṇa to allow for the depiction of more than two līlās, the Kāliyamardana and the Keśīvadha.

It will be instructive at this point to contrast the activity in Uttar Pradesh, especially at Mathurā, with that in Karnataka, especially at Bādāmī during the sixth and seventh centuries. The first extended program of sculptures depicting Gopāla-Kṛṣṇa's exploits on both banks of the Jumnā occurs in Caves II and III at Bādāmī (*c.* AD 578) and somewhat later (*c.* 7th century AD) at the gate of the Bādāmī Northern Fort. Taken together, the Bādāmī panels provide the main sculptural parameters of the legend. These include: the birth of Kṛṣṇa; imprisonment of Devakī and Vasudeva and Kaṃsa's visit; transfer to Gokula; killing of Kṛṣṇa's elder sister; Kṛṣṇa and Balarāma with Yaśodā and Rohiṇī; scene in Gokula; the butter thief; Pūtanā episode; the cart incident; uprooting the Yamalārjuna trees; killing of Vatsa and Arishṭa; coronation of Kṛṣṇa; subjugation of Kāliya; slaughter of Dhenuka by Balarāma; Kṛṣṇa Govardhana; slaughter of Kuvalayāpīḍa; Kṛṣṇa's fight with Cāṇūra; Kṛṣṇa and the *gopīs* sporting; Subhadrā-haraṇa; the Mathurā wrestling arena; the conflict with Kaṃsa.[19] In effect, Bādāmī offers the first comprehensive sculptural statement on the meaning of Gopāla-Kṛṣṇa.

To return to Mathurā, its unremarkable role in the sculptural formulation of the Gopāla-Kṛṣṇa legend supports a penetrating series of studies made by C. Vaudeville.[20] From analysis of selected texts, sculptural material, and site observations, Vaudeville is able to show that the town of Mathurā was not central to Purāṇic legends of Gopāla-Kṛṣṇa[21] and that Gopāla-Kṛṣṇa was not a major Vaiṣṇava deity in the Gangetic area by the end of the Gupta period. He may have been "the great yakṣa of Mount Govardhana and the protector of cowherds living in the area of Mathurā."[22] His popularity among cowherders and pastoral people promotes the generally accepted view that the concept of Gopāla-Kṛṣṇa originated with the Ābhīras.[23] Their homeland may have been in the eastern Punjab;[24] in the *Mahābhārata,* Ābhīras are associated with Vinaśana, the present Sirhind in that part of the State. The *Periplus of the Erythraean Sea* (second half of first century AD) locates them in the Kathiawar area.[25] Ptolemy's *Geography,* a century later, places the Ābhīras in the lower Indus Valley. At this time, they also figure as generals under the Śaka satraps of western India.[26] Further movement of the Ābhīras into the Gangetic Valley and the Deccan is variously recorded. An inscription from Nasik, dated *c.* AD 248–49 mentions the Ābhīra king Māṭharīputra Īśvarasena.[27] Another inscription attributed to Ābhīra Vasushena (AD 278) has been found at Nāgārjunakoṇḍa.[28] The *Harivaṃśa* (5161–5163) associates the land from Madhuvana near Mathurā to Anūpa and Ānarta near Dvāraka as territory occupied by Ābhīras.[29] It is therefore theorized that the Ābhīras, and other pastoral tribes they contacted in their wanderings, fostered and developed a cult featuring devotion to a cowherd god. It is quite likely that the Doab nurtured the early stages of this cult. However, the cult seems to have matured outside of that region. In sum, is it not possible that the dearth of Kṛṣṇa-līlā images at Mathurā and elsewhere in north India towards the close of the Gupta period accurately reflects Gopāla-Kṛṣṇa's position as a minor folk deity during these ages? Taken as such, the near absence of Kṛṣṇa-līlā scenes in Mathurā during the Kuṣāṇa period and their continued scarcity and limited range in the Gupta period is more readily understandable.

Whereas Mathurā was probably not a center for Gopāla-Kṛṣṇa worship until much later,[30] it was the locale intimately connected with the Kṛṣṇa of the epic, Vāsudeva-Kṛṣṇa. It is generally agreed that the story of the man-god Vāsudeva-Kṛṣṇa did not begin to join with that of Gopāla-Kṛṣṇa until the *Harivaṃśa* and *Viṣṇu Purāṇa,* and it is usual to trace the rise of Kṛṣṇaism from the merging of legends connected with these two[31] Kṛṣṇas. In isolating the human aspect of Vāsudeva-Kṛṣṇa's story in pre-Purāṇic sources, Mathurā figures importantly. Vāsudeva-Kṛṣṇa's family ties, on his father's side, are with the Vṛṣṇis of Mathurā. In the epic, Vāsudeva-Kṛṣṇa is the son of Vasudeva, king of the Vṛṣṇis. The Vṛṣṇis are already known in the later Vedic period; their descendants (i.e., Vārshṇa, Vārṣṇeya, Vārshṇya) are mentioned in the Brāhmaṇas.[32] Pāṇini (VI. 2. 34) cites the Vṛṣṇis and Andhakas (with whom they were allied to form a branch of the Yādava clan) as *kṣatriya* names. We know from the *Mahābhārata* that at times these people controlled the rulership of Mathurā (e.g., II. 13. 29–30; V. 126. 36ff). The town should have been their ancestral home, to which they are drawn to return after the momentary retreat of Jarāsaṃdha.[33] Local power may be attributed to Vāsudeva-Kṛṣṇa in the epic.[34] Indeed the combination of geopolitical factors influences his character and actions. He is considered the protector of the Vṛṣṇis.[35] In addition, a series of epithets show that his identity is closely connected with his lineage.[36] As scion of the Vṛṣṇis, the appellation 'Vārshṇeya' is enough to designate him,[37] or it can be associated with him as a sort of paternal surname (e.g., Kṛṣṇa Vārṣṇeya *MhBh.* III. 187.51). This Vṛṣṇi potentate is motivated into alliances and maneuvers which promote the interests of his faction of the Vṛṣṇis.[38] A case in point is the killing of Kaṃsa to whom he is related on his mother's side. Kṛṣṇa says that he punished the usurper "for the good of his kinsmen,"[39] presumably a faction outside of Kaṃsa's party. This conflict, already known to the *Mahābhāṣya,* the *Ghaṭa Jātaka* and possibly the *Arthaśāstra,*[40] must belong to the oldest core not of the Gopāla-Kṛṣṇa legend, but of the Vṛṣṇi myth cycle that should have developed around the deified hero. Resolution of this conflict forms the early motive for the Supreme Lord to descend to earth and take on human form as Kṛṣṇa in Mathurā.[41]

The divinity of Vāsudeva-Kṛṣṇa, already assumed by the author of the *Mahābhāṣya,* permeates the epic. That is not to deny that there are changes in the scope of his divinity. Rather it is to echo the belief of Dhṛitarāshṭra who knows the Vṛṣṇi hero to be the eternal Viṣṇu.[42] The absorption of the Vṛṣṇi hero into the Vaiṣṇava mainstream is very gradual. The amalgamation process was preceded and concurrent with a cult of several Vṛṣṇi heroes. Inscriptional evidence indicates the existence of such a cult in Mathurā. The Morā Well inscription *(c.* AD 10–25), found 11 km west of Mathurā, records that a stone shrine housed images *(pratimā)* of the blessed *(bhagavat)* five heroes *(pañcavīras)* of the Vṛṣṇis. The identification of these five apotheosized *kṣatriyas* is accepted as being Saṃkarṣaṇa (Balarāma, Baladeva), Vāsudeva, Pradyumna, Sāmba, and Aniruddha. Since they are all related to each other through their relationship to Vāsudeva-Kṛṣṇa,[43] it may be inferred that he is the main object of worship. Indeed, a cult of Vāsudeva, known as Bhāgavatism, was already in existence by the second century BC.[44]

The above literary and epigraphical sources suggest that Mathurā was pivotal in formulating the legend and worship associated with the hero-god Vāsudeva-Kṛṣṇa. Interestingly, adherents of Brahmanic traditions in Mathurā[45] may not have felt hostile to a local cult of Vṛṣṇi heroes, nor have been excluded from participation. Several references show that a spirit of accommodation existed between the two. For example, in the *Mahābhārata*, Kṛṣṇa himself undergoes the Vedic *dikṣā* ceremony.[46] Two pre-Christian inscriptions also indicate that no clear distinctions existed between followers of Vedic ritual practices and devotees of Vṛṣṇi heroes. The Nānāghāṭ (Maharashtra) inscription of the first century BC begins with an invocation to several gods, including Saṃkarṣaṇa and Vāsudeva, and then continues to describe the amounts of sacrificial fees the donor paid to the priests who performed a number of Vedic sacrifices.[47] From the Ghosūṇḍī inscription (Rajasthan) of the same age, it is learned that the Vedic *Aśvamedha* sacrifice was performed in honor of Saṃkarṣaṇa and Vāsudeva.[48]

Thus, the thrust of the pre-Purāṇic material, including the passages cited at the outset of this paper, is to ally Vāsudeva-Kṛṣṇa, not the cowherd Kṛṣṇa, with Mathurā. In consequence, a paradox would indeed exist if Mathurā, patronizing as it did a stone shrine with Vṛṣṇi images in the pre-Kuṣāṇa period, did not continue in its artistic heyday to fashion such images. And this is what we should consider next.

A look at Gupta iconographic references certainly reinforces our expectation. The *Bṛhat Saṃhitā* (LVII. 37) states that Ekānaṃśā (the sister of Balarāma and Kṛṣṇa[49]) is to be placed between Baladeva and Kṛṣṇa; if she is two-armed, her left hand should rest at the hip and her right carries a lotus. The *Viṣṇu-dharmottara Purāṇa* confirms this description (III. 85. 72), which is, significantly, contained within a series (III. 85. 71–79) describing representations of the following eleven deities: Devakī, Yaśodā, Ekānaṃśā, Balarāma, Kṛṣṇa, Rukmiṇī, Satyabhāmā, Pradyumna, Aniruddha, Sāmba, Yayudhāna.[50] Except for Yaśodā, they are all Vṛṣṇis by blood or marriage; and all are related in one way or another to Vāsudeva-Kṛṣṇa. With the acknowledgement, in both pre- and post-Kuṣāṇa sources, of icons representing Vṛṣṇi stock, the probability of their occurrence in the Kuṣāṇa period is of course quite high.

Indeed from Mathurā come four small Kuṣāṇa kinship triads.[51] Artistically they are not impressive, but iconologically they are very important. The least damaged piece (Mathurā Museum No. 67. 529; h. 18.4 cm) is of red mottled sandstone (Fig. 11.1). It depicts three figures, much effaced, though originally carved in high relief. The center figure is a short female. She has two arms; the

Fig. 11.1. Triad consisting of Saṃkarṣaṇa/Balarāma, Ekānaṃśā, and Vāsudeva-Kṛṣṇa. Mathura Museum No. 67.529.

right hand is probably poised in the fear-allaying gesture *(abhaya mudrā)*. A "canopy" is arched over her head. The larger male figures flanking her are four-armed. The male on her right holds a mace *(gadā)* in the upper right hand and a plough *(hala)* surmounted by a small lion in the upper left hand. The natural right hand is in *abhaya mudrā* while the natural left rests at the waist. The male on the left seems to hold his natural hands in the same position as the other male; it is no longer possible to determine if the right hand carried another emblem. His raised right and left hands hold the *gadā* and discus *(cakra)* respectively. All three figures are deities, as the *abhaya mudrā* indicates. The attributes of the god on the right clearly belong to Saṃkarṣaṇa/Balarāma.[52] The *gadā* and *cakra,* held by the other god, are of course attributes of Viṣṇu. However, the same attributes can also be associated with Vāsudeva-Kṛṣṇa. It may be remembered that in the famous epiphany section of the *Bhagavad Gītā,* Arjuna, overwhelmed upon seeing the *viśvarūpa* form of Kṛṣṇa, asks to see him instead "with crown, mace, discus in hand" (XI. 46). The *gadā* and *cakra* bespeak of sovereignty aad strength and are therefore entirely appropriate as attributes for this Vṛṣṇi hero-god. Another passage in the *Mahābhārata* mentions Vāsudeva-Kṛṣṇa bearing the conch *(śaṅkha)* in addition to the *cakra* and *gadā*.[53] A later Pāñcarātra text, the *Sāttvata-Saṃhitā* (5.9-21) describes, for purposes of meditation, the four *vyūhas,* associated with four deified Vṛṣṇi heroes. Herein, Vāsudeva, as the first *vyūha,* is likewise said to bear the *cakra, gadā* and *śaṅkha.*[54] Probably such icons of Vāsudeva-Kṛṣṇa remain to be identified in the art of the Kuṣāṇa period.[55(*)] From the Gupta period two examples exist. Holding *śaṅkha* and *gadā* in the raised hands and *cakra* in the lowered left, a four-armed Vāsudeva-Kṛṣṇa is represented on a fragment of a Garhwa lintel now in the Lucknow Museum.[56] The lintel depicts a scene from the *Mahābhārata;* Arjuna and Vāsudeva-Kṛṣṇa watch the fatal wrestling match between Bhīma and Jarāsaṃdha, Another relief in the Deogarh style shows a four-armed Vāsudeva-Kṛṣṇa seated, as a spectator on a low throne; again Arjuna is by his side.[57] Here *gadā* and *cakra* are held in the extra hands while the natural left holds the *śaṅkha.* It thus seems very probable that the male god on the small Kuṣāṇa relief from Mathurā (No. 67. 529) is Vāsudeva-Kṛṣṇa, Saṃkarṣaṇa/Balarāma's younger brother, and not Viṣṇu.[58] The female in the center should be, according to the *Bṛhat Saṃhitā* and the *Viṣṇudharmottara,* Ekānaṃśā.[59]

Fig. 11.2. Triad fragment. Mathura Museum No. U45.

The second triad (Fig. 11.2) from Mathurā (Mathurā Museum No. U45), shows only Saṃkarṣaṇa/Balarāma and Ekānaṃśā standing side by side; probably it is a fragment. This piece is 19 cm high. The male figure is four-armed, holding mace and plough surmounted by a lion. His right hand is in *abhaya mudrā;* the left rests at the hip—it may have held a flask.[60] Ekānaṃśa has a "canopy" over her head. She also displays the *abhaya mudrā* and rests the left hand on the hip. The relief, much worn, is of red mottled sandstone.

The third piece (Fig. 11.3) is a buff sandstone fragment (Mathurā Museum No. 15. 912). It is only 17.8 cm in height and shows a four-armed Vāsudeva-Kṛṣṇa with Ekānaṃśā standing to his right. She is completely defaced. The god and his attributes can be distinguished. Wearing a cylindrical crown, he holds the *gadā* and *cakra* in the extra right and left hands; the natural right is in *abhaya* and the natural left holds what looks like a long-necked flask.

Fig. 11.3. Triad fragment. Mathura Museum No. 15.912. Photograph: Government Museum, Mathura.

From the Gayā District comes the only other known Vṛṣṇi kinship triad dating to an early period (Figs. 11.4–11.6). It shows intriguing similarities and differences from the Mathurā series. This trio consists of three separate statues representing Saṃkarṣaṇa/Balarāma, Ekānaṃśā, and Vāsudeva-Kṛṣṇa.[61] Each statue is large. Balarāma as elder brother stands 150 x 40 cm; Vāsudeva-Kṛṣṇa as younger brother is 140 x 40 cm; Ekānaṃśā's size is 127 x 37 cm. They are made of local buff sandstone probably quarried at Kaimur Hill. The figures themselves were found at Devangarh, in the Nawad subdivision of Gayā. Briefly, Saṃkarṣaṇa/Balarāma is two-armed and is identified by the plough in his left hand; the right is in *abhaya.* Also the protective serpent canopy, characteristic of this deity, appears overhead.[62] He wears a turban knotted on the left side, two earrings, a necklace and a *dhotī* gathered in front and tied in loops at the hips. His sister is also two-armed. Her right hand is raised in *abhaya mudrā* while the left rests at the hip and holds an unidentified object. Her robust and rounded form is decked with jewelry including a tiara, ear-pendants, hair ornaments, a necklace, bangles, anklets and a heavy girdle, which secures a fine, thin sari draped in front and gathered in the center. Vāsudeva-Kṛṣṇa is four-armed. The upper raised right hand holds a ribbed *gadā;* the left bears the *cakra.* The natural right is in *abhaya* and the natural left holds the *śaṅkha* at the hip. He is adorned with a central crested turban, long earrings, a necklace and bangles. His *dhotī* is draped like that of his brother. Both males have broad, fleshy torsos. All three figures stand, *samapada,* on plain pedestals.

The Gayā trio represents an early phase of Bihar sculpture which received its inspiration from the Mathurā school; the trio seems to reflect the late Kuṣāṇa and early Gupta stylistic developments at Mathurā.[63]

All the above triads have one thing in common; they stress kinship relationship more than theological hierarchy.[63a(*)] From a theological point of view, probably Vāsudeva-Kṛṣṇa is the most important of the three divinities. Evidence of a cult

Fig. 11.4. Saṃkarṣaṇa/Balarāma of the Gayā Trio. Patna Museum No. 11300. Photograph: Patna Museum.

Fig. 11.5. Ekānaṃśā of the Gayā Trio. Patna Museum No. 11269. Photograph: Patna Museum.

of Vāsudeva in pre-Christian times has already been mentioned above. In addition, the *vyūha* doctrine, giving greater metaphysical dominance to Vāsudeva than Saṃkarṣaṇa/Balarāma, is already attested in the art and literature from the pre-Christian period onward.[64] Yet these triads unmistakably emphasize the importance of Saṃkarṣaṇa/Balarāma over Vāsudeva-Kṛṣṇa. In the Gayā trio, Saṃkarṣaṇa/Balarāma is the tallest. In the Mathurā triads he is, or would be if the piece were complete, the male to the right of Ekānaṃśā. Clearly, the whole series is meant to portray the elder brother, the older sister and the younger brother.[65]

Fashioned during the Kuṣāṇa period, these kinship triads should have been made in response to the Bhāgavatas' worship of ancestral heroes in Mathurā. It may be noted that even though Saṃkarṣaṇa/Balarāma and Vāsudeva-Kṛṣṇa are heroes *(vīras)* of a *kṣatriya* line that exercised some local power and rulership, the hero gods of these pieces do not appear as "royal" gods. They are modeled to resemble neither the indigenous *cakravartin* type nor the imperial Kuṣāṇa images of more foreign inspiration.[65a(*)] Represented as deified warriors, they recall the words of the Morā Well inscription. This inscription also indicates that the gods received a *bhakti* mode of worship, for focus was on their enshrined icons. The apotheosis of heroes, attested to in this inscription, is not an unusual religious phenomenon. The process is already intimated in the *Aṣṭādhyāyī;* according to IV. 3.99, distinguished *kṣatriya* heroes had become objects of religious *bhakti* even before Pāṇini's time. That the process operated upon Vṛṣṇi heroes can be surmised from a variety of early sources. In addition to the aforementioned Nānāghāṭ and Ghosūṇḍī inscriptions, there are coins, sculptures, literary references, and other inscriptions indicating that the Vṛṣṇi heroes, especially Saṃkarṣaṇa/Balārama and Vāsudeva-Kṛṣṇa were already objects of Bhāgavata worship by the Śuṅga period. Additional evidence for the presence of the Bhāgavata cult in Mathurā may come from another inscription of the time of Śoḍāsa. It records the gift of a *toraṇa* (gateway) and *vedikā* (railing) at a temple which some scholars believe was dedicated to Bhagavān Vāsudeva.[66] Vṛṣṇi females were also deified as the above cited *Viṣṇudharmottara* passage reveals. In the case of Ekānaṃśā, epic and purāṇic legends describe not only her deification but also her worship among the Vṛṣṇi people; S. Jaiswal directs our attention to Vṛṣṇi genealogies in the *Harivaṃśa* and *Viṣṇu Purāṇa,* which may disclose an early matriarchal substratum among the Vṛṣṇis.[67] However that may be, it does seem clear that prominent male and female Vṛṣṇi ancestors were deified and worshipped in northern India from pre-Christian times onward; probably their apotheosis is part of a larger *bhakti* trend which apotheosized distinguished *kṣatriya* ancestors. The carved triads affirm that Mathurā, legendary ancestral home of the Vṛṣṇis, continued to support such a cult during Kuṣāṇa times.

That Mathurā encouraged the development of this ancestor cult, which would have had to compete for support and patronage with many other sectarian cults, probably pertains to factors beyond local pride and family zeal. The triads from Mathurā and Gayā reveal a very strong interrelationship between *bhakti* worship of ancestral heroes and brahmanic reverence to ancestral spirits. The main brahmanic ritual performed for the benefit of one's ancestors is called *śrāddha*. The Vedic *śrāddha* ceremony is meant to transform the dead *(preta)*, a rather harmful spirit, into a friendly and helpful ancestor.[68] There are both domestic *(gṛhya)* and public *(śrauta) śrāddha* rites for the dead.[69] Basic to *śrāddha* ceremonies is the offering of balls of food *(piṇḍa)* to the departed, especially the closest direct ancestors (viz., the father, grandfather and great-grandfather). The *smṛti* literature speaks of Gayā as one of the most suitable and auspicious places to perform *śrāddha*.[70] Indeed this city is an ancient holy place *(tīrtha)* associated with the performance of obsequies to ancestors.[71] There is also a special *Gayāśrāddha* characteristic to that place.[72] *Gayāśrāddha* "can be celebrated by anybody for any deceased person at any time of the year although the fortnight ending with the Mahālayā-Amāvasya (i.e., the new moon day in *amānta* Bhadrapada or *pūrṇimānta* Āśvina) is regarded the best time for it...."[73]

A noteworthy correlation exists between some of the basic features of *śrāddha* and the Vṛṣṇi heroes, especially the deities on the kinship triads. First, in a passage of the *Viṣṇudharmottara* quoted by *Śrāddhasāra* (p. 6) and *Śrāddhaprakāśa* (pp. 11–12) it is said that the *piṇḍa* offered to the great-grandfather is the god Vāsudeva himself, the one to the grandfather is designated Saṃkarṣaṇa, that to the father is known as Pradyumna and the offerer of the *piṇḍas* is himself in the position of Aniruddha.[74] Second, the name Ekānaṃśā signifies "the single portionless one or the new moon".[75] As noted above, the new moon day is appropriate for the performance of *śrāddha*. In a *Mahābhārata* passage (III. 208. 7–8), Ekānaṃśā is associated

Fig. 11.6. Vāsudeva-Kṛṣṇa of the Gayā Trio. Patna Museum No. 11299. Photograph: Patna Museum.

with Kuhū; Kuhū is the presiding deity of the fifteenth day of the dark-half when the moon is invisible.[76] The passage relates the lineage of the great seer Aṅgiras. Ekānaṃśā is proclaimed his seventh daughter and is called by the name Mahāmatī at the great fiery sacrifices, as well as by the name Kuhū. The same passage also notes that Sinīvālī is the third daughter of Aṅgiras. These daughters bear names of propitious days for performing *śrāddha*. "Those who keep *śrauta* fires should perform *śrāddha* on Sinīvālī day while those who do not keep *śrauta* fires and Śudras should offer *śrāddha* on Kuhū day."

In view of the foregoing it does not seem accidental that the large Vṛṣṇi kinship trio was found in the region of Gayā. The find may represent a rapproachment between modes of Bhāgavata and Brahmanical worship. Though highly speculative, it may be worthwhile to ponder whether the small Mathurā triad slabs represent a rapproachment between Bhāgavata and *gṛhya śrāddha* rites and the large Gayā trio represents an affinity between Bhāgavata and *śrauta śrāddha* rites. In any case it does seem apparent that the Bhāgavata cult, involving the worship of Vṛṣṇi ancestors, exhibits respect and recognition of Vedic *śrāddha* rites and traditions. This is but another instance in what seems to be a recurring pattern of accommodation between Vedic and Bhāgavata religious systems.[77] In a place such as Mathurā, stronghold of Brahmanic sentiments, that accommodating tendency should have fostered a climate wherein the Bhāgavata cult could grow.

Upon reflection, it could be argued that four Kuṣāṇa triad slabs from Mathurā do not convincingly indicate that the Bhāgavata cult, and worship of Vāsudeva-Kṛṣṇa, was any more prevalent in Mathurā than worship of Gopāla-Kṛṣṇa for whom at least two Kuṣāṇa reliefs and three Gupta reliefs from Mathurā are known to date. However, it can be demonstrated in another paper,[78] that on the basis of the identification of Vāsudeva-Kṛṣṇa on the kinship triads, it is possible to identify many more Kuṣāṇa icons from Mathurā as representing Vāsudeva-Kṛṣṇa. Indeed, it can be shown that he is among the most important deities, within emerging Hinduism, to be worshipped at Mathurā during the Kuṣāṇa period.

NOTES AND REFERENCES

1. V.S. Agrawala, *A Catalogue of the Brahmanical Images in Mathurā Art*, Lucknow, 1951, p. 42. Since Agrawala's *Catalogue*, two Mathura Kuṣāṇa weight stones have been found which are decorated with representations of Kṛṣṇa fighting Keśī. For the one in the Mathura Museum (No. 58. 4476), see N.P. Joshi, *Mathura Sculptures*, Mathura, 1966, p. 68 and Fig. 64. For the one in a private Pakistani collection, see J.E. van Lohuizen-de Leeuw, "Gandhara and Mathura: Their Cultural Relationship," *Aspects of Indian Art*, P. Pal (ed.), Leiden, 1972, p. 30. P. XIa.
2. *Mārkaṇḍeya Purāṇa* 4.56. This interesting passage is translated in C. Dimmitt and J.A.B. van Buitenen, *Classical Hindu Mythology*, Philadelphia, 1978, p. 66.
3. E.g. *Mahābhārata*, 2.13 which narrates Jarāsaṃdha's avenging attacks on Mathurā. After Jarāsaṃdha's temporary retreat, Kṛṣṇa states, "all of us lived again happily in

Mathurā"; ultimately however, he and his people "had to abandon Mathurā, for fear of Jarāsaṃdha ... and leave for Dvāraka city." J.A.B. vah Buitenen, *The Mahābhārata* II, Chicago, 1975, pp. 50 and 59.

4. Norvin Hein, *The Miracle Plays of Mathurā*, New Haven and London, 1972, Chap. 9. Cf. R.G. Bhandarkar, "Allusions to Kṛṣṇa in Patañjali's Mahābhāsya," *The Indian Antiquary* III (1874), 14–16. Mid-second century BC is the date usually assigned to the *Mahābhāsya*. A date in the first century AD is suggested in the recent studies of S.D. Joshi and J.A.F. Roodbergen, *Patañjali's Vyākarana-Mahābhāsya*, Poona, 1976 (see Introduction).
5. D. Srinivasan, "Early Vaiṣṇava Imagery: Caturvyūha and Variant Forms," *Archives of Asian Art XXXII* (1979), 50. Page 145 in this volume.
6. The date of the *Harivaṃśa* is still a matter of debate. The general consensus, with which Daniel H.H. Ingalls agrees ("The Harivaṃśa as a Mahākāvya" in *Mélanges d'Indianisme à la mémoire de Louis Renou* [Paris, 1968], 381–94) places the text between the birth of Christ and the third century AD. C. Vaudeville would date it between the eight and tenth century AD ("Aspects du mythe de Kṛṣṇa-Gopāla dans l'Inde ancienne" in the same Festschrift, p. 753). The material in this paper seems to support the later dating.
I understand Charlotte Vaudeville to suggest that the Mathurā relief No. 1344 could represent a cowherd (Nanda?) carrying the babe which was set down on the riverbank by a Nāga (Balarāma ?); see "The Cowherd God in Ancient India" in *Pastoralists and Nomads in South Asia*, edited by L.S. Leschnik and G-D. Sontheimer, Weisbaden, 1975, pp. 101–02.
7. "See fig. 86 in K. Desai, *Iconography of Viṣṇu*, New Delhi, 1973. From approximately the same period, a Garhwa pillar fragment representing the transfer scene also does not illustrate a river crossing. See B.H. Bourdillon, "Kṛṣṇa Obelisks at Garhwa," *Journal of the Uttar Pradesh Historical Society*, I: 2 (1918), 37. In the post-Gupta temple at Paharpur, Bengal (*c.* 7th–8th century), the transfer is still not depicted as a river crossing (see K.N. Dikshit, *Excavations at Paharpur*, Bengal, in *A.S.I. Memoirs*, No. 55, Delhi, 1938, pl. XXIX b).
8. Mathurā Museum no. D. 47.A.K. Coomaraswamy, *History of Indian and Indonesian Art*, Dover (ed.), New York, 1965, p. 66 and fig. 102.
9. V.S. Agrawala, *A Catalogue*, p. 18; N.P. Joshi, *Mathura Sculptures*, p. 87; R.C. Sharma, *Mathura Museum and Art*, 2nd ed., Allahabad, 1976, p. 102.
10. See H. Goetz, "The Earliest Representations of the Myth Cycle of Kṛṣṇa Govinda," *Journal of the Oriental Institute*, Baroda, 1:1 (1951), 51–59; U.P. Shah, "Terracottas from former Bikaner State," *Lalit Kalā VIII* (1960), 55–62; V.S. Agrawala, "The Religious Significance of the Gupta Terracottas from Rang Mahal," *Idem.*, pp. 63–68.
11. See S. Jaiswal, *The Origin and Development of Vaiṣṇavism*, Delhi, 1967, p. 186; *A.S.I.A.R., 1909–1910* (Calcutta, 1914), Pl. 44b; D.R. Bhandarkar, "Two Sculptures at Mandor," *A.S.I.A.R.*, 1905–06 (Calcutta, 1909), 135–40.
12. The possibility of a new thematic representation has been suggested by Vaudeville. She proposes that the Ahichattra terracotta of Jumnā in the Delhi National Museum also shows Dāmodara-Kṛṣṇa, the child god of Gokula beside the figure of the river goddess; see "The Cowherd God," p. 102.
13. They are, respectively, No. 147 in the Bharat Kala Bhavan and No. AM 259 in the Allahabad Museum.
14. One fragment is now in the Baroda Museum; see fig. 1 in H. Goetz, "Myth Cycle of Kṛṣṇa Govinda." Another representation occurs on the top panel of a railing now in a private Paris collection; see M. Beniste, *Rapports entre le premier art khmer et l'art indien* Paris, 1970, Tome II, fig. 141. A third fragmentary relief is cited by Krishna Deva in

"Kṛṣṇa-Līlā Scenes in the Lakshmaṇa Temple, Khajuraho," *Lalit Kalā* VII (1960), fn. 2, p. 86, as illustrated by K.D. Bajpai, "Images of Kṛṣṇa and Balarāma in Mathurā Art," *Kalānidhi* (Hindi), I:2, fig. 3. This journal was not available to me.

15. R.C. Agrawala, "Unpublished Sculptures and Terracottas in the National Museum, New Delhi and Some Allied Problems," *East and West* XVII: 3–4 (1967), 279; fig. 11.
16. R.C. Singh, "Bhitargaon Brick Temple," *B.M.A.U.P.*, 2 (1968), 30–35.
17. Bourdillon, "Kṛṣṇa Obelisks," pp. 36–37, identifies the following: Kāliyamardana; Kṛṣṇa preparing for the encounter with Cāṇūr and Mushṭika; Kṛṣṇa and Yaśodā (?); the two wrestlers awaiting Kṛṣṇa, Kṛṣṇa stealing butter; the river Jumnā; Yaśodā churning butter; Kṛṣṇa Govardhana; Vasudeva transporting baby Kṛṣṇa; Pūtanā-vadha.
18. Helpful compilations have been offered by K. Desai, *Viṣṇu*, pp. 123–40 and Michael W. Meister, "Kṛṣṇa-līlā from Wadhwān and Osian," *J.I.S.O.A.*, Vol. V (1972–73), see Appendix.
19. See R.D. Banerji, *Basreliefs of Badami, A.S.I. Memoirs,* No. 25 (Calcutta, 1928); Goetz, "Myth Cycle," 56. The sequence cited above does not correspond to actual sequences at the site.
20. "Aspects du mythe Kṛṣṇa-Gopāla dans l'Inde ancienne"; "The Cowherd God in Ancient India"; "Braj, Lost and Found," *Indo-Iranian Journal,* XVIII: 3/4 (1976), 195–213.
21. She notes that his association with the city of Mathurā is but a fleeting one. He was born there but was immediately whisked away to be brought to Braj and Gokula. When he re-enters Mathurā, his childhood is behind him and his link with Braj is severed. Also, in the *Ghaṭa Jātaka,* Kṛṣṇa is born in the village of Govaḍḍhamāna, not in Mathurā; "Braj, Lost and Found," 198–99.
22. Vaudeville, "The Cowherd God," p. 100.
23. This view was advanced by R.G. Bhandarkar, *Vaiṣṇavism, Śaivism and Minor Religious Systems (1913),* Chap. IX. Cf. S. Jaiswal *(Vaiṣṇavism,* p. 81) who finds in the *Harivaṃśa* and the *Bālacarita* strong evidence for the origin of the cowherd-god among the Ābhīras.
24. Jaiswal, *Vaiṣṇavism,* pp. 80–84; Vaudeville, "Cowherd God," 104–05; fn. 20. Cf. B. Suryavanshi, *The Abhiras,* Baroda, 1962, pp. 1–5.
25. B. Suryavanshi, *The Abhiras,* pp. 7–8.
26. R.C. Majumdar, gen. ed., *The Age of Imperial Unity,* Vol. II, 4th ed., Bombay, 1968, p. 221.
27. *Ibid.*, p. 222.
28. D.C. Sircar, *Select Inscriptions* I, 2nd ed., Calcutta, 1965, p. 525.
29. R.G. Bhandarkar, *Vaiṣṇavism, Śaivism,* p. 37.
30. See discussion in Vaudeville, "The Cowherd God" pp. 103–104; also note the later Purāṇic references to Mathurā in connection with Kṛṣṇa worship in P.V. Kane, *History of Dharmaśāstra,* Vol. IV, Poona, 1953, p. 690 and in the article entitled "Nārada Purāna—A Study," *Purāna* XXI: 1 (1979), 418. I wish to thank Prof. Cornelia Dimmitt for bringing this article to my attention.
31. For a brief reference to the interpolated passages of the Gopāla-Kṛṣṇa legend in the *Mahābhārata*, see R.G. Bhandarkar, *Vaiṣṇavism, Śaivism*, pp. 35–36; C. Vaudeville, "The Cowherd God," pp. 94–95. It should be noted that there is an often cited third component, namely Vedic Kṛṣṇa, who may have merged with Vāsudeva-Kṛṣṇa before the latter joined with Gopāla-Kṛṣṇa. See H. Raychaudhuri, *Materials for the Study of the Early History of the Vaishnava Sect,* 2nd ed. (reprint), New Delhi, 1975, pp. 21–22 for a discussion on the identity of Vedic Kṛṣṇa and Epic Vāsudeva. Cf. S.K. De, "The Vedic and the Epic Kṛṣṇa," *The Indian Historical Quarterly,* XVIII (1942), 297–301.
32. A.A. MacDonell and A.B. Keith, *Vedic Index* II (reprint), Delhi, 1958, 289–90.

33. *Mahābhārata* II. 13.44.
34. D.C. Sircar, *(Studies in the Religious Life of Ancient and Medieval India,* Delhi, 1971, p. 17) notes that "the *Mahābhārata* sometimes mentions Vāsudeva as *Saṅghamukhya* or Elder of the Republican Confederacy of the Vṛṣṇi, Andhaka and other associate peoples."
35. See S. Sorensen, *Index to the Names in the Mahābhārata*, London, 1904, p. 755.
36. Kṛṣṇa is: Vṛishṇiśārdūla; Vṛishṇiśreshṭha; Vṛishṇikulaśreshṭha; Vṛishṇikulodvaha; Vṛishṇinandana; Vṛishṇipati; Vṛishṇipravara; Vṛishṇipravīra; Vṛishṇipuṃgava; Vṛishṇisattama; Vṛishṇisiṃha; Vṛishṇivīra; Vṛishṇy-Andhakapati; Vṛishṇy-Andhakottama, See Sorenson, *Index*, pp. 755–56.
37. Although some other kinfolk may be called *vārṣṇeya (i),* or bear an epithet containing the term *vṛṣṇi-,* these are preponderately applied to Vāsudeva-Kṛṣṇa.
38. See discussions in J.A.B. van Buitenen, *The Mahābhārata,* Vol. I, Chicago, 1973, pp. 10–11; Vol. II, pp. 14–17; Vol. III, Chicago, 1978, pp. 138–40.
39. van Buitenen, *The Mahābhārata* Vol. III (5.126.36 ff), pp. 422–23. After this ouster, Kaṃsa's father is reinstated as king of Mathurā, he having been apparently allied to Kṛṣṇa's faction.
40. B.P. Sinha, *Readings in Kauṭilya's Arthaśāstra,* Delhi, 1976, p. 172.
41. The Supreme Lord, in the Nārāyaṇīya section of the *Mahābhārata,* is Nārāyaṇa. He is an important cosmic god in Vedic literature who later comes to be identified with Viṣṇu. See discussion and bibliography in D. Srinivasan, "God as Brahmanical Ascetic: A Colossal Kuṣāṇa Icon of the Mathura School", *Journal of the Indian Society of Oriental Art*, N.S., Vol. X, 1978-79: 1-16. It may be noted that this passage *(Mahābhārata* 12. 340) explains both the *vyūha* and *avatāra* doctrines and reserves the name Vāsudeva for the first *vyūha.* So also the *Mārkaṇḍeya* passage (4.44–58) mentioned in n. 2, above.
42. *Mahābhārata* 5.22.31. This passage would imply that Vāsudeva-Kṛṣṇa is identical to Viṣṇu. In the *Bhagavad Gītā,* where this identity is not apparent, Kṛṣṇa as the Supreme, says that he is the foremost of each class of beings and as such is Vāsudeva among the Vṛṣṇis (10.37). In the Nārāyaṇīya passage mentioned above, Kṛṣṇa is an *avatāra.* Concerning the developmental stages associated with Kṛṣṇa's divinity, J. Gonda observes that the identification between Kṛṣṇa and Viṣṇu should have occurred between the time of the *Bhagavad Gītā* (*Mahābhārata* 6.25–42; *c.* 200 BC) where he is not yet an *avatāra* of Viṣṇu and *Mahābhārata* 14.53 where he is (*Die Religionen Indiens* I., Stuttgart, 1960, p. 243).
43. Saṃkarṣaṇa (Balarāma) is the older brother of Vāsudeva-Kṛṣṇa; Pradyumna and Sāmba are his sons, and Aniruddha is his grandson, being the son of Pradyumna.
44. This cult is indicated by the Besnagar Garuḍa Pillar Inscription; see D.C. Sircar, *Select Inscriptions,* pp. 88–89.
45. Two Mathurā inscriptions may be cited as indicative of Brahmanic activity there during the Kuṣāṇa period. The inscription on a *yūpa* (Mathura Museum No. Q 13) states that the Vedic Dvādaśarātra *sattra* was celebrated. The Puṇyaśālā Pillar inscription (Mathura Museum No. 1913) records an endowment to the Puṇyaśālā to feed, among others, one hundred Brahmins on a monthly basis; V.S. Agrawala, *Mathura Museum Catalogue* IV, Varanasi, 1963, pp. 136–40.
46. *Dikṣā* is a rite performed as an initiation or consecration for a particular ceremony; *dikṣā* was the means enabling the sacrificer to enter into a higher state of existence. J. Gonda, "Dikṣā" in *Change and Continuity in Indian Religion,* The Hague, 1965, 315ff. Reference to Kṛṣṇa's performance of *dikṣā* is in J. Gonda, *Viṣṇuism and Śivaism,* London, 1970, p. 89.

47. D.C. Sircar, *Select Inscriptions*, pp. 192–97.
48. Sircar, *Ibid.*, pp. 90–91. The Ghosūṇḍī inscription offers important evidence for the early merging tendencies within Vaiṣṇavism, Cf. D. Srinivasan, "Early Vaiṣṇava Imagery," p. 51. Page 146 in this volume. Sircar (*Religious Life*, p. 21) makes the interesting observation that these inscriptions testify to the spread of the Bhāgavata religion among performers of Vedic sacrifices outside of the Mathurā region and Vāsudeva's own clan.
49. *Harivaṃśa* II. 101. 18. One wonders whether a family connection between Ekānaṃśā and Kṛṣṇa is already implied in earlier texts. For example, *Kauṣītaki Brāhmaṇa* XXX. 9 speaks of a Kṛṣṇa Āṅgirasa, and *Mahābhārata* 3.208. 7–8 states that Ekānaṃśā is the seventh daughter of Aṅgiras.
50. Rukmuṇī and Satyabhāmā are wives of Kṛṣṇa; Yayudhāna is another Vṛṣṇi warrior.
51. Three of these reliefs have been discussed in several very informative papers: P.L. Gupta, "Ekānaṁśā and Her Images," *J.B.R.S.*, 54 (1968), 229–44; N.P. Joshi, "Ekānaṁśā in Early Kuṣāṇa Art," *J.I.S.O.A.*, n.s. II (1967/68), 34–36. I would like to express my sincere appreciation to Dr. N.P. Joshi for valuable discussions in this area which stimulated my interest in Kuṣāṇa triads. The fourth relief comes to my attention through the kindness of Professor van Lohuizen-de Leeuw, who will soon publish the piece. She has informed me that the triad is carved on a weight stone (47 x 25.4 x 5.7 cm) made of the red Mathura sand-stone. Of importance in the present context is that the relief depicts, from right to left, Balarāma, Ekānaṁśā and a four-armed Vāsudeva-Kṛṣṇa.
52. Cf. Mathura Museum Nos. 39.2856; C 19; Lucknow Museum No. S758; from the Gupta period, see Lucknow Museum No. J89.
53. *Mahābhārata 6.66.*
54. F. Otto Schrader, *Introduction to the Pāñcarātra and the Ahirbudhnya Saṃhitā*, Madras, 1916, pp. 152–53.
55. This subject will be considered in a forthcoming paper "Vaiṣṇava Art and Iconography at Mathurā" to be presented at the seminar "The Cultural History of Ancient Mathura" (Jan. 1980).

    * ADDENDUM: The paper has been published in *Mathura: The Cultural Heritage*, gen. ed. Doris Meth Srinivasan, South Asia Publications / American Institute of Indian Studies, New Delhi, 1989, pp. 383-92.
56. Museum No. H88; N.P. Joshi, *Catalogue of the Brahmanical Sculptures in the State Museum, Lucknow*, Lucknow, 1972, pp. 89–90.
57. The relief (No.1. 18) is in the Museum für Indische Kunst Berlin. It has been given the same identification as No. H88, above. See the Museum's *Katalog 1971* (Berlin, 1971), number 98.
58. This identification is also proposed by P.L. Gupta, "Ekānaṃśā," 243–44; cf. N.P. Joshi, "Ekānaṃśā," 35. W.E. Begley, *Viṣṇu's Flaming Wheel: The Iconography of the Sudarśana-Cakra*, New York, 1973, p. 39, comes to a similar conclusion.
59. However, the lotus which the Gupta texts prescribe is not found on Kuṣāṇa icons of Ekānaṃśā.
60. N.P. Joshi ("Ekānaṃśā," 35) notices these additional features: a single earring in the left ear and a triple crested headgear.
61. C.R.P. Sinha, "Some Important Sculptural Acquisitions of the Patna Museum," *J.B.R.S.*, LIII (1967), 155–60; C.R.P. Sinha, "The Kuṣāṇa Art of Bihar," *J.B.R.S.*, LIX (1973), 65–74; this trio in the Patna Museum has the following Museum numbers: 11300, 11269, 11301.

62. Cf. Mathura Museum Nos. C19; C15; 392–5; and the Tumain (M.P.) standing Balarāma.
63. P. Chandra, "Some Remarks on Bihar Sculpture from the Fourth to the Ninth Century," *Aspects of Indian Art*, Leiden, 1972, p. 60.
63a. ADDENDUM: It is interesting that a Vṛṣṇi Triad dating to c. 11th-12th century AD and coming from Patnitola, present-day Bangladesh, has been found in 2010. See the following brief article for picture and description: Mokammal H. Bhuiyan, "The Unpublished Balarāma-Ekānaṃśā-Vāsudeva Image from Patnitola", *Journal of Bengal Art*, Vol. 17, 2012; 211-13.
64. D. Srinivasan, "Early Vaiṣṇava Imagery," 39–54. Chapter 8 in this volume.
65. Note that both the Ghosūṇḍi and Nānāghāṭ inscriptions also record the genealogical, not the metaphysical, order of the Vṛṣṇi hero gods.
65a. ADDENDUM: Whereas Saṃkarṣaṇa / Balarāma is not represented with royal attributes, I no longer believe the same can be said for Vāsudeva / Kṛṣṇa. True, he is not represented with a cakravartin's Seven Jewels of office, nor does he look like a Kuṣāṇa dynastic ruler; he does however have some emblems of a sovereign seen in early Indian art. Vāsudeva-Kṛṣṇa can be shown with a crown (Fig. 11.3) and the mace (Fig. 11.6); both are emblematic of royalty. These stand in contrast to the cakra and conch (both instruments used in battle) and recall the god's heroic nature. The combination of heroic and royal symbols pertain well to the god of the *Bhagavad Gītā*, being the Great God as deified royal hero.
66. Mathura Museum No. 367; H. Lüders, "Seven Brahmi Inscriptions from Mathura and Vicinity," *E.I.* XXIV, 208–10; D.C. Sircar, "Two Brāhmī Inscriptions," *J.B.R.S.*, XXXIX, 1–2 (1953), 45–48.
67. Cf. S. Jaiswal, *Vaiṣṇavism*, pp. 66–67.
68. L. Renou, *Vedic India*, Vol. III, in *Classical India;* translated by P. Spratt, Delhi, Varanasi, 1971, pp. 119–20.
69. See A.B. Keith, *The Religion and Philosophy of the Veda and Upanishads*, II, (reprint), Delhi, 1976, 425–32.
70. P.V. Kane, *History of Dharmaśāstra*, IV, 654–56; 662ff .
71. *Mahābhārata* 3. 82.84: "If one dwells for both the dark and light fortnights at Gayā, he doubtlessly purifies his lineage to seven generations" (van Buitenen, *The Mahābhārata* II, p. 390).
72. Kane, *History of Dharmaśāstra*, IV, 669ff.
73. D.C. Sircar, "Inscriptions from Gayā," *E.I.* XXXIII; 3 (1959), 103.
74. Kane, *History of Dharmaśāstra* IV, pp. 350–51.
75. M. Monier-Williams, *A Sanskrit-English Dictionary*, Oxford, 1899, p. 230.
76. S.K. Lal, "Lunar Deities *Sinīvālī Kuhū, Anumati* and *Rākā*," *CASS Studies*, No. 2 (1974), 130.
77. See the stimulating remarks of S. Jaiswal, *Vaiṣṇavism*, p. 45.
78. See note 55.

12

Saṃkarṣaṇa/Balarāma and the Mountain: A New Attribute

Balarāma is a minor yet complex Hindu god. In all the Vaiṣṇava Purāṇas, he is mentioned alongside his more important brother Kṛṣṇa. Both may be considered partial incarnations of Viṣṇu, or when Kṛṣṇa is regarded as the manifestation of Viṣṇu, Balarāma is Viṣṇu's seventh *avatāra*. However, Balarāma was not always in the shadow of the beguiling Dark Lord. Originally he was more important. In the *Mahābhārata,* Rāma is likely to refer to Balarāma (Parpola 2002: 367). There is every indication that Balarāma started out as a deity possessing powerful aspects derived from distinct spheres : the agricultural, the subterranean and the heroic. The god's original complexity is due to his fusing aspects stemming from folklore and hero mythology into a richly nuanced personality. The earliest images of the god reflect this fusion : symbols relate to ploughing the earth, to snakes below the earth and to authority and heroic strength. This paper adds a new attribute which demonstrates that originally Balarāma was associated with a mountain that figured in one of Kṛṣṇa's most famous miracles.

Purāṇic Balarāma has many facets. He is known to be a heavy drinker, addicted to wine. He exerts no control over his temper. He is irascible, and even had a serious fight with his younger brother Kṛṣṇa over the Syamantaka jewel (*Viṣṇu Purāṇa* 4.13.99–101; Wilson 1979: 343–44). His strength annihilates enemies and accounts for three of his names: Balarāma, 'Rāma the Strong'; Baladeva, 'the god of strength'; Balabhadra, 'skilful in strength'. Saṃkarṣaṇa is another of his names. Once while Saṃkarṣaṇa/Balarāma was intoxicated, he ordered the

Originally published in *Religion and Art: New Issues in Indian Iconography and Iconology,* Claudine Bautze-Picron (ed.), London 2008, pp. 93-104, reprinted with stylistic changes, additions and with permission of the British Association for South Asian Studies.

Fig. 12.1 Balarāma diverting the course of the Yamuna River with his plough, Punjab Hills, Chamba, *c.*1760-65 (© Brooklyn Museum inv. no. 36.250).

Yamuna River to come closer so that he could bathe. When his command was not obeyed, he threw his ploughshare into the river in order to drag the waters to him (*Viṣṇu Purāṇa* 5.25.8–24; Wilson 1979: 452–53).

A Chamba miniature of *c.*1760–65 (Fig. 12.1) illustrates the event perfectly. Saṃkarṣaṇa/Balarāma wears blue clothes. He holds the mace symbolic of authority and leadership in his left hand and, with his plough grasped in the right, he digs below the soil in order to form a furrow, which the diverted Yamuna waters begin to fill. This *Viṣṇu Purāṇa* story connects the god to authority and leadership pertaining to the heroic realm, and to agriculture and water pertaining to the fertile earth and the subterranean region, that is, the chthonic realm. The chthonic realm can be inhabited by snakes. Indeed Purāṇic Balarāma is believed to be the incarnation of the cosmic serpent, a form of Viṣṇu. The *Viṣṇu Purāṇa* expresses the Vaiṣṇavas' belief that Balarāma is the embodiment of the Serpent Śeṣa (The Remainder), upon whom Viṣṇu sleeps between world aeons (*Viṣṇu Purāṇa* 5.37.54–56; Wilson 1979: 479–80).

These characteristics, admittedly painted with broad brush strokes, do help to introduce Balarāma's standard depiction. If, by the time of the medieval period, an image consists of a god who is protected by a snake canopy and holds a plough, a club or pestle/mace, and often a wine cup, that image can only represent Saṃkarṣaṇa/Balarāma. This mode of representing the god had become standardized earlier. Post-Gupta (e.g. Asher 1980: pl. 220) and Gupta icons (e.g. Joshi 1979: pl. 26) depict the god in this manner. This iconographic formula had actually been worked out by pre-Gupta times. This is not surprising since Balarāma

Fig. 12.2 Saṃkarṣaṇa/Balarāma, coin of Agathocles, from Ai Khanoum, obverse, 2nd century BC (© Délégation Archéologique Française en Afghanistan).

is an ancient god; worship of Kṛṣṇa and his elder brother Saṃkarṣaṇa/Balarāma can be traced back to the 2nd century BC, as both appear on the silver coins of the Indo-Greek king Agathocles (Fig. 12.2), on petroglyphs of the first half of the 1st century AD in Chilas, Pakistan (Jettmar 1989: pl. 4), and on a Madhya Pradesh rock painting that may date to about the 2nd century BC (Neumayer 1992–93: 58, Fig. 2). Balarāma also occurs on the obverse of coppers assigned to Maues, the Scythian king in Gandhāra, dated *c.*70 BC (Cribb in Errington and Cribb 1992: 80, no. 74). These north-western and central Indian depictions show Saṃkarṣaṇa/Balarāma with the plough and the mace or club, but without the snake canopy and wine cup.

Given this stable iconographic history, how are we to explain the way he is depicted in an exceptional Kangra miniature in the former collection of Mr Jeff Chandler (Fig. 12.3). In the centre sits the four-armed Saṃkarṣaṇa/Balarāma. He is seated on an open lotus covering most of the low hexagonal table. The four-armed deity is assuredly Saṃkarṣaṇa/Balarāma since he holds the mace and ploughshare in two of his hands, and serpents spread all over his crown. But what is on top of the serpents? The painting came on the market in 1999 and this is how Sotheby's catalogue described Lot 219:

> Balarāma seated on a terrace. Kangra. *c.*1780—the four-armed divinity ... has a mass of writhing serpents emerging from his head supporting an island, flanked by four maidservants offering him food and wine and caressing his arms, noblemen and rulers observing from the corners (Sotheby's 1999: 218).

The image is $8\frac{5}{8}$ x $6\frac{3}{8}$ in (21.9 x 16.2 cm). It has an "oval format with pink spandrels decorated with gold floral arabesques, dark blue foliate inner border, beige and pink-speckled outer border...". This painting is the only example I know that adds a raised ground, be it a hill, a mountain, an embankment or a mound, to the standard iconography I have just outlined.

The standard iconography, typical from the Gupta period onwards, is the result of multiple attributes pertaining to the different spheres that coalesce to define the god's nature. Saṃkarṣaṇa/Balarāma is a Vīra, that is, a hero of Mathurā. The town is the ancestral home of the Vṛṣṇi clan. This is a *kṣatriya* clan, which at times ruled Mathurā, and Saṃkarṣaṇa/Balarāma as well as Vāsudeva-Kṛṣṇa were born into Mathurā's Vṛṣṇi clan. By the early 1st century AD, there is written evidence that five heroes of this clan were deified and worshipped. The

Morā Well inscription, found 11 km west of Mathurā and dated to *c.* AD 10–25, records that a shrine was set up for the worship of images of five deified Vṛṣṇi Vīras. Possibly some Vīras could have been deified and worshipped earlier, as the depictions on coins and rocks in the north-west and Madhya Pradesh would seem to indicate. The most renowned Vṛṣṇi Vīras are Saṃkarṣaṇa/Balarāma and his younger brother Vāsudeva-Kṛṣṇa. These two heroes, together with their sister Ekānaṃśā, are depicted on small red sandstone reliefs made in Mathurā during the Kuṣāṇa period. I call these diminutive reliefs 'kinship triads', since they focus on three family members of the local Vṛṣṇi clan who became deified (Srinivasan, 1981; paper is in this volume). On these reliefs, Saṃkarṣaṇa/Balarāma is consistently shown with four arms (e.g. Srinivasan 1997: Fig. 16.5). His upper right holds the mace emblematic of his leadership status. His upper left reminds that he is also associated with agriculture; in this hand he balances a plough topped by a small lion. Perhaps the lion surmounting the plough indicates that the god could also have used the plough as a weapon. Saṃkarṣaṇa/Balarāma's natural right hand is in the *vyāvṛtta* position, while the natural left rests at the waist or hip. The relief, formerly in the Robert Ellsworth Collection, is the best preserved of the kinship triads; it confirms that the same iconography also appears in a more damaged Mathurā kinship triad featuring Saṃkarṣaṇa/Balarāma (Srinivasan 1981: Fig. 1).

Fig. 12.3 Balarāma seated on a terrace, Kangra, *c.*1780, private collection (© Mr. Jeff Chandler).

All five deified Vṛṣṇi Vīras can be seen in a 4th century relief from Kondamotu, Andhra Pradesh. They are clustered around the theriomorphic image of Narasiṃha (Srinivasan 1997: pl. 18.1). The eldest Vīra, Saṃkarṣaṇa/Balarāma, is at the head of the row. Again he is depicted with emblems that speak of the god's heroic and agricultural natures, namely the mace and the lion-topped plough. Neither the snake hood nor the wine cup appears in any of the depictions featuring the *vīra*-cum-agrarian symbols on these Kuṣāṇa and post-Kuṣāṇa kinship reliefs. It may be proposed that the kinship reliefs and the earlier coins, as well as petroglyphs and rock painting, depict Saṃkarṣaṇa/Balarāma as a ploughman

Fig. 12.4 Balarāma from Kukargaon, Kuṣāṇa period, Mathurā Museum inv. C15 (© Government Museum, Mathurā).

and a hero. The god's heroic aspect is already portrayed on the Agathocles coins where both Vṛṣṇi Vīras are dressed as warriors. Saṃkarṣaṇa/Balarāma appears on the obverse, which has the Greek legend; this is the preferred side in the Indo-Greek context and it is reserved for the elder brother. The rationale for the brothers' appearance may well be that the heroes of Mathurā meshed well with the ancient Greeks' hero cult, making the deities acceptable over a large geographic terrain.

The snake and the wine cup, attributes missing on the several representations mentioned above, are beautifully carved on large Kuṣāṇa sculptures depicting the chthonic aspect of Balarāma's nature. These attributes figure prominently on a Kuṣāṇa image of Balarāma produced in Mathurā and found at Kukargaon (Fig. 12.4). A seven-hooded snake canopy surmounts the characteristic triple crested headgear of the god. His right arm is bent and raised above the head and the left hand holds the wine cup to the chest. Very similar in form and stance is the over life-size sculpture from Chargaon showing the same symbols. It bears an inscription on the back that identifies the deity. It is not Balarāma. It is an image of *bhagavā nāgo,* that is, a Nāga, or Snake Lord, who was set up by the side of his own lotus pool in the 40th year of the Kuṣāṇa king Huviṣka (Joshi 1979: pl. 3). The Chargaon Nāga illustrates just how close Balarāma's chthonic aspect is to that of snakes and the subterranean region they inhabit. So, how do we know that the Kukargaon statue represents Balarāma and not some Nāgarāja, or Snake King? In addition to Balarāma's triple-crested crown, the deity wears one earring and the Vaiṣṇava *vanamālā,* all iconographic emblems pertaining to that god. Clearly, an image of Balarāma must have a certain threshold of identifiable emblems that pertain to aspects of his complex persona: the snake and wine cup refer to his chthonic character, which imply that he is (or has aspects of) a snake deity; the plough and pestle connect him to the earth and its fertility, and suggest that he is an agricultural god of generation; and the mace reminds that he is a Vīra, a local hero of Mathurā.

These well-defined iconographic features fuse, as we have seen, from Gupta times onwards. The fusion does not begin suddenly. Even pre-Kuṣāṇa (e.g. Joshi

1979: pls 8.a-c, 9) and Kuṣāṇa images can show some combination of emblems pertaining to these various powers in the god's nature. For example, a late Kuṣāṇa/ early Gupta kinship triad from Gayā, Bihar (Srinivasan 1981: Fig. 4), consists of three separate, large images. The elder brother's head is protected by the serpent canopy; he is two-armed and carries the plough in his left hand while the right is poised in *abhayamudrā*. See Fig. 11.4 in this volume.

Fig. 12.5 Balarāma from the Sāñcī region, *c.* 1st century BC, private collector (© private collection).

An earlier, heretofore unpublished, example from the Madhya Pradesh region is in a private collection. Carved in the creamy sandstone associated with the Sāñcī region, it dates to about the end of the 1st century BC (Fig. 12.5). The turban, facial features and modelling invite comparison with the sculptures of Sāñcī Stūpa I. Saṃkarṣaṇa/ Balarāma, now 30 in (76.2 cm) tall, would have been even taller were the part below the knees still intact. The god has two hands. He holds the faceted mace in his right and the plough topped by the lion in his left hand. A five-headed serpent canopy extends over his double-knotted turban. The back highlights the unmistakable shape of the rearing snake and its spreading hood.

Another M.P. image—combining the heroic, agrarian and chthonic aspects in Saṃkarṣaṇa/Balarāma's nature—is an over life-size statue *in situ* at Andher, a site 8 miles (12.9 km) south-east of Sāñcī (Fig. 12.6). When I saw this image in 1999, I considered the currently transfigured icon as originally that of Saṃkarṣaṇa/Balarāma, and discussed the identification with Michael Willis who knows the site. The image measures about 7 ft 6 in (2.3 m); its plastered front has been remodelled and painted brightly as an image of four-armed Śiva. At Śiva's feet lies a part of the original sandstone image; it is a fragment of Saṃkarṣaṇa/ Balarāma preserved above the chest (Fig. 12.7), not above the waist (Shaw 2004: 26). A close look at the damaged fragment, probably dating to the early 1st century AD, reveals the assimilated iconography that we have been following. Some indication of the original snake hood remains at the right elbow and near the god's turban; for some reason not specified, Shaw considers this image 'with no serpent attributes' (Shaw 2004: 26). The faceted mace, similar to the Sāñcī example

Fig. 12.6 Transfigured image of Saṃkarṣaṇa/ Balarāma, in situ at Andher, Madhya Pradesh, c. 1st century AD (© author).

Fig. 12.7 Fragment of Saṃkarṣaṇa/Balarāma, presumably upper part (originally belonging to Figure 12.6; © author).

in Fig. 12.5 and the *gadā* held by Vīra Vāsudeva-Kṛṣṇa (Srinivasan 1981: pl. 6; fig 11.6 in this volume; cf. Balarāma's mace in Neumayer 1992–3: fig. 2)—and therefore not a pestle (Shaw 2004: 26) – is lifted overhead by the right hand; on the left, a portion of the lion can be made out, which originally would have topped the ploughshare. The back of the large sculpture, which has not been reconfigured, shows a huge sandstone serpent, somewhat similar in shape to that of the serpent at the back of Fig. 12.5. If additional confirmation is needed on the primacy of Saṃkarṣaṇa/Balarāma at this spot, it is provided by the presence of water that should have been in the ancient stone tank, some 30 ft (9 m) from the statue. Recent studies have indicated that the Sāñcī area was dotted in antiquity with icons of *nāgas, nāga* couples and a few Balarāmas, installed after the completion of dams and other irrigation works constructed for agricultural projects (Shaw and Sutcliffe 2003: 73–104). The occurrence of Balarāma amidst predominantly *nāga* statuary near to water emphasizes the strong connection this god had to snakes even when his iconography incorporates the additional *vīra* and agricultural aspects. It should be registered that when I saw the image (Figs. 12.6–12.7) I took the Saṃkarṣaṇa/ Balarāma fragment to have been part of the original and to have been replaced by the reconstructed Śiva image, whereas Shaw believes that there were originally two images at this Andher location: Fig. 12.6, as Balarāma in his serpent form, which now 'has been obscured by recent clay remodelling of the face and upper torso' (Shaw 2004: 25), and Fig. 12.7, as Balarāma in his non-serpent form, according to Shaw. Short of revisiting the site to re-inspect and compare fractures, etc., it seems reasonable to conjecture that there would have been no need (and no precedent) for two Balarāmas with the serpent attribute standing at the same place and dated to the same period.

In this selective but representative overview of Saṃkarṣaṇa/Balarāma's standard iconography, spanning the centuries between the Agathocles coins and the medieval Vaiṣṇava icons, and covering wide regions above the Vindhya hills, I do not know of any example that incorporates a hill, a mountain or a mound. It is doubtful that the raised ground in the Kangra miniature is due to a painter's desire to innovate. Vogel cites a few ancient Buddhist stories perhaps stemming from folklore that mention mountains as abodes of snakes (Vogel 1972: 33, 119, 146). And snakes emerge from underneath the raised ground in the Kangra miniature. Moreover, the attribute is assimilated to the standard emblems associated with Balarāma for centuries, nay, for over a millennium. It is hard to imagine that a form as prominent as the raised ground situated above the god's crown should have been placed there by the whim of a Kangra artist. Why, then, is this attribute there? If deliberately included, what does it mean?

Though early icons displaying aspects of Balarāma's nature encompass a broad swathe across northern India, the region that takes precedence when seeking an interpretation must center around Mathurā. It is here that the origins of Saṃkarṣaṇa/Balarāma's *vīra* aspect can be traced; it is here that he continues to be a popular god to this day; it is here that a contemporary ritual remembers his agrarian aspect; and indeed, it is here that contemporary shrines dedicated to Balarāma provide initial insight into the meaning of the raised piece of earth.

The town of Mathurā together with the surrounding rural areas are today part of what is called Braj. Balarāma is an extremely popular god here, affectionately worshipped as 'Dāūjī', meaning 'elder brother' in the local Braj dialect. Therefore, whatever other associations his shrines and/or icons may elicit, they figure in addition to his status as 'Dāūjī', namely the divine elder brother within the Vṛṣṇi Vīra clan.

Just outside of Mathurā town, in the village of Baldeo (Braj for Baladeva), is a large modern Dāūjī temple. The image of Baladeva, still in worship, is said to have been extracted from a pond and is considered to be one of the most ancient *mūrtis* in all of Braj (Vaudeville 1989: 113). The *mūrti* depicts the god holding the cup in his left hand and raising his right over the serpent hood above his head (compare with Fig. 12.4). The priests who attend this temple belong to the ancient Mathurā tribe called 'Ahivāsīs'. They call themselves Brahmans and snake worshippers, as the Sanskrit term *ahi* in their name recalls. The Dāūjī temple at Baldeo exemplifies the easy intermingling of Balarāma's chthonic and heroic aspects.

The village of Anyor, near Mount Govardhan, boasts of two Dāūjī shrines. The first contains an image with the standard iconography as seen in the Baladeva image. The second represents Dāūjī aniconically by five Govardhan stones

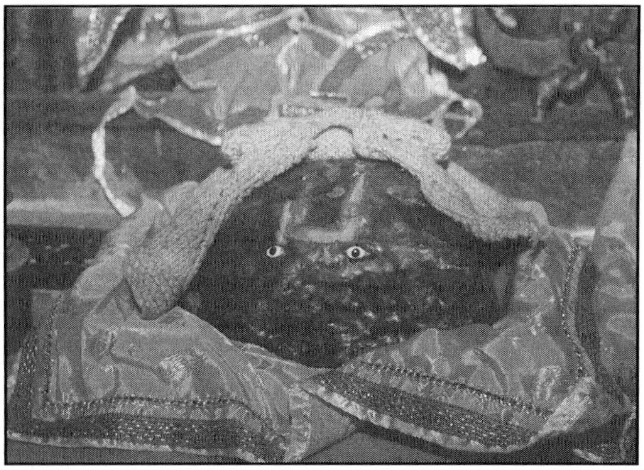

Fig. 12.8 A piece of Govardhan rock on the altar, modern Dāūjī shrine, Mathurā City (© author).

arranged in an arc on the ground. Another modern Dāūjī shrine located by the side of the large Mathurā Bhūteśvar temple also contains a referent to Mount Govardhan. Inside, Dāūjī is portrayed as in the Baldeo and Anyor shrines. Revatī, his consort, stands by his side. However, on the altar and at the feet of the gods is a large piece of the Govardhan rock. The rock has been made fit for worship (Fig. 12.8). Its large eyes indicate that the presence of that mountain has been installed within. This shrine and the one at Anyor are our first indications that Balarāma's assimilated iconography can include a mountain. Further, these contemporary shrines provide its likely identification. It is Mount Govardhan, the sacred hill still worshipped today by devout Vaiṣṇavas. The introduction of Mount Govardhan into the worship of Saṃkarṣaṇa/Balarāma is rather unexpected. We usually associate Kṛṣṇa with Mount Govardhan, remembering, of course, the Purāṇic (and *Harivaṃṣa*) legend of Kṛṣṇa's feat in lifting this mountain.

A clue as to the connection between Mount Govardhan and Balarāma comes from the Govardhanapūjā festival celebrated by the Braj folk (Vaudeville 1989: 110–12). The Braj are mainly a pastoral people who have made only 'superficial adjustments with upper caste sectarian Vaiṣṇavism' (Vaudeville 1989: 114). The Govardhanapūjā is interpreted differently by the upper caste (Vallabhite and Gauḍīya) Vaiṣṇavas and the Brajvāsī cowherd people. The Braj folk sculpt a 'cowdung Govardhan', which has some anthropomorphic elements. The Govardhan effigy has a squarish 'body' surmounted by a rounded head. It can have two 'arms', raised from the 'body' (Vaudeville 1989: 111); it can also have just the right arm raised, recalling the raised right hand of the Nāga and Balarāma icons and the left in 'the *abhaya* posture' (Vaudeville 1989: 112). Between the parallel feet hangs down what looks like an oversized penis. Notably the Sanskrit word for plough, *lāṅgala,* also has the meaning of 'penis', according to local lexicons (Monier-Williams 1960: 900; Vaudeville 1989: 111).

We are reminded of another rock engraving at Chilas, northern Pakistan (Group 7, no. 3, dated 50 BC–AD 50), bearing the label 'Valadebo' (= Baladeva; Fig. 12.9). The iconography that Fussman (1989: 15) found enigmatic – 'un personnage masculin nu, au sexe (ou *dhotī?)* pendant, brandissant une (lance?) de la droite mi-tendue' – is actually the god's *lāṅgala* depicted twice: as his penis and as his plough affixed to the end of a spear. (Interestingly, native lexicons also assign the meaning 'palm tree' to *lāṅgala,* which is of course an ancient emblem of Balarāma; *lāṅgūla* signifies 'tail', a concept used in serpent lore, see below). To

Fig. 12.9 Valadebo (Baladeva), Chilas rock engraving in situ, 50 BC–AD 50 (photograph © Gérard Fussman).

return to the *pūjā,* in the middle of the Govardhan effigy, there is a large hole interpreted as the 'navel' or 'mouth' into which milk is poured to feed the snakes in the lower regions. And it is through the *lāṅgala* that subterranean waters are drawn up to fertilize the earth. The Govardhanapūjā of the Braj folk is of twofold importance in seeking the significance of the Kangra attribute: the rite connects Mount Govardhan with snakes residing underneath, and the effigy of Mount Govardhan shares some aspects with Balarāma's imagery. Even an essential element of the Purāṇic story cited at the beginning of this paper—Saṃkarṣaṇa/ Balarāma with his *lāṅgala* (plough) causing water to fill a furrow—reverberates with the power of the effigy's *lāṅgala* (penis) to fertilize and irrigate the earth from waters below.

It is now time to observe that the god's other name Saṃkarṣaṇa, derived from the verb root *saṃ√ kṛṣ,* means 'ploughing', 'drawing out', etc. (Monier-Williams 1960: 1126). The appellation Saṃkarṣaṇa/Balarāma seems to focus on the god's two important powers: he is the one who ploughs and who is strong. Therefore, in this paper I have referred to the god as Saṃkarṣaṇa (and Balarāma) when he is associated with the plough and when his *vīra* status is evident (Srinivasan 1997: 211). However, the question of when to call this god Saṃkarṣaṇa and/or Balarāma still needs to be worked out more closely, since on the Chilas petroglyph he is 'Baladeva' and his symbols are the plough, spear and large penis (Fig. 12.9).

The appellation 'the plougher' refers not only to the agrarian and heroic aspects of the god; a 'ploughing god' has sexual overtones. Śiva, the most erotic god in Hinduism, whose sign is the raised *liṅga*, is worshipped as Lāṅgaleśvara in a region of Orissa and is described as 'Lord of the Plough' in some Bengali literature (Smith 1999: 208–28). Parpola would like to go back to Megasthenes to connect Śiva's sexuality with agrarian generation and the plough (Parpola 2002: 369–70). We may ask ourselves—once aware of the interplay between Śiva and Balarāma—whether it is mere chance that the ancient Andher icon of Balarāma has been converted into a modern icon of Śiva? Do the folk in the Sāñcī region remember some connection between the two? Most noteworthy is that both Vaudeville (1989: 113–14) and Parpola (2002: 369) have proposed that Balarāma has an ancient Śaivite background. Of related interest are the pre-Kuṣāṇa fragmentary finds of a Śivaliṅga, a Nāginī and a *yakṣa* in the Sāñcī area (probably not 2nd century AD: Shaw 2004, 29–30; see and compare Mitterwallner 1984: 19, Fig. 9a; Srinivasan 1984: Figs. 19, 21, 24; see Figs. 4.3, 4.5, 4.8 in this volume and Srinivasan 2007: Figs. 13, 15, 17, 19; see Figs. 15.13, 15.15, 15.17, 15.19 in this volume).

Folk beliefs appear to be critical in establishing an association between Mount Govardhana and Balarāma. The *Mahābhārata* may clarify the connection. In 2.38.9, Śiśupāla, Kṛṣṇa's foe, denigrates Kṛṣṇa's lifting of the mountain in this way: 'If he held up the mountain Govardhana for seven days, that I think, is hardly a miracle, Bhīṣma; it is as big as an anthill!' (van Buitenen 1975: 98). The comparison between Mount Govardhan and an anthill is significant. Snakes make their abodes in anthills. When John Irwin studied Indian anthill rites and worship, he reported that in most cases the worshippers were not worshipping the anthill but the serpent living inside (Irwin 1982: 350-51; cf. G.D. Sontheimer, quoted by Vaudeville 1989: 105). Vaudeville (1992: 5–6) also remarks on the resemblance between an anthill and the strange shape of the Govardhan hillock.

Current place names in Braj support a local belief that a giant snake resides within Mount Govardhan and that its head and tail surface above ground. Charlotte Vaudeville identified the name of the village that recalls the emerging tail of the snake; this is the village of Puchrī (lit. 'the tail'). She states: "The prevailing local belief seems to have been that the Nāgarāja underlying Mount Govardhan had its head ('mouth') at Mānasī Gaṅgā and its tail at Puchrī" (Vaudeville 1980: 8).

How did the elder brother of the Vṛṣṇi Heroes (Dāūjī of later times) come to be associated with a snake residing under Mount Govardhan? Judging by the antiquity of anthropomorphic snake imagery, it is probable that the worship of Nāgarājas, or Snake Lords, may be older than the worship of the Vṛṣṇi Heroes in the Mathurā region. There is the example of a large Nāgarāja from the Mathurā region (Joshi, 1979: pl. 1), who probably dates between the 3rd and 2nd century BC. The figure may even represent Balarāma (a break by the ear might have been the one earring, and possibly the broken left arm held a wine cup at the chest—observations conveyed to me by Sonya Quintanilla). Recalling the correlation between the snake cult and anthills in contemporary lore and the epic's comparison of Mount Govardhan to an anthill, the possibility exists that quite early, perhaps even from the post-Mauryan period onwards, some Mathurā folk believed that a giant snake lived under Mount Govardhan and they began to worship it.

The next postulate seems unavoidable. Probably before the Christian era, the giant snake believed to live under Mount Govardhan became identified with the Vīra Saṃkarṣaṇa/Balarāma. It is most provocative to consider the well-known Saṃkarṣaṇa/Balarāma icon from Jansutī in the light of this assumption (Fig. 12.10). It was found on the road to Govardhan 6 miles (9.7 km) from Mathurā. This is one of the oldest icons of the god, dating to about the 2nd to 1st century BC. It belongs to the group of images combining the heroic, the agrarian and chthonic (or serpentine) aspects of the god. Saṃkarṣaṇa/Balarāma stands with the right knee slightly flexed. He wears a single earring and a large Śuṅga-style turban, over which looms the serpent canopy. His two arms hold the club in the right and the plough in the left. Could this be an early visual record of the Vṛṣṇi Vīra's assimilation to Govardhana's giant Nāga? I find it equally instructive that the location of all three early Balarāma images in the Sāñcī region are on or near raised ground: the snake-backed Balarāmas from Chandna, Andher (Fig. 12.6) and Mehgaon, found *in situ*, are located on an embankment, at the base of a hill and on the embankment of a dried-up tank, respectively (Shaw 2004: 24-28). In all these cases Saṃkarṣaṇa/Balarāma, the darling of the folk and the hero with sexual energies, serpentine features and fertilizing powers, is placed in localities where he can draw up water and retain it on earth so that fertilization, agriculture and generation can flourish anew.

Fig. 12.10 Saṃkarṣaṇa/Balarāma from Jansutī, U.P.; 2nd to 1st centuries BC, State Museum, Lucknow, inv. G215 (photograph © State Museum, Lucknow).

In conclusion, the overarching aspects that form the nature of this complex deity appear before the Kuṣāṇa period, and for the most part before the Christian era. From the Aï Khanoum coins, the Tikula, M.P. rock painting and the Chilas II petroglyphs, it is apparent that between the 2nd century BC and early 1st century AD, both the *vīra* and agricultural aspects defined the powers of Saṃkarṣaṇa/Balarāma. Also before AD 50, judging from the Chilas II Valadebo image, his

Fig. 12.11 Balarāma from Mathurā, Kuṣāṇa period, Los Angeles County Museum of Art, from the Nasli and Alice Heeramaneck Collection, Museum Associates Purchase inv. M 73.4.7 (© Los Angeles County Museum of Art, from the Nasli and Alice Heeramaneck Collection, Museum Associates Purchase).

agricultural aspect, symbolized in part by the plough, also included the fertilizing powers of the penis, perhaps punningly derived from local meanings associated with *lāṅgala* as well as Balarāma's ancient Śaivite association. The Jansutī image, found on the road to Mount Govardhan, is probably the earliest image with the serpentine attribute, possibly fostered by proximity to the mountain. A mix of the agricultural, subterranean and heroic aspects began early—and stayed—with some combinations surfacing from time to time, as seen in the virile Kuṣāṇa Balarāma image from Mathurā (Los Angeles County Museum of Art, inv. M.73.4.7; Fig. 12.11). The god has one earring, holds the wine cup in his left hand and is addorsed with a giant snake. His raised right arm and his prominent male member are both reminiscent of the Braj Govardhan effigy.

Devotional Vaiṣṇavism, we all know, soon annexed and subordinated local cults and local lore into the 'Greater Tradition' at Mathurā and elsewhere. In this realignment, Kṛṣṇa not only came to dominate Balarāma, but also his elder brother's association with Mount Govardhan. But a lingering connection remained. A Kangra artist remembered. Mathurā's contemporary Dāūjī shrines have not forgotten; neither had Sūr Dās, the 16th-century Braj poet who wove together an unforgettable, poetic image of Balarāma that resonates deeply with the full panoply of his powers (trans. Sanford 2000: 382):

> Gopal sent out a call:
> Proud Haladhar does not speak to anyone. He changed the course of the Yamuna. His eyes spin. His movements lurch. Just as if he took the form of a mountain.
> He wears blue clothes, his blouse hangs. He swallows from a gold cup.
> He brings 1,000 young women with him, singing songs from forest to forest.
> The pure hand of Balabhadra killed Dvivid, the kin of Kaṃsa.
> Jay-jay Rāma, the gods say. Countless Kusum flowers rain down.
> Paramānand says, the brother of the lord, his support, carries the snake's gem.
> (Sāgar 1162)

REFERENCES

Asher, Frederick M. (1980), *The Art of Eastern India, 300–800,* Minneapolis: Univ. of Minnesota Press.

Errington, E. and J. Cribb with M. Claringbull. (1992), *The Crossroads of Asia: Transformation in Image and Symbol in the Art of Ancient Afghanistan and Pakistan,* Cambridge: The Ancient India and Iran Trust.

Fussman, G. (1989), 'Les Inscriptions Kharoṣṭhī de la Plaine de Chilas' in K. Jettmar, *Antiquities of Northen Pakistan,* Vol. 1, text.

Irwin, J. (1982), 'The Sacred Anthill and the Cult of the Primordial Mound', *History of Religions* 21, 339-60.

Jettmar, K. *et al.* (1989), *Antiquities of Northern Pakistan, Vol. 1: Rock Inscriptions in the Indus Valley. Plates,* Mainz: von Zabern.

Joshi, N.P. (1979), *Iconography of Balarāma,* New Delhi: Abhinav Publications.

Mitterwallner, G. von. (1984), 'Evolution of the Liṅga', in M.W. Meister (ed.), *Discourses on Śiva: Proceedings of a Symposium on the Nature of Religious Imagery,* Philadelphia: Univ. of Pennsylvania Press, 12-31.

Monier-Williams, Sir Monier. (1960), *Sanskrit-English Dictionary,* [reprint:] Oxford: Clarendon Press.

Neumayer, E. (1992-93), 'On the Identification of Bhakti-Deities in Rock Pictures', *Purātattva* 23, 53-60.

Parpola, A. (2002), 'ΠΑΝΔΑΙΗ and Sītā: On the Historical Background of the Sanskrit Epics', *Journal of the American Oriental Society* 122, 361-73.

Sanford, A.W. (2000), 'Uneasy partners. Balarāma as Embodiment of Wilderness' in Offredi, M, *The Banyan Tree: Essay on Early Literature in New Indo-Aryan Languages, Proceedings of the Seventh International Conference on Early Literature in New Indo-Aryan Languages,* Venice, Università degli Studi di Venezia, New Delhi: Manohar, Vol. II, 363-87.

Shaw, J. (2004), 'Nāga Sculptures in Sanchi's Archaeological Landscape: Buddhism, Vaiṣṇavism and Local Agricultural Cults in Central India, First Century BCE to Fifth Century CE', *Artibus Asiae* LXIV/I, 5-59.

Shaw, J. and J. Sutcliffe. (2003), 'Water Management, Patronage Networks and Religious Change: New Evidence from the Sanchi Dam Complex and Counterparts in Gujarat and Sri Lanka', *South Asian Studies 19,* 73-104.

Smith, W.L. (1999), 'Śiva, Lord of the Plough' in R.P. Das (ed.), *Essays on Middle Bengali Literature,* Calcutta: Firma KLM, 208-28.

Sotheby's. (1999), *Indian and Southeast Asian Art Sales Catalogue, Sale 7280; March* 25, 1999, New York.

Srinivasan, D. (1981), 'Early Kṛishṇa Icons: The Case at Mathurā', in J.G. Williams (ed.), *Kalādarśana: American Studies in the Art of India,* New Delhi: Oxford & IBH Publishing Co, 127-36.

Srinivasan, D.M. (1984), 'Significance and Scope of Pre-Kuṣāṇa Śaivite Iconography', in M.W. Meister (ed.), *Discourses on Śiva: Proceedings of a Symposium on the Nature of Religious Imagery,* Philadelphia: Univ. of Pennsylvania Press, 32-46.

Srinivasan, Doris Meth. (1997), *Many Heads, Arms and Eyes: Origin, Meaning and Form of Multiplicity in Indian Art,* Leiden: E.J. Brill.

Srinivasan, D.M. (2007), 'Monumental Nāginīs from Mathurā', in D.M. Srinivasan (ed.), *On the Cusp of an Era: Art in the Pre-Kuṣāṇa World,* Leiden: E.J. Brill.

Vaudeville, C. (1980), 'The Govardhan Myth in Northern India', *Indo-Iranian Journal* 22, 1-45

Vaudeville, Ch. (1989), 'Multiple Approaches to a Living Hindu Myth: The Lord of the Govardhan Hill', in G.D. Sontheimer and H. Kulke (eds.), *Hinduism Reconsidered*, Delhi: Manohar, 105-25.

Vaudeville, Ch. (1992), 'Govardhan, the Eater hill', in R.S. McGregor (ed.), *Devotional Literature in South Asia*, Cambridge: Cambridge University Press, 3-10.

Vogel, J.Ph. (1972), *Indian Serpent-Lore*, [reprint:] Varanasi/Delhi: Indological Book House.

Wilson, H.H. (trans.). (1979), *Viṣṇu Purāṇa*, [reprint:] Calcutta: Punthi Pustak, 3rd edition.

13

Royalty's Courtesans and God's Mortal Wives: Keepers of Culture in Precolonial India

The Indian courtesan pervades precolonial art, literature, mythology, texts on rituals, polity, pleasure, and law books in the three major religions founded on Indian soil. Yet as much as she captivates, she also eludes. Why? Because her actions, her character, her mystique, are relayed to us by outsiders to her world, or to traditional India. Her own voice has remained faint until fairly modern times. This essay introduces different voices that describe the Indian courtesan over a vast stretch of history. What becomes clear is that two options for power were open to the precolonial Indian woman: that of the sexually liberated and educated courtesan or the pure, sexually controlled, uneducated wife.

THE WIFE/COURTESAN DICHOTOMY

Abbé Dubois, a French missionary who lived and worked in India from 1792 to 1823, made up his mind that the cultivated Indian female existed, but she was not the Indian wife:

> A young girl's mind remains totally uncultivated though many of them have good abilities. In fact, what use would learning or accomplishments be to women who are still in such a state of domestic degradation and servitude? All that a Hindu woman need know is how to grind and boil rice and look after her household affairs which are neither numerous nor difficult to manage. Courtesans, whose business in life is to dance in the temples and at public ceremonies, and prostitutes, are the only women who are allowed to learn to read, sing or dance.

Originally published in *Courtesans' Arts: Cross Cultural Perspectives*, M. Feldman and B. Gordon (eds.), 2006, pp. 161-81 incl. figures. Reprinted with stylistic changes, additions and by permission of Oxford University Press, USA.

The Abbé's observations are corroborated by a contemporary Indian, Abdul Halim Sharar. In his history of the north Indian kingdom of Awadh, Sharar notes that it was the courtesans who sustained the high culture at Lucknow, the kingdom's capital. They kept alive the distinctive manners of Lucknow society and were instrumental in the development of Kathak dance and Hindustani music.[1]

I am prompted to cite these two testimonies by far more than a need to document the cultivated nature of courtesans in early nineteenth-century India. The Abbé's observations pertain to southern, or peninsular, India. His description of southern Indian mores is contained in his book *Hindu Manners, Customs, and Ceremonies.*[2] the operative word is "Hindu." Sharar, a novelist and journalist, wrote about the Muslim kingdom of Awadh in north India. These two observers, living and working in contrasting religious spheres at considerable geographic distance from each other, both imagined the courtesan as the keeper of culture. This overarching theme describes the courtesan not only of the precolonial period but also of prior ages.

Were all courtesans in India cultivated? Of course not. There were courtesans and prostitutes, as Abbé Dubois noted, and throughout Indian history specific Sanskrit terms were used to highlight distinctions between them.[3] The exceptionally civilized public woman, proficient in arts and endowed with winsome qualities, is called a *gaṇikā.* A *veśyā,* or specifically a woman called a *rūpajīvā,* is a prostitute, ranked below the *gaṇikā,* whose artistic talents she does not possess. A very low-grade prostitute (a "whore") is a *puṃścalī,* and a prostitute who is a slave is a *dāsī,* such as a *kumbhadāsī,* a "pots-and-pans" prostitute consigned to the most menial of tasks. A temple dancer, or religious courtesan, is called a *devadāsī.* The institution of the *devadāsī* can be traced in India from the third century BC[4] until it was finally outlawed in 1947. Unless otherwise stated, this essay concentrates on the *gaṇikā,* a secular courtesan, often associated with a royal court,[5] and the *devadāsī,* the temple courtesan, dedicated to the temple as god's mortal wife.

As may already be surmised, Indians liked nothing better than to name and classify, and this predilection extends to listing the arts that a *gaṇikā* should master. The *Kāmasūtra,* composed sometime between the early Christian era and the fourth and fifth centuries AD, is perhaps the best-known source on courtesans and prostitutes of ancient India. Being a text with aphoristic rules on sexual relations between men and women, it devotes one section, part VI, to the courtesan *(veśyā).* Herein, the legendary author, Vātsyāyana, advises the courtesan to be skilled in the sixty-four arts that define a cultured person.[6] He lists them all and the list is daunting. Topping it are singing, playing on musical instruments, dancing, writing, drawing. Picture-making, trimming, and decorating are also to be studied. Some unexpected skills include knowledge of magic, tailoring, carpentry, architecture, chemistry, minerology, cock-, quail-, and ram-fighting, rules of society, and how to pay respects and compliments to others. In the aggregate, the sixty-four arts form a remarkable portrait of the civilized and knowledgeable elite in society. In fact, the text states this by saying that when the *veśyā* is proficient in these arts, and imbued with beauty, politeness, and virtue, she becomes a *gaṇikā,* and "receives a seat of honour in the assembly of men"; that is, she can discourse with men as their equal. The *Kāmasūtra* goes further: "She is moreover always respected by the king, and praised by learned men and her favour being sought for by all, she becomes an object of universal regard."[7]

Fig. 13.1. One side of double-faced relief possibly depicting the courtesan Vasantasena (Kuṣāṇa Period, 2nd century AD).

Molding the sexualized female into a courtesan of character preceded the account in the *Kāmasūtra.* The *Arthaśāstra,* a text on Indian polity dating perhaps to the first or second century AD but containing information that may go back as far as the third century BC, discusses the *gaṇikā's* education because the state is to invest in her training and to profit from her success. *Gaṇikās, dāsīs,* and actresses are to be taught singing, playing on instruments like the *vīṇā,* pipe, and drum, reciting, dancing, acting, writing, painting, reading the thoughts of others, manufacturing scents and garlands, shampooing, and the art of attracting and captivating the mind of others. The text proposes that the state bear the cost of this education and directly employ the recipients; in effect, the *gaṇikā* of the *Arthaśāstra* is to turn over her earnings to the state and to receive, besides the accoutrements of a glamorous lifestyle, a monthly salary from the king's treasury.[8] The *gaṇikā* in the play entitled *The Little Clay Cart* epitomizes the educated courtesan: independent, wealthy—and generous (see Fig. 13.1).[9]

Her rigorous education can be inferred by the fact that she speaks Sanskrit whereas the others cannot, not even a brahman recently dragged into poverty. Her taste in architecture and the decorative arts is opulent and self-assured, as a visit to her mansion in act 4 of the play demonstrates. The mansion is preceded by eight courts. *Gaṇikās* strolling through the third court have picture-boards in hand that are covered with all manner of scenes.[10] The fourth court reveals courtesans being trained in the arts of singing, dancing, playing musical instruments, and performing erotic plays. A visitor entering this court is amazed:

> Oh, oh, oh! The drums are thundering like rain clouds under the hands of young women. Brass cymbals are falling like the stars that fall from heaven when their merit is exhausted, and the reed flute sighs sweetly like the humming of honey bees. There with a blow of the hand a vīṇā is made to run like a mistress enraged by her lover's jealous querulousness. And there the courtesans of the first degree, singing sweetly like honey bees drunk with the attar of flowers, are dancing, and plays are rehearsed, love plays all.[11]

Though none of the texts cited thus far (with the exception of that in n. 4) furnishes an objective, historical account, each contains overlapping information regarding the cultivated courtesan, indicating thereby that they may bear some semblance to reality in these early periods. The *Viṣṇudharmottara Purāṇa,* a bit later, touches on the connection between courtesans and painting.[12] It alludes to the way courtesans (the *veśyā*) should be depicted in paintings; their proportions and their manner of attire ("flamboyant and erotic") are specified in III–43.24–25. The cumulative evidence from these various sources has prompted one scholar to suggest that courtesans both practiced (perhaps "dabbled in" would be more accurate) and fostered Indian fresco paintings of the pre-medieval periods.[13] I would add that they also appeared in the genre.[14]

Temple courtesans, *devadāsīs,* can also be traced back to early times. The third-century BC. Jogīmārā Inscription in Central India is perhaps the first to mention a *devadāsī*. The lettering is engraved inside a cave and underneath paintings that cover the vault of the cave.[15] And the *Arthaśāstra* says that when the temple service of *devadāsīs* is finished, they can take up spinning (2.23.2). According to Desai's reading of the few available literary and travel accounts from about the eighth to twelfth centuries AD, the likely services these girls gave to the temple were singing, dancing, and sexual gratification.[16]

In sum, the areas wherein literature claims that the secular and temple courtesans excelled during the first millenium AD appear to be the same as those they still excelled in towards the end of the second millenium, when the Abbé Dubois made his observations. The dichotomy he observed between the cultivated public woman and the domestic wife is founded on customs long prevalent in traditional India. For example, the *Kāmasūtra* has a separate section about the wife (part IV) that precedes and contrasts notably with the section on the courtesan. Until colonial times, there does seem to have been a split between females who are keepers of culture and females who are keepers of the home.[17] The former are considered to be unmarried, unchaste, attached to a matrilineal kin group, economically independent, and educated to a degree; the latter are recognized as being married, chaste, embedded in a patrilineal kin group upon which the wife is economically dependent, and uneducated in spheres unrelated to the home.[18] Whether, through the ages, this situation has a significant or insignificant basis in reality depends upon how much credence one gives to literary sources and traditional treatises on polity, law, love, the arts, and so forth, which may express theoretical ideals or criteria more than factual realities.[19]

One such treatise, *The Law Book of Manu*, dating to around the second century AD, warns the virtuous on the evils of the virtueless: "Drinking (spirituous liquor), associating with wicked people, separation from the husband, rambling abroad, sleeping (at unseasonable hours), and dwelling in other men's houses, are the six causes of the ruin of women."[20] The evils *Manu* cites—drinking, promiscuity, and inattentiveness to the home—are infractions that narrow the gap between the world of the wife and that of the courtesan. These are, however, symptoms, not causes, of the dichotomy between wife and courtesan, just as education is symptomatic of a far greater divide. The apparent contrast between domestic degradation and urbane cultivation noted by the Abbé obscured the fact that the Hindu wife, confined though she was, had status in his day and throughout the first and second millennia AD, according to traditional law. The same *Law of Manu* reveals the basis of her stature in a male-dominated society: "He who carefully guards his wife, preserves (the purity of) his offspring, virtuous conduct, his family, himself, and his (means of acquiring) merit" (*dharma*)."[21] This passage recognizes that, from the point of view of the male, a married woman's power is her sexual purity. The commentator, who takes "*dharma*" as "religion" in the above verse, views an "unchaste woman" as one not "entitled to being associated in the performance of religious rites. For these reasons, if a man guards his wife, he preserves all these."[22] Herein lies the fundamental difference between the wife and courtesan, no matter how civilized the latter may be. Because of the bride's (or wife's) sexual purity, the husband knows his offspring are his, and the family he rears can maintain the necessary traditions that bring merit to his lineage: "As the male is to whom a wife cleaves, even so is the son whom she brings forth; let him therefore carefully guard his wife, in order to keep his offspring pure."[23]

To lead a traditional Hindu life, it is essential to be married and carry out familial obligations. The role of the wife is to continue the family line and enable it to perform life-cycle ceremonies. Upon these depend the social and religious merit (*dharma*) of the family. The traditional outlook was to consider only the virgin as marriageable. Since a woman was thought to be naturally libidinous, the unmarried girl, after puberty, needed to be guarded by the parents;[24] after marriage, the job passed on to the husband. Only the pure wife could prepare food for the family and cook the balls of rice offered in the all-important ancestor rites (*śrāddha*). Ideally, the legitimate son born out of a sanctified marriage could perform the *śrāddha* rites for the family's ancestors; if these rites were not done it was believed that at least three generations of ancestors would find no peace in the afterlife.[25] Traditional Hindu life is punctuated by other mandated life-cycle rites (*saṁskāras*),[26] which depend upon the proper behavior and actions of the wife, so that she may help her husband in performing domestic rituals.[27] Though familial rites revolve mainly around the male, the husband and/or sons, a wife is needed who is qualified to enable traditional rites, values, and social customs to survive. And survive they have. The *śrāddha* rite, still practiced today, goes back to ancient Hinduism; the same can be said of the *saṁskāras* and domestic rituals. The indispensable need for the sexual purity of the wife should have been her source of power for over two millennia—beginning sometime within the first millennium BC (with the formulation of the ancient Hindu rites, which were subsequently enshrined as duties in the theoretical law book of *Manu*), and continuing into contemporary times, as research conducted in the late twentieth century shows.[28] The basic dichotomy, in short, between the wife and the courtesan rests on the opposition between the keeper of the (pure) lineage and the keeper of culture, and this divide seems to describe the bookends of diametrically opposed realms of power open to the Indian female up to the colonial period and beyond.

It may surprise the Western reader that a cultivated courtesan could wield so much power and prestige throughout the millennia. The high regard accorded her in the *Kāmasūtra,* noted above, hints in that direction.[29] as do other literary works. In a Sanskrit farce attributed to King Mahendravarman I, who ruled in south India at the beginning of the seventh century AD, the *gaṇikā* and her entourage are not the butt of ridicule; rather it is the ascetic brahman.[30] In Somadeva's eleventh-century work, *The Ocean of Story,* a tale called "King Vikramāditya and the Courtesan" re-counts how Madanamālā's sensuality and magnanimity capture the heart of a king; but what prompts him to ask her to live with him is her loyalty, constancy, and selfless love for him.[31] Just as the power of the wife stems from the traditional values, customs, myths, and fantasies embedded in pan-Indic norms, so too do those of the courtesan. In the few instances where records reflecting the courtesan's thinking exist, a perspective becomes apparent which is quite different from the one revealed in traditional sources. Many ancient (and contemporary) societies considered the sexually awakened female as both auspicious and dangerous. The second section of this essay indicates that the Indian tradition had three archetypes so considered: the *gaṇikā,* the *devadāsī,* and the wife. This situation lasted until colonial times, when India was ruled by foreigners whose norms and codes were so different from those of traditional India that the latter lost ground. Then the courtesan's power was broken and her sphere of cultivation passed onto the virtuous wife and her daughters.

THE POWER OF THE SEXUALIZED FEMALE

Courtesans, especially the *gaṇikā* and *devadāsī,* had extraordinary customers. Kings and brahmans have already been mentioned. These are men from the two highest castes. Brahmans belong to the top, or priestly, caste, emphasizing learning, especially ritual knowledge; kings and lesser royalty formed the second, or ruling caste. Fact, fantasy, ritual exigencies, and poetic license, all lead various sources to recount other, unusual paramours of courtesans as well.

An ascetic *(brahmacārin)* cavorts with a low-grade courtesan *(puṃścalī)* in an ancient Hindu (i.e., Vedic) ritual, the *Mahāvrata,* which probably celebrated the winter solstice. A *brahmacārin* is a high-born student of Vedic sacred knowledge; during the years of his studentship he is supposed to live a life of sexual abstinence. In one part of the *Mahāvrata* rite, the *brahmacārin* must exchange obscene insults with the whore. The *puṃścalī* cries to him: "you who have misbehaved! who have violated your vow of continence!," to which the *brahmacārin* answers: "shame upon you, depraved one! harlot! who washes off the village community, who washes off man's member!"[32] The sexual jibes may substitute for the act itself, for this part of the rite was supposed to promote fertility.[33] The procreative benefit resulting from an ascetic's encounter with a seductive female is a frequent motif in Indian mythology.[34] The seduction of Ṛṣyaśṛṅga (Sage "Antelope-horn") was so popular that versions are found in early Buddhist texts, in the Hindu epic (i.e., the *Mahābhārata),* in ancient stories (e.g., the *Padma Purāṇa),* in Chinese texts, and in Indian art.[35] The Sage was born when a doe ingested the seed of a Brahman ascetic living in the forest. She became pregnant and gave birth to a boy with a horn on his head (Fig. 13.2).

Fig. 13.2. Probably Ṛṣyaśṛṅga on a railing pillar (Kuṣāṇa Period. 2nd century AD).

Ṛṣyaśṛṅga grew up practicing strict asceticism; so innocent and removed from females was he that he thought a seductress sent to break his chastity was some marvelous ascetic. In some versions the enticing female is actually an *apsaras* (heavenly nymph), or a princess, or a princess with her entourage of courtesans (as in Fig. 13.3), or a courtesan with a troupe of prostitutes.

In all but the earliest versions, the continence of Ṛṣyaśṛṅga is so prolonged and strenuous that it causes drought in the land; for the release of rain, either Ṛṣyaśṛṅga's presence alone or the release of his seed is needed. To cause the latter is the job of the enticing female(s). Mythopoeic logic formulates an analogy, on the one hand, between the retention of sexual fluid and the withholding of fertilizing waters in nature, and on the other, the spilling of seed and the release of fertilizing rain. As part of this analogous thinking, courtesans, because of their unrestrained sexual life, can be regarded, in the Ṛṣyaśṛṅga legend and in other

Fig. 13.3. Ṛṣyaśṛṅga is surrounded by a princess and courtesans. Begram ivory. Afghanistan (*c.* 2nd century AD).

contexts, as valuable promoters of fecundity in nature, as well as in the human sphere. Thus, according to one Purāṇa, the *Viṣṇudharmottara Purāṇa* (II.21.6; 104.87), "the earth dug away from the housedoor of a prostitute was held to have absorbed her beneficent potency."[36] The same *Purāṇa* (II.163.20) includes *gaṇikās* of the first degree among a list of auspicious objects. And in another text of approximately similar age (*Viṣṇusmṛti* 63.29), courtesans are counted among those that cause good luck.

Frequent sexual coupling and the potency associated with that frequency seem to be a source of the courtesan's power. Myth, rite, and traditional lore recognize that sexual intercourse activates fertility and procreation. It follows therefore that the courtesan's carnal life promotes her own empowerment.

A glimpse at another source of her power can be caught in the late medieval songs sung by courtesans in parts of south India. A collection of short musical compositions, or *padams,* recently translated from the Telugu, were composed mainly by the seventeenth-century poet Kṣetrayya for the sophisticated and talented courtesans who sang and danced in temples and courts before gods and kings.[37] These professionals were the *devadāsīs,* and possibly the *veśyās* and *gaṇikās* of the day. The poetry is devotional yet of a highly erotic content. As the courtesan sings, we ought to imagine the king, and even the god, cast in the role of lover. The poet voices, through the person of the courtesan, his own longing for a personal experience with god, giving the *padams* a highly charged eroticism:

> Don't you know my house
> garland in the palace of the Love God
> where flowers cast their fragrance everywhere?

Don't you know the house
hidden by tamarind trees,
in that narrow space marked by the two golden hills?

That's where you lose your senses,
where the Love God hunts without fear.[38]

The translators explain the reason why the courtesan is the perfect instrument by which the poet can express his hunger to experience god. It is not so much her boldness, her freedom from conventional constraints, her spontaneity and sensuality, as it is her particular knowledge of her lover that appealed greatly to the devotee's wishes. "Bodily experience becomes the crucial mode of knowing... the courtesan experiences her divine client by taking him physically into her body... there is this fascination with bodily knowledge of god."[39] Here, then, is another source of the courtesan's power, still based on her sexuality, though not only on the procreative energies released by her action, but also on the immediacy of the—erotically induced—knowledge of the divine she could claim.

A twentieth-century field study of the *devadāsīs* in the temple town of Puri, Orissa (in eastern India), describes the erotic atmosphere during a ritual temple dance, which I think sheds light on what actually happened when a dancer danced in the Hindu temple. The description is offered here as a way to explore how a dancer's sexuality can translate into physical knowledge of a king or a god. It is not offered as a direct explanation of the power of Kṣetrayya's courtesans since the time and circumstances between seventeenth-century south Indian temples and royal courts and the institutions and practices of nineteenth- and twentieth-century north India ought to be considerable.[40]

The Puri *devadāsīs* performed a daily midday ritual that brought them into intimate contact with the divine and his partial incarnation on earth, the king. The temple *devadāsīs,* also known as *gaṇikās* or *veśyās,* are themselves considered mortal embodiments of the god whose temple they serve. Indeed, they undergo an initial induction ceremony, after which they consider themselves married to the main deity of the temple. Thereupon they are believed to possess a share of divine sovereignty and to be the earthly embodiment of the god's divine consort. The god has absolute sovereignty over the temple land. Earthly temple servants have a share of that authority, and the king has the biggest earthly share. As such, a *devadāsī* can have sexual relations with those mortal men who partake of the divinity of her divine lord.

During sexual intercourse, the *devadāsī* produces the auspicious female life force; the female life force is her sexual fluid. The creative powers released by this life force assure prosperity, fertility, and well-being of the land. Just as, in myth, an ascetic, such as Ṛṣyaśṛṅga, can cause rain, good crops, and so on by finally spilling his powerful seed, so too it was believed that in dance the *devadāsī* brings on rains, harvests, and welfare by emitting her sexual fluid. Whereas the married woman's fluid makes her family and lineage thrive, the fluid of the *devadāsī* produced during her dance is available for the welfare of the devotees and embodiments of her divine lord.

"The dance is a divine sexual intercourse."[41] The way the dancer arouses eroticism is illustrated by the *devadāsī's* sexual activity in the midday ritual at the Puri Temple. The dancer's active sexuality, her role as a courtesan, is announced by her costume, her ornaments, and her movements. All that she wears, from her tight-fitting choli (blouse) to the girdle upholding her sari skirt, clings to and accentuates her curves. Yet during the midday ritual, the *devadāsī* is not looked upon as a seductive woman but as a female power, a goddess. The Puri Temple is dedicated to the god Viṣṇu, whose presence resides in the temple's stationary icon. The *devadāsī* is referred to as the "mobile goddess," just as the king, the partial embodiment of Viṣṇu, is considered the "mobile Viṣṇu."[42] During the midday ritual, the goddess, dancing for the assembled pilgrims, lets her potent sexual fluid fall to the ground. At the end of the dance, many of the pilgrims roll in the ground where her leavings have mixed with the dust. Marglin, the anthropologist who documents this midday ritual, offers an interpretation of the events: the *devadāsī,* transformed into the mobile goddess, has cosmic intercourse with her god; the production of sexual leftover is auspicious and beneficial for the land and its people.[43] Thus, the sexualized female during the midday ritual not only transforms into a goddess, but experiences union with god and produces, as a result, an actual substance charged with life-giving powers.

An early Buddhist text suggests that a courtesan achieves extraordinary power by doing her job faultlessly. The *Milindapañha,* probably composed at the beginning of our era, contains the story of Bindumatī, a courtesan who has the power to make the Ganges River flow back upstream.[44] She performed this feat by making a "Truth Act." A "Truth Act" is a formal declaration of the perfect execution of one's duties in life, prescribed according to one's particular position in the traditional social hierarchy. The king, who witnessed the miracle of the Ganges flowing upstream, exclaimed: "You possess the Power of Truth! You, a thief, a cheat, corrupt, cleft in twain, vicious, a wicked old sinner who have broken the bonds of morality and live on the plunder of fools."[45 & 45a(*)] What gives you the Power, the King asks. Her reply is that whoever gives her money, regardless of his caste, she treats them all exactly alike. Free from fawning and contempt, she serves the payer. This, she says, is the basis of her power to make the Ganges flow back upstream. The story not only connects the courtesan with the power that Indian custom ascribes to the potency of truth, but it also implies that the courtesan's job did not lie outside of the religiously sanctioned view regarding the different duties *(dharma)* for different strata of Hindu society.

There is an intriguing association, made in story and scholarship, between the courtesan and members of Hindu society who renounce all worldly connections in their quest of spiritual goals. The link probably rests on the fact that both courtesans and ascetics renounce family ties. As Marglin observes, with

Fig. 13.4. Dancer and musicians. Cave 7 at Aurangabad, Maharashtra (*c.* 6th century AD). Note that this sensuous female group is located on the left wall inside the main Buddha shrine.

some surprise, the Puri *devadāsīs* are not referred to as outcastes; rather, her interviews conclude, once the women, recruited from different castes, had become *devadāsīs,* they were equated with the ascetic stage of life. This is the fourth stage of life, mentioned in such ancient Hindu treatises as *The Law of Manu,* wherein asceticism is described as being open only to males and considered to be an ideal that most men would not follow in their own lifetime. Likewise, Veena Talwar Oldenburg, who between 1976 and 1986 interviewed the descendants of Lucknow courtesans, finds that the stage of life closest to the courtesan's lifestyle is that of the fourth, or the ascetic's stage.[46] The divide between the courtesan and Buddhist renouncers could be narrow too (see Fig. 13.4). The Buddhist Verses of the Eldresses *(Therīgāthā)* contain verses attributed to the courtesan Ambapālī (vv, 252–70). It was she who received the Buddha in the city of Vaiśālī as he toured and taught in northern India. The Buddha and his entourage stayed at Ambapālī's mango grove, and when she came to the garden and invited the Buddha and the brethren to take a meal at her house, he consented.[47] The commentary explains that she became a courtesan because in a former life she called an eldress *(therī,* a lady disciple of the Buddha) a *gaṇikā.*[48] According to the commentary, Ambapālī charged fifty pieces and so made her city of Vaiśālī very rich. (We are reminded of the prescription in the *Arthaśāstra* that a *gaṇikā* should turn over her earnings to the government.) In the ca. sixth-century AD. Tamil text *Maṇimēkalai,* the eponymous heroine decides to become a Buddhist nun just as her mother, the courtesan Mādavi, had decided earlier. Mādavi, a dancer in the great fifth-century Tamil poem *Śilappadigāram* ("The Jewelled Anklet"), vows to become a Buddhist nun when her beloved is executed for a theft he did not commit. *Maṇimēkalai,* more of a disputation on the ultimate worthiness of Buddhist doctrines than a narrative, sees the daughter follow the same religious path as the mother did.

The literature cited above, both fable and factual, and very varied—representing different religions, regions, and periods—nevertheless shows the tendency to emphasize the courtesan's sexuality. The focus of most of these accounts links a courtesan's power to her presence as a sexualized female. She is the temptress par excellence, and her faultless performance as a courtesan/prostitute correlates with the respect, cultivation, magic potency, even godliness she can achieve. Most of these accounts, it must be noted, are not primarily about the courtesan; when they focus on her, it is from an ahistorical point of view that sees her as a type, not a specific person. The *Kāmasūtra* belongs to this category, and so too do the *Arthaśāstra,* the *Mahāvrata* rite, *The Law of Manu,* the *Purāṇas,* the fictional accounts, and probably the Buddhist accounts. They are, most probably, masculine writings on the subject of a fascinating type—the powerful, dangerous female, not anchored to stabilizing and conventional norms. Even Marglin's interviews with the Puri *devadāsīs* and the Puri ritual specialists sustain the view that a cultivated courtesan's power is derived mainly from her sexual activity. Another anthropologist, Saskia C. Kersenboom-Story, draws similar conclusions in her rather subjective book on the south Indian *devadāsī.*[49] The title of her work, *Nityasumaṅgalī,* announces the idealized orientation of the author. "Nityasumaṅgalī" means "a female who remains ever auspicious," and brings to mind the traditional view of the Indian wife who is considered auspicious while her husband lives and inauspicious upon his death. A *devadāsī,* being dedicated or "married" to a divine lord, has, as such, a husband who can never die, and is thus considered in Kersenboom-Story's book as "nityasumaṅgalī." Kersenboom-Story allies the *devadāsī's* powers to her femininity in the ritual, connecting the *devadāsī* herself to the supreme goddess of the temple. Kersenboom-Story interviewed one *devadāsī* concerning her "marriage" ceremony, and others regarding the various arts they studied, which include (in addition to dance) literary texts and several languages.[50] In the end, she maintains that a *devadāsī* is not *like* a goddess but actually is a divinity. The *devadāsī-nityasumaṅgalī,* she says, is "a woman whose auspiciousness is lasting because she is the goddess."[51]

This view does not represent the total picture. A more complex image of the cultivated courtesan emerges from the few sources that analyze historical records or candid revelations provided by the courtesans themselves. Were it not for three such sources known to me, it would be easy to maintain that the unchanging power of the cultivated courtesan throughout Indian history relates to her function as a sexualized female. But this seems to be an incomplete assessment.

The first of these studies examines the conditions of south Indian temple women in the context of temple life during the Chola period, 850–1300 AD.[52] The analysis is based on an exhaustive corpus of all Chola inscriptions that mention temple women. There are 304 pertinent inscriptions and they disclose a rather different story. First, it is noteworthy that in these Chola inscriptions, the temple women are not referred to as "dancers"; rather, the terms applied to them had meanings such as "devotee of God," "daughter of God," or, "woman of the temple."[53] The names reflect a relationship between the women and the temple that does not, apparently, hinge on feminine sexuality. "Temple women's relationships with the temple were secured not as a consequence of ritual function or professional skill—nor through inheritance or ceremonies of initiation or 'marriage' to the temple deity—but through their donations."[54] The inscriptions indicate that during the Chola period the most important undertaking of temple women was to make gifts to the temple. Orr, the author of the study, does not deny that Chola temple women were sexually active. Clearly they were, "given the references to their children in the inscriptions, but there is no hint that their sexual activity was significant to their identities or to their roles in the temple."[55] In their capacity as donors they established networks within the temple and could gain some rights and privileges; royal patronage was not a factor in their attainment of privileges. As such, the oft-quoted Chola inscription of Rājarāja I at the Tanjore Temple, used to indicate royal largesse and patronage since it mentions the king's transfer of four hundred dancing girls to this temple, is an anomaly. It is the only such event recorded in a Chola inscription, and therefore cannot be used as evidence of royal support for Chola temple women.[56] The inscriptions do suggest that Chola temple women had positions inflected by gender in the sense that they were different and more marginal than the positions occupied by temple males. But their identity as females was not due to their sexuality or their association or identification with female divine power. Indeed, Orr finds that the economic freedom of temple women, plus the limited power and connections they garnered for themselves within the temple structures, allowed them in later centuries "to have a continuing role in the life of the temple, eventually establishing themselves in hereditary positions as specialists in dance."[57] The results of Orr's study are quite different and more nuanced than studies of south Indian courtesans that are based on literary or theoretical writings.[58] Orr's findings caution that little about the life of the precolonial courtesan may actually be known until more rigorous historical accounts can be uncovered, or until credibly sensitive fieldwork can be undertaken for later periods.

Oldenburg's interactions and penetration into the world of the descendants of Lucknow courtesans represents just this kind of fieldwork. The *tawa'if* were patronized and became part of the powerful elite of Lucknow in precolonial times. These were certainly sexualized women who enjoyed luxury, privileges, property, and cultural engagement because of their liaisons with males in authority

Fig. 13.5. Nobleman and courtesan on an upper terrace. Opaque watercolor on paper (Lucknow, *c.* 1820). Photograph courtesy of James Ivory.

at Lucknow. As Oldenburg notes, these women, debased by the British, had consorted with kings and courtiers, enjoyed a fabulously opulent living, manipulated men and means for their own social and political ends, and had been the custodians of culture and the trendsetters of fashion (Fig. 13.5).[59] Their descendants revealed to Oldenburg how these women had transformed themselves from diffident, fearful females at the time they entered a "salon" into assertive, propertied, independent, educated, and fiercely proud women.

The power they achieved resulted from a process implemented by the older women of a salon, who completely reversed the social perceptions (and thereby raised the confidence level) of the younger members. Instead of seeing themselves as objects dependent on the whims of males, they turned their outlook around. Through intense friendships among themselves leading to confessions of past grief, through private plays, jokes, raunchy songs downgrading heterosexual marriage, by mastering the art of deception with clients, the courtesans of a given salon freed themselves of the perceptions and expectations they encountered as children growing up in a society that fostered the role of the subservient female, be she daughter, wife, daughter-in-law, mother, widow. Yet the need for intimacy and love remained in their reconfigured world wherein they only pretended to love men. The extent to which Oldenburg was able to penetrate their private lives is perhaps most vividly demonstrated by the tawa'if admission to lesbian practices among themselves. In today's language, we might say that the source of power of these Lucknow courtesans stems from a recognition of their self-worth in private lives that they concealed from outsiders. Their pretense of succumbing to male fantasies would be hard to uncover were it not for the unusual interviewer who gains their confidence, or from their own literary writings.

The third source is one such rare literary voice. Binodini Dasi was a prominent actress of the Bengali theater at a time when the theater was undergoing extraordinary change. During the late nineteenth century, Bengali theater productions appeared on permanent, public stages; they were financed by financiers and presented by paid professional actors and actresses. Many of the latter were recruited from the prostitute quarters, as was Binodini Dasi. At the age of ten or eleven she was recruited, and worked as a successful actress for twelve years, starring in over fifty plays. At the age of twenty-four she retired, and spent more than the next three decades involved in a writing career during which she wrote two accounts of her life: *My Story* (1912) and *My Life as an Actress* (1924). Her works must be considered courageous, honest, and remarkable. Though she had little formal education, she mustered sufficient stamina to open her heart to an indifferent public whose hypocritical ways she did not hesitate to criticize.

Dasi reveals not only her personal pain but also a fallacy in the wife/courtesan dichotomy. In *My Story* she tells of her grief and despair after the death of her patron of thirty-one years, whom she characterizes as having loved her, protected her, and introduced financial stability into her life:

> Innumerable sighs hold together the heart of this luckless woman. An intolerable burden of pain has been covered by smiles, as despair fights hopelessness relentlessly day and night. How many are the unfulfilled longings, the wounds burning with pain that are alight in her heart; has anyone ever seen any of this? They become prostitutes forced by circumstances, lacking shelter, lacking space; but they too, first come into this world with the heart of a woman. The woman who is a loving mother, she too belongs to the same species! But we have been struck against stone from the very beginning and like the bit of iron which becomes magnetized having been repeatedly struck against a magnet, likewise, we have been struck against stone, have turned into stone ourselves![60]

Dasi does not attribute the difference between the life of the wife and that of the courtesan to a difference of caste, deeds of a previous life and thus retribution, nor to moral superiority of the former over the latter. She blames economic and circumstantial inequalities between women who are otherwise sisters, some being luckier than others. Dasi's words stand in such sharp contrast with the other writings cited on this issue that we can only wonder how representative the others are. Accurate information, it would seem, on women's socio-economic positions may differ vastly and can well depend upon the gender and aim of the writer. Dasi is aware that in her own time some of the bourgeois lovers of courtesans by night turn into their severest denouncers by day. It is such hypocrites, writes Dasi, who prey on the defenselessness of courtesans, keeping them down, and thus unable to break out of their existence: "And it is these tempters of the helpless who become leaders of society and pass moral judgement on these insecure women in order to crush them at every step of their existence! ...Nothing

Fig. 13.6. Raja Sawant Singh and Bani Thani in a mango grove (Kishangarh Miniature, *c.* 1735–50).

Fig. 13.7. Courtesan. Painting on ivory (*c.* 1825).

is lost for a man even if a hundred mistakes are made, but a woman is doomed if her step but falter one bit."[61]

Binodini Dasi was a remarkable actress, chosen to star in a play after only one previous theatrical appearance. She is also a courageous, captivating author.[62] Yet hers are not the proud, defiant words of a cultivated courtesan who conquered adversity and had the guts to write about her trials. Something had changed, and it is evident in Dasi's self-deprecating tone. The time is the early twentieth century, and the late nineteenth through early twentieth centuries are times when the cultivated courtesan is caught in a crossfire that reassigns traditional Indian culture away from its two archetypes, the courtesan and the *devadāsī,* to the third archetype, the wife.

One consistent feature in the precolonial texts examined above is that the cultivated courtesan and the *devadāsī* were both necessary and celebrated as keepers of, or contributors to, the artistic, cultural, and religious life of India. One nearly forgotten example of such an all-encompassing function is the eighteenth-century (so-called) Bani Thaniji, a poetess and courtesan or co-wife of Raj Singh (alias Nagari Das). Bani Thaniji was initiated into a temple in Vrindaban, near Mathura, Uttar Pradesh,[63] and she may have been the inspiration for the

Fig. 13.8. Courtesan with attendant.

extraordinary female in Kishangarh paintings (Fig. 13.6). What seems equally consistent is that India tended to link artistic and cultural involvement with sexual activity. Thus, an outlook running through precolonial literature, no matter what the genre, is that the cultivated woman is the public woman (Fig. 13.7). The situation had not yet changed in the early nineteenth century in either the North or the South, according to the observations of Abbé Dubois and Abdul Halim Sharar, whose remarks opened this essay. But in 1856, the British captured Lucknow and annexed Tanjore, the cultural center of the South. They caused royal patronage to stop. The courtesans in the North lost employment in the sumptuous royal courts and the *devadāsīs* in both the North and the South lost prestige and employment. Under law, the British considered the *devadāsīs* as "temple prostitutes," and the courtesans and dancing girls ("*nautch* girls") in the North also came to be considered as prostitutes. Photographs taken of courtesans during this period represent them garbed as erotic curiosities with trapped, vacuous stares facing a heartless lens (Fig. 13.8). These photographs capture the cultivated courtesan in the process of becoming objectified (Fig. 13.9). Not only do the new rulers of India reduce her to the category of prostitute, but local reformers also work to ostracize her and boycott her artistic appearances. Perhaps the most serious development towards elimination of the cultivated courtesan's power occurred after 1912, with the decoupling of art and sex. Leaders in the

Fig. 13.9. Courtesan with attendant.

Theosophical Society and A.K. Coomaraswamy, the father of Indian art history, were actively engaged in transforming the erotic dances of the *devadāsīs* into Bharata Natyam ("Dance of the Nation"), and they encouraged girls from good families to learn and perform the dance.[64] A trend was set in motion whereby the definition of the cultivated woman would enter a new phase: the keeper of culture and the keeper of the (pure) lineage was to become one and the same.

NOTES AND REFERENCES

1. Abdul Halim Sharar, *Lucknow: The Last Phase of an Oriental Culture,* trans. and ed. E.S. Harcourt and Fakhir Hussain (London: Paul Elek, 1975), 142, 145–47, 196, 276.
2. 3d ed. (Oxford: Clarendon Press, 1906), 336–37.
3. For a general discussion of these and other terms, see Moti Chandra, *The World of the Courtesans* (Bombay: Vikas Publishing House, 1973),23–24,33,44–45; and Devangana Desai, *Erotic Sculpture of India:* A *Socio-Cultural Study* (2d rev. ed., New Delhi: Tata-McGraw Hill, 1975) (and see index therein for discussion of terms).
4. T. Bloch, "Jogīmārā Inscription," *Archaeological Survey of India, Annual Report, 1903–4* (Calcutta, 1906), 128–31.
5. Note that in the Muslim court of Lucknow cited above she is called *tawa'if.*
6. See *The Kāmasūtra of Vātsyāyana,* trans. Sir Richard F. Burton and F.F. Arbutknot (Mumbai: Jaico, 1976), 137 ff.; also 12–16. Jaina literature lists seventy-two arts (see Chandra, *The World of the Courtesans,* 38 ff.). These lists ought probably to be understood as

conventionalized tropes intended to delineate, in broad strokes, the highly cultivated person.

7. *Kāmasūtra,* trans. Burton.
8. Cf. Chandra, *The World of the Courtesans,* 43–55; P.K. Gode, 'The Role of the Courtezan in the Early History of Indian Painting," *Annals of the Bhandarkar Oriental Research Institute* 22 (1941): 24–37. For a ca. third-century BC statue of a royal courtesan exhibiting features mentioned in the *Arthaśāstra,* see my article entitled "The Mauryan Gaṇikā from Dīdargañj (Pāṭaliputra)," in the Maurizio Taddei Memorial Issue of *East and West* (2005), pp. 345-62 and pp. 278-95 in this volume.
9. The date of the play is ca. AD 400, but it seems to be an expansion of an earlier version written by another playwright. See J.A.B. van Buitenen, *Two Plays of Ancient India* (New York: Columbia University Press, 1968), 30–31, n. 10. The identification of the female on this second-century AD relief with the courtesan who is the heroine of this play has been made by C. Sivaramamurti, *Sources of History Illumined by Literature* (New Delhi: Kanak, 1979), 9–11.
10. Cf. van Buitenen, *Two Plays of Ancient India,* 102; Gode, "Courtezans," 30.
11. Van Buitenen, *Two Plays.*
12. Cf. *The Citrasūtra of the Viṣṇudharmottara Purāṇa,* ed. and trans. Parul Dave Mukherji (New Delhi: Indira Gandhi National Centre for the Arts, 2001).
13. Gode, "Courtesans," 24–34.
14. For example, Cave 16 at Ajanta, sixth century, shows the remains of the Ṛṣyaśṛṅga story featuring the Ṛṣi, a princess, and her retinue of courtesans. See Klaus Fischer, *Erotik und Askese in Kult und Kunst der Inder* (Cologne: Du Mont, 1979), 136, fig. 85.
15. See Bloch, "Jogīmārā," 128–31. Note that the information in Desai, *Erotic Sculpture,* 107, differs from Bloch's analysis.
16. See Desai, *Erotic Sculpture,* 107, 201.
17. A clear statement of the opposing worlds in the nineteenth century is found in *When God is a Customer: Telugu Courtesan Songs by Kṣetrayya and Others,* ed. and trans. A.K. Ramanujan, Velcheru Narayana Rao, and David Shulman (Berkeley: University of California Press, 1994). Telugu is a Dravidian language dominant in the region from Chennai (Madras) to the borders of Orissa. See pp. 27–28.
18. See Frédérique Apffel Marglin, *Wives of the God-King* (Delhi: Oxford University Press, 1985), 2–6, 177–78; cf. *Kāmasūtra,* trans. Burton, chaps. 4 and 6; Veena Talwar Oldenberg, "Lifestyle as Resistance: The Case of the Courtesans of Lucknow, India," *Feminist Studies* 16 (1990): 259–87.
19. The uneven portrayal of the courtesan is evident in the compilation of hundreds of Classical Sanskrit texts by Ludwik Sternbach, *Gaṇikā-vṛtta-sangrahah, or Texts on Courtezans in Classical Sanskrit* (Hoshiapur: Viśveśvarānandasamsthāna-Prakāśanamandalam, 1953). Unfortunately, the author does not date his texts, but they generally agree on the dangerous, greedy, duplicitous character of the courtesan.
20. *The Laws of Manu,* in *Sacred Books of the East,* F. Max Müller (ed.), 50 vols., vol. 25, trans. Georg Bühler (Oxford: Clarendon Press, 1886), IX.I3, p. 329.
21. *Manu,* IX.7, p. 328. Note that the Sanskrit term translated as "merit" is *dharma.*
22. *Manusmṛti with Manubhāṣya of Medhātithi,* Vol. 7, trans. Ganganath Jha (Calcutta: University of Calcutta, 1920–26), 6.
23. *Manu,* trans. Bühler, IX.9, p. 329.
24. Cf. A.L. Basham, *The Wonder that Was India,* third ed. rev. (London: Sidgwick and Jackson, 1967), 167.

25. Substitute provisions are possible, though less desirable; cf. A.L. Basham, *A Cultural History of India* (Oxford: Oxford University Press, 1975), 130.
26. Some of these rites take place at the birth of a child and celebrate the name-giving ceremony, the first feeding of solid food, the first haircut, then educational rites for boys, next marriage rites, funeral rites, and *śrāddha.*
27. Ram Gopal, *India of Vedic Kalpasūtras* (Delhi: National Publishing House, 1959), 444.
28. Marglin, *Wives,* gives a fine analysis, based on interviews in Puri during the 1970s and 1980s on the contemporary basis of power of both the wife and the temple courtesan; see chaps. 2 and 3.
29. For a summary on the housewife in the *Kāmasūtra,* see Chandra, *The World of the Courtesans,* 78–79, and 85–93 for the courtesan in that text.
30. See King Mahendravarman, *The Farce of the Pious Courtesan; and A Farce of Drunken Sport,* ed. and trans. Michael Lockwood and A. Visnu Bhat (Madras: Tambaram Research Associates, 1991).
31. Somadeva's Kathā Sarit Sāgara, *The Ocean of Story,* trans. C.H. Tawney (London, 1924), vol. 3, chap. 38. Tawney cites references to inscriptions of courtesans as donors to temples, and to literary passages of courtesans as "intellectual, generous and of noble character" (p. 207). Madanamālā, the courtesan, is referred to as a *veśyā;* Tawney assumes she is a *gaṇikā,* the highest type of *veśyā.*
32. J. Gonda, "Ascetics and Courtesans," *Adyar Library Bulletin* 25 (1961): 78–102, at p. 80.
33. Ibid.
34. For treatment of the motif in early Indian mythology, see Wendy Doniger O'Flaherty, *Asceticism and Eroticism in the Mythology of Śiva* (Delhi: Oxford University Press, 1973), chap. 2.
35. Ibid.
36. Gonda, "Ascetics," 91.
37. See *When God Is a Customer.*
38. Ibid., 18.
39. Ibid.
40. The following account is based on the analysis of Frédérique Apffel Marglin, "Refining the Body: Transformative Emotion in Ritual Dance," in *Divine Passions: The Social Construction of Emotion in India,* ed. Owen Lynch (Berkeley: University of California Press, 1990), 212–36. Marglin analyzes the experience, knowledge, and reminiscences of the last quarter of the twentieth century from ritual specialists, practitioners, and informants.
41. Marglin, "Refining the Body," 224. It should be noted by those acquainted with South Asian religious developments that the midday ritual is part of a Tantric offering, and the followers of the Puri rituals are worshippers of female divine power, *Śakti.*
42. "Mobile" is to be understood as not fixed in one place, i.e. the *devadāsī* can move around in the dance.
43. This is a partial summary of the author's interpretation; it is condensed and abbreviated here for the non-specialist in South Asian religion and culture. For further details, see Marglin, "Refining the Body," 224, 230–32.
44. See E. W. Burlingame, 'The Act of Truth *(Saccakiriya)*: A Hindu Spell and Its Employment as a Psychic Motif in Hindu Fiction," *Journal of the Royal Asiatic Society (1917)*: 430–67. The Bindumatī charm is in *Milindapañha* 122–23; Bindumatī is considered a *gaṇikā.*
45. W. Norman Brown, "The Basis for the Hindu Act of Truth," *Review of Religion 5/1* (Nov. 1940): 37.

45a. ADDENDUM: For a more recent treatment of the truth act see: George Thompson, "On Truth-Acts in Vedic", *Indo-Iranian Journal* 41, 1998; 125-153.

46. Oldenburg, "Lifestyle as Resistance," 277–79.

47. See *The Mahā-parinibbāna Suttanta* II. 16–20, in *Buddhist Suttas,* trans. T.W. Rhys Davids in *The Sacred Books of the East,* Vol. II (1881).

48. Ria Kloppenborg, "Female Stereotypes in Early Buddhism: The Women of the Therīgathā," in *Female Stereotypes in Religious Traditions,* ed. Ria Kloppenborg and Wouter J. Hane-graaff (Leiden: Brill, 1995), 151–69.

49. Saskia C. Kersenboom-Story, *Nityasumaṅgalī: Devadāsī Tradition in South India* (Delhi: Motilal Banarsidass, 1987).

50. Ibid., 191.

51. Ibid., 197. The same author maintains this position in a subsequent short and well-intentioned essay on the function of the *devadāsī;* see Saskia C. Kersenboom, "Devadāsī Murai," *Rasamañjari* 2/2 (Aug. 1997),55–64, at p. 60.

52. Leslie C. Orr, *Donors, Devotees, and Daughters of God: Temple Women in Medieval Tamilnadu* (New York: Oxford University Press, 2000).

53. Ibid., 162.

54. Ibid.

55. Ibid., 174.

56. Kersenboom-Story, *Nityasumaṅgalī,* 25–30. Perhaps the latest source to draw this erroneous conclusion is John Guy, "Indian Dance in the Temple Context," in Pratapaditya Pal, *Dancing to the Flute* (Sidney: The Art Gallery of New South Wales, Australia, 1997), 29.

57. Orr, *Donors, Devotees,* 171.

58. Compare, for example, Chandra, *The World of the Courtesans,* chap. 10, or Desai, *Erotic Sculpture,* 161–62, with Orr, *Donors, Devotees.*

59. Oldenburg, "Lifestyle as Resistance," 260.

60. Anupama Taranath, "Disrupting Colonial Modernity: Indian Courtesans and Literary Cultures, 1888–1912" (Ph.D. diss., University of California at San Diego, 2000), 300–01. Taranath is quoting from Binodini Dasi, *My Story and My Life as an Actress* (1912), trans. and ed. Rimla Bhattacharya (New Delhi: Kali for Women Press, 1998).

61. Taranath, "Disrupting Colonial Modernity," 305, quoting Dasi, 104–05.

62. Ibid., 306.

63. See A. W. Entwistle, Brāj: *Centre of Kṛṣṇa Pilgrimage* (Groningen: E. Forsten, 1982), 209–10.

64. Taranath, "Disrupting Colonial Modernity," 306.

14

The Mauryan Gaṇikā from Dīdārgañj (Pāṭaliputra)

To Honor the Memory of Maurizio Taddei,
an Exceptional Colleague who became a Friend.

What, or better who, is a *gaṇikā?* Among Indologists, the Sanskrit term is not yet a household word. A *gaṇikā* is a special type of courtesan. She is not a prostitute. Indeed, the Indian tradition seems to have classified, and specified, the difference between the two. The civilized public woman, proficient in the arts, winsome in her ways, and endowed with exceptional beauty and taste is called a *gaṇikā.* Below her are ranked women who do not possess the talents of a *gaṇikā; veśyā, rūpajīvā, puṃścalī, dāsī,* etc. are some of the terms applied to women who are considered prostitutes[1]. The *gaṇikā* of ancient India, like the hetaera of ancient Greece or the Japanese geisha, is the exceptionally refined and cultivated courtesan. And we know quite a bit about her.

The *Kāmasūtra,* composed sometime between the early Christian era and the 4th/5th century AD, is perhaps the most well known source on courtesans and prostitutes in ancient India. Part VI is devoted to the courtesan. Herein, Vātsyāyana advises the courtesan to be skilled in the sixty-four arts that define a cultured person[2]. He lists them all and the list is daunting. Topping the list are singing, playing musical instruments, dancing, writing, drawing, picture-making, trimming and decorating. Some unexpected skills are knowledge of magic, tailoring, carpentry, architecture, chemistry, mineralogy, cock- quail- and ram-fighting, rules of society and how to pay respects and compliments to others. In the aggregate, the sixty-four arts are a remarkable portrait of the civilized and

Originally published in *East and West* (Rome), Vol. 55, Nos. 1-4 (December 2005); pp. 345-62. Reprinted with stylistic changes, additions and permission from IsIAO.

knowledgeable elite in society. The *Kāmasūtra* avows this by saying that when a *veśyā* is proficient in these arts and is imbued with beauty, politeness and virtues, she becomes a *gaṇikā,* and 'receives a seat of honour in the assembly of men'; that is, she can discourse with men as their equal. The text goes further: 'She is moreover always respected by the king and praised by learned men and her favour being sought for by all, she becomes an object of universal regard'[3]. Vātsyāyana was not the first to describe and instruct in the courtesans' arts. Dattaka who lived before Vātsyāyana wrote a special guide for courtesans[4].

The *gaṇikā* in the play the *Mṛcchakaṭika* (The Little Clay Cart), approximately contemporaneous with the *Kāmasūtra,* encapsules Vātsyāyana's ideal, and permits an (albeit fictionalized) glimpse of the life of an educated courtesan. Vasantasenā is an independent woman who is also wealthy and generous. Her tastes in architecture and the decorative arts are opulent and self-assured. She lives in a mansion preceded by eight courts, some of which are occupied by fledgling courtesans being trained in the various arts, possibly including 'picture-making'.

This image may not be entirely a literary conceit. A *gaṇikā,* in ancient days, was politically protected and that afforded her a certain degree of security and financial independence. She probably could lay claim to considerable status in antiquity. Aside from a queen, the *gaṇikā* was a secular female who derived status and power directly from the ruler. The *gaṇikā's* main duty, as described in the *Arthaśāstra,* is to attend to the king, assuring her of royal protection. Besides the pleasures she afforded the king, a *gaṇikā's* person and purse were overseen by an administrative system that stood to benefit when she yielded herself to others upon the order of the king (cf. *AŚ* 2.27.19). The manner in which politics and economics converged is set forth in the *Arthaśāstra,* a text on Indian polity dating perhaps to the 1st or 2nd century AD but containing information that may well go back as far as the 3rd century BC[5]. The text discusses the *gaṇikā's* education. *Gaṇikās, dāsīs* and actresses are to be taught singing, playing instruments like the *vīṇā,* pipe and drum, recitation, dancing, acting, writing, painting, reading the thoughts of others, manufacture of scents and garlands, shampooing and the art of attraction and captivating the minds of others (*AŚ* 2.27.28)[6]. The list probably formed the basis of the later sixty-four arts enumerated in the *Kāmasūtra.* The *Arthaśāstra* proposes that the state bears the cost of this education and directly employs the recipients; in effect, the *gaṇikā* of the *Arthaśāstra* is to turn over her earnings to the state and to receive, besides the accouterments of a glamorous life-style, a monthly salary from the king's treasury. A *gaṇikā,* it seems, is attached primarily to the king's court and there is a special royal officer (the *gaṇikādhyakṣa AŚ* 2.27.1) appointed to regulate her duties and her finances. This Superintendent pays a 1000 *paṇas* per annum to a *gaṇikā* (*AŚ* 2.27.1). The same section dealing with the *gaṇikādhyakṣa* (2.27), gives indication that a *gaṇikā* could receive and keep goods (i.e. ornaments) and belongings (i.e. property) in her own name. But, legally, the *gaṇikā* does not appear to be a free or independent agent since the

Arthaśāstra sets forth the amount she, or her son, must pay to gain freedom (*AŚ* 2.27.6). Yet, the fact that the *Arthaśāstra* sets fines if the courtesan gives her jewels to anyone but her mother (*AŚ* 2.27.11), or if she sells or mortgages her property (*AŚ* 2.27.12), would seem to indicate that a courtesan could accumulate such belongings. Rights applicable to the profession are passed along matrilinear lines[7] (cf. 2.27.2), in addition to the personal belongings. The possibility for transmission of wealth through a courtesan's female family members may well have a feature in administrative systems in North India around the several centuries of the Christian era. How else can one explain a 1st century AD. Mathurā inscription detailing the large donation offered by Vasu, a junior (?)[8] *gaṇikā?* The inscription is carved on a fairly large Mathurā *Śilāpaṭa,* possibly from Maholi. Vasu, also the daughter of a *gaṇikā* named Loṇaśobhikā, presents to the Jain Nirgranta *arhats* a shrine *(devikula),* an assembly hall, a cistern and the stone slab (the *śilāpaṭa*)[9].

The term, *gaṇikā,* provides an additional avenue for gaining insight into the reasons for her prestige. *Gaṇikā* is derived from the term *gaṇa* + the feminine suffix *ikā*[10]. Meanings for *gaṇa* range from 'group, troop' etc. to 'company, association, or corporation'[11]. The *Vinayavastu* of the *Mūlasarvāstivāda* tells a story about Āmrapālī which goes a long way towards understanding which connotation of *gaṇa* operates in the term *gaṇikā*[12].

Āmrapālī was the adopted daughter of Mahānāma, a rich citizen of Vaiśālī. Many suitors, including princes, having sought her hand, her father brought the matter to the notice of the Lichchhavi *gaṇa* and it was discussed in the Assembly. When the members saw Āmrapālī, they decided that she was a *strīratna* (a jewel of a woman), and so, according to the convention already laid down, it was decided that she was not be married to anybody but was to be enjoyed by the *gaṇa.*

It would follow from this account that a *gaṇikā* is a female associated with a governing group *(gaṇa),* or, acting for, or, enjoyed by the *gaṇa.* The reference to the Lichchhavi *gaṇa* signals that *gaṇa* in this instance refers to a non-monarchical form of government which existed alongside monarchies[13]. The *Arthaśāstra* mentions the Lichchhavis (AŚ 11.1.5), among other oligarchies. It may be deduced that the term *gaṇikā* was applied to a public woman so exceptionally endowed ('a jewel of a woman'), that she was reserved and enjoyed by the ruling elite of a particular locality.

Another story involving Āmrapālī confirms that the *gaṇikā* is a credit to her town. It was in Āmrapālī's mango grove that the Buddha chose to stop with his entourage while preaching in Vaiśālī[14]. When the courtesan came to know that the Buddha was in her grove, Āmrapālī proceeded to her garden and invited the Blessed One and his brethren to take a meal in her house the next day. The Buddha consented. The next day, after the meal that Āmrapālī served with her own hands was over, the courtesan made a gift of the mansion, saying 'Lord, I present this mansion to the order of the mendicants, of which the Buddha is the chief' *(Mahā-*

Parinibhāna-Sutta, II 24). According to the *Vinayapiṭaka,* Ambapālikā/Āmrapālī charged fifty pieces a night, and so made her city of Vaiśālī (and presumably herself), very rich[15]. We are reminded of the prescription in the *Arthaśāstra* that a *gaṇikā* should relinquish her earnings to the government in return for a salary and personal possessions which then belong to her. The *Arthaśāstra* also itemizes the various fines and fees a courtesan would need to pay the state for specified transgressions[16], so we may assume that these financial arrangements were meant to be requirements, not mere speculations, and that she could, in theory, accumulate suffient funds in her own name to pay.

The wide spectrum of ancient accounts—political treatise, theatrical play, guide to lovemaking, Buddhist religious texts, Jain religious art—indicate the degree to which the image of the *gaṇikā* stirred the lives and thoughts of Indians during ancient times. No wonder the image of the *gaṇikā* strides through antiquity's literature as a dazzling female, combining as she does a glamourous, yet dangerous, but cultivated persona[17]. So it is that the *Lalitavistara* (XII 11)[18], dating towards the beginning of our era[19], has King Śuddhodana wishing to secure a bride for Siddhārtha who is as accomplished as a *gaṇikā,* or that the legendary author Bharata of the *Nāṭyaśāstra* (dated between the 2nd century BC–2nd century AD) describes a *gaṇikā* as one of four types of heroines. A *gaṇikā,* he states, 'should have the qualities of light-heartedness, exaltedness and expertise in dance, music and other arts'[20]. No wonder that Kālidāsa, writing the *Meghadūta* in the 5th century, has the 'Cloud' view, as it drifts over the Mahākāla temple, *veśyās* whose hands grow weary from flicking fly whisks *(camaras)* during the time of a temple service (I 34–35), or, that King Mahendravarman I, writing *The Farce of the Pious Courtesan* in the 7th century, makes the *brahman,* not the *gaṇikā,* the object of the play's mockery. So too in Somadeva's tale called 'King Vikramāditya and the Courtesan', within his 11th century work *The Ocean of Story,* there is a description of the courtesan Madanamālā which highlights her integrity in addition to her other charms[21].

Concomitant with a *gaṇikā's* physical and cultural attributes is her connection to a particular group in a particular locality, the idiosyncratic feature embedded in her name. Therefore another of her defining qualities seems to be the geographical region in which she operates. Although, in time, a *gaṇikā's* association is not solely tied to a specific *gaṇa*[22], a random sampling reveals that her name is often cited together with a specific town or city. Āmrapālī's connection with Vaiśālī in Buddhist literature has already been noted[23]. Then there is the beautiful *gaṇikā* Sirimā of Rājagṛha mentioned in the *Dhammapāda Commentary* (iii 308–309)[24]. Sālavatī, also of Rājagṛha 'was elected a *gaṇik-thāna* and she was counted among the important citizens'[25]. Vāsavadattā is the most famous courtesan of Mathurā; she charges 500 *purāṇaśata* ('old' or gold)[26] coins a night, but falls in love with the Buddhist ascetic Upagupta from whom she asks no money (see the *Divyāvadāna,* Chapter 26)[27]. Banaras, or Kāśī, has a courtesan whose fee was thought to equal half the day's revenue of Kāśī. But she had so few clients that she was forced to reduce her fee to half and thereby also earned notoriety as Ardha Kāśī (Half Kāśī)[28]. The Jain text *Nāyādhammakahāo* describes Devadattā, a rich courtesan of Campa city[29]; Jain literature also knows of a renowned Ujjaini courtesan named Devadattā *(Uttarāhdhyana Ṭīkā,* 3, 59–65)[30]. It is interesting to observe with Moti Chandra that 'a *gaṇikā's* position was respected by the king to such an extent that she was considered a jewel of his capital and almost all big towns had a chief courtesan'[31].

A story recounted in the *Milindapañha* illustrates king Aśoka's regard for a *gaṇikā* in his capital. When the king inquired whether anyone possessed the power to perform an Act of Truth, none could make this claim except the courtesan Bindumatī. A 'Truth Act' is a formal declaration of the perfect execution of one's duties in life, prescribed according to one's particular position in the Indian traditional social hierarchy[32]. Bindumatī, a *gaṇikā,* could make the Ganges River flow back upstream. Aśoka was astounded by this miracle and asked Bindumatī how she, a courtesan, could possess the power of Truth. Her reply is that she treats all customers alike, 'free from fawning and contempt, she serves the payer'[33]. In effect, her claim to miraculous power is her perfect execution as a courtesan.

Aśoka's imperial capital was Pāṭaliputra, and although the king's encounter with Bindumatī may be regarded by some as a curious story, there is other evidence indicating that Pāṭaliputra in ancient times was famous for its courtesans. Desai observes that there is a connection between prosperous urban trade centers in antiquity, and a preoccupation with sex[34]. Pāṭaliputra was not only a thriving center of trade, but it was the metropolis of the powerful Mauryan dynasty during the 4th through 3rd centuries BC; from this *entrepôt,* the famous Mauryan 'Royal Road' proceeded northward. In addition, the Central Trunk-Route connected Pāṭaliputra to towns lying on the Ganges[35]. As such, Pāṭaliputra was probably a hub of Mauryan political and economic activities, whose élite could seek and support women of pleasure. Dattaka, who preceded Vātsyāyana, wrote a *Kāmaśāstra* as a guide for the courtesans of Pāṭaliputra[36]. The *Kaumudīmahotsava* seems to confirm this, relating that Dattaka's manual was studied by the learned courtesans[37]. Further, Jain literature preserves the name of one, Kośā, a famous courtesan of Pāṭaliputra *(Uttarāhdhyana Ṭīkā,* 2.29 ff.)[38]. Above all, since the royal court had its seat in Pāṭaliputra, the city would be likely to have a chief *gaṇikā* in residence. The *Arthaśāstra* specifies that the royal Superintendent for *gaṇikās* should appoint both a *gaṇikā* (who may or may not come from the family of a *gaṇikā)* and a *pratigaṇikā* (a rival[39], or deputy[40] *gaṇikā)* for a lesser salary (cf. *AŚ* 2.27.1).

I propose that an ancient Pāṭaliputra sculpture represents an image of a royal *gaṇikā.* A beauteous female image, carved in the environs of the Mauryan capital, is imbued with the characteristics that mark her as a *gaṇikā,* possibly the chief *gaṇikā*—or the *pratigaṇikā*—attached to the imperial court.

Fig. 14.1. Female image from Dīdārgañj, Pāṭaliputra. Front. Mauryan Period. The Patna Museum. (Photograph, courtesy The American Institute of Indian Studies (AIIS).

Fig. 14.2. Female image from Dīdārgañj, Pāṭaliputra. Back. Mauryan period. The Patna Museum. (Photograph, courtesy AIIS).

For nearly a century, that is, ever since she was found in 1917, the female image from Dīdārgañj (a suburb of Pāṭaliputra), has been recognized as being pivotal to the understanding of early Indian art (Figs. 14.1–14.2). Though much appreciated for her commanding presence, physical beauty and accomplished carving in sandstone, the Dīdārgañj female continues to be studied, not merely cited, because she teases. The basic questions she poses have defied satisfactory answers. All who mention the Dīdārgañj female are puzzled by at least two aspects. Scholars question whether a monumental sculpture exhibiting superb modeling could arise during the Mauryan period, that is, at the beginning of the Indian sculptural tradition. One of the main reasons she is placed in this early period is technical. The high polish of the sandstone and crispness of execution are also found in other Mauryan works. Many of these, such as the Lohānīpur (Pāṭaliputra) torso, the Pāṭaliputra *caurī* bearer, all the lion Aśokan pillars except the one at Vaiśālī[41], and the Rāmpurvā Bull capital, are often considered royal art, receiving patronage from the Mauryan dynasty[42]. If the Dīdārgañj figure were ascribed to this early date, she would need to be interpreted as a monumental female *caurī* bearer, probably produced under royal patronage. However, since a *caurī* is held by attending figures, this interpretation raises a seeming set of contradictions. Why would a royal atelier lavish so much talent and expenditure on a monumental image of an attendant, that is, a minor figure? One scholarly opinion casts a new light on this conundrum by suggesting that the so-called Mauryan polish, though probably a trait of Pāṭaliputra, need not necessarily designate the early period. Following this hypothesis with detailed stylistic comparisons, the Dīdārgañj figure has been dated much later than the Mauryan age (that is, into the Kuṣāṇa period by some scholars, or, to the 1st century AD by other investigators)[43]. The mystery of her identity has not been clarified by these attempts at a later dating. This is an iconographic problem whose difficulty stems from the fact that there are not many other early, pre-Kuṣāṇa (or Kuṣāṇa) life-size female images with which to compare the Dīdārgañj female. In addition, the figure herself offers her admirers hardly any iconographic clues as to who she might be.

Most often, she is labled as the Dīdārgañj Yakṣī, probably because a *yakṣī* is a fertility figure and the female's large globular breasts, tiny waist and broad hips are the typical attributes associated with the fecund female. However, this identification can be easily contested. Asher and Spink simply call her the Dīdārgañj figure and point out that the fly whisk held by the image is not associated with the early *yakṣīs* from Bhārhut[44]. This is an important objection, for this fanning device is the figure's only hand-held attribute. The fly whisk is, of course, the second puzzling aspect of the female. It seems almost inconceivable that one of the first life-size female statues in the history of Indian art should be an attendant. Huntington, who dates the image to the Mauryan period, makes an observation with which I agree, namely, that the statue has 'none of the usual accoutrement of a *yakṣī*'[45]. R.N. Misra, who also places the statue into the Mauryan period, considers the image to represent Hārīti, but concedes that 'The iconic attributes of Hārīti associated with her late images are entirely absent in this image [...]'[46]. At minimum, it has been assumed that she is a goddess, or godling since a *yakṣī* is a religious, albeit minor, divinity[47]. In an intersting study relating to the Aśvamedha type of Gupta coin[48], Pal discusses significant deities associated with the *caurī*. Yet even the divine nature of the Dīdārgañj female can be easily challenged by the fact that the fly whisk is a prerogative of royal rank and therefore it cannot be ruled out that she could stem from the secular sphere.

To date, neither her identity nor her date of execution has been agreed upon. I believe that in this case these two issues go together. Understanding who is likely to be represented may promote the likely date for the representation. Therefore, without once again giving a complete description of the oft-described sculpture, I propose to concentrate straightaway on the problem of identity.

The few distinquishing characteristics on which to hang an idenfication, nevertheless, go far towards identifying the Dīdārgañj female as a *gaṇikā* of Pāṭaliputra.

First there is the matter of size and stance. The statue, carved mostly in the round, measures 163 x 49 cm (64 1/4 x 19/4 in.). Not many large sculptures of free (or nearly free-) standing females can be bracketed between the Mauryan and Kuṣāṇa Periods, and the few that do exist do not, as will be seen below, offer a threshold of comparisons. The frontal stance of the Dīdārgañj figure is not quite in *samapada* (weight equally distributed on both straight legs); her right knee bends slightly while her weight shifts onto the left leg. It is important to note that the posture of the legs gently carries through to a distinctive movement in the upper body. Accordingly, the Dīdārgañj female bends her torso with its beauteous breasts slightly forward. This posture is sharply distinguishable from the *tribhaṅga* pose so often assumed by *yakṇīs*. Another noteworthy feature is seen in the lower garment. The folds of the fine material drape easily and cling closely to the legs; but at center, the folds fall thick and heavy, thereby not only covering, but eliminating any outline of the pudendum. In contrast, the attire of early *yakṣīs* displays, more than hides, the female's sexual parts. The *combination* of the characteristics associated with the Dīdārgañj figure – life-size, almost fully disengaged from the stone, standing frontally, but without the *tribhaṅga* pose, and drapery over the pudendum – clearly belongs to an iconographic realm far removed from that the early *yakṣīs*[49].

There is a small group of monumental females from the pre-Kuṣāṇa period that share a number of these combined characteristics. Four known life-size Snake Goddesses, and one example of a colossal Tree Goddess, all carved in the round in or around Mathurā, and dating between 100 BC-1st century AD, exhibit some similar features. They have been recently analyzed[50]. The imposing size and rounded, sensuous volumes of these females convey their exceptional nature (see Fig. 14.3). They are meant to represent females imbued with exceptional powers. Perhaps the Snake Goddesses were believed to assure fertility as well as safety from poisonous snakes; possibly the Tree Goddess was believed to bestow the sap of life. These females were probably worshipped by the folk who believed they embodied forces in nature. Whereas the specific powers yielded by these folk

Fig. 14.3. Nāginī (Snake Goddess). 62 3/4 x 23 x 12 1/2 inches. Sandstone. Carved in Mathurā. 1st century AD. The Nelson-Atkins Museum of Art, No. 79.2I. (Photograph, courtesy The Nelson-Atkins Museum of Art).

goddesses may be conjectural, what is less left to speculation is that the ancients used recognizable conventions—monumental size, rigid frontality, equal (or near equal) distribution of weight on both legs—to indicate beings of extraordinary powers. These characteristics are also exhibited by the, as yet, unidentified female figure from Besnagar/Vidiśā dated to *c.* 100 BC[51]. The size, frontality and manner in which the Dīdārgañj female is draped ally her to the way special female types were rendered in pre-Kuṣāṇa times[52]. The Dīdārgañj figure presents one notable distinction, not to mention the *caurī* attribute: whereas the other female figures stand in *samapada* (or nearly *samapada* fashion), only the Dīdārgañj female executes the graceful movement, described above, consisting of the gentle shift of weight from the right to the left leg, causing her upper body to bow slightly forward.

The problematic flywhisk she holds actually helps to identify the figure, for a fan is the *sine qua non* of a courtesan. Quite possibly the close connection between the fly whisk and a courtesan explains the choice of Kālidāsa's imagery, mentioned above. The *Arthaśāstra,* in the section dealing with the Royal Superintendent of the *gaṇikās,* provides insight into a royal *gaṇikā's* paraphernalia:

> saubhāgyālaṅkāravṛddhyā sahasreṇa vāraṃ kaniṣṭhaṃ madyamamuttamam vāropayet chatrabhṛṅgāravyajanaśibikāpīṭhikāratheṣu ca viśeṣārtham // (*AŚ* 2.27).

According to (their) superiority in beauty and ornaments, he (i.e. the Superintendent of the *gaṇikās)* should set (i.e. fix) 1000 *paṇas* for the lowest, middling, and uppermost turn (i.e. attending royal service?), (given) in order to add lustre (to the royal presence) with respect to the umbrella *(chatra),* the golden pitcher *(bhṛṅgāra),* the whisk *(vyajana),* the palanquin *(śibikā),* the royal seat (i.e. throne, *pīṭhikā),* and the chariot *(ratha).*

Fig. 14.4. Procession Scene. Ht. 38 cm, w. 50 cm. Terracotta. Candraketugarh. Śuṅga Period. (Private collection).

The *gaṇikās,* it seems, are appointed primarily for attendance on the king, for holding the umbrella over his head, or carrying the water-jug[53] for him or fanning him or accompanying him on processions and so on (2.27.1–4)[54].

Thus, we may expect that royal processions or audiences during Mauryan and subsequent times were spectacular to behold. Surrounding the king, whether seated on his throne or riding in some royal conveyance, were the beauteous *gaṇikā* and *pratigaṇikā* holding attributes that added lustre to the sovereign's regal presence.

A rather large terracotta from eastern India lets us imagine what such a procession may have looked like during that time[55]. From the site of Candraketugarh, 23 miles northeast of Calcutta in Bengal, comes a plaque vividly portraying a procession with two large elephants and a cortege of females (Fig. 14.4). The women, depicted in rows across the entire terracotta, play musical instruments, cast flowers, clap, carry flags and banners, and pay obeisance with folded hands to a personage possibly represented in an accompaying plaque, for no such one is found in this piece. The main personages in this plaque are the females seated on the elephants. On the first elephant sits a female drummer, another who carries a flower, and an attendant holds a banner. It is the set of

Fig. 14.5. Bhājā, Maharashtra. Vihāra XIX. *c.* 100–70 BC. Carved entrance to monk's cell. (Photograph, courtesy AIIS).

three females on the second elephant that is of particular interest. This group, somewhat larger and occupying more space than the other group, is evidently the more important of the two sets of elephant riders. The first female holds a *caurī,* the second, associated with (although not holding), a large *chatra,* extends the palms of her hands (possibly as if clapping as do other females in the top and bottom rows); the third female holds a large pot. In seeing these three damsels, it is hard not to think of *Arthaśāstra,* 2.27.4 (above), mentioning the *gaṇikās* appointed to accompany royalty on processions with the umbrella, the golden pitcher and the flywhisk.

Another scene tantalizingly close to the *Arthaśāstra's* pronouncement actually exists. It appears in a relief on the verandah of Buddhist Vihāra XIX at Bhājā (Maharashtra). On the east end of the verandah are two reliefs flanking the doorway to the cell chamber. Both carvings have tentative identifications. The scene on the right is usually understood to represent the Vedic god Indra riding on his elephant; the theme on the left is taken to be Sūrya riding his quadriga across the heavens and over a hugely inflated female demonic form (Fig. 14.5). A major hesitation in accepting these identifications has been the difficulty to explain why Brahmanic deities should occupy such dominant positions in a Buddhist monk's cell. Whereas the following observations will neither answer this concern,

Fig. 14.6. Bhājā. Close-up of carving on the left side of entrance to monk's cell. (Photograph, courtesy AIIS).

nor fully identify both scenes, they will, I hope, clarify one section of the so-called Sūrya relief.

The male figure in the quadriga wears the large, elaborate turban also associated with royalty (Fig. 14.6). Indeed, the royal *chatra* is held above his head by a female on his right who stands close to his side on the chariot. To his left stands another maiden prominently holding the *vyajana,* or fly whisk. As such, the scene quite resembles the *Arthaśāstra's* description in 2.27.4: a royal personage (the king) in his chariot flanked by his *gaṇikā* and *pratigaṇikā,* each holding a symbol of royalty mentioned in the text. The Bhājā monastery is one of India's oldest *vihāras.* It was excavated during the Śuṅga Period, inaugurated by Puṣyamitra Śuṅga, the military officer who caused the fall of the Mauryan Empire. The Bhājā complex, including Vihāra XIX, is dated to 100–70 BC[56 & 56a(*)]. As such, the Bhājā royal scene, carved possibly more than 200 years after parts of the *Arthaśāstra* were composed, exemplifies the text's description of palace courtesans. The correlation between a textual description perhaps based on an aspect of courtly life in one part of the country and its (unexplained) appearance clear across the subcontinent about two centuries later need not be considered problematic. Courtesans in the service of kings and aristocrats were part of ancient Indian society[57], and *gaṇikās* would be employed wherever the ruling élite of a particular region were located. What remains difficult to understand is why a king in a quadriga with his courtesans should appear in this religious context unless, of course, this relief depicts a legendary king with his courtly retinue. Such an identification has been proposed, and continues to be duly noted[58] together with the meaning of the entire scene including the demonic female below the royal group. An unexpected source hints at a new way to tackle and interpret the context. A bronze vase from Himachal Pradesh extends the royal evidence and offers some clues from the Northwest. As the Bhājā scene, the vase (in the collection of the British Museum; Acc. No. OA 1880–22) can probably be associated with a similar religious context[59]. It was found in one of the structures of a Buddhist monastery, either a vaulted shrine or a vaulted store room, and it probably had a ritual and not a funerary function. The scene of a royal procession is incised around the globular body between the shoulder and base of the vase. The royal personage is depicted twice, once riding an elephant with a female sitting behind him holding the royal umbrella and the flywhisk. The second time the same royal figure appears in a horse-drawn chariot, again protected by the umbrella and accompanied by the *caurī*-bearing female. She is bare-breasted and clad only in a *dhoti.* The dress of these and the other figures compares with 1st century representations. This is the date assigned to this vase which also has numerous auspicious symbols evocative of a *mahāpuruṣa* and *cakravartin* incised in the processional field. Elizabeth Errington who wrote the entry for this object comes to the original conclusion that although the vessel was found in a Buddhist context, it may relate to the concept of a *cakravartin.* Perhaps this line of interpretation can be equally applied to the Bhājā Vihāra.

The information supplied by the *Arthaśāstra* and illustrated by the Bhājā relief provide sufficient evidence to propose that the Dīdārgañj female be identified as a *gaṇikā.* As the Bhājā *gaṇikā* in the chariot, the Dīdārgañj *gaṇikā* is decked with jewels and has but one attibute, namely the fan. Whereas the Bhājā *gaṇikā* dons a fine turban for the outing, the hair of the Dīdārgañj female is dressed in an elaborate coiffure. The style is composed of three features: there is the small, round bun on the forehead; a braid over the back of the head, and a chignon at the back of the neck joined by the braid to the bun[60]. The entire coiffure is crowned by a small tiara. Whereas some scholars had compared this hairstyle to Roman hairstyles prevailing in *circa* the mid 1st century BC to *circa* the 1st century AD, and therefore posited a Kuṣāṇa date for the Dīdārgañj sculpture, Morris has shown conclusively the several and distinct variations in hairstyles in Roman, Kuṣāṇa and the Dīdārgañj examples. She concludes that the hairstyle in Kuṣāṇa sculptures is a separate and parallel development from the Roman examples. And since both exhibit distinct differences from the hairstyle of the Dīdārgañj female, the latter may be left 'where she has traditionally been placed, in the Mauryan period'[61].

I concur with that dating. As further indication of the high level of artisanship available in Pāṭaliputra of the Mauryan Period, terracotta figurines should be considered. Indeed, I find it unusual that the Bulandibagh terracottas, stemming from within the confines of ancient Pāṭaliputra, are not regularly cited as proof of the fine craftsmanship available in the region at that time. These can mitigate the question of expert modeling regularly raised when a Mauryan date is given to the Dīdārgañj image. The Bulandibagh type of terracotta figurines are not found outside of Pāṭaliputra[62], and the female representations are considered among the finest specimens of Indian terracotta art[63]. They are generally large (for a terracotta), standing and executed in a more naturalistic style; they often include the (so-called) female dancers whose pose and dress contrast with that of the Dīdārgañj courtesan[64].

The pose of the Mauryan *gaṇikā* from Dīdārgañj suits her position at court. The particular stance of this *gaṇikā* is one of deference. In slightly bending one knee and lowering the torso forward, she executes a gracious bow almost in the manner of a courtsey[65].

Towards whom does she show this deference? Most probably the king. Indeed, it may be proposed that a royal figure, either seated or standing would have been flanked by two courtesans, the *gaṇikā* and the *pratigaṇikā*. One of these, I propose, is the Dīdārgañj female; the other one, though no longer known, may have been holding the umbrella and/or vase. Already Susan Huntington made a similar suggestion on the basis that the Dīdārgañj *caurī*-bearer must be an attendant to someone, and since attendants in later Indic art come in pairs, there may have existed a second similar sculpture[66]. My quite similar suggestion stems from different reasoning based on the identification, the dating and royal context of this image. In concluding that the Dīdārgañj female is a royal courtesan at the Mauryan court, there is every reason to believe that the sculpture would have been executed in a royal atelier, just as the other sculptures mentioned above, which exhibit similar stylistic and technical traits and are considered imperial art.

The Dīdārgañj female may be the earliest known, but probably not the only, courtesan glorified in the ancient art of India[67]. The courtesan should have been a sufficiently frequent artistic subject, for she was included in the major early treatise on Indian painting. *Adhyāya* 42 of *The Citrasūtra of the Viṣṇudharmottara Purāṇa* describes the manner in which a large number of significant beings ought to be represented. Among these, the proportion for the courtesan *(veśyā)* is given. Although the date of this text is still a matter of considerable debate, it may be that the mid-5th century AD will come to be seen as a reasonable position[68].

When the Dīdārgañj female is identified as a *gaṇikā* then so many aspects of her heretofore puzzling iconography fall into place. The presence of the fly whisk, the reason for the slight bow, the general stylistic similarity with other pieces produced by royal ateliers in Pāṭaliputra, the size of the figure, perhaps even the small tiara on the head[68a(*)], to say nothing of her exceptional beauty, all these become signposts designating the *gaṇikā*. As such, there is no conflict with proposing a Mauryan date; indeed these signposts would be expected of an imperial *gaṇikā* sculpted in the area around the capital, Pāṭaliputra. However, this identification may require some scholarly readjustments. That the earliest known life-size female statue should be that of a royal *gaṇikā* indicates the importance the courtesan had in the ancient social life of the times. But historians of Indian art do not usually include the possibilty of a *gaṇikā's* image when deciding on the identification of a feminine representation. Confronted with a problematic female image, we routinely make some initial assessments in order to decide on the possible category wherein the specific identity may lie. We ask ourselves if the image is sacred or secular; if the image is of a major or a minor godling, belonging to a folk, or Hindu, Buddhist or Jain cult, or derived from a transplanted foreign belief system? We apply terms to any of these, and other possibilities, using terms such as *yakṣī, nāginī, yoginī, devī, ḍākinī, tyche, vṛkṣadevatā,* etc. The terms designate generic female types wherefrom may be winnowed the specific persona. Let *gaṇikā* be added to these generic terms. Perhaps it would be the only designation, thus far, to refer to an important, indigenous type who is a secular female. Yet who knows, perhaps if we make this term a household word, other images of courtesans would come into our line of vision. Worse things could happen.

NOTES AND REFERENCES

1. For an overall survey of courtesans and *devadāsīs* in pre-Colonial India, see my paper "Royalty's Courtesans and God's Mortal Wives: Keepers of Culture in Pre-Colonial India", in *The Courtesan's Arts: Cross-cultural Perspectives,* M. Feldman & B. Gordon (ed.), New York 2006. See n. 3 there for further references to these terms. Chapter 13 in this volume.
2. See *The Kāmasūtra of Vātsyāyana,* transl. Sir R.F. Burton & F.F. Arbutknot, Mumbai 1976, pp. 137 ff.
3. Ibid.
4. Cf. D. Desai, *Erotic Sculpture of India. A Socio-Cultural Study,* New Delhi 1975, p. 17.
5. Kangle regards the text as the work of Kauṭilya who helped Candragupta come to power in Magadha. See R.P. Kangle, ed. and transl., *The Arthaśāstra,* Part III, repr. Delhi 1986, 1988, p. 106.
6. M. Chandra, *The World of Courtesans,* Delhi 1973, p. 46. See Kangle, *Arthaśāstra,* pp. 163–64.
7. Cf. Sh. Arora, 'Position of Women in India in the 4th Century BC', *JIH,* 62, 1–3r, 1984, p. 16.
8. Suggested reading of J.P. Vogel, *Catalogue of the Archaeological Museum at Mathurā,* Allahabad 1910, p. 185. This reading is followed by S. Rhie Quintanilla, 'Āyāgapaṭas: Characteristics, Symbolism, and Chronology', *Artibus Asiae,* LX, 1, 2000, pp. 121–22.
9. Note here the Q2 Āyāgapaṭa is well analyzed by Quintanilla, 'Āyāgapaṭas...', *cit.*
10. See W.D. Whitney, *Sanskrit Grammar,* Cambridge 1950, p. 446, ¶ 1181c; for a similar example, Whitney cites *nāya* > *nāyikā.*
11. Sir M. Monier-Williams, *A Sanskrit-English Dictionary,* repr. Oxford 1960, p. 343; cf. P.M. Upadhye, 'The Gaṇikā in Buddisth and Jaina Literature', *Sangeet Natak,* 97, 1990, p. 10.

12. The account occurs in the *Civara-vastu*, See N. Dutt, *Gilgit Manuscripts*, Vol. III, Part 2, Srinagar-Kashmir 1942, pp. 16–22. In this account, Āmrapālī is called a *veśyā*. See R.C. Majumdar, gen. ed., *The Age of Imperial Unity*, Bombay 1951, pp. 568–69, for a summary. Majumdar adds: 'The Pāli Vinaya Texts tell us that a merchant, after having described the charms of Ambapālī of Vaiśālī to king Bimbisāra, requested him "to install a courtesan" in Rājagṛiha, and this was done'.
13. For details on this form of government in ancient India, see Majumdar, *op. cit.*, pp. 330–34.
14. See, for example, Mahā-Parinibbāna-Sutta, II 12–25, in *Buddhist Suttas* translated from the Pāli by T.W. Rhys Davids, *Sacred Books of the East*, Vol. XI, Oxford 1881.
15. See H. Oldenberg, ed., *Vinayapiṭaka*, Vol. I, London 1879–1883, p. 268.
16. O.N. Tripathi, *Taxation and Fiscal Administration in Ancient India*, Lucknow 1985, p. 112.
17. The uneven portrayal of the courtesan is evident in the compilation of hundreds of classical Sanskrits texts compiled by L. Sternbach in his *Gaṇikā-vṛtta-sangrahaḥ, or Texts on Courtezans in Classical Sanskit*, Hoshiapur, 1953.
18. R. Mitra, ed., *The Lalita Vistara*, Bibliotheca Indica Series, Vol. 15, Calcutta 1877, p. 156.
19. É. Lamotte, *Histoire du bouddhisme indien*, Louvain 1958, pp. 723–24.
20. *Nāṭyaśāstra*, Vol. III, transl. N.P Unni, Nag Publishers, 1988, Chapter 34.26, p. 1064.
21. This idealized description continues both in the arts and, amazingly, in accounts attributed to actual courtesans. For details, see Srinivasan, 'Royalty's Courtesans...', *cit.*
22. Cf. Chandra, op. cit., p. 24.
23. The following citations are found in Upadhye, op. cit., pp. 10–14.
24. Chandra, op. cit., p. 28. See n. 12 on installing a courtesan in Rājagṛha.
25. Ibid., p. 23.
26. Jaini translates the pieces of money as 'old' coins in P.S. Jaini, 'Political and Cultural Data in References to Mathurā in the Buddhist Literature', in D.M. Srinivasan (ed.), *Mathurā: The Cultural Heritage*, New Delhi, 1989, p. 217. J.S. Strong considers the coins pieces of gold in his *The Legend and Cult of Upagupta*, Princeton, 1992, p. 77.
27. The *Divyāvadāna*, E.B. Cowell & R.A. Neil (ed.), Cambridge 1886, pp. 352–54; also *Divyāvadāna*, ed. P.L. Vaidya, Darbhanga, 1959, pp. 218–19.
28. Chandra, op. cit., p. 28, referring to *Vin. Texts*, iii 360–61.
29. Upadhye, op. cit., p. 13. The term is *ganiyā*, Prakrit for *gaṇikā*. See Mani Jambūvijaya, *Ṇāyādhammakahāo*, Jaina-Agama-Series, 5, Bombay, 1989, p. 276.
30. Reference cited by Chandra, op. cit., p. 33, n. 4.
31. Ibid., p. 33.
32. For details see Srinivasan, 'Royalty's Courtesans...', *cit.*, p. 170 (p. 266 in this volume) and nn. 44 and 45.
33. Ibid.
34. Desai, op. cit., p. 17. She notices that terracottas and similar objects representing sex have been collected from ancient urban sites.
35. See Sh.G. Bajpai, 'Mathurā: Trade Routes, Commerce and Communication Patterns, from Post-Mauryan Period to the End of the Kuṣāṇa Period', in Srinivasan (gen. ed.), *Mathurā: The Cultural Heritage, cit.*
36. Desai, op. cit., p. 17. Also S. Goel, 'Public and Professional Life of Women in the Gupta Age (300 A–600 AD)', *Indian Journal of Social Research*, 36, 1–2, 1995, p. 9.
37. *Kaumudīmahotasavaḥ*, Dakshina Bharati Sanskrit Series, 4, Madras 1929, p. 37.
38. Reference cited by Chandra, op. cit., p. 33, n. 3.
39. According to the translation of R. Shamasastry, *Kauṭilya's Arthaśāstra*, Mysore 1929[3], p. 136.

40. According to the translation of Kangle, *Arthaśāstra*, Part II, p. 158.
41. F. Asher & W. Spink, 'Maurya Figural Sculpture Reconsidered', *Ars Orientalis*, 19, 1989, p. 3 and n. 21.
42. For illustrations, see *ibid.*, figs. 15 and 18; and S.L. Huntington, *The Art of Ancient India...* with contributions by J.C. Huntington, New York-Tokyo 1985, figs. 4.3–4.5.
43. See Spink & Asher, *op. cit.*, esp. pp. 5–6; writing in 1989, the Kuṣāṇa Period probably meant 2nd–3rd century AD. J.C. Harle, *The Art and Architecture of the Indian Subcontinent*, New Haven-London 1994[2], assigns the image to the 1st century AD, p. 33 citing H. Plaeschke, 'Zur Datierung der "Caurī-Trägerin" von Dīdargañj', *Wissenschaftliche Zeitschrift der Martin-Luther-Universität Halle-Wittemberg*, XII, 3–4, 1963, pp. 319–30. Plaeschke makes several assumptions which prevent him from looking at all aspects of the problem. He assumes that the figure is a *yakṣī*. Therefore his strictly stylistic analysis is based almost totally on a comparative study between the Dīdārgañj female and other female statues that are mainly *yakśīs*. Notably, he omits a comparison with Mauryan terracotta female figures. Further, he assumes that the Indian sculptural tradition developed in a linear fashion, going from archaic forms (via additive delineations) to organic forms (via more naturalistic delineations). The notion of a royal school is not introduced; neither is the concept of uneven pockets of artistry at the center of a school, or at its periphery, etc. His paper is a classic example of the limits of the stylistic method in solving art historical problems. Although a complete critique of this paper is not warranted here, it should be noted that this dated paper can no longer be cited as a reliable basis for dating the Dīdārgañj image.
44. Asher & Spink, op. cit., p. 7, n. 1.
45. Huntington, op. cit., pp. 53–54.
46. R.N. Misra, *Yaksha Cult and Iconography*, New Delhi 1981, p. 109.
47. See P. Chandra, *The Sculpture of India. 3000 B.C.–1300 A.D.*, National Gallery of Art, Washington 1985, p. 49. This scholar also believes that the sculpture probably dates to the 3rd century BC.
48. P. Pal, 'The Chowrie-Bearing Goddess on the Aśvamedha Type of Samudragupta's Coin', *Ars Orientalis*, XVIII, 1988, pp. 197–205.
49. Misra, op. cit., figs. 43, 46–48, 51–53.
50. D.M. Srinivasan, 'Monumental Nāginīs from Mathurā', in *On the Cusp of an Era: Art in the Pre-Kuṣāṇa World*, Doris Meth Srinivasan (ed.), Leiden, 2007, pp. 351-84 and pp. 296-328 in this volume.
51. See Huntington, op. cit., fig. 5.4.
52. The heavy drapery fold over the pudendum compares best to the Śuṅga Besnagar female statue and the pre-Kuṣāṇa Nāga Queen on the lintel of the Sonkh Naga Temple. See H. Härtel, *Excavations at Sonkh. 2500 Years of a Town in Mathura District*, Berlin, 1993, pl. 4, p. 438.
53. It is perhaps useful to notice that Monier-Williams, *Dictionary, cit.*, indicates, on p. 765, the lexicographer's meaning for *bhṛṅgāra* is 'a vase used at the inauguration of a king'.
54. Kangle, *Arthaśāstra*, Part. III, p. 164.
55. The plaque, in a Private Collection, dates to the Śuṅga period, a date corroborated by thermoluminescence analysis performed by Oxford Authentication Ltd. The report, dated in 2001, estimated that the date of the last firing of the terracotta was between 1400 and 2300 years ago. The plaque (38 x 50 cm) had been previously in a private Indian collection.
56. For the latest discussion on Bhājā, with selected prior analyses, see R. De Caroli, 'Reading Bhājā: A Non-Narrative Interpretation of the Vihāra 19 Reliefs', *EW*, 50, 1–4,

2000, pp. 259–80. De Caroli does not reconsider the iconography of the females in the 'Sūrya panel', because he accepts the Sūrya/Indra identification. For additional perspectives and references, see Huntington, op. cit., pp. 77–80.

56a. ADDENDUM: For my review of De Caroli's book, see *JAOS* 127.1; 2007; 95-99.

57. See Desai, op. cit., pp. 170 ff.

58. See G.R. Gyani, 'Identification of the So-called Sūrya and Indra Figures in Cave No. 20 [*sic.*] of the Bhājā Group', *Bulletin of the Prince of Wales Museum of Western India,* Vol. I, 1950–51, pp. 15–21; Huntington, op. cit., p. 78.

59. The following description is based on the excellent entry provided by Elizabeth Errington in E. Errington & J. Cribb, with M. Claringbull, eds., *The Crossroads of Asia. Transformation in Image and Symbol,* Cambridge 1992, pp. 162–64.

60. For an excellent analysis of this hairstyle see R. Morris, 'The Dīdārgañj Yakṣī and the "Coque ou Bouffant de Chevelure" Hairstyle: A Reassessment', *AAA,* 42, 1989, pp. 77–81.

61. Morris, op. cit., p. 79. This paper contains a full bibliography on the subject as does R. Morris, 'Roman Hairstyle in Kuṣāṇa-Period Art of Mathurā?', in M. Taddei & P. Callieri, eds., *South Asian Archaeology* 1987, Rome 1990, pp. 787–800. Coming out at about the same time as the papers by Morris is the article by Asher & Spink which is not included in Morris' analysis. Asher & Spink also discuss the hairstyle and hair ornament in the context of Kuṣāṇa Period sculptures.

62. N. Verma, *The Terracottas of Bihar,* Delhi, 1986, p. 10.

63. Huntington, op. cit., p. 55; Verma, op. cit., p. 46.

64. See A.G. Poster, *From Indian Earth. 4,000 Years of Terracottas Art,* New York 1986, pl. 2.

65. The movement is noted in Huntington, op. cit., p. 53; middle photo on that page.

66. Ibid., p. 53.

67. For other examples, see Srinivasan, 'Royalty's Courtesans...', *cit.* In addition, a marble slab in the Ajitanatha Temple in Taranga (northern Gujarat), depicts the emperor Kumarapala riding a horse. He is accompanied by an umbrella-holding female and a *caurī*-holding female, who could represent the *gaṇikā* and the *pratigaṇicā* at court. I wish to thank Shri M.A. Dhaky for the reference to this marble slab.

68. See discussion in the following review article: *The Citrasūtra of the Viṣṇudharmottara Parāṇa,* critically edited and translated by P.D. Mukherji, New Delhi 2001, reviewed by D.M. Srinivasan for the *JAOS,* 124.3, 2004, pp. 369–72. Several texts and objects are cited in this review which favour a c. fifth century date.

68a. ADDENDUM: The fact that the *gaṇikā* wears a small tiara is another indication that possibly she was made in an earlier (i.e. Mauryan) period. Pāṇini notes that the chief queen was crowned jointly with the king who wears a *paṭṭa*, a fillet. Queens on some Gupta gold coins wear the *paṭṭa*. Prior to Gupta times, females, be they queens or goddesses are hardly ever depicted wearing a *paṭṭa* or a crown. The one instance known to me is of an actual Ikṣvāku royal, Queen Varmabhattā, rendered on a memorial pillar at Nāgārjunakoṇḍa dated to the early part of the fourth century AD. She may be wearing a headdress that does not look like a *paṭṭa*. The pillar relief shows multiple foreign influences. (On all the above, see my "Queens and Crowns and Sorrowful Queen Māyā-Part III", in press in the *Proceedings of the International Conference on the Archaeology of Buddhism in Asia,* Archaeological Survey of India, New Delhi, February 17th-19th, 2012. The paper will also be in Volume II, *Listening to Icons*). The Mauryan period was influenced by western art from the Achamenian Empire. Possibly, the small tiara on the Dīdārgañj gaṇikā is due to foreign influence.

15

Monumental Nāginīs from Mathurā

A UNIQUE SET

This paper analyses a set of life-size Snakes Goddesses (Nāginīs) dating to the first century AD. They were probably made in Mathurā and shipped, for worship, to Nandan, U.P. These Nāginīs open a new subject category in early Indian art because they are: 1) a life-size 2) group of 3) goddesses not originating from the sphere of Hinduism, Buddhism or Jainism, and 4) dating to the 1st century AD. These four characteristics, taken together, have so far not been associated with other early imagery. As such, there is no precedent on which to base the analysis. However, the likelihood that such a set could occur can be anticipated. For example, the slightly later Mathurā life-size Nāginī in the Cleveland Museum of Art (No. 68.104), which may be coupled with a Nāgarāja in The Brooklyn Museum of Art (No. 67.202), raises the possibility that, as elsewhere, there could have been earlier attempts in Mathurā.[1] Also, as will be shown below, archaeological, iconographic and textual indicators suggest the worship of Nāginīs within the Nāga Cult to be prevalent in antiquity. Therefore, even though the Nāginī set described in this paper is presently anomalous, it is not a cultural impossibility for its time. However, before providing evidence in support of that contention, the onus of any anomaly is proof of authenticity; it is with this issue that we should start.

AUTHENTICITY

This section opens with detailed descriptions of the Nāginīs' physical properties, including their place of discovery and point of dispersal, all of which

---

Originally published in *On the Cusp of an Era: Art in the Pre-Kuṣāṇa World*, Doris Meth Srinivasan (ed.), Leiden-Boston, 2007; pp. 351-84. Reprinted with stylistic changes, additions and permission from Brill.

Fig. 15.1. Nāginī from Nandan, U.P. 1st century AD. National Museum, New Delhi (Acc. No. Safe Custody Object). Photograph courtesy, National Museum, New Delhi.

Fig. 15.2. Nāginī from Nandan, U.P. 1st century AD. Tokyo Private Collection. Photograph, courtesy Katolec Corporation Collection.

relate to the question of authenticity, to be addressed in the second part of this section.

DESCRIPTION

Today the Nāginīs stand apart, one in New Delhi (Fig. 15.1), one in Tokyo (Fig. 15.2), and one in Kansas City (Fig. 15.3). But in Pre-Kuṣāṇa times, they should have formed a unit at Nandan, circa 100–110 kilometers from Mathurā, where I believe they were made.

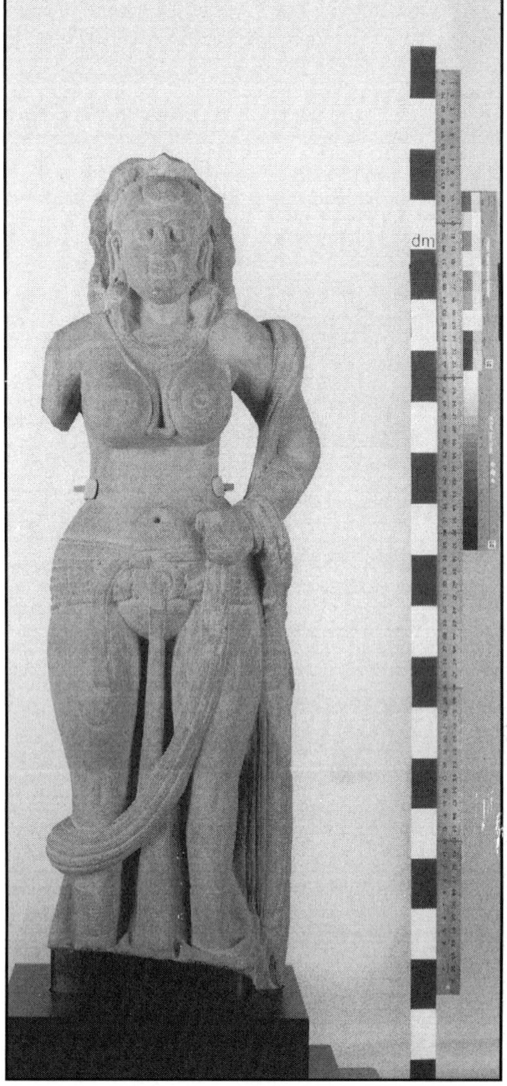

Fig. 15.3. Nāginī from Nandan, U.P. 1st century AD. The Nelson-Atkins Museum of Art (Acc. No. 79–21). Photograph courtesy The Nelson-Atkins Museum of Art.

Fig. 15.4. Reverse of Fig. 15.1, National Museum Nāginī. Photograph courtesy, National Museum, New Delhi.

Discovery of the New Delhi Nāginī, now in the National Museum, New Delhi, was announced in "A note on A Red Sandstone Nāgini from Nadan, District Agra (Uttar Pradesh)."[2] The Figure, sculpted in the round, came into the Museum in two fragments the combined height of which the Museum recorded as 5′2" (1 m. 58 cm).[3] The split occurs at the Nāginī's waist. The part from the waist up measures 71 cms.; the part below the waist measures 99 cms. The figure faces straightforward with a slight bend in the right leg. The right arm is missing and the left, also subject to the split (see Figs. 15.1 & 15.4), is now repaired and held akimbo. Although the New Delhi Nāginī suffered considerable damage, her salient identifying feature remains. The snakehood can clearly be seen from the back where the thinly incised lines indicate that the serpent hood is comprised of nine or more heads (Fig. 15.5). The center part of this hood is treated like tresses that are ornamented with a double-strand garland held together by a broad ribbon at each of the four sides. The interior of the garland has netting indicated by cross-hatching. Draped over the female's flat back and buttocks is a long scarf, going over the left shoulder and then cascading downward through the crook in the left arm (Fig. 15.4). In front, the scarf moves diagonally upward, held at the hip by the (chipped) left hand; it then wraps around the wrist. The Nāginī wears a thin lower garment held up by a beaded girdle composed of four strands. The garment is gathered in frontal folds that descend to the knees. The Nāginī's ornaments are limited to a flat torque; the beginnings of a longer, thinner, outer necklace can be seen by the strand to the right, above the breast. Heavy earrings, now broken off, would have hung from distended lobes.

Fig. 15.5. Reverse. Close-up of Snakehood of Fig. 15.1. Photograph courtesy The Nelson-Atkins Museum of Art.

Both the slightly mottled red sandstone and the physical appearance of the Nāginī conform well to the female type fashioned in the early Mathurā school of art. She should have had large breasts, a thick waist, a rounded belly, wide hips and firm, ample thighs. The loss of the breasts and belly are not due to vandalism, as opined by the Museum.[4] Rather, the sculptured surface of the stone detached itself along the weak strata in the bedding planes of the sandstone. Her face is rather full and fleshy; the eyes, with the little groove at the outer corners, protrude, and her lower lip is thick.

The general appearances of the Tokyo Nāginī in the Katolec Corporation Collection, and the Nāginī in The Nelson-Atkins Museum of Art, Kansas City, are similar to the Nāginī in the National Museum, New Delhi.

The Kansas City (KC) Nāginī, also of slightly spotted sandstone, achieves a height of 62 3/4" (Fig. 15.3). Her feet have been broken off around the ankles, further down therefore than the break of the New Delhi (ND) Nāginī. The KC Nāginī is also carved in the round, but she has no bends in the body; therefore, her weight is equally distributed on both straight legs. From the front, vestiges of the snakehood remain. Attributes of feminine beauty associated with Mathurā art are like those exhibited by the ND Nāginī. The KC Nāginī also wears a long scarf draped much the same way as the other Nāginī. The right arm is broken off just below the shoulder. The back of the KC Nāginī echoes the flat, finished

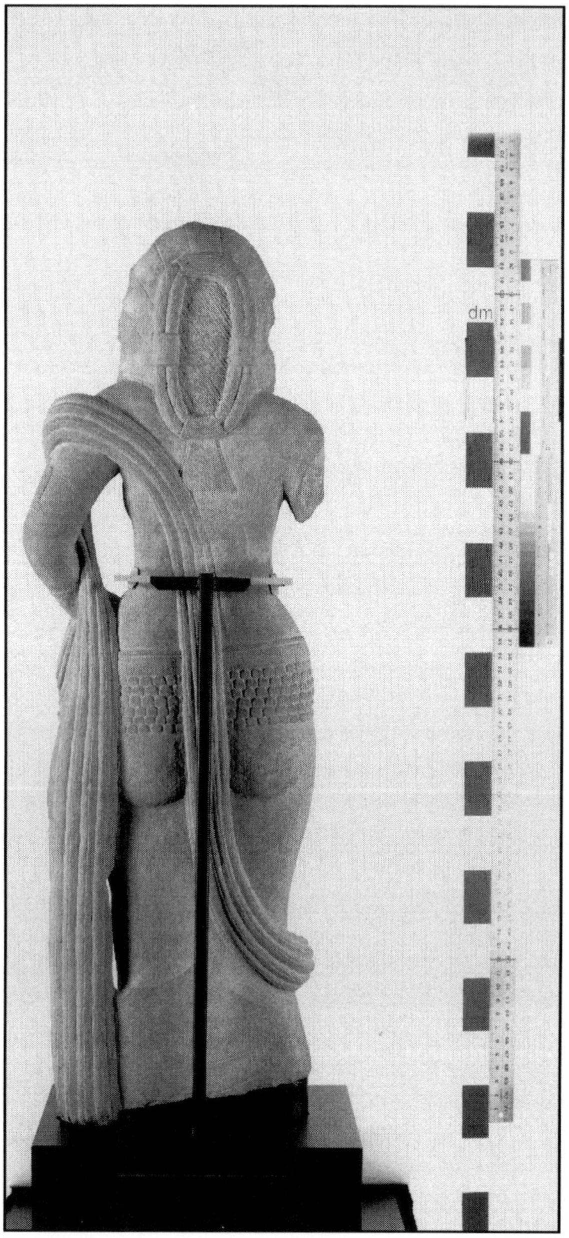

Fig. 15.6. Reverse of Fig. 15.3, the Kansas City Nāginī. Photograph courtesy The Nelson-Atkins Museum of Art, Kansas City.

treatment of the ND sculpture (Fig. 15.6). This view also reveals a hood composed of possibly nine serpent heads, counting, again, the lines demarcating the separate serpent heads (Fig. 15.7). The back shows how the artist rendered the transformation from human legs to snake coils. Nāgas, some believed, are creatures that appear as humans and only reveal their true serpent nature under special circumstances.[5] The sculptor of the KC Nāginī separated the two human legs by a thin wedge that thickens, progressively, to become coils wrapping around the lower legs. The KC Nāginī sustained a split similar to that of the ND Nāginī, and the former has been repaired in the West.

Indeed, all the Nāginīs were split at the waist. The upper and lower sections of the Tokyo Nāginī were joined in Europe; today, this Nāginī stands 65 3/8" tall.[6] As with the KC Nāginī, the ankles and feet of the Tokyo Nāginī are broken off and missing. The Tokyo Nāginī's stone, posture, and dress resemble that of the KC Nāginī. But her face, though recognizably sculpted in the Mathurā style, is somewhat slimmer and more off center than the other two. She resembles the other Nāginīs by her snakehood (Fig. 15.8)[7] and also by a wedge in the back that originally represented snake coils (Fig. 15.9).

Design of jewelry and apparel further unite the three Nāginīs. All have nearly identical long ears with perforated lobes from which hang heavy earrings. Close to the neck, the KC Nāginī wears a flat torque with a central square containing a flower with open petals. A longer necklace lies between the breasts. She also displays an armlet and bangles on the left arm together with anklets on both lower legs. But for the absence of the armlets, the Tokyo Nāginī wears nearly the same jewelry as the KC Nāginī. Breakage of the ND Nāginī's lower legs precludes verification of the original presence of anklets. She wears no armlets, but her two necklaces appear to be quite similar to those of

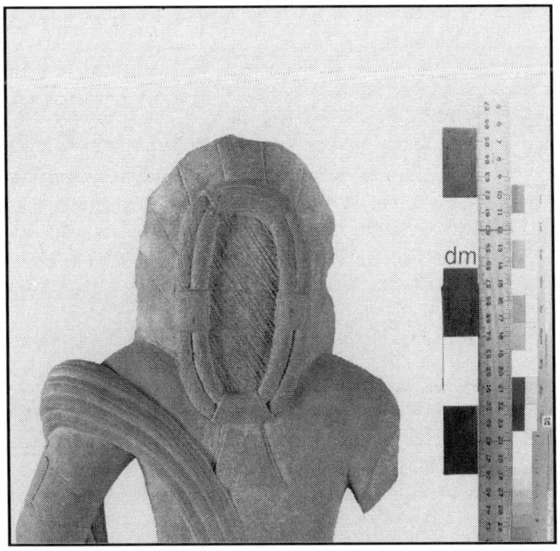

Fig. 15.7. Reverse. Close-up of Snakehood of Fig. 15.3. Photograph courtesy The Nelson-Atkins Museum of Art.

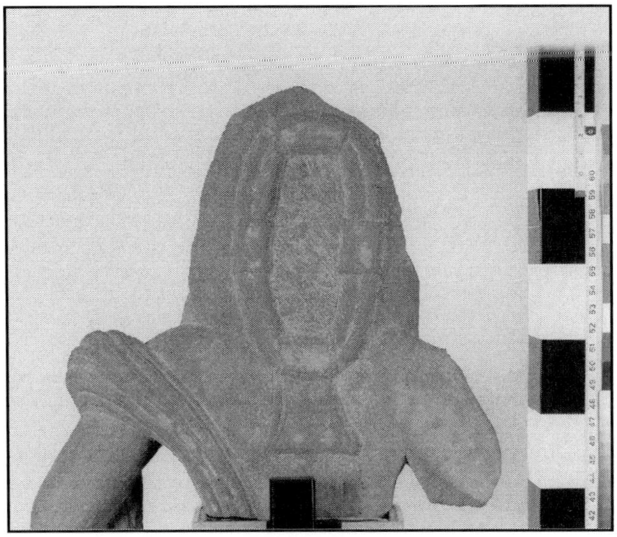

Fig. 15.8. Reverse. Close-up of Snakehood of Fig. 15.2. Photograph courtesy Katolec Corporation Collection.

the Tokyo and KC Nāginīs. All three females are clothed in the same sort of diaphanous lower skirt held below the deep navel by a cloth ribbon tied in the same manner in the KC and Tokyo Nāginīs—the two having this section still intact.[8] Beneath the ribbon, each Nāginī wears a wide beaded girdle having a circular floral clasp in the middle (i.e., the Tokyo and KC examples). However, the Nāginīs are by no means identical. The breasts of the Tokyo Nāginī are somewhat smaller and higher, and her waist is thinner. The girdle of the KC Nāginī contains two more strands of beads than the others. The drapery, though rendered in similar fashion, does not relate similarly to the body in each case. The KC Nāginī has softly folded drapery, tied together and falling down on the lower left side; it is reminiscent of the tactile pliancy of wraps and scarves of the two doorkeepers made in Mathurā District during the Kṣatrapa Period (*c.* 1st century AD).[9]

The unusual breakage sustained by all three sculptures is explained by the National Museum in connection with the acquisition of their Nāginī.

> This sculpture is reported to have been discovered in the village Nadan, Ferozabad, Agra. It was captured by the Police and brought to the National Museum for safe custody.[10] ...The sculpture seems to have been fairly intact before and, in any case, not broken into two fragments as at present. It seems to have been deliberately split at the waist along a grooved line indented for that purpose. The sculpture broke into two fragments as a result of the blows delivered along the grooved line but some part of the groove remained unaffected which indicates the *modus operandi* of the vandals. The fresh scars and planes of cleavage are ample proof of this phenomenon. The feet and the pedestal were broken earlier and are missing. The purpose of this dastardly act attempted was no doubt to simplify the problem of

transporting such a heavy figure over human shoulders over a track that no vehicle can negotiate.[11]

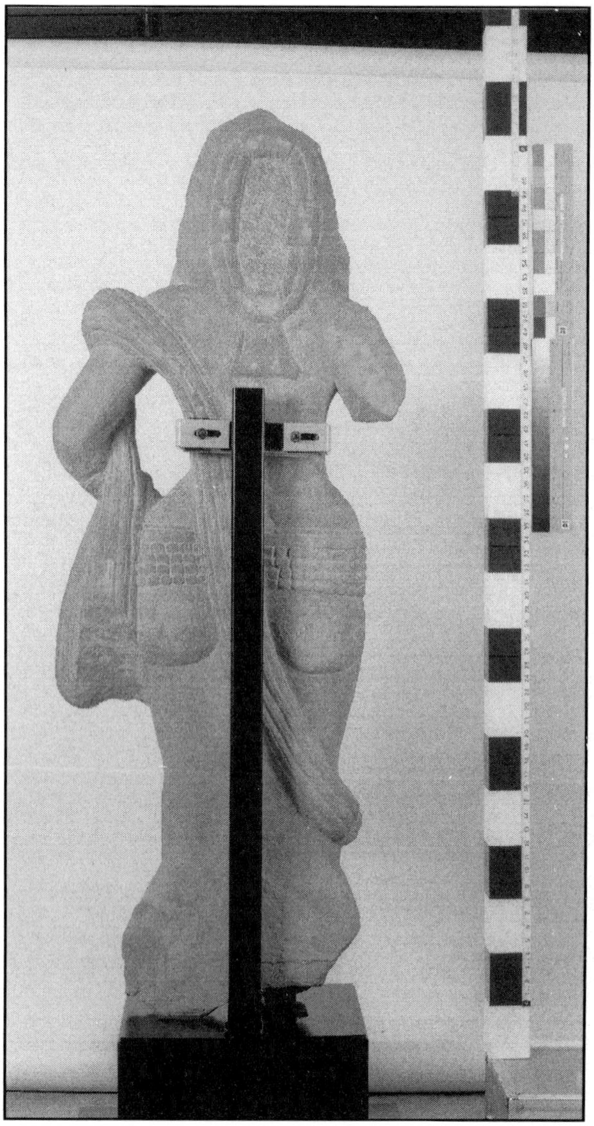

Fig. 15.9. Reverse of Fig. 15.2, the Tokyo Nāginī. Photograph courtesy Katolec Corporation Collection.

These two accounts, published by the Museum, clearly establish the background for the advent of the Nāginī into the National Museum. Evidently, she was found by vandals in the village of Na[n]dan, at a place inaccessible to any sort of vehicle. In an effort to get the heavy, life-size stone sculpture out of that village, the vandals cut her in two. However, the police captured the booty and deposited it in the National Museum.

It seems that the police did not capture all the booty. Several eyewitnesses have reported to me that both the KC and Tokyo Nāginīs arrived in the West, split at the waist and across the left arm, that is, damaged just like the ND Nāginī was, when first captured.[12] The late Dr. René Russek, a well-known collector of Indian sculpture, told me that sometime in the 70s he, Willi Wolff, the dealer, and Mr. Willy Frei, a friend and also a collector, saw the two upper portions of the two Nāginīs in the Zürich Free Zone.[13] He said this may have been around 1976 and that both pieces were not cleaned at the time. I recently talked with the only surviving member of this group, Mr. Willy Frei, who did remember seeing the upper portion of the KC Nāginī around 1975.[14] The split of the Tokyo Nāginī can be verified further by the Rossis, the art dealers who offered the Tokyo Nāginī to the Japanese collector.[15] According to René Russek, it was not until one to two years later that the lower parts of the two sculptures arrived. Dr. Russek observed that whereas it is not unusual for a genuine piece to be broken and shipped in parts staggered a year or two apart, it is unheard of for a fake. In his experience, all fakes come out in one transport.

More than two decades after the vandalism, in November 2000, the three Nāginīs stood reunited and on display in an exhibition at The Nelson-Atkins Museum of Art. By this time, they had all been repaired. Repairs had been made in India and Europe, quite probably using different techniques to join and retouch surfaces. The varying conditions of repair and restoration must be kept in mind when comparisons of heights are made. Even so, the current height measurements of the three Nāginīs, taken while they were exhibited in Kansas City, are not very far apart:

ND Nāginī	:	62 1/4"
Tokyo Nāginī	:	65 3/4"
KC Nāginī	:	62 3/4"

In sum, the *Description* section has presented three sculptures sharing many physical properties, including a man-made breakage inflicted around the mid-70s. The National Museum accounts implicate vandals probably involved in the art market. The National Museum accounts leave no doubt but that the Nāginī in safekeeping with that Museum is genuine. It now remains to establish the genuiness of the other two.

Fig. 15.10. The Tokyo Nāginī in Fig. 15.2, prior to cleaning. Photograph courtesy Anna Maria Rossi and Fabio Rossi.

Documentary, scientific and site data

As Dr. Russek indicated, the upper part of the Tokyo Nāginī arrived in the West before being cleaned. The lower part apparently also arrived uncleaned, since I have the photograph of the entire statue taken prior to cleaning (Fig. 15.10). The photograph was taken in or before October 1980 since the Italian writing on the back has been translated for me: "On the month of October 1980, I have removed the calcareous incrustatins [sic] (scales) of the sculpture at the residence of Mr. Rossi in Passerano." (Signed) Pia Sarzina Sciacca.[16] The photograph shows the joined upper and lower parts of the female sculpture. As such, this photograph is the important predecessor of Fig. 15.2, the Tokyo Nāginī after cleaning. Indeed, in a document dated 27/08/2001, and written in Turin, Ms. Sciacca, whose letterhead states 'expert in conservation of works of art', reiterates that she and an assistant removed "completely the calcareous incrustations (scales) which had deposited on the sculpture depicted in the enclosed photograph." She goes on the describe the way the cleaning was performed, and that the job took twenty-one working days.

Thus, partial evidence for the probable authenticity of the Tokyo Nāginī includes:

(a) the photo of this piece prior to cleaning;
(b) the first-hand observations of René Russek regarding this sculpture and his general remark regarding staggered shipments;
(c) the declaration of Ms. Sciacca, who cleaned the sculpture.

Additional evidence will be cited below under Scaled Photography.

The KC Nāginī was subjected to a number of scientific tests carried out by John Twilley in 1998 at the request of The Nelson-Atkins Museum of Art. Mr. Twilley examined the sculpture and submitted to me on June 27, 1998, a report entitled "Scientific and Technical Investigations of a Kuṣāṇa Nāginī in Spotted Red Sandstone."[17] His work involved examination of the piece, including observations made using directional lighting and ultraviolet fluorescent light, and microscopic examination. Samples of surface accretions were removed from the Nāginī for analysis by x-ray diffraction and Fourier Transform Infrared Spectroscopy in order to determine their composition, and thin section petrography was used to verify their microstructure.[18] According to Twilley, "No evidence was found for the use of modern tools, for the imposition of false weathering features or the application of man made materials intended to simulate burial deposits."[19] In addition, Twilley, who is familiar with Kuṣāṇa and classical sculpture, writes, "A very important observation is that the sides of the torso both retain a faint ridge which is a remnant left from the sculpting of the stone at the stage where the open spaces under the arms were being created. This can be observed on a number of sculptures from the classical world of Greece and Rome and results from the intersection of curving lines from front and rear when they meet beneath a limb which precludes thorough finishing of the surface."[20] The resulting ridge can be found on the right side of the torso and implies that the right arm was in place when that part of the torso was carved. "By far the most prominent example of this feature is present in the gap between the left leg and the outer fall of the drapery."[21]

The report emphasizes the importance of both the scientific and art historical methods to establish authenticity. From the scientific perspective, Twilley could not find any compelling evidence that would preclude an ancient date for the KC Nāginī. As such, the scientific tests performed on this Nāginī favored assessing the sculpture as both authentic and ancient.

This assessment supports the implication resulting from the fact, mentioned above, that part of the KC Nāginī landed in the West in *c.* 1975.

The remembrances of the older villagers at Nandan tend to support the likely authenticity of both the Tokyo and KC sculptures. Twilley and I were told that the older villagers remember the presence of the sculptures at Nandan. Since their recollection is not a foolproof endorsement, the background for this testimony needs to be relayed.

Twilley and I, accompanied by a junior officer of the Archaeological Survey of India, made a site visit to Nandan in February 2000. It took most of the day to get from Agra to Nandan, and, once there, to make the villagers comfortable with our presence and questions. Our questions, in English, were translated into Hindi by the ASI officer, who then translated and transmitted their responses back to us. Close to sunset, we were led to a large disturbed area close to the Jumna River, but at considerable walking distance from the habitational grounds. The area, perhaps an acre in size, was bound on one side by a sandy slope suggesting that an excavation may have occurred there in the past. A huge depression existing near the slope may be connected to the 'excavation' work. It was in this area that some villagers said they saw the Nāginīs before they were taken away. The difficulty with this information is that: 1) some data could have been lost in the translation process; 2) possibly the responses were conditioned by what the villagers opined we, the visitors, came to hear; 3) the ASI officer could have misunderstood the specificity of the question I relayed to him, causing the villagers to have provided answers relating to a part of the disturbed area (i.e., the excavation/depression/tank), rather than to the sculptures.

Fig. 15.11. Red Sandstone Fragment of Nāginī's Feet. *In situ* at Nandan. Photograph by John Twilley.

One fact stands. Two Nāginī pieces can unequivocally be considered authentic and assigned to Nandan. The first is, of course, the sculpture in the National Museum. The second is, presumably, still in Nandan. It was shown to Twilley and myself in February 2000. After we left the disturbed area and walked, for about twenty-five minutes, back to the inhabited part of the village, the villagers showed us a large sandstone fragment of a Nāginī's feet resting on a base supported by a tang (Fig. 15.11). Identification is assured because the back of the stone retains the bottom part of twisted snake coils (Fig. 15.12). The actual feet and ankles are slender and therefore female (Fig. 15.13). The fragment, lying in a muddy path, was not used in worship but apparently was a curiosity in the village. I was given no explanation as to how it got there, or from which part of Nandan it might have come.

Does the fragment belong to one of the three known Nāginīs, or to a fourth? Evidence suggests it belongs to a fourth. Measurements of the dimensions of the top of the fragment show that the feet could belong to a Nāginī from this set but not necessarily from one of the three. The fragment's top length, end to end,

Fig. 15.12. Reverse of Fig. 15.11. Author's Photograph.

measures 20". The bottom breakage point of the KC Nāginī measures 20 3/4". The widest surviving width at the bottom of the Tokyo Nāginī, which is not quite at the same place as the KC Nāginī's breakage point, is 17 3/4". The bottom breakage point of the ND Nāginī is closer to the knees, so a comparison of its measurements to that of the Nandan fragment is irrelevant. Since the measurements of the Nandan fragment could align with either the Tokyo or KC Nāginī, it cannot be ruled out that the feet could belong to one of the two.

However, iconographic comparisons eliminate this possibility. The Nandan feet have anklets on both feet, though only worn circles now remain (Figs. 15.11 & 15.13). The circles originally could have formed one or two heavy anklets around each foot.[22] The Tokyo Nāginī retains the remains of two heavy anklets around the left ankle (Fig. 15.2). The KC Nāginī has traces of double heavy anklets also on the left foot (Fig. 15.3). Therefore, the Nandan feet are unlikely to belong to either of these statues since the norm seems to be two heavy anklets per ankle. Again, nothing can be ventured regarding the ND Nāginī broken closer to the knees. True, a chunk of sandstone could have broken off below the knees and above the ankles of the ND Nāginī. But neither Twilley nor I saw any other chunk of stone in the entire Nandan region we traversed. To quote Twilley's site observations,

Fig. 15.13. Side View of Fig. 15.11. Photograph by John Twilley.

> ... there is no evidence that any rock exists in the area. The sculpture base was literally the only piece of rock in the entire area. None appeared in the village buildings. If rock existed in the area, it should have been exposed by erosion in the river valleys,

which we didn't see. However, all the sand that we saw being hauled out of the river was grey, not red, so we can be pretty sure that red sandstone isn't exposed in the river valley below the site....[23]

As such, no meaningful connection can be made, at this time, between the Nandan fragment and the ND Nāginī.

I propose that the snake feet found at Nandan belong to a fouth Nāginī in the set comprising the ND, the KC, and the Tokyo Nāginī, for the following reasons:

(a) The Nandan fragment cannot belong to the KC Nāginī because the anklets don't match.
(b) The Nandan fragment cannot belong to the Tokyo Nāginī for the same reason, in addition to the fact that the Nandan fragment preserves the form of the central fold between the feet (Fig. 15.14), whereas the central folds terminate between the ankles of the Tokyo Nāginī.
(c) It is likely, for reasons given above, that the Nandan feet do not belong to the ND Nāginī. Note also, that the feet of the fragment are poised in a way that could accommodate straight or bent legs, and that the ND Nāginī's right leg shows a slight bend.

Scaled Photography

To determine the degree of similarity or difference between the proportions of the three Nāginīs, two procedures were undertaken. First, a comparison was made of the measurements of seven facial features taken from close-up photographs of each Nāginī shot under similar conditions. Second, and based on the first procedure, three separate, complete frontal photographs (one of each the Nāginī) taken under similar conditions were scanned into a computer and the resultant composite image was scaled.[24] The results from these two procedures reveal surprising correlations in proportions, as will be demonstrated next. But first, it should be noted that the accuracy of both results rests on the fact that all three sculptures came together for the exhibition at The Nelson-Atkins Museum of Art.[25] During the time the Nāginīs were in Kansas City, they were under the scrutiny of the Museum's Photography and Conservation Departments.[26]

1. Photos and measurements of the Nāginīs' face

Dale Benson in the Museum's Conservation Department took very accurate measurements of the Nāginīs' faces. Jamison Miller, the Museum's chief photographer, took full-length slides of each Nāginī using the same lighting, distance, film, camera, lens, and camera height for each statue. The three full-length slides were enlarged so that each image could accommodate Benson's measurements of each face. The photographer then "plugged Paul Benson's face measurements into a computer and made fresh printouts of each Nāginī. These

Fig. 15.14. Close-up of Feet in Fig. 15.11. Author's Photograph.

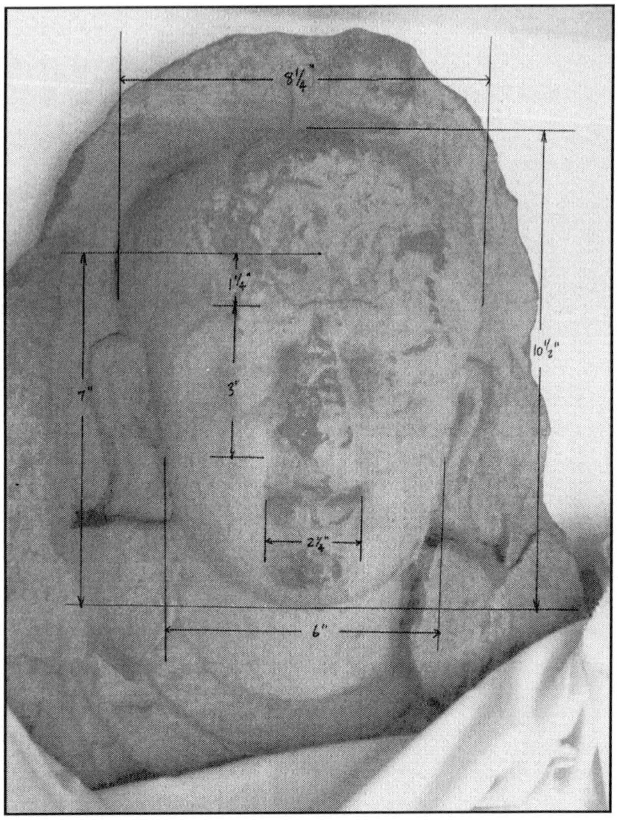

Fig. 15.15. Face of the National Museum Nāginī, Fig. 15.1, with measurements. Photograph courtesy The Nelson-Atkins Museum of Art.

accurate measurements did not change the size of the printouts much at all....[27]" The prints, reproduced here in reduced format (Figs. 15.15–15.17), will now be compared and analyzed.

(a) Measurement from top of the head at the hairline to bottom of the chin

ND Nāginī	10 1/2"
KC Nāginī	10"
Tokyo Nāginī	10"

(b) Measurement from beginning of the hairline (i.e., top of the forehead) to bottom of the chin

ND Nāginī	7"
KC Nāginī	7"
Tokyo Nāginī	6 3/4"

(c) Measurement of jaw width

ND Nāginī	6"
KC Nāginī	5 1/2"
Tokyo Nāginī	5"

(d) Measurement of cranial width

ND Nāginī	8 1/4"
KC Nāginī	7 1/4"
Tokyo Nāginī	6 3/4"

(e) Measurement of mouth width

ND Nāginī	2 1/4"
KC Nāginī	2"
Tokyo Nāginī	2"

(f) Meaurement of top of eyebrow to bottom of the nose

ND Nāginī	3"
KC Nāginī	3"
Tokyo Nāginī	2 1/2"

(g) Measurement of top of eyebrow to beginning of hairline (i.e., top of forehead)

ND Nāginī	1 1/4"
KC Nāginī	1"
Tokyo Nāginī	1 1/2"

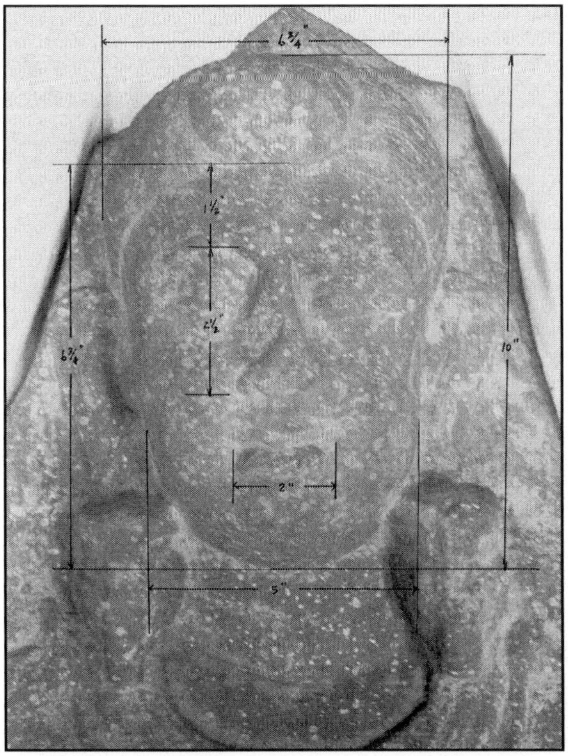

Fig. 15.16. Face of the Tokyo Nāginī, Fig. 15.2, with measurements. Photograph courtesy of The Nelson-Atkins Museum of Art.

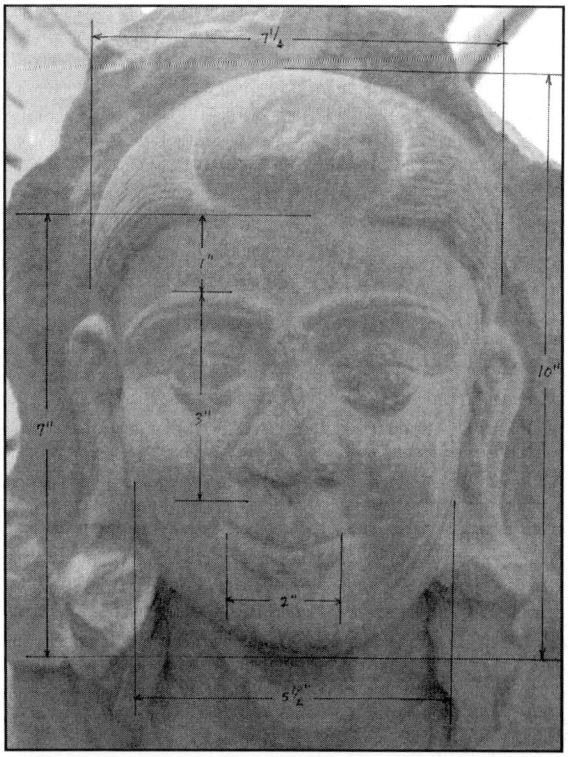

Fig. 15.17. Face of the Kansas City Nāginī, Fig. 15.3, with measurements. Photograph courtesy The Nelson-Atkins Museum of Art.

It is no exaggeration to say that the facial dimensions of the three sculptures, made by hand in the 1st century AD, are remarkably close. In most of the categories, the ND Nāginī's head is larger than the others by a small degree, and the Tokyo Nāginī's head is smaller, also not by much. In sum, the difference in facial measurements is sufficiently slight to suggest that the three sculptures, found together, were made to belong together. However, judging from the differences and overall facial expressions, it seems likely that more than one carver worked on the statues. I do believe we have just what we might expect when three separate statues are hand-carved as a set during the 1st century AD, namely slight variations due to different hands, and/or the impossibility of exact duplication even by the same hand.

2. Scaled frontal, full-length photographs of the Nāginīs

The comparative scaled imagery of the Nāginīs (Fig. 15.18), is a composite constructed according to specific steps. Ms. Mary Sorrentino, a graphic designer affiliated with the University of Memphis, scanned into her computer three slides of the three Nāginīs taken by Jamison Miller during the exhibition period. Mr. Miller had made a special set of slides on which he placed a center vertical

Fig. 15.18. Comparative Scaled Image of the Three Nāginīs. Photograph by Mary Sorrentino.

line running the entire length of the figure. (Presumably, Mr. Miller was guided by the belly button to determine the center, and he probably extrapolated coordinates for the ND Nāginī to determine the position of its belly button, now missing.) Next, Ms. Sorrentino scanned in the printouts of the three measured faces. She reduced and overlaid each printout until it coordinated with the face of the matching full figure scanned in from the slide. This step insured that the three full-length figures adhere to the 'golden rule' of the accurately measured faces. A composite was then made of the three full-length Nāginī figures. These were lined up according to a secure horizontal reference point, namely the chin. A line was made by Ms. Sorrentino which connects all the Nāginīs' chins on the composite image. The other horizontal lines going through the composite image were established relative to the chin (horizontal) and the belly button (vertical) coordinates. Let us now read the results:

(a) closely correlated features: the chin, necklace (note outer end of collier), hips, Mont of Venus, left fist, placement of girdle, and center drapery fold (close for Tokyo and KC Nāginīs).

(b) fairly closely correlated features: eyes, barrel-shaped bead on long necklace, girdle tie on right thigh, knee cap (fairly close in ND and KC statues);
(c) not closely correlated features: drapery swag circling right leg, start of leg anklets, extended width of left arm (i.e., distance from center vertical line to point inside left arm), perhaps the breasts, and probably the nose.

There are numerous closely correlated features; when these are added to the fairly closely correlated features, the tally far exceeds the number of features that do not correlate closely. The tally of correlated features together with the similarity of facial measurements contribute significant information pertinent to the question of authenticity.

The significant contribution made by the scaled photographs relates to the proportions of the ND Nāginī as compared to the other two Nāginīs. The ND Nāginī is broken in the middle of the drapery swag around the right leg and below the knee of the left leg; the other two sculptures continue down to the anklets. On the composite image, the three Nāginīs line up rather well to the upper thighs; it is around the knee area that variations occur. The kneecaps of the Tokyo Nāginī are considerably higher that those of the ND and KC Nāginīs (indeed, the latter two have been noted as being fairly closely correlated features). Accordingly, the supposition is that the ND Nāginī is not very much taller than the KC Nāginī. Corroborating this supposition is the fact that the seven facial features of the ND Nāginī never exceed by more than 1 1/2" those of the other Nāginīs.

The scaled photographs lend further support to the hypothesis that the ancient sculptor(s) intended to create a set of visually similar statues.

STYLISTIC ANALYSIS

The stylistic analysis is undertaken to determine the date and provenance of the Nāginī statues. The analysis is based on a comparison between the three statues and other pieces of assured authenticity. As such, the ensuing comparisons can also be read as additional evidence relating to the Nāginīs' authenticity. The main features to be compared are the face, posture, kneecaps and hairstyle.

The three Nāginīs share pronounced facial features even though their expressions are subtly different due to the slight variations in facial proportions described above. The head of the well-known 'Bodhisattva' statue, from Sārnāth, dedicated by Friar Bala in the year 3 of Kaniṣka's reign has a face similar in structure and expression to the faces of the ND and KC Nāginīs. Probably made in Mathurā the statue may be dated to the first quarter of the second century AD. It serves here as the *terminus ad quem* for the Nāginīs' facial type. The head serving as the *terminus a quo* belongs to the female divinity standing in the center of the Amohini Āyavati (or Āyāgapaṭa) found at Kaṅkālī Ṭīlā, Mathurā (State Museum, Lucknow J1; Fig. 15.19). Both her face, stance, body type and modelling quite

Fig. 15.19. Amohini Āyavati from Kaṅkālī-Ṭīlā, Mathurā. *c.* 14 AD. State Museum, Lucknow (Acc. No. J 1). Photograph after Vincent A. Smith, *The Jain Stūpa and other Antiquities of Mathurā.* (Allahabad, 1901). Pl. XIV.

anticipate the Nāginīs. The Amohini Āyavati is inscribed in the 42nd, or in the 72nd, year of Mahākṣatrapa Śoḍāsa. The number seems to be a dynastic year, but its reading is under debate. Many favor reading the year '72',[28] although '42' is maintained by others. Her dates, accordingly, vary between 14/15 BC or 15 AD if allied to the Vikrama era; but the latter part of the first century AD is also possibly based on another dynastic reckoning (favored by H. Falk; personal communication 2/23/06). The Yakṣī from Akrur (Mathura Museum No. F 6, Fig. 15.20), also resembles the female divinity on the Amohini tablet. In a study surveying a particular hairstyle also found on the Nāginīs, the Akrur Yakṣī has been placed between the late first century BC and the early first century AD. When first analyzed, this hairstyle was termed *coque ou bouffant de chevelure.*[29] In sum, comparative indicators relating to facial structure and features tend to place our Nāginīs in the Mathurā region between *c.* the mid first century AD to early second century AD.

All the above pieces used for comparison also share the posture of the three Nāginīs. Among females in our sample, it is immediately apparent how close the stance of the Akrur Yakṣī and the Amohini tablet divinity is to that of the Nāginīs. But for their smaller waists, the body proportions of these two, especially the globular breasts and full hips, are remarkably similar to the Snake Goddesses. The Akrur Yakṣī also has a long necklace, a cloth ribbon above the beaded girdle tied like that of the Nāginīs, and, also like the three Nāginīs, flat yet finished carving on the reverse. Another early example of a female with this posture is the Goddess Vasudhārā on a first century AD relief from Bajna (near to Bhūteśvar, Mathurā; Mathura Museum No. 18.1411).[30] Fortunately, the right hand of all the abovementioned three females is still intact. Raised at the elbow, the Amohini divinity makes the *abhaya-mudrā* gesture. But the hand of Vasudhārā and the Akrur Yakṣī is turned inward. This may be the way the Nāginīs held the right arm, especially since proof of appropriateness of this inward raised gesture for

Nāginīs comes from a small, near contemporaneous Nāginī recovered at Sonkh, Mathurā District.[31]

It may be well to pause a moment and reflect just how unusual this posture is for pre-Kuṣāṇa and early Kuṣāṇa females. No intact female sculpture from the Sonkh Apsidal Temple No. 2, the Snake temple, assumes this hieratic standing pose, nor does any female depicted on the Mathurā railing pillars found at Sanghol.[32] A completely frontal female, whose pudendum is covered and who exhibits no, or only the slightest, movement in the body, is a rare phenomenon in this early period. One example, albeit a seated example, is the Nāga Queen on the middle lintel of the bottom architrave of the Sonkh Apsidal Temple No. 2. This Nāginī sits on the right side of her consort, exhibiting a more balanced posture than he, and she has drapery covering her pudendum (see Härtel, *Sonkh*, p. 420, No. 4.

Another feature which bespeaks of an early dating is the peanut-shaped kneecap so prominently carved on the KC Nāginī. Actually, the Tokyo Nāginī displays the bulges, too. A less prominent, more natural kneecap appears on the right knee of ND Nāginī. This bone, which becomes more rounded and integrated on the legs of some of the Sanghol maidens,[33] may, when exaggerated as a peanut-shaped kneecap, be an indicator of the pre-Kuṣāṇa period. The best comparative example is found on the pre-Kuṣāṇa monumental Tree Goddess in the Los Angeles County Museum of Art (No. M 86.21; Fig. 15.21).

Fig. 15.20. The Akrur Yakṣī. Mathurā. Between late 1st century BC – early 1st century AD. Mathurā Museum (Acc. No. F 6). Photograph courtesy The Government Museum, Mathurā.

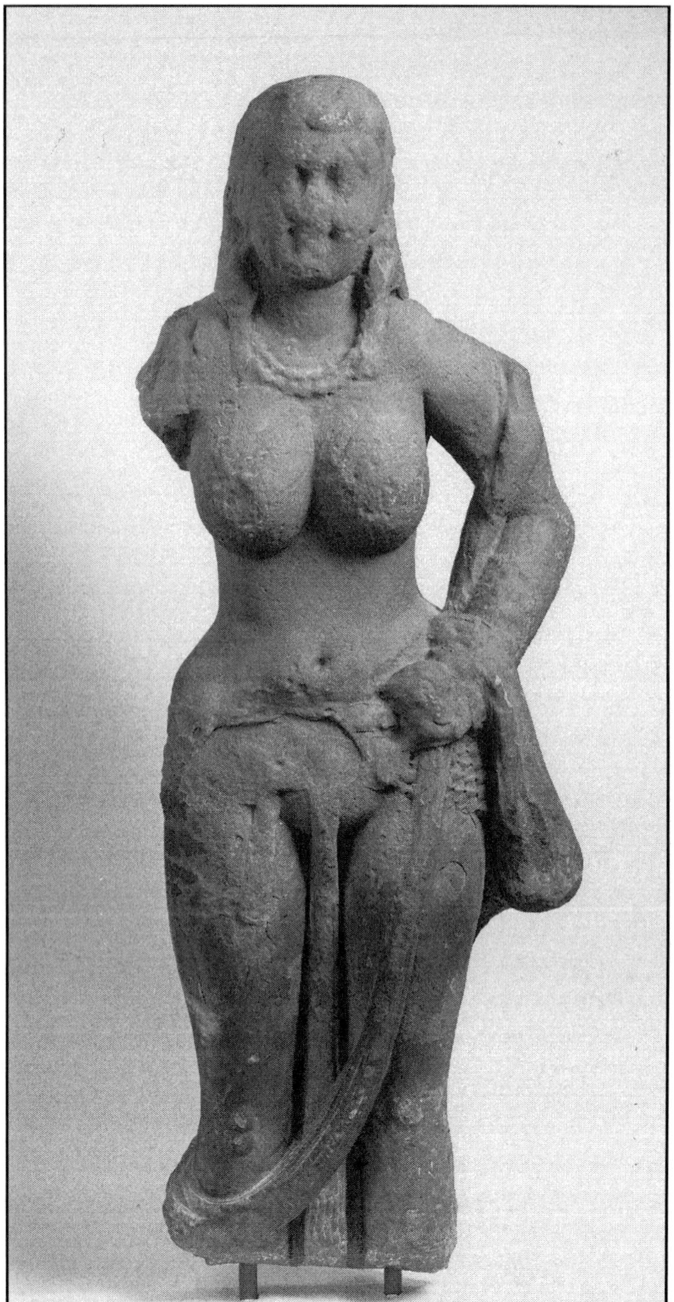

Fig. 15.21. Tree Goddess, Uttar Pradesh, Mathurā. 1st century AD. Los Angeles County Museum of Art (M 86.21), Purchased with funds provided by Mr. and Mrs. Allan C. Balch. Photograph copyright 2004 Museum Associates/LACMA.

The figure appears to be made in Mathurā, although the Museum has no record of its find place. The treatment of her legs, particularly the broad thighs and bulging kneecaps, are astonishingly like those of our Nāginīs. The Tree Goddess has been assigned to the first century AD.[34] A few decades later, the same bulging kneecap can be noticed on the reverse of the middle architrave of the Sonkh Apsidal Nāga Temple: the playful Nāga sprite who places his foot into the jaws of the *makara* shows the same convention at the knee.[35]

Regarding the question of dating, it is noteworthy that several stylistic comparisons can be made between our Nāginīs and sculptures connected to the excavated Sonkh Nāga Temple. Since the Temple can be fairly accurately dated between the third quarter of the first century AD and the beginning of the second century, the implication is that the Nāginīs also fit into this time frame. The likelihood of the Nāginīs being made in Mathurā is also advanced; thereby their authenticity continues to be affirmed.

The hairstyle of the Nāginīs can be placed between the first and beginning of the second ceutury AD. Following the distinctions Morris attributes to the bouffant hairstyle, the bun and side sections of the three Nāginīs conform more to the way the hairstyle is depicted on sculptures "that range approximately between the first century AD and the second century AD..."[36] In a somewhat earlier depiction of this bouffant style, the bun is not only more raised, but also wider, stretching almost across the whole forehead. In this grouping, Morris places the divinity on the Amohini Āyavati and the Akrur Yakṣī. While I am not entirely convinced that these variations can always be used as discrete dating tools,[37] they do seem to work for our Nāginīs. A first century AD date seems to be warranted. Perhaps the Nāginīs date several decades after the Akrur Yakṣī and the Amohini relief; approaching more closely the time of the Sonkh sculptures. I therefore propose to place the Nāginīs around the third quarter of the first century AD.[38]

The side strands of hair are not treated in the same manner on all three Nāginīs and this difference made me review the issue of provenance. In the KC and ND sculptures, the strands, delineated by incised lines, are combed straight back behind the ears. The Tokyo Nāginī does not have all the strands pulled back; a mass of strands escapes to curl unto both cheeks. Side curls are not frequent in pre-Kuṣāṇa art from Mathurā, but they do occur. The Akrur Yakṣī has side strands which are not curled. A large, first century AD female of red sandstone looks like the KC Nāginī and has side curls (Mathura Museum No. F5). The Museum's label states that the provenance of No. F5 is Vrindavan, Mathura District. This information posits the appearance of the side curl within the Mathurā circle during pre-to-early Kuṣāṇa times; it therefore helps to anchor all the Nāginīs to Mathurā,[39] and the possibility that the Snake Goddesses were made in Mathurā and transported to Nandan.

The absence of stone at Nandan makes importation all the more probable. As mentioned earlier, no rock or stone rubble was seen in the village during my site visit in 2000. There was no stone rubble in the construction of village houses, nor was red sand hauled out of the Jumna during my visit, only grey sand. Apparently, no red sandstone is to be found in the river valley below the site. At minimum, the red sandstone used to carve the Nāginīs must have come from outside Nandan.

Sandstone quarries were located reasonably close to Mathurā.[40] This factor plus the characteristic Mathurā style reflected in the carving of the Nāginīs convince me that the Snake Goddesses were made in Mathurā and shipped, probably via the Jumna River, to Nandan. The riverine route between Delhi and Agra was navigable throughout the year, facilitating commerce and contact between Mathurā and Nandan. Nandan seems to have had sufficient resources to make a stop worthwhile. In ancient times, wealthy persons living there patronized the Mathurā School of Art. We know that a huge Kuṣāṇa image of Bhagavān Nārāyaṇa (Mathurā Museum No. 77.4),[41] was exported from Mathurā to Nandan. The patrons of Nandan should have paid handsomely to cover the cost of shipping a sandstone icon of Nārāyaṇa that was over 8′ tall.

WORSHIP OF NĀGINĪS

Although Snake Goddesses are folk deities, indications are that the Nāginīs were worshipped, at Nandan, as major deities, not as minor godlings.

First, their importance is underscored by their size. In the several centuries around the Christian era, a life-size or greater than life-size statue represents a deity of superior rank. Only a few divinities are conceived as colossi in early Indian art, and most of these are male. A large statue of a goddess is rare indeed. The aforementioned pre-Kuṣāṇa Tree Goddess in the Los Angeles County Museum of Art is one such rarity. Thus, in the first century AD, a *set* of life-size Nāginīs should have signified an unusual gathering of female power.

Did the Nandan Nāginīs share power with a Nāgarāja? Are we to imagine that originally one or several Nāgarājas stood with the Nāginīs? Such couples do exist in pre-Kuṣāṇa, Kuṣāṇa and Gupta times,[42] but I do not believe that our Nāginīs formed part of such couples. For one, no Nāgarāja has been associated with the site. Second, and most noteworthy, the iconography of the Nāginīs bespeaks of their own pre-eminence.

The number of snake heads in the hoods of the Nāginīs marks their superior cult status. All three Nāginīs exhibit the remains of nine or more snake heads in the hood. This is the highest number yet to be associated with either a Nāga's or a Nāginī's snakehood. The Tokyo Nāginī shows the remains of a nine-headed hood (Fig. 15.8). The KC Nāginī also appears to have a nine-headed snakehood (Fig. 15.7). To be sure, broken edges and faintness of some lines in both statues necessitate gauging and guestimating distances between incised lines demarcating separate hoods. The ND Nāginī seems to have nine or more snake heads in her hood (Fig. 15.5). A relief from the Sonkh Nāga Temple clearly establishes a connection between the number of snake heads in a hood and the rank of the associated figure. The so-called Court Scene (see p. 420, No. 4) in H. Härtel's *Sonkh*, indicates that minor Nāgas can be easily differentiated from major ones by the lesser number of snake heads in their hoods. The Nāga Queen and the Nāgarāja both are crowned with a seven-headed snakehood while the attendants have one head in theirs. The count of heads in the hoods of the Nandan Nāginīs indicates their high status. Interestingly, a nine-headed hood is seen on another Nāginī head made in Mathurā and dating to the Kuṣāṇa period.[43]

The third iconographic feature to designate the Nāginīs as major cult deities is the way their bodies are represented. It is far more common in early Indian art to render the female body in *contrapposto* than to represent it in the stiff, straight, and frontal manner of the Nāginīs. It may be argued that the females compared to the Nāginīs, namely the female on the Amohini tablet, the Akrur Yakṣī, and Vasudhārā also have this posture and that they are not major deities in the aforementioned images. The difference, however, between the females in those images and the Nāginīs is that the latter are a free-standing, life-size set and these converging features assure their superior status. Lest it be speculated that the Nāginīs need not have constituted a set and could have been erected at separate points in Nandan, it ought to be remembered that early Mathurā art was not adverse to creating sets, if beliefs so mandated it. For example, Lokapālas, or

Guardians of the Four Cardinal Directions, are depicted by this date. Literary evidence shows that they are popular godlings in the several centuries around the Christian era.[44] In the art of Mathurā, they are shown as four identical figures standing in horizontal alignment on small stone and terracotta panels.[45] In the Buddhist art of Gandhāra, they occur in narrative reliefs, again as identically conceived personages.[46]

The Nandan Nāginīs are not, it would appear, allied to man's preoccupation with poisonous snakes, fear of snake bites, or other destructive aspects of snakes. Magical incantations to safeguard against harmful snakes are found in Vedic texts,[47] but this does not seem to be the context from which the Nāginīs' imagery and conceptualization arose.

The Nandan Nāginīs, like the deities of the Sonkh Nāga Temple, are a paean to a wondrous realm filled with enchanting beings whose human bodies sport but the slightest reference to their true serpentine nature.[48] A glimpse into this fantastic world is provided in some Vedic and Buddhist literature, the latter containing lore on the beauty of serpent maidens.[49] A story related by Xuanzang about 'The Śākya Youth who married a Snake Maiden...' alludes not only to the Nāginī's beauty but also to the reason she lost her human form.[50] Her previous bad deeds caused her to be reborn as a Snake Maiden. A Śākya Youth uses all of his accrued religious merit to restore her human body. He becomes a king and they marry, although he is unaware that her human body could not be fully restored. At night, as she sleeps, a nine-headed snakehood sprouts from her head. Could this detail lead us towards an understanding of the nine-headed hoods belonging to the Nandan Nāginīs? Is this number a sign of a Nāginī's beauty, dignity, and majesty?

The Nandan Nāginīs come from a region in north India where Nāga worship was particularly prevalent. The cult flourished in an area around Mathurā, as well as at sites to the south in the Sāñcī, Vidiśā, and Allahabad[51] areas, and at sites to the east in Bihar[52] and Orissa.[53] Perhaps the reason for the cult's prevalence in this broad stretch, comprising both the heartland of Brahmanism, the heterodoxies, and tribal regions, is that the Nāga Cult, obviously a folk cult, was able to coexist and even penetrate the other religions in these lands.[54] So for example, a Nāga desiring to learn the *dhamma* and free himself of his serpent status takes the form of a Brahman youth to join the order of monks.[55] Or, a later Buddhist text refers to a Nāgarāja who belongs to the Brahman caste.[56] Significant for our interest in Nāginī worship in the Gangetic Valley is the *Mahābhārata's* citation of a *tīrtha,* or holy place of pilgrimage, named Sarpadevī (Serpent Goddess).[57] The passage suggests that Sarpadevī is a pilgrimage center located between the Jumna and Ganges Rivers, thus in the greater territory that includes Nandan. Sarpadevī is not an anomaly; a look at Kane's list of *tīrthas* contains about ten sacred places in this northern part of India that seem to be connected with snakes.[58]

A remarkable description of a sacrificial session in the *Pañcaviṁśa Brāhmaṇa* gives further indication of the rapprochement between Nāga worship and the Brahmanic mainstream.[59] The passage (XXV. 15) describes a *sattra* in which some of the officiating ritual specialists are Nāgas. The rite, also noted in the *Baudhāyana Śrauta Sūtra* (17.18), and in the *Baudhāyana Gṛhya Sūtra* (3.10), is performed so that nāgas can conquer death, that is, so that they can attain immortality. Some of the Gṛhya Sūtras also contain accounts of the Sarpabali ritual, an annual rite lasting four months; the Sarpabali seems to have a twofold aim, namely to ward off snakes in the rainy season, and to honour divine serpents.[60]

An inscribed Mathurā image from the time of Kaniṣka II is an actual depiction of Nāga and Nāginī worship (Mathura Museum Nos. 210–11). The image, a sandstone relief from Rāl Bhaḍār, shows a row of devotees: five males, five females and two children. They pay homage to a group of Nāgas; the large Nāga is flanked by two shorter Nāginīs. They are all depicted as humans but with the addition of snakehoods; the male has a seven-headed hood, the females' hoods contain three. At the bottom of the relief is an inscription that reads, "...a tank and a garden (were caused to be made) for the holy Nāga Bhumo (as) the donation of...".[61] This relief offers two points important for the interpretation of the Nandan set. First, here is an example where snake deities are worshipped as a group. Although the literature attests to this sort of worship (see below), it can often be overlooked if an uncritical eye is cast on the pre-Kuṣāṇa and Kuṣāṇa sculptural remains. During these ages, single representations of Nāgas or Nāginīs undoubtedly predominate, but not always as this example of a group shows. (The occasional example of a Nāga and Nāginī couple has already been mentioned.) Second, the inscription specifies that the place of worship is outdoors, near a body of water. An outdoor setting by a tank is mentioned in two other Kuṣāṇa inscriptions (one from Mathurā, one from Gandhāra) associated with snakes.[62] And, of course, the Sonkh Nāga Temple (Apsidal Temple No. 2) supports such a linkage for it seems to have originally stood by the banks of a river.[63] The evidence from the Rāl Bhaḍār image can be applied to the Nandan images, supporting as it does the notion that a group, or a set of Nāginīs, is not conceptually improbable. Furthermore, their probable find place near to the Jumna river, according to the Nandan villagers, is precisely where one would expect to find them.

Establishment of Snake deities near water may not be characteristic of the Nandan's Snake images alone; the connection exists farther south in the area of Sāñcī. A recent study has found that of the sixteen groups of Nāga sculptures dating between the 2nd century BC and the 10th century AD whose provenance is known, "seven are associated with irrigation reservoirs, five with village tanks and four with rivers or streams."[64]

From Gandhāra to Sāñcī, then, with Mathurā in between, we have direct evidence that images of Nāgas and presumably Nāginīs were formally erected close to a temple, a garden, and/or a body of water. Some of these icons are large, masterfully carved and engraved with an inscription. They should have been costly to erect, and someone or some group should have derived considerable benefits in so doing. It is hard to imagine a more sophisticated type of 'folk cult'. Even so, the Nāga Cult in Mathurā's environs with its Nāga Temple and superbly crafted Nāga sculptures does not seem to have left texts or ritual manuals. There is, to the best of my knowledge, no direct, relevant documentation regarding the manner in which pre-Kuṣāṇa Nāginīs would have been set up and the type of ritual worship such icons may have received. The only approach I can propose is to peruse the texts of religions which incorporated Nāga/Nāginī worship, thereby determining if rituals are described in ways that could reflect ancient modes of practice.

Fortunately, both the Hindu and Buddhist textual traditions contain a few useful descriptions, albeit in later works. The *Rauravāgama,* a south Indian Śaivite ritual text probably dating to the 7th century AD presents detailed descriptions in two chapters (38 and 57), on the proper rituals to install Nāga images, and the fruits to be gained from nāga worship.[65] Chapter 38 describes the way the Nāgarāja image should look; the actions to be taken to 'open the eyes of the image'; where it should be placed, and the type of mantras and oblations that should be offered to it. The latter appear to be taken from the Śaivite tantric realm. The tendency to place Nāga images in formal settings, as noted in the ancient Mathurā inscriptions, continues here. The chapter states that the image is installed on an altar situated in the center of a pavillion, fronting the temple which is built to specific dimensions. Interestingly, the entire rite is undertaken to rid a person of any injuries coming from snakes. In other words, there is an intermingling between the theriomorphic and anthropomorphic nature and power of Nāgas. The description of the installation of a Nāga image in Chapter 57 is much longer and more complex. Even though the main image to be installed in Chapter 57 seems to be a theriomorphic icon of a serpent, features of this rite may help in contextualizing the Nandan Nāginīs. Of considerable interest is that this ritual reflects a remarkable number of Vedic tendencies; it has thus absorbed some of the religious atmosphere predominant in ancient Mathurā, a stronghold of Brahmanism, that emphasized Vedic culture and religious practices. In the *Rauravāgama* rite, the officiating priests are Brahmans; recitations are from the Vedas or recall Vedic models (i.e., a Nāgagāyatrī is recited), and the appropriate places where an image can be installed is highly reminiscent of Brahmanic cultural traits. It may be well to think of the pre-Kuṣāṇa Brahmanic environment in the Gangetic Valley as I quote this section of Chapter 57 from the *Rauravāgama:*

> Le sage doit faire l'installation de Mahānāga dans un temple. Il faut construire un temple qui lui est propre ou bien il faut faire l'installation de Nāga dans un temple de Śiva (ou) de Viṣṇu, ou au bord d'une rivière ou d'un étang ou dans un lieu sacré *(tīrtha)* ou bien encore dans des endroits purs, ou encore à proximité d'un banyan.[66]

In citing that the placement of a Mahānāga (i.e. Great Nāga) image may be near a river, or a tank, or a sacred place, or near pure places, or near a banyan tree, this 7th century text recalls that the location of the Rāl Bhaḍār image (see above) and the huge Nāgarāja of Chargaon in Mathurā District are by tanks of water (see also Footnote 62). Clearly, images of snake deities in and around Mathurā, in the Sāñcī area (as noted above), and presumably in southern India (if we are guided by the *Rauravāgama),* from pre-Kuṣāṇa, to Kuṣāṇa, to Gupta times and beyond, could be set up outdoors near water or trees, or inside a temple.

The Nandan fragment found at the site in 2000 reveals which of these options—outdoors or indoors—applies to the Nāginī set. The fragment of a Nāginī's feet rests on a rectangular base, beneath which appears a roughly hewn and tapered tang (Fig. 15.13). It is evident that the tang was the part stuck into the earth, and that the part above the ground started with the rectangular base. Apparently, the Nāginīs stood outdoors on a base supported by a tang. Twilley's work on the KC Nāginī confirms this. He found surface features on the sandstone that are the natural result of the stone's weathering above ground and its exposure to the elements over long periods of time.[67] Other features that he found on the KC Nāginī would indicate that the sculpture may have been buried at some point.[68] Presupposing that the fragment discovered at Nandan implies that all the Nandan Nāginīs would have terminated in a tang, it can only be assumed that initially the tang secured each Goddess firmly into the ground. This technique was commonly used to erect images outdoors; it can be noticed in both Kuṣāṇa sectarian and folk deities. For example, a Maheśa in the University Museum, Philadelphia, rests on a tang,[69] as does the huge (2 meter 40), Chargaon Nāgarāja (Fig. 15.22; Mathurā Museum No. C 13). So too was Bhikṣu Bala's 'Bodhisattva' image installed outdoors along a *caṅkrama,* or promenade taken by the Buddha. To these we may now add the Nāgas from the Sāñcī region which stood out-of-outdoors. The strong indication is that the Nandan Nāginīs would also have stood outdoors and probably near to a source of water, be it either the Jumna, or perhaps the large depression (in the area where the villagers placed the Nāginīs) which may originally have been a tank of water. Did trees shelter them? Did a garden exist in the vicinity? Today there are no clues to answer such specific questions.

What is likely, when the information from the surface treatment of the KC Nāginī and the tang at the bottom of the Nandan fragment are combined with known locations of other ancient Nāga sculptures is that the Nāginīs were probably worshipped outdoors at Nandan.

CONCLUSION: CONTEXTUALIZING THE NANDAN NĀGINĪS

At the outset, I listed four charateristics that render the Nandan Nāginīs unique. To repeat, the Nandan Nāginīs are an anomaly because they represent a 1st century AD set of life-size Snake Goddesses, that is, a group of monumental deities

Fig. 15.22. Nāgarāja from Chargaon, deinstalled in 2000 and lying on the Museum's floor. Kuṣāṇa Period. The Government Museum, Mathura (Acc. No. C 13). Author's photograph.

from the popular religious sphere. Having discussed their probable authenticity, dating, their status as major divinities, and the likelihood of their worship outdoors near water, it remains to show that this unique set is not a cultural anomaly, since the four characteristics I listed can be credibly anticipated and applied to Nāginīs.

The rarity of life-size female images in early art has already been noted, and the pre-Kuṣāṇa LACMA Tree Goddess has already been mentioned as belonging to this special category; the Mathurā Tree Goddess, though broken somewhat below the knees stands 6 feet, 3 inches. Now, however, is the time to indicate that a life-size Nāginī from Mathurā, earlier than either the Tree Goddes or the Nandan Serpent maidens, has come to light. Dating between the 2nd–1st century BC, a red sandstone Nāginī housed in the National Museum, New Delhi (Acc. No. 72.71) measures 135 X 43 X 37 cms., though her feet are missing.[70] Much of the carving is effaced, but it is still possible to discern that the Nāginī stands straight, faces forward, has no bends in the body, and that the pleating of her lower garment covers the pudendum. She represents therefore *one* of the earliest monumental Snake Goddesses known to date. Just recently another, equally ancient Nāginī probably from Sāñcī has been published (No. P.2004.02 in the Norton Simon Museum).[71] The Sāñcī Snake Goddess shares the posture, the monumentality (57 in./144.8 cm), and modestly draped pleating of the Mathurā Goddess. These are among the earliest colossi, but not *the* earliest female colossus if the Dīdārgañj *caurī*-bearer is placed into the Mauryan period, as is my inclination. The Nandan Nāginī set therefore does have precedents. Though these early Nāginīs and the

Nandan Nāginīs, together with the Tree Goddess are rareties, they exemplify a pattern. It cannot go unnoticed that the examples of early monumental female sculptures[72] represent folk deities—a Tree Goddess, Snake Goddesses—as well as the Dīdārgañj *caurī*-bearer who probably belongs to the secular realm.[73] The reason is not hard to find. India's sculptural tradition begins with stone carvings representing official art and images worshipped by the folk. Worship of deities representing powers in nature (such as rain, rivers, trees, mountains, caves, the ocean, etc.) as well as those causing fertility, strength, well-being, victory dominion, etc. probably existed from prehistoric times onward; the worship continued along with, and influenced, later sectarian (and secular) imagery. Indeed, when the need for devotional icons arose, among the first to become concretized were the folk deities. The Nāga Cult fits this paradigm. Worship of Nāgas, maintains V.S. Agrawala "was there [in India] even prior to Yakṣa worship."[74]

Though the discovery of a set of life-size Nāginīs may be surprising to some, those acquainted with Vedic, Hindu and Buddhist literature will not find the appearance of such a set unusual. Quite a number of religious texts in these traditions cite lists of Nāga groups.[75] *Atharva Veda* (*AV*) hymns mention groups of four[76] or six snakes, and these may be connected with the directions in the sky.[77] Vogel notes that the group of six in *AV* 3.27 is regarded as *dikpālas* prior to the standard four or eight *lokapālas* (i.e., both terms referring to guardians of the directions, in the sky and on earth) in later Hindu mythology.[78] The *Mahābhārata* (*MhBh.*) contains several long lists of Nāgas of which the following are but a sampling: *MhBh.* 1.31.1 ff. lists seventy-six names as "the chief Nāgas". Five Nāga groups comprising eighty-seven separate names are listed in *MhBh.* 1.52; and sixty-seven Nāgas are enumerated in *MhBh.* 5.101.8 ff. The Purāṇas also give long lists; forty-one Nāgas are given in *Vāyu Purāṇa* 2.8.66–71; fifteen names occur in *Bhāgavata Purāṇa* 5.24.29–31; and eight Nāgas are listed in the *Agni Purāṇa* (Chapter 294 If). A list of groups of Nāgas in Buddhist literature includes the *Saddharmapuṇḍarīka* which cites the names of eight Nāgarājas;[79] eighty Nāgarājas and fifty-five common Nāgas are given in the *Mahāvyutpatti.* In addition, Witzel provides a list of Nepalese Nāgas together with a multitude of Nāga names listed in the Kashmiri *Nīlamata Purāṇa.* A quick overview of all the material collected by Witzel is presented here mainly to show that it is a common pan-Indic phenomenon to group Nāgas together. Also, it may be recalled that numerous human royal families traced their lineage to the union of a male and a beauteous Nāginī.[80]

A specific reference to a ritual sequence involving a group of Nāginī Powers occurs in the *Rauravāgama.* An ancillary ceremony performed during the rite on installation of a Nāga image (Chapter 57) is to the "huit jeunes filles commençant par Śakti et terminant par Śakti"[81] (Chapter 57, vss. 53–63). The names of the eight females recall serpentine connections: Kamalā, Utpalā, Padmā, Nāgakanyā, Śyamalā, Dehinī, Pādasarpā and Śeṣabālā. Contained within this ceremony is a meditation upon the cult of Nāgeśvarī. Just before this ceremony involving what may be termed as eight Nāginī Śaktis, a group of eight Nāgas receive homages. They form four pairs acting as door guardians disposed on the sides of the pavillion's portals which houses the main deities (see Chapter 57, vss. 39–52 and fn. 27 in Dagens et Barazer-Billoret, *Le Rauravāgama,* 380). The *Rauravāgama* ceremonies, in this paper, illustrate that it is not uncommon to worship Nāgas and Nāginīs in groups, and that it is usual for such groups to be positioned in some kind of pattern. Nāginīs occurring in certain Buddhist rituals are also placed in specific positions.[82] A ritual, preserved in a Tibetan source, can be helpful in contextualizing Nāgas of an earlier age, since it, too, has elements reminiscent of Vedic ceremonies. The ritual attributed to Śrī Dīpaṅkarabhadra requires the drawing of a circular *maṇḍala* wherein the action takes place.[83] Eight Nāgas and eight Nāginīs are made of barley flour and set within the sacred space; the wives of the eight Nāgas are placed at the outer rim of the *maṇḍala.* As for the Nāgas, four face in the cardinal directions and the others face the interstices. Additionally, four Nāgas are stationed at the four entrances to the *maṇḍala.* Again, the notion is reinforced that Nāga and Nāginī images, whether of flour or stone, are placed in the ritual arena according to specific patterns deemed ritually efficacious. Specific placement of Nāgas and Nāginīs is upheld in yet another Buddhist ritual also attributed to Śrī Dipaṅkarabhadra. Here, the ritual arena is a *maṇḍala* in the form of a lotus. On its open petals are placed the Nāgas, their wives, or Nāginīs, and their sons. One pattern that reoccurs in these descriptions is placement of the Nāgas as doorkeepers facing the quadrants. We are reminded of the set of guardians mentioned above, namely the Gods of the Four Directions. In the art of Gandhāra during the 5th–6th century AD, these Gods of the Four Directions assume the same positioning, that is, they face each of the quadrants.[84]

The close relationship between Nāgas, Nāginīs and sets of directional gods has surfaced several times in both the religious literature and the early art. This is an important point. Reference to a connection between snakes and the directions in *AV* 3.27 has already been mentioned. The *Śatapatha Brāhmaṇa* (1.2.5.17) delegates serpents *(sarpa)* to the West when allocating different classes of beings to the different quadrants. According to Witzel, "groups of Nāgas as *lokapālas* are also found in later literature, but, interestingly, with quite different names."[85] He cites fairly early texts: *Lalitavistara* (ed. Lefman, pp. 387–91) and the *Cullavagga* 5.6 85. The connection between Nāgas/Nāginīs and the directions in early religious art allows for a comparison between the depiction of snake deities and directional deities during similar periods. Like the Nandan Nāginīs, *lokapālas* are not distinguished from one another by iconographic details. Just as the Nandan Nāginīs stand in the rigid *samapāda* pose, so too do the *lokapālas.* And, of course, both groups belong to the category of 'folk cults'. *Lokapālas* are the only group of figures in early Indian art and literature known to me that have so many discreet characteristics overlapping with the Nāginī set. There are, to be sure, some important differences—*lokapālas* are minor deities carved standing in a row on small stone or terracotta panels, and only in the Gupta period do they face the four quarters; Nāginīs are major cult divinities individually carved for probable positioning into some spatial arrangement.

Theoretically, the same options are possible for the placement of the early Nāginīs as exist for the early *lokapālas*. The Nāginīs could have been positioned in some linear fashion along a water's edge. However, if we accept that there were originally four Nāginīs, then the possibility is strong that each one would have faced in one of the cardinal directions. The numerous connections between Nāgas/ Nāginīs and doorkeepers, guardians,[86] and Gods of the Four Directions lead me to conjecture that the four Nāginīs were set up so that each female faced a quadrant. Possibly even stronger confirmation for this disposition of the Nāginīs is that a Sonkh icon, which originally may have been the main icon of the Sonkh Nāga Temple, is a four-sided Nāga image showing identical Nāgarājas on the obverse and reverse.[87]

The Nandan Nāginīs, beauteous and powerful, may well have stood outdoors by some body of water; facing the four directions, they would have received the circumambulating worshippers desirous of the safety and fertility they believed that the Goddesses could bestow.

NOTES AND REFERENCES

1. For illustrations of both sculptures, see S.J. Czuma and R. Morris, *Kuṣāṇa Sculptures: Images from Early India*, (Cleveland, 1985); Plates 25 & 26. The authors propose that the two sculptures form a Nāga couple, which may be the case. See Endnote 42, for an earlier Nāga couple.
2. N.R. Banerjee wrote the note in *National Museum Bulletin* Nos. 4, 5 and 6 (1983), 71; Fig. 64. See also Late Dr. Shashi Prabha Asthana, *Mathurā Kalā* (A Catalogue of Mathura Sculptures in the National Museum), National Museum, (New Delhi, 1999), 55–56. An earlier, less informative mention of the sculpture is by B.N. Sharma, "A Nāginī Image from Nadan," *Oriental Art*, N.S. XXV (1979), 248–50. My thanks to Dr. R.D. Choudhury, Director, National Museum, for providing facilities to study the National Museum Nāginī.
3. This height is independently verified by John Twilley, Art Conservation Scientist, who accompanied me in 2000 to the National Museum to prepare for the exhibition of the Nāginī that year in Kansas City. Twilley noted: 4'10" is the surviving height from top of the head to top of the deteriorating wood base below; estimated length of statue inside base = 2 1/2" – 3 1/2". Estimated total surviving height is 5'1 1/2" +/– 1".
4. Asthana 1999, 56.
5. The story in *Mahāvagga* 1.63, to which Professor O.v. Hinüber drew my attention, implies that Nāgas look like humans except in certain situations. Also in the Vedic snake sacrifice *(sarpasattra)*, kings and princes of the snakes in human form officiated as priests (according to *Baudh. ŚS* 17, 18); cf. *Pañcaviṃśa-Brāhmaṇa 25.15* and fn. 1, p. 641 in W. Caland, *Pañcaviṃśa-Brāhmaṇa*, Delhi, 1931.
6. As measured in Tokyo by Twilley in 2000; 65 3/4" as measured in KC.

7. Twilley and I could determine by counting the incised lines, that the hood probably had nine heads, but certainly more than seven. Patterned hairnets occasionally can be noticed on Mathurā females. See Mathura Museum No. 36.2665, a Nāginī of the Gupta Period.
8. Both these figures even share the same sort of casually incised arrows on the cloth espied above the girdle, best seen in the back.
9. See Doris Meth Srinivasan, with Lore Sander, "Newly Discovered Inscribed Mathurā Sculptures of Probable Doorkeepers, Dating to the Kṣatrapa Period", *Archives of Asian Art* XLIII (1990), Figs. 1A & 3A.
10. Asthana 1999, 56.
11. Banerjee 1983, 71.
12. This is, of course, the stone's thinnest cross section, where it is easiest to cut and snap, thereby facilitating transport.
13. This information comes from notes I took of a conversation I had with René Russek in February 1996.
14. My discussion with Mr. Frei took place in Zürich in 2002. I wish to thank Mr. Frei for sharing his knowledge of the situation with me.
15. My thanks to the Rossis and to Mr. T. Kaku, Taiyo Ltd. for assistance in gathering this information.
16. The photograph and translation were passed on to me by Mr. T. Kaku, via the Rossis. Their help is gratefully acknowledged.
17. At the time, I was Curator of South and Southeast Asian Art at The Nelson and this sculpture was in my charge.
18. Twilley 1998 (unpublished report), 8.
19. Twilley 1998, 1.
20. Twilley 1998, 7.
21. Twilley 1998, 7.
22. Note that what is now seen as one worn form may have originally been differentiated by distinctly, modeled surfaces. Today's worn circle was probably differentiated into drapery and anklet forms. It must be remembered that the Nandan fragment has been lying in the village for a very long time with children and animals milling around it, and without anyone particularly concerned about its preservation.
23. E-mail I received from Twilley on Nov. 16, 2000, on the subject of Nanden [*sic*] Notes.
24. For this phase of the work, I wish to thank Professor Robert Lewis, Art Department at the University of Memphis, and also Ms. Mary Sorrentino, graphic designer.
25. I wish to acknowledge the assistance I received from this Museum in supporting the exhibition of these sculptures.
26. I am thankful for the efforts of Ms. Elisabeth Batchelor, Head of Conservation, and Paul Benson in the same department.
27. E-mail, dated February 15, 2001, from Jamison Miller to me.
28. At the beginning of the century, Lüders argued for the reading of 72. See H. Lüders, "Three early Brāhmī inscriptions", *Epigraphia Indica* 9, (1907–'08), 239–48. See J.E. van Lohuizen-de Leeuw, *The "Scythian" Period,* (Leiden, 1949), 239–48. See D.C. Sircar, "Paleographic and Epigraphical Evidence on Kaniṣka's date" in *Papers on the Date of Kaniṣka,* A.L. Basham (ed.), (Leiden, 1968), 278ff., and D.C. Sircar, *Select Inscriptions I,* 2nd ed. (Calcutta, 1965), 120. Cf. S.-R. Quintanilla, "Āyāgapaṭas: Characteristics, Symbolism and Chronology", *Artibus Asiae* LX.1, 79–137. See J. Rosenfield, *The Dynastic Arts of the Kushans* (Berkeley, 1967), 299, fn. 11; he prefers to read 42. For additional

discussions, see Doris Meth Srinivasan (ed.), *Mathurā, The Cultural Heritage* (New Delhi, 1989), 403, under 'Śoḍāsa'.

29. Rekha Morris, "Roman Hairstyle in Kuṣāṇa-Period Art of Mathurā?," *South Asian Archaeology* 1987 (Rome, 1990). 787ff. See also her "Didargañj Yakṣī and the 'Coque, ou Bouffant de Chevelure' Hairstyle: A Reassessment," *Archives of Asian Art* 42 (1989), 77–81. These two excellent studies, in which the author implies that French art historical premises have been made and perpetuated by those disregarding visual nuances, have not received sufficient attention. I favor dating the Akrur Yakṣī closer to the first century AD.
30. See N.P. Joshi, *Mathura Sculptures* (Mathura, 1966), Fig. 34.
31. The upper part of the Nāginī was recovered in an area adjoining the Sonkh Apsidal Temple No. 2 (the Nāga Temple). See Herbert Härtel, *Excavations at Sonkh, 2500 of a Town in Mathurā District* (Berlin, 1993), 431–32. On the basis of coin evidence, the author dates Phase 2 of the Temple to the pre-to-early Kuṣāṇa Period.
32. Härtel 1993, 430; S.P. Gupta, *Kuṣāṇa Sculptures from Sanghol* (New Delhi, 1985), 108; see Crossbar 42, side A. Note that the Sanghol pillars are contemporaneous with the Apsidal Temple, Phase 2.
33. Gupta 1985, Figs. 6.3, 14.8, 11, 12, 24.
34. P. Pal, *Indian Sculpture* I (Los Angeles, 1986), 176–77.
35. See Härtel 1993, 437, Fig. 2 Reverse.
36. Morris 1990, 797. Characteristic of this style is that the bun is rather small and lies flat, as do the side strands that are pulled back.
37. For example, on the basis of hairstyle Morris places the Cleveland Museum Nāginī (No. 68.104) and the National Museum Śrī Lakṣmi (Figs. 16 and 15, respectively, in her 1990 article), into the same group as the Amohinī divinity and the Akrur Yakṣī. She dates this group between the late first century BC and the early first century AD. I would place her Figs. 16 and 15 into the middle of the 2nd century AD and posterior to the Nandan Nāginīs made in Mathurā. The features of the Cleveland Nāginī that suggest a later date are: a more integrated transition from convex to concave forms, the slight slimming down of volumes, and softer modeling. Also these other specific features should be taken into account: the more elaborate hair decoration in the back; necklaces that are less stiff, more pliant and more responsive to the contours of the upper torso; an open left hand; and a less static frontal pose.
38. We are reminded that an Indian ivory statuette found in Pompeii and therefore of a date no later than 79 AD, and probably closer to the mid first century AD, has a hair ornament somewhat similar to that of the Nāginīs. The latest discussion relating to this well-known find is by Sanjyot Mehendale. "The Ivory Statuette from Bhokardan and its Connection to the Ivory Statuettes from Pompeii and Ter", *South Asian Archaeology 1991* (Stuttgart, 1993), 529–38.
39. Interestingly side locks, continue into the Kuṣāṇa Period. Note the female head, ostensibly made by the Mathurā School and displayed in the National Museum, New Delhi (No. 230).
40. Information on sandstone quarries feeding into Mathurā's ateliers comes from several discussions with Shri M.C. Joshi in New Delhi during January and February 2000.
41. See Doris Meth Srinivasan, "God as Brahmanical Ascetic. A Colossal Kushān Icon of the Mathurā School", *Journal of the Indian Society of Oriental Arts* n.s X (1978–79), 1ff. Further bibliography is in Doris Meth Srinivasan, *Many Heads, Arms and Eyes: Origin, Meaning and Form of Multiplicity in Indian Art,* (Leiden, New York, Köln, 1997), 243–45. See also chapter 7 in this volume.

42. A pre-Kuṣāṇa example is illustrated in *Indian Archaeology* 1972–73—*A Review*, 59 and Fig. A, being a Nāga and Nāginī from Gulgaon. One late Kuṣāṇa—early Gupta example from Mathurā is in Herbert Härtel, *Indische Sculpturen I* (Berlin, 1960), Fig. 20. Two separate Gupta sculptures comprising a Nāga/Nāginī pair, are in the Metropolitan Museum of Art (No. 1987.415.2). Of course, another possible Kuṣāṇa pair is the Cleveland/Brooklyn example mentioned at the outset of this paper.
43. See Rekha Morris, "Buddha Under a Ficus tree and two Sculptures from Mathura in the Sackler Museum, Harvard University", *Archives of Asian Art*, LI (1998–99) 82, Fig. 4. Morris dates this head of a Nāginī to the late 1st century AD. I would assign a date of late 2nd century AD.
44. See references in Corinna Wessels-Mevissen, *The Gods of the Directions in Ancient India. Origin and Early Development in Art and Literature* (Berlin, 2001), 21.
45. Wessels-Mevissen. 2001, 21, Figs. 4 and 5. Cf. N.P. Joshi, *Catalogue of the Brahmanical Sculptures in the State Museum, Lucknow* (Lucknow, 1972), 53–54.
46. E.g. see W. Zwalf, *Catalogue of Gandhāra Sculpture in the British Museum* (London, 1996), Vol. 2, Nos. 189–92. Sir John Marshall, *The Buddhist Art of Gandhāra* (Cambridge, 1960), Fig. 77.
47. E.g. *Atharva Veda Saṃhitā* 6.56.1; *Āśvalāyana Gṛhya Sūtra* II.1.9–10. Further references in unpublished ms. of Michael Witzel, *The Nāgas of Kashmir.* Section 5 on The Nature of the Nāgas; In the Vedas and in the Epics. I wish to thank the author for generously sharing this ms. with me.
48. Härtel (1993, 425–26) expresses this idea well in his outline on the development leading to the Nāga Cult in Mathurā.
49. See J. Ph. Vogel, *Indian Serpent-Lore* (Varanasi, Delhi, 1972), 134.
50. Vogel 1972, 123–25.
51. Joanna Williams, "New Nāga Images from the Sāñcī Area", *Oriental Art* 22 (1976), 174–79. Julia Shaw and John Sutcliffe, "Ancient irrigation works in the Sanchi area: an archaeological and hydrological investigation", *South Asian Studies 17* (2001), 55–75.
52. Note Dr. H.K. Prasad, "The Nāga-Cult in Bihar", *Journal of the Bihar Research Society* 46 (1960) 129–34.
53. See S.C. Panda, *Nāga Cult in Orissa*, (Delhi, 1986).
54. See Vogel 1972, for a good overview of the integration of the Nāga Cult into Hinduism and Buddhism. Also see Richard S. Cohen, "Nāga, Yakṣiṇī, Buddha: Local Deities and Local Buddhism at Ajanta", *History of Religion* 37.4 (1998), 360–400.
55. *Mahavāgga.* Vinaya Piṭaka No. 63.
56. Marcelle Lalou, "Le Culte des Naga et la Thérapeutique", *Journal Asiatique* (1938), 6, fn. 3.
57. 3 (33) 81.13–14. It should be noticed that M. Monier-Williams, *A Sanskrit-English Dictionary* (Oxford, 1960), 1184, cites 'Sarpadevī' as a name of a *Tīrtha*, as does Ved Kumari, *Nīlamata Purāṇa*, (Delhi, 1968–72) 183, and J.A.B. van Buitenen (*The Mahābhārata.* Books 2 & 3 [Chicago, 1975] 379, translates "Sarpadarvī" [*sic*], "the greatest ford of the Snakes."
58. P.V. Kane, *History of Dharmaśāstras* 4 (Poona, 1953), 783.
59. My thanks to Michael Witzel for pointing out this passage to me.
60. Āśvalāyana Gṛhya Sūtra II.1; Pāraskara Gṛhya Sūtra II.14.
61. H. Lüders, *Mathurā Inscriptions*, K.L. Janert (ed.) (Göttingen, 1961), # 102.
62. Lüders 1961, # 137. From Gandhāra we get a Kharoṣṭhī inscription stating that a tank was made for the worship of all snakes. See George Bühler, "A New Kharoṣṭhī Inscription from Swat", *Indian Antiquary* 25 (May, 1896), 141–42.

63. Härtel 1993, 413.
64. Shaw and Sutcliffe 2001, 68.
65. Chapter 52 in the same Āgama contains a ceremony to appease snakes in case a person has injured the young or the eggs of a snake. Here is another instance where the ritual has the animal, not the divinity in mind.
66. B. Dagens et M.-L. Barazer-Billoret, *Le Rauravāgama*, II, (Pondichéry, 2000), 375.
67. J. Twilley, 1998, 6. The author refers to a process of 'spalling' noticed on the stone. This process, he adds, does not occur during burial.
68. Twilley 1998, 11.
69. University of Pennsylvania, University Museum. Mathurā Maheśa.
70. See Asthana, 1999, Entry No. 59; 54.
71. Pratapaditya Pal, *Durga: Avenging Goddess Nuturing Mother (Pasadena,* 2005), Fig. 12.
72. The subject of monumental sculptures of male personages is not taken up here.
73. Please see my "The Mauryan Gaṇikā from Dīdārgañj (Paṭaliputra)" *East and West*, Vol. 55, Nos. 1–4 (December 2005), 345–62. Also in this volume.
74. *Ancient Indian Folk Cults* (Varanasi, 1970) 105. Agrawala insinuates the great antiquity of the cult by illustrating its near primordial nature from a passage in the *Śatapatha Brāhmaṇa* (3.6.2.2): "Surasā, the mother of the gods, was an epithet used for Mother Earth. Kadrū, the mother of the Nāgas, was also a term for Mother Earth."
75. The following discussion owes much to Witzel's ms., "The Nāgas of Kashmir". I also rely on Vogel, 1972.
76. See *AV* 6.56.2; 5.13.5–6; 10.4.13.
77. See *AV* 3. 26 and 27 for a group of six snakes. Cf. Taittirīya Saṃhitā 5.5.10.
78. Vogel 1972, 8–9.
79. Witzel cites the reference as "Kern, Bunyiu Nanjio, p. 4, line 11. Witzel notes that the Buddhist lists of Nāgas differ considerably from the Brahmanic ones. He remarks that the difference is probably due to the different centers of these religions. Obviously, a comparison of names and the resultant interpretation of differing lists falls outside the purview of this paper.
80. Further discussion in Witzel, "Nāgas".
81. Dagens et Barazer-Billoret 2000, 382.
82. Cited by Lalou 1933. 1–19.
83. This ritual, in the Tibetan, is called *klu'i gdon-las grol-bar-byed-pa sbrul 'jin gsaṅ-ba źes-bya-ba.*
84. Wessels-Mevissen 2001, 19.
85. M. Witzel, "Nāgas". Cf. Wessels-Mevissen, 2001, 5.
86. The role of Guardian continued in the art; see for example the beauteous Nāga couple guarding the portals of the Buddha's sanctuary at Ajanta, Cave 19.
87. Härtel 1993, 432 and Fig. 22 on page 443.

16

Mathurā's 'Personality' and the Development of Narrative Art*

"Mathurā actually appears to have had no interest in narrative at all - the exceptions often bear the sign of Gandhāran stylistic influence".[i]

— Maurizio Taddei

What a provocative statement! Is it possible that India's first school of art, so creative in inventing icons, had little interest in depicting narratives? Or, is something else—something peculiar to Mathurā- operating?

Beginning the first century BC/AD through the third century AD, Mathurā was special. Before then, religion and art set Mathurā apart. But afterwards more than these dominated, giving Mathurā an exceptional personality. Two sources framing the periods of our concern, illustrate great change. The Buddha is reputedly to have said that there are five disadvantages in Mathurā. "What five? The ground is uneven; there is much dust; there are fierce dogs; bestial yakhās; and alms are got with difficulty" (*Aṅguttaranikāya* in the *Sutta Piṭaka*; part of the earliest Pāli canon of the Theravada school). The description is famously interpreted as a negative obsevation, although I think it need not altogether be (more on that later). Bhāsa, probably of the post-Kusāṇa age, captures the spirit of a totally different Mathurā in Act 5, v.15 of his *Bālacarita*: "The best of deities guard Mathurā this city with its rows of mansions adorned with gold, with its spacious palaces and markets, its gates and towers..."[1]. Even if poetic licence is disregarded, Bhāsa describes a wealthy, bustling, fortified urban center. Indeed carved on Mathurā reliefs perhaps of the 1st century AD[2], gates, towers and multi-storied

Originally published in *Art, Icon and Architecture in South Asia: Essays in Honour of Dr. Devangana Desai*, Anila Verghese and Anna L. Dallapiccola (eds.), New Delhi, 2015; pp. 57-78. Reprinted with stylistic changes, addenda and permission from Aryan Books International.

mansions breathe reality into Bhāsa's words. A burst of activity should have occurred prior to Bhāsa's time.

A series of circumstances prior to the post-Kusāṇa age coalesced and succeeded in transforming this "town of the gods" (Ptolemy's likely translation[3]) into a prosperous, cosmopolitan and cultured urban center. Economic vibrancy was certainly a transformative factor. Mathurā's markets, as we can infer from Bhāsa, exuded wealth. A great variety of local, inter-regional and international goods were to be found in Mathurā during the centuries around the Christian era.

Various industries, crafts and artisanal activities developed locally. Inscriptional references and visual sources testify to weapon-making, brass and iron goods, pottery manufacture, guild of flour makers, textile manufacture (Mathurā cotton is mentioned in *Arthaśastra* II.11.115), oil & perfume manufacture, weavers & tailors (the latter especially for foreign tailored clothes), artisans (such as construction workers & sculptors) and entertainers, to mention some of the local activities.[4] Noticeably absent is prosperity due to agricultural production. Mathurā's economic success was generated by the industriousness of its inhabitants and its pivotal position on a series of trade routes, allowing for the import and export of goods.

Mathurā was directly linked to routes in the Western regions going through Rajasthan to Sind and Gujarat. Three branches of the Uttarāpatha met at Mathurā. The town was directly connected by a branch of the Uttarāpatha, or Northern Route, leading to Tāmralipti, the active seaport in the East[5]. Southern feeder routes passed through Mathurā on the way to flourishing western ports and central emporia such as Vidiśā, Ujjayinī and several others, wherefrom pathways continued which joined Mathurā to southern commercial and political centers, including Pratiṣṭhāna, the capital of the imperial Sātavāhanas.[6] The Uttarāpatha had an unmistakable effect on shaping the character of the city. This pathway connected Mathurā to thriving mercantile, political and intellectual centers: the route went through Taxila – Sagala – Mathurā – Pāṭaliputra unto Tāmralipti. Beyond Taxila, overland routes extended to Kabul, Begram, Bactria plus points farther West, ultimately connecting with the Mediterranean world.[7] Feeding into the Uttarāpatha, from the East were routes through Central Asia; thus the Silk Route, and routes over the Karakoram, Hindu Kush and Pamir Mountains could ultimately lead into the Gangetic Valley. Here lay the magnet attracting a stream of foreign invaders: fertile lands watered by great river systems, terrain promising natural resources. Outsiders – especially in post-Mauryan through pre-Gupta times – braved arduous northern and eastern routes often through mountain passes to reach Northern India. Here lay the Gaṅgā-Yamunā *doab*; its heartland was *Āryāvarta* – "Land of the Aryas", antithesis of the northern borderlands along the Uttarāpatha, where Brahmanic practices were less strictly (or not at all) maintained. Mathurā lay within this stronghold of Brahmanic tradition. Yet with the advent of incoming foreign settlers, especially the invading Śākas and

Kuṣāṇas (beginning around the first century BC until the waning of Kuṣāṇa power in the third century AD), the town gained a cosmopolitan veneer. However, the appearance of physical comfort and ease could already be noted before their advent.[8] These invaders established themselves as ruling powers in the northwestern borderlands and by extending their rule to Mathurā, they brought a degree of multiculturalism and a diverse population into Mathurā.[9] Indeed Mathurā served as the Kuṣāṇas' chief center of rule in the upper Doab.

"An overwhelming amount of evidence in imperishable materials", writes J.E van Lohuizen-de Leeuw, "indicates that there was cultural contact between Mathurā and the Northwest, the region of Gandhāra."[10] To cite two of her Kuṣāṇa examples: six Mathurā stool-querns were found in houses at Taxila[11] and two Mathurā weight stones were sent to the Northwest, where they were found. The weight stones show a male pushing against the chest of a prancing horse. The scene is often (to my mind, unconvincingly) identified as Kṛṣṇa fighting Keśin. It is hard to explain why this scene should be illustrated and episodes relating to Kṛṣṇa's birth, childhood and characteristic *līlās* would not be illustrated. Even before the Kuṣāṇa Period, Mathurā was in contact with the Northwest and important Gangetic towns as indicated by the dispersal pattern of etched beads.[12]

Operating as a distribution hub already in the post-Mauryan period, Mathurā became by the Kuṣāṇa period an active, profitable clearing center.[13] Mathurā sculpture was exported far and wide (e.g. Taxila, Sāñchī, Amarāvati, Nandan, Sanghol, Śrāvastī), adding renown and funds to the city's coffers. As this commercial trend is generally known and widely published, I shall add only one other example which comments anew on commerce within Mathurā. The example is found in Chapter 26 of the *Divyāvadāna* (dating approximately from the beginning of the common era[14]) and concerns Vāsavadattā, Mathurā's famous courtesan and the pious Buddhist ascetic Upagupta, also a native of the town. The courtesan's misfortune begin when she takes up with a trader travelling along the Uttarāpatha and stopping in Mathurā with 500 horses for sale. His profits embolden him to celebrate with the best courtesan in town, namely Vāsavadattā.[15] Two economic verities are hidden in this story. The first is that Mathurā was a clearing house for the horse trade, a function that could only have picked up with the approach and arrival of the Yüeh-chih/Kuṣāṇas. These horse-riding people were known as suppliers of good horses from the steppes. Second is the likelihood that Vāsavadattā was an expensive courtesan. We know that Mathurā housed courtesans of different ranks including a *gaṇikā;* the latter would need to turn over a portion of her considerable earnings to the political adminstration which gave her protection[16]. Here again, Mathurā stood to benefit monetarily.

As a hub of growing political influence and economic affluence, Mathurā's cultural life accelarated. Patañjali (dated c. 150 BC) in his *Mahābhāṣya* V.3.57 (with possible later interpolations[17]), could remark that the residents of Mathurā were more cultured than those of Śaṅkāsya and Pāṭaliputra. A glimpse into the range of cultural activities can be gleaned from Mathurā inscriptions and art dating within the 1st century BC – 3rd century AD (i.e. during the time of the Indo-Scyhthians, the Indo-Parthians and the Kuṣāṇas). Already in pre- Kuṣāṇa times, the inhabitants saw dance performances, accompanied by instrumental groups. Solo performances probably also existed; a pre-Kuṣāṇa inscription records a donation by the wife of a dancer (*nataka = nartaka*)[18]. One can only imagine that such actual events inspired the lively imagery of dancers with an ensemble of musicians found on the reverse of a 1st century gateway (*toraṇa*) architrave from the Jaina site of Kāṇkālī Tīlā.[19] Some instruments such as cymbals[20], drum and harp[21] can be recognized in reliefs. B.N. Mukherjee also notes the *vīnā*, flute, conch.[22] A small Mathurā terracotta shows a female dancer in conjunction with another female holding a *vīnā* in one hand and placing the other around the neck of a male companion[23]. Dramatic performances requiring groups of actors (*śailālaka*) can be inferred by a Kuṣāṇa donative inscription from Jamālpur mound. The slab was set up by "the sons of actors of Mathurā", namely the Cāndaka brothers who were apparently sufficiently busy and remunerated to afford the donation.[24] Sports events could also entertain the people of Mathurā. Wrestling seems to have been popular. Weight stones carved in Mathurā and also exported to Gandhāra can show athletes engaged in wrestling matches or contests. The so-called Keśin/Kṛṣṇa weight stones could have been simply lifting devices. Bhāsa's *Bālacarita* includes an episode of physical combat at Mathurā's court. In Act V—prior to being killed—Mathurā's King Kaṁsa sends two wrestlers to smash both Kṛṣṇa and Balarāma, his brother. In sum, the recorded cultural events which entertained the people of Mathurā appear to be staged performances. Dancing, music, theater, sporting contests can all be labled as "performing arts", although there may have been others which are unrecorded.

A threshold was reached as political, economic, diverse religio-cultural and ethnic forces aligned with the burgeoning skills of Mathurā's artisans. A surge in creativity produced a vast artistic output recognized as a school of art—India's first. The school fulfilled the devotional needs of Mathurā's different devotees so well that the newly invented icons attained the status of benchmarks for the Kuṣāṇa age and beyond. Specifically, Mathurā art produced the standard icons of Buddhist, Jain, Hindu, Nāga, Yakṣa and other folk deities. Leaving aside the considerable Buddhist, Jain and folk images since this paper will concentrate (though not entirely) on ancient Hinduism in Mathurā, a quick overview of the Hindu icons developed by Mathurā's craftsmen may be itemized[25]. Iconographies were invented or standardized for the following divinities: Saṃkarṣaṇa/Balarāma[26]; the Vaiṣṇava Caturvyūha icon[27]; Vāsudeva-Kṛṣṇa[28]; Varāha, Hayagrīva[29] and Trivikrama[30]; Ekānamśā and the Vṛṣṇi Vīras[31]; Gaṇeśa[32]; Nārāyaṇa[33]; Agni[34]; the Warrior Goddess[35]; Divine Matṛkas[36]; Ardhanārī[37]; Kuvera; standing Sūrya; Indra, Brahmā[38], the 'southern' type of Skanda-

Kārttikeya (in contradistinction to the northwestern type)[39]. This is an extraordinary achievement. Within the span of a few centuries mainly in the Kuṣāṇa Period, a new iconographic vocabulary was conceived, concretized and accepted by the worshipful populace[40]. I cannot think of another time in India's artistic history that such a burst of artistic innovation occurred.

These dynamic forces developed around a fulcrum. Brahmanism had dominant prestige in Mathurā. If this is postulated a number of anomalies find their rationale. The first might be why the Buddha found it difficult to get alms in a locale dominated by Brahmanic culture. To substantiate the fundamental position of Brahmanism in Mathurā, the hallmarks of Brahmanism need to be defined in order to assess both its presence and cultural effect upon Mathurā.

Obviously, adherence to the Vedic canon, and concomitantly, the prestige of Sanskrit, the language of the Vedic and Brahmanic texts, were vital aspects of Brahmanism. Promotion of religious beliefs flowing from these sacred texts, to wit, adherence to Vedic sacrifices (foisting an early predilection for divine symbols instead of anthropomorphic figures), and subsequent adherence to developing ancient Hindu gods were to be supported. Emphasis on oral rather than written communication of customs, sacred texts, transactions, sagas was fostered by the Brahmanic tradition. Upholding the social system described in the Dharmaśāstras—with its codification of the norms and duties of the four classes of man—was incumbent upon an individual for it marked his place in Brahmanic society.[41]

Brahmanism's strong presence in Mathurā existed in spite of, or in reaction to, the non-Brahmanic populace in its midst. Of all the early north Indian territories, the most complete record of inscriptions comes from Mathurā; these plus the information gleaned from its art provide data relevant to the position of Brahmanism in the town during the period of the invasions. Among Mathurā inscriptions, the overwhelming records touch on Buddhist and Jain topics; only a few relate to Hinduism. An indicator of Mathurā's role as bulwark against the 'polluting' influences of the non-Brahmanic populace is announced by Patañjali, who probably came from the Mathurā area[42]. The introduction to his *Mahābhāṣya* makes clear his grammar's objectives and the prestige of Sanskrit in a traditional culture. Witzel summarizes the aims of the introduction "a catechism of traditionalism, protection of the Vedas, proper pronunciation and adherence to correct grammar, avoidance of 'popular' words, behaving properly, not killing brahmins, not drinking alcohol, which everybody around him was doing, as the Mathurā inscriptions—and Patañjali himself—indicate."[43]

Usage of Sanskrit, the language of Brahmanic culture, in Mathurā's inscriptions is therefore a tool to shed light on the position of Brahmanism there. Notably, it is only after the arrival of the Kṣatrapas from the Northwest, towards the end of the first century BC, that Sanskritization occurs in Mathurā inscriptions.[44] One of the first inscriptions was written by a Brahman, the treasurer (*gañjavara*), of Śoḍāsa (c. first quarter of 1st century AD), the Śāka ruling in Mathurā.[45] Several other Sanskrit inscriptions written during this time and connected to the Kṣatrapa court are Nos. 113, 115, 178 in Luders, *Mathurā Inscriptions.*[46]

The occurrence of written Sanskrit and its apperance in inscriptions at a time when foreigners and outside rulers established themselves in Mathurā supports Witzel's theory[47], namely that a Brahmanic reaction set in due to the presence of a foreign and/or non-Brahmanic populace. The fact that Sanskrit should, in part, be a symbol of Mathurā's distinctiveness, or what I have designated as her "personality" is also due to Mathurā's location within the region of Āryāvarta. Situated within the boundaries of exemplary Brahmanical life and culture, Mathurā could employ language to stress a hierarchic difference in education and position between the Brahmanic and the rest of the population in its midst.[48]

Backing up these inferences are specific inscriptional references to a Vedic sacrifice, the *varṇāśrama* system and high respect for Brahmans among administrative officials. A reference to *yūpa*, or a Vedic sacrificial pillar, can be cited. It occurs on a seal dating before the close of the first century BC. The legend reads *yūpalaṭhikasa.*[49] Two actual remains of *yūpas* were found in the bed of the Yamunā at Mathurā. One dating to the reign of Vāsiṣka commemorates a Brahman's performance of the Dvādaśarātra rite and the setting up of the *yūpa.*[50] The Brahman states that he belongs to the Bhāradvāja *gotra*. Śoḍāsa's treasurer, mentioned above, states that he belongs to the Śegrava (i.e. Śaigrava) *gotra.* A *gotra* separates Brahmanic society into exogamous clans and to this day it is an important feature in connection with matrimonial choices. It bespeaks of the Brahmanical social system, which could be adopted by the other twice-born classes or *varṇas* (i.e. the *kṣatriyas* and *vaiśyas varṇas*). Inherent in belonging to a particular *gotra* is therefore suscribing to the norms of a particular Brahmanic *varṇa* (later caste). Such social divisions existed in Mathurā. A Kuṣāṇa inscription refers to *kṣatriyas*, stating that four Kṣatriya brothers installed an image of Kārttikeya.[51] The Vṛṣṇis, surely present in Mathurā, belong to the *kṣatriya varṇa.*[52] In addition, there are inscriptions showing that government officials held Brahmans in high regard and provided for them (see No. 99 in Lüders, *Mathurā Inscriptions*). An inscription dating to the reign of Huviṣka declares that Brahmans were regularly fed at an "alms-house" constructed for meritorious deeds.[53] We may deduce from the mention of *brahmans* and *kṣatriyas* that *vaiśya* and *śūdras* also lived in Mathurā; mention of a guild of flour workers implies the presence of *vaiśyas*. In sum, even though there is sparse reference to Hindu or Brahmanic content in Mathurā's early inscriptions[54], the above indicators leave little doubt that Mathurā's traditional society arranged itself according to, and followed, the tenets of, the *varṇāśrama* system as codified in brahmanic Dharma texts[55]. Subscribing to this system and its laws and duties means that there is a preference for orality among some in communicating important aspects of personal identity.

A person who identifies with a particular *gotra* cannot help but be reminded, often, of the importance and prestige of oral transmission. A person of the upper three classes recites his lineage before and/or during *gṛhya* and *śrauta* rites he undertakes; some can be performed daily. Certainly lineage recitation occurs in marriage and *śrāddha* rites. One's *gotra* is committed to memory and is passed on orally to succeeding generations. Such recitations, their retention, and transmission reinforce through the ages the power and cultural prestige of oral dissemination of knowledge and information.

The disparity between the number of inscriptions relating to Vedic or Hindu matters vs. Buddhist, Jain and Nāga matters can probably be explained by Brahmanism's preference for oral transmission. This preference is already noticed, according to Witzel, in the formulation of Pāṇini's grammar.[56] Further, the origin of the *padapāṭha* of the *Rig Veda* by Śakalya, also around the middle of the first millenium BC is a mnemonic device which assures correct pronunciation of this Veda, and in effect, creates the fixed *RV* text.[57] Possibly a foray to write down, for the first time, the *White Yajur Veda* occurred during the Kānva Period (c. 50 BC). The Kānvas were Brahmans and belonged to this Veda. But this endeavor was soon abandoned "in favor of the exclusively oral preservation of the texts".[58] However, <u>written</u> injunctions against setting down a saced text are only found later.[59]

I consider Brahmanism's emphasis on oral transmission most significant in affecting Mathurā's output of visual narratives. One good argument in favour of this conjecture is the representation of Kṛṣṇa of the Vṛṣṇi clan, Mathurā's 'home-grown' divinity. Textual evidence shows the esteem in which Vāsudeva-Kṛṣṇa was held. A Mathurā inscription dating to the time of Śoḍāsa records the erection of a gateway, a terrace, and a *devakula* at the *mahāsthāna* of Vāsudeva (-Kṛṣṇa[60]). From the same period comes the Morā Well Inscription mentioning the installation of images of the blessed five Vṛṣṇi Vīras, among whom we must surely count Vāsudeva-Kṛṣṇa. So too does the *Mahābhāṣya* refer to notions that could only be located in Mathurā: it speaks of "the antagonism between the *Kaṁsa-bhaktas* who were *kāla-mukha* (dark-faced) and the *Vāsudeva-bhaktas* who were *rakta-mukha* (red-faced), although the reference may be to a dramatic representation of the slaying of Kaṁsa."[61] Indeed more than a century ago, R.G. Bhandarkar interpreted these passages as evidence in the *Mahābhāṣya* for the killing of Kaṁsa and the narration and presentation of dramas presumably in Mathurā on the life of Vāsudeva- Kṛṣṇa.[62] Yet no narrative depiction of this major event exists in early Mathurā art! The few Kṛṣṇa narratives that have been proposed are problematic and could be interpreted differently, like the Kṛṣṇa/Keśin weight stones. Another example, the Mathurā Kuṣāṇa fragment identified as Vāsudeva crossing the river Yamunā with baby Kṛṣṇa (indistinct, at best) shows a *nāga* in the waters who closely reminds of the *nāga* in the waters of the Varāha relief in Cave 5, Udayagiri[63]; the similarity suggests the possibility of incorrectly identifying this fragment as a Kṛṣṇa narrative. A Mathurā narrative depicting Kṛṣṇa lifting Mt. Govardhana, formerly assigned to the Kuṣāṇa period by A.K. Coomaraswamy, has for sometime been recognized as a Mathurā Gupta production.[64] The later date is totally comprehensible since it is Saṃkarṣaṇa/ Balarāma—and not his younger brother Kṛṣṇa - who is first associated with Mt. Govardhana, probably before the Kuṣāṇa age. Folklore hints at this earlier association.[65] Yet Vāsudeva-Kṛṣṇa, the god of the Bhagavad Gītā, claims in that text, that his devotees always recount his stories (X.9). If there are stories of Mathurā's god at this time, why cannot we identify them? If however we dispense searching for Kṛṣṇa's narratives, and look for icons, then, clearly, Bhagavān Vāsudeva, alone and in Vṛṣṇi kinship reliefs, dominates as one of the most important gods worshipped in Mathurā during Kuṣāṇa times[66]. It could be said, as I did following Vaudeville, that Mathurā was not central to the legends surrounding Gopāla-Kṛṣṇa. Narrative reliefs of Gopala-Kṛṣṇa's *līlās* were conceived later.[67] The dearth of narratives is evident not only with respect to Kṛṣṇa, but also with respect to other Hindu gods.

Among the Hindu icons invented by Mathurā's ateliers several are attached to stories. Trivikrama, Varāha, Hayagrīva all arise within narrative contexts. Whereas the icons of these divinities were fashioned, the deities were not depicted within their narrative contexts. By the 5th century, the narratives are visually rendered—but not in Mathurā's Gupta corpus! (See the Trivikrama narrative on the Pawāya toraṇa lintel and the Varāha story at Cave 5, Udayagiri).[68] This summary virtually cancels out the existence of undisputed pre-Gupta Vaiṣṇava narratives at Mathurā.

The earliest Gaṇeśa, conceived in Mathurā, is a post- Kuṣāṇa work not related to any narrative (see fn. 32). The earliest unambiguous narrative relief of the slaying of the Buffalo Demon is dated c. 3rd-4th century AD. It comes from Gandhāra, not Mathurā and shows the Warrior God Skanda/Kārttikeya performing this feat! Again, this is comprehensible because the ealiest reference to this feat is in the *Mahābhārata* where it is attributed to Skanda/Kārttikeya and not to a Devī[69].

Narratives were spun around the other Hindu god, Rudra - Śiva, since Vedic times. There are *śaivite* legends in the Saṃhitās and Brāhmaṇas. As already noted in an earlier work[70], the *Kauṣītaki Brāhmaṇa* (VI. 1-9), tells how Rudra received all his names. Another story relates how Rudra punishes incestuous Prajāpati and distributes the seed (*Śatapatha Brāhmaṇa* I.7.41-8). The *Taittirīya Saṃhitā* (II.6.8.2) and the *Aitareya Brāhmaṇa* (III. 34) recount events that foreshadow the story of Śiva's exclusion from Dakṣa's sacrifice. His destruction of the three cities is already in the *Mahābhārata* (VIII.24.3ff). Thus the absence of *śaiva* narratives in Mathurā art cannot be attributed to the lack of pre-purāṇic stories.[71]

The thrust of Mathurā's Hindu art is on the icon, not the narrative. This preference during pre-Gupta times appears to reflect a theological orientation. That is, an icon focuses more on the might and nature of a deity than on miracles and playful actions, or *līlās*. The former tends to be visually expressed by an hieratic image with its attributes; the latter is expressed better by narrative. A theological orientation is itself allied to subjects explored in Brāhmaṇical texts.[72]

Assuming the above rationale for the dearth of Hindu narratives is correct, does it follow that only Hindu narratives are affected? To say it another way, does the scope of Mathurā's Buddhist and Jain narratives compensate for the lack of Hindu narratives? Or is Mathurā's general narrative output as negligible as Taddei believed, writing in 1999, or Dehejia writing in 1997?[73] The question is not irrelevant since Sonya Rhie Quintanilla, in 2007, brought together for discussion a few Buddhist and Jain narratives that she alleges were made in Mathurā between c. 100 BC – early 1st century AD[74]. The Jain narrative depicts the dance of Nīlāñjanā and the renunciation of Ṛṣabhanātha; it appears on the architrave "reportedly" from the Jain site of Kāṇkali Tīlā, dated by Quintanilla to c. 100 BC. Early Buddhist narratives include the *parinirvāṇa* scene carved on a column from a Buddhist stūpa. It is dated by both Pal[75] and Quintanilla to the first century AD, and can be counted as coming from Mathurā since Pal informs that "its mate" is in the Mathurā Museum. Offer of the bowls by four *lokapālas*, seen on the Isāpur railing is a Buddhist narrative long identified[76]. Whereas there is agreement that it preceeds the Kuṣāṇa age, Quintanilla pushes it back to the time of Śoḍāsa's reign; this is debatable. Also uncertain is whether to include a representation of Māyā's dream featured in a roundel from a Hathīn (Haryana) rail post dated to c. 100 BC by Quintanilla; neither the use of spotted red sandstone nor its find place between Mathurā and Delhi is sufficient to indicate that the rail post is a Mathurā export.[77] These few but early narrative reliefs remind that Buddhism, and stories about the Buddha began in Gangetic India—not the Northwest.

However when a comparison is made between Buddhist narratives from Mathurā and Gandhāra produced during the first through third century AD (i.e. the time of the Kuṣāṇa hegemony in these regions) the result comes as a surprise, even when one remembers that Mathurā is one town and Gandhāra is a large area. The surprise is the overwhelming expansion of themes pertaining to the life of the Buddha in Gandhāra. I am not comparing numbers of narrative works produced. I am solely comparing the portrayal of narrative themes in Mathurā vs. Gandhāra during pre-Gupta times. Jātaka themes are not compared.[78] The comparison is based on themes described in two sources. For Gandhāran art the source is Alfred Foucher, *L'Art gréco-bouddhique du Gandhāra* (Paris, 1905-1951; Deuxieme Partie; Chapitres IV-VIII). For Mathurā art a convenient list is in Joan Anastasia Raducha, *Iconography of Buddhist Relief Scenes from Kushan Mathurā* (PhD Thesis; University of Wisconsin-Madison; 1982; Appendix II). I am well aware that for Gandhāra there are more up-to-date resources, especially as a result of the Italian excavations. I am also not sure how inclusive the Raducha study is since I happen to have published and interpreted a Mathurā relief with scenes of the life of the Buddha (State Museum, Lucknow B 208[79]); some scenes are not on Raducha's List. A comprehensive corpus of all Gandhāra and Mathurā narrative examples is therefore a desideratum. The ensuing comparison however does not need to be based on a comprehensive corpus. The fairly large sample is a tool to gauge Mathurā's general interest in producing narrative art—irrespective of its religious content. As will be seen below, the imbalance between Gandhāran and Mathurā themes is so overwhelming that were a comprehensive study accomplished, it would undoubtedly refine the findings given below but not the overall skew.

THEME 1: Birth of the Buddha-to-be

- Mathurā Reliefs : Sūrya seated on his chariot [this is SML B. 208[80]]; Māyā under the tree and child emerges from right side. Śakra receives babe
- Gandhāra Reliefs: Dream of Māyā; Interpretation of Dream; Birth scene (as Mathurā), The Seven Steps

THEME 2: The Bath

- Mathurā Reliefs : Babe stands on platform, nāgas on either side
- Gandhāra Reliefs: First bath scene, iconography somewhat different from Mathurā; Return from Lumbinī Park, Asita's visit; Births coinciding with the birth of Siddhārtha

THEME 3: Childhood and Youth of the Bodhisattva

- Mathurā Reliefs : absent
- Gandhāra Reliefs: Schooling & learning to write; Physical exercise (archery); Choice of a Bride; Death and Disposal of Elephant; Archery Contest; Fighters and Wrestlers; Marriage Ceremony; Pleasures of the Palace.

THEME 4: Becoming a Buddha

- Mathurā Reliefs : Renunciation scene with women asleep; Leaving Kapilavāstu; Removing the cūḍā; Farewell of Chandaka and Kaṇṭhaka; Māra, Vajrapāṇi present at Departure.
- Gandhāra Reliefs: First Meditation; Four Encounters; Sleep of the Palace Women; Leaving the Palace and Kapilavāstu; Farewell to Chandaka and Kaṇṭhaka; Cutting the Hair or cūḍā; Exchange of clothes; Chandaka returns.

THEME 5: Steps Towards Enlightenment

- Mathurā Reliefs : Approaching Bodhi Tree with the Grass; Defeat of Māra
- Gandhāra Reliefs: First Interview with Bimbisāra; Meeting Brahmanic Ascetics; Six Years Performing Penances; Hommage of Nāga Kālika; Meeting the Grass Cutter; Preparing the Seat of Enlightenment; Defeat of Māra.

THEME 6: Enlightenment

Mathurā Reliefs : Four *lokapālas* Offer Four Bowls; First Sermon

Gandhāra Reliefs: Four *lokapālas* Offer Four Bowls; Entreaty to Preach; First Sermon

THEME 7: Career of the Buddha

Mathurā Reliefs : Indra visits the Buddha in the Cave; Subjugation of Nalagiri; Descent from the Trāyastriṃśa Heaven; Ambush of Devadatta; Offering of Dust.

Gandhāra Reliefs: Conversion of Kāśyapas; Walking on Water; Miracle of Fire; Victory over the Snake; Conversion of the Black Snake; Entering Rājagṛha; Buddha among the Śākyas; Nanda's Conversion; Nanda's Ordination; Gift of the Jetavana; Teaching in the Trayastriṃśa Heaven; Āmrapālī's Gift; Indra Visits the Buddha in the Cave; Nāga Elāpatra's Visit; Conversion of Yakṣa Āṭavida; Monkey's Offering; Offering of Dust; Conversion of Ugrasena; the Measure of the Buddha; the Angry White Dog; Subjugation of Nalagiri; Descent from the Trāyastriṃśa Heaven; Ambush of Devadatta; Submission of Nāga Apalāla.

THEME 8: Mahā Parinirvāṇa

Mathurā Reliefs : Mahā Parinirvāṇa (showing Buddha lying on right side, monk and lay mourners, and Subhadra; Vajrapāṇi; Māra; Śāla trees with tree sprites) [Raducha: yakṣas which is wrong].

Gandhāra Reliefs: Mahā Parinirvāṇa (showing same elements as in Mathurā reliefs); Buddha's Coffin; Cremation; Relics Return to Kuśinagara; Guarding the Relics; Distribution of Relics; Transport of Relics; Depositing Relics in Stūpa.

It must be asked whether the Mathurā region would be aware/have access to a fuller range of stories connected to the life of the Buddha, for if the stories were extant but ostensibly beyond the ken of Mathurā, then Mathurā's more limited scope could be a possible explanation for the limited depictions. This however is not the case. The early Sanskrit poem, the *Buddhacarita* by Aśvaghoṣa relates the sage's life from birth through to enlightenment. The work is usually dated to circa 1st century AD and the poet is believed to come from Saketa. Thanks to the fairly recent discovery and translation of the Rabatak inscription attributed to a high official of Kaniṣka I, we know that the north Indian town of Saketa (in south central U.P.) was in the Kuṣāṇa hegemony as well. Therefore the likelihood that the great poet's work—composed in Sanskrit—would be unknown in the Mathurā region is minimal.

The next critical question is whether this work, contemporary or even slightly prior to some of Mathurā's Buddhist narratives, is closer to Mathurā's limited or Gandhāra's elaborate treatment. Astonishingly, although Aśvaghoṣa's locality is closer to Mathurā, the *Buddhacarita* account is considerably closer to the themes depicted in Gandhāran art. The subjects taken up in the *Buddhacarita* are given below for the convenience of the reader:

Birth
1. Dream of Māyā; Interpretation
2. Birth in the Lumbinī Grove; emergence from Māyā's right side
3. Takes 7 steps
4. the Bath
5. Brahman's prophesy
6. Asita's Visit and prophesy

Life in the Palace
1. Marriage
2. Pleasures of the Palace
3. Birth of Rāhula

The Prince's Perturbation
1. The 4 encounters
2. 1st Meditation
3. Resolve to Leave Palace

Departure
1. Sleeping Women
2. Leaves, riding on Kaṇṭhaka
3. Yakṣas Muffle noise of hoofs with their hands
4. Farewell to Kaṇṭhaka (who licks Master's feet) and Chandaka
5. Cutting off turban and hair underneath
6. Exchange of clothes
7. Chandaka Returns to Kapilavāstu

Practice and Rejection of Ascetics' Penances
1. Visit of Bimbisāra
2. 6 years of Austerities, including starvation
3. Visit of Arāḍa

Resolve and Vow
1. Eats Food Given by Nandabalā
2. Takes grass from grasscutter
3. Vow to achieve enligthenment
4. Sits in meditation pose
5. Appearance of Māra's monstrous army
6. Defeat of Māra, who has a bow

Enlightenment
1. Meditation and final enlightenment during 4 watches
2. Continued deep meditation for 7 days
3. Buddha decides to teach
4. 4 *lokapālas* each offer a begging bowl
5. 2 merchants give the first alms
6. Buddha goes to Kāśi to teach

Fig. 16.1 Mathura relief with scenes from the life of the Buddha, Kuṣāṇa period, from State Museum, Lucknow (No. B 208) (Photo courtesy: State Museum, Lucknow).

Roughly twenty-two themes depicted in Gandhāran narratives are mentioned in the *Buddhacarita* vs. c. eleven themes in Mathurā's assemblage.

There is however one subject portrayed at Mathurā (and Bodh Gayā, see below) but not at Gandhāra though it is mentioned in the *Buddhacarita*. Nowhere does the art of Gandhāra begin the story of the Buddha with the scene of Sūrya riding his chariot. Siddhārtha's family originated from the Sun (e.g. see *Buddhacarita* X.23). The poem can refer to the family's lineage by *'ādityapūrva'* X.23), thus directly descended from Ikṣvāku, son of Manu the first mortal of Sūrya and Aditi.[81] Pāli texts can refer to the Buddha's lineage by the term *adiccabandhu* (Skt. Ādityabandhu, kinsman of Āditya, i.e. kinsman of the Sun).[82] The image of Sūrya on the chariot precedes the Buddha's Temptation and Enlightenment in the Mathura relief (Fig. 16.1).[82a(*)] In effect, the image functions as an ideograph announcing Siddhārtha's genealogy, namely the Sūryavaṃśa[83]. This placement of the Sūrya image in the narrative sequence is equivalent to the narrative itself saying 'Hear now the story of the scion of the Śākya clan'. The other example is on a Śuṅga railing at the site of Bodh Gayā, not an accidental choice (Fig. 16.2). The choice is under the influence of its surrounding. There is, as is well known, Buddhist (Bodh) Gayā and Hindu Gayā. Hindu Gayā is an auspicious place to perform the ancient *śraddha* ceremony, already mentioned by Pāṇini as the rite devoted to the worship of ancestors.[84] The ritual aims to transform the dead *(preta)* from a harmful spirit to a friendly ancestor. Recitation of one's lineage is part of the rite ensuring that Hindu Gayā keeps alive—nay,

Fig. 16.2 Bodh Gaya railing with Surya relief, Śuṅga period (Photo courtesy of the Archaeological Survey of India, New Delhi).

emphasizes—the importance of lineage. Committing to memory the knowledge of one's ancestors together with the ability to recite one's lineage recognizes the importance of the oral tradition which enables one to do so. It is proposed that the Gayā environment was influenced by the promience given to ancestors at Hindu Gayā, resulting in the visual reference to Siddhārtha's Sūryavaṃśa at Bodh Gayā. Interestingly, the *śrāddha* ceremony also has a strong relation to Mathurā. *Śrāddha*'s basic ritual mentions the ancestral Vṛṣṇi lineage. A fundamental offering in the ceremony is balls of food (*piṇḍa*) to the departed, especially the closest direct ancestors (the father, the grandfather and great-grandfather). "In a passage of the *Vishṇudharmottara* quoted by *Śrāddasāra* (page 6) and *Śrāddhaprakāśa* (pp. 11-12), it is said that the *piṇḍa* offered to the great-grandfather is the god Vāsudeva himself, the one to the grandfather is designated Saṃkarshaṇa, that to the father is known as Pradyumna and the offerer of the *piṇḍa* is himself in the position of Aniruddha".[85] The four names are those of the Vṛṣṇis of Mathurā. The centrality of a famous Mathurā lineage occurring in Vedic *śrāddha* sheds light on the environment in which Siddhārtha's Sūryavaṃśa lineage becomes part of the Mathurā narrative sequence in his life.

Identification by lineage, its articulation in ritual, the *śrāddha* ritual itself, these are all recognizable Brahmanic customs. And, as already indicated, they all rely on the strength of orality practiced in a place. This is important for the overarching question posed at the outset because orality, I maintain, has an effect on the flow of narratives.

When David McMahan, an historian of South Asian Buddhism, set out to explain the difference in the literary styles of the Pāli canon and the Mahāyāna sutras, he puts considerable emphasis on the former being works of literature that are "written versions of a vast corpus of orally transmitted sayings" and the latter being works of a "written tradition"[86]. The distinctions he observes as well as his findings can be, I believe, fruitfully applied also to the visual arts; I know of no study that factors orality into the nature of narrative art in ancient Greater India. McMahan compares two introductory passages to Buddhist teachings, one from an early Pāli text, the *Saḷāyatana-vibhaṅga Suttam* and the other from the Mahāyāna text, the *Gaṇḍavyūha* which he dates to c. the second or third century AD. The Mahāyāna introduction is far lengthier, containing lavish scenes, elaborate descriptions, sumptuous details full of rich imagery, coloration and wondrous forms. The Pāli introduction is terse, straightforward, direct. Early Buddhist culture was an oral culture and the Pāli textual example represents, according to McMahan, the written version of what was originally heard. Hearing teachings meant the words had to be focussed, not florid. And to be orally preserved they would have had mnemonic features, usually repetitions. When reading rather than hearing became a significant mode for gaining access to Buddhist teachings, the literary form of presentation was free to change. The lesson which can be applied to visual narratives is that an oral culture fosters more limited thematic expressions than a literary one which fosters greater elaborations—precisely the artistic difference between Mathurā's life of the Buddha and that of Gandhāra.

You may however reasonably object, noting that writing seems to have been very prevalent in Mathurā at the time the narratives were conceived. You would certainly call attention to the large number of Mathurā inscriptions, and the fact that one dated in the year 93 mentions the term for a writer or scribe (*kāyastha),* indicative of persons trained and employed for the purpose of writing in Mathurā[87]. This is true. But whereas writing was practiced, orality, because of its association with the esteemed Brahmanic tradition, had greater prestige and considerable presence. Recall the above noted emphasis on orality in the numerous recorded cultural events which the people of Mathurā enjoyed. To these indicators of the pervasiveness of an oral culture may be added oral recitation—sometimes practiced daily—by priests and sacrificers alike in public and domestic Vedic rites (e.g. Saṃdhyā, Śrāddha etc.). Another contributor to the oral culture is the role of the ancient story teller who gathered the town's people around him and recounted the tales of Brahmanic and Bhagavata deities—tales which were probably woven into the epics, including the *Bhagavad Gītā*.[88] Other evidence for the respect paid Brahmans is the lip-service given them and their customs by foreign or non-orthodox persons in Mathurā. Support to Brahmans given by Śāka and Kuṣāṇa rulers has already been noted. Another, subtle indicator of Brahmanism's magnet is that the Andhaka-Vṛṣṇis of Mathurā adopted the *gotra* system. As Romila Thapar notes, "Intially it [i.e. the *gotra* system] appears in more frequent association with the *brāhmaṇs* and was to remain essentially a *brāhmaṇ* identity. Later sources mention certain *kṣatriyas* such as the Andhaka-

Vṛṣṇis... using *gotra* identities. ...For *kṣatriyas* to adopt the *gotra* system was something of an anomaly since they were identified by lineage or *vaṃśa*, preferred endogamy and are known to have made cross-cousin marriages as well as to have married into collateral lineages."[89] (i.e. customs opposed to by brahmanic *gotra* rules).

It has been argued in this paper that central to Mathurā's 'personality' was Brahmanism and that it, through its emphasis on orality, conditioned the School's limited rendering of narratives. This position I think has not been advanced before. Therefore it should be tested and I believe there is a way to do that. It is fascinating to read a remark—similar to the one quoted at the outset by Taddei—this time referring to narrative depictions in Āndha. I shall quote Monika Zin's remarks in full because her observations may serve as the basis for a test case.

In a Round Table Discussion, following an International Symposium on Buddhism and Art in Gandhāra and Kucha, Professor Zin, a specialist of Buddhist narrative art mainly below the Gangetic Doab, commented that at Nāgārjunakoṇḍa there are "...122 archaeological sites... 33 among them were Buddhist monasteries and stūpas. Now, what is really exciting with these 33 monasteries: narrative reliefs have been found in only 5 of them. In addition to this, those 5 monasteries have exactly the same plan. Each one has a stūpa, two caitya-shrines standing facing each other door to door: inside one the Buddha image, inside the other the stūpa—and a monastery with monk's [*sic*] residences in three sides. In one of these monasteries an inscription was discovered. It belonged to monks of the Aparamahāvinaseliya... part of the Mahāsaṃghika. There were also different monasteries in Nāgārjunakoṇḍa—they have different plans, and narrative reliefs have not been found in them. So it looks to me that there were particular schools which were interested in narrative depictions, while others were not."[90]

It looks to me as if some cultural similarities between Nāgārjunakoṇḍa and Mathurā may be studied in depth for possibly shedding light on the use of narratives at the Āndhra site, and the role of Brahmanism there in promoting or suppressing the development of visual narrative scenes. It is well known that the Ikṣvāku, under whose rule the Buddhist site of Nāgārjunakoṇḍa was built, followed the Hindu religion. The first known Ikṣvāku king, Śantamūla I practised the '*Vaidika-dharma*' detailed in inscriptions of his descendents. He is said to have performed the *Agnihotra, Agnistoma, Vājapeya,* and *Aśvamedha* and *dānas* like *Hiraṇya-koṭi-dāna, Go-śatasahasra-dāna* and *Hala-śata-sahasra-dāna*.[91] "Though his descendents... are not known to have performed these *Vaidika* deeds, they do not appear to have deviated from the path trodden by Śāntamūla I."[92] Ikṣvāku inscriptions are mainly in Prākrit; a few are in Sanskrit.[93] The inscriptions mainly cite women who patronized Buddhism, including the magnificent monument at Nāgārjunakoṇḍa. So it needs to be determined whether the Sanskrit inscriptions pertained to Hindu information and the Prakrit ones Buddhist information. It is also known that the Ikṣvāku built Hindu temples, but most have either been submerged or not yet carefully studied.[94] The Ikṣvākus of Nāgārjunakoṇḍa were feudatories under the Sātavāhanas and when that Empire declined, the Ikṣvāku carved out a power base in the Guntur district. Noteworthy is that Sātāvahanas were also promoters of Brahmanism[95]. A very large number of Vedic sacrifices performed by a member of the Sātavāhana Dynasty is already recorded, according to Sircar, on the Nanaghat cave inscription (c. second half of the first century BC).[96] In Āndhra, the Ikṣvāku were followed by kings of the Bṛhatphalāyana *gotra* who also made donations to Brahmans[97]. In short, was the promotion of Brahmanism practiced by the Ikṣvāku part of a religious continuum in the area, raising the possibility that here too prevailed—as at Mathurā—an oral tradition based on the established prestige of Brahmanic culture? Such an investigation, while interesting in and of itself, would offer greater clarification in the proposal postulated here, namely that narrative choices in art can be conditioned by a culture that emphasizes the prestige of orality.

Another possible postulate is latent in my application of the McMahan thesis [that an oral Buddhist literary tradition results in terse, direct, limited stylistic discourse and a Buddhist textual tradition results in an expanded, more elaborate stylistic discourse] to early Indian narrative art. This postulate needs further philological investigation to answer the following question more fully.

1) To repeat—if one result of Mathurā's core Brahmanic culture—namely the prestige of oral communication—could have resulted in the School's limited rendering of narrative visual scenes (Hindu, Jain, Buddhist), and if
2) a comparison of Mathurā and Gandhāra Buddhist visual narratives determines that there is greater elaboration on the Life of the Buddha in Gandhāran art during the same period, then
3) would that imply that the Northwest may have had an earlier (probably secular) writing tradition than Mathurā?

The answer to that question seems to be a provisional 'yes'. Michael Witzel together with (in part) Steve Farmer have provided (in a paper dealing with the larger theme of canon formation[98]) the following chronological sequence relating to the introduction of script and writing in Gandhāra:

1. Introduction of Aramaic script and language occurred in Gandhāra during the last half of the sixth century BC when Gandhāra, conquered by the Achemenids, became a satrapy of the Persians.
2. The Persians used Aramaic for secular (i.e. administrative) purposes. Although the Kharoṣṭhī script may well have developed from the Aramaic script in Gandhāra, there was stiff resistance from the Brahmans of the Northwest to use Kharoṣṭhī in writing down their sacred texts, the Vedas.

3. Pāṇini (c. 350 BC?), working in the Northwest, knows of the use of writing and books, but composed and taught his grammar for oral use only.
4. By the time Patañjali (c. 150 BC), composed his grammar, he could no longer depend on the oral tradition for Pāṇini's *Aṣṭādhyāyī*. Indeed, the writing tradition for texts in Gandhāra may have begun in c. 250 BC (with the possibility that Patañjali's predecessor, Kātyāyana received Pāṇini's work in written form).
5. By c. 50 AD, the earliest Buddhist texts, probably based on earlier copies, were written on birch bark in Gandhāra.

All these indicators—of script and writing known in Gandhāra from the 6th century BC through the beginning of our era—may be balanced with the first evidence of writing in Mathurā around the time of our era (during the reign of the Kṣatrapas of Mathurā).

In sum there are art historical as well as philological avenues that need much further explorations. Nevertheless, the proposition whether or not orality vs. writing impacts the output of early narrative art in India seems to open up a whole new field for investigating the problems posed in this paper. Hindu narratives do begin to flourish above the Deccan [not notably in Mathurā!] in the Gupta and post-Gupta periods, just as the stress on Brahmanism weakens and the dawn of the so-called golden Gupta age is ushered in.[99]

NOTES AND REFERENCES

* I wish to express my thanks to Michael Witzel for his helpful comments on an earlier Draft of this paper. The paper was first read at the Mathurā Workshop at the Freie Universität in Berlin, organized by Monika Zin, during April 11-13, 2014.

i. "Oral Narrative, Visual Narrative, Literary Narrative in Ancient Buddhist India", in *India, Tibet and China. Genesis and Aspects of Traditional Narrative*, edited by Alfredo Cadonna, Firenze Leo Olschki, 1999; reprinted in Giovanni Verardi and Anna Filigenzi, (eds.), *On Gandhara. Collected Articles*, Collana "Collectanea" 3, Vol. 2, Naples, 2003, p. 515.

1. I am working with the assumption that Bhāsa is pre- Kālidāsa. Numerous events in this play are not depicted in Mathurā's art of the Kuṣāṇa Period. van Buitenen in *The Little Clay Cart* speculates (pp. 31-32) that Śūdraka may have found Bhāsa's play called *Carudatta* incomplete and set out to complete it. These clues suggest that Bhāsa is probably post-Kuṣāṇa and pre- Gupta (i.e. pre- Śūdraka and pre-Kālidāsa). Christopher Austin writes that Bhāsa is normally dated to the fourth century AD. See his "The Fructification of the Tale of the Tree: The Pārijātaharaṇa in the Harivaṃśa and its Appendices", *JAOS* 133.2 (2013) 253. I would agree with this date. However Michael Witzel believes his dramas were composed by 150 AD. See his "Brahmanical Reaction to Foreign Influences and to Social and Religious Change", in P. Olivelle, *Between the Empires. Society in India 300 BCE to 400 CE*; Oxford University Press, New York, 2006, p. 467, fn. 40. The date of Bhāsa seems still to be an open question for Sanskritists. In *JAOS* 127.4 (2007), Stephanie W. Jamison in her review of *Théâtre de l'Inde anncienne*, (eds.) L. Bansat - Boudon, et al. (pp. 517-519) finds dates ranging from c. 2nd century AD

to c. 8th century in various parts of the book which treat Bhāsa, and she herself does not speculate.

2. See J. Ph. Vogel, *La Sculpture de Mathurā, Ars Asiatica* XV, Paris et Bruxelles, 1930. Plate XXIII a & b.
3. See J.E. van Lohuizen-de Leeuw, *The "Scythian" Period*, Leiden, 1949, p. 146 for a brief discussion on the moniker.
4. Please see details in R.S. Sharma, "Trends in the Economic History of Mathurā (c. 300 BC-300 AD)" in Doris Meth Srinivasan (ed.), *Mathurā: The Cultural Heritage*, New Delhi, 1989, pp. 31-38.
5. See Jason Neelis, *Early Buddhist Transmission and Trade Networks. Mobility and Exchange within and Beyond the Northwestern Borderlands of South Asia*, Brill, Leiden, Boston 2011; Chapter 3; especially pp. 198-200.
6. These highlights are from Shiva G. Bajpai, "Mathurā: Trade Routes, Commerce and Communication Patterns, from the Post-Mauryan Period to the End of the Kuṣāṇa Period", in Doris Meth Srinivasan (ed.), *Mathurā: The Cultural Heritage*, New Delhi, 1989, pp. 46-58.
7. Bajpai, "Trade Routes", p. 49. See Maps in Saifur Rahman Dar, "Pathways Between Gandhāra and North India During Second Century BC – Second Century AD" in Doris Meth Srinivasan (ed.), *On the Cusp of an Era. Art in the Pre-Kuṣāṇa World*, Brill, Leiden, London 2007, pp. 29-54. Figs. 2.1, 2.2.
8. Härtel speaks of the archaeological findings in the Mitra level at Sonkh (i.e. 100 B.C.-20 BC) as a threshold marking a change in the direction of greater wealth. See Herbert Härtel, "The Pre-Kuṣāṇa and Early Kuṣāṇa Levels at Sonkh", in Doris Meth Srinivasan (ed.), *On the Cusp of an Era. Art in the Pre-Kuṣāṇa World*, Brill, Leiden, London 2007, p. 347.
9. See J ason Neelis, "Passage to India", in Doris Meth Srinivasan (ed.), *On the Cusp of an Era. Art in the Pre-Kuṣāṇa World*, Brill, Leiden, London 2007, pp. 55-93.
10. "Gandhāra and Mathurā: Their Cultural Relationship", P. Pal (ed.), *Aspects of Indian Art*, Leiden, 1972, pp. 27-43.
11. See John Marshall, *Taxila*, Reprint, New Delhi, 1975, Vol. II, p. 486.
12. For details see Doris Meth Srinivasan, *Many Heads, Arms and Eyes: Origin, Meaning and Form of Multiplicity in Indian Art*, Brill, Leiden, New York, Köln, 1997, pp. 308-309.
13. Cf. Romila Thapar, "The early History of Mathurā: Up to and Including the Mauryan Period", in Doris Meth Srinivasan (ed.), *Mathurā: The Cultural Heritage*, New Delhi, 1989, pp. 12-18.
14. H. Akira, *A History of Indian Buddhism. From Śākyamuni to Early Mahāyāna*. Reprint, Delhi, 1993, p. 268.
15. The story and references to other versions are in John S. Strong, *The Legend and Cult of Upagupta*, Princeton, 1992, pp. 76-80.
16. See Q2 Ayagapatta in J.Ph. Vogel, *Archaeological Museum at Mathurā*, pp. 184-85. Note Doris Meth Srinivasan, "The Mauryan Gaṇikā from Dīdārgañj (Pāṭaliputra)", *East and West*, Vol. 55, 2005, 345-362.
17. See D.C. Sircar, *Studies in the Religious Life of Ancient and Medieval India*, Delhi, 1971, p. 13, fn. 77.
18. See *Epigraphia Indica*, Vol. II, p. 200 or H. Lüders, A List of Brāhmī Inscriptions from earliest times to about AD 400 with the exception of those of Aśoka, in *Epigraphia Indica*, Vol. X; # 100, p. 18.
19. See Fig. 294 in Sonya Rhie Quintanilla, *History of Early Stone Sculpture at Mathurā*, Leiden, Boston, 2007, and pp. 229-233.

20. See Plate XXXII in Vincent A. Smith, *The Jain Stūpa and other Antiquities of Mathurā*; 2nd edition, Varanasi, 1969.
21. See Figs. 14 and 30 in N.P. Joshi, *Mathurā Sculpture*, Mathurā, 1966.
22. B.N. Mukherjee, *Mathurā and Its Society. The Śaka-Pahlava Phase*, Calcutta, 1981, p. 176, fn. 160.
23. K.D. Bajpai, "Some New Mathurā Finds", *Journal of the U.P Historical Society*, Vol. XXI, 1948, Fig. 13, pp. 128-9 and fn 29A.
24. H. Lüders, *Mathurā Inscriptions*, (ed.) by Klaus L. Janert; Göttingen, 1961, pp. 61-63, Par. 27.
25. Please see, in addition to the references cited below, V.S. Agrawala, *A Catalogue of the Brahmanical Images in Mathurā Art*, U.P. Historical Society, Lucknow, 1951.
26. See Doris Meth Srinivasan, "Vaiṣṇava Art and Iconography at Mathurā" in Srinivasan (ed.), *Mathurā: The Cultural Heritage*, pp. 383-392. Also Doris Meth Srinivasan, "Saṃkarṣaṇa/Balarāma and the Mountain: A New Attribute" in Claudine Bautze-Picron (ed.), *Religion and Art: New Issues in Indian Iconography and Iconology*, Vol. I of the Proceedings of the 18th Conference of the European Association of South Asian Archaeologists, London 2005, London 2008, pp. 93-104. Plus bibliography in these papers. See also this volume for the seond paper.
27. Doris Meth Srinivasan, "Early Vaiṣṇava Imagery: Caturvyūha and Variant Forms", *Archives of Asian Art* XXXII, 1979, 39-54. Plus bibliography. Doris Meth Srinivasan; with Lore Sander, "Viśvarūpa Vyūha Avatāra. Reappraisals Based on an Inscribed Bronze from the Northwest Dated to the Early 5th Century AD", East and West, Vol. Nos. 1-4, 1997, 105-170.
28. Doris Meth Srinivasan, "Vaiṣṇava Art and Iconography at Mathurā" in Srinivasan (ed.), *Mathurā: The Cultural Heritage*, New Delhi, 1989, pp. 383-392.
29. Ibid.
30. Doris Meth Srinivasan, "A Unique Mathurā Eight-Armed Viṣṇu of the 4th Century AD", *Oriental Art*, Vol. XXXIV, No. 4, Winter 1988/89, 276-281, see Fig. 2.5.
31. Doris M. Srinivasan, "Early Kṛṣṇa Icons: The Case at Mathurā", in J. Williams (ed.), *Kalādarśana: American Studies in the Art of India*, New Delhi, 1981, pp. 127-136.
32. Doris Meth Srinivasan and Vinay Kumar Gupta, "Reflecting from Hindsight: Thoughts on a New Post-Kuṣāṇa Mathurā Panel of Gaṇeśa and Śrī-Lakṣmī", M.N.P. Tiwari & K. Giri (eds.), *Bilvapatra. Treasures of Indian Art*, Dr. N.P. Joshi Felicitation Volume, New Delhi, 2013, pp. 188-198.
33. Doris M. Srinivasan, "God as Brahmanical Ascetic: A Colossal Kushan Icon of the Mathurā School, *Journal of the Indian Society of Oriental Art*, N.S. Vol. X('78-'79) 1-16; Doris M. Srinivasan "Bhagavān Nārāyana: A Colossal Kushan Icon", *Pakistan Archaeology*, No. 26, 1991, 263-271. Also see chapter 7 in this volume.
34. Besides V.S. Agrawala, above, see Doris Meth Srinivasan, with Lore Sander, "Newly Discovered Inscribed Mathurā Sculptures of Probable Doorkeepers Dating to the Kṣatrapa Period", *Archives of Asian Art* XLIII, 1990, 63-68.
35. Doris Meth Srinivasan, *Many Heads, Arms and Eyes: Origin, Meaning and Form of Multiplicity in Indian Art*, Brill, Leiden, New York, Köln, 1997, see Chapter 20.
36. N.P. Joshi, "Māṭṛkā Figures in Kuṣāṇa Sculptures at Mathurā", M. Yaldiz and W. Lobo (eds.), *Investigating Indian Art*, Berlin, 1987, pp. 159-171.
37. V.S. Agrawala, *A Catalogue of the Brahmanical Images in Mathura Art*, U.P. Historical Society, Lucknow, p. 41.
38. For these four, see V.S. Agrawala, *A Catalogue of the Brahmanical Images in Mathura Art*, U.P. Historical Society, Lucknow.

39. Doris Meth Srinivasan, "Skanda/Kārttikeya in the Early Art of the Northwest", *Silk Road Art and Archaeology 5*, Kamakura, 1997/98, 233-268.
40. The icons listed are all firsts. Such images as the *liṅga, mukha liṅga, Śiva, abhiṣeka* Lakṣmī are fashioned first elsewhere and therefore are not cited.
41. Please see further discussion, especially as Brahmanism relates to the culture of ancient Mathurā, Srinivasan, *Many Heads, Arms and Eyes*. Chapter 21.
42. Michael Witzel, "Brahmanical Reaction to Foreign Influences and to Social and Religious Change", in P. Olivelle, *Between the Empires. Society in India 300 BCE to 400 CE*; Oxford University Press, New York, 2006, see pp. 477 and 480. H. Scharfe, "A Second 'Index Fossil' of Sanskrit Grammarians" *Journal of the American Oriental Society*, Vol. 96.2, 1976; see p. 274.
43. Witzel, "Brahmanical Reaction", pp. 481-482 and fn. 84.
44. Damsteegt, "The Pre- Kuṣāṇa and Kuṣāṇa Inscriptions and the Supercession of the Prākrit by Sanskrit in North India in General and at Mathurā in Particular", D.M. Srinivasan (ed.), *Mathurā: The Cultural Heritage*, New Delhi, 1989, pp. 302-303.
45. D.C. Sircar, *Select Inscriptions bearing on Indian History and Civilization*, Vol. I, Calcutta, 1965, No. 26, p. 121.
46. Ibid.
47. Already voiced by me in *Many Heads, Arms and Eyes*, in the 'Why Mathurā' chapter, pp. 312-313.
48. A definition of Āryāvarta is given by Patañjali (2.4.10: I.475.2-10) which is quite similar to the definition contained in the Manusmṛti (2.21-22). See wording in Witzel, "Brahmanical Reaction", pp. 478-479 and fns. 70 and 71.
49. See M.C. Joshi, "Mathurā as an Ancient Settlement" in D.M. Srinivasan (ed.), *Mathurā: The Cultural Heritage*, New Delhi, 1989; pp. 165-170; see p. 168. For interpretation see Srinivasan, *Many Heads, Arms and Eyes*, p. 312, fn. 41.
50. Lüders, *Mathurā Inscriptions*, No. 94, pp. 125-126.
51. Mukherjee, *Mathurā and Society*, p. 130 and fn. 185. See also no. 32, p. 230 in S.J. Czuma with R. Morris, *Kushan Sculpture. Images from Early India*, Cleveland; 1985. Note that the 'converted date' of AD 188 is not valid.
52. V.S. Agrawala, *India as Known to Pāṇini*, 2nd edition, 1963, p. 79. It will be remembered that seven miles from Mathurā the Morā Well inscription, dating to the early decades of the first century AD, was found. It mentions the Vṛṣṇi Vīras, one of the five being Vāsudeva-Kṛṣṇa.
53. See details in Srinivasan, *Many Heads, Arms and Eyes*, pp. 312-313.
54. Ibid, p. 314.
55. The term *varṇāśramadharma* can be summed up as doing your duty (*dharma*) according to your class (*varṇa*-i.e. Brahman, Kṣatriya, Vaiśya, or Śūdra) and the stage of life (*āśrama*) you are in at any given time.
56. Witzel, "Brahmanical Reaction", p. 461. Dates for Pāṇini are usually given as c. 500-400 BC. The latest review on his dates is in Neelis, *Early Buddhist Transmission and Trade Networks*, fn. 7 pp. 187-188. See also Witzel's latest position in his paper cited in fn. 98, below.
57. See also pp. 322-324 of Michael Witzel, "The Development of the Vedic Canon and its Schools: The Social and Political Milieu", in Michael Witzel (ed.), *Inside the Texts. Beyond the Texts*, Cambridge, 1997; pp. 257-345.
58. Witzel, "Brahmanical Reaction", p. 472. All this information regarding the White Yajur Veda is from Witzel's paper.
59. Ibid, p. 477, fn. 58.

60. D.C. Sircar, *Studies in the Religious Life of Ancient and Medieval India*, Delhi, 1971, p. 19.
61. Sircar, *Religious Life*, p. 20.
62. R.G. Bhandarkar, "Allusions to Kṛṣṇa in Patañjali's Mahābhāṣya", *The Indian Antiquary III* (1874), 14-16.
63. Cf. N.P. Joshi, *Mathurā Sculptures*, Mathurā, 1966, Fig. 58 with J.C. Harle, *Gupta Sculpture*, Oxford, 1974, Fig. 14.
64. See Charlotte Schmid, *Le Don de Voir*, Paris, 2010, Fig. 59.
65. See Doris Meth Srinivasan, "Saṃkarṣaṇa/Balarāma and the Mountain", 2008.
66. See D.M. Srinivasan, "Early Kṛṣṇa Icons", pp. 127-136.
67. Ibid.
68. For an analysis of the 5th century Vākāṭaka inscription, a Trivikrama sculpture and the Trivikrama Temple of Ramtek, see Hans Bakker, "The Trivikrama Temple: A New Interpretation of Rāmagiri Evidence (3)", *South Asian Studies*, 2013, Vol. 29.2, 169-176.
69. See Doris Meth Srinivasan, "Hindu Deities in Gandhāra" in *Gandhāra. The Buddhist Heritage of Pakistan. Legends, Monasteries, and Paradise*, Mainz, 2008, pp. 132-133 and Plate Cat. No. 111, on p. 160, and, Srinivasan, *Many Heads, Arms and Eyes*, p. 302 ff.
70. Srinivasan, *Many Heads, Arms and Eyes*, p. 238. I did not mention in this work that the Kaṭha Āraṇyaka, ed. and translated by Michael Witzel (Harvard Oriental Series, 2004) also describes how Rudra got all his names.
71. Phyllis Granoff published in 2006, so I am told, the paper on *śaiva* narratives I invited her to write for the Symposium *On the Cusp of an Era. Art in the Pre-Kuṣāṇa World*. (The symposium papers were published under the same title by Brill, Leiden, London 2007). Granoff did not concentrate on Pre-Kuṣāṇa or Kuṣāṇa evidence and instead used purāṇic and medieval texts to establish her explanation as to why early narrative scenes relating to Śiva are lacking in the early art. I critiqued her position extensively in an Addendum to my paper "Significance and Scope of Pre-Kuṣāṇa Śaivite Iconography" in *Discourses on Śiva*, ed. Michael W. Meister Philadelphia 1984, pp. 32-46. The paper with Addendum is reprinted in this anthology. See pages 70-71 fn. 45a. Her position can be summarized: 1) hesitancy to portray the god anthropomorphically, 2) late appearance of Śiva himself in narrative exploits, because, 3) relevant narratives, as early Purāṇas show, have others, especially Śiva's *gaṇas*, and not Śiva as the main actor in a story. These positions skirt the problem of Mathurā's dearth of narrative art in general, plus the evidence she gives for lack of early *śaiva* narratives are unfortunately at variance with the art (see details in Addendum).
72. For discussion on this idea see Chapters I and 21 in Srinivasan, *Many Heads, Arms and Eyes*.
73. Vidya Dehejia, *Discourse in Early Buddhist Art: Visual Narratives of India*, Delhi, 1997, pp. 141-142, 149. The author made this assessment for Mathurā's Buddhist narrative output during the first century BCE.
74. Sonya Rhie Quintanilla, *History of Early Stone Sculpture at Mathurā ca 150 BCE-100 CE*, Leiden, Boston, 2007, pp. 41-47, 66-67, 78-79, 199, 196.
75. Pratapaditya Pal, *Asian Art at the Norton Simon Museum; Vol. I: Art from the Indian Subcontinent*, New Haven and London, 2003. No. 38, pp. 74-75.
76. J.E. van Lohuizen-de Leeuw, *The "Scythian" Period*, Leiden, 1949, pp. 157-158 and fn. 45; also Quintanilla, *Early Stone Sculpture at Mathurā*, p. 200, fn. 60.
77. Quintanilla, *Early Stone Sculpture at Mathurā*, pp. 65-66.
78. A paper to be published in March 2014 takes up the differences between Gandhāran versions of literary and visual narratives of the Buddha's previous births. Many of the points in this paper compliment the discussion in the present paper. Please see Jason

Neelis, "Literary and Visual Narratives in Gandhāran Buddhist Manuscripts and Material Cultures: Localization of Jātakas, Avadānas and previous-Birth Stories" in *History and Material Culture in Asian Religions*, edited by Benjamin Fleming and Richard Mann. Studies in Religion, Media, and Culture. New York: Routledge, pp. 252-264.

79. Doris Meth Srinivasan, "Genealogy of the Buddha in Early Indian Art" in *Eastern Approaches*, T.S. Maxwell (ed.), Delhi, 1992, pp. 38-44.
80. Reference in preceeding footnote.
81. Srinivasan, "Genealogy of the Buddha", p. 40.
82. Ibid. and p. 43, fn. 7.

82a. ADDENDUM: I have revised this sentence so that the description of the relief (Fig. 16.1) reads as in my original analysis of relief SML No. B 208, cited in footnote 79. Also please see M. Frenger , "Sun Images from Mathura - Cult Icons or Emblems ?" in *South Asian Archaeology* 2003, Band 1, Ute F. Vogt and Hans-Joachim Weisshaar (eds.); Aachen 2005; 443-449, especially 444.

83. Srinivasan, "Genealogy of the Buddha", p. 40 and p. 43, fn.7.
84. Agrawala, *India as Known to Pāṇini*, p. 388.
85. Srinivasan, "Early Kṛṣṇa Icons: The Case at Mathurā", p. 132. For my arguments in favor of a c. 5th century date for the Vishṇudharmottara, please see my review of *The Citrasūtra of the Viṣṇudhamottara Purāṇa*, by Parul Dave Mukherji, Delhi, Indira Gandhi National Center for the Arts, 2001 in the *Journal of the American Oriental Society* 124.3 (2004) 569-572.
86. David McMahan, "Orality, Writing, and Authority in South Asian Buddhism: Visionary Literature and the Struggle for Legitmacy in the Mahāyāna", *History of Religions*, Vol. 37, No. 3 (1998), 249-274.
87. Satya Shrava, *The Dated Kushāṇa Inscriptions*, New Delhi, 1993, p. 121, No. 153.
88. For an expanded treatment on these aspects of oral transmission in Mathurā, please see my *Many Heads, Arms and Eyes*, 316-320.
89. Romila Thapar, *From Lineage to State, Social Formations in the Mid-First Millennium* BC *in the Ganga Valley, Bombay*, 1984, pp. 45-46. A.L. Basham, *The Wonder That was India*, Third Revised Edition, London, 1967, p. 154.
90. Symposium: *Buddhism and Art in Gandhāra and Kucha. Buddhist Culture along the Silk Road: Gandhāra, Kucha and Turfan*. Section I; edited by Akira Miyaji, Ryukoku University, March 2013, p. 182.
91. P.R. Srinivasan and S. Sankaranarayanan, *Inscriptions of the Ikshvāku Period*, Hyderabad, 1979, pp. 3-4.
92. Ibid.
93. Ibid.
94. Elizabeth Rosen Stone, *The Buddhist Art of Nāgārjunakoṇḍa*, Delhi, 1994, p. 11.
95. See details in Witzel, "Brahmanical Reaction", pp. 474, 476.
96. Sircar, *Select Inscriptions*, Vol. I, 1965, p. 192. Cf. Witzel, "Brahmanical Reaction", p. 468, fn. 45.
97. Nilakanta Sastri, *A History of South India*, Fourth Edition, Madras, 1976, p. 101.
98. "Gandhāra and the formation of the Vedic and Zoroastrian canons". *Traveaux de symposium international. Le Livre. La Roumanie. L'Europe. Troisième edition, 20-24 Septembre 2010. Tome III. Etudes euro- et afro-asiatiques*. Bucharest: Bibliothèque de Bucarest 2011, 490-532.
99. The following examples can be cited: the *śaiva* relief panels at Elephanta; the *vaiṣṇava* reliefs at Udayagiri; the Kṛṣṇa Līlā Scenes on north Indian Pillars for which see Donald M. Stadtner, "The Tradition of Kṛṣṇa Pillars in North India", *Archives of Asian Art*, Vol. 40 (1987), pp. 56-68.